Volume Five

X Toolkit Intrinsics
Reference Manual

Third Edition for X11,
Release 4 and Release 5

Edited by David Flanagan

O'Reilly & Associates, Inc.

X Toolkit Intrinsics Reference Manual

Edited by David Flanagan

X Series Editor: Adrian Nye

Printing History

January 1990:	First Edition.
September 1990:	Second Edition. Revised for R4.
June 1991:	Minor corrections.
April 1992:	Third Edition. Revised to cover R4 and R5.
June 1993:	Minor corrections. Appendix H, *Changes Between Release 4 and Release 5,* added.

This document is based in part on *X Toolkit Intrinsics—C Language Interface*, by Joel McCormack, Paul Asente, and Ralph Swick, and *X Toolkit Athena Widgets—C Language Interface* by Ralph Swick and Terry Weissman, both of which are copyright © 1985, 1986, 1987, 1988, 1989, 1990 the Massachusetts Institute of Technology, Cambridge, Massachusetts, and Digital Equipment Corporation, Maynard, Massachusetts.

We have used this material under the terms of its copyright, which grants free use, subject to the following conditions:

> "Permission to use, copy, modify and distribute this documentation (*i.e., the original MIT and DEC material*) for any purpose and without fee is hereby granted, provided that the above copyright notice appears in all copies and that both that copyright notice and this permission notice appear in supporting documentation, and that the name of MIT or Digital not be used in advertising or publicity pertaining to distribution of the software without specific, written prior permission. MIT and Digital make no representations about the suitability of the software described herein for any purpose. It is provided 'as is' without expressed or implied warranty."

Note, however, that those portions of this document that are based on the original X11 documentation and other source material have been significantly revised, and that all such revisions are copyright © 1990 O'Reilly & Associates, Inc. Inasmuch as the proprietary revisions can't be separated from the freely copyable MIT source material, the net result is that copying of this document is not allowed. Sorry for the doublespeak!

Many of the designations used by manufacturers and sellers to distinguish their products are claimed as trademarks. Where those designations appear in this book, and O'Reilly and Associates, Inc. was aware of a trademark claim, the designations have been printed in caps or initial caps.

While every precaution has been taken in the preparation of this book, the publisher assumes no responsibility for errors or omissions, or for damages resulting from the use of the information contained herein.

This book is printed on acid-free paper with 50% recycled content, 10-15% post-consumer waste. O'Reilly & Associates is committed to using paper with the highest recycled content available consistent with high quality.

Volume 5, Third Edition: ISBN 1-56592-007-4

X Toolkit Intrinsics
Reference Manual

Table of Contents

About the X Toolkit

The X Toolkit is the collective name for two C-language subroutine libraries (Xt and Xaw) designed to simplify the development of X Window System applications using reusable components called *widgets*. Typical widgets include scrollbars, menus, dialog boxes, text-editing areas, drawing areas, etc. Each widget is made up of its own X window, but most of the work that goes on in that window has already been taken care of—all the application programmer has to do is assemble the widgets and write application-specific code that will be called in response to events in the widgets.

The Xt library (the Intrinsics) consists of routines for using and building widgets. Widgets are defined using an object-oriented classing mechanism. The Xaw widget library is based on Xt and provides a small number of widgets that can be used to write simple application programs.

The Xt Intrinsics are written using Xlib, the lowest level C language interface to the X Window System. Both the Xt Intrinsics and Xlib are required by the X standard (established by the X Consortium) on any system that allows programming of X applications.

Xaw is the Athena Widget set, the early development of which took place at MIT's Project Athena. Primarily, Xaw was designed as a simple demonstration and test of the Intrinsics—not as a complete set of widgets for writing demanding applications. There are numerous other widget sets provided by system vendors to implement particular user-interface styles. The two dominant widget sets are OSF/*Motif*, which has a user interface similar to IBM's Presentation Manager, and AT&T and Sun's *OPEN LOOK* Widget set.

The X Toolkit Intrinsics will work the same way with any of these Xt-compatible widget sets. In fact, it is possible, though not always aesthetically or economically desirable, to combine widgets from different widget sets in the same application.*

---

*Note that there are other X toolkits (note the lowercase "t" in "toolkits") that have nothing whatever to do with the X Toolkit (Xt), except that they have similar goals—namely, to make it easier to write standard X applications. These toolkits include Andrew (from Carnegie-Mellon University), InterViews (from Stanford), and XView (from Sun). These are not merely different widget sets but are entirely different toolkits. They are not compatible with Xt.

About This Book

This book is the fifth volume in the O'Reilly & Associates X Window System Series. It includes reference pages for each of the Xt Intrinsics functions and macros, for all the prototype procedures, for Intrinsics classes and methods, for the Athena Widgets, and for the Xmu functions useful to Xt programmers. Within each section, reference pages are organized alphabetically for ease of access; a permuted index and numerous appendices and quick reference aids are also provided.

Volumes Four and Five are designed to be used together. Volume Four provides an explanation of the X Toolkit, including tutorial material and numerous programming examples. Arranged by task or topic, each chapter brings together a group of X Toolkit functions, describes the conceptual foundation they are based on, and illustrates how they are most often used in writing applications. This volume is structured so as to be useful as a tutorial and also as a task-oriented reference.

To get the most out of the examples in Volume Four, you will need the exact calling sequences of each function from Volume Five. To understand fully how to use each of the functions described in Volume Five, all but the most experienced Toolkit "hacker" will need the explanation and examples in Volume Four.

If you are using the OSF/Motif widget set, you will find Volume Six, *Motif Programming Manual*, an invaluable information source on how to use this commercial widget set to build real applications. Volume Six is a fine companion to Volumes Four and Five, because it discusses the widget set in detail, while Volume Four provides the details on the Xt Intrinsics, including information on how to write custom widgets.

Even though the Toolkit is intended to hide the low-level X interface provided by Xlib, there are times in writing widgets when Xlib functions will be necessary because no Xt feature exists to do the same thing. Volume Four describes the most common occasions for using Xlib but does not provide a reference to the particular functions involved. For that, see Volume One, *Xlib Programming Manual*, and Volume Two, *Xlib Reference Manual*.

How This Book is Organized

Volume Five consists of reference pages for Toolkit functions. It also contains numerous helpful appendices.

The book is organized as follows:

Preface   Describes the organization of the book and the conventions it follows.

Permuted Index   Provides a standard UNIX permuted index for all reference pages, regardless of section.

Section 1   *Xt Functions and Macros*, contains reference pages for all the Intrinsics functions and macros.

Assumptions

This book makes no assumptions about the reader's knowledge of object-oriented programming or the X Window System. It does assume familiarity with the C programming language and the concepts and architecture of the X Toolkit, which are presented in Volume Four, *X Toolkit Intrinsics Programming Manual*. For some advanced topics, the reader may also need to consult Volume One, *Xlib Programming Manual*, and Volume Two, *Xlib Reference Manual*.

Related Documents

Ten other books on the X Window System are available from O'Reilly & Associates, Inc.:

Volume Zero   *X Protocol Reference Manual*

Volume One   *Xlib Programming Manual*

Volume Two   *Xlib Reference Manual*

Volume Three   *X Window System User's Guide*

Volume Four   *X Toolkit Intrinsics Programming Manual*

Volume Six A   *Motif Programming Manual*

Volume Six B   *Motif Reference Manual*

Volume Seven   *XView Programming Manual* with accompanying reference volume.

Volume Eight   *X Window System Administrator's Guide.*

Quick Reference *The X Window System in a Nutshell*

The following documents are included on the X11 source tape:

X Toolkit Intrinsics—C Language Interface, by Joel McCormack, Paul Asente, and Ralph Swick
Athena Widget Set—C Language Interface, by Chris D. Peterson
Xlib—C Language X Interface, by Jim Gettys and Robert Scheifler
Xmu Library X Version 11, Release 5

The following Nutshell Handbooks published by O'Reilly and Associates, Inc. are useful when programming in C:

Checking C Programs with lint, by Ian Darwin
Practical C Programming, by Steve Oualline
Managing Projects with make, by Andrew Oram and Steve Talbott
Using C on the UNIX System, by Dave Curry
Posix Programmer's Guide, by Donald Lewine
Power Programming with RPC, by John Bloomer

The following is the classic introduction to C programming:

The C Programming Language, by B. W. Kernighan and D. M. Ritchie

Conventions Used in This Book

Italics are used for:

- UNIX pathnames, filenames, program names, user command names, and options for user commands.

- New terms where they are defined.

`Typewriter Font` is used for:

- Anything that would be typed verbatim into code, such as examples of source code and text on the screen.

- The contents of include files, such as structure types, structure members, symbols (defined constants and bit flags), and macros.

- Xt, Xlib, POSIX, and any other C function name.

`Italic Typewriter Font` is used for:

- Arguments to functions, since they could be typed in code as shown but are arbitrary names that could be changed.

Helvetica Italics are used for:

- Titles of examples, figures, and tables.

Boldface is used for:

- Chapter and section headings.

Request for Comments

Please write to tell us about any flaws you find in this manual or how you think it could be improved in order to help us provide you with the best documentation possible.

Our U.S. mail address, e-mail address, and telephone numbers are as follows:

O'Reilly and Associates, Inc.
103 Morris Street, Suite A
Sebastopol, CA 95472
800-998-9938
international +1 707-829-0515

UUCP: uunet!ora.com!adrian Internet: adrian@ora.com

Bulk Sales Information

This manual is being resold by many workstation manufacturers as their official X Window System documentation. For information on volume discounts for bulk purchase, call O'Reilly and Associates, Inc., at 800-998-9938, or send e-mail to linda@ora.com (uunet!ora.com!linda).

For companies requiring extensive customization of the book, source licensing terms are also available.

Obtaining the X Window System Software

The X Window System is copyrighted but freely distributed. The only restriction this places on its use is that the copyright notice identifying the author and the terms of use must accompany all copies of the software or documentation. Thanks to this policy, the software is available for nominal cost from a variety of sources. See Appendix F, *Sources of Additional Information*, in Volume Four, *X Toolkit Intrinsics Programming Manual*, for a listing of these sources.

Acknowledgements

As mentioned above, this manual is based in large part on the *X Toolkit Intrinsics—C Language Interface*, by Joel McCormack, Paul Asente, and Ralph Swick, and on the *Athena Widget Set—C Language Interface*, by Chris Peterson and on *Xmu Library X Version 11, Release 5*. We have done our best to incorporate all the useful information from these documents, while reorganizing them into alphabetical reference manual pages. We have clarified and expanded the descriptions of Intrinsics functions, added examples and cross references, and in general tried to make it more useful for reference purposes.

We would like to thank the authors of these documents, and the X Consortium, for the copyright policy that allows others to build upon their work. Their generosity of spirit not only has made this book possible, but is the basis for the unparalleled speed with which the X Window System has been adopted as a *de facto* standard.

We would also like to thank the reviewers of the companion volume, *X Toolkit Intrinsics Programming Manual*. Even though they didn't directly review this book, their comments are often reflected in its pages. They were David Lewis, Peter Winston of Integrated Computer Solutions (ICS), Wendy Eisner of Sunquest Information Systems, Dan Heller of Island Graphics, Inc. (now working with O'Reilly and Associates), Miles O'Neal of Systems and Software Solutions, Inc., Chris Peterson of ICS, and Ian Darwin of SoftQuad. Extra thanks are due to Ralph Swick and Chris Peterson, who answered many questions during the development of these books.

We are grateful to Sony Microsystems for the loan of a Sony NEWS workstation running their implementation of the X Window System. The speed and power of the Sony workstation, and the support of their staff, was a great help in developing these books. Additional development was done on a Sun-3 workstation running MIT's sample server, a Visual 640 X Display Station, and an NCD16 Network Display Station.

Mark Langley edited an early version of this book. His help is greatly appreciated.

Many staff members of O'Reilly and Associates Inc. worked on this book: Ellie Cutler, Jean Diaz, David Flanagan, Edie Friedman, Daniel Gilly, Dan Heller, Eileen Kramer, Kismet McDonough, Lenny Muellner, Adrian Nye, Tim O'Reilly, Chris Reilley, Susan Sarkes Dalton, Mike Sierra, Lesley Strother, Sue Willing, and Donna Woonteiler.

Of course, the editors alone take responsibility for any errors or omissions that remain.

Permuted Index

The permuted index takes the brief descriptive string from the title of each command page and rotates (permutes) the string so that each keyword will at one point start the second, or center, column of the line. The beginning and end of the original string are indicated by a slash when they are in other than their original position; if the string is too long, it is truncated.

To find the command you want, simply scan down the middle of the page, looking for a keyword of interest on the right side of the blank gutter. Once you find the keyword you want, you can read (with contortions) the brief description of the command that makes up the entry. If things still look promising, you can look all the way over to the right for the name of the relevant command page. The number in parentheses is the section in which that command page can be found.

Permuted Index

How to Use the Permuted Index

The permuted index takes the brief descriptive string from the title of each command page and rotates (permutes) the string so that each keyword will at one point start the *second*, or center, column of the line. The beginning and end of the original string are indicated by a slash when they are in other than their original position; if the string is too long, it is truncated.

To find the command you want, simply scan down the middle of the page, looking for a keyword of interest on the right side of the blank gutter. Once you find the keyword you want, you can read (with contortions) the brief description of the command that makes up the entry. If things still look promising, you can look all the way over to the right for the name of the relevant command page.

The Permuted Index

XtParseAcceleratorTable: compile an	accelerator table into its internal/	XtParseAcceleratorTable(1)
Core method to display current	accelerators display_accelerator:	display_accelerator(4)
descendants onto a/ /install all	accelerators from a widget and its	XtInstallAllAccelerators(1)
/install a widget's	accelerators on another widget	XtInstallAccelerators(1)
accepting or rejecting the/	accept_focus: Core class method for	accept_focus(4)
/interface definition for the	accept_focus() method	XtAcceptFocusProc(2)
accept_focus: Core class method for	accepting or rejecting the keyboard/	accept_focus(4)
XtMenuPopdown: built-in	action for popping down a widget	XtMenuPopdown(1)
XtMenuPopup: built-in	action for popping up a widget	XtMenuPopup(1)
/interface definition for	action hook procedure.	XtActionHookProc(2)
XtRemoveActionHook: unregister an	action hook procedure	XtRemoveActionHook(1)
a procedure to be called before any	action is invoked /register	XtAppAddActionHook(1)
interface definition for	action procedure XtActionProc:	XtActionProc(2)
explicitly invoke a named	action procedure XtCallActionProc:	XtCallActionProc(1)
XtRegisterGrabAction: register an	action procedure as one that needs/	XtRegisterGrabAction(1)
XtGetActionList: get the	action table of a widget class	XtGetActionList(1)
Manager XtAddActions: register an	action table with the Translation	XtAddActions(1)
XtAppAddActions: register an	action table with the Translation/	XtAppAddActions(1)
Command: command button	activated by pointer click	Command(5)
XtUngrabKeyboard: release an	active keyboard grab	XtUngrabKeyboard(1)
XtUngrabPointer: release an	active pointer grab	XtUngrabPointer(1)
XtGrabKeyboard:	actively grab the keyboard	XtGrabKeyboard(1)

a child is created insert_child: Composite class method called when .... insert_child(4)
a child is destroyed delete_child: Composite class method called when .... delete_child(4)
a child requests/ geometry_manager: Composite class method called when .... geometry_manager(4)
to a change in a/ change_managed: Composite class method to respond .... change_managed(4)
children Composite: fundamental widget with .... Composite(3)
a widget is a subclass of the Composite widget class /whether .... XtIsComposite(1)
/RectObj class method to negotiate compromise geometries .... set_values_almost(4)
/an event handler, or change the conditions under which it is called .... XtRemoveEventHandler(1)
/a raw event handler, or change the conditions under which it is called .... XtRemoveRawEventHandler(1)
a modal widget XtAddGrab: constrain or redirect user input to .... XtAddGrab(1)
constraint resources for its/ Constraint: a widget that provides .... Constraint(3)
handle/ Constraint set_values: Constraint class method called to .... Constraint set_values(4)
resources/ Constraint destroy: Constraint class method for freeing .... Constraint destroy(4)
Constraint get_values_hook: Constraint class method for/ .... Constraint get_values_hook(4)
initialize/ Constraint initialize: Constraint class method to .... Constraint initialize(4)
resources associated with a child's constraint record /for freeing .... Constraint destroy(4)
a child object or widget's constraint record /to initialize .... Constraint initialize(4)
/resources that do not appear in the Constraint resource list .... Constraint get_values_hook(4)
for a particular widget/ /get the constraint resource list structure .... XtGetConstraintResourceList(1)
method called to handle changes to constraint resources /class .... Constraint set_values(4)
Constraint: a widget that provides constraint resources for its/ .... Constraint(3)
/method for obtaining values of constraint resources that do not/ .... Constraint get_values_hook(4)
a widget is a subclass of the Constraint widget class /whether .... XtIsConstraint(1)
class method for freeing resources/ Constraint destroy: Constraint .... Constraint destroy(4)
Constraint class method for/ Constraint get_values_hook: .... Constraint get_values_hook(4)
class method to initialize a child/ Constraint initialize: Constraint .... Constraint initialize(4)
class method called to handle/ Constraint set_values: Constraint .... Constraint set_values(4)
/widget implementing constraints on children .... Form(5)
SimpleMenu: menu container widget .... SimpleMenu(5)
handled by XtDispatchEvent() that contains a timestamp /recent event .... XtLastTimestampProcessed(1)
converter in a single application context /a "new-style" type .... XtAppSetTypeConverter(1)
and remove it from an application context /close a display .... XtCloseDisplay(1)
/create an application context .... XtCreateApplicationContext(1)
and add it to an application context /initialize a display .... XtDisplayInitialize(1)
and add a display to an application context /open, initialize, ... XtOpenDisplay(1)
/destroy an application context and close its displays .... XtDestroyApplicationContext(1)
/retrieve the application context associated with a Display .... XtDisplayToApplicationContext(1)
/get the application context for a given widget .... XtWidgetToApplicationContext(1)
/internals, create an application context, open and initialize a/ .... XtAppInitialize(1)
/type converter for all application contexts in a process .... XtSetTypeConverter(1)
XtAppMainLoop: continuously process events .... XtAppMainLoop(1)
XtMainLoop: continuously process events .... XtMainLoop(1)
Simple: Core subclass with cursor control and insensitivity/ .... Simple(5)
in another/ Scrollbar: widget to control scrolling of viewing area .... Scrollbar(5)
/fundamental widget class that controls the interaction between/ .... Shell(3)
/emit boilerplate string conversion error message .... XtStringConversionWarning(1)
/issue a warning message during conversion of string resource/ .... XtDisplayStringConversionWarning(1)
XtConvert: convert resource type .... XtConvert(1)
/definition for procedure to convert the case of keysyms .... XtCaseProc(2)
register an "old-style" resource converter XtAddConverter: .... XtAddConverter(1)
register an "old-style" resource converter XtAppAddConverter: .... XtAppAddConverter(1)
obtain an argument for a resource converter /for procedure to .... XtConvertArgProc(2)
definition for old-style resource converter XtConverter: interface .... XtConverter(2)

obtain the resource database for a display XtDatabase: .... XtDatabase(1)
context associated with a Display /retrieve the application .... XtDisplayToApplicationContext(1)
for a particular Display /to XtDisplayInitialize() .... XtGetApplicationNameAndClass(1)
initialize toolkit and display XtInitialize: .... XtInitialize(1)
XtMapWidget: map a widget to its display .... XtMapWidget(1)
Label: widget to display a non-editable string .... Label(5)
StripChart: widget to display a real-time graphic chart .... StripChart(5)
XtDisplayInitialize: initialize a display and add it to an/ .... XtDisplayInitialize(1)
/context, open and initialize a display, and create the initial/ .... XtAppInitialize(1)
XtCloseDisplay: close a display and remove it from an/ .... XtCloseDisplay(1)
display_accelerator: Core method to display current accelerators .... display_accelerator(4)
XtDisplayOfObject: return the display pointer for the nearest/ .... XtDisplayOfObject(1)
widget XtDisplay: return the X Display pointer for the specified .... XtDisplay(1)
/translate a window and display pointer into a widget ID .... XtWindowToWidget(1)
/open, initialize, and add a display to an application context .... XtOpenDisplay(1)
display current accelerators display_accelerator: Core method to .... display_accelerator(4)
/interface definition for the display_accelerator() method .... XtStringProc(2)
application context and close its displays /destroy an .... XtDestroyApplicationContext(1)
/values of constraint resources that do not appear in the Constraint/ .... Constraint get_values_hook(4)
/obtaining values of resources that do not appear in the resource list .... get_values_hook(4)
head of/ XtPeekEvent: return, but do not remove the event at the .... XtPeekEvent(1)
of an/ XtAppPeekEvent: return, but do not remove the event at the head .... XtAppPeekEvent(1)
built-in action for popping down a widget XtMenuPopdown: .... XtMenuPopdown(1)
Grip: attachment point for dragging other widgets .... Grip(5)
expose: Core class method that draws a widget's graphics .... expose(4)
to be called when a specified time elapses /register a procedure .... XtAddTimeOut(1)
to be called when a specified time elapses /register a procedure .... XtAppAddTimeOut(1)
XtNumber: determine the number of elements in a fixed-size array .... XtNumber(1)
error/ XtStringConversionWarning: emit boilerplate string conversion .... XtStringConversionWarning(1)
Sme: base class for menu entries .... Sme(5)
SmeBSB: basic menu entry .... SmeBSB(5)
in the translation table entry /final event specification .... XtGetActionKeysym(1)
/interface definition for low-level error and warning handler/ .... XtErrorHandler(2)
/interface definition for high-level error and warning handler/ .... XtErrorMsgHandler(2)
/obtain the default error database .... XtAppGetErrorDatabase(1)
text of a named message from the error database /get the .... XtAppGetErrorDatabaseText(1)
XtGetErrorDatabase: obtain the error database .... XtGetErrorDatabase(1)
text of a named message from the error database /get the .... XtGetErrorDatabaseText(1)
XtAppError: call the low-level error handler .... XtAppError(1)
call the high-level fatal error handler XtAppErrorMsg: .... XtAppErrorMsg(1)
/set the high-level error handler .... XtAppSetErrorMsgHandler(1)
XtError: call the low-level fatal error handler .... XtError(1)
call the high-level fatal error handler XtErrorMsg: .... XtErrorMsg(1)
/set the low-level error handler procedure .... XtAppSetErrorHandler(1)
/set the low-level error handler procedure .... XtSetErrorHandler(1)
/set the high-level error handler procedure .... XtSetErrorMsgHandler(1)
/emit boilerplate string conversion error message .... XtStringConversionWarning(1)
/interface definition for a filename evaluation procedure .... XtFilePredicate(2)
handler without selecting for the event /register an event .... XtAddRawEventHandler(1)
input event and return the next X event /dispatch timer and alternate .... XtAppNextEvent(1)
/dispatch timer and alternate input event and return the next X event .... XtAppNextEvent(1)
/return, but do not remove the event at the head of an/ .... XtPeekEvent(1)
/return, but do not remove the event at the head of an/ .... XtAppPeekEvent(1)

/but do not remove the event at the	head of an application's input/	XtAppPeekEvent(1)
handler/ /interface definition for	high-level error and warning	XtErrorMsgHandler(2)
XtAppSetErrorMsgHandler: set the	high-level error handler	XtAppSetErrorMsgHandler(1)
XtSetErrorMsgHandler: set the	high-level error handler procedure	XtSetErrorMsgHandler(1)
XtAppErrorMsg: call the	high-level fatal error handler	XtAppErrorMsg(1)
XtErrorMsg: call the	high-level fatal error handler	XtErrorMsg(1)
XtAppSetWarningMsgHandler: set the	high-level warning handler	XtAppSetWarningMsgHandler(1)
XtAppWarningMsg: call the	high-level warning handler	XtAppWarningMsg(1)
XtWarningMsg: call the	high-level warning handler	XtWarningMsg(1)
XtSetWarningMsgHandler: set the	high-level warning handler/	XtSetWarningMsgHandler(1)
interface definition for action	hook procedure. XtActionHookProc:	XtActionHookProc(2)
unregister an action	hook procedure XtRemoveActionHook:	XtRemoveActionHook(1)
/widget class for vendor-specific	hooks for interaction with custom/	VendorShell(3)
widget for vertical or	horizontal /geometry-managing	Paned(5)
/widget class that interacts with an	ICCCM-compliant window manager	WMShell(3)
and display pointer into a widget	ID /translate a window	XtWindowToWidget(1)
to be called when the event loop is	idle /register a procedure	XtAddWorkProc(1)
to be called when the event loop is	idle /register a procedure	XtAppAddWorkProc(1)
called when the event loop is	idle /definition for procedure	XtWorkProc(2)
and determine order of two strings,	ignoring case /compare	XmuCompareISOLatin1(6)
Form: geometry-managing widget	implementing constraints on/	Form(5)
/definition for procedure to cancel	incremental selection transfer	XtCancelConvertSelectionProc(2)
/for procedure called when an	incremental selection transfer/	XtSelectionDoneIncrProc(2)
/to other clients using the	incremental transfer interface	XtOwnSelectionIncremental(1)
/obtain the selection value using	incremental transfers	XtGetSelectionValueIncremental(1)
multiple selection values using	incremental transfers /obtain	XtGetSelectionValuesIncremental(1)
procedure to return selection data	incrementally /definition for a	XtConvertSelectionIncrProc(2)
cursor control and insensitivity	indication /Core subclass with	Simple(5)
/set WM_COLORMAP_WINDOWS property to	inform window manager of custom/	XtSetWMColormapWindows(1)
/a display, and create the	initial application shell instance	XtAppInitialize(1)
class method for one-time class	initialization /Object	class_initialize(4)
/Constraint class method to	initialize a child object or/	Constraint initialize(4)
an/ XtDisplayInitialize:	initialize a display and add it to	XtDisplayInitialize(1)
/an application context, open and	initialize a display, and create/	XtAppInitialize(1)
creating/ XtInitializeWidgetClass:	initialize a widget class without	XtInitializeWidgetClass(1)
application/ XtOpenDisplay: open,	initialize, and add a display to an	XtOpenDisplay(1)
fields /Object class method to	initialize class part structure	class_part_initialize(4)
/allocate memory for an array and	initialize its bytes to zero	XtCalloc(1)
interface definition for the	initialize() methods XtInitProc:	XtInitProc(2)
initializing a widget or object/	initialize: Object class method for	initialize(4)
XtToolkitInitialize:	initialize the X Toolkit internals	XtToolkitInitialize(1)
create an/ XtAppInitialize:	initialize the X Toolkit internals,	XtAppInitialize(1)
using varargs/ XtVaAppInitialize:	initialize the X Toolkit internals,	XtVaAppInitialize(1)
XtInitialize:	initialize toolkit and display	XtInitialize(1)
interface definition for the	initialize_hook() and XtArgsProc:	XtArgsProc(2)
method for initializing subpart/	initialize_hook: obsolete Object	initialize_hook(4)
initialize: Object class method for	initializing a widget or object/	initialize(4)
/obsolete Object method for	initializing subpart data	initialize_hook(4)
event /dispatch timer and alternate	input event and return the next X	XtAppNextEvent(1)
/get and process one	input event of a specified type	XtAppProcessEvent(1)
XtProcessEvent: get and process one	input event of a specified type	XtProcessEvent(1)
XtCallAcceptFocus: offer the	input focus to a child widget	XtCallAcceptFocus(1)
normal/ XtRemoveGrab: redirect user	input from modal widget back to	XtRemoveGrab(1)

to obtain an/ XtConvertArgProc:	interface definition for procedure	XtConvertArgProc(2)
accept_focus()/ XtAcceptFocusProc:	interface definition for the	XtAcceptFocusProc(2)
class_initialize() method XtProc:	interface definition for the	XtProc(2)
XtWidgetClassProc:	interface definition for the/	XtWidgetClassProc(2)
expose() method XtExposeProc:	interface definition for the Core	XtExposeProc(2)
XtStringProc:	interface definition for the/	XtStringProc(2)
initialize() methods XtInitProc:	interface definition for the	XtInitProc(2)
initialize_hook() and XtArgsProc:	interface definition for the	XtArgsProc(2)
realize() method XtRealizeProc:	interface definition for the	XtRealizeProc(2)
set_values()/ XtSetValuesFunc:	interface definition for the	XtSetValuesFunc(2)
set_values_almost()/ XtAlmostProc:	interface definition for the	XtAlmostProc(2)
set_values_hook()/ XtArgsFunc:	interface definition for the	XtArgsFunc(2)
an accelerator table into its	internal representation /compile	XtParseAcceleratorTable(1)
a translation table into its	internal representation /compile	XtParseTranslationTable(1)
initialize the X Toolkit	internals XtToolkitInitialize:	XtToolkitInitialize(1)
context,/ /initialize the X Toolkit	internals, create an application	XtAppInitialize(1)
style /initialize the X Toolkit	internals, using varargs argument	XtVaAppInitialize(1)
mapping table maintained by the	Intrinsics /keysym in the keyboard	XtKeysymToKeycodeList(1)
/get the current	Intrinsics selection timeout value	XtAppGetSelectionTimeout(1)
XtAppSetSelectionTimeout: set the	Intrinsics selection timeout value	XtAppSetSelectionTimeout(1)
/get the current	Intrinsics selection timeout value	XtGetSelectionTimeout(1)
XtSetSelectionTimeout: set the	Intrinsics selection timeout value	XtSetSelectionTimeout(1)
SmeLine: menu	item separator	SmeLine(5)
XtUngrabKey: cancel a passive	key grab	XtUngrabKey(1)
XtGrabKey: passively grab a single	key of the keyboard	XtGrabKey(1)
XtSetKeyTranslator: register a	key translator	XtSetKeyTranslator(1)
passively grab a single key of the	keyboard XtGrabKey:	XtGrabKey(1)
XtGrabKeyboard: actively grab the	keyboard	XtGrabKeyboard(1)
for accepting or rejecting the	keyboard focus /Core class method	accept_focus(4)
XtUngrabKeyboard: release an active	keyboard grab	XtUngrabKeyboard(1)
XtSetKeyboardFocus: redirect	keyboard input to a widget	XtSetKeyboardFocus(1)
/map to a particular keysym in the	keyboard mapping table maintained/	XtKeysymToKeycodeList(1)
keysym in the/ /return the list of	keycodes that map to a particular	XtKeysymToKeycodeList(1)
/return a pointer to the	keycode-to-keysym mapping	XtGetKeysymTable(1)
XtKeyProc: interface definition for	keycode-to-keysym translation/	XtKeyProc(2)
XtTranslateKey: the default	keycode-to-keysym translator	XtTranslateKey(1)
/invoke the currently registered	keycode-to-keysym translator	XtTranslateKeycode(1)
and lowercase versions of a	keysym /determine uppercase	XtConvertCase(1)
XtGetActionKeysym: retrieve the	keysym and modifiers that matched/	XtGetActionKeysym(1)
keycodes that map to a particular	keysym in the keyboard mapping/ /of	XtKeysymToKeycodeList(1)
procedure to convert the case of	keysyms /interface definition for	XtCaseProc(2)
non-editable string	Label: widget to display a	Label(5)
appear in the Constraint resource	list /resources that do not	Constraint get_values_hook(4)
that do not appear in the resource	list /obtaining values of resources	get_values_hook(4)
procedure to a named callback	list XtAddCallback: add a callback	XtAddCallback(1)
procedures to a named callback	list /add an array of callback	XtAddCallbacks(1)
on a widget's named callback	list /execute the procedures	XtCallCallbacks(1)
data structure to an argument	list /values from a subpart	XtGetSubvalues(1)
the status of a widget's callback	list XtHasCallbacks: determine	XtHasCallbacks(1)
all procedures from a callback	list XtRemoveAllCallbacks: delete	XtRemoveAllCallbacks(1)
remove a callback from a callback	list XtRemoveCallback:	XtRemoveCallback(1)
a list of callbacks from a callback	list XtRemoveCallbacks: remove	XtRemoveCallbacks(1)
standard substitutions in a path	list /search for a file using	XtResolvePathname(1)

XtSetKeyboardFocus:	redirect keyboard input to a widget	XtSetKeyboardFocus(1)
widget back to/ XtRemoveGrab:	redirect user input from modal	XtRemoveGrab(1)
widget XtAddGrab: constrain or	redirect user input to a modal	XtAddGrab(1)
resources obtained/ /decrement the	reference counts for cached	XtAppReleaseCacheRefs(1)
and GraphicsExpose events into a	region /merge Expose	XtAddExposureToRegion(1)
XtRegisterCaseConverter:	register a case converter	XtRegisterCaseConverter(1)
XtSetKeyTranslator:	register a key translator	XtSetKeyTranslator(1)
converter for/ XtSetTypeConverter:	register a "new-style" type	XtSetTypeConverter(1)
converter/ XtAppSetTypeConverter:	register a "new-style" type	XtAppSetTypeConverter(1)
before any/ XtAppAddActionHook:	register a procedure to be called	XtAppAddActionHook(1)
when a specified/ XtAddTimeOut:	register a procedure to be called	XtAddTimeOut(1)
when a specified/ XtAppAddTimeOut:	register a procedure to be called	XtAppAddTimeOut(1)
when specified/ XtAddEventHandler:	register a procedure to be called	XtAddEventHandler(1)
when the event loop/ XtAddWorkProc:	register a procedure to be called	XtAddWorkProc(1)
when the event/ XtAppAddWorkProc:	register a procedure to be called	XtAppAddWorkProc(1)
when there is activity/ XtAddInput:	register a procedure to be called	XtAddInput(1)
when there is/ XtAppAddInput:	register a procedure to be called	XtAppAddInput(1)
that needs a/ XtRegisterGrabAction:	register an action procedure as one	XtRegisterGrabAction(1)
Translation Manager XtAddActions:	register an action table with the	XtAddActions(1)
Translation/ XtAppAddActions:	register an action table with the	XtAppAddActions(1)
that/ XtInsertEventHandler:	register an event handler procedure	XtInsertEventHandler(1)
that/ XtInsertRawEventHandler:	register an event handler procedure	XtInsertRawEventHandler(1)
selecting/ XtAddRawEventHandler:	register an event handler without	XtAddRawEventHandler(1)
converter XtAddConverter:	register an "old-style" resource	XtAddConverter(1)
converter XtAppAddConverter:	register an "old-style" resource	XtAppAddConverter(1)
/dispatch an event to	registered event handlers	XtDispatchEvent(1)
before or after all previously	registered event handlers /events	XtInsertEventHandler(1)
/before or after all previously	registered event handlers, without/	XtInsertRawEventHandler(1)
translator /invoke the currently	registered keycode-to-keysym	XtTranslateKeycode(1)
/Core class method for accepting or	rejecting the keyboard focus	accept_focus(4)
free read-only GCs XtDestroyGC:	Release 2 compatible function to	XtDestroyGC(1)
/callback function to	release a cached resource value	XtCallbackReleaseCacheRef(1)
/callback function to	release a list of cached values	XtCallbackReleaseCacheRefList(1)
XtUngrabKeyboard:	release an active keyboard grab	XtUngrabKeyboard(1)
XtUngrabPointer:	release an active pointer grab	XtUngrabPointer(1)
XmuReleaseStippledPixmap:	release pixmap created with/	XmuReleaseStippledPixmap(6)
list XtRemoveCallback:	remove a callback from a callback	XtRemoveCallback(1)
callback list XtRemoveCallbacks:	remove a list of callbacks from a	XtRemoveCallbacks(1)
parent/ XtUnmanageChildren:	remove a list of children from a	XtUnmanageChildren(1)
change/ XtRemoveRawEventHandler:	remove a raw event handler, or	XtRemoveRawEventHandler(1)
managed list XtUnmanageChild:	remove a widget from its parent's	XtUnmanageChild(1)
from a/ XtUninstallTranslations:	remove all existing translations	XtUninstallTranslations(1)
the/ XtRemoveEventHandler:	remove an event handler, or change	XtRemoveEventHandler(1)
XtCloseDisplay: close a display and	remove it from an application/	XtCloseDisplay(1)
XtPeekEvent: return, but do not	remove the event at the head of an/	XtPeekEvent(1)
XtAppPeekEvent: return, but do not	remove the event at the head of an/	XtAppPeekEvent(1)
accelerator table into its internal	representation /compile an	XtParseAcceleratorTable(1)
translation table into its internal	representation /compile a	XtParseTranslationTable(1)
/return property name string	represented by an AtomPtr	XmuNameOfAtom(6)
and/ /RectObj method called to	request a widget's preferred size	query_geometry(4)
geometry XtMakeGeometryRequest:	request parent to change child's	XtMakeGeometryRequest(1)
size XtMakeResizeRequest:	request parent to change child's	XtMakeResizeRequest(1)
XtGetSelectionValue:	request the value of a selection	XtGetSelectionValue(1)

procedure to be called when a/ XtAppAddTimeOut: register a .... XtAppAddTimeOut(1)
procedure to be called when the/ XtAppAddWorkProc: register a .... XtAppAddWorkProc(1)
widget at the root of a widget/ XtAppCreateShell: create a shell .... XtAppCreateShell(1)
error handler XtAppError: call the low-level .... XtAppError(1)
fatal error handler XtAppErrorMsg: call the high-level .... XtAppErrorMsg(1)
default error database XtAppGetErrorDatabase: obtain the .... XtAppGetErrorDatabase(1)
text of a named message from the/ XtAppGetErrorDatabaseText: get the .... XtAppGetErrorDatabaseText(1)
current Intrinsics selection/ XtAppGetSelectionTimeout: get the .... XtAppGetSelectionTimeout(1)
Toolkit internals, create an/ XtAppInitialize: initialize the X .... XtAppInitialize(1)
events XtAppMainLoop: continuously process .... XtAppMainLoop(1)
alternate input event and return/ XtAppNextEvent: dispatch timer and .... XtAppNextEvent(1)
remove the event at the head of an/ XtAppPeekEvent: return, but do not .... XtAppPeekEvent(1)
events are in an application's/ XtAppPending: determine whether any .... XtAppPending(1)
one input event of a specified/ XtAppProcessEvent: get and process .... XtAppProcessEvent(1)
the reference counts for cached/ XtAppReleaseCacheRefs: decrement .... XtAppReleaseCacheRefs(1)
low-level error handler procedure XtAppSetErrorHandler: set the .... XtAppSetErrorHandler(1)
high-level error handler XtAppSetErrorMsgHandler: set the .... XtAppSetErrorMsgHandler(1)
a default set of resource values XtAppSetFallbackResources: specify .... XtAppSetFallbackResources(1)
Intrinsics selection timeout value XtAppSetSelectionTimeout: set the .... XtAppSetSelectionTimeout(1)
"new-style" type converter in a/ XtAppSetTypeConverter: register a .... XtAppSetTypeConverter(1)
low-level warning handler XtAppSetWarningHandler: set the .... XtAppSetWarningHandler(1)
high-level warning handler XtAppSetWarningMsgHandler: set the .... XtAppSetWarningMsgHandler(1)
warning handler XtAppWarning: call the low-level .... XtAppWarning(1)
high-level warning handler XtAppWarningMsg: call the .... XtAppWarningMsg(1)
for the set_values_hook() method XtArgsFunc: interface definition .... XtArgsFunc(2)
for the initialize_hook() and XtArgsProc: interface definition .... XtArgsProc(2)
nondestructively merge new/ XtAugmentTranslations: .... XtAugmentTranslations(1)
widget's event mask XtBuildEventMask: retrieve a .... XtBuildEventMask(1)
focus to a child widget XtCallAcceptFocus: offer the input .... XtCallAcceptFocus(1)
a named action procedure XtCallActionProc: explicitly invoke .... XtCallActionProc(1)
function to pop up a widget XtCallbackExclusive: callback .... XtCallbackExclusive(1)
to pop up a widget XtCallbackNone: callback function .... XtCallbackNone(1)
function to pop up a widget XtCallbackNonexclusive: callback .... XtCallbackNonexclusive(1)
function to popdown a widget XtCallbackPopdown: callback .... XtCallbackPopdown(1)
definition for callback procedure XtCallbackProc: interface .... XtCallbackProc(2)
function to release a cached/ XtCallbackReleaseCacheRef: callback .... XtCallbackReleaseCacheRef(1)
callback function to release a/ XtCallbackReleaseCacheRefList: .... XtCallbackReleaseCacheRefList(1)
procedures in a callback list,/ XtCallCallbackList: execute the .... XtCallCallbackList(1)
procedures on a widget's named/ XtCallCallbacks: execute the .... XtCallCallbacks(1)
for cached resources obtained from XtCallConverter() /reference counts .... XtAppReleaseCacheRefs(1)
a "new-style" resource converter/ XtCallConverter: explicitly invoke .... XtCallConverter(1)
array and initialize its bytes to/ XtCalloc: allocate memory for an .... XtCalloc(1)
interface definition for procedure/ XtCancelConvertSelectionProc: .... XtCancelConvertSelectionProc(2)
for procedure to convert the case/ XtCaseProc: interface definition .... XtCaseProc(2)
class, if compiled with DEBUG/ XtCheckSubclass: verify an object's .... XtCheckSubclass(1)
XtClass: obtain a widget's class .... XtClass(1)
remove it from an application/ XtCloseDisplay: close a display and .... XtCloseDisplay(1)
resize widget XtConfigureWidget: move and/or .... XtConfigureWidget(1)
XtConvert: convert resource type .... XtConvert(1)
a resource converter, copying the/ XtConvertAndStore: look up and call .... XtConvertAndStore(1)
definition for procedure to obtain/ XtConvertArgProc: interface .... XtConvertArgProc(2)
and lowercase versions of a keysym XtConvertCase: determine uppercase .... XtConvertCase(1)
for old-style resource converter XtConverter: interface definition .... XtConverter(2)

values from a subpart data/ XtGetSubvalues: copy resource .... XtGetSubvalues(1)

values XtGetValues: query widget resource .... XtGetValues(1)

single pointer button XtGrabButton: passively grab a .... XtGrabButton(1)

key of the keyboard XtGrabKey: passively grab a single .... XtGrabKey(1)

keyboard XtGrabKeyboard: actively grab the .... XtGrabKeyboard(1)

pointer XtGrabPointer: actively grab the .... XtGrabPointer(1)

status of a widget's callback list XtHasCallbacks: determine the .... XtHasCallbacks(1)

and display XtInitialize: initialize toolkit .... XtInitialize(1)

a widget class without creating/ XtInitializeWidgetClass: initialize .... XtInitializeWidgetClass(1)

for the initialize() methods XtInitProc: interface definition .... XtInitProc(2)

definition for procedure to handle/ XtInputCallbackProc: interface .... XtInputCallbackProc(2)

event handler procedure that/ XtInsertEventHandler: register an .... XtInsertEventHandler(1)

an event handler procedure that/ XtInsertRawEventHandler: register .... XtInsertRawEventHandler(1)

widget's accelerators on another/ XtInstallAccelerators: install a .... XtInstallAccelerators(1)

all accelerators from a widget and/ XtInstallAllAccelerators: install .... XtInstallAllAccelerators(1)

a widget is a subclass of the/ XtIsApplicationShell: test whether .... XtIsApplicationShell(1)

widget is a subclass of the/ XtIsComposite: test whether a .... XtIsComposite(1)

widget is a subclass of the/ XtIsConstraint: test whether a .... XtIsConstraint(1)

widget is managed by its parent XtIsManaged: determine whether a .... XtIsManaged(1)

is a subclass of the Object widget/ XtIsObject: test whether a widget .... XtIsObject(1)

widget is a subclass of the/ XtIsOverrideShell: test whether a .... XtIsOverrideShell(1)

widget has been realized XtIsRealized: determine whether a .... XtIsRealized(1)

is a subclass of the RectObj/ XtIsRectObj: test whether a widget .... XtIsRectObj(1)

sensitivity state of a widget XtIsSensitive: check the current .... XtIsSensitive(1)

a subclass of the Shell widget/ XtIsShell: test whether a widget is .... XtIsShell(1)

widget is a subclass of a class XtIsSubclass: determine whether a .... XtIsSubclass(1)

widget is a subclass of the/ XtIsTopLevelShell: test whether a .... XtIsTopLevelShell(1)

widget is a subclass of the/ XtIsTransientShell: test whether a .... XtIsTransientShell(1)

widget is a subclass of the/ XtIsVendorShell: test whether a .... XtIsVendorShell(1)

is a subclass of the Core widget/ XtIsWidget: test whether a widget .... XtIsWidget(1)

is a subclass of the WMShell/ XtIsWMShell: test whether a widget .... XtIsWMShell(1)

keycode-to-keysym translation/ XtKeyProc: interface definition for .... XtKeyProc(2)

list of keycodes that map to a/ XtKeysymToKeycodeList: return the .... XtKeysymToKeycodeList(1)

the timestamp from the most recent/ XtLastTimestampProcessed: retrieve .... XtLastTimestampProcessed(1)

definition for a procedure called/ XtLoseSelectionIncrProc: interface .... XtLoseSelectionIncrProc(2)

definition for procedure to notify/ XtLoseSelectionProc: interface .... XtLoseSelectionProc(2)

events XtMainLoop: continuously process .... XtMainLoop(1)

parent to change child's geometry XtMakeGeometryRequest: request .... XtMakeGeometryRequest(1)

to change child's size XtMakeResizeRequest: request parent .... XtMakeResizeRequest(1)

XtMalloc: allocate memory .... XtMalloc(1)

its parent's geometry management XtManageChild: bring a widget under .... XtManageChild(1)

widgets under their parent's/ XtManageChildren: bring an array of .... XtManageChildren(1)

display XtMapWidget: map a widget to its .... XtMapWidget(1)

popping down a widget XtMenuPopdown: built-in action for .... XtMenuPopdown(1)

popping up a widget XtMenuPopup: built-in action for .... XtMenuPopup(1)

arrays XtMergeArgLists: merge two ArgList .... XtMergeArgLists(1)

its parent XtMoveWidget: move a widget within .... XtMoveWidget(1)

instance name of the specified/ XtName: return a pointer to the .... XtName(1)

XtNameToWidget: find a named widget .... XtNameToWidget(1)

/interface definition for an XtNcreatePopupChildProc procedure .... XtCreatePopupChildProc(2)

instance of a data type XtNew: allocate storage for one .... XtNew(1)

string XtNewString: copy an instance of a .... XtNewString(1)

input queue XtNextEvent: return next event from .... XtNextEvent(1)

Section 1

Intrinsics Functions and Macros

This section contains alphabetically-organized reference pages for each Intrinsics function and macro. Some are used by application programmers, some by widget writers, and some by both.

The first reference page, Introduction, explains the format and contents of each of the following pages.

In This Section:

☞

XtDisplay	XtIsWMShell	XtResolvePathname
XtDisplayInitialize	XtIsWidget	XtScreen
XtDisplayOfObject	XtKeysymToKeycodeList	XtScreenDatabase
XtDisplayStringConversionWarning	XtLastTimestampProcessed	XtScreenOfObject
XtDisplayToApplicationContext	XtMainLoop	XtSetArg
XtError	XtMakeGeometryRequest	XtSetErrorHandler
XtErrorMsg	XtMakeResizeRequest	XtSetErrorMsgHandler
XtFindFile	XtMalloc	XtSetKeyTranslator
XtFree	XtManageChild	XtSetKeyboardFocus
XtGetActionKeysym	XtManageChildren	XtSetLanguageProc
XtGetActionList	XtMapWidget	XtSetMappedWhenManaged
XtGetApplicationNameAndClass	XtMenuPopdown	XtSetMultiClickTime
XtGetApplicationResources	XtMenuPopup	XtSetSelectionTimeout
XtGetConstraintResourceList	XtMergeArgLists	XtSetSensitive
XtGetErrorDatabase	XtMoveWidget	XtSetSubvalues
XtGetErrorDatabaseText	XtName	XtSetTypeConverter
XtGetGC	XtNameToWidget	XtSetValues
XtGetKeysymTable	XtNew	XtSetWMColormapWindows
XtGetMultiClickTime	XtNewString	XtSetWarningHandler
XtGetResourceList	XtNextEvent	XtSetWarningMsgHandler
XtGetSelectionRequest	XtNumber	XtStringConversionWarning
XtGetSelectionTimeout	XtOffset	XtSuperclass
XtGetSelectionValue	XtOffsetOf	XtToolkitInitialize
XtGetSelectionValueIncremental	XtOpenDisplay	XtTranslateCoords
XtGetSelectionValues	XtOverrideTranslations	XtTranslateKey
XtGetSelectionValuesIncremental	XtOwnSelection	XtTranslateKeycode
XtGetSubresources	XtOwnSelectionIncremental	XtUngrabButton
XtGetSubvalues	XtParent	XtUngrabKey
XtGetValues	XtParseAcceleratorTable	XtUngrabKeyboard
XtGrabButton	XtParseTranslationTable	XtUngrabPointer
XtGrabKey	XtPeekEvent	XtUninstallTranslations
XtGrabKeyboard	XtPending	XtUnmanageChild
XtGrabPointer	XtPopdown	XtUnmanageChildren
XtHasCallbacks	XtPopup	XtUnmapWidget
XtInitialize	XtPopupSpringLoaded	XtUnrealizeWidget
XtInitializeWidgetClass	XtProcessEvent	XtVaAppCreateShell
XtInsertEventHandler	XtQueryGeometry	XtVaAppInitialize
XtInsertRawEventHandler	XtRealizeWidget	XtVaCreateArgsList
XtInstallAccelerators	XtRealloc	XtVaCreateManagedWidget
XtInstallAllAccelerators	XtRegisterCaseConverter	XtVaCreatePopupShell
XtIsApplicationShell	XtRegisterGrabAction	XtVaCreateWidget
XtIsComposite	XtReleaseGC	XtVaGetApplicationResources
XtIsConstraint	XtRemoveActionHook	XtVaGetSubresources
XtIsManaged	XtRemoveAllCallbacks	XtVaGetSubvalues
XtIsObject	XtRemoveCallback	XtVaGetValues
XtIsOverrideShell	XtRemoveCallbacks	XtVaSetSubvalues
XtIsRealized	XtRemoveEventHandler	XtVaSetValues
XtIsRectObj	XtRemoveGrab	XtWarning
XtIsSensitive	XtRemoveInput	XtWarningMsg
XtIsShell	XtRemoveRawEventHandler	XtWidgetToApplicationContext
XtIsSubclass	XtRemoveTimeOut	XtWindow
XtIsTopLevelShell	XtRemoveWorkProc	XtWindowOfObject
XtIsTransientShell	XtResizeWidget	XtWindowToWidget
XtIsVendorShell	XtResizeWindow	

This page describes the format and contents of each reference page in Section 1, which covers the Xt Intrinsics functions and macros.

Name

Function – a brief description of the function.

Synopsis

This section shows the signature of the function: the names and types of the arguments, and the type of the return value. The header *<X11/Intrinsic.h>* declares all of the public Intrinsics functions and macros.

Inputs

This subsection describes each of the function arguments that pass information to the function.

Outputs

This subsection describes any of the function arguments that are used to return information from the function. These arguments are always of some pointer type, so you should use the C address-of operator (**&**) to pass the address of the variable in which the function will store the return value. The names of these arguments are usually suffixed with _return to indicate that values are returned in them. Some arguments both supply and return a value; they will be listed in this section and in the "Inputs" section above. Finally, note that because the list of function arguments is broken into "Input" and "Output" sections, they do not always appear in the same order that they are passed to the function. See the function signature for the actual calling order.

Returns

This subsection explains the return value of the function, if any.

Availability

This section appears for functions that were added in Release 4 or Release 5, and also for functions that are now superseded by other, preferred, functions.

Description

This section explains what the function does and describes its arguments and return value. If you've used the function before and are just looking for a refresher, this section and the synopsis above should be all you need.

Usage

This section appears for most functions and provides less formal information about the function: when and how you might want to use it, things to watch out for, and related functions that you might want to consider.

Example

This section appears for some of the most commonly used Xt functions, and provides an example of their use.

Background

This section presents detailed technical material related to the function. It is usually derived directly from the Xt specification, and is therefore definitive. You should not often have to refer to this section, but the material here is necessary for a complete understanding of the workings of the Intrinsics.

Algorithm

This section explains the details of the algorithm followed by some of the Intrinsics functions. Like the material in the "Background" section, it is very technical and generally derived directly from the specification.

Structures

This section shows the definition of any structures, enumerated types, typedefs, or symbolic constants used by the function.

See Also

This section refers you to related functions, prototype procedures, Intrinsics widget classes, or widget methods. The numbers in parenthesis following each reference refer to the sections of this book in which they are found.

XtAddActions

Name

XtAddActions – register an action table with the Translation Manager.

Synopsis

```
void XtAddActions(actions, num_actions)
    XtActionList actions;
    Cardinal num_actions;
```

Inputs

actions   Specifies the action table to register.

num_actions Specifies the number of entries in this action table.

Availability

Superseded by XtAppAddActions().

Description

XtAddActions() registers *actions*, an array of *num_actions* XtActionsRec structures with the Translation Manager. Each element of the array contains an action name and an action procedure pointer. When a named action is invoked through a translation table, the procedure to be called is looked up in the action tables that have been registered.

Usage

XtAddActions() has been superseded by XtAppAddActions(), which performs the same function on a per-application context basis. XtAddActions() now calls XtAppAdd-Actions() passing the default application context created by XtInitialize(). Very few programs need multiple application contexts, and you can continue to use XtAdd-Actions() if you initialize your application with XtInitialize(). We recommend, however, that you use XtAppInitialize(), XtAppAddActions(), and the other Xt-App*() application context specific functions.

See XtAppAddActions() for more information about how to use actions.

See Also

XtAppAddActions(1),
XtActionProc(2).

Xt Functions and Macros

Name

XtAddCallback – add a callback procedure to a named callback list.

Synopsis

```
void XtAddCallback(object, callback_name, callback, client_data)
    Widget object;
    String callback_name;
    XtCallbackProc callback;
    XtPointer client_data;
```

Inputs

object   Specifies the object which owns the callback list; may be of class Object or any subclass thereof.

callback_name
             Specifies the resource name of the callback list to which the procedure is to be added.

callback   Specifies the procedure to be added.

client_data Specifies data to be passed to *callback* when it is invoked, or NULL.

Description

XtAddCallback() adds the procedure *callback* and the data *client_data* to the callback list named by *callback_name* in the widget or object *object*. If the procedure already appears on the list, with the same or with different data, it will be added to the list again, and when the callback list is invoked, the procedure will be called as many times as it has been added.

The *callback* procedure must be of type XtCallbackProc. This procedure type expects three arguments and does not return anything. The arguments are the widget or object that caused the callback to be invoked, the untyped data (*client_data*) that was registered with the procedure, and another untyped argument, *call_data* which generally points to a structure which contains data particular to the callback list and object class. See XtCallback-Proc(2).

Usage

The order that callback procedures are invoked in is, unfortunately, not specified by the Xt Intrinsics. If you have several operations that must be executed in a particular order, you should not register them as separate callbacks. Instead you should register a single callback that invokes each of the operations sequentially.

If you want to register several callback procedures at the same time, you can use XtAdd-Callbacks(). Callbacks can also be set on a callback list by specifying a XtCallback-List as a resource when the widget is created. A callback list should not be set with XtSet-Values() once a widget is created, however, because this replaces the entire list of procedures rather than simply adding new procedures to the list. The Intrinsics do not define a String-to-XtCallbackList converter, but if you write one and use it in your application, then you can also specify callbacks from a resource file. Finally, note that callback lists in a widget are compiled into an internal form by the Intrinsics, so attempting to examine a callback list with `XtGetValues()` will not work.

Background

Generally speaking, a widget expecting to interact with an application will declare one or more callback lists as resources; the application adds functions to these callback lists, which will be invoked whenever the predefined callback conditions are met. Callback lists have resource names, so that the application can add and remove functions to a callback list by name.

Callbacks are not necessarily invoked in response to any event; a widget can call the specified routines at any arbitrary point in its code, whenever it wants to provide a "hook" for application interaction. For example, all widgets provide an `XtNdestroyCallback` resource to allow applications to interpose a routine to be executed when the widget is destroyed.

Widgets can define additional callback lists as they see fit. For example, the Athena Command widget defines the `XtNcallback` callback list to notify clients when the widget has been activated (by the user clicking on it with the pointer). (This is actually a poor choice of names. It should have been given a more specific name, such as `XtNnotifyCallback`.)

Callbacks differ from actions in the way that the registered function is invoked. For callbacks, the trigger is an abstract occurrence defined by the widget, which may or may not be event-related. The routines on a widget's callback lists are invoked by the widget code, using a call to `XtCallCallbacks()`. Actions, on the other hand, are invoked directly by Xt, as the result of an event combination specified by the translations mechanism.

See Also

XtAddCallbacks(1), *XtCallCallbacks*(1), *XtRemoveAllCallbacks*(1), *XtRemoveCallback*(1), *XtRemove-Callbacks*(1),
XtCallbackProc(2).

Xt Functions and Macros

Name

XtAddCallbacks – add an array of callback procedures to a named callback list.

Synopsis

```
void XtAddCallbacks(object, callback_name, callbacks)
    Widget object;
    String callback_name;
    XtCallbackList callbacks;
```

Inputs

object   Specifies the object which owns the callback list; may be of class Object or any subclass thereof.

callback_name

Specifies the resource name of the callback list to which the procedures are to be added.

callbacks   Specifies a NULL-terminated array of callback procedures and corresponding client data.

Description

XtAddCallbacks() adds the procedure/data pairs specified in *callbacks* to the callback list named *callback_name* in the widget or object *object*. Each element of *callbacks* is a structure of type XtCallbackRec and contains a pointer to a callback procedure and the data to be registered with and passed to that procedure. Because XtAddCallbacks() does not have an argument that specifies the length of this array, the last element of the array must contain NULL in both of its fields.

A procedure may appear multiple times in the *callbacks* array, and may be added to a callback list more than once, with different or even with the same data. When the callback list is invoked, each procedure will be called as many times as it appears on the list.

Each procedure to be added to the callback list must be of type XtCallbackProc. This procedure type expects three arguments and does not return anything. The arguments are the widget or object that caused the callback to be invoked, the untyped data that was registered with the procedure, and another untyped argument, *call_data* which generally points to a structure which contains data particular to the callback list and object class. See Xt-CallbackProc(2).

Usage

The order that callback procedures are invoked in is, unfortunately, not specified by the Xt Intrinsics. If you have several operations that must be executed in a particular order, you should not register them as separate callbacks. Instead you should register a single callback that invokes each of the operations sequentially.

If you want to register only a single callback procedure, XtAddCallback() is easier to use. You may find this function easier even if you are registering several functions, because it does not require you to declare and initialize an array of XtCallbackRec.

Callbacks can also be set on a callback list by specifying a `XtCallbackList` as a resource when the widget is created. A callback list should not be set with `XtSetValues()` once a widget is created, however, because this replaces the entire list of procedures rather than simply adding new procedures to the list. The Intrinsics do not define a String-to-XtCallbackList converter, but if you write one and use it in your application, then you can also specify callbacks from a resource file. Finally, note that callback lists in a widget are compiled into an internal form by the Intrinsics, so attempting to examine a callback list with `XtGetValues()` will not work.

Background

Generally speaking, a widget expecting to interact with an application will declare one or more callback lists as resources; the application adds functions to these callback lists, which will be invoked whenever the predefined callback conditions are met. Callback lists have resource names, so that the application can add and remove functions to a callback list by name.

Callbacks are not necessarily invoked in response to any event; a widget can call the specified routines at any arbitrary point in its code, whenever it wants to provide a "hook" for application interaction. For example, all widgets provide an `XtNdestroyCallback` resource to allow applications to interpose a routine to be executed when the widget is destroyed.

Widgets can define additional callback lists as they see fit. For example, the Athena Command widget defines the `XtNcallback` callback list to notify clients when the widget has been activated (by the user clicking on it with the pointer). (This is actually a poor choice of names. It should have been given a more specific name, such as `XtNnotifyCallback`.)

Callbacks differ from actions in the way that the registered function is invoked. For callbacks, the trigger is an abstract occurrence defined by the widget, which may or may not be event-related. The routines on a widget's callback lists are invoked by the widget code, using a call to `XtCallCallbacks()`. Actions, on the other hand, are invoked directly by Xt, as the result of an event combination specified by the translations mechanism.

Example

When calling `XtAddCallbacks()`, you will generally use a statically initialized array like the following:

```
XtCallbackRec button_callback_list[] = {
    {dispatch_function, (XtPointer) 1},
    {dispatch_function, (XtPointer) 2},
    {do_something_else, NULL},
    {(XtCallbackProc) NULL, (XtPointer) NULL},
};
```

Structures

```
typedef struct _XtCallbackRec {
    XtCallbackProc  callback;
    XtPointer       closure;
} XtCallbackRec, *XtCallbackList;
```

See Also
    XtAddCallback(1), *XtCallCallbacks*(1), *XtRemoveAllCallbacks*(1), *XtRemoveCallback*(1), *XtRemove-*
    Callbacks(1),
    XtCallbackProc(2).

Name

XtAddConverter – register an "old-style" resource converter.

Synopsis

```
void XtAddConverter(from_type, to_type, converter, convert_args, num_args)
    String from_type;
    String to_type;
    XtConverter converter;
    XtConvertArgList convert_args;
    Cardinal num_args;
```

Inputs

from_type   Specifies the resource name of the datatype that the converter converts from.

to_type   Specifies the resource name of the datatype that the converter converts to.

converter   Specifies the converter procedure. See XtConverter(2).

convert_args

    Specifies how to obtain any additional arguments needed for the conversion.

num_args   Specifies the number elements in *convert_args*.

Availability

Superseded by XtAppAddConverter().

Description

XtAddConverter() registers *converter* as a procedure to convert data of resource type *from_type* to resource type *to_type*. The *convert_args* array is registered with the converter, and will be used to obtain arguments to pass to the converter each time it is invoked.

Usage

XtAddConverter() has been superseded by XtAppAddConverter(), which allows the registration of converter functions on a per-application context basis. XtAddConverter() now calls XtAppAddConverter() passing the default application context created by Xt-Initialize(). Very few programs need multiple application contexts, and you can continue to use XtAddConverter() if you initialize your application with Xt-Initialize(). We recommend, however, that you use XtAppInitialize(), XtApp-AddConverter(), and the other XtApp*() application context specific functions.

See XtAppAddConverter() for more information about converters and the XtConvert-ArgList data type.

XtAddConverter() and XtAppAddConverter() register "old-style" converters which are still in common use, but are not as flexible as the (incompatible) "new-style" converters added in Release 4. If you must register an existing old-style converter, use XtAppAdd-Converter(), but if you are writing a converter of your own, consider using a new-style converter. See XtAppSetTypeConverter().

See Also

XtAppAddConverter(1), *XtAppSetTypeConverter*(1), *XtSetTypeConverter*(1),
XtConverter(2), *XtTypeConverter*(2).

XtAddEventHandler

Name

XtAddEventHandler – register a procedure to be called when specified events occur on a widget.

Synopsis

```
void XtAddEventHandler(w, event_mask, nonmaskable, proc, client_data)
    Widget w;
    EventMask event_mask;
    Boolean nonmaskable;
    XtEventHandler proc;
    XtPointer client_data;
```

Inputs

w	Specifies the widget for which this event handler is being registered. Must be of class Core or any subclass thereof.
event_mask	Specifies the event type that will trigger the handler.
nonmaskable	Specifies whether this procedure should be called on nonmaskable event types.
proc	Specifies the handler procedure.
client_data	Specifies additional data to be passed to the event handler.

Description

XtAddEventHandler() registers the procedure *proc* and the data *client_data* with the Intrinsics event dispatching mechanism. When an event of one of the types set in *event_mask* occurs on the window of the widget *w*, *proc* will be invoked and *client_data* passed as one of its arguments. If the window of the widget is not already receiving events of the specified types, XtAddEventHandler() calls XSelectInput() to ensure that they will be delivered. Additionally, if the handler is registered with the *nonmaskable* argument True, then it will also be invoked when any of the nonmaskable event types occur. These events are GraphicsExpose, NoExpose, SelectionClear, SelectionRequest, SelectionNotify, ClientMessage, and MappingNotify. Ordinarily, nonmaskable events are of interest only to the Intrinsics.

If the specified procedure/data pair has already been registered for this widget, then the *event_mask* argument augments the event mask already registered for the handler, and the procedure will only be called once for any particular event. The same procedure may be registered multiple times with different values of *client_data*, and each instance will be treated as a separate handler.

See XtEventHandler(2) for an explanation of how to write an event handler procedure.

Usage

Neither applications nor widgets often need to use event handlers. Using action procedures and translation tables provides a more flexible way to respond to input events.

Xt Functions and Macros (side tab)

The Intrinsics do not specify the order in which event handlers will be called when an event arrives. As of Release 4, however, the function `XtInsertEventHandler()` will register an event handler that will be called before or after all *previously* registered handlers.

An event handler can be removed with `XtRemoveEventHandler()`.

Structures

Each of the event mask symbols listed in the table below set a single bit in an event mask. The *event_mask* argument is formed by combining these symbols with the bitwise OR operator (|). Note that the nonmaskable event types do not appear in this table and cannot be requested in an event mask.

NoEventMask	Button1MotionMask	StructureNotifyMask
KeyPressMask	Button2MotionMask	ResizeRedirectMask
KeyReleaseMask	Button3MotionMask	SubstructureNotifyMask
ButtonPressMask	Button4MotionMask	SubstructureRedirectMask
ButtonReleaseMask	Button5MotionMask	FocusChangeMask
EnterWindowMask	ButtonMotionMask	PropertyChangeMask
LeaveWindowMask	KeymapStateMask	ColormapChangeMask
PointerMotionMask	ExposureMask	OwnerGrabButtonMask
PointerMotionHintMask	VisibilityChangeMask	

See Appendix C, *Event Reference*, for more information on event types and masks.

See Also

XtAddRawEventHandler(1), *XtInsertEventHandler*(1), *XtRemoveEventHandler*(1), *XtEventHandler*(2).

XtAddExposureToRegion

XtAddExposureToRegion — merge `Expose` and `GraphicsExpose` events into a region.

Synopsis

```
void XtAddExposureToRegion(event, region)
    XEvent *event;
    Region region;
```

Inputs

event   Specifies a pointer to a `Expose` or `GraphicsExpose` event.

region   Specifies a region to be added to.

Outputs

region   Returns the specified region merged with the rectangle of the expose event.

Description

`XtAddExposureToRegion()` computes the union of the exposed rectangle specified by *event* and the region specified by *region* and stores the results back into *region*. If the *event* argument is not an `Expose` or `GraphicsExpose` event, `XtAddExposureTo-Region()` returns without an error and without modifying *region*.

Usage

This is a utility function that allows the caller to merge expose events into a region that can be processed all at once instead of as a series of individual rectangles. It is used by the Intrinsics exposure compression mechanism, and could be of use within event handlers, action procedures, or a widget's `expose()` method.

Structures

`Region` is a pointer to an opaque type.

See Also

expose(4).

XtAddGrab

Name

XtAddGrab – constrain or redirect user input to a modal widget.

Synopsis

```
void XtAddGrab(w, exclusive, spring_loaded)
    Widget w;
    Boolean exclusive;
    Boolean spring_loaded;
```

Inputs

w
Specifies the widget that is to be made modal. Must be of class Core or any subclass thereof.

exclusive
Specifies whether user events should be dispatched exclusively to this widget or also to modal parent widgets.

spring_loaded
Specifies whether this widget was popped up because the user pressed a pointer button.

Description

XtAddGrab() makes a widget *modal*. When a modal widget exists, XtDispatchEvent() will not deliver events that occur outside of the modal widget (unless, perhaps, they occur in the modal widget's modal parent) or will redirect events that occur outside of the modal widget to the modal widget.

A modal popup dialog box may itself have popup children, and a popup menu may have sub-menus that popup. A modal widget and all of its descendants are referred to as the *modal cascade*. If the *exclusive* argument to XtAddGrab() is True, then events should be delivered only to the specified widget, not to any previous widgets in the modal cascade. If it is False, then events will be delivered to the specified widget and any ancestors in the modal cascade until one is found that has *exclusive* True.

Some popups (menus, for example) popup when the user presses a mouse button, and must pop down when the user releases that button, even if it is released outside of the popup. This sort of popup should call XtAddGrab() with the *spring_loaded* argument set to True. XtDispatchEvent() will dispatch key and button events to a spring-loaded popup regardless of where those events occur in the application. Note that if *spring_loaded* is True, then *exclusive* must also be True.

Usage

You do not often need to call XtAddGrab() explicitly. XtPopup() will pop up a dialog box and call XtAddGrab() appropriately, and the predefined callback procedures XtCallbackExclusive(), XtCallbackNone(), and XtCallbackNonexclusive() will do the same and are suitable for registering on widget callback lists. The predefined action named XtMenuPopup will pop up a spring-loaded widget and can be called directly from a translation table.

If you call `XtAddGrab()` then you should call `XtRemoveGrab()` when you are done with your modal widget.

Note that `XtAddGrab()` does not issue an X button or key grab as `XtGrabButton()` and `XtGrabKey()` do (although there is a button grab implicitly made while any mouse button is held down over a popup menu, for example). Its name refers to the fact that it uses event remapping to simulate the effect of a grab without locking out input to other applications running on the same display.

Background

Modal widgets are widgets that, except for the input directed to them, lock out user input to the application.

When a modal menu or modal dialog box is popped up using `XtPopup()`, user events (keyboard and pointer events) that occur outside the modal widget should be delivered to the modal widget or ignored. In no case will user events be delivered to a widget outside the modal widget.

Menus can pop up submenus, and dialog boxes can pop up further dialog boxes, to create a popup cascade. In this case, user events may be delivered to one of several modal widgets in the cascade.

Display-related events should be delivered outside the modal cascade so that exposure events and the like keep the application's display up-to-date. Any event that occurs within the cascade is delivered as usual. The user events delivered to the most recent spring-loaded shell in the cascade when they occur outside the cascade are called remap events and are `KeyPress`, `KeyRelease`, `ButtonPress`, and `ButtonRelease`. The user events ignored when they occur outside the cascade are `MotionNotify` and `EnterNotify`. All other events are delivered normally. In particular, note that this is one way in which widgets can receive `LeaveNotify` events without first receiving `EnterNotify` events; they should be prepared to deal with this, typically by ignoring any unmatched `LeaveNotify` events.

`XtAddGrab()` appends the widget to the modal cascade and checks that *exclusive* is `True` if *spring_loaded* is `True`. If this condition is not met, `XtAddGrab()` generates a warning message.

The modal cascade is used by `XtDispatchEvent()` when it tries to dispatch a user event. When at least one modal widget is in the widget cascade, `XtDispatchEvent()` first determines if the event should be delivered. It starts at the most recent cascade entry and follows the cascade up to and including the most recent cascade entry added with the *exclusive* parameter `True`.

This subset of the modal cascade along with all descendants of these widgets comprise the active subset. User events that occur outside the widgets in this subset are ignored or remapped. Modal menus with submenus generally add a submenu widget to the cascade with *exclusive* `False`. Modal dialog boxes that need to restrict user input to the most deeply nested dialog box add a subdialog widget to the cascade with *exclusive* `True`. User events that occur within the active subset are delivered to the appropriate widget, which is usually a child or further descendant of the modal widget.

Regardless of where in the application they occur, remap events are always delivered to the most recent widget in the active subset of the cascade registered with `spring_loaded` `True`, if any such widget exists. If the event occurred in the active subset of the cascade but outside the spring-loaded widget, it is delivered normally before being delivered also to the spring-loaded widget. Regardless of where it is dispatched, the Intrinsics do not modify the contents of the event.

See Also

XtCallbackExclusive(1), *XtCallbackNone*(1), *XtCallbackNonexclusive*(1), *XtCallbackPopdown*(1), *Xt-CreatePopupShell*(1), *XtDispatchEvent*(1), *XtMenuPopup*(1), *XtPopdown*(1), *XtPopup*(1), *XtRemove-Grab*(1).

XtAddInput

Name

XtAddInput – register a procedure to be called when there is activity on a file descriptor.

Synopsis

```
XtInputId XtAddInput(source, condition, proc, client_data)
    int source;
    XtPointer condition;
    XtInputCallbackProc proc;
    XtPointer client_data;
```

Inputs

source   Specifies the file descriptor (on a POSIX-based system) to monitor.

condition   Specifies a mask that indicates a read, write, or exception condition or some operating-system-dependent condition.

proc   Specifies the procedure that is to be called when *condition* occurs on *source*.

client_data Specifies data to be passed to *proc* when it is invoked.

Returns

A handle of type XtInputId that can be passed to XtRemoveInput() to unregister this input procedure.

Availability

Superseded by XtAppAddInput().

Description

XtAddInput() registers a file descriptor *source* to be monitored by XtAppNext-Event() and a procedure *proc* to be called with data *client_data* when the condition (such as "input ready" or "error") *condition* arises.

On a POSIX-based system, the supported values for *condition* are XtInputReadMask, XtInputWriteMask, or XtInputExceptMask. These values cannot be ORed together.

Usage

XtAddInput() has been superseded by XtAppAddInput(), which performs the same function on a per-application context basis. XtAddInput() now calls XtAppAddInput() passing the default application context created by XtInitialize(). Very few programs need multiple application contexts, and you can continue to use XtAddInput() if you initialize your application with XtInitialize(). We recommend, however, that you use Xt-AppInitialize(), XtAppAddInput(), and the other XtApp*() application context specific functions.

See XtAppAddInput() for more information.

See Also

XtAppAddInput(1), *XtRemoveInput*(1),
XtInputCallbackProc(2).

Name

XtAddRawEventHandler – register an event handler without selecting for the event.

Synopsis

```
void XtAddRawEventHandler(w, event_mask, nonmaskable, proc, client_data)
    Widget w;
    EventMask event_mask;
    Boolean nonmaskable;
    XtEventHandler proc;
    XtPointer client_data;
```

Inputs

w   Specifies the widget for which this event handler is being registered. Must be of class Core or any subclass thereof.

event_mask   Specifies the event type that will trigger the handler.

nonmaskable Specifies whether this procedure should be called on nonmaskable event types.

proc   Specifies the handler procedure.

client_data Specifies additional data to be passed to the event handler.

Description

XtAddRawEventHandler() registers the procedure *proc* and the data *client_data* with the Intrinsics event dispatching mechanism. When an event of one of the types set in *event_mask* occurs on the window of the widget *w*, *proc* will be invoked and *client_data* passed as one of its arguments. Additionally, if the handler is registered with the *nonmaskable* argument True, then it will also be invoked when any of the nonmaskable event types occur. These events are GraphicsExpose, NoExpose, SelectionClear, SelectionRequest, SelectionNotify, ClientMessage, and MappingNotify. Ordinarily, nonmaskable events are of interest only to the Intrinsics.

XtAddRawEventHandler() is similar to XtAddEventHandler() except that it never causes an XSelectInput() call to be made for its events. The event mask in XtAddRawEventHandler() indicates which events the handler will be called in response to, but only when these events are selected elsewhere.

If the specified procedure/data pair has already been registered for this widget, then the *event_mask* argument augments the event mask already registered for the handler, and the procedure will only be called once for any particular event. The same procedure may be registered multiple times with different values of *client_data*, and each instance will be treated as a separate handler.

See XtEventHandler(2) for an explanation of how to write an event handler procedure.

Usage

You rarely need to register a raw event handler. XtAddEventHandler is sufficient in most cases. In particular, you do not need to use raw event handlers to avoid redundant calls to

XSelectInput(). The Intrinsics keep track of the event mask of each widget and calls XSelectInput() only when necessary.

The Intrinsics do not specify the order in which event handlers will be called when an event arrives. As of Release 4, however, the function XtInsertRawEventHandler() will register a raw event handler that will be called before or after all *previously* registered handlers.

Raw event handlers are removed with a call to XtRemoveRawEventHandler().

Structures

Each of the event types listed in the table below set a single bit in an event mask. The *event_mask* argument is formed by combining these symbols with the bitwise OR operator (|). Note that the nonmaskable event types do not appear in this table and cannot be requested in an event mask.

NoEventMask	Button1MotionMask	StructureNotifyMask
KeyPressMask	Button2MotionMask	ResizeRedirectMask
KeyReleaseMask	Button3MotionMask	SubstructureNotifyMask
ButtonPressMask	Button4MotionMask	SubstructureRedirectMask
ButtonReleaseMask	Button5MotionMask	FocusChangeMask
EnterWindowMask	ButtonMotionMask	PropertyChangeMask
LeaveWindowMask	KeymapStateMask	ColormapChangeMask
PointerMotionMask	ExposureMask	OwnerGrabButtonMask
PointerMotionHintMask	VisibilityChangeMask	

See Appendix C, *Event Reference*, for more information on event types and masks.

See Also

XtAddEventHandler(1), *XtInsertRawEventHandler*(1), *XtRemoveRawEventHandler*(1), *XtEventHandler*(2).

Name

XtAddTimeOut – register a procedure to be called when a specified time elapses.

Synopsis

```
XtIntervalId XtAddTimeOut(interval, proc, client_data)
    unsigned long interval;
    XtTimerCallbackProc proc;
    XtPointer client_data;
```

Inputs

interval   Specifies the time interval in milliseconds.

proc   Specifies the procedure to be called when the time expires.

client_data Specifies data to be passed to *proc* when it is called.

Returns

A handle of type `XtIntervalId` that can be used to unregister the timeout procedure with `XtRemoveTimeOut()`.

Availability

Superseded by `XtAppAddTimeOut()`.

Description

`XtAddTimeOut()` registers a procedure *proc*, to be called by `XtAppNextEvent()` with *client_data* after *interval* milliseconds elapse. The procedure is called once and automatically unregistered; it will not be called repeatedly every *interval* milliseconds.

Usage

`XtAddTimeOut()` has been superseded by `XtAppAddTimeOut()`, which performs the same function on a per-application context basis. `XtAddTimeOut()` now calls `XtAppAddTimeOut()` passing the default application context created by `XtInitialize()`. Very few programs need multiple application contexts, and you can continue to use `XtAddTimeOut()` if you initialize your application with `XtInitialize()`. We recommend, however, that you use `XtAppInitialize()`, `XtAppAddTimeOut()`, and the other `XtApp*()` application context specific functions.

See `XtAppAddTimeOut()` for more information.

See Also

XtAppAddTimeOut(1), *XtAppNextEvent*(1), *XtRemoveTimeOut*(1),
XtTimerCallbackProc(2).

XtAddWorkProc

Name

XtAddWorkProc – register a procedure to be called when the event loop is idle.

Synopsis

```
XtWorkProcId XtAddWorkProc(proc, client_data)
    XtWorkProc proc;
    XtPointer client_data;
```

Inputs

proc   Specifies the procedure to be called when the application is idle.

client_data Specifies data to be passed to *proc* when it is called.

Returns

A handle of type XtWorkProcId that can be passed to XtRemoveWorkProc() to unregister the work procedure.

Availability

Superseded by XtAppAddWorkProc().

Description

XtAddWorkProc() registers the procedure *proc* and the data *client_data* to be called by XtAppNextEvent() when there are no pending input events and it would otherwise block.

Usage

XtAddWorkProc() has been superseded by XtAppAddWorkProc(), which performs the same function on a per-application context basis. XtAddWorkProc() now calls XtApp-AddWorkProc() passing the default application context created by XtInitialize(). Very few programs need multiple application contexts, and you can continue to use XtAdd-WorkProc() if you initialize your application with XtInitialize(). We recommend, however, that you use XtAppInitialize(), XtAppAddWorkProc(), and the other Xt-App*() application context specific functions.

See XtAppAddWorkProc() for more information.

See Also

XtAppAddWorkProc(1), *XtRemoveWorkProc*(1),
XtWorkProc(2).

XtAllocateGC

Name

XtAllocateGC – obtain a sharable GC with modifiable fields.

Synopsis

```
GC XtAllocateGC(object, depth, value_mask, values, dynamic_mask,
        dont_care_mask)
    Widget object;
    Cardinal depth;
    XtGCMask value_mask;
    XtGCValues *values;
    XtGCMask dynamic_mask;
    XtGCMask dont_care_mask;
```

Inputs

object   Specifies an object; may be of class Object or any subclass thereof.

depth   Specifies the depth for which the returned GC is valid, or 0.

value_mask   Specifies the fields of the GC which must have fixed values.

values   Specifies the values for the fields in *value_mask*.

dynamic_mask
                  Specifies fields of the GC which may be modified.

dont_care_mask
                  Specifies fields of the GC which will never be used.

Returns

A GC with fields as specified in *value_mask* and *values*.

Availability

Release 5 and later.

Description

XtAllocateGC() returns a sharable GC with values as specified in *values* for each field set in *value_mask*. The GC is valid for the screen of the specified object (the screen of the nearest widget ancestor if the specified object is not itself a widget) and for drawable depth *depth*. If *depth* is 0, the depth is taken from the XtNdepth resource of the object (or from its nearest widget ancestor). The *dynamic_mask* and *dont_care_mask* arguments specify more information about the intended usage of the GC which influences how the GC may be shared. These arguments are explained below.

When returned, the GC may already be in use by other widgets, and it may be passed to other widgets in the future. For this reason, none of the fields specified in *value_mask* should ever be modified. The *dynamic_mask* argument specifies fields of the GC that may be modified by the widget. Because this is a shared GC, other widgets may also modify those fields, and a widget cannot rely on them to remain unchanged. For this reason, these fields must be explicitly set prior to every use.

The *dont_care_mask* argument specifies fields of the GC that the widget does not care about (i.e., fields that will never be used by any of the graphic functions called with this GC). The returned GC may have any values for these fields.

GC fields that are not specified in *value_mask*, *dynamic_mask*, or *dont_care_mask* will always have their default values in the returned GC. If a field is specified in both *value_mask*, and in *dynamic_mask*, then the field is modifiable, but will also be initialized to the appropriate value specified in *values*. If a field is set in *dont_care_mask* and is also set in one of the other masks, the *dont_care_mask* is ignored for that field.

Usage

XtAllocateGC() is a generalization of XtGetGC(). Calling XtAllocateGC() with *depth*, *dynamic_mask*, and *dont_care_mask* all 0 is equivalent to calling XtGetGC() with the remaining arguments.

There are several common situations in which a modifiable GC is necessary. If you are drawing complex text with XDrawText(), the font field of your GC will be automatically changed to each of the font values in your text description. Also, if you use clip masks to protect or speed up drawing in a widget's expose method, you will need to modify the clipping fields of the GC. Using XtAllocateGC() with a *dynamic_mask* argument means that you can share a GC, with other instances of the same widget at least, instead of allocating a private GC with XCreateGC().

Furthermore, specifying a *dont_care_mask* when allocating a shared GC can make that GC much more sharable. For example, if a widget draws text with XDrawString() only, then it is only interested in the font and foreground fields of a GC. If it allocates its GC and specifies that it doesn't care about the background field, then it can share its GC with another widget that uses the same font and foreground, but draws with XDrawImageString() and so *does* care about the background field. This kind of sharing is not possible with XtGetGC().

Note that XtAllocateGC() is new in Release 5. If you use it in a widget, you will lose portability to Release 4. If you have a Release 4 widget that uses a private GC, you may be able to add conditional compilation directives to make it use the more efficient XtAllocateGC() when compiled with X11R5.

When done with a GC obtained with XtAllocateGC(), it should be freed with Xt-ReleaseGC().

Structures

The XtGCMask type is simply an unsigned long:

```
typedef unsigned long  XtGCMask; /* Mask of values that are used by widget*/
```

Each of the symbols in the table below sets a single bit in an XtGCMask. The *value_mask*, *dynamic_mask*, and *dont_care_mask* arguments are formed by combining these symbols with the bitwise OR operator (|):

GCArcMode	GCFillRule	GCLineWidth
GCBackground	GCFillStyle	GCPlaneMask
GCCapStyle	GCFont	GCStipple
GCClipMask	GCForeground	GCSubwindowMode
GCClipXOrigin	GCFunction	GCTile
GCClipYOrigin	GCGraphicsExposures	GCTileStipXOrigin
GCDashList	GCJoinStyle	GCTileStipYOrigin
GCDashOffset	GCLineStyle	

The XGCValues structure has one field for each of the GC fields:

```
typedef struct {
        int function;                   /* logical operation */
        unsigned long plane_mask;       /* plane mask */
        unsigned long foreground;       /* foreground pixel */
        unsigned long background;       /* background pixel */
        int line_width;                 /* line width */
        int line_style;                 /* LineSolid, LineOnOffDash,
                                           LineDoubleDash */
        int cap_style;                  /* CapNotLast, CapButt,
                                           CapRound, CapProjecting */
        int join_style;                 /* JoinMiter, JoinRound, JoinBevel */
        int fill_style;                 /* FillSolid, FillTiled,
                                           FillStippled, FillOpaqueStippled */
        int fill_rule;                  /* EvenOddRule, WindingRule */
        int arc_mode;                   /* ArcChord, ArcPieSlice */
        Pixmap tile;                    /* tile pixmap for tiling operations */
        Pixmap stipple;                 /* stipple 1 plane pixmap for stippling */
        int ts_x_origin;                /* offset for tile or
        int ts_y_origin;                 * stipple operations */
        Font font;                      /* default text font for text operations */
        int subwindow_mode;             /* ClipByChildren, IncludeInferiors */
        Bool graphics_exposures;        /* should exposures be generated? */
        int clip_x_origin;              /* origin for clipping */
        int clip_y_origin;
        Pixmap clip_mask;               /* bitmap clipping; other calls for rects */
        int dash_offset;                /* patterned/dashed line information */
        char dashes;
} XGCValues;
```

See Also

XtGetGC(1), *XtReleaseGC*(1).

Name

XtAppAddActionHook – register a procedure to be called before any action is invoked.

Synopsis

```
XtActionHookId XtAppAddActionHook(app, proc, client_data)
      XtAppContext app;
      XtActionHookProc proc;
      XtPointer client_data;
```

Inputs

app   Specifies the application context.

proc   Specifies the action hook procedure.

client_data   Specifies data to be passed to the procedure.

Returns

A handle of type `XtActionHookId` that can be passed to `XtRemoveActionHook()` to unregister the action hook procedure.

Availability

Release 4 and later.

Description

`XtAppAddActionHook()` registers a procedure *proc* to be called by the translation manager with data `client_data` just before any action procedure is dispatched in the application context `app`. Any number of action hook procedure/data pairs may be registered in an application context, and they will be called in reverse order of registration (i.e., the most recently registered will be the first called).

See `XtActionHookProc`(2) for an explanation of how to write an action hook procedure.

Usage

Action hooks can be used to record user actions for later playback using `XtCallAction-Proc()`. This is one way to implement keyboard macros.

An action hook procedure can be unregistered with `XtRemoveActionHook()`.

Structures

`XtActionHookId` is an opaque type.

See Also

XtRemoveActionHook(1),
XtActionHookProc(2).

XtAppAddActions

Name

XtAppAddActions – register an action table with the Translation Manager.

Synopsis

```
void XtAppAddActions(app_context, actions, num_actions)
    XtAppContext app_context;
    XtActionList actions;
    Cardinal num_actions;
```

Inputs

app_context Specifies the application context.

actions Specifies the action table to register.

num_args Specifies the number of entries in this action table.

Description

XtAppAddActions() registers *actions*, an array of *num_actions* XtActionsRec structures with the Translation Manager for the application context *app_context*. Each element of the array contains an action name and an action procedure pointer. When a named action is invoked through a translation table, the procedure to be called is looked up in the action tables that have been registered.

If more than one action is registered with the same name, the most recently registered action is used. If duplicate actions exist in an action table, the first is used. XtAppAddActions() registers actions globally to an application context. This is in contrast to actions placed in the Core widget class part actions field which are defined locally to a widget class only.

See XtActionProc(2) for an explanation of how to write an action procedure.

Usage

Note that there is no way to unregister actions. Registering an new definition for an action name will simply make the old definition inaccessible.

Action procedures should not assume that the widget in which they are invoked is realized; an accelerator can cause an action to be called for a widget that does not yet have a window.

You should never need to call XtAppAddActions() when writing a widget. Widget's actions are registered locally to the widget through the Core class part actions field.

Background

The translation manager provides an interface to specify and manage the mapping of X event sequences into procedure calls, for example, calling procedure Yes() when the 'Y' key is pressed.

The translation manager uses two kinds of tables to perform translations:

- Action tables, which specify the mapping of externally available procedure name strings to the corresponding procedure.

- A translation table, which specifies the mapping of event sequences to procedure name strings.

The translation manager uses a simple algorithm to resolve the name of a procedure specified in a translation table into the actual procedure specified in an action table. When the widget is realized, the translation manager performs a search for the name in the following tables, in order:

- The widget's class and all superclass action tables, in subclass-to-superclass order.

- The parent's class and all superclass action tables, in subclass-to-superclass order, then on up the ancestor tree.

- The action tables registered with `XtAppAddActions()` and `XtAddActions()` from the most recently added table to the oldest table.

As soon as it finds a name, the translation manager stops the search. If it cannot find a name, the translation manager generates a warning message.

The Intrinsics reserve all action names and parameters starting with the characters "Xt" for future standard enhancements. Users, applications, and widgets should not declare action names or pass parameters starting with these characters except to invoke specified built-in Intrinsics functions.

Example

An action table is generally declared as a statically initialized array. By convention, the name of an action and the C function name are identical except that the function name begins with an uppercase letter:

```
static XtActionsRec global_actions[] = {
    {"confirm", Confirm},
    {"quit", Quit},
};
```

This action table could be registered with the following command:

```
XtAppAddActions(app, global_actions, XtNumber(global_action);
```

Structures

The `XtActionsRec` structure and the `XtActionList` type are defined as follows:

```
typedef struct _XtActionsRec{
    String string;
    XtActionProc proc;
} XtActionsRec;

typedef struct _XtActionsRec *XtActionList;
```

See Also

XtActionProc(2).

XtAppAddConverter

Name

XtAppAddConverter – register an "old-style" resource converter.

Synopsis

```
void XtAppAddConverter(app_context, from_type, to_type, converter, con-
        vert_args, num_args)
    XtAppContext app_context;
    String from_type;
    String to_type;
    XtConverter converter;
    XtConvertArgList convert_args;
    Cardinal num_args;
```

Inputs

app_context	Specifies the application context.
from_type	Specifies the source type of the resource to be converted.
to_type	Specifies the destination type to which the resource is to be converted.
converter	Specifies the converter procedure. See XtConverter(2).
convert_args	Specifies how to obtain additional arguments needed for the conversion; if no arguments are provided, this should be NULL. See the Structures section below for a detailed description of the format of convert_args.
num_args	Specifies the number of additional arguments to the converter or zero.

Description

XtAppAddConverter() registers converter in application context app_context as a procedure to convert data of resource type from_type to resource type to_type.

Each element of convert_args is an XtConvertArgRec. It is not the argument actually passed to the converter procedure, but specifies how to obtain an XrmValue argument which will be passed to the converter. The "Background" section below explains the XtConvertArgRec structure in detail.

See XtConverter(2) for an explanation of how to write an "old-style" converter.

Usage

XtAppAddConverter() registers an "old-style" converter. This kind of converter is still in common use, but are not as flexible as the (incompatible) "new-style" converter added in Release 4. If you must register an existing old-style converter, use XtAppAdd-Converter(), but if you are writing a converter of your own, consider using a new-style converter. See XtAppSetTypeConverter().

If you write a widget that has a resource which is of some enumerated type, you should write a converter routine which will convert between the symbolic names of each value and the values themselves. This converter should then be registered in your widget's class_initial-ize() method.

If you are writing a programming library or an application that defines non-standard types, it may be useful to provide string converters for those types. This allows resources of that type to be specified from a resource file. An application that supported user-configurable popup menus, for example, might include a String-to-Menu converter.

Some converters need additional arguments, such as a screen or colormap in order to correctly perform the conversion. These converters are registered with an `XtConvertArgList`. Generally the author of the converter will also define a static array of `XtConvertArgRec` to be registered with the converter. There are also two `XtConvertArgLists` predefined by the Intrinsics: `screenConvertArg` passes the widget's screen field to the converter in `args[0]`, and `colorConvertArgs` passes the widget's screen field to the converter in `args[0]` and the widget's colormap field in `args[1]`.

The Intrinsics define a number of standard converters which do not need to be registered. See `XtConvertAndStore()` for a list of these predefined converters. There are also a number of other useful converters defined in the Xmu library which do need to be registered explicitly. See `XmuCvtStringToMisc`(6).

Example

You can register the String-to-Widget converter from the Xmu library with the following:

```
static XtConvertArgRec parentCvtArg[] = {
    {XtBaseOffset, (XtPointer)XtOffset(Widget, core.parent), sizeof(Widget)
};

XtAppAddConverter(app, XtRString, XtRWidget, XmuCvtStringToWidget,
                  parentCvtArg, XtNumber(parentCvtArg));
```

Background

For the few type converters that need additional arguments, the Intrinsics conversion mechanism provides a method of specifying how these arguments should be computed. Before a converter is called, each element of the `XtConvertArgList` is interpreted to determine the sizes and values of the arguments. These computed arguments are passed to the converter as an array of `XrmValue`. The enumerated type `XtAddressMode` and the structure `XtConvertArgRec` specify how each argument is derived.

```
typedef enum {
        /* address mode                 parameter representation */
        XtAddress,              /* address */
        XtBaseOffset,           /* offset */
        XtImmediate,            /* constant */
        XtResourceString,       /* resource name string */
        XtResourceQuark,        /* resource name quark */
        XtWidgetBaseOffset,     /* offset */
        XtProcedureArg          /* procedure to call */
} XtAddressMode;

typedef struct {
        XtAddressMode address_mode;
        XtPointer address_id;
```

```
    Cardinal size;
} XtConvertArgRec, *XtConvertArgList;
```

The `size` field of an `XtConvertArgRec` specifies the length of the data in bytes. The `address_mode` field specifies how the `address_id` field should be interpreted. The possible values of `XtAddressMode` have the following meanings:

`XtAddress`
 causes `address_id` to be interpreted as the address of the data.

`XtBaseOffset`
 causes `address_id` to be interpreted as the offset from the widget base.

`XtImmediate`
 causes `address_id` to be interpreted as a constant.

`XtResourceString`
 causes `address_id` to be interpreted as the name of a resource that is to be converted into an offset from the widget base.

`XtResourceQuark`
 causes `address_id` to be interpreted as the result of an `XrmStringToQuark()` conversion on the name of a resource, which is to be converted into an offset from the widget base.

`XtWidgetBaseOffset`
 is similar to `XtBaseOffset` except that it searches for the closest windowed ancestor if the object is not of a subclass of Core.

`XtProcedureArg`
 specifies that `address_id` is a pointer to a procedure of type `XtConvertArgProc` to be invoked to return the conversion argument. See `XtConvertArgProc`(2) for an explanation of how to write a procedure of this type.

Structures

The `XtConvertArgRec` structure and the related `XtAddressMode` type are shown in the "Background" section above.

See Also

XtAppSetTypeConverter(1), *XtCallConverter*(1), *XtConvertandStore*, *XtDirectConvert*(1), *XtSetType-Converter*(1),
XtConverter(2), *XtTypeConverter*(2), *XtConvertArgProc*(2),
XmuCvtStringToMisc(6).

Name

XtAppAddInput – register a procedure to be called when there is activity on a file descriptor.

Synopsis

```
XtInputId XtAppAddInput(app_context, source, condition, proc, client_data)
    XtAppContext app_context;
    int source;
    XtPointer condition;
    XtInputCallbackProc proc;
    XtPointer client_data;
```

Inputs

app_context Specifies the application context.

source Specifies the file descriptor (on a POSIX-based system) to monitor.

condition Specifies a mask that indicates a read, write, or exception condition or some operating-system-dependent condition.

proc Specifies the procedure that is to be called when *condition* occurs on *source*.

client_data Specifies data to be passed to *proc* when it is invoked.

Returns

A handle of type XtInputId that can be passed to XtRemoveInput() to unregister this input procedure.

Description

XtAddInput() registers a file descriptor *source* to be monitored by XtAppNext-Event() and a procedure *proc* to be called with data *client_data* when the condition (such as "input ready" or "error") *condition* arises.

On a POSIX-based system, the supported values for *condition* are XtInputReadMask, XtInputWriteMask, or XtInputExceptMask. These values cannot be ORed together. On non-POSIX systems, the types of *source* and *condition* will be operating-system dependent.

See XtInputCallbackProc(2) for an explanation of how to write an input callback.

See the POSIX select() system call for more information on the possible file descriptor conditions that can be selected for.

Usage

XtAppAddInput() allows an Xt application to receive non-X based events through the same event loop that delivers X events. File descriptors in POSIX are a very general mechanism, and XtAppAddInput() can be used to receive notification when the user types a command to stdin, when a child process closes a pipe, or when there is data available on an RPC socket, for example.

An input callback can be unregistered by calling XtRemoveInput() and passing the Xt-InputId returned by this function.

Note that when reading from a socket, you should be careful not to close the end of the socket that is waiting before exiting `XtAppMainLoop()`. If you do this, you will get an infinite loop, in which the callback is called repeatedly, while the Intrinsics wait for an EOF to be read.

Structures

The `XtInputId` type is defined as follows:

```
typedef unsigned long XtInputId;
```

See Also

XtRemoveInput(1),
XtInputCallbackProc(2).

XtAppAddTimeOut — register a procedure to be called when a specified time elapses.

Synopsis

```
XtIntervalId XtAppAddTimeOut(app_context, interval, proc, client_data)
    XtAppContext app_context;
    unsigned long interval;
    XtTimerCallbackProc proc;
    XtPointer client_data;
```

Inputs

`app_context` Specifies the application context in which the timer is to be set.

`interval` Specifies the time interval in milliseconds.

`proc` Specifies the procedure that is to be called when the time expires. See `Xt-TimerCallbackProc`(2).

`client_data` Specifies data to be passed to `proc` when it is called.

Returns

A handle of type `XtIntervalId` that can be used to unregister the timeout procedure with `XtRemoveTimeOut()`.

Description

`XtAppAddTimeOut()` registers, in application context `app_context`, a procedure `proc`, to be called by `XtAppNextEvent()` with `client_data` after `interval` milliseconds elapse. The procedure is called once and automatically unregistered; it will not be called repeatedly every `interval` milliseconds.

See `XtTimerCallbackProc`(2) for an explanation of how to write a timer callback.

Usage

Timer callbacks are automatically unregistered after they are triggered. To have a callback called at a regular interval, call `XtAppAddTimeOut()` again from within the timer callback.

A timer callback can be explicitly unregistered before it is invoked by calling `XtRemove-TimeOut()` with the `XtIntervalId` returned by this function.

Structures

The `XtIntervalId` type is defined as follows:

```
typedef unsigned long XtIntervalId;
```

See Also

XtAppNextEvent(1), *XtRemoveTimeOut*(1), *XtTimerCallbackProc*(2).

XtAppAddWorkProc — register a procedure to be called when the event loop is idle.

Synopsis

```
XtWorkProcId XtAppAddWorkProc(app_context, proc, client_data)
    XtAppContext app_context;
    XtWorkProc proc;
    XtPointer client_data;
```

Inputs

app_context Specifies the application context.

proc Specifies the procedure that is to be called when the application is idle.

client_data Specifies data to be passed to *proc* when it is called.

Returns

A handle of type `XtWorkProcId` that can be passed to `XtRemoveWorkProc()` to unregister the work procedure.

Description

`XtAddWorkProc()` registers the procedure *proc* and the data *client_data* to be called by `XtAppNextEvent()` or `XtAppProcessEvent()` when there are no pending input events and it would otherwise block. Multiple work procedures can be registered, and the most recently added one is always the one that is called. However, if a work procedure itself adds another work procedure, the newly added one has lower priority than the current one.

A work procedure returns a `Boolean`. If it returns `True`, it will automatically be unregistered and will not be called again. If it returns `False` it will be called the next time the application is idle. See `XtWorkProc(2)` for more information.

Usage

`XtAppAddWorkProc()` implements a limited form of background processing. Most applications spend most of their time waiting for input; to do useful work during this idle time, you can register a work procedure that will run when the application is idle.

A work procedure must return quickly or the application will not be able to promptly respond to user events. If a large task needs to be done in the background, the work procedure should periodically save its state and return `False`. Work procedures should not be used to do frivolous work in the background. In a multi-tasking system, an idle application should generally actually be idle, and not steal CPU time from other processes.

A work procedure can be explicitly removed by calling `XtRemoveWorkProc()` with the `XtWorkProcId` returned by this function.

Structures

The `XtWorkProcId` type is defined as follows:

```
typedef unsigned long XtWorkProcId;
```

See Also

XtAppNextEvent(1), *XtAppProcessEvent*(1), *XtRemoveWorkProc*(1),
XtWorkProc(2).

XtAppCreateShell

Name

XtAppCreateShell – create a shell widget at the root of a widget tree.

Synopsis

```
Widget XtAppCreateShell(application_name, application_class, widget_class,
        display, args, num_args)
    String application_name;
    String application_class;
    WidgetClass widget_class;
    Display *display;
    ArgList args;
    Cardinal num_args;
```

Inputs

application_name

Specifies the resource name of the shell widget, or NULL.

application_class

Specifies the resource class to be used for the shell widget if it is of `applicationShellWidgetClass` or a subclass thereof.

widget_class

Specifies the widget class of the created widget. (normally `applicationShellWidgetClass`).

display Specifies the display on which the shell is to be created.

args Specifies the argument list to override other resource specifications.

num_args Specifies the number of arguments in the argument list.

Description

`XtAppCreateShell()` creates a shell widget of class *widget_class* on display *display*. The created widget has no parent—it is at the root of a widget tree and at the top of the resource name hierarchy. The resource name of the widget is either *application_name*, or, if that is NULL, the name that was passed to `XtDisplayInitialize()` or `XtOpenDisplay()` when the display was initialized. The resource class of the widget is either *application_class*, if the `widget_class` is `applicationShellWidgetClass` or a subclass, or the normal class name of the widget otherwise. The widget is created on the screen specified by the `XtNscreen` resource or on the default screen of *display* if no such resource is found.

In X11R4, the `XtNscreen` and other resources are all obtained from *args* and from the database of *display*. In X11R5, however, there is a resource database for each screen of a display, and the resources for the created shell widget are obtained somewhat differently: the argument list *args* is first scanned for a resource named `XtNscreen`, and if none is found, the database of the default screen of *display* is searched for this resource. If the `XtNscreen` resource is found the database from the specified screen is used for all the remaining resources of the widget. If the `XtNscreen` resource is not found, the database of the default screen continues to be used. In either case, the resources in *args* override values in the database.

Usage

Most applications can simply use `XtAppInitialize()` which initializes the toolkit, creates an application context, opens a display, and then calls `XtAppCreateShell()` to create a shell on that display.

An application that wishes to have multiple toplevel windows on the same screen (a mail reader and a mail composer, for example) should generally use `XtCreatePopupShell()` to create additional shells within the widget tree and resource hierarchy of the original shell. Creating multiple root shells with different names is generally not a good idea because then your application will have resources specified under several different hierarchies. It is sometimes useful to create multiple root shells with the *same* name, however, if your application is capable of creating multiple instances of itself. Each of these instances will find the same resources in the same database and will appear to be "clones" of each other.

To create shells on multiple displays, open each display with `XtOpenDisplay()` and use the resulting `Display *` in a call to `XtAppCreateShell()`. If all displays are initialized in the same application context, then all events will be correctly handled by `XtAppMainLoop()`.

`XtAppCreateShell()` can also be used to create toplevel shells on multiple screens. Note that prior to X11R5, however, it is not possible to maintain separate resource databases for each screen.

The specified widget class for the new shell widget should almost always be `applicationShellWidgetClass` or some subclass.

`XtVaAppCreateShell()` behaves identically to `XtAppCreateShell()`, but takes a NULL-terminated variable-length argument list of resource name/resource value pairs rather than an array of `Arg`.

See Also

XtAppInitialize(1), *XtCreatePopupShell*(1), *XtDisplayInitialize*(1), *XtOpenDisplay*(1), *XtVaAppCreateShell*(1).

XtAppError

Name

XtAppError – call the low-level error handler.

Synopsis

```
void XtAppError(app_context, message)
    XtAppContext app_context;
    String message;
```

Inputs

app_context   Specifies the application context.

message   Specifies the error message to be reported.

Returns

XtAppError() terminates the application and does not return.

Description

XtAppError() passes its arguments to the installed low-level error handler. On POSIX systems, the default handler is _XtDefaultError(). It prints the message to the stderr stream and calls exit().

Usage

To report non-fatal error messages or warnings without exiting, use XtAppWarning() or XtAppWarningMsg(). To change the low-level error handler, use XtAppSetError-Handler().

XtAppError() calls the "low-level" error handler. It is better to use XtAppErrorMsg() which calls the "high-level" error handler. The high-level handler looks up the error message in a resource database and so allows for customization and internationalization of error messages.

Although the Intrinsics interface allows separate error and warning handlers for each application context, most implementations will support only a single set of handlers. When a new handler is installed, it will be used in all application contexts.

See Also

XtAppErrorMsg(1), *XtAppSetErrorHandler*(1), *XtAppSetErrorMsgHandler*(1), *XtAppSetWarning-Handler*(1), *XtAppSetWarningMsgHandler*(1), *XtAppWarning*(1), *XtAppWarningMsg*(1), *XtErrorHandler*(2). *XtErrorMsgHandler*(2).

Name

XtAppErrorMsg – call the high-level fatal error handler.

Synopsis

```
void XtAppErrorMsg(app_context, name, type, class, default, params,
        num_params)
    XtAppContext app_context;
    String name;
    String type;
    String class;
    String default;
    String *params;
    Cardinal *num_params;
```

Inputs

app_context	Specifies the application context.
name	Specifies the general kind of error.
type	Specifies the detailed name of the error.
class	Specifies the resource class of the error.
default	Specifies the default message to use if no message is found in the database.
params	Specifies an array of values to be inserted into the message.
num_params	Specifies the number of elements in *params*.

Returns

XtAppErrorMsg() terminates the application and does not return.

Description

XtAppErrorMsg() passes all of its arguments except *app_context* to the installed high-level error handler. The default high-level error handler is _XtDefaultErrorMsg(). It calls XtAppGetErrorDatabaseText() to lookup an error message of the specified *name*, *type*, and *class* in the error database. If no such message is found, XtAppGetErrorDatabaseText() returns the specified *default* message. In either case, _XtDefaultErrorMsg() does a printf-style substitution of *params* into the message, and passes the resulting text to the low-level error handler by calling XtError().

See XtAppGetErrorDatabaseText() for details on how messages are looked up in the error database.

Usage

To report non-fatal error messages or warnings without exiting, use XtAppWarningMsg(). To change the high-level error handler, use XtAppSetErrorMsgHandler().

Note that the *num_params* argument to this function is a Cardinal *, not a Cardinal.

Although the Intrinsics interface allows separate error and warning handlers for each application context, most implementations will support only a single set of handlers. When a new handler is installed, it will be used in all application contexts.

Example

The following code is from the Intrinsics internal function _XtCreateWidget():

```
String params[2];
Cardinal num_params = 2;

params[0] = name;
params[1] = XtName(parent);
XtAppErrorMsg(XtWidgetToApplicationContext(parent),
    "nonWidget", XtNxtCreateWidget, XtCXtToolkitError,
    "attempt to add non-widget child to parent which supports only widgets",
    params, &num_params);
```

See Also

XtAppError(1), *XtAppSetErrorHandler*(1), *XtAppSetErrorMsgHandler*(1), *XtAppSetWarningHandler*(1), *XtAppSetWarningMsgHandler*(1), *XtAppWarning*(1), *XtAppWarningMsg*(1), *XtErrorMsgHandler*(2).

XtAppGetErrorDatabase

Name

XtAppGetErrorDatabase – obtain the default error database.

Synopsis

```
XrmDatabase *XtAppGetErrorDatabase(app_context)
    XtAppContext app_context;
```

Inputs

app_context Specifies the application context.

Returns

The address of an XrmDatabase.

Description

XtAppGetErrorDatabase() returns the address of the XrmDatabase error message database used by the default high-level error and warning handlers for *app_context*. This database may be empty until XtAppGetErrorDatabaseText() is called for the first time.

While the X Toolkit specification permits individual error databases for each application context, most implementations will only support a single database. In the MIT implementation, the error database file is */usr/lib/X11/XtErrorDB*.

Usage

You should never need to call this function if you simply want to report error and warning messages through the standard handlers.

Because the Intrinsics do not support the customization and internationalization of error messages very well, some applications may want to override values in the default database with their own customized messages. The default database can be obtained for this purpose by making a single dummy call to XtAppGetErrorDatabaseText() and then calling XtAppGetErrorDatabase().

See Also

XtAppErrorMsg(1), *XtAppGetErrorDatabaseText*(1), *XtAppWarningMsg*(1), *XtErrorMsgHandler*(2).

Xt Functions and Macros

Name

XtAppGetErrorDatabaseText – get the text of a named message from the error database.

Synopsis

```
void XtAppGetErrorDatabaseText(app_context, name, type, class, default,
        buffer_return, nbytes, database)
    XtAppContext app_context;
    String name, type, class;
    String default;
    String buffer_return;
    int nbytes;
    XrmDatabase database;
```

Inputs

app_context	Specifies the application context.
name	Specifies the name or general kind of the message.
type	Specifies the type or detailed name of the message.
class	Specifies the resource class of the error message.
default	Specifies the default message to use if an error database entry is not found.
nbytes	Specifies the size of *buffer_return* in bytes.
database	Specifies the database to be used, or NULL if the application's database is to be used.

Outputs

buffer_return	Specifies the buffer into which the error message is to be returned.

Description

XtAppGetErrorDatabaseText() looks up the message named by *name*, *type*, and *class* in *database* or in the database returned by XtAppGetErrorDatabase() for *app_context* if *database* is NULL. If such a message is found, it is stored into *buffer_return*, otherwise the message in *default* is stored into *buffer_return*.

The resource name of the message is formed by concatenating *name* and *type* with a single "." between them. The resource class of the message is *class* if it already contains a ".", or otherwise is formed by concatenating *class* with itself with a single "." between the strings.

Usage

You should not need to call XtAppGetErrorDatabaseText() unless you are writing a customized high-level error or warning handler.

Because the Intrinsics do not support the customization and internationalization of error messages very well, some applications may want to read a customized error database (found with XtResolvePathname() or named by an application resource, for example) and provide customized error and warning handlers that call XtAppGetErrorDatabaseText() specifying this custom database explicitly.

While the X Toolkit specification permits individual error databases for each application context, most implementations will only support a single database. In the MIT implementation, the error database file is */usr/lib/X11/XtErrorDB*.

See Also

XtAppGetErrorDatabase (1),
XtErrorMsgHandler (2).

XtAppGetSelectionTimeout

Name

XtAppGetSelectionTimeout – get the current Intrinsics selection timeout value.

Synopsis

```
unsigned long XtAppGetSelectionTimeout(app_context)
    XtAppContext app_context;
```

Inputs

app_context Specifies the application context.

Returns

The selection timeout interval for the application context.

Description

XtAppGetSelectionTimeout() returns the current selection timeout value for the specified application context, in milliseconds. The selection timeout is the time within which the
two communicating applications must respond to one another. The initial timeout value is set
by the selectionTimeout application resource, which defaults to 5000 milliseconds (5
seconds).

Usage

A new timeout value can be set by a call to XtAppSetSelectionTimeout(). You should
rarely need to query or set this value. In particular, an application generally should not change
this value except under the explicit request of the user.

See Also

XtAppSetSelectionTimeout(1).

Name

XtAppInitialize – initialize the X Toolkit internals, create an application context, open and initialize a display, and create the initial application shell instance.

Synopsis

```
Widget XtAppInitialize(app_context_return, application_class, options,
        num_options, argc_in_out, argv_in_out, fallback_resources, args,
        num_args)
    XtAppContext *app_context_return;
    String application_class;
    XrmOptionDescList options;
    Cardinal num_options;
    int *argc_in_out;                /* was type Cardinal * in R4 */
    String *argv_in_out;
    String *fallback_resources;
    ArgList args;
    Cardinal num_args;
```

Inputs

application_class Specifies the class name of the application.

options Specifies an array of XrmOptionDescRec which describe how to parse the command line.

num_options Specifies the number of elements in *options*.

argc_in_out Specifies the address of the number of command line arguments. This argument is of type int * in Release 5 and of type Cardinal * in Release 4.

argv_in_out Specifies the array of command line arguments.

fallback_resources

Specifies a NULL-terminated array of resource specification strings to be used if the application class resource file cannot be opened or read, or NULL if no fallback resources are desired.

args Specifies an argument list to override any other resource specifications for the created shell widget.

num_args Specifies the number of elements in *args*.

Outputs

app_context_return

Returns the newly created application context, if non-NULL.

argc_in_out Returns the number of command line arguments remaining after the command line is parsed by XtDisplayInitialize().

argv_in_out Returns the command line as modified by XtDisplay-Initialize().

Returns

A toplevel shell widget of class `applicationShellWidgetClass`.

Availability

Release 4 and later.

Description

`XtAppInitialize()` is a convenience procedure that most applications will use to initialize themselves. It does the following:

- Calls `XtToolkitInitialize()` to do Intrinsics internal initialization.

- Calls `XtCreateApplicationContext()` to create an application context for the application. If *app_context_return* is non-NULL, the newly created application context is stored at the address it points to.

- Calls `XtAppSetFallbackResources()` passing the application context and *fallback_resources*, unless that argument is NULL.

- Calls `XtOpenDisplay()` passing the application context, *application_class*, *options*, *num_options*, *argc_in_out*, and *argv_in_out*. `XtOpenDisplay()` determines the display name and the application name from the command line or environment variables, opens a connection to the display, and calls `XtDisplayInitialize()` to parse the command line and build the resource database. The command line as modified by `XtDisplayInitialize()` is returned in *argc_in_out* and argv_in_out. See the "Background" section below for more details on all of these steps.

- Calls `XtAppCreateShell()` to create an applicationShellWidgetClass shell, passing *args* and *num_args* to override any resources found in the database.

If the display cannot be opened, an error message is issued and `XtAppInitialize()` terminates the application.

Usage

Most applications can `XtAppInitialize()` to initialize themselves. Most programmers will not need to understand the details of initialization described in the "Background" section below. Applications that open multiple displays or create multiple application contexts will have to use the lower-level initialization functions explicitly.

Most applications can have all their command-line options automatically parsed by declaring an `XrmOptionDescList` and passing it to `XtAppInitialize()` which will convert values on the command line into values in the resource database which can then be retrieved into a structure with `XtGetApplicationResources()`. This is a good idea, because if your application supports customization through application resources (which it should if there is anything to customize) then customization through the command line comes essentially for free.

If all your command line options are parsed this way, then `XtAppInitialize()` should remove everything except *argv[0]* from the command line and should set *argc* to 1. If this is not the case when `XtAppInitialize()` returns, then the user has requested an unrecognized option. If you parse some command line options manually, you should parse them after calling `XtAppInitialize()`.

The "Background" section below explains how to declare an `XrmOptionDescList` and the example below shows the one used by *viewres*.

The `fallback_resources` argument is an array of strings, each string equivalent to a line in a resource file. If your application relies on an app-defaults file, you can use fallback resources as a backup to be used in case the app-defaults file is installed incorrectly or otherwise cannot be found. If the application needs many resources to function properly, your fallback resources might simply set a label widget to display an error message which informs the user that the app-defaults file could not be found. The example below shows a simple fallback resource list.

In Release 4, the `argc_in_out` argument is of type `Cardinal *`, and in Release 5, this argument is of type `int *`. This is a minor incompatibility that may result warnings from ANSI-C compilers when porting from one release to another. The example below shows a way around this problem.

`XtVaAppInitialize()` performs the same function as `XtAppInitialize()`, but accepts a `NULL`-terminated variable-length argument list of resource name/resource value pairs instead of an *ArgList*.

Example

The following initialization code is adapted from the X11R5 *viewres* application.

```
static XrmOptionDescRec Options[] = {
    { "-top", "*topObject", XrmoptionSepArg, (XPointer) NULL },
    { "-variable", "*showVariable", XrmoptionNoArg, (XPointer) "on" },
    { "-vertical", "*Tree.Gravity", XrmoptionNoArg, (XPointer) "north" }
};

static char *fallback_resources[] = {
    "*allowShellResize: true",
    "*Porthole.top: ChainTop",
    "*Porthole.left: ChainLeft",
    "*Porthole.bottom: ChainBottom",
    "*Porthole.right:  ChainRight",
    "*Porthole.resizable: on",
    (char *) NULL
};

main (argc, argv)
    int argc;
    char **argv;
{

    Widget toplevel;
    XtAppContext app_con;

    toplevel = XtAppInitialize(&app_con, "Viewres",
                               Options, XtNumber (Options),
#if XtSpecificationRelease > 4
```

```
                                        &argc,
#else
                                        (Cardinal *)&argc,
#endif
                                        argv,
                                        fallback_resources,
                                        (ArgList) NULL, (Cardinal) 0);

        if (argc != 1) display_usage_message();
                .
                .
                .
    }
```

Background

Initializing an application is a complex process. It involves determining the display to be opened, determining the name of the application, setting the locale of the application, determining the screen on which to create the shell widget, parsing the command line, and building the resource database. Each of these tasks is described in detail below. Some of the details have changed between Release 4 and Release 5. Release 5 is described below.

Determining Which Display to Open

XtAppInitialize() calls XtOpenDisplay() with NULL for its *display_name* argument. XtOpenDisplay() determines which display to open by first checking the command line (note that the command line has not been parsed at this point) for a *–display* command line option, and if that is not found, using the value of the DISPLAY environment variable (on POSIX systems). The name is used in a call to XOpenDisplay().

Determining the Application Name

XtOpenDisplay() also determines the name of the application. It checks for the name in the following four locations and uses the first one it finds:

* the value of the *–name* command line option.

* the value of its *application_name* argument. Note that XtAppInitialize() always passes NULL for this value.

* the value of the RESOURCE_NAME environment variable.

* the first word on the command line, *argv[0]*, stripped of any leading directories.

If the name is not found in any of these sources, "main" is used. This name is passed to XtDisplayInitialize() to be used in building the resource database, and will later be used by XtAppCreateShell() to name the application's toplevel shell widget.

Establishing the Application's Locale

XtDisplayInitialize() determines an application's "language string" by searching for the *–xnlLanguage* command line option, an *–xrm* command line option that sets the xnlLanguage resource, or a value for the xnlLanguage option in the user's personal resource database (i.e., the resources set on the display with *xrdb*, or the resources in the *.Xdefaults* file.)

In Release 5, if a language procedure has been registered (see `XtSetLanguageProc()`) then the language string is passed to this language procedure. The language procedure localizes the application, usually by calling `setlocale()`, and returns a string which becomes the new value of the application's language string. If a language procedure has not been set, and in Release 4, the LANG environment variable is used for the language string if no command line argument or resource value is found.

In either Release 4 and Release 5, the language string is associated with the display and used in future calls to `XtResolvePathname()` so that file customized for a particular language can be found. See `XtDisplayInitialize()` and `XtSetLanguageProc()` for more detail on this process.

Parsing the Command Line

`XtDisplayInitialize()` parses the application command line by merging *options* into the standard Xt command line options table and calling `XrmParseCommand()`. Each element in *options* and the Xt options table is a `XrmOptionDescRec` structure (shown in the "Structures" section below) which describes how to parse a single command line argument. The fields of this structure are as follows:

option
> The string to be searched for on the command line. As with standard command-line options, Xt will automatically accept any unique abbreviation of the option specified here. For example, the option *–pixmapWidthInPixels* will be recognized if typed on the command line as *–pixmapW*. However, if you wanted the option *–pw* to set the same resource, then you would need another entry, since *pw* is not the leading string of `pixmapWidthInPixels`.

specifier
> The resource specification. This string must identify a widget resource or an application resource, but not provide a value. Since it has the same form as allowed in the resource databases, it may apply to a single widget or to many widgets. If it applies to no widgets, no error message will be issued.

argKind
> The argument style. This field is of type `XrmOptionKind` which describes how the option is to be interpreted. These constants are described below.

value
> If `argKind` is `XrmOptionNoArg`, this field specifies the resource value (a string) to be inserted into the database. If `argKind` is `XrmOptionSkipNArgs`, this field specifies the number of arguments to skip (you'll need to use a cast to set this field to an integer). For other values of `argKind`, this field is not used.

The possible values for `XrmOptionKind` and their meanings are as follows:

`XrmoptionNoArg`
> Take the value in the `value` field of the options table. For example, this is used for Boolean fields, where the option might be *–debug* and the default value `False`.

`XrmoptionIsArg`
> The flag itself is the value without any additional information. For example, if the option were *–on*, the value would be "on." This constant is infrequently used, because the desired value such as "on" is usually not descriptive enough when used as an option (*–on*).

`XrmoptionStickyArg`
> The value is the characters immediately following the option with no white space intervening. This is the style of arguments for some POSIX utilities such as *uucico* where *–sventure* means to call system *venture*.

`XrmoptionSepArg`
> The next item after the white space after this flag is the value. For example, *–fg blue* would indicate that *blue* is the value for the resource specified by *–fg*.

`XrmoptionResArg`
> The resource name and its value are the next argument in *argv* after the white space after this flag. For example, the flag might be
>
>   -res basecalc*background:white;
>
> then the resource name/value pair would be used as is. This form is rarely used because it is equivalent to *–xrm*, and because the C shell requires that special characters such as * be quoted.

`XrmoptionSkipArg`
> Ignore this option and the next argument in *argv*.

`XrmoptionSkipNArgs`
> Ignore this option and the next `XrmOptionDescRec.value` options

`XrmoptionSkipLine`
> Ignore this option and the rest of *argv*.

The standard command line options parsed by `XtDisplayInitialize()` are shown in the table below.

Option	Resource	Value	Sets
–background	`*background`	Next argument	Background color.
–bd	`*borderColor`	Next argument	Border color.
–bg	`*background`	Next argument	Background color.
–bordercolor	`*borderColor`	Next argument	Color of border.
–borderwidth	`.borderWidth`	Next argument	Width of border in pixels.
–bw	`.borderWidth`	Next argument	Width of border in pixels.
–display	`.display`	Next argument	Server to use.
–fg	`*foreground`	Next argument	Foreground color.

Option	Resource	Value	Sets
–fn	`*font`	Next argument	Font name.
–font	`*font`	Next argument	Font name.
–foreground	`*foreground`	Next argument	Foreground color.
–geometry	`.geometry`	Next argument	Size and position.
–iconic	`.iconic`	"on"	Start as an icon.
–name	`.name`	Next argument	Name of application.
–reverse	`*reverseVideo`	"on"	Reverse video.
–rv	`*reverseVideo`	"on"	Reverse video.
+rv	`*reverseVideo`	"off"	No reverse video.
–selectionTimeout	`.selectionTimeout`	Null	Selection timeout.
–synchronous	`.synchronous`	"on"	Synchronous debug mode.
+synchronous	`.synchronous`	"off"	Synchronous debug mode.
–title	`.title`	Next argument	Title of application.
–xnlLanguage	`.xnlLanguage`	Next argument	Language.
–xrm	Value of argument	Next argument	Depends on argument.

Building the Resource Database

`XtDisplayInitialize()` builds the application's resource database by merging in resources from a number of sources. The merges are all done to augment rather than override, so if a resource from one of these sources conflicts with a resource in the database, the conflicting value is ignored. The sources are:

- The application command line, parsed as described above.

- The file named by the XENVIRONMENT environment variable, or, if that does not exist, the file *.Xdefaults-<host>* in the user's home directory, where *<host>* is the name of the machine on which the application is running.

- The per-screen resources, stored in the SCREEN_RESOURCES property on the root window of the screen, and returned by the function `XScreenResourceString()`

- The per-display resources stored in the RESOURCE_MANAGER property on the root window of the default screen of the display, and obtained with `XResourceManager-String()`. These resources are set by the user with *xrdb*. If no RESOURCE_MANAGER property exists, the contents of the instead.

- The user's application-specific resource file, which is found with `XtResolve-Pathname()` and the path specified in the XUSERFILESEARCHPATH environment variable. If this environment variable is not defined, an implementation-defined default path is used. This default path will be relative to the directory specified in the XAPPLRESDIR environment variable, if it exists, or the user's home directory otherwise.

- The application class-specific resource file (the "app-defaults" file), which is found with `XtResolvePathname()`.

For more details on the precise algorithm used by the Intrinsics to build the database, see `Xt-DisplayInitialize()`.

Determining the Screen

In Release 5, XtAppCreateShell() checks its *args* argument for the XtNscreen resource. If that is not found, it looks for the resource in the database of the default screen of the display. If no screen is found, the default screen of the display is used. If a value for the screen resource is found, the shell widget is created on the specified screen, and the database for that screen of the display is obtained with XtScreenDatabase() and used for all the remaining resources of the widget. Note that this database will have to be built using the steps described above.

In Release 4, only the default screen of a display has a resource database, and widget resources come from that database regardless of the which screen the shell widget is created on.

Structures

An XrmOptionDescList describes how to parse command line resources. Prior to Release 5, the value field of the XrmOptionDescRec structure was of type caddr_t. It was changed in Release 5 for portability reasons.

```
typedef enum {
    XrmoptionNoArg,     /* Value is specified in OptionDescRec.value    */
    XrmoptionIsArg,     /* Value is the option string itself            */
    XrmoptionStickyArg, /* Value is characters immediately following option */
    XrmoptionSepArg,    /* Value is next argument in argv                */
    XrmoptionResArg,    /* Resource and value in next argument in argv   */
    XrmoptionSkipArg,   /* Ignore this option and the next argument in argv */
    XrmoptionSkipLine,  /* Ignore this option and the rest of argv       */
    XrmoptionSkipNArgs  /* Ignore this option and the next
                           OptionDescRes.value arguments in argv */
} XrmOptionKind;

typedef struct {
    char          *option;      /* Option abbreviation in argv             */
    char          *specifier;   /* Resource specifier                      */
    XrmOptionKind argKind;      /* Which style of option it is             */
    XPointer      value;        /* Value to provide if XrmoptionNoArg      */
} XrmOptionDescRec, *XrmOptionDescList;
```

An ArgList is an array of resource name/resource value pairs:

```
typedef struct {
    String    name;
    XtArgVal  value;
} Arg, *ArgList;
```

See Also

XtAppCreateShell(1), *XtAppSetFallbackResources*(1), *XtCreateApplicationContext*(1), *XtDisplayInitialize*(1), *XtOpenDisplay*(1), *XtResolvePathname*(1), *XtScreenDatabase*(1), *XtSetLanguageProc*(1), *XtToolkitInitialize*(1), *XtVaAppInitialize*(1).

Name

XtAppMainLoop – continuously process events.

Synopsis

```
void XtAppMainLoop(app_context)
    XtAppContext app_context;
```

Inputs

app_context Specifies the application context that identifies the application.

Returns

XtAppMainLoop() enters an infinite loop and never returns.

Description

XtAppMainLoop() enters an infinite loop which calls XtAppNextEvent() to wait for an events on all displays in *app_context* and XtDispatchEvent() to dispatch that event to the appropriate code.

Usage

Most applications will call XtAppNextEvent() as the last line of their main() procedure. Some applications may provide their own versions of this loop, however. A custom event loop might test an application-dependent global flag or other termination condition before looping back and calling XtAppNextEvent(). If the number of top-level widgets drops to zero, the application may be able to exit safely, for example.

Applications that use multiple application contexts or that use internal event loops will have to build their own event loop.

Background

XtAppNextEvent() looks for X events in the input queue, and also handles timer events (see XtAppAddTimeOut()) and events from alternate input sources (see XtAppAdd-Input()). If none of these events are pending and a work procedure (see XtAppAddWork-Proc()) is registered, XtAppNextEvent() invokes that work procedure to do background processing, otherwise it blocks waiting for an event. Note that XtAppNextEvent() dispatches timer and input events directly, but returns any X events that occur. Within XtApp-MainLoop(), these X events are always passed to XtDispatchEvent().

XtDispatchEvent() dispatches an event to the appropriate event handlers (see XtAdd-EventHandler()). Note that the translation manager registers an event handler, and that events that are dispatched to the translation manager will be further dispatched through the translations-to-actions mechanism.

Example

XtAppMainLoop() is implemented as follows:

```
void XtAppMainLoop(app)
        XtAppContext app;
{
    XEvent event;
```

Xt Functions and Macros

```
for (;;) {
    XtAppNextEvent(app, &event);
    XtDispatchEvent(&event);
}
}
```

See Also

XtAddEventHandler(1), *XtAppAddInput*(1), *XtAppAddTimeOut*(1), *XtAppAddWorkProc*(1), *XtAppNextEvent*(1), *XtAppProcessEvent*(1), *XtDispatchEvent*(1).

Name

XtAppNextEvent – dispatch timer and alternate input event and return the next X event.

Synopsis

```
void XtAppNextEvent(app_context, event_return)
    XtAppContext app_context;
    XEvent *event_return;
```

Inputs

app_context   Specifies the application context.

Outputs

event_return   Returns the dequeued event structure.

Description

If there is an X event pending on any of the Displays in *app_context*, XtAppNext-
Event() returns that event in *event_return*. Otherwise, it flushes the X output buffer of
each Display, and if there is a background work procedure registered (see XtAppAddWork-
Proc()), XtAppNextEvent() calls it and starts over by checking for pending events. If
there are no pending events and no work procedures, XtAppNextEvent() blocks while
waiting for input on any of the Display connections, activity on any of the alternate input
sources registered with XtAppAddInput(), or the expiration of any timers registered with
XtAppAddTimeOut().

If there is activity on an alternate input source or if a timeout interval elapses, XtAppNext-
Event() calls the callback that was registered with the input source or with the timer. If an X
event occurs, XtAppNextEvent() removes that event from the queue and returns it in
event_return.

Usage

Programs rarely need this much control over the event dispatching mechanism. Most programs
use XtAppMainLoop(). If you want to process a single X, input, or timer event, consider
XtAppProcessEvent().

See Also

XtAppAddInput(1), *XtAppAddTimeOut*(1), *XtAppAddWorkProc*(1), *XtAppMainLoop*(1), *XtAppPeek-
Event*(1), *XtAppPending*(1), *XtAppProcessEvent*(1), *XtDispatchEvent*(1).

*Xt Functions
and Macros*

XtAppPeekEvent

Name

XtAppPeekEvent – return, but do not remove the event at the head of an application's input queue; block if no events are available.

Synopsis

```
Boolean XtAppPeekEvent(app_context, event_return)
    XtAppContext app_context;
    XEvent *event_return;
```

Inputs

app_context   Specifies the application context.

Outputs

event_return

Returns the event from the head of the queue, if that event is an X event.

Returns

True if the event at the head of the queue is an X event; False if it is a timer event or an alternate input source event.

Description

If there are X events pending on any of the displays in app_context, XtAppPeek-Event() copies the event from the head of the application event queue into event_return (without removing the event from the queue) and returns True. If there are no events, it flushes the output buffers of each display and checks again. If there are still no pending X events on any of the displays, but there are timer or alternate input events ready, XtAppPeek-Event() returns False.

If there are no events of any kind, XtAppPeekEvent() blocks until one occurs, and then if it is an X event, copies the event (without removing it from the queue) and returns True or returns False otherwise. Note that XtAppPeekEvent() never calls background work procedures registered with XtAppAddWorkProc().

Usage

Programs rarely need this much control over the event dispatching mechanism. Most programs use XtAppMainLoop().

If you want to get X events *and* remove them from the input queue, consider XtAppNext-Event(). This function also dispatches timer and alternate input events.

If you want to check for input events without blocking, use XtAppPending(). This function returns a value that indicates which types of events are pending for an application context, or 0 if no events are pending.

See Also

XtAppMainLoop(1), *XtAppNextEvent*(1), *XtAppPending*(1).

XtAppPending

Name

XtAppPending – determine whether any events are in an application's input queue.

Synopsis

```
XtInputMask XtAppPending(app_context)
    XtAppContext app_context;
```

Inputs

app_context   Specifies the application context.

Returns

An `XtInputMask` which indicates what kind of events, if any, are pending on *app_context*.

Description

`XtAppPending()` returns a nonzero value if there are pending events from the X server, timer, or other input sources.

The return value is a bit mask that is the OR of `XtIMXEvent` (an X event), `XtIMTimer` (a timer event—see `XtAppAddTimeOut()`), and `XtIMAlternateInput` (an alternate input event—see `XtAppAddInput()`). As a convenience, the symbolic name `XtIMAll` is defined as the bitwise inclusive OR of all event types. If no events are pending, `XtAppPending()` flushes the output buffers of each display in the application context and returns zero. This call is the Intrinsics equivalent to the Xlib call `XPending()`.

`XtAppPending()` never blocks.

Usage

Programs rarely need this much control over the event dispatching mechanism. Most programs use `XtAppMainLoop()`.

Structures

The `XtInputMask` type and its possible values are defined as follows:

```
typedef unsigned longXtInputMask;

#define XtIMXEvent1
#define XtIMTimer2
#define XtIMAlternateInput4
#define XtIMAll (XtIMXEvent | XtIMTimer | XtIMAlternateInput)
```

See Also

XtAppAddInput(1), *XtAppAddTimeOut*(1), *XtAppMainLoop*(1), *XtAppNextEvent*(1), *XtAppPeekEvent*(1), *XtAppProcessEvent*(1), *XtDispatchEvent*(1).

Xt Functions and Macros

Name

XtAppProcessEvent – get and process one input event of a specified type.

Synopsis

```
void XtAppProcessEvent(app_context, mask)
    XtAppContext app_context;
    XtInputMask mask;
```

Inputs

`app_context` Specifies the application context for which to process events.

`mask` Specifies what types of events to process.

Description

`XtAppProcessEvent()` processes one X event, alternate input source event or timer event in `app_context`. The `mask` argument specifies which types of events are to be processed; it is the bitwise inclusive OR (|) of any of the values `XtIMXEvent`, `XtIMTimer`, or `Xt-IMAlternateInput`, or the value `XtIMAll` which specifies all three event types.

If there is no event or input of the appropriate type to process, if there is a background work procedure registered (see `XtAppAddWorkProc()`) `XtAppProcessEvent()` calls that procedure and checks again for input from all specified sources. If there are no pending events and no work procedures registered, `XtAppProcessEvent()` blocks until an event of one of the specified types occurs.

If X events are specified in `mask`, and no events are immediately available, `XtAppProcess-Event()` flushes the output buffer of each of the Displays in `app_context`. If there is more than one of the requested types of input available, it is undefined which will be processed.

`XtAppProcessEvent()` handles timer and alternate input events by calling the callback procedures registered for those events (see `XtAppAddTimeOut()` and `XtAppAdd-Input()`). It handles X events by passing them to `XtDispatchEvent()`. `XtDispatch-Event()` handles an event by passing it to the appropriate event handlers (see `XtAdd-EventHandler()`) or to the Translation Manager (which is itself an event handler).

Usage

Programs rarely need this much control over the event dispatching mechanism. Most programs use `XtAppMainLoop()`.

Structures

The `XtInputMask` type and its possible values are defined as follows:

```
typedef unsigned longXtInputMask;

#define XtIMXEvent1
#define XtIMTimer2
#define XtIMAlternateInput4
#define XtIMAll (XtIMXEvent | XtIMTimer | XtIMAlternateInput)
```

See Also

XtAppAddInput(1), *XtAppAddTimeOut*(1), *XtAppAddWorkProc*(1), *XtAppMainLoop*(1), *XtAppNext-Event*(1), *XtAppPeekEvent*(1), *XtAppPending*(1), *XtDispatchEvent*(1).

Name

XtAppReleaseCacheRefs – decrement the reference counts for cached resources obtained from
XtCallConverter().

Synopsis

```
void XtAppReleaseCacheRefs(app, refs)
      XtAppContext app;
      XtCacheRef *refs;
```

Inputs

app   Specifies the application context.

refs   Specifies a NULL-terminated array of cache references to be decremented.

Availability

Release 4 and later.

Description

XtAppReleaseCacheRefs() decrements the reference count for each XtCacheRef in
the NULL-terminated array *refs*. If any reference count reaches zero, the destructor registered with XtSetTypeConverter() for that resource type, if any, will be called and the
resource removed from the conversion cache.

An XtCacheRef is a handle to a cached resource value. It is obtained in a call to XtCall-
Converter().

Usage

Applications and widgets should very rarely need to call this function. The Intrinsics provide
two predefined callbacks which can be registered with an XtCacheRef or an array of Xt-
CacheRef on the destroy callback of a widget or object to automatically call XtApp-
ReleaseCacheRefs() when the resources are no longer needed. See XtCallback-
ReleaseCacheRef() and XtCallbackReleaseCacheRefList().

Additionally, the function XtConvertAndStore() which is a higher-level interface to
resource converters than XtCallConverter() is passed a widget or object and automatically registers XtCallbackReleaseCacheRef() on the object's destroy callback if
needed. XtCreateWidget() may also register such callbacks.

Structures

XtCacheRef is an opaque type.

See Also

XtCallbackReleaseCacheRef(1), *XtCallbackReleaseCacheRefList*(1), *XtCallConverter*(1), *XtConvertAnd-
Store*(1), *XtSetTypeConverter*(1),
XtDestructor(2).

Name

XtAppSetErrorHandler – set the low-level error handler procedure.

Synopsis

```
XtErrorHandler XtAppSetErrorHandler(app_context, handler)
    XtAppContext app_context;
    XtErrorHandler handler;
```

Inputs

app_context Specifies the application context.

handler Specifies the new fatal error procedure, which should not return.

Returns

A pointer to the previously installed low-level error handler.

Description

XtAppSetErrorHandler() registers the procedure *handler* in *app_context* as the procedure to be invoked by XtAppError(). It returns a pointer to the previously installed low-level fatal error handler. *handler* must terminate the application; if it returns the subsequent behavior of the Intrinsics is undefined.

The default low-level error handler provided by the Intrinsics is _XtDefaultError(). On POSIX-based systems, it prints the message to standard error and terminates the application.

Usage

Note that application-context-specific error handling is not implemented on many systems. Most implementations will have just one set of error handlers. If they are set for different application contexts, the one performed last will prevail.

See Also

XtAppError(1), *XtAppErrorMsg*(1), *XtAppSetErrorMsgHandler*(1), *XtAppSetWarningHandler*(1), *XtAppSetWarningMsgHandler*(1), *XtAppWarning*(1), *XtAppWarningMsg*(1), *XtErrorHandler*(2).

Name

XtAppSetErrorMsgHandler – set the high-level error handler.

Synopsis

```
XtErrorMsgHandler XtAppSetErrorMsgHandler(app_context, msg_handler)
    XtAppContext app_context;
    XtErrorMsgHandler msg_handler;
```

Inputs

app_context   Specifies the application context.

msg_handler   Specifies the new high-level fatal error message handling procedure, which should not return.

Returns

A pointer to the previously installed high-level error handler.

Description

XtAppSetErrorMsgHandler() registers the procedure *msg_handler* in *app_context* as the procedure to be invoked by XtAppErrorMsg(). It returns a pointer to the previously installed high-level error handler.

The default high-level fatal error handler provided by the Intrinsics is named _XtDefaultErrorMsg(). It looks up a message in the error resource database (see XtAppGetErrorDatabaseText()), substitutes the supplied parameters into the message, and calls XtError(). See XtErrorMsgHandler(2) for an explanation of how to write a customized high-level error handler.

msg_handler should generally invoke the low-level error handler to display the message and exit. Fatal error message handlers should not return. If one does, subsequent X Toolkit behavior is undefined.

Usage

Note that application-context-specific error handling is not implemented on many systems. Most implementations will have just one set of error handlers. If they are set for different application contexts, the one performed last will prevail.

See Also

XtAppError(1), *XtAppErrorMsg*(1), *XtAppGetErrorDatabaseText*(1), *XtAppSetErrorHandler*(1), *XtAppSetWarningHandler*(1), *XtAppSetWarningMsgHandler*(1), *XtAppWarning*(1), *XtAppWarningMsg*(1), *XtErrorHandler*(2), *XtErrorMsgHandler*(2).

XtAppSetFallbackResources

Name

XtAppSetFallbackResources – specify a default set of resource values.

Synopsis

```
void XtAppSetFallbackResources(app_context, specification_list)
    XtAppContext app_context;
    String *specification_list;
```

Inputs

app_context Specifies the application context in which the fallback resources will be used.

specification_list

Specifies a NULL-terminated array of resource specifications to pre-load the database, or NULL.

Availability

Release 4 and later.

Description

XtAppSetFallbackResources() registers *specification_list* as a default set of resource values that will be used in *app_context* to initialize the resource database if the application-specific class resource file (i.e., the *app-defaults* file) cannot be found.

specification_list is an array of strings, each string a single resource specification in resource file format. If XtDisplayInitialize() is not able to find or read an application-specific class resource file then the resource database for the display will be initialized with the values most recently registered with XtAppSetFallbackResources().

XtAppSetFallbackResources() is not required to copy *specification_list*; the caller must ensure that the contents of the list and of the strings addressed by the list remain valid until all displays are initialized, or until XtAppSetFallbackResources() is called again. Passing NULL for *specification_list* removes any previous fallback resource specification for the application context.

Usage

XtAppInitialize() provides an argument for specifying the fallback resources, so few applications need to call XtAppSetFallbackResources() directly. Note that XtAppSetFallbackResources() should be called before XtOpenDisplay() or XtDisplayInitialize() if they are to take effect for that display.

The intended use of fallback resources is to provide a minimal number of resources that make the application usable (or at least terminate with helpful diagnostic messages) when some problem exists in finding and loading the application-defaults file.

See Also

XtAppInitialize(1), *XtDisplayInitialize*(1), *XtOpenDisplay*(1).

Xt Functions and Macros

Name
XtAppSetSelectionTimeout – set the Intrinsics selection timeout value.

Synopsis
```
void XtAppSetSelectionTimeout(app_context, timeout)
    XtAppContext app_context;
    unsigned long timeout;
```

Inputs
app_context   Specifies the application context.

timeout   Specifies the selection timeout in milliseconds.

Description
XtAppSetSelectionTimeout() sets the Intrinsics selection timeout value for the specified application context. The selection timeout is the time within which two communicating applications must respond to one another. The initial timeout value is set by the selection-Timeout application resource, which has a default value of 5000 milliseconds (5 seconds).

Usage
The current timeout value can be retrieved by a call to XtAppGetSelectionTimeout(). You should rarely need to query or set this value. In particular, an application generally should not change this value except under the explicit request of the user.

See Also
XtAppGetSelectionTimeout(1).

Name

XtAppSetTypeConverter – register a "new-style" type converter in a single application context.

Synopsis

```
void XtAppSetTypeConverter(app_context, from_type, to_type, converter,
        convert_args, num_args, cache_type, destructor)
    XtAppContext app_context;
    String from_type;
    String to_type;
    XtTypeConverter converter;
    XtConvertArgList convert_args;
    Cardinal num_args;
    XtCacheType cache_type;
    XtDestructor destructor;
```

Inputs

app_context Specifies the application context.

from_type Specifies the source type.

to_type Specifies the destination type.

converter Specifies the resource type converter procedure.

convert_args
Specifies additional conversion arguments, or NULL.

num_args Specifies the count of additional conversion arguments, or zero.

cache_type Specifies whether or not resources produced by this converter are sharable or display-specific and when they should be freed.

destructor Specifies a destroy procedure for resources produced by this conversion, or NULL if no additional action is required, to deallocate resources produced by converter.

Availability

Release 4 and later.

Description

XtAppSetTypeConverter() registers *converter* in *app_context* as a procedure to convert data of resource type *from_type* to resource type *to_type*.

Each element of *convert_args* is an XtConvertArgRec. It is not the argument actually passed to the converter procedure, but specifies how to obtain an XrmValue argument which will be passed to the converter. The "Background" section below explains the XtConvertArgRec structure in detail.

Converted resource values returned by *converter* will automatically be cached according to the argument *cache_type*, which can be XtCacheNone, XtCacheAll, or XtCacheByDisplay. The meanings of these types are described in the "Background" section below. In addition, the qualifier XtCacheRefCount can be ORed with any of these values and specifies that references to cached values produced by this converter should be counted, and if the count ever drops to zero, the value should be removed from the cache, and the procedure *destructor* should be called to free any memory or resources associated with that value.

If the same *from_type* and *to_type* are specified in multiple calls to `XtAppSetType-Converter()`, the most recent overrides the previous ones.

See `XtTypeConverter(2)` for an explanation of how to write a "new-style" converter. See `XtDestuctor(2)` for an explanation of how to write a destructor procedure. See `XtCall-Converter()` for an explanation of how reference counting of cached values is performed.

Usage

`XtAppSetTypeConverter()` registers a resource converter of a type added to the Intrinsics in Release 4. If you need to register an "old-style" converter which was written before Release 4, use `XtAppAddConverter()`.

`XtSetTypeConverter()` is identical to `XtAppSetTypeConverter()` except that it registers the converter in all application contexts, including application contexts that are created in the future.

If you write a widget that has a resource which is of some enumerated type, you should write a converter routine which will convert between the symbolic names of each value and the values themselves. This converter should then be registered in your widget's `class_initialize()` method.

If you are writing a programming library or an application that defines non-standard types, it may be useful to provide string converters for those types. This allows resources of that type to be specified from a resource file. An application that supported user-configurable popup menus, for example, might include a String-to-Menu converter.

Some converters need additional arguments, such as a screen or colormap in order to correctly perform the conversion. These converters are registered with an `XtConvertArgList`. Generally the author of the converter will also define a static array of `XtConvertArgRec` to be registered with the converter. There are also two `XtConvertArgLists` predefined by the Intrinsics: `screenConvertArg` passes the widget's `screen` field to the converter in `args[0]`, and `colorConvertArgs` passes the widget's `screen` field to the converter in `args[0]` and the widget's `colormap` field in `args[1]`.

The Intrinsics define a number of standard converters which do not need to be registered. See `XtConvertAndStore()` for a list of these predefined converters. There are also a number of other useful converters defined in the Xmu library which do need to be registered explicitly. See `XmuCvtStringToMisc(6)`.

Example

You can register the XmuCvtStringToColorCursor from the Xmu library with the following:

```
static XtConvertArgRec colorCursorConvertArgs[] = {
  {XtWidgetBaseOffset, (XtPointer) XtOffsetOf(WidgetRec, core.screen),
    sizeof(Screen *)},
  {XtResourceString, (XtPointer) XtNpointerColor,sizeof(Pixel)},
```

```
    {XtResourceString, (XtPointer) XtNpointerColorBackground, sizeof(Pixel)},
    {XtWidgetBaseOffset, (XtPointer) XtOffsetOf(WidgetRec,core.colormap),
        sizeof(Colormap)}
};

XtSetTypeConverter(XtRString, XtRColorCursor, XmuCvtStringToColorCursor,
                colorCursorConvertArgs, XtNumber(colorCursorConvertArgs),
                XtCacheByDisplay, NULL);
```

Background

Specifying Arguments to a Converter

For the few type converters that need additional arguments, the Intrinsics conversion mechanism provides a method of specifying how these arguments should be computed. Before a converter is called, each element of the XtConvertArgList is interpreted to determine the sizes and values of the arguments. These computed arguments are passed to the converter as an array of XrmValue. The enumerated type XtAddressMode and the structure XtConvertArgRec specify how each argument is derived.

```
typedef enum {
        /* address mode          parameter representation */
        XtAddress,               /* address */
        XtBaseOffset,            /* offset */
        XtImmediate,             /* constant */
        XtResourceString,        /* resource name string */
        XtResourceQuark,         /* resource name quark */
        XtWidgetBaseOffset,      /* offset */
        XtProcedureArg           /* procedure to call */
} XtAddressMode;

typedef struct {
        XtAddressMode address_mode;
        XtPointer address_id;
        Cardinal size;
} XtConvertArgRec, *XtConvertArgList;
```

The size field of an XtConvertArgRec specifies the length of the data in bytes. The address_mode field specifies how the address_id field should be interpreted. The possible values of XtAddressMode have the following meanings:

XtAddress
    causes address_id to be interpreted as the address of the data.

XtBaseOffset
    causes address_id to be interpreted as the offset from the widget base.

XtImmediate
    causes address_id to be interpreted as a constant.

`XtResourceString`
> causes `address_id` to be interpreted as the name of a resource that is to be converted into an offset from the widget base.

`XtResourceQuark`
> causes `address_id` to be interpreted as the result of an `XrmStringToQuark()` conversion on the name of a resource, which is to be converted into an offset from the widget base.

`XtWidgetBaseOffset`
> is similar to `XtBaseOffset` except that it searches for the closest windowed ancestor if the object is not of a subclass of Core.

`XtProcedureArg`
> specifies that `address_id` is a pointer to a procedure of type `XtConvertArgProc` to be invoked to return the conversion argument. See `XtConvertArgProc`(2) for an explanation of how to write a procedure of this type.

Caching Converted Values

The possible values for the *cache_type* argument are as follows:

`XtCacheNone`
> Specifies that the results of a previous conversion may not be reused to satisfy any other resource requests; the specified converter will be called each time the converted value is required.

`XtCacheAll`
> Specifies that the results of a previous conversion should be reused for any resource request that depends upon the same source value and conversion arguments.

`XtCacheByDisplay`
> Specifies that the results of a previous conversion should be used as for `XtCacheAll` but that the value should be removed from the cache and the destructor, if any, should be called, when `XtCloseDisplay()` is called for the display connection associated with the converted value.

The qualifier `XtCacheRefCount` may be ORed with any of the above values. If `XtCache-RefCount` is specified, calls to `XtCreateWidget()`, `XtCreateManagedWidget()`, `XtGetApplicationResources()` and `XtGetSubresources()` that use the converted value will be counted. When a widget using the converted value is destroyed, the count is decremented, and if the count reaches zero, the destructor procedure *destructor* will be called and the converted value will be removed from the conversion cache.

Structures

The `XtConvertArgRec` structure and the related `XtAddressMode` type are shown in the "Background" section above. The `XtCacheType` type and its legal values are defined as follows:

```
typedef int          XtCacheType;

#define               XtCacheNone        0x001
#define               XtCacheAll         0x002
#define               XtCacheByDisplay   0x003
#define               XtCacheRefCount    0x100
```

See Also

XtAppReleaseCacheRefs(1), *XtCallbackReleaseCacheRef*(1), *XtCallbackReleaseCacheRefList*(1), *XtCall-Converter*(1), *XtConvertAndStore*(1), *XtSetTypeConverter*(1), *XtConvertArgProc*(2), *XtDestructor*(2), *XtTypeConverter*(2).

Xt Functions
and Macros

Name

XtAppSetWarningHandler – set the low-level warning handler.

Synopsis

```
XtErrorHandler XtAppSetWarningHandler(app_context, handler)
    XtAppContext app_context;
    XtErrorHandler handler;
```

Inputs

`app_context` Specifies the application context.

`handler`   Specifies the new nonfatal error procedure.

Returns

A pointer to the previously installed low-level error handler.

Description

`XtAppSetWarningHandler()` registers the procedure `handler` in `app_context` as the procedure to be invoked by `XtAppWarning()`. It returns a pointer to the previously installed low-level warning handler.

The default low-level warning handler provided by the Intrinsics is `_XtDefaultWarning()`. On POSIX-based systems, it prints the message to standard error and returns to the caller.

Usage

Note that application-context-specific error and warning handling is not implemented on many systems. Most implementations will have just one set of error handlers. If they are set for different application contexts, the one performed last will prevail.

See Also

XtAppError(1), *XtAppErrorMsg*(1), *XtAppSetErrorHandler*(1), *XtAppSetErrorMsgHandler*(1), *XtAppSetWarningMsgHandler*(1), *XtAppWarning*(1), *XtAppWarningMsg*(1), *XtErrorHandler*(2).

XtAppSetWarningMsgHandler

Name

XtAppSetWarningMsgHandler – set the high-level warning handler.

Synopsis

```
XtErrorMsgHandler XtAppSetWarningMsgHandler(app_context, msg_handler)
    XtAppContext app_context;
    XtErrorMsgHandler msg_handler;
```

Inputs

app_context   Specifies the application context.

msg_handler   Specifies the new high-level warning handler.

Returns

A pointer to the previously installed high-level warning handler.

Description

XtAppSetWarningMsgHandler() registers the procedure *msg_handler* in *app_context* as the procedure to be invoked by XtAppWarningMsg(). It returns a pointer to the previously installed high-level warning handler.

The default high-level warning handler provided by the Intrinsics is named _XtDefaultWarningMsg(). It looks up a message in the error resource database (see XtAppGetErrorDatabaseText()), substitutes the supplied parameters into the message, and calls XtWarning(). See XtWarningMsgHandler(2) for an explanation of how to write a customized high-level warning handler.

msg_handler should generally invoke the low-level warning handler to display the message.

Usage

Note that application-context-specific error and warning handling is not implemented on many systems. Most implementations will have just one set of error handlers. If they are set for different application contexts, the one performed last will prevail.

See Also

XtAppError(1), *XtAppErrorMsg*(1), *XtAppGetErrorDatabaseText*(1), *XtAppSetErrorHandler*(1), *XtAppSetErrorMsgHandler*(1), *XtAppSetWarningHandler*(1), *XtAppWarning*(1), *XtAppWarningMsg*(1), *XtErrorHandler*(2), *XtErrorMsgHandler*(2).

XtAppWarning

Name

XtAppWarning – call the low-level warning handler.

Synopsis

```
void XtAppWarning(app_context, message)
    XtAppContext app_context;
    String message;
```

Inputs

app_context Specifies the application context.

message Specifies the warning message that is to be reported.

Description

XtAppWarning() passes its arguments to the installed low-level warning handler. On POSIX systems, the default handler is _XtDefaultWarning(). It prints the message to the stderr stream and returns.

Usage

To report fatal error messages and exit, use XtAppError() or XtAppErrorMsg(). To change the low-level warning handler, use XtAppSetWarningHandler().

XtAppWarning() calls the "low-level" warning handler. It is better to use XtApp-WarningMsg() which calls the "high-level" warning handler. The high-level handler looks up the warning message in a resource database and so allows for customization and internationalization of warning messages.

Although the Intrinsics interface allows separate error and warning handlers for each application context, most implementations will support only a single set of handlers. When a new handler is installed, it will be used in all application contexts.

See Also

XtAppError(1), *XtAppErrorMsg*(1), *XtAppSetErrorHandler*(1), *XtAppSetErrorMsgHandler*(1), *XtAppSet-WarningHandler*(1), *XtAppSetWarningMsgHandler*(1), *XtAppWarningMsg*(1), *XtErrorHandler*(2), *XtErrorMsgHandler*(2).

XtAppWarningMsg

Name

XtAppWarningMsg – call the high-level warning handler.

Synopsis

```
void XtAppWarningMsg(app_context, name, type, class , default, params,
        num_params)
    XtAppContext app_context;
    String name;
    String type;
    String class;
    String default;
    String *params;
    Cardinal *num_params;
```

Inputs

app_context Specifies the application context.

name   Specifies the general kind of error.

type   Specifies the detailed name of the error.

class   Specifies the resource class.

default   Specifies the default message to use if no message is found in the database.

params   Specifies an array of values to be inserted into the message.

num_params   Specifies the number of elements in *params*.

Description

XtAppWarningMsg() passes all of its arguments except *app_context* to the installed high-level warning handler. The default high-level warning handler is _XtDefault-WarningMsg(). It calls XtAppGetErrorDatabaseText() to lookup a message of the specified *name*, *type*, and *class* in the error database. If no such message is found, Xt-AppGetErrorDatabaseText() returns the specified *default* message. In either case, _XtDefaultWarningMsg() does a printf-style substitution of *params* into the message, and passes the resulting text to the low-level warning handler by calling XtWarning().

See XtAppGetErrorDatabaseText() for details on how messages are looked up in the error database.

Usage

To report fatal error messages and exit, use XtAppErrorMsg(). To change the high-level warning handler, use XtAppSetWarningMsgHandler().

Note that the *num_params* argument to this function is a Cardinal *, not a Cardinal.

Although the Intrinsics interface allows separate error and warning handlers for each application context, most implementations will support only a single set of handlers. When a new handler is installed, it will be used in all application contexts.

Example

The following code is from `XtDisplayStringConversionWarning()`:

```
String params[2];
Cardinal num_params = 2;

params[0] = (String)from;
params[1] = (String)toType;
XtAppWarningMsg(XtDisplayToApplicationContext(dpy),
            XtNconversionError, "string", XtCXtToolkitError,
            "Cannot convert string to type %s",
            params, &num_params);
```

See Also

XtAppError(1), *XtAppErrorMsg*(1), *XtAppSetErrorHandler*(1), *XtAppSetErrorMsgHandler*(1), *XtAppSet-WarningHandler*(1), *XtAppSetWarningMsgHandler*(1), *XtAppWarning*(1),
XtErrorHandler(2), *XtErrorMsgHandler*(2).

Name

XtAugmentTranslations – nondestructively merge new translations with widget's existing ones.

Synopsis

```
void XtAugmentTranslations(w, translations)
    Widget w;
    XtTranslations translations;
```

Inputs

w   Specifies the widget into which the new translations are to be merged. Must be of class Core or any subclass thereof.

translations   Specifies the compiled translation table to merge in.

Description

XtAugmentTranslations() merges a compiled translation table translations into a widget's internal compiled translation table, ignoring any new translations that conflict with existing translations. The table translations is not altered by this process. Any "#replace", "#augment", or "#override" directives in translations are ignored by this function.

Usage

Use XtParseTranslationTable() to convert a string representation of a translation table to the XtTranslations compiled form.

To merge translations into a widget and replace existing translations where there are conflicts, use XtOverrideTranslations(). To completely replace a widget's translation table, use XtSetValues() to set a compiled translation table on the widget's XtNtranslations resource. To remove all of a widget's translations, use XtUninstallTranslations().

Translation tables can also be specified in string from a resource file. By default, specifying a value for the translations resource will completely replace the existing translations. If the string form of the translation table begins with the directives "#augment" or "#override", however, then the specified translations will be merged with the widget's existing translations, and new translations that conflict with existing translations will be ignored or will override the existing translations, respectively.

See Also

XtOverrideTranslations(1), *XtParseTranslationTable*(1), *XtUninstallTranslations*(1).

*Xt Functions
and Macros*

XtBuildEventMask

Name

XtBuildEventMask – retrieve a widget's event mask.

Synopsis

```
EventMask XtBuildEventMask(w)
    Widget w;
```

Inputs

w   Specifies the widget. Must be of class Core or any subclass thereof.

Returns

An event mask with a bit set for each event type the widget is receiving.

Description

XtBuildEventMask() returns a widget's event mask. The mask reflects the events the widget is currently selecting. (If the widget is unrealized, then the mask reflects the events the widget will select when it is realized.) This event mask is the logical OR of all event masks selected by adding event handlers and event translations (including accelerators). It is updated whenever event handlers or translations are installed or removed for the specified widget.

Structures

The event_mask is formed by combining the event mask symbols listed in the table below using the bitwise OR operator (|). Each mask symbol sets a bit in the event_mask.

NoEventMask	Button1MotionMask	StructureNotifyMask
KeyPressMask	Button2MotionMask	ResizeRedirectMask
KeyReleaseMask	Button3MotionMask	SubstructureNotifyMask
ButtonPressMask	Button4MotionMask	SubstructureRedirectMask
ButtonReleaseMask	Button5MotionMask	FocusChangeMask
EnterWindowMask	ButtonMotionMask	PropertyChangeMask
LeaveWindowMask	KeymapStateMask	ColormapChangeMask
PointerMotionMask	ExposureMask	OwnerGrabButtonMask
PointerMotionHintMask	VisibilityChangeMask	

See Also

XtAddEventHandler(1), *XtAddRawEventHandler*(1), *XtRealizeWidget*(1).

XtCallAcceptFocus

Name

XtCallAcceptFocus – offer the input focus to a child widget.

Synopsis

```
Boolean XtCallAcceptFocus(w, time)
    Widget w;
    Time *time;
```

Inputs

w   Specifies the widget; must be of class Core or any subclass thereof.

time   Specifies the X time of the event that is causing the accept focus.

Returns

True if *w* took the input focus; False if *w* did not take the input focus.

Description

XtCallAcceptFocus() calls the specified widget's Core class accept_focus() method, passing it the specified widget and time, and *True* if the widget took the input focus, or *False* otherwise. If the accept_focus() method is NULL, XtCallAcceptFocus() returns False.

Usage

Generally, only widgets should call XtCallAcceptFocus(), and generally only on their descendants.

Note that calling a widget's accept_focus() method does not automatically assign the input focus, and does not mean that the widget will necessarily take the input focus. The accept_focus() method must decide whether or not to take the focus and then take it with XSetInputFocus() or XtSetKeyboardFocus().

Background

Widgets that need the input focus can call XSetInputFocus() explicitly, pursuant to the restrictions of the *Inter-Client Communications Convention Manual*. To allow outside agents, such as the parent, to cause a widget to take the input focus, every widget exports an accept_focus() method. The widget returns a value indicating whether it actually took the focus or not, so that the parent can give the focus to another widget. Widgets that need to know when they lose the input focus must use the Xlib focus notification mechanism explicitly (typically by specifying translations for FocusIn and FocusOut events). Widget classes that never want the input focus should set the accept_focus() method to NULL.

See Also

XtSetKeyboardFocus(1),
accept_focus(4).

XtCallActionProc

Name

XtCallActionProc – explicitly invoke a named action procedure.

Synopsis

```
void XtCallActionProc(widget, action, event, params, num_params)
      Widget widget;
      String action;
      XEvent *event;
      String *params;
      Cardinal num_params;
```

Inputs

widget   Specifies the widget in which the action is to be invoked; must be of class Core or any subclass thereof.

action   Specifies the name of the action routine.

event   Specifies the event to pass to the action procedure.

params   Specifies parameters to pass to the action procedure.

num_params Specifies the number of elements in the *params* array.

Description

XtCallActionProc() looks up the action procedure named *action* and invokes it, passing *widget*, *event*, *params*, and *num_params* as arguments. Before calling the named action, XtCallActionProc() invokes any action hook procedures that have been registered with XtAppAddActionHook().

It is the responsibility of the caller to ensure that the contents of the *event*, *params*, and *num_params* arguments are appropriate for the specified action routine and, if necessary, that the specified widget is realized and/or sensitive. If the named action routine cannot be found, XtCallActionProc() generates a warning message and returns.

When searching for the action procedure, XtCallActionProc() looks in the following places:

• The widget's class and all superclass action tables, in subclass-to-superclass order.

• The parent's class and all superclass action tables, in subclass-to-superclass order, then on up the ancestor tree.

• The action tables registered with XtAppAddActions() and XtAddActions() from the most recently added table to the oldest table.

See Also

XtAppAddActionHook(1), *XtRemoveActionHook*(1),
XtActionHookProc(2).

XtCallbackExclusive

Name

XtCallbackExclusive – callback function to pop up a widget.

Synopsis

```
void XtCallbackExclusive(w, client_data, call_data)
    Widget w;
    XtPointer client_data;
    XtPointer call_data;
```

Inputs

w   Specifies the widget.

client_data   Specifies the popup shell.

call_data   Specifies the callback data, which is not used by this procedure.

Description

XtCallbackExclusive() calls XtPopup() on the widget passed in the *client_data* argument with *grab_mode* set to XtGrabExclusive. Then it calls XtSetSensitive() on *w* to make that widget insensitive.

XtCallbackExclusive() is a convenience procedure designed to be registered on a widget's callback list (which is why it has a third, unused argument). The widget to be popped up should be registered as *client_data* for the callback. The reason that this callback makes its invoking widget insensitive is so that the use cannot request to popup the shell again while it is already up.

Usage

To popup a shell with a non-exclusive grab or with no grab at all, you can use XtCallback-Nonexclusive() or XtCallbackNone(). To popdown a shell from a callback, use Xt-CallbackPopdown().

Note that this function does not attempt to place the popup shell at any particular location, and for that reason may not be appropriate in many circumstances.

It is also possible to pop up a shell with the XtMenuPopup action.

Example

To arrange for the shell pshell to be popped up when the use clicks on the button widget button, you would use code like the following:

```
XtAddCallback(button,XtNcallback,XtCallbackExclusive,pshell);
```

A companion example is presented on the XtCallbackPopdown() reference page.

See Also

XtCallbackNone(1), *XtCallbackNonexclusive*(1), *XtCallbackPopdown*(1), *XtMenuPopdown*(1), *XtMenu-Popup*(1), *XtPopdown*(1), *XtPopup*(1), *XtSetSensitive*(1).

Xt Functions and Macros

XtCallbackNone

Name

XtCallbackNone – callback function to pop up a widget.

Synopsis

```
void XtCallbackNone(w, client_data, call_data)
    Widget w;
    XtPointer client_data;
    XtPointer call_data;
```

Inputs

w   Specifies the widget.

client_data   Specifies the popup shell.

call_data   Specifies the callback data, which is not used by this procedure.

Description

XtCallbackNone() calls XtPopup() on the widget passed in the *client_data* argument with *grab_mode* set to XtGrabNone. Then it calls XtSetSensitive() on *w* to make that widget insensitive.

XtCallbackNone() is a convenience procedure designed to be registered on a widget's callback list (which is why it has a third, unused argument). The widget to be popped up should be registered as *client_data* for the callback. The reason that this callback makes its invoking widget insensitive is so that the use cannot request to popup the shell again while it is already up.

Usage

To popup a shell with an exclusive grab or with no grab at all, you can use XtCallback-Exclusive() or XtCallbackNone(). To popdown a shell from a callback, use Xt-CallbackPopdown().

Note that this function does not attempt to place the popup shell at any particular location, and for that reason may not be appropriate in many circumstances.

It is also possible to pop up a shell with the XtMenuPopup action.

Example

To arrange for the shell pshell to be popped up when the use clicks on the button widget button, you would use code like the following:

```
XtAddCallback(button,XtNcallback,XtCallbackNone,pshell);
```

A companion example is presented on the XtCallbackPopdown() reference page.

See Also

XtCallbackExclusive(1), *XtCallbackNonexclusive*(1), *XtCallbackPopdown*(1), *XtMenuPopdown*(1), *Xt-MenuPopup*(1), *XtPopdown*(1), *XtPopup*(1), *XtSetSensitive*(1).

Name

XtCallbackNonexclusive – callback function to pop up a widget.

Synopsis

```
void XtCallbackNonexclusive(w, client_data, call_data)
    Widget w;
    XtPointer client_data;
    XtPointer call_data;
```

Inputs

w　　　　　　Specifies the widget.

client_data　Specifies the popup shell.

call_data　Specifies the callback data, which is not used by this procedure.

Description

XtCallbackNonexclusive() calls XtPopup() on the widget passed in the *client_data* argument with *grab_mode* set to XtGrabNonexclusive. Then it calls XtSetSensitive() on *w* to make that widget insensitive.

XtCallbackNonexclusive() is a convenience procedure designed to be registered on a widget's callback list (which is why it has a third, unused argument). The widget to be popped up should be registered as *client_data* for the callback. The reason that this callback makes its invoking widget insensitive is so that the use cannot request to popup the shell again while it is already up.

Usage

To popup a shell with a non-exclusive grab or with no grab at all, you can use XtCallbackNonexlusive() or XtCallbackNone(). To popdown a shell from a callback, use XtCallbackPopdown().

Note that this function does not attempt to place the popup shell at any particular location, and for that reason may not be appropriate in many circumstances.

It is also possible to pop up a shell with the XtMenuPopup action.

Example

To arrange for the shell pshell to be popped up when the use clicks on the button widget button, you would use code like the following:

```
XtAddCallback(button,XtNcallback,XtCallbackNonexclusive,pshell);
```

A companion example is presented on the XtCallbackPopdown() reference page.

See Also

XtCallbackNone(1), *XtCallbackExclusive*(1), *XtCallbackPopdown*(1), *XtMenuPopdown*(1), *XtMenuPopup*(1), *XtPopdown*(1), *XtPopup*(1), *XtSetSensitive*(1).

Name

XtCallbackPopdown – callback function to popdown a widget.

Synopsis

```
void XtCallbackPopdown(w, client_data, call_data)
    Widget w;
    XtPointer client_data;
    XtPointer call_data;
```

Inputs

w   Specifies the widget.

client_data Specifies a pointer to an XtPopdownID structure.

call_data   Specifies the callback data, which is not used by this procedure.

Description

XtCallbackPopdown() casts is *client_data* argument to an XtPopdownIDRec *, calls XtPopdown on the widget in the shell_widget field, and then resensitizes the widget in the enable_widget field by calling XtSetSensitive().

XtCallbackPopdown() is a convenience procedure designed to be registered on a widget's callback list (which is why it has third, unused argument) and used on a shell widget popped up with XtCallbackExclusive(), XtCallbackNone(), or XtCallback-Nonexclusive(). The widget to be popped down and the widget that was desensitized when the shell was popped up should be stored into the XtPopdownID structure that is registered with XtCallbackPopdown().

Usage

It is also possible to pop down a shell with the XtMenuPopdown action.

Example

The following code registers XtCallbackPopdown() to popdown the widget pshell when the button ok is pressed. It assumes that pshell was popped up by XtCallback-Exclusive() registered on the widget button.

```
XtPopdownIDRec pop_rec;

pop_rec.shell_widget = pshell;
pop_rec.enable_widget = button;
XtAddCallback(ok, XtNcallback, XtCallbackPopdown, &pop_rec);
```

Structures

XtCallbackPopdown() expects a XtPopdownID as its *client_data* argument.

```
typedef struct {
    Widget shell_widget;
    Widget enable_widget;
} XtPopdownIDRec, *XtPopdownID;
```

See Also

XtCallbackExclusive(1), *XtCallbackNone*(1), *XtCallbackNonexclusive*(1), *XtMenuPopup*(1), *XtMenu-Popdown*(1), *XtPopdown*(1), *XtPopup*(1), *XtSetSensitive*(1).

Xt Functions and Macros

XtCallbackReleaseCacheRef

Name

XtCallbackReleaseCacheRef – callback function to release a cached resource value.

Synopsis

```
void XtCallbackReleaseCacheRef(object, client_data, call_data)
    Widget object;
    XtPointer client_data;
    XtPointer call_data;
```

Inputs

object   Specifies the object with which the resource is associated.

client_data   Specifies the conversion cache entry to be released.

call_data   Is ignored.

Availability

Release 4 and later.

Description

XtCallbackReleaseCacheRef() casts its *client_data* argument to an XtCache-Ref, places it in a NULL-terminated array of XtCacheRef and passes this array to XtApp-ReleaseCacheRefs(). XtAppReleaseCacheRefs() decrements the reference count on the specified object in the resource conversion cache, and if the count reaches zero it removes the object from the cache and calls the appropriate destructor procedures.

XtCallbackReleaseCacheRef() is a convenience procedure designed to be registered on the destroy callback list of a widget or object (which is why it has third, unused argument).

Usage

XtCacheRef values are returned from calls to XtCallConverter(). The higher-level converter function XtConvertAndStore() performs the conversion and automatically registers this function on the object's destroy callback list if necessary.

To release an array of XtCacheRef, you can use XtCallbackReleaseCache-RefList().

Structures

XtCacheRef is an opaque type.

See Also

XtAppReleaseCacheRefs(1), *XtCallbackReleaseCacheRefList*(1), *XtCallConverter*(1), *XtConvertAnd-Store*(1).

XtCallbackReleaseCacheRefList

Name

XtCallbackReleaseCacheRefList — callback function to release a list of cached values.

Synopsis

```
void XtCallbackReleaseCacheRefList(object, client_data, call_data)
      Widget object;
      XtPointer client_data;
      XtPointer call_data;
```

Inputs

object   Specifies the object with which the resources are associated.

client_data   Specifies the conversion cache entries to be released.

call_data   Is ignored.

Availability

Release 4 and later.

Description

XtCallbackReleaseCacheRefList() casts its *client_data* argument to a NULL-terminated array of XtCacheRef and passes this array to XtAppReleaseCacheRefs(). XtAppReleaseCacheRefs() decrements the reference count on the specified objects in the resource conversion cache, and if the count reaches zero on any of them it removes the object from the cache and calls the appropriate destructor procedures.

XtCallbackReleaseCacheReList() is a convenience procedure designed to be registered on the destroy callback list of a widget or object (which is why it has third, unused argument).

Usage

XtCacheRef values are returned from calls to XtCallConverter(). The higher-level converter function XtConvertAndStore() performs the conversion and automatically registers XtCallbackReleaseCacheRef() on the object's destroy callback list if necessary.

To release a single XtCacheRef, you can use XtCallbackReleaseCacheRef().

Structures

XtCacheRef is an opaque type.

See Also

XtAppReleaseCacheRefs(1), *XtCallbackReleaseCacheRef*(1), *XtCallConverter*(1), *XtConvertAndStore*(1).

Xt Functions and Macros

XtCallCallbackList

Name

XtCallCallbackList – execute the procedures in a callback list, specifying the callback list by address.

Synopsis

```
void XtCallCallbackList(object, callbacks, call_data)
     Widget object;
     XtCallbackList callbacks;
     XtPointer call_data;
```

Inputs

object   Specifies the object which contains the callback list; may be of class Object or any subclass thereof.

callbacks   Specifies the callback list to be invoked.

call_data   Specifies data to pass to each of the callback procedures in the list as their call_data arguments.

Availability

Release 4 and later.

Description

XtCallCallbackList() calls the procedures on the callbacks callback list. It invokes each procedure with object as the first argument, the data registered with the procedure as the second argument and call_data as the third argument.

callbacks must be of type XtCallbackList, and must be a widget or object resource of resource type XtRCallback.

Usage

XtCallCallbackList() should only be called by widgets and objects; applications will never need to call it.

XtCallCallbacks() calls the procedures on a callback list specified by name. XtCall-CallbackList() is generally a little faster because it does not have to look up the callback list by name.

The call_data argument is untyped value. The caller must be sure to pass correctly initialized data of the type expected by callbacks registered on the specified callback list. This type may be an int, or some other type that fits in 32 bits, but is often a pointer to a structure.

Widgets maintain XtCallbackLists in a compiled internal form, for this reason, you cannot call XtCallCallbackList() on a statically initialized array of XtCallbackRec or any other XtCallbackList that is not a widget or object resource.

See Also

XtAddCallback(1), *XtCallCallbacks*(1).

Name

XtCallCallbacks – execute the procedures on a widget's named callback list.

Synopsis

```
void XtCallCallbacks(object, callback_name, call_data)
    Widget object;
    String callback_name;
    XtPointer call_data;
```

Inputs

object   Specifies the object; may be of class Object or any subclass thereof.

callback_name
                 Specifies the resource name of the callback list to be executed.

call_data   Specifies the value to pass to each callback procedure as its third argument.

Description

XtCallCallbacks() calls the procedures registered on the callback list named by *callback_name* on the widget or object *object*. It invokes each procedure with *object* as the first argument, the data registered with each procedure as the second argument, and *call_data* as the third argument.

Usage

XtCallCallbacks() should only be called by widgets and objects; applications will never need to call it.

XtCallCallbackList() calls the procedures on a callback list specified directly as an XtCallbackList. This is generally a little faster because it does not have to look up the callback list by name.

The *call_data* argument is untyped value. The caller must be sure to pass correctly initialized data of the type expected by callbacks registered on the specified callback list. This type may be an int, or some other type that fits in 32 bits, but is often a pointer to a structure.

See Also

XtAddCallback(1), *XtCallCallbackList*(1).

Xt Functions and Macros

XtCallConverter

Name

XtCallConverter – explicitly invoke a "new-style" resource converter and cache result.

Synopsis

```
Boolean XtCallConverter(display, converter, args, num_args, from,
        to_in_out, cache_ref_return)
    Display* display;
    XtTypeConverter converter;
    XrmValuePtr args;
    Cardinal num_args;
    XrmValuePtr from;
    XrmValuePtr to_in_out;
    XtCacheRef *cache_ref_return;
```

Inputs

display   Specifies the display with which the conversion is to be associated.

converter   Specifies the new-style conversion procedure to be called.

args   Specifies the additional conversion arguments needed to perform the conversion, or NULL.

num_args   Specifies the number of additional arguments.

from   Specifies the source value to be converted.

to_in_out   Specifies the address at which the converted value is to be stored, and the number of bytes allocated at that address.

Outputs

to_in_out   Returns (in the size field) the actual size of the converted value.

cache_ref_return
                 Returns a conversion cache ID if the converter was registered with reference counting. NULL may be passed for this argument if the caller is not interested in reference counting of cached conversion values.

Returns

True if the conversion was performed successfully, False otherwise.

Availability

Release 4 and later.

Description

XtCallConverter() converts the value from as appropriate for the conversion procedure converter by looking a converted value up in the cache, or by invoking the converter with the *display*, *args*, *num_args*, *from*, and *to_in_out* arguments.

to_in_out->addr should contain the address at which the converted value is to be stored, and *to_in_out*->size should contain the number of bytes allocated at that address.

See the "Background" section below for more details.

Usage

XtConvertAndStore() is a higher level interface to resource conversion, and is easier to use in most cases.

You do not often need, in applications or widgets, to convert between resource types directly. Generally you can rely on the Intrinsics resource management code to perform all necessary conversions for you. When writing a resource converter, however, you may find that you need to invoke another converter.

If XtCallConverter() returns an XtCacheRef value you must store it and decrement the reference count (with XtAppReleaseCacheRefs()) when you no longer need the converted value. The easiest way to do this is to register the predefined callback XtCallback-ReleaseCacheRef() on the destroy callback of the widget or object that is using the converted value.

Background

XtCallConverter() looks up the specified type converter in the application context associated with the display. If the converter was not registered or was registered with cache type XtCacheAll or XtCacheByDisplay, XtCallConverter() looks in the conversion cache to see whether this conversion procedure has been called with the specified arguments. If so, XtCallConverter() checks the success status of the prior call. If the conversion failed, XtCallConverter() returns False immediately; otherwise it checks the size specified in the *to_in_out* argument.

If this size is greater than or equal to the size stored in the cache, XtCallConverter():

* Copies the information stored in the cache to the location specified by the *to_in_out* argument.

* Stores the cache size in to_in_out->size.

* Returns True.

If the size specified in the *to_in_out* argument is smaller than the size stored in the cache, XtCallConverter() copies the cache size into to->size and returns False. If the converter was registered with cache type XtCacheNone or if no value was found in the conversion cache, XtCallConverter() calls the converter and, if it was not registered with cache type XtCacheNone, enters the result in the cache. XtCallConverter() then returns what the converter returned.

cache_ref_return specifies storage allocated by the caller in which an opaque value will be stored. If the type converter has been registered with the XtCacheRefCount modifier and if the value returned in *cache_ref_return* is non-NULL, then the caller should store the *cache_ref_return* value in order to decrement the reference count when the converted value is no longer required. *cache_ref_return* should be specified as NULL if the caller is unwilling or unable to store the value.

Structures

```
typedef struct {
    unsigned int    size;
    XPointer        addr;
} XrmValue, *XrmValuePtr;
```

See Also

XtCallbackReleaseCacheRef(1), *XtConvertAndStore*(1), *XtSetTypeConverter*(1), *XtTypeConverter*(2).

Name

XtCalloc – allocate memory for an array and initialize its bytes to zero.

Synopsis

```
char *XtCalloc(num, size);
    Cardinal num;
    Cardinal size;
```

Inputs

num   Specifies the number of array elements to allocate.

size   Specifies the size of an array element in bytes.

Returns

A pointer to allocated memory.

Description

XtCalloc() allocates memory for an array of *num* elements each of `size` bytes and initializes each allocated byte to zero. If there is insufficient memory, XtCalloc() terminates by calling XtErrorMsg().

Usage

Note that in most cases, you will have to cast the return value of XtCalloc() to the type appropriate for the array elements you are allocating.

XtNew() and XtNewString() provide slightly higher-level approaches to memory allocation.

The function XtCalloc() is implemented by the Toolkit independently of the particular environment, so programs ported to a system not supporting calloc will still work.

See Also

XtErrorMsg(1), *XtFree*(1), *XtMalloc*(1), *XtNew*(1), *XtNewString*(1), *XtRealloc*(1).

Xt Functions and Macros

XtCheckSubclass

Name

XtCheckSubclass – verify an object's class, if compiled with DEBUG defined.

Synopsis

```
void XtCheckSubclass(object, object_class, message)
    Widget object;
    WidgetClass object_class;
    String message;
```

Inputs

object   Specifies the object; may be of class Object or any subclass thereof.

object_class   Specifies the widget class to test against; may be objectClass or any sub-
                  class thereof.

message   Specifies the message to be displayed if object is not a subclass of
                  object_class.

Description

XtCheckSubclass() checks that object is of class object_class or a subclass. If it
is not, XtCheckSubclass() calls XtErrorMsg() passing message as the default message to be displayed. XtErrorMsg() displays the message and terminates the application.

XtCheckSubclass() is implemented as a macro which only performs the check if compiled with the symbol DEBUG defined (i.e., if the C compiler is invoked with the flag
–DDEBUG).

Usage

XtCheckSubclass() is intended for use similar to the POSIX assert() macro while
developing and debugging a widget or an application. It should be used in all application and
widget-internal functions that might inadvertently be passed an object of the wrong type. Public functions exported by a widget should always check a widget's class (not just when DEBUG
is defined) using XtIsSubclass() or a related function because even if a widget is bug-
free, an application programmer may still pass an object of the wrong type to the widget.

See Also

XtClass(1), *XtIsSubclass*(1), *XtSuperclass*(1),
Core(3).

Name

XtClass – obtain a widget's class.

Synopsis

```
WidgetClass XtClass(object)
    Widget object;
```

Inputs

object   Specifies the object; may be of class Object or any subclass thereof.

Returns

a pointer to the class structure for *object*.

Description

XtClass() returns a pointer to the specified object's class structure.

XtClass() is implemented as a function when called from application code, but is replaced by a more efficient macro when called from widget code including the file *<X11/IntrinsicP.h>*.

See Also

XtCheckSubclass(1), *XtIsSubclass*(1), *XtSuperclass*(1).

Name

XtCloseDisplay – close a display and remove it from an application context.

Synopsis

```
void XtCloseDisplay(display)
    Display *display;
```

Inputs

display   Specifies the display.

Description

XtCloseDisplay() calls XCloseDisplay() to close *display* as soon as it is safe to do so. If called from within an event dispatch (for example, a callback procedure), XtClose-Display() does not close the display until the dispatch is complete.

The closed display is removed from its application context. Any converted resources associated with that display which are cached with an XtCacheType of XtCacheByDisplay are removed from the conversion cache and have their destructors, if any, called.

Usage

Note that applications need only call XtCloseDisplay() if they are to continue executing after closing the display; otherwise, they should call XtDestroyApplicationContext() or just exit.

See Also

XtAppInitialize(1), *XtDestroyApplicationContext*(1), *XtOpenDisplay*(1), *XtSetTypeConverter*(1).

XtConfigureWidget

Name

XtConfigureWidget – move and/or resize widget.

Synopsis

```
void XtConfigureWidget(w, x, y, width, height, border_width)
    Widget w;
    Position x;
    Position y;
    Dimension width;
    Dimension height;
    Dimension border_width;
```

Inputs

w   Specifies the widget; must be of class RectObj or any subclass thereof.

x, y   Specify the widget's new x and y coordinates.

width, height, border_width
         Specify the widget's new dimensions.

Description

XtConfigureWidget() sets the size and position of a widget. If the new size and position are the same as the widget's current values, it returns immediately. Otherwise Xt-ConfigureWidget() writes the new x, y, width, height, and border_width values into instance fields of the object and, if the object is a widget and is realized, calls XConfigureWindow() on the widget's window.

If either the new width or the new height is different from its old value, XtConfigure-Widget() calls the widget's resize() method to notify it of the size change.

Usage

XtConfigureWidget() should be used only by a parent widget on one of its children widget. If you want to set a widget size or position from an application, use XtSetValues() to set the XtNx, XtNy, XtNwidth, and XtNheight resources. If widget wants to change its own size or location, it must use XtMakeGeometryRequest().

XtResizeWidget() and XtMoveWidget() are similar to XtConfigureWidget() but are simpler for the cases when you need only to resize or only to move a widget.

See Also

XtMakeGeometryRequest(1), *XtMakeResizeRequest*(1), *XtMoveWidget*(1), *XtResizeWidget*(1).

Xt Functions and Macros

Name

XtConvert – convert resource type.

Synopsis

```
void XtConvert(object, from_type, from, to_type, to_return)
    Widget object;
    String from_type;
    XrmValuePtr from;
    String to_type;
    XrmValuePtr to_return;
```

Inputs

object	Specifies the object to use for additional arguments (if any are needed); may be of class Object or any subclass thereof.
from_type	Specifies the source type.
from	Specifies the value to be converted.
to_type	Specifies the destination type.

Outputs

to_return	Returns the address and the size of the converted value.

Availability

Superseded by `XtConvertAndStore()`.

Description

`XtConvert()` looks up the appropriate resource converter registered to convert *from_type* to *to_type*, computes any additional arguments required by that converter (see `XtSet-TypeConverter()` for an explanation of how these arguments are computed) and then calls `XtDirectConvert()` or `XtCallConverter()` depending on whether the converter procedure is an "old-style" or a "new-style" converter.

If the conversion is successful, *to_return*->addr will be non-NULL. The data at this address must be copied immediately by the caller, because it may be in static storage owned by the type converter procedure.

Usage

As of Release 4, `XtConvert()` is superseded by the more general function `XtConvert-AndStore()`.

You do not often need, in applications or widgets, to convert between resource types directly. Generally you can rely on the Intrinsics resource management code to perform all necessary conversions for you. When writing a resource converter, however, you may find that you need to invoke another converter.

Structures

```
typedef struct {
    unsigned int    size;
    XPointer        addr;
} XrmValue, *XrmValuePtr;
```

See Also

XtConvertAndStore(1).

Name

XtConvertAndStore – look up and call a resource converter, copying the resulting value.

Synopsis

```
Boolean XtConvertAndStore(object, from_type, from, to_type, to_in_out)
    Widget object;
    String from_type;
    XrmValuePtr from;
    String to_type;
    XrmValuePtr to_in_out;
```

Inputs

object   Specifies the object to use for additional arguments, if any are needed, and the destroy callback list; may be of class Object or any subclass thereof.

from_type Specifies the source type.

from   Specifies the value to be converted.

to_type   Specifies the destination type.

to_in_out Specifies the address at which the converted value is to be stored, or NULL, and the number of bytes allocated for the value at that address.

Outputs

to_in_out Returns the address at which the converted value was stored, and the actual number of bytes occupied by that value.

Returns

True if the conversion was successful; False otherwise.

Availability

Release 4 and later.

Description

XtConvertAndStore() looks up the type converter registered to convert *from_type* to *to_type*, computes any additional arguments needed (see XtSetTypeConverter() for an explanation of how these arguments are computed), and then calls XtCallConverter() (or XtDirectConvert() for old-style converters) with the *from* and *to_in_out* arguments.

When converting from a string, *from_type* should be XtRString, *from->addr* should be the address of the first character of the string (a char *, not a char **), and *from->size* should be the length of the string plus one.

Generally, the caller will initialize the *to_in_out* argument to specify the location at which the converted value will be stored and the number of bytes of memory allocated at that location. The *to_in_out* argument is passed directly to the converter which stores the data at the requested location and modifies the size field to the actual size of the converted data.

If instead *to_in_out*->addr is NULL on entry to XtConvertAndStore(), it will be replaced with a pointer to private storage which contains the converted value. As in the previous case, the size of the converted value will be returned in *to_in_out*->size. A value returned in this way is stored in memory that is static to the converter, and the caller is expected to copy it immediately and must not modify it in any way.

XtCallConverter() returns True if the conversion succeeds, and returns False otherwise.

XtConvertAndStore() adds XtCallbackReleaseCacheRef() to the destroy-Callback list of the specified widget or object if the conversion returns an XtCacheRef value. This will automatically decrement the reference count on the cached value of the resource when the object no longer needs it. The resulting resource should not be referenced after the object has been destroyed.

Usage

You do not often need, in applications or widgets, to convert between resource types directly. Generally you can rely on the Intrinsics resource management code to perform all necessary conversions for you. When writing a resource converter, however, you may find that you need to invoke another converter.

The Intrinsics define a number of pre-registered converters, most of them between String and other common Xt types. The table below describes these predefined converters. The Xmu library also contains a number of useful converters, which are not pre-registered. See Xmu-CvtStringToMisc(6).

from_type	*to_type*	Description
XtRString	XtRAcceleratorTable	Compiles a string accelerator table into internal accelerator table format (no need to call XtParseAcceleratorTable()).
	XtRBoolean	Converts strings "true," "false," "yes," "no," "on," "off" to corresponding Boolean value (case insensitive).
	XtRBool	Same as for XtRBoolean.
	XtRCursor	Given a standard X cursor name, returns a cursor ID.
	XtRDimension	Converts a width or height value to a Dimension.
	XtRDisplay	Given a display name, opens the display and returns a Display structure.
	XtRFile	Given a filename, opens the file and returns the file descriptor.
	XtRFloat	Converts a numeric string to floating point.
	XtRFont	Given a font name, loads the font (if it is not already loaded) and returns the font ID. The value Xt-DefaultFont will return the default font for the screen.
	XtRFontStruct	Given a font name, loads the font (if it is not already loaded) and returns a pointer to the FontStruct containing font metrics. The value XtDefaultFont returns the default font for the screen.
	XtRInt	Converts a numeric string to an integer.

from_type	to_type	Description
	XtRPixel	Converts a color name string (e.g., "red" or "#FF0000") into the pixel value that will produce the closest color possible on the hardware. See Appendix C, *Specifying Fonts and Colors*, for more information on legal values. The two values XtDefault-Background and XtDefaultForeground are always guaranteed to exist, and to contrast, on any server.
	XtRPosition	Converts an x or y value to a Position.
	XtRShort	Converts a numeric string to a short integer.
	XtRTranslationTable	Compiles string translation table into internal translation table format (no need to call XtParse-TranslationTable()).
	XtRUnsignedChar	Converts a string to an unsigned char.
XtRColor	XtRPixel	Converts an XColor structure to a pixel value.
XtRPixel	XtRColor	Converts a pixel value to an XColor structure.
XtRInt	XtRBoolean	Converts an int to a Boolean.
	XtRBool	Converts an int to a Bool.
	XtRColor	Converts an int to an XColor.
	XtRDimension	Converts an int to a Dimension.
	XtRFloat	Converts an int to a float.
	XtRFont	Converts an int to a Font.
	XtRPixel	Converts an int to a pixel value.
	XtRPixmap	Converts an int to a Pixmap.
	XtRPosition	Converts an int to a Position.
	XtRShort	Converts an int to a short.
	XtRUnsignedChar	Converts an int to an unsigned char.

Structures

```
typedef struct {
    unsigned int    size;
    XPointer        addr;
} XrmValue, *XrmValuePtr;
```

See Also

XtAppSetTypeConverter(1), *XtCallbackReleaseCacheRef*(1), *XtCallConverter*(1), *XtDirectConvert*(1), *Xt-SetTypeConverter*(1).

XtConvertCase

Name

XtConvertCase – determine uppercase and lowercase versions of a keysym.

Synopsis

```
void XtConvertCase(display, keysym, lower_return, upper_return)
    Display *display;
    KeySym keysym;
    KeySym *lower_return;
    KeySym *upper_return;
```

Inputs

display   Specifies the display that the keysym came from.

keysym   Specifies the keysym to convert.

Outputs

lower_return   Returns the lowercase equivalent of the keysym.

upper_return   Returns the uppercase equivalent of the keysym.

Description

XtConvertCase() calls the case converter procedure most recently registered for a range of keysyms that includes *keysym* to obtain uppercase and lowercase versions of the supplied keysym.

Usage

You will probably never need to call this function unless you are writing a customized keycode-to-keysym translator. The Translation Manager uses case converters as part of its keycode-to-keysym translation process.

You can register a case converter for a range of keysyms with XtRegisterCase-Converter().

See Also

XtRegisterCaseConverter(1), *XtSetKeyTranslator*(1), *XtTranslateKey*(1), *XtTranslateKeycode*(1), *XtCaseProc*(2), *XtKeyProc*(2).

Xt Functions and Macros

Name

XtCreateApplicationContext – create an application context.

Synopsis

```
XtAppContext XtCreateApplicationContext()
```

Description

`XtCreateApplicationContext()` creates and returns an application context, which is an opaque type. Every application must have at least one application context.

Usage

`XtAppInitialize()` calls `XtCreateApplicationContext()` as part of its initialization sequence, so you should not often need to use this function.

The superseded routines that use an implicit context (like `XtMainLoop()` and `XtAddTimeOut()`) depend on a default context created by `XtInitialize()`. You cannot use these routines if you initialize a specific application context.

See Also

XtAppInitialize(1).

XtCreateApplicationShell

Name

XtCreateApplicationShell – create an additional top-level widget.

Synopsis

```
Widget XtCreateApplicationShell(application_name, widget_class, args,
        num_args)
    String application_name; /*unused*/
    WidgetClass widget_class;
    ArgList args;
    Cardinal num_args;
```

Inputs

application_name
> This argument is unused.

widget_class
> Specifies the widget class for the shell widget to be created.

args   Specifies an argument list to override any other resource specifications.

num_args   Specifies the number of elements in *args*.

Returns

A newly created shell widget of class *widget_class*.

Availability

Superseded by XtAppCreateShell().

Description

XtCreateApplicationShell() creates and returns a shell widget of class *widget_class*. The created widget has no parent—it is at the root of a widget tree and at the top of the resource name hierarchy.

XtCreateApplicationShell() creates the widget by calling XtAppCreateShell() passing a NULL *application_name*, the *application_class* that was passed to Xt-Initialize(), the display that was opened by XtInitialize() and the *widget_class*, *args*, and *num_args* arguments.

Usage

XtCreateApplicationShell() has been superseded by XtAppCreateShell(), which is substantially more flexible. You can continue to use XtCreateApplication-Shell() only if you initialize your application with XtInitialize(). We recommend that you use XtAppInitialize(), XtAppCreateShell(), and the other XtApp*() application context specific functions.

See XtAppCreateShell() for more information.

See Also

XtAppCreateShell(1).

XtCreateManagedWidget

Name

XtCreateManagedWidget – create and manage a child widget.

Synopsis

```
Widget XtCreateManagedWidget(name, widget_class, parent, args, num_args)
    String name;
    WidgetClass widget_class;
    Widget parent;
    ArgList args;
    Cardinal num_args;
```

Inputs

name   Specifies the resource name for the created widget.

widget_class   Specifies the widget class pointer for the created widget; must be rectObj-
                  Class or any subclass.

parent   Specifies the parent widget; must be of class Composite or any subclass
                  thereof.

args   Specifies the argument list to override the resource defaults.

num_args   Specifies the number of arguments in the argument list.

Returns

The newly created and managed child widget.

Description

XtCreateManagedWidget() creates a widget by passing all of its arguments to Xt-
CreateWidget(), and then calling XtManageChild() on the resulting widget. It returns
the created and managed widget.

Usage

You can use XtVaCreateManagedWidget() to do the same thing, except that resource
names and values are passed in a variable length argument list, rather than an ArgList.

If you are creating a number of children of an already realized parent, it is more efficient to create them and then manage them all in a single call to XtManageChildren().

See Also

XtCreateWidget(1), *XtManageChild*(1), *XtManageChildren*(1), *XtVaCreateManagedWidget*(1).

XtCreatePopupShell

Name

XtCreatePopupShell – create a popup shell widget.

Synopsis

```
Widget XtCreatePopupShell(name, widget_class, parent, args, num_args)
    String name;
    WidgetClass widget_class;
    Widget parent;
    ArgList args;
    Cardinal num_args;
```

Inputs

name   Specifies the resource name for the created shell widget.

widget_class   Specifies the widget class pointer for the created shell widget; must be shellClass or any subclass.

parent   Specifies the parent widget; must be of class Core or any subclass thereof.

args   Specifies the argument list to override the resource defaults.

num_args   Specifies the number of arguments in the argument list.

Returns

A widget of class *widget_class* created as a popup child of *parent*.

Description

XtCreatePopupShell() checks that *widget_class* is a subclass of Shell, and, if it is, creates a widget of that class. The widget is not stored in the children array (maintained by Composite widgets), but rather in the popup_list array (which all widgets have).

The screen resource for this widget is determined by first scanning *args* for the XtNscreen resource. If it is not found, the resource database associated with the parent's screen is queried. If both queries fail, the parent's screen is used. Once the screen is determined, the resource database associated with that screen is used to retrieve all remaining resources for the widget not specified in *args*.

Usage

All shell widgets other than those created by XtAppInitialize() and XtAppCreate-Shell() must be created with XtCreatePopupShell(). Popup shells can be a child of any widget, not just Composite widgets. Remember that shell widgets can only have a single child, which will generally be the layout widget that arranges whatever grandchildren widgets are to appear in the popup.

Creating and realizing a popup shell widget is not enough to make it visible. To make a shell pop up, use XtPopup() or one of the predefined callback procedures or menu actions that call this function. To make it popdown, call XtPopdown().

Rather than initializing an ArgList to pass to XtCreatePopupShell(), you can call XtVaCreatePopupShell() which accepts a NULL-terminated variable length argument list of resource names and resource values.

See Also

XtCallbackExclusive(1), *XtMenuPopup*(1), *XtPopdown*(1), *XtPopup*(1), *XtVaCreatePopupShell*(1).

Name

XtCreateWidget – create an instance of a widget.

Synopsis

```
Widget XtCreateWidget(name, object_class, parent, args, num_args)
    String name;
    WidgetClass object_class;
    Widget parent;
    ArgList args;
    Cardinal num_args;
```

Inputs

name Specifies the resource name for the created object.

object_class

Specifies the widget class pointer for the created widget; may be objectClass or any subclass.

parent Specifies the parent widget; may be of class objectClass or any subclass thereof.

args Specifies the argument list to override the resource defaults.

num_args Specifies the number of arguments in the argument list.

Returns

An child widget or object of *parent* of class *object_class*.

Description

XtCreateWidget() creates a new instance of class *object_class* named *name*, as a child of *parent*. The resource name/resource value pairs in *args* are used to set resources in the widget and override resources from the resource database. The details of the widget creation procedure are explained in the "Algorithm" section below.

Usage

A created widget will not be visible until it is managed. You can manage a child widget with XtManageChild(), and you can combine the call to XtCreateWidget() and XtManageChild() by calling XtCreateManagedWidget(). Note that you cannot manage direct subclasses of Object.

A created and managed widget will not be visible unless it has been realized (i.e., had an X window created). You realize a widget by calling XtRealizeWidget(), which realizes the specified widget and all of its children. If you create a child of a realized widget, the child is automatically realized. You will generally call XtRealizeWidget() once in an application, just before entering your main event loop.

Rather than initialize an ArgList and pass it to XtCreateWidget(), you can call XtVaCreateWidget() or XtVaCreateManagedWidget() which both accept a NULL-terminated variable length argument list of resource names and resource values.

To create a popup widget, you must use `XtCreatePopupShell()` rather than `XtCreate-Widget()`.

You may give your widgets any *name* you want, and may give multiple widgets the same name. If two sibling widgets have the same name, however, they will get the same resources from the resource database, and it is undefined which will be returned by a call to `XtNameTo-Widget()`.

`XtCreateWidget()` allows you to create child widgets of non-Composite widgets. If you do this, the child widget will not appear on any `children` list in the parent and will not be automatically realized when its parent is realized or destroyed when its parent is destroyed. The only time you should do this is when writing a non-Composite widget that explicitly creates and manages its own children.

Algorithm

`XtCreateWidget()` does the following when creating a widget or an object:

- Checks to see if the `class_initialize()` method has been called for this class and for all superclasses and, if not, calls those necessary in a superclass-to-subclass order.

- If the specified class is not `coreWidgetClass` or a subclass thereof, and the parent's class is a subclass of `compositeWidgetClass` and either no extension record in the parent's composite class part extension field exists with the `record_type` NULLQUARK or the `accepts_objects` field in the extension record is False, `XtCreate-Widget()` issues a fatal error.

- Allocates memory for the widget instance.

- If the parent is a member of the class `constraintWidgetClass`, allocates memory for the parent's constraints and stores the address of this memory into the `constraints` field.

- Initializes the Core nonresource data fields (for example, `parent` and `visible`).

- Initializes the resource fields (for example, `background_pixel`) by using the `Core-ClassPart` resource lists specified for this class and all superclasses.

- If the parent is a member of the class `constraintWidgetClass`, initializes the resource fields of the constraints record by using the `ConstraintClassPart` resource lists specified for the parent's class and all superclasses up to `constraintWidget-Class`.

- Calls the `initialize()` methods for the widget in superclass-to-subclass order.

- If the parent is a member of the class `compositeWidgetClass`, puts the widget into its parent's children list by calling its parent's `insert_child()` method.

- If the parent is a member of the class `constraintWidgetClass`, calls the `ConstraintClassPart initialize()` methods, in superclass-to-subclass order.

`XtCreateWidget()` converts and caches resources in a way equivalent to `XtConvert-AndStore()` when initializing the object instance. Because there is extra memory overhead required to implement reference counting, clients may distinguish those objects that are never destroyed before the application exits from those that may be destroyed and whose resources should be deallocated.

To specify whether reference counting is to be enabled for the resources of a particular object when the object is created, the client can specify a value for the `Boolean` resource `XtNinitialResourcesPersistent`, class `XtCInitialResourcesPersistent`.

When `XtCreateWidget()` is called, if this resource is not specified as `False` in either the arglist or the resource database, then the resources referenced by this object are not reference-counted, regardless of how the type converter may have been registered. The effective default value is `True`; thus clients that expect to destroy one or more objects and want resources deallocated must explicitly specify `False` for `XtNinitialResourcesPersistent`

The resources are still freed and destructors called when `XtCloseDisplay()` is called if the conversion was registered as `XtCacheByDisplay`.

See Also

XtCreateManagedWidget(1), *XtVaCreateWidget*(1), *XtVaCreateManagedWidget*(1).

Name

XtCreateWindow – create widget's window.

Synopsis

```
void XtCreateWindow(w, window_class, visual, value_mask, attributes)
    Widget w;
    unsigned int window_class;
    Visual *visual;
    XtValueMask value_mask;
    XSetWindowAttributes *attributes;
```

Inputs

w   Specifies the widget that is to have a window created; must be of class Core or a subclass thereof.

window_class   Specifies the Xlib window class (InputOutput, InputOnly, or CopyFromParent).

visual   Specifies the Xlib visual type (usually CopyFromParent).

value_mask   Specifies which attribute fields to use.

attributes   Specifies the window attributes to use in the XCreateWindow() call.

Description

XtCreateWindow() copies the depth, screen, x, y, width, height and border_width fields of the core part of the specified widget into the *attributes* structure. Then it passes *attributes* and an appropriately modified *value_mask* along with the widget's display, the widget's parent's window, *window_class*, and *visual* to the Xlib function XCreateWindow(). It stores the newly created Window in the widget's core part window field.

Usage

This is a convenience function intended for use in the realize() method of widgets. It should never be called by an application.

Structures

The XSetWindowAttributes structure is as follows:

```
typedef struct {
    Pixmap background_pixmap;       /* background or None or ParentRelative * /
    unsigned long background_pixel;/* background pixel */
    Pixmap border_pixmap;           /* border of the window */
    unsigned long border_pixel;     /* border pixel value */
    int bit_gravity;                /* one of bit gravity values */
    int win_gravity;                /* one of the window gravity values */
    int backing_store;              /* NotUseful, WhenMapped, Always */
    unsigned long backing_planes;   /* planes to be preserved if possible */
    unsigned long backing_pixel;    /* value to use in restoring planes */
    Bool save_under;                /* should bits under be saved (popups) */
    long event_mask;                /* set of events that should be saved */
    long do_not_propagate_mask;     /* set of events that should not propagate */
```

```
    Bool override_redirect;       /* boolean value for override-redirect */
    Colormap colormap;            /* colormap to be associated with window */
    Cursor cursor;                /* cursor to be displayed (or None) */
} XSetWindowAttributes;

/* Definitions for valuemask argument.  These control which fields in
 * XSetWindowAttributes structure should be used.
 */

#define CWBackPixmap          (1L<<0)
#define CWBackPixel           (1L<<1)
#define CWBorderPixmap        (1L<<2)
#define CWBorderPixel         (1L<<3)
#define CWBitGravity          (1L<<4)
#define CWWinGravity          (1L<<5)
#define CWBackingStore        (1L<<6)
#define CWBackingPlanes       (1L<<7)
#define CWBackingPixel        (1L<<8)
#define CWOverrideRedirect    (1L<<9)
#define CWSaveUnder           (1L<<10)
#define CWEventMask           (1L<<11)
#define CWDontPropagate       (1L<<12)
#define CWColormap            (1L<<13)
#define CWCursor              (1L<<14)
```

See Also

realize(4).

XtDatabase

Name

XtDatabase – obtain the resource database for a display.

Synopsis

```
XrmDatabase XtDatabase(display)
    Display *display;
```

Inputs

display   Specifies the display for which the resource database should be returned.

Returns

The database for the specified display, or NULL.

Description

In Release 4 and previous releases, XtDatabase() returns the resource database built by XtDisplayInitialize() for the display. In Release 5, which supports a resource database for each screen, XtDatabase() returns the resource database built by XtDisplay-Initialize() for the default screen of the display.

In Release 4 and previous releases, the results are undefined if *display* has not been initialized by XtDisplayInitialize(). In Release 5, XtDatabase() returns NULL if no database has been set for the display.

Usage

In Release 5, the function XtScreenDatabase() returns the resource associated with a specified screen.

You should rarely need to obtain the database of a display or screen. XtGetApplication-Resources() and related functions provide a more manageable approach to obtaining resource values.

Structures

XrmDatabase is an opaque data type.

See Also

XtAppInitialize(1), *XtDisplayInitialize*(1), *XtScreenDatabase*(1).

XtDestroyApplicationContext

Name

XtDestroyApplicationContext – destroy an application context and close its displays.

Synopsis

```
void XtDestroyApplicationContext(app_context)
    XtAppContext app_context;
```

Inputs

app_context Specifies the application context.

Description

XtDestroyApplicationContext() destroys the specified application context and closes any display connections in it as soon as it is safe to do so. If called from within an event handler or a callback procedure, XtDestroyApplicationContext() does not destroy the application context until the dispatch is complete.

Usage

X Toolkit applications need not call XtDestroyApplicationContext() unless they use multiple application contexts and want to destroy one. Most applications can exit using the standard method for their operating system (typically, by calling exit for POSIX-based systems). The quickest way to make the windows disappear while exiting is to call XtUnmap-Widget() on each top-level shell widget. The X Toolkit has no resources beyond those in the program image, and the X server will free its resources when its connection to the application is broken.

See Also

XtCreateApplicationContext(1).

Xt Functions and Macros

Name

XtDestroyGC – Release 2 compatible function to free read-only GCs.

Synopsis

```
void XtDestroyGC(w, gc)
    Widget w;
    GC gc;
```

Inputs

w   Specifies any object on the display for which the GC was created.

gc   Specifies the GC to be deallocated.

Availability

XtDestroyGC() is superseded by XtReleaseGC().

Description

XtDestroyGC() deallocates a shared (read-only) Graphics Context. References to sharable GCs are counted, and a free request is generated to the server when the last user of a given GC destroys it.

Note that some earlier versions of XtDestroyGC() had only a gc argument. Therefore, this function is not very portable. In addition, XtDestroyGC() is only guaranteed to work properly if there is exactly one open display in the application.

Usage

You should never use this function. Programs running under Release 3 and later should be converted to use XtReleaseGC().

See Also

XtAllocateGC(1), *XtGetGC*(1), *XtReleaseGC*(1).

XtDestroyWidget

Name

XtDestroyWidget – destroy a widget instance.

Synopsis

```
void XtDestroyWidget(object)
    Widget object;
```

Inputs

object   Specifies the object to be destroyed; may be of class Object or any subclass thereof.

Description

XtDestroyWidget() destroys *object* and all of its normal and popup descendants. It frees all resources associated with that widget and its descendants, and calls the Xlib function XDestroyWindow() to destroy the windows (if any) of the affected objects. The details this procedure are explained in the "Algorithm" section below.

Usage

Most applications simply exit, causing widgets to be destroyed automatically. Applications that create and destroy widgets dynamically should call XtDestroyWidget().

XtDestroyWidget() can be used by widgets that need to destroy themselves. It can be called at any time, including from a callback routine of the widget being destroyed.

When an application needs to perform additional processing during the destruction of a widget, it should register a callback procedure on the XtNdestroyCallback list of the widget.

Applications that use multiple displays and want to destroy all the widgets on one of them can simply call XtCloseDisplay(). Applications that use multiple application contexts and want to destroy all the widgets in one of them can call XtDestroyApplication-Context(). A widget's windows can be destroyed without destroying the widget data structures by calling XtUnrealizeWidget().

Algorithm

Widget destruction occurs in two phases to prevent dangling references to destroyed widgets.

In phase 1, XtDestroyWidget() performs the following:

- If the being_destroyed field of the widget is True, it returns immediately.

- Recursively descends the widget tree and sets the being_destroyed field to True for the widget and all normal and popup children.

- Adds the widget to a list of widgets (the destroy list) that should be destroyed when it is safe to do so.

Entries on the destroy list satisfy the invariant that if w2 occurs after w1 on the destroy list, then w2 is not a descendent, either normal or popup, of w1.

Phase 2 occurs when all procedures that should execute as a result of the current event have been called, including all procedures registered with the event and translation managers, that is, when the current invocation of `XtDispatchEvent()` is about to return, or immediately if not in `XtDispatchEvent()`.

In phase 2, `XtDestroyWidget()` performs the following on each entry in the destroy list in the order specified:

- Calls the destroy callback procedures registered on the widget and all normal and popup descendants in postorder (it calls child callbacks before parent callbacks).

- If the widget is not a popup child and the widget's parent is a subclass of `composite-WidgetClass`, and if the parent is not being destroyed, it calls `XtUnmanageChild()` on the widget and then calls the widget's parent's delete_child procedure (see Section 3.3).

- If the widget is not a popup child and the widget's parent is a subclass of `constraint-WidgetClass`, it calls the `ConstraintClassPart` destroy procedure for the parent, then for the parent's superclass, until finally it calls the `ConstraintClassPart` destroy procedure for `constraintWidgetClass`.

- Calls the destroy procedures for the widget and all normal and popup descendants in postorder. For each such widget, it calls the `CoreClassPart` destroy procedure declared in the widget class, then the destroy procedure declared in its superclass, until finally it calls the destroy procedure declared in the Object class record.

- Calls `XDestroyWindow()` if the specified widget is realized (that is, has an X window). The server recursively destroys all normal descendant windows.

- Recursively descends the tree and destroys the windows for all realized popup descendants, deallocates all popup descendants, constraint records, callback lists, and if the widget's class is a subclass of `compositeWidgetClass`, children.

`XtCreateWidget()` and `XtConvertAndStore()` automatically register `Xt-CallbackReleaseCacheRef()` as a destroy callback on all widgets that use reference-counted resources from the conversion cache. In this way, destroying a widget also invokes the appropriate resource destructors when the reference count of a converted resource reaches 0.

See Also

XtCloseDisplay(1), *XtDestroyApplicationContext*(1), *XtUnrealizeWidget*(1).

XtDirectConvert

Name

XtDirectConvert – explicitly invoke an "old-style" resource converter and cache result.

Synopsis

```
void XtDirectConvert(converter, args, num_args, from, to_return)
    XtConverter converter;
    XrmValuePtr args;
    Cardinal num_args;
    XrmValuePtr from;
    XrmValuePtr to_return;
```

Inputs

converter   Specifies the "old-style" conversion procedure to be called.

args   Specifies the argument list that contains the additional arguments needed to perform the conversion (often NULL).

num_args   Specifies the number of additional arguments (often zero).

from   Specifies the value to be converted.

Outputs

to_return   Returns the converted value.

Description

XtDirectConvert() looks in the converter cache to see if the named conversion procedure has previously been called with the specified arguments. If so, it sets the cached resource address and size in *to_return* and returns. If no cached value is found, it sets *to_return->addr* to NULL and *to_return->size* to zero and calls *converter* with its remaining arguments. The results of the conversion are stored in the cache and returned in *to_return*.

If the conversion is successful, *to_return->addr* will be non-NULL. The data at this address must be copied immediately by the caller, because it may be in static storage owned by the type converter procedure.

Usage

XtDirectConvert() invokes an "old-style" converter of type XtConverter. In Release 4, more flexible (and incompatible) "new-style" converters of type XtTypeConverter were added. Old-style converters are still in use, and if you have to invoke one explicitly, you must use XtDirectConvert(). If you are writing your own converter, you should use the new style.

XtConvertAndStore() provides a higher level interface to resource conversion, and is easier to use in most cases. It works with both old-style and new-style converters.

You do not often need, in applications or widgets, to convert between resource types directly. Generally you can rely on the Intrinsics resource management code to perform all necessary conversions for you. When writing a resource converter, however, you may find that you need to invoke another converter.

Xt Functions and Macros

Structures

```
typedef struct {
    unsigned int    size;
    XPointer        addr;
} XrmValue, *XrmValuePtr;
```

See Also

XtAppAddConverter(1), *XtCallConverter*(1), *XtConvertAndStore*(1), *XtSetTypeConverter*(1), *XtConverter*(2), *XtTypeConverter*(2).

Name

XtDisownSelection – indicate that selection data is no longer available.

Synopsis

```
void XtDisownSelection(w, selection, time)
    Widget w;
    Atom selection;
    Time time;
```

Inputs

w　　　　　　　Specifies the widget relinquishing selection ownership.

selection　　Specifies which selection the widget is giving up (usually XA_PRIMARY or XA_SECONDARY).

time　　　　　Specifies the timestamp that indicates when the request to relinquish selection ownership was initiated.

Description

XtDisownSelection() informs the Intrinsics selection mechanism that the specified widget is to lose ownership of the specified selection as of the specified time. If the widget does not currently own the selection, either because it lost the selection or because it never had the selection to begin with, XtDisownSelection() does nothing.

After a widget has called XtDisownSelection(), its XtConvertProc is not called even if a request arrives later with a timestamp during the period that this widget owned the selection. However, its XtDoneProc will be called if a conversion that started before the call to XtDisownSelection() finishes after the call to XtDisownSelection(). See XtOwnSelection() for more information.

Usage

Usually, a selection owner maintains ownership indefinitely until some other client requests ownership, at which time the Intrinsics selection mechanism informs the previous owner that it has lost ownership of the selection. However, in response to some user actions (for example, when a user deletes the information selected), the application may with to explicitly inform the Intrinsics that it no longer is to be the selection owner by calling XtDisownSelection().

When the selection changes hands because another client has claimed it (rather than as a result of a call to XtDisownSelection()), the Intrinsics inform the application that it has lost the selection ownership by calling its XtLoseSelectionProc.

See Also

XtGetSelectionValue(1), *XtOwnSelection*(1),
XtConvertProc(2), *XtDoneProc*(2), *XtLoseSelectionProc*(2).

**Xt Functions
and Macros**

Name

XtDispatchEvent – dispatch an event to registered event handlers.

Synopsis

```
Boolean XtDispatchEvent(event)
    XEvent *event;
```

Inputs

event   Specifies a pointer to the event structure to be dispatched to the appropriate event handlers.

Returns

True if the event was dispatched to one or more event filters or event handlers. False if no handler could be found.

Description

XtDispatchEvent() sends events to Xlib event filters (new in Release 5) and to handler functions previously registered with XtAddEventHandler(). Since the entire translation manager is an event handler, XtDispatchEvent() results in action functions being called if a translation matches the event being dispatched. XtDispatchEvent() calls the appropriate handler functions and passes them the widget, the event, and client-specific data. See the "Background" section below for details on how events are dispatched.

If no handlers for the event are registered, the event is ignored. If there are multiple handlers registered for an event, the order in which handlers are called is undefined. (But see XtInsertEventHandler().)

XtDispatchEvent() returns True if it dispatched the event to some filter (in Release 5) or handler and False if it found no handler to dispatch the event to.

XtDispatchEvent() records the timestamp of the last event dispatched which contains a timestamp (see XtLastTimestampProcessed()) and also is responsible for implementing the grab semantics of XtAddGrab().

Usage

In most applications, XtAppMainLoop() is used to dispatch events transparently. XtAppProcessEvent() can also be used to get and dispatch a single event. XtAddEventHandler() and XtInsertEventHandler() are used to register event handlers.

The most common use of XtDispatchEvent() is to dispatch events acquired with XtAppNextEvent(). However, it also can be used to dispatch user-constructed events.

Background

In Release 5, the function XFilterEvent() was added to Xlib to support event filtering for international input methods. The Release 5 Intrinsics support internationalized input by calling XFilterEvent() from within XtDispatchEvent(). Note that there is no public Xlib interface for registering an event filter.

In Release 5, XtDispatchEvent() behaves as follows.

XtDispatchEvent() first calls XFilterEvent() with the *event* and the window of the widget to which the Intrinsics intend to dispatch the event (the subsections below explain how XtDispatchEvent() decides which widget to dispatch to), or the event window if the Intrinsics would not dispatch the event to any handlers. If XFilterEvent() returns True and the event activated a server grab as identified by a previous call to XtGrabKey() or Xt-GrabButton(), XtDispatchEvent()calls XtUngrabKeyboard() or XtUngrab-Pointer() with the timestamp from the event and immediately returns True. If XFilter-Event() returns True and a grab was not activated, XtDispatchEvent() just immediately returns True.

Otherwise, if XFilterEvent() returns False, XtDispatchEvent() sends the event to the event handler functions that have been previously registered with the dispatch routine. Xt-DispatchEvent() returns True if XFilterEvent() returned True, or if the event was dispatched to some handler, and returns False if it found no handler to which to dispatch the event. XtDispatchEvent() records the last timestamp in any event that contains a timestamp (see XtLastTimestampProcessed()), regardless of whether it was filtered or dispatched.

If a modal cascade is active with *spring_loaded* True, and if the event is a remap event as defined by XtAddGrab(), XtDispatchEvent() may dispatch the event a second time. If it does so, XtDispatchEvent() will call XFilterEvent() again with the window of the spring-loaded widget prior to the second dispatch and if XFilterEvent() returns True, the second dispatch will not be performed.

Dispatching Events to a Modal Cascade

XtAddGrab() (which is called by XtPopup()) adds a widget to the *modal cascade*. When there is a modal cascade, events that occur outside of the cascade must not be delivered, or must be remapped to one of the widgets in the cascade. XtDispatchEvent() does this as follows.

When at least one modal widget is in the widget cascade, XtDispatchEvent() first determines if the event should be delivered. It starts at the most recent cascade entry and follows the cascade up to and including the most recent cascade entry added with the *exclusive* parameter True.

This subset of the modal cascade along with all descendants of these widgets comprise the active subset. User events that occur outside the widgets in this subset are ignored or remapped. User events that occur within the active subset are delivered to the appropriate widget, which is usually a child or further descendant of the modal widget.

Regardless of where in the application they occur, remap events (events of type KeyPress, KeyRelease, ButtonPress and ButtonRelease) are always delivered to the most recent widget in the active subset of the cascade registered with *spring_loaded* True, if any such widget exists. If the event occurred in the active subset of the cascade but outside the spring-loaded widget, it is delivered normally before being delivered also to the spring-loaded widget. Regardless of where it is dispatched, the Intrinsics do not modify the contents of the event.

Dispatching Events with Redirected Keyboard Focus

XtSetKeyboardFocus() causes XtDispatchEvent() to remap keyboard events occurring within the specified subtree and dispatch them to the specified descendant widget or to an ancestor. If the descendant's class is not a subclass of Core, the descendant is replaced by its closest windowed ancestor.

When there is no modal cascade, keyboard events can be dispatched to a widget in one of four ways. Assume the server delivered the event to the window for widget E (because of X input focus, key or keyboard grabs, or pointer position).

- If neither E nor any of E's ancestors have redirected the keyboard focus, or if the event activated a grab for E as specified by a call to XtGrabKey() with any value of *owner_events*, or if the keyboard is actively grabbed by E with *owner_events* False via XtGrabKeyboard() or XtGrabKey() on a previous key press, the event is dispatched to E.

- Beginning with the ancestor of E closest to the root that has redirected the keyboard focus or E if no such ancestor exists, if the target of that focus redirection has in turn redirected the keyboard focus, recursively follow this focus chain to find a widget F that has not redirected focus.

  - If E is the final focus target widget F or a descendant of F, the event is dispatched to E.

  - If E is not F, an ancestor of F, or a descendant of F, and the event activated a grab for E as specified by a call to XtGrabKey() for E, XtUngrabKeyboard() is called.

  - If E is an ancestor of F, and the event is a key press, and either

    + E has grabbed the key with XtGrabKey() and *owner_events* False, or

    + E has grabbed the key with XtGrabKey() and *owner_events* True, and the coordinates of the event are outside the rectangle specified by E's geometry,

    then the event is dispatched to E.

  - Otherwise, define A as the closest common ancestor of E and F:

    + If there is an active keyboard grab for any widget via either XtGrabKeyboard() or XtGrabKey() on a previous key press, or if no widget between F and A (noninclusive) has grabbed the key and modifier combination with XtGrabKey() and any value of *owner_events*, the event is dispatched to F.

    + Else, the event is dispatched to the ancestor of F closest to A that has grabbed the key and modifier combination with XtGrabKey().

When there is a modal cascade, if the final destination widget as identified above is in the active subset of the cascade, the event is dispatched; otherwise the event is remapped to a spring-loaded shell or discarded. Regardless of where it is dispatched, the Intrinsics do not modify the contents of the event.

When *subtree* or one of its descendants acquires the X input focus or the pointer moves into the subtree such that keyboard events would now be delivered to the subtree, a FocusIn event is generated for the descendant if focus change events have been selected by the descendant. Similarly, when *subtree* loses the X input focus or the keyboard focus for one of its ancestors, a `FocusOut` event is generated for descendant if focus change events have been selected by the descendant.

See Also

XtAddEventHandler(1), *XtAddGrab*(1), *XtAppMainLoop*(1), *XtInsertEventHandler*(1).

XtDisplay

Name

XtDisplay – return the X Display pointer for the specified widget.

Synopsis

```
Display *XtDisplay(w)
    Widget w;
```

Inputs

w   Specifies the widget; must be of class Core or any subclass thereof.

Returns

The Display of the specified widget.

Description

XtDisplay() returns the display pointer for the specified widget.

Usage

XtDisplay() is implemented as a function when called from application code, but is replaced by a more efficient macro when called from widget code that includes the file *<X11/IntrinsicP.h>*.

Use XtDisplayOfObject() to return the display of a widget or the nearest widget ancestor of a non-widget object.

See Also

XtDisplayOfObject(1), *XtScreen*(1).

Name

XtDisplayInitialize – initialize a display and add it to an application context.

Synopsis

```
void XtDisplayInitialize(app_context, display, application_name, applica-
        tion_class, options, num_options, argc, argv)
    XtAppContext app_context;
    Display *display;
    String application_name;
    String application_class;
    XrmOptionDescRec *options;
    Cardinal num_options;
    int *argc;                /* was Cardinal * in Release 4 */
    String *argv;
```

Inputs

app_context Specifies the application context.

display Specifies the display. Note that a display can be in at most one application context.

application_name
Specifies the name of the application instance.

application_class
Specifies the class name of this application. This name is usually the generic name for all instances of this application.

options Specifies how to parse the command line for any application-specific resources. The *options* argument is passed as a parameter to XrmParseCommand().

num_options Specifies the number of entries in the options list.

argc Specifies a pointer to the number of command line arguments. In Release 4 and previously, this argument was of type Cardinal *. In Release 5 it is an int *.

argv Specifies the command line arguments.

Outputs

argc Returns the number of command line arguments remaining after the command line is parsed.

argv Returns a modified command line containing only the application name and any arguments that were not recognized as standard Xt options or options specified in *options*.

Description

In Release 5, XtDisplayInitialize() first retrieves the language string to be used for the specified display and calls the language procedure (if any was registered) with that language string. In all releases, XtDisplayInitialize() parses the command line using the

Xlib XrmParseCommand() function, builds the resource database, and performs other per-display initialization. See XtAppInitialize() for information on how the language string is handled and how the command line is parsed. See the "Background" section below for detail on how the resource database is built.

If the synchronize resource is True, XtDisplayInitialize() calls the Xlib XSynchronize() function to put Xlib into synchronous mode for this display connection and any others currently open in the application context.

In Release 5, XtDisplayInitialize() calls XrmSetDatabase() to associate the resource database of the default screen with the display.

Usage

XtDisplayInitialize() does not actually open a display connection. XtOpenDisplay() opens a display and then calls XtDisplayInitialize(). Most applications need not use either of these functions; they can use XtAppInitialize() instead.

In Release 4, the *argc* argument is of type Cardinal *, and in Release 5, this argument is of type int *. This is a minor incompatibility that may result warnings from ANSI-C compilers when porting from one release to another.

After XtDisplayInitialize() has been called, *argc* and *argv* contain only those arguments that were not in the standard option table or in the table specified by the *options* argument. If the modified *argc* is not zero, most applications simply print out the modified *argv* along with a message listing the allowable options.

Background

The algorithm for building the resource database has changed significantly between Release 4 and Release 5, with the introduction of per-screen databases, internationalization and the customization resource. The process followed by XtDisplayInitialize() in Release 5 is described below.

XtDisplayInitialize() first determines the language string to be used for the specified display and then creates resource databases as needed for each screen of the display by combining the following sources in order, with the entries in the first named source having highest precedence:

- Application command line (argv).

- Per-host user environment resource file on the local host.

- Per-screen resource specifications from the server.

- Per-display resource specifications from the server or from the user preference file on the local host.

- Application-specific user resource file on the local host.

- Application-specific class resource file on the local host.

When the resource database for a particular screen on the display is needed (either internally, or when `XtScreenDatabase()` is called), `XtDisplayInitialize()` creates the resource database for the screen in the following manner:

- A temporary database, the "server resource database", is created from the string returned by `XResourceManagerString()` or, if `XResourceManagerString()` returns `NULL`, the contents of a resource file in the user's home directory. On POSIX-based systems, the usual name for this user preference resource file is `$HOME/`*.Xdefaults*.

- If a language procedure has been set, `XtDisplayInitialize()` first searches the command line for the option "–xnlLanguage", or for a –xrm option that specifies the xnlLanguage/XnlLanguage resource. If such a resource is found, the value is assumed to be entirely in XPCS, the X Portable Character Set. If neither option is specified on the command line, `XtDisplayInitialize()` queries the server resource database (which is assumed to be entirely in XPCS) for the resource *name*`.xnlLanguage`, class *Class*`.XnlLanguage` where *name* and *Class* are the `application_name` and `application_class` specified to `XtDisplayInitialize()`. The language procedure is then invoked with the resource value if found, else the empty string. The string returned from the language procedure is saved for all future references in the Intrinsics that require the per-display language string.

- The screen resource database is initialized by parsing the command line. (See `XtAppInitialize()` for information on how the command line is parsed.)

- If a language procedure has not been set, The initial database is then queried for the resource *name*`.xnlLanguage`, class *Class*`.XnlLanguage` as specified above. If this database query fails, the server resource database is queried; if this query also fails, the language is determined from the environment; on POSIX-based systems, this is done by retrieving the value of the `LANG` environment variable. If no language string is found, the empty string is used. This language string is saved for all future references in the Intrinsics that require the per-display language string.

- After determining the language string, the user's environment resource file is then merged into the initial resource database if the file exists. This file is user-, host-, and process-specific and is expected to contain user preferences that are to override those specifications in the per-display and per-screen resources. On POSIX-based systems, the user's environment resource file name is specified by the value of the `XENVIRONMENT` environment variable. If this environment variable does not exist, the user's home directory is searched for a file named *.Xdefaults-host* , where *host* is the host name of the machine on which the application is running.

- The per-screen resource specifications are then merged into the screen resource database, if they exist. These specifications are the string returned by `XScreenResourceString()` for the respective screen and are owned entirely by the user.

- Next, the server resource database created earlier is merged into the screen resource database. The server property, and corresponding user preference file, are owned and constructed entirely by the user.

- The application-specific user resource file from the local host is then merged into the screen resource database. This file is owned by the application and typically stores user customizations in a directory owned by the user. Its name is found by calling `XrmSet-Database()` with the current screen resource database, after preserving the original display-associated database, then calling `XtResolvePathname()` with the parameters (*display*, NULL, NULL, NULL, *path*, NULL, 0, NULL) where *path* is defined in an operating-system-specific way. On POSIX-based systems, *path* is defined to be the value of the environment variable XUSERFILESEARCHPATH if this is defined. If XUSER-FILESEARCHPATH is not defined, an implementation-dependent default value is used. This default value is constrained in the following manner:

  - If the environment variable XAPPLRESDIR is not defined, the default XUSER-FILESEARCHPATH must contain at least six entries. These entries must contain $HOME as the directory prefix, plus the following substitutions:

    1. %C, %N, %L or %C, %N, %l, %t, %c

    2. %C, %N, %l

    3. %C, %N

    4. %N, %L or %N, %l, %t, %c

    5. %N, %l

    6. %N

    The order of these six entries within the path must be as given above. The order and use of substitutions within a given entry is implementation dependent.

  - If XAPPLRESDIR is defined, the default XUSERFILESEARCHPATH must contain at least seven entries. These entries must contain the following directory prefixes and substitutions:

    1. $XAPPLRESDIR with %C, %N, %L or %C, %N, %l, %t, %c

    2. $XAPPLRESDIR with %C, %N, %l

    3. $XAPPLRESDIR with %C, %N

    4. $XAPPLRESDIR with %N, %L or %N, %l, %t, %c

    5. $XAPPLRESDIR with %N, %l

    6. $XAPPLRESDIR with %N

    7. $HOME with %N

    The order of these seven entries within the path must be as given above. The order and use of substitutions within a given entry is implementation dependent.

- Lastly, the application-specific class resource file from the local host is merged into the screen resource database. This file is owned by the application and is usually placed in a system directory (*/usr/lib/X11/app-defaults* in most implementations) when the application is installed. It may contain site-wide customizations specified by the system manager. The name of the application class resource file is found by calling `XtResolvePathname()`

with the parameters (*display*, "app-defaults", NULL, NULL, NULL, NULL, 0, NULL). This call will look in the default system directory, or in the directories specified by XFILESEARCHPATH environment variable. See XtResolvePathname() for details on how this variable is used.

This file, the application class "app-defaults" file, should be provided by the developer of the application and may be required for the application to function properly. A simple application that wants to be assured of having a minimal set of resources in the absence of its class resource file can declare fallback resource specifications with XtAppSetFallbackResources().

Note that the customization substitution string is retrieved dynamically by XtResolve-Pathname() so that the resolved file name of the application class resource file can be affected by any of the earlier sources for the screen resource database, even though the contents of the class resource file have lowest precedence.

Structures

The XrmOptionDescRec structure is as follows. See XtAppInitialize() for information on how it is used.

```
typedef enum {
                               /* Value is ... */
    XrmoptionNoArg,            /* specified in OptionDescRec.value */
    XrmoptionIsArg,            /* the option string itself */
    XrmoptionStickyArg,        /* characters immediately following option */
    XrmoptionSepArg,           /* next argument in argv */
    XrmoptionResArg,           /* next argument is input to XrmPutLineResource *
                               /* Ignore this option and ... */
    XrmoptionSkipArg,          /* the next argument in argv */
    XrmoptionSkipNArgs,        /* Ignore this option and ... */
                               /* the next value arguments in argv */
    XrmoptionSkipLine          /* the rest of argv */
} XrmOptionKind;

typedef struct {
    char *option;              /* Option name in argv */
    char *specifier;           /* Resource name (without application name) */
    XrmOptionKind argKind;     /* Which style of option it is */
    caddr_t value;             /* Value to provide if XrmoptionNoArg */
} XrmOptionDescRec, *XrmOptionDescList;
```

See Also

XtAppCreateShell(1), *XtAppInitialize*(1), *XtCreateApplicationContext*(1), *XtDatabase*(1), *XtOpenDisplay*(1), *XtResolvePathname*(1).

XtDisplayOfObject

Name

XtDisplayOfObject – return the display pointer for the nearest ancestor of object that is of class Core.

Synopsis

```
Display *XtDisplayOfObject(object)
     Widget object;
```

Inputs

object   Specifies the object; may be of class Object or any subclass thereof.

Returns

The display of *object* or of its nearest widget ancestor.

Availability

Release 4 and later.

Description

XtDisplayOfObject() is identical in function to XtDisplay() if the *object* is a widget; otherwise XtDisplayOfObject() returns the display pointer for the nearest ancestor of *object* that is of class Core.

Usage

If you are working with windowed objects, use XtDisplay() rather than XtDisplay-OfObject(). XtDisplay() may be implemented as an efficient macro for widget code that includes the file *<X11/IntrinsicP.h>*.

See Also

XtScreenOfObject(1), *XtWindowOfObject*(1).

XtDisplayStringConversionWarning

Name
XtDisplayStringConversionWarning – issue a warning message during conversion of string resource values.

Synopsis
```
void XtDisplayStringConversionWarning(display, from_value, to_type)
    Display *display;
    String from_value, to_type;
```

Inputs
display Specifies the display connection with which the conversion is associated.

from_value Specifies the string that could not be converted.

to_type Specifies the target representation type requested.

Availability
Release 4 and later.

Description
XtDisplayStringConversionWarning() issues a warning message using XtApp-WarningMsg() with *name* set to conversionError, *type* set to string, *class* set to XtToolkitError and the *default* message string set to:

Cannot convert *from_value* to type *to_type*

Usage
This function is intended for use within "new-style" string resource converters. To issue other types of warning or error messages, the type converter should use XtAppWarningMsg() or XtAppErrorMsg() directly.

XtDisplayStringConversionWarning() supersedes XtStringConversion-Warning() which does not take a Display * argument and can therefore be used in "old-style" converters.

See Also
XtAppErrorMsg(1), *XtAppWarningMsg*(1).

XtDisplayToApplicationContext

Name

XtDisplayToApplicationContext – retrieve the application context associated with a Display.

Synopsis

```
XtAppContext XtDisplayToApplicationContext( display )
      Display *display;
```

Inputs

display   Specifies an open and initialized display connection.

Returns

The application context of *display*.

Description

XtDisplayToApplicationContext() returns the application context in which the specified display was initialized. If the display has not been initialized with XtDisplay-Initialize() (which is called by XtOpenDisplay() and XtAppInitialize()), an error message is issued.

See Also

XtCreateApplicationContext(1), *XtDisplayInitialize*(1).

XtError

Name

XtError – call the low-level fatal error handler.

Synopsis

```
void XtError(message)
    String message;
```

Inputs

message   Specifies the message to be reported.

Returns

XtError() terminates the application and does not return.

Availability

XtError() has been superseded by XtAppError().

Description

XtError() passes its arguments to the installed low-level error handler. On POSIX systems, the default handler is _XtDefaultError(). It prints the message to the stderr stream and calls exit().

Usage

XtError() has been superseded by XtAppError(), which performs the same function on a per-application context basis. XtError() now calls XtAppError() passing the default application context created by XtInitialize(). Very few programs need multiple application contexts, and you can continue to use XtError() if you initialize your application with XtInitialize(). We recommend, however, that you use XtAppInitialize(), Xt-AppError(), and the other XtApp*() application context specific functions.

See XtAppError() for more information.

XtError() calls the "low-level" error handler. It is better to use XtAppErrorMsg() which calls the "high-level" error handler. The high-level handler looks up the error message in a resource database and so allows for customization and internationalization of error messages.

See Also

XtErrorMsg(1), *XtSetErrorHandler*(1), *XtSetWarningMsg*(1), *XtWarning*(1), *XtWarningMsg*(1).

XtErrorMsg

Name

XtErrorMsg – call the high-level fatal error handler.

Synopsis

```
void XtErrorMsg(name, type, class, default, params, num_params)
    String name;
    String type;
    String class;
    String default;
    String *params;
    Cardinal *num_params;
```

Inputs

name   Specifies the general kind of error.

type   Specifies the detailed name of the error.

class   Specifies the resource class of the error.

default   Specifies the default message to use if no message is found in the database.

params   Specifies an array of values to be inserted into the message.

num_params Specifies the number of elements in *params*.

Returns

XtErrorMsg() terminates the application and does not return.

Availability

XtErrorMsg() has been superseded by XtAppErrorMsg().

Description

XtErrorMsg() passes all of its arguments to the installed high-level error handler. The default high-level error handler is _XtDefaultErrorMsg(). It calls XtAppGetError-DatabaseText() to lookup an error message of the specified *name*, *type*, and *class* in the error database. If no such message is found, XtAppGetErrorDatabaseText() returns the specified *default* message. In either case, _XtDefaultErrorMsg() does a printf-style substitution of *params* into the message, and passes the resulting text to the low-level error handler by calling XtError().

Usage

XtErrorMsg() has been superseded by XtAppErrorMsg(), which performs the same function on a per-application context basis. XtErrorMsg() now calls XtAppErrorMsg() passing the default application context created by XtInitialize(). Very few programs need multiple application contexts, and you can continue to use XtErrorMsg() if you initialize your application with XtInitialize(). We recommend, however, that you use Xt-AppInitialize(), XtAppErrorMsg(), and the other XtApp*() application context specific functions.

See XtAppErrorMsg() for more information.

See Also

XtAppErrorMsg(1), *XtAppWarningMsg*(1).

XtFindFile

Name

XtFindFile – search for a file using substitutions in a path.

Synopsis

```
String XtFindFile(path, substitutions, num_substitutions, predicate)
    String path;
    Substitution substitutions;
    Cardinal num_substitutions;
    XtFilePredicate predicate;
```

Inputs

path   Specifies a path of file names including substitution characters.

substitutions
                  Specifies a list of substitutions to make into the path.

num_substitutions
                  Specifies the number of substitutions passed in.

predicate   Specifies a procedure called to judge each potential file name, or NULL.

Returns

A filename, or NULL if no file was found.

Availability

Release 4 and later.

Description

XtFindFile() performs the substitutions specified by *substitutions* on each colon-separated element of *path* in turn, and passes the resulting string to *predicate*. If *predicate* returns *True*, XtFindFile() returns the string. If *predicate* never returns True, XtFindFile() returns NULL.

Each element in *substitutions* is a structure that contains a character and a string. If any element in *path* contains a percent sign followed by a character that appears in *substitutions*, then that two-character sequence will be replaced by the corresponding string in *substitutions*. The "Background" section below provides more details about the substitution process.

If *predicate* is NULL, then an internal predicate is used that returns True if the string is the name of a readable file (and is not a directory), and returns False otherwise. See XtFilePredicate(2) for more details on how to write a file predicate procedure.

The caller must free the returned string with XtFree() when it is no longer needed.

Usage

XtFindFile() is intended as a way to find a file that depends on variables such as the current setting of the locale, or the number of bitplanes available on a screen. Most applications can use the higher-level function XtResolvePathname() which provides a number of standard substitutions and a default path.

The default predicate procedure is sufficient for most uses. An application that wanted to find a directory rather than a file, for example, would have to specify a custom predicate, as would an application that wanted to verify that a file was readable and that the contents of the file were reasonable would also have to provide a custom predicate procedure.

Background

There are two substitution sequences that are treated specially:

- The character sequence %: (percent colon) specifies an embedded colon that is not a delimiter; the sequence is replaced by a single colon.

- The character sequence %% (percent percent) specifies a percent character that does not introduce a substitution; the sequence is replaced by a single percent character.

A substitution string entry of NULL is equivalent to a pointer to an empty string.

If the operating system does not interpret multiple embedded name separators in the path (i.e., "/" in POSIX) the same way as a single separator, XtFindFile() will collapse multiple separators into a single one after performing all string substitutions. Except for collapsing embedded separators, the contents of the string substitutions are not interpreted by XtFindFile() and may therefore contain any operating-system-dependent characters, including additional name separators.

Structures

The Substitution type is defined as follows:

```
typedef struct {
    char match;
    String substitution;
} SubstitutionRec, *Substitution;
```

See Also

XtResolvePathname(1),
XtFilePredicate(2).

XtFree

Name

XtFree – free allocated memory.

Synopsis

```
void XtFree(ptr);
    char *ptr;
```

Inputs

ptr   Specifies the address of the allocated memory to be freed.

Description

XtFree() frees a block of memory previously allocated by XtMalloc(), XtRealloc(), XtCalloc(), XtNew() or XtNewString() so that it can be reused by the system.

If *ptr* is NULL, XtFree() returns immediately.

Usage

The *ptr* argument is of type char *. In many cases, you will have to cast the data you are freeing to this type in order to avoid warning messages from your compiler.

A number of Xt functions return strings or other values that must be freed with XtFree() when the caller will no longer need them. You should be sure to check the documentation of any function that returns a value to find out who "owns" the memory and who is expected to free it.

Calling the Toolkit's XtMalloc() and XtFree() is more portable and provides better error checking than calling system-specific malloc and free. You should not use XtFree() on memory that was allocated with malloc() or other non-Xt memory allocation routines.

See Also

XtCalloc(1), *XtMalloc*(1), *XtNew*(1), *XtNewString*(1), *XtRealloc*(1).

Name

XtGetActionKeysym – retrieve the keysym and modifiers that matched the final event specification in the translation table entry.

Synopsis

```
KeySym XtGetActionKeysym(event, modifiers_return)
      XEvent *event;
      Modifiers *modifiers_return;
```

Inputs

event   Specifies the event pointer passed to the action procedure by the Intrinsics.

Outputs

modifiers_return

Returns the modifier state actually used to generate the returned keysym. You may pass NULL if you are not interested in the modifiers.

Returns

The keysym of the final event specification in the translation table entry that dispatched the current action, or NoSymbol.

Availability

Release 4 and later.

Description

XtGetActionKeysym() returns the keysym of the final event specification in the translation table entry that invoked the current action, provided that:

*   XtGetActionKeysym() is called after an action procedure has been invoked by the Intrinsics and before that action procedure returns,

*   the event pointer has the same value as the event pointer passed to that action routine, and

*   the event is a KeyPress or a KeyRelease.

XtGetActionKeysym() also returns the modifiers actually used to generate this keysym if *modifiers_return* is non-NULL.

If XtGetActionKeysym() is not called from an action procedure, or if event does not match the event that invoked the action, but if the event is a KeyPress or KeyRelease, then XtGetActionKeysym() calls XtTranslateKeycode() and returns the results.

If the event is not a KeyPress or KeyRelease, then XtGetActionKeysym() returns NoSymbol and does not examine *modifiers_return*.

Note that if an action procedure which was invoked by the Intrinsics invokes a subsequent action procedure (and so on) via XtCallActionProc(), the nested action procedure may also call XtGetActionKeysym() to retrieve the Intrinsics' keysym and modifiers.

Usage

You should only call XtGetActionKeysym() from within an action procedure. When an action procedure is invoked on a KeyPress or KeyRelease event, it often has a need to retrieve the keysym and modifiers corresponding to the event that caused it to be invoked. In order to avoid repeating the processing that was just performed by the Intrinsics to match the translation entry, the keysym and modifiers are stored for the duration of the action procedure and can be obtained with this function.

Structures

A KeySym is an X server resource:

```
typedef XID KeySym;
```

The Modifiers type and its possible values are as follows:

```
typedef unsigned int Modifiers;

#define ShiftMask          (1<<0)
#define LockMask           (1<<1)
#define ControlMask        (1<<2)
#define Mod1Mask           (1<<3)
#define Mod2Mask           (1<<4)
#define Mod3Mask           (1<<5)
#define Mod4Mask           (1<<6)
#define Mod5Mask           (1<<7)
```

See Also

XtActionProc(1), *XtAppAddActions*(1), *XtTranslateKeycode*(1).

Name

XtGetActionList – get the action table of a widget class.

Synopsis

```
void XtGetActionList(widget_class, actions_return, num_actions_return)
    WidgetClass widget_class;
    XtActionList *actions_return;
    Cardinal *num_actions_return;
```

Inputs

widget_class   Specifies the widget class whose action table is to be returned; must be coreWidgetClass or any subclass.

Outputs

actions_return   Returns the action table of the widget class.

num_actions_return   Returns the number of elements in the action table.

Availability

Release 5 and later.

Description

XtGetActionList returns the action table defined by *widget_class* in *actions_return*. This table does not include actions defined by the superclasses.

If *widget_class* is not initialized, or is not coreWidgetClass or a subclass thereof, or if the class does not define any actions, NULL will be returned in *actions_return* and zero will be returned in *num_actions_return*. If a non-NULL action table is returned, the application is responsible for freeing the table using XtFree() when it is no longer needed.

Structures

The XtActionsRec structure and the XtActionList type are defined as follows:

```
typedef struct _XtActionsRec{
    String string;
    XtActionProc proc;
} XtActionsRec;

typedef struct _XtActionsRec *XtActionList;
```

See Also

XtActionProc(2).

Xt Functions and Macros

XtGetApplicationNameAndClass

Name

XtGetApplicationNameAndClass – return the application name and class as passed to Xt-DisplayInitialize() for a particular Display.

Synopsis

```
void XtGetApplicationNameAndClass(display, name_return, class_return)
    Display *display;
    String  *name_return;
    String  *class_return;
```

Inputs

display Specifies an open display connection that has been initialized with Xt-DisplayInitialize().

Outputs

name_return Returns the application name.

class_return
        Returns the application class.

Availability

Release 4 and later.

Description

XtGetApplicationNameAndClass() returns the application name and class passed to XtDisplayInitialize() for the specified display. If the display was never initialized or has been closed, the result is undefined. The returned strings are owned by the Intrinsics and must not be modified or freed by the caller.

See Also

XtDisplayInitialize(1).

XtGetApplicationResources

Name

XtGetApplicationResources – set application variables from the resource database.

Synopsis

```
void XtGetApplicationResources(object, base, resources, num_resources,
        args, num_args)
    Widget object;
    XtPointer base;
    XtResourceList resources;
    Cardinal num_resources;
    ArgList args;
    Cardinal num_args;
```

Inputs

object   Specifies the object that identifies the resource database to search; may be of class Object or any subclass.

base   Specifies the base address of the structure into which the resource values will be written.

resources   Specifies the application's resource list.

num_resources

       Specifies the number of resources in the resource list.

args   Specifies the argument list to override other resource specifications, or NULL.

num_args   Specifies the number of arguments in the argument list.

Outputs

base   Returns the resource values from the argument list, the resource database, or the resource list defaults.

Description

`XtGetApplicationResources()` retrieves resource settings that apply to an overall application, rather than to a particular widget. For each resource in *resources*, `XtGet-ApplicationResource()` sets a value in the structure pointed to by *base*. This value comes from the argument list *args*, or if no value for the resource is found in the argument list, from the resource database associated with *object*, or if no value is found in the database, from the *default_addr* field of the resource itself. Once the value is determined, it is copied into the structure at *base* using the `resource_offset` and `resource_size` fields of the resource.

The search of the database is done using the `resource_name` and `resource_class` fields of the resource. Resources are searched for at the level in the resource name hierarchy at which *object*'s resources are found, i.e., application resources are set in a resource database in the same way as the specified object's resources are set.

`XtGetApplicationResources()` may overwrite the specified resource list with an equivalent representation in an internal format that optimizes access time if the list is used repeatedly. The resource list must be allocated in writable storage and the caller must not modify the list contents after the call if the same list is to be used again. Any per-display resources fetched by XtGetApplicationResources() will not be freed from the resource cache until the display is closed.

The use of each of the fields in the XtResource structure is explained in detail in the "Background" section below.

Usage

Any application that has any configurability should define application resources as an alternative to command line options and configuration files. To do this, you declare a structure that contains a field for each of the resource values you want to look up in the database. Then you statically initialize an array of XtResource structures which describe the name, class, type and default of each resource, and also specify the size of the resource value and the location within your structure at which it should be stored. Next you call XtGetApplication-Resources() with the address of your structure and your application resource list, and possibly an argument list of values to override the database. When XtGetApplication-Resources() returns, your structure will be initialized with values from the argument list, the resource database, or from the resource list defaults. The "Example" section below shows an example of this process, and the "Background" section explains each of the fields of an Xt-Resource structure in more detail.

Usually, you will pass a the shell widget returned by XtAppInitialize() as *object*. This will make XtGetApplicationResources() look up resources of the form *application_name.resource_name*. You may use any other widget or object, but this will make Xt-GetApplicationResources() look up resources that are deeper in the hierarchy, resources that appear to be resources of the specified widget.

Example

Here is a short program that declares and initializes an application resource list and uses it to get the value of some application resources.

```
#include <X11/StringDefs.h>
#include <X11/Intrinsic.h>

/*
 * fields to be filled in from resources
 */
typedef struct {
    Pixel highlight_color;
    XFontStruct *bold_font;
    Boolean palette_on_left;
} application_variable_rec;

static XtResource resources[] = {
    {"highlightColor", XtCForeground, XtRPixel, sizeof(Pixel),
     XtOffsetOf(application_variable_rec, highlight_color),
     XtRString, XtDefaultForeground
     },
    {"boldFont", XtCFont, XtRFontStruct, sizeof(XFontStruct *),
```

```
    XtOffsetOf(application_variable_rec, bold_font),
    XtRString, XtDefaultFont
    },
    {"paletteOnLeft", "PaletteOnLeft", XtRBoolean, sizeof(Boolean),
     XtOffsetOf(application_variable_rec, palette_on_left),
     XtRImmediate, True
    }
};

main(argc, argv)
int argc;
char **argv;
{
    XtAppContext app_context;
    Widget toplevel;
    application_variable_rec app_vars;

    toplevel = XtAppInitialize(&app_context, "XDraw",
            NULL, 0, &argc, argv,
            NULL, NULL, 0);

    XtGetApplicationResources(toplevel,                /* widget */
            &app_vars,              /* base address */
            resources,              /* resource list */
            XtNumber(resources),    /* how many */
            NULL, 0);               /* ArgList */
    .
    .
    .
}
```

If the application name is "xdraw", then the application resources can be set with lines like the following in a resource file:

```
xdraw.highlightColor: blue
xdraw.boldFont: *-helvetica-bold-r-*-*-*-180-*
xdraw.paletteOnLeft: False
```

Background

To use `XtGetApplicationResources()`, you must initialize an array of `XtResource` structures which describe the resources you want to obtain. The `XtResource` structure is shown in the "Structures" section below. The fields of this structure are used as follows:

resource_name

This field specifies the name of the resource, i.e., the name that must appear in a resource file to set this resource. By convention, the first letter of a resource name is lowercase, and any subsequent words are capitalized and concatenated without a hyphen or under-score—"background" and "backgroundPixmap", for example. If you define a symbolic constant for the resource name, it should be the same as the resource name, with a prefix, which should end with an 'N'—XtNbackground or XmNbackgroundPixmap, for example. It is also convention that the field in which this resource's value will be stored has the same name as the resource, using all lowercase letters, and underscores to separate words—`background` and `background_pixmap`, for example. Resource names beginning with "xt" are reserved by the Intrinsics.

resource_class

This field specifies the class name of the resource. If a number of resources have the same class, you can specify a value for all those resources with a single line in a resource file. The "normalFont" and "boldFont" resources might both be of class "Font", for example. Class names conventionally begin with capital letters, and, as with resource names, subsequent words are capitalized and underscores are not used. Symbolic names for class names are conventionally spelled the same way as the class name with a prefix which ends with 'C'—XtCFont, for example. If there is no general category to use for a resource's class, the class should be the same as the resource name, but capitalized. Class names beginning with "Xt" are reserved by the Intrinsics.

resource_type

This field is a string that identifies the type of the resource. By convention, it is spelled the same way as the type of the field that this resource will set, but begins with a capital letter. Symbolic names for resource types are spelled the same as the type name, but begin with a prefix which end with 'R'—XtRInt and XmRFontList, for example. The Intrinsics predefine a number of types which are shown in the table below. Type names are used to identify which resource converter should be used to convert a string value from the resource database into the appropriate type. If one of your fields is not of one of the standard types listed below, use a type of your own, but be aware that you will have to write and register a converter procedure if you want to get values for that field from the resource database.

resource_size

This field specifies the size in bytes of the field in your structure that this resource will set. Use the `sizeof()` operator to compute this value.

resource_offset

This field specifies the offset of this resource's field from the beginning of the structure. This value is added to the *base* argument passed to `XtGetApplication-Resources()` in order to determine where the resource value is to be stored. This field plus the `resource_size` field provide enough information to correctly store the resource value. Use the `XtOffsetOf()` macro to determine the offset of a field in a structure.

default_type

This is a string which specifies the type of the default value in the `default_addr` field. It is the same sort of type as the `resource_type` field explained above. The type of the default does not have to be the same as the type of resource. If they do not match, an appropriate resource converter will be invoked to convert the default value when it is required. In addition to the types listed in the table below, and any types of your own definition, there are two special values that can be set in this field. If `default_type` is `XtRImmediate`, then `default_addr` is interpreted as the resource value itself, rather than a pointer to the value. This is useful for resources that are integers, Booleans, or other scalar types. If `default_type` is `XtRCallProc`, then `default_addr` is pointer to a procedure of type `XtResourceDefaultProc` which is responsible for storing the default value in the correct location. See `XtResourceDefaultProc(2)` for details on the responsibilities of such a procedure.

`default_addr`

This field specifies a pointer to the default value of the resource, which must be of the type identified by `default_type`. This field is interpreted differently for types `XtRImmediate` and `XtRCallProc`, as explained above. Also, if `default_type` is `XtRString`, then `default_addr` is the string itself, not the address of the string (i.e., it is a `char *`, not a `char **`).

The Intrinsics define symbolic names for a number of strings which represent commonly used types. These symbolic names and the types they represent are shown in the table below.

Resource Type	C Type	Resource Type	C Type
XtRAcceleratorTable	XtAccelerators	XtRInitialState	int
XtRAtom	Atom	XtRInt	int
XtRBitmap	Pixmap, depth=1	XtRLongBoolean	long
XtRBoolean	Boolean	XtRObject	Object
XtRBool	Bool	XtRPixel	Pixel
XtRCallback	XtCallbackList	XtRPixmap	Pixmap
XtRCardinal	Cardinal	XtRPointer	XtPointer
XtRColor	XColor	XtRPosition	Position
XtRColormap	Colormap	XtRScreen	Screen*
XtRCursor	Cursor	XtRShort	short
XtRDimension	Dimension	XtRString	String
XtRDisplay	Display*	XtRStringArray	String*
XtREnum	XtEnum	XtRStringTable	String*
XtRFile	FILE*	XtRTranslationTable	XtTranslations
XtRFloat	float	XtRUnsignedChar	unsigned char
XtRFont	Font	XtRVisual	Visual*
XtRFontSet	XFontSet	XtRWidget	Widget
XtRFontStruct	XFontStruct*	XtRWidgetClass	WidgetClass
XtRFunction	(*)()	XtRWidgetList	WidgetList
XtRGeometry	char*	XtRWindow	Window

Structures

`XtResource` is defined as follows:

```
typedef struct _XtResource {
    String    resource_name;   /* Resource name */
    String    resource_class;  /* Resource class */
    String    resource_type;   /* Representation type desired */
    Cardinal  resource_size;   /* Size in bytes of representation */
    Cardinal  resource_offset; /* Offset from base to put resource value */
```

Xt Functions and Macros

```
    String    default_type;   /* Representation type of specified default */
    XtPointer default_addr;   /* Address of resource default value */
} XtResource, *XtResourceList;
```

The `ArgList` type is defined as follows:

```
typedef struct {
    String    name;
    XtArgVal  value;
} Arg, *ArgList;
```

See Also

XtGetSubresources(1), *XtOffsetOf*(1).

XtGetConstraintResourceList

Name

XtGetConstraintResourceList – get the constraint resource list structure for a particular widget class.

Synopsis

```
void XtGetConstraintResourceList(object_class, resources_return,
        num_resources_return)
    WidgetClass object_class;
    XtResourceList *resources_return;
    Cardinal *num_resources_return;
```

Inputs

`object_class` Specifies the object class to be queried; may be of class objectClass or any subclass thereof.

Outputs

`resources_return` Returns the constraint resource list.

`num_resources_return`
Returns the number of entries in the constraint resource list.

Availability

Release 4 and later.

Description

XtGetConstraintResources() returns the resource list of the constraintClassPart of the widget class `object_class`. If it is called before the widget class is initialized, the resource list as specified in the widget class record will be returned. If it is called after the widget class has been initialized, the merged resource list for the class and all constraint superclasses is returned. If the specified `object_class` is not a subclass of constraintWidgetClass, *resources_return* is set to NULL and *num_resources_return* is set to zero. The list returned by XtGetConstraintResourceList() should be freed using XtFree() when it is no longer needed.

Usage

Most applications will never need to query a widget class for the resources it supports. This function is intended to support interface builders and applications like *editres* which allow the use to view the available resources and set them interactively.

To get the normal resources of a widget rather than the constraint resources, use XtGet-ResourceList().

See Also

XtGetResourceList(1).

XtGetErrorDatabase

Name

XtGetErrorDatabase – obtain the error database.

Synopsis

```
XrmDatabase *XtGetErrorDatabase()
```

Inputs

Returns

The address of an `XrmDatabase`.

Availability

`XtGetErrorDatabase()` has been superseded by `XtAppGetErrorDatabase()`.

Description

`XtGetErrorDatabase()` returns the address of the error database used by high-level error and warning handlers. This database may be empty until `XtGetErrorDatabaseText()` is called for the first time.

Usage

`XtGetErrorDatabase()` has been superseded by `XtAppGetErrorDatabase()`, which performs the same function on a per-application context basis. `XtGetError-Database()` now calls `XtAppGetErrorDatabase()` passing the default application context created by `XtInitialize()`. Very few programs need multiple application contexts, and you can continue to use `XtGetErrorDatabase()` if you initialize your application with `XtInitialize()`. We recommend, however, that you use `XtApp-Initialize()`, `XtAppGetErrorDatabase()`, and the other `XtApp*()` application context specific functions.

See `XtAppGetErrorDatabase()` for more information.

See Also

XtAppGetErrorDatabase(1), *XtAppGetErrorDatabaseText*(1), *XtGetErrorDatabaseText*(1), *XtErrorMsgHandler*(2).

Name

XtGetErrorDatabaseText – get the text of a named message from the error database.

Synopsis

```
void XtGetErrorDatabaseText(name, type, class, default, buffer_return,
        nbytes)
    String name, type, class;
    String default;
    String buffer_return;
    int nbytes;
```

Inputs

name   Specifies the name or general kind of the message.

type   Specifies the type or detailed name of the message.

class   Specifies the resource class of the error message.

default   Specifies the default message to use if an error database entry is not found.

nbytes   Specifies the size of *buffer_return* in bytes.

Outputs

buffer_return

Specifies the buffer into which the error message is to be returned.

Availability

XtGetErrorDatabaseText() has been superseded by XtAppGetErrorDatabase-Text().

Description

XtGetErrorDatabaseText() looks up the message named by *name*, *type*, and *class* in the database returned by XtGetErrorDatabase(). If such a message is found, it is stored into *buffer_return*, otherwise the message in *default* is stored into *buffer_return*.

The resource name of the message is formed by concatenating *name* and *type* with a single "." between them. The resource class of the message is *class* if it already contains a ".", or otherwise is formed by concatenating *class* with itself with a single "." between the strings.

Usage

XtGetErrorDatabaseText() has been superseded by XtAppGetErrorDatabase-Text(), which performs the same function on a per-application context basis. XtGet-ErrorDatabaseText() now calls XtAppGetErrorDatabaseText() passing the default application context created by XtInitialize(). Very few programs need multiple application contexts, and you can continue to use XtGetErrorDatabaseText() if you initialize your application with XtInitialize(). We recommend, however, that you use XtAppInitialize(), XtAppGetErrorDatabaseText(), and the other XtApp*() application context specific functions.

See `XtAppGetErrorDatabaseText()` for more information.

See Also

XtAppGetErrorDatabase(1), *XtAppGetErrorDatabaseText*(1),
XtErrorMsgHandler(2).

Name

XtGetGC – obtain a read-only, sharable GC.

Synopsis

```
GC XtGetGC(object, value_mask, values)
    Widget object;
    XtGCMask value_mask;
    XGCValues *values;
```

Inputs

object   Specifies the object with which the GC is to be associated; may be of class Object or any subclass thereof.

value_mask   Specifies which fields of the GC are to be filled in with widget data.

values   Specifies the actual values for this GC.

Returns

A read-only GC with fields as specified in value_mask and values.

Description

XtGetGC() returns a sharable, read-only GC with values as specified in values for each bit set in value_mask. The GC is valid for the screen and depth of object, or the nearest widget ancestor if object is not a subclass of Core.

XtGetGC() shares only GCs in which all values in the GC are the same. In particular, it does not use the value_mask provided to determine which fields of the GC a widget considers relevant. value_mask is used only to tell the server which fields should be filled in with widget data and which it should fill in with default values.

Usage

The Intrinsics provide a mechanism whereby widgets can share a graphics context (GC), reducing the number of GCs created and thereby improving server performance. The mechanism is a simple caching scheme, and all GCs obtained by means of this mechanism must be treated as read-only.

If a GC with modifiable fields is needed, in Release 4 or previous releases the Xlib XCreate-GC() function must be used. In Release 5, XtAllocateGC() allows a widget to allocate a shared GC with modifiable fields.

Generally only widgets will need to allocate GCs, though some applications may also want to do so. When done with a shared GC, free it with XtReleaseGC().

Structures

The XtGCMask type is defined as follows:

```
typedef unsigned long  XtGCMask; /* Mask of values that are used by widget*/
```

Each of the symbols in the table below sets a single bit in an XtGCMask. The *value_mask*, argument is formed by combining these symbols with the bitwise OR operator (|):

GCArcMode	GCFillRule	GCLineWidth
GCBackground	GCFillStyle	GCPlaneMask
GCCapStyle	GCFont	GCStipple
GCClipMask	GCForeground	GCSubwindowMode
GCClipXOrigin	GCFunction	GCTile
GCClipYOrigin	GCGraphicsExposures	GCTileStipXOrigin
GCDashList	GCJoinStyle	GCTileStipYOrigin
GCDashOffset	GCLineStyle	

The XGCValues structure contains the GC fields:

```
typedef struct {
    int function;                   /* logical operation */
    unsigned long plane_mask;       /* plane mask */
    unsigned long foreground;       /* foreground pixel */
    unsigned long background;       /* background pixel */
    int line_width;                 /* line width */
    int line_style;                 /* LineSolid, LineOnOffDash,
                                       LineDoubleDash */
    int cap_style;                  /* CapNotLast, CapButt,
                                       CapRound, CapProjecting */
    int join_style;                 /* JoinMiter, JoinRound, JoinBevel */
    int fill_style;                 /* FillSolid, FillTiled,
                                       FillStippled, FillOpaqueStippled */
    int fill_rule;                  /* EvenOddRule, WindingRule */
    int arc_mode;                   /* ArcChord, ArcPieSlice */
    Pixmap tile;                    /* tile pixmap for tiling operations */
    Pixmap stipple;                 /* stipple 1 plane pixmap for stippling */
    int ts_x_origin;                /* offset for tile or
    int ts_y_origin;                 * stipple operations */
    Font font;                      /* default text font for text operations */
    int subwindow_mode;             /* ClipByChildren, IncludeInferiors */
    Bool graphics_exposures;        /* should exposures be generated? */
    int clip_x_origin;              /* origin for clipping */
    int clip_y_origin;
    Pixmap clip_mask;               /* bitmap clipping; other calls for rects */
    int dash_offset;                /* patterned/dashed line information */
    char dashes;
} XGCValues;
```

See Also

XtAllocateGC(1), *XtReleaseGC*(1).

Name

XtGetKeysymTable – return a pointer to the keycode-to-keysym mapping table of a display.

Synopsis

```
KeySym *XtGetKeysymTable(display, min_keycode_return,
      keysyms_per_keycode_return)
    Display *display;
    KeyCode *min_keycode_return;
    int *keysyms_per_keycode_return;
```

Inputs

display   Specifies the display whose table is required.

Outputs

min_keycode_return
> Returns the minimum keycode valid for the display.

keysyms_per_keycode_return
> Returns the number of keysyms stored for each keycode.

Returns

The keycode-to-keysym table for *display*.

Availability

Release 4 and later.

Description

XtGetKeysymTable() returns a pointer to the Intrinsics' copy of the X server's keycode-to-keysym table, which must not be modified by the application. This table is simply an array of KeySym. The number of keysyms associated with each keycode is returned in *keysyms_per_keycode_return*. The first keysyms in the table are for the keycode returned in *min_keycode_return*. The keysyms for a keycode *k* begin at index:

k - min_keycode_return) * keysyms_per_keycode_return

Any entries in the table that have no keysyms associated with them contain the value No-Symbol.

Usage

The Intrinsics maintains a table internally to map keycodes to keysyms for each open display. The Translation Manager uses this table, and custom keycode-to-keysym translator procedures (see XtSetKeyTranslator()) and other clients may also need to use it. Most applications and widgets will never need to use this function.

You should not cache this keysym table but should call XtGetKeysymTable() each time the value is needed, because the table may change at any time.

See Also

XtConvertCase(1), *XtKeysymToKeycodeList*(1), *XtRegisterCaseConverter*(1), *XtSetKeyTranslator*(1), *XtTranslateKeycode*(1).

Xt Functions and Macros

Name
XtGetMultiClickTime – read the multi-click time.

Synopsis
```
int XtGetMultiClickTime(display)
    Display *display;
```

Inputs
display   Specifies the display connection.

Returns
The multi-click time for *display*, in milliseconds.

Availability
Release 4 and later.

Description
XtGetMultiClickTime() returns the time in milliseconds that the translation manager uses to determine if multiple events are to be interpreted as a repeated event for purposes of matching a translation entry containing a repeat count.

Translation table entries may specify actions that are taken when two or more identical events occur consecutively, separated by a short time interval called the multi-click time. The multi-click time value can be specified as an application resource with name multiClickTime and class MultiClickTime and can also be modified dynamically by the application (see XtSetMultiClickTime()). The multi-click time is unique for each Display and is retrieved from the resource database by XtDisplayInitialize(). If no value is specified, the initial value is 200 milliseconds.

See Also
XtSetMultiClickTime(1).

XtGetResourceList

Name

XtGetResourceList – get the resource list of a widget class.

Synopsis

```
void XtGetResourceList(object_class, resources_return,
        num_resources_return);
    WidgetClass object_class;
    XtResourceList *resources_return;
    Cardinal *num_resources_return;
```

Inputs

object_class
Specifies the object class to be queried; may be objectClass or any subclass.

Outputs

resources_return
Returns the resource list.

num_resources_return
Returns the number of entries in the resource list.

Description

XtGetResourceList() returns the corePart resource list of the specified widget or object class. If it is called before the widget class is initialized it returns the resource list as specified in the widget class record. If it is called after the widget class has been initialized, it returns a merged resource list that includes the resources for all superclasses. The list returned by Xt-GetResourceList() should be freed using XtFree() when it is no longer needed.

Usage

Most applications will never need to query the a widget class for the resources it supports. This function is intended to support interface builders and applications like *editres* which allow the use to view the available resources and set them interactively.

To get the constraint resources of a widget class, use XtGetConstraintResource-List().

Structures

XtResource is defined as follows:

```
typedef struct _XtResource {
    String     resource_name;  /* Resource name */
    String     resource_class; /* Resource class */
    String     resource_type;  /* Representation type desired */
    Cardinal   resource_size;  /* Size in bytes of representation */
    Cardinal   resource_offset;/* Offset from base to put resource value */
    String     default_type;   /* Representation type of specified default */
    XtPointer  default_addr;   /* Address of resource default value */
} XtResource, *XtResourceList;
```

See Also

XtGetConstraintResourceList(1).

XtGetSelectionRequest

Name

XtGetSelectionRequest – retrieve the SelectionRequest event that triggered a Xt-ConvertSelectionProc.

Synopsis

```
XSelectionRequestEvent *XtGetSelectionRequest(w, selection, request_id)
    Widget w;
    Atom selection;
    XtRequestId request_id;
```

Inputs

w   Specifies the widget which currently owns this selection.

selection   Specifies the selection being processed.

request_id   Specifies the requestor ID in the case of incremental selections, or NULL in the case of atomic transfers.

Returns

A pointer to a SelectionRequest event structure.

Availability

Release 4 and later.

Description

XtGetSelectionRequest() may only be called from within an XtConvert-SelectionProc and returns a pointer to the SelectionRequest event which caused the procedure to be invoked. *request_id* specifies a unique ID for the individual request in the case that multiple incremental transfers are outstanding. For atomic transfers, *request_id* must be specified as NULL. If no SelectionRequest event is being processed for the specified widget, selection and ID, XtGetSelectionRequest() returns NULL.

Usage

An XtConvertSelectionProc is not passed the event that triggered it, but it needs the timestamp of this event in order to comply with the ICCCM. XtGetSelectionRequest() was added in Release 4 as a work-around to this problem.

See Also

XtGetSelectionValue(1), *XtGetSelectionValueIncremental*(1), *XtOwnSelection*(1), *XtConvertSelectionProc*(2).

XtGetSelectionTimeout

Name

XtGetSelectionTimeout – get the current Intrinsics selection timeout value.

Synopsis

```
unsigned long XtGetSelectionTimeout()
```

Inputs

Returns

The selection timeout value.

Availability

XtGetSelectionTimeout() has been superseded by XtAppGetSelection-
Timeout().

Description

XtGetSelectionTimeout() returns the current selection timeout value, in milliseconds.
The selection timeout is the time within which the two communicating applications must
respond to one another. The initial timeout value is set by the selectionTimeout application resource, which defaults to 5000 milliseconds (5 seconds).

Usage

XtGetSelectionTimeout() has been superseded by XtAppGetSelection-
Timeout(), which performs the same function on a per-application context basis. XtGet-
SelectionTimeout() now calls XtAppGetSelectionTimeout() passing the default
application context created by XtInitialize(). Very few programs need multiple application contexts, and you can continue to use XtGetSelectionTimeout() if you initialize
your application with XtInitialize(). We recommend, however, that you use XtApp-
Initialize(), XtAppGetSelectionTimeout(), and the other XtApp*() application context specific functions.

See XtAppGetSelectionTimeout() for more information.

See Also

XtAppGetSelectionTimeout(1), *XtAppSetSelectionTimeout*(1).

XtGetSelectionValue

Name

XtGetSelectionValue – request the value of a selection.

Synopsis

```
void XtGetSelectionValue(w, selection, target, callback, client_data, time)
    Widget w;
    Atom selection;
    Atom target;
    XtSelectionCallbackProc callback;
    XtPointer client_data;
    Time time;
```

Inputs

w
Specifies the widget that is making the request. Must be of class Core or any subclass thereof.

selection
Specifies the particular selection desired (usually XA_PRIMARY or XA_SECONDARY).

target
Specifies the type of information about the selection that is being requested.

callback
Specifies the callback procedure to be called when the selection value has been obtained. Note that this is how the selection value is communicated back to the client.

client_data
Specifies an argument to be passed to *callback* when it is called.

time
Specifies the timestamp that indicates when the selection is desired. This should be the timestamp of the event that triggered this request; the value CurrentTime is not acceptable.

Description

XtGetSelectionValue() initiates an ICCCM-compliant request to the owner of the selection identified by *selection* to convert that selection to the type identified by *target*, and registers *callback* as the procedure to be called (with *client_data* as one of its arguments) when the converted value is ready.

callback will be called some time after XtGetSelectionValue() is called. It may be called before or after XtGetSelectionValue() returns. If there is no owner for the selection or if the owner could not convert to the requested type, *callback* will be called with a value of NULL and length zero.

If multiple calls to the server are required to get all the data, this will be transparent to the widget; the Intrinsics perform all the necessary fragmentation and reassembly of the selection.

See XtSelectionCallbackProc(2) for information on how to write a callback appropriate to register with this function.

Usage

Because of the asynchronous nature of interclient communication, it is not possible to call a function that returns the value of the selection immediately. When you need the value of the selection, to paste it into a widget, for example, you must call `XtGetSelectionValue()` and supply a callback which will be called at some later time. It is in this callback that you can actually perform your paste.

To determine the target types that the selection owner will be willing to return, intern the string "TARGETS" using `XInternAtom()`, and send the corresponding Atom as *target*.

To (atomically) request that a selection value be converted to several target types, use `XtGet-SelectionValues()`.

See Also

XtGetSelectionValues(1), *XtGetSelectionValueIncremental*(1), *XtOwnSelection*(1), *XtSelectionCallbackProc*(2).

XtGetSelectionValueIncremental

Name

XtGetSelectionValueIncremental – obtain the selection value using incremental transfers.

Synopsis

```
void XtGetSelectionValueIncremental(w, selection, target, callback,
        client_data, time)
    Widget w;
    Atom selection;
    Atom target;
    XtSelectionCallbackProc callback;
    XtPointer client_data;
    Time time;
```

Inputs

w   Specifies the widget that is making the request. Must be of class Core or any subclass thereof.

selection   Specifies the particular selection desired (usually XA_PRIMARY or XA_SECONDARY).

target   Specifies the type of the information that is needed about the selection.

callback   Specifies the callback procedure that is to be called to receive each data segment.

client_data Specifies client-specific data that is to be passed to the specified callback procedure when it is invoked.

time   Specifies the timestamp that indicates when the selection request was initiated. This should be the timestamp of the event which triggered this request; the value CurrentTime is not acceptable.

Availability

Release 4 and later.

Description

XtGetSelectionValueIncremental() initiates an ICCCM-compliant request to the owner of the selection identified by *selection* to convert the selected value to the type identified by *target*, and registers *callback* with the Intrinsics incremental selection interface as the procedure to call when segments of the requested value are delivered.

callback will be called some time after XtGetSelectionValue() is called. It may be called before or after XtGetSelectionValue() returns. It will be called once for each segment of the selection value, and a final time with a non-NULL value (which must be freed) and a zero length. This final call is simply an indication that the transfer is complete.

If the transfer times out or is otherwise aborted before it completes, callback will be called with *type* pointing to the atom XT_CONVERT_FAIL. In this case, the requestor must decide whether to abort the entire transfer or to proceed with the partially transferred selection.

If there is no owner for the selection or if the owner could not convert to the requested type, *callback* will be called with a value of NULL and length zero.

See XtSelectionCallbackProc(2) for more information on how to write a callback appropriate to register with this function.

Usage

Because of the asynchronous nature of interclient communication, it is not possible to call a function that returns the value of the selection immediately. When you need the value of the selection, to paste it into a widget, for example, you must request the value of the selection and supply a callback which will be called at some later time. It is in this callback that you can actually perform your paste.

Most applications and widgets can use XtGetSelectionValue() which will call the specified callback exactly once with the value. Some selection *owners* will find it more natural to supply the selection value in an incremental fashion, delivering one piece at a time. This could be the case when the selection is large disjoint pieces of text in a text editor widget, for example. The selection *requestor* may request selections incrementally, but is never required to do so—the Intrinsics will coalesce an incrementally transferred value if the requestor requests it through the atomic XtGetSelectionValue() interface.

In some cases, however, it may be more natural to receive selection values through the incremental interface. Note that there is information in the boundaries of each segment that is transferred incrementally. This information is lost if the selection is coalesced into a single value.

See XtGetSelectionValue() for more information.

See Also

XtGetSelectionValue(1), *XtGetSelectionValuesIncremental*(1), *XtOwnSelectionIncremental*(1).

XtGetSelectionValues

Name

XtGetSelectionValues – obtain selection data in multiple formats.

Synopsis

```
void XtGetSelectionValues(w, selection, targets, count, callback,
        client_data, time)
    Widget w;
    Atom selection;
    Atom *targets;
    int count;
    XtSelectionCallbackProc callback;
    XtPointer *client_data;
    Time time;
```

Inputs

w
Specifies the widget that is making the request. Must be of class core or any subclass thereof.

selection
Specifies the particular selection desired (usually XA_PRIMARY or XA_SECONDARY).

targets
Specifies the types of information about the selection that are being requested.

count
Specifies the length of the *targets* and *client_data* arrays.

callback
Specifies the callback procedure to be called with each selection value obtained. Note that this is how the selection values are communicated back to the client.

client_data
Specifies an array of client data (one for each target type) each element of which will be passed to *callback* when it is called for the corresponding element of *targets*.

time
Specifies the timestamp that indicates when the selection value is desired. This should be the timestamp of the event that triggered this request; the value CurrentTime is not acceptable.

Description

XtGetSelectionValues() is similar to XtGetSelectionValue() except that it takes an array of target types and an array of client data and requests the current value of the selection converted to each of the targets. The callback is called once for each element of *targets*, and is passed the corresponding element of *client_data*. The effect is as if each target were specified in a separate call to XtGetSelectionValue(), except that XtGetSelectionValues() guarantees that all the conversions will use the same selection value because the ownership of the selection cannot change in the middle of the list, as could happen when calling XtGetSelectionValue() repeatedly.

See XtGetSelectionValue() for more information.

See Also

XtGetSelectionValue(1), *XtGetSelectionValueIncremental*(1), *XtGetSelectionValuesIncremental*(1), *XtSelectionCallbackProc*(2).

XtGetSelectionValuesIncremental

Name

XtGetSelectionValuesIncremental – obtain multiple selection values using incremental transfers.

Synopsis

```
void XtGetSelectionValuesIncremental(w, selection, targets, count,
     callback, client_data, time)
   Widget w;
   Atom selection;
   Atom *targets;
   int count;
   XtSelectionCallbackProc callback;
   XtPointer *client_data;
   Time time;
```

Inputs

w   Specifies the widget that is making the request.

selection   Specifies the particular selection desired (usually XA_PRIMARY or XA_SECON-DARY).

targets   Specifies the types of information about the selection that are being requested.

count   Specifies the length of the *targets* and *client_data* arrays.

callback   Specifies the callback procedure that is to be called to receive each selection value.

client_data   Specifies an array of client data (one for each target type) each element of which will be passed to *callback* when it is called for the corresponding element of *targets*.

time   Specifies the timestamp that indicates when the selection request was initiated. This should be the timestamp of the event which triggered this request; the value CurrentTime is not acceptable.

Availability

Release 4 and later.

Description

XtGetSelectionValuesIncremental() is similar to XtGetSelectionValue-Incremental() except that it takes an array of target types and an array of client data and requests the current value of the selection be converted to each of the targets. The effect is as if each target were specified in a separate call to XtGetSelectionValueIncremental(), except that XtGetSelectionValuesIncremental() guarantees that all the conversions will use the same selection value because the ownership of the selection cannot change in the middle of the list, as could happen when calling XtGetSelectionValue-Incremental() repeatedly.

Note that the callback procedure passed to XtGetSelectionValuesIncremental()
must be prepared to receive a segment of data for any of the requested values. It is not
guaranteed that all segments for one target will be delivered before any segments for the next
target are delivered.

See XtGetSelectionValueIncremental() for more information.

See Also

XtGetSelectionValue(1), *XtGetSelectionValueIncremental*(1), *XtGetSelectionValues*(1),
XtSelectionCallbackProc(2).

XtGetSubresources

Name

XtGetSubresources – get subpart values from the resource database.

Synopsis

```
void XtGetSubresources(object, base, subpart_name, subpart_class,
        resources, num_resources, args, num_args)
    Widget object;
    XtPointer base;
    String subpart_name;
    String subpart_class;
    XtResourceList resources;
    Cardinal num_resources;
    ArgList args;
    Cardinal num_args;
```

Inputs

object
Specifies the object used to qualify the subpart resource name and class; may be of class Object or any subclass thereof.

base
Specifies the base address of the subpart data structure into which the resource values will be written.

subpart_name
Specifies the resource name of the subpart.

subpart_class
Specifies the resource class name of the subpart.

resources
Specifies the resource list for the subpart.

num_resources
Specifies the number of resources in the resource list.

args
Specifies the argument list to override any other resource specifications.

num_args
Specifies the number of arguments in the argument list.

Outputs

base
Returns the resource values from the argument list, the resource database, or the resource list defaults.

Description

XtGetSubresources() is similar to XtGetApplicationResources(). It retrieves resource values for "subparts" of a widget or object that are not themselves widgets or objects. For each resource in *resources*, XtGetSubresources() sets a value in the structure pointed to by *base*. This value comes from the argument list *args*, or if no value for the resource is found in the argument list, from the resource database associated with *object*, or if no value is found in the database, from the *default_addr* field of the resource itself. Once the value is determined, it is copied into the structure at *base* using the resource_offset and resource_size fields of the resource.

The database is searched for resources that appear beneath the specified object in the name hierarchy—subpart resources should be specified in a database as if as if the subpart were a child `object`, with name `subpart_name` and class `subpart_class`.

`XtGetSubresources()` may overwrite the specified resource list with an equivalent representation in an internal format that optimizes access time if the list is used repeatedly. The resource list must be allocated in writable storage and the caller must not modify the list contents after the call if the same list is to be used again. Any per-display resources fetched by `XtGetSubresources()` will not be freed from the resource cache until the display is closed.

See `XtGetApplicationResources()` for an explanation and example of how to create a resource list.

Usage

Using subparts in a widget or object can be a useful way to modularize that object. The Release 3 Athena Text widget, for example, had subparts for its data source and data sink. In Release 4 and later, however, it is often easier to use non-widget objects instead of subparts. The Athena Text widget now uses this approach.

If you use subpart resources, the user will see the subpart hierarchy and will automatically be able to set subpart resources from a resource file. To allow the user to set and query subpart resources using the standard C `XtSetValues()`/`XtGetValues()` interface, however, your widget's `set_values()` (or `set_values_hook()` prior to Release 4) method must call `XtSetSubvalues()` and your `get_values_hook()` method must call `XtGet-Subvalues()`. An alternative is to provide public functions with your widget to set and query subpart values.

Note that `XtGetSubresources()` differs from `XtGetApplicationResources()` in that it looks for resources in a named "subpart" of `object`, rather than resources that appear at the same level in the hierarchy as `object`'s own resources.

You can use `XtVaGetSubresources()` to get subpart resource values using a variable length argument list rather than a single `ArgList` argument.

Structures

`XtResource` is defined as follows:

```
typedef struct _XtResource {
    String    resource_name;   /* Resource name */
    String    resource_class;  /* Resource class */
    String    resource_type;   /* Representation type desired */
    Cardinal  resource_size;   /* Size in bytes of representation */
    Cardinal  resource_offset;/* Offset from base to put resource value */
    String    default_type;    /* Representation type of specified default */
    XtPointer default_addr;    /* Address of resource default value */
} XtResource, XtResourceList;
```

An `Arg` is defined as follows:

```
typedef struct {
    String name;
    XtArgVal value;
} Arg, *ArgList;
```

See Also

XtGetApplicationResources(1), *XtGetSubvalues*(1), *XtSetSubvalues*(1), *XtVaGetSubresources*(1), *get_values_hook*(4), *set_values*(4).

XtGetSubvalues

Name

XtGetSubvalues – copy resource values from a subpart data structure to an argument list.

Synopsis

```
void XtGetSubvalues(base, resources, num_resources, args, num_args)
    XtPointer base;
    XtResourceList resources;
    Cardinal num_resources;
    ArgList args;
    Cardinal num_args;
```

Inputs

base   Specifies the base address of the subpart data structure for which the resources should be retrieved.

resources   Specifies the subpart resource list.

num_resources
         Specifies the number of resources in the resource list.

args   Specifies an array of name/address pairs that contain the resource names and the addresses into which the resource values are to be stored.

num_args   Specifies the number of arguments in the argument list.

Description

For each argument in *args*, XtGetSubvalues() uses the argument name field to look up the resource in *resources*, and uses the information in that resource structure to copy the resource value from the subpart structure pointed to by *base* to the location specified by the argument value field.

If the argument list contains a resource name that is not found in the *resources*, the memory pointed to by the argument *value* field will not be modified.

The value field of each element in *args* must contain the address into which to store the corresponding resource value. It is the caller's responsibility ensure that there is enough memory at the given location for the requested resource, and to free this memory if it was dynamically allocated.

See XtGetApplicationResources() for a description of the various fields of a XtResource structure and an example of initializing an XtResourceList.

Usage

XtGetSubvalues() is normally called in the get_values_hook() method of a widget with a subpart in order to get the values of requested subpart resources that cannot be automatically fetched by the widget. See XtSetSubvalues() for more information.

Note that an application cannot call XtGetSubvalues() for a widget because it does not have access to a widget's subpart resource list.

To set a widget's subpart resource values, see XtSetSubvalues().

See `XtGetSubresources()` for more explanation of subpart resources.

To get subpart resource values using a variable-length argument list rather than a single `Arg-List` array, use `XtVaGetSubvalues()`.

Structures

`XtResource` is defined as follows:

```
typedef struct _XtResource {
    String     resource_name;  /* Resource name */
    String     resource_class; /* Resource class */
    String     resource_type;  /* Representation type desired */
    Cardinal   resource_size;  /* Size in bytes of representation */
    Cardinal   resource_offset;/* Offset from base to put resource value */
    String     default_type;   /* Representation type of specified default */
    XtPointer default_addr;    /* Address of resource default value */
} XtResource, XtResourceList;
```

See `XtGetApplicationResources()` for an explanation of the fields of this structure.

An `Arg` is defined as follows:

```
typedef struct {
    String name;
    XtArgVal value;
} Arg, *ArgList;
```

See Also

XtGetSubresources(1), *XtVaGetSubvalues*(1),
get_values_hook(4).

XtGetValues

Name

XtGetValues – query widget resource values.

Synopsis

```
void XtGetValues(object, args, num_args)
    Widget object;
    ArgList args;
    Cardinal num_args;
```

Inputs

object   Specifies the object whose resource values are to be returned; may be of class Object or any subclass thereof.

args   Specifies the argument list of name/address pairs that contain the resource names and the addresses into which the resource values are to be stored.

num_args   Specifies the number of arguments in the argument list.

Description

XtGetValues() retrieves the current values of one or more resources associated with a widget instance. Each element in *args* is an Arg structure which contains the resource name in the name field, and a pointer to the location at which the resource is to be stored in the *value* field. It is the caller's responsibility to ensure that the value field points to a value of the correct type. If the value field points to allocated memory, the caller is also responsible for freeing that memory.

If *args* contains a resource name that is not found in any of the resource lists searched, the value at the corresponding address is not modified.

Many widget resource values are simply copied from the widget to the specified address. When the resource is a pointer type (such as a string or pointer to a structure) some widgets will make a copy of the pointed to value and store the address of this copy at the specified address. If a copy is made, the caller is responsible for freeing the value when done with it. If no copy is made, then the returned value points to memory owned by the widget, and the caller must not modify or free this value in any way. None of the Intrinsics defined classes copy values in this way, nor do widgets in the Athena Widget set. See the documentation for the particular resource of the particular widget you are using to determine if a copy is made.

If a resource value which is a pointer type is returned without being copied, then the returned value may not remain valid indefinitely. The Intrinsics specify lifetimes for the following resources: The XtNchildren resource of Composite widgets and any callback list resource are only valid until some operation (such as XtCreateWidget() or XtAddCallback()) modifies the resource. The XtNtranslations and XtNaccelerators Core resources remain valid at least until the widget is destroyed. The XtNscreen Core resource remains valid until the Display is closed. See the documentation for the particular resource of the particular widget you are using to determine its lifetime.

The "Background" section below explains in detail how XtGetValues() finds the requested resource values.

Usage

Generally you will use the `XtSetArg()` macro to initialize the `ArgList` passed to this function. You can also use `XtVaGetValues()` pass it a variable-length argument list instead of an `ArgList` array. The "Example" section below shows an example use of this function.

Note that some widgets provide public functions to query the value of commonly used resources. These functions are generally faster, and it is usually better specified whether or not the caller must free the returned value.

You can *set* a widget's resources with `XtSetValues()` or `XtVaSetValues()`.

Example

You can use `XtGetValues()` as follows to get widget resources:

```
Arg args[10];
int i;
String label;
Dimension margin;
Pixel color;

/* set up an argument list */
i = 0;
XtSetArg(args[i], XtNlabel, &label); i++;
XtSetArg(args[i], XtNmargin, &margin); i++;
XtSetArg(args[i], XtNforeground, &color); i++;

/* query the values */
XtGetValues(s, args, i);

/* label, margin, and color now contain the requested values */
printf("Widget's label is %s; margin is %d.\n", label, margin);
printf("Widget's label is %s; margin is %d.\n", label, margin);

/* In some widget sets we'd have to free label now. */
/* XtFree(label); */
```

Background

`XtGetValues()` looks for resources named in *args* using the following procedure:

- It searches the normal resource lists for the object, starting with the resources of the Object class and proceeding down the subclass chain to the class of the object.

- If the object's parent is a subclass of constraintWidgetClass, it searches the constraint resource lists of the parent, starting at constraintWidgetClass and proceeding down the subclass chain to the constraint resources of the parent's class.

Once all the resources have been fetched from the widget's normal and constraint resources list, `XtGetValues()` calls the widget's `get_values_hook()` methods. `get_values_hook()` procedures can be used to return subpart resource values or constraint subpart resource values through the `XtGetValues()` interface (see `XtGetSubvalues()`) and may modify the data stored at the location addressed by the `value` field of the argument. This means that a `get_values_hook()` may be used to make copies of data (such as strings) whose resource representation is a pointer. The get_values_hook() methods are called as follows:

- If any get_values_hook() methods in the object's class or superclass records are non-NULL, they are called in superclass-to-subclass order.

- If the object's parent is a subclass of constraintWidgetClass, and if any of the parent's class or superclass records have declared ConstraintClassExtension records in the Constraint class part extension field with a record type of NULLQUARK and if the get_values_hook() field in the extension record is non-NULL, then XtGetValues() calls these get_values_hook() procedures in superclass-to-subclass order.

Structures

An Arg is defined as follows:

```
typedef struct {
    String name;
    XtArgVal value;
} Arg, *ArgList;
```

See Also

XtSetArg(1), *XtSetValues*(1), *XtVaGetValues*(1), *XtVaSetValues*(1),
get_values_hook(4).

XtGrabButton

Name

XtGrabButton – passively grab a single pointer button.

Synopsis

```
void XtGrabButton(widget, button, modifiers, owner_events, event_mask,
        pointer_mode, keyboard_mode, confine_to, cursor)
    Widget widget;
    int button;
    Modifiers modifiers;
    Boolean owner_events;
    unsigned int event_mask;
    int pointer_mode, keyboard_mode;
    Window confine_to;
    Cursor cursor;
```

Inputs

widget   Specifies the widget in whose window the button is to be grabbed. Must be of class Core or any subclass thereof.

button   Specifies the mouse button which is to be grabbed.

modifiers   Specifies the modifiers that must be down to trigger the grab.

owner_events
                  Specifies whether pointer events generated during the grab are reported normally within the application (True) or only to the specified widget (False).

event_mask   Specifies the event mask to take effect during the grab.

pointer_mode
                  Controls processing of pointer events during the grab. Either GrabMode-Sync or GrabModeAsync.

keyboard_mode
                  Controls processing of keyboard events during the grab. Either GrabMode-Sync or GrabModeAsync.

confine_to   Specifies the ID of the window to confine the pointer, or None.

cursor   Specifies the cursor to be displayed during the grab, or None.

Description

XtGrabButton() calls XGrabButton() to establish a passive button grab. It specifies the widget's window as the *grab_window*, and passes its remaining arguments directly to XGrabButton(). If the widget is not realized, the call to XGrabButton() will be performed when the widget is realized and its window becomes mapped. If the widget is unrealized and later realized again, the call to XGrabButton() will be performed again.

The *button* argument may be Button1, Button2, Button3, Button4, Button5, or AnyButton. The constant AnyButton is equivalent to issuing the grab request for all possible buttons. The button symbols cannot be ORed together.

Xt Functions and Macros (side tab)

The *modifiers* argument is a bitwise OR of one or more of the following symbols: Shift-Mask, LockMask, ControlMask, Mod1Mask, Mod2Mask, Mod3Mask, Mod4Mask, Mod5Mask, or AnyModifier. AnyModifier is equivalent to issuing the grab key request for all possible modifier combinations (including no modifiers).

See XtGrabPointer() for an explanation of the *owner_events*, *event_mask*, *pointer_mode*, *keyboard_mode*, *confine_to*, and *cursor* arguments.

See the "Background" section below for a description of event handling when a passive button grab is triggered.

Usage

When you passively grab a button/modifiers combination, all events that occur when that button and those modifiers are down will be delivered to the window you specify or to your application, regardless of the location of the pointer. Button grabs can be used by applications like *xmag* and window managers which need to use the pointer to indicate a point on or a region of the screen, regardless of the applications that are under the pointer.

You should rarely need to use this function. An automatic grab takes place between a ButtonPress event and the corresponding ButtonRelease event, so this call is not necessary in some of the most common situations. It may be necessary for some styles of menus, however.

Note that XtAddGrab() and spring-loaded popups perform a similar function, but without issuing any X server grabs.

To cancel a passive button grab, use XtUngrabButton().

Background

After making this call, if XtDispatchEvent() is called with a ButtonPress event matching the specified *button* and *modifiers* (which may be AnyButton or AnyModifier, respectively) for the widget's window, the Intrinsics will undo the grab by calling XtUngrabPointer() with the timestamp from the ButtonPress event if either of the following conditions is true:

• There is a modal cascade and the widget is not in the active subset of the cascade and the pointer was not previously grabbed, or

• XFilterEvent() returns True.

Otherwise, after making this call, the pointer will be actively grabbed (as for XtGrabPointer()), the last-pointer-grab time will be set to the time at which the button was pressed (as transmitted in the ButtonPress event), and the ButtonPress event will be reported if all of the following conditions are true:

• The pointer is not grabbed, and the specified button is logically pressed when the specified modifier keys are logically down, and no other buttons or modifier keys are logically down.

• The *grab_window* contains the pointer.

• The *confine_to* window (if any) is viewable.

- A passive grab on the same button/key combination does not exist on any ancestor of `grab_window`.

The active grab is terminated automatically when the logical state of the pointer has all buttons released (independent of the state of the logical modifier keys).

Note that the logical state of a device (as seen by client applications) may lag the physical state if device event processing is frozen.

This request overrides all previous grabs by the same client on the same button/key combinations on the same window. A modifiers of `AnyModifier` is equivalent to issuing the grab request for all possible modifier combinations (including the combination of no modifiers). It is not required that all modifiers specified have currently assigned `KeyCodes`. A button of `AnyButton` is equivalent to issuing the request for all possible buttons. Otherwise, it is not required that the specified button currently be assigned to a physical button.

If some other client has already issued a `XGrabButton()` with the same button/key combination on the same window, a `BadAccess` error results. When using `AnyModifier` or `AnyButton`, the request fails completely, and a `BadAccess` error results (no grabs are established) if there is a conflicting grab for any combination. `XGrabButton()` has no effect on an active grab.

See Also

XtAddGrab(1), *XtGrabKey*(1), *XtGrabKeyboard*(1), *XtGrabPointer*(1), *XtRegisterGrabAction*(1), *XtUngrabButton*(1), *XtUngrabKey*(1), *XtUngrabKeyboard*(1), *XtUngrabPointer*(1).

XtGrabKey

Name

XtGrabKey – passively grab a single key of the keyboard.

Synopsis

```
void XtGrabKey(widget, keycode, modifiers, owner_events, pointer_mode,
        keyboard_mode)
    Widget widget;
    KeyCode keycode;
    Modifiers modifiers;
    Boolean owner_events;
    int pointer_mode, keyboard_mode;
```

Inputs

widget Specifies the widget in whose window the key is to be grabbed. Must be of class Core or any subclass thereof.

keycode Specifies the keycode to be grabbed. It may be a modifier key. Specifying AnyKey is equivalent to issuing the request for all key codes.

modifiers Specifies a set of modifiers that must be down to trigger the grab.

owner_events

    Specifies whether events generated during the grab are reported normally within the application (True) or only to the specified widget (False).

pointer_mode

    Controls processing of pointer events during the grab. Either GrabMode-Sync or GrabModeAsync.

keyboard_mode

    Controls processing of keyboard events during the grab. Either GrabMode-Sync or GrabModeAsync.

Description

XtGrabKey() calls XGrabKey() to establish a passive grab on the key specified by *keycode*. It specifies the widget's window as the *grab_window* and passes its remaining arguments unmodified. If the widget is not realized, the call to XGrabKey() will be performed when the widget is realized and its window becomes mapped. If the widget is unrealized and later realized again, the call to XGrabKey() will be performed again.

The *modifiers* argument is a bitwise OR of one or more of the following symbols: Shift-Mask, LockMask, Control Mask, Mod1Mask, Mod2Mask, Mod3Mask, Mod4Mask, Mod5Mask, or AnyModifier. AnyModifier is equivalent to issuing the grab key request for all possible modifier combinations (including no modifiers).

See XtGrabKeyboard() for a description of the *owner_events*, *pointer_mode*, and *keyboard_mode* arguments.

See the "Description" section below for details of event processing when an passive key grab is triggered.

Usage

When you passively grab a key/modifiers combination, all events that occur when that button and those modifiers are down will be delivered to your widget's window or to your application, regardless of the location of the pointer. Key grabs can be used by applications like window managers that want to define keyboard "hot keys" that invoke a particular function regardless of which application is currently in use.

Most applications will never need to issue a grab. `XtAddGrab()` (called by `XtPopup()`) can be used to implement modal popups inside an application, and `XtSetKeyboard-Focus()` can be used to redirect keyboard focus within an application. Neither function actually issues a grab, and so does not interrupt event processing by other clients.

To cancel a passive key grab, use `XtUngrabKey()`.

Background

After this call, if `XtDispatchEvent()` is called with a `KeyPress` event matching the specified `keycode` and `modifiers` (which may be `AnyKey` or `AnyModifier`, respectively) for the widget's window, the Intrinsics will undo the grab by calling `XtUngrab-Keyboard()` with the timestamp from the `KeyPress` event if either of the following conditions is true:

- There is a modal cascade and the widget is not in the active subset of the cascade and the keyboard was not previously grabbed, or

- `XFilterEvent()` returns `True`.

Otherwise, after this call, the keyboard will be actively grabbed (as for `XGrabKeyboard()`), the last-keyboard-grab time will be set to the time at which the key was pressed (as transmitted in the `KeyPress` event), and the `KeyPress` event will be reported if all of the following conditions are true:

- The keyboard is not grabbed and the specified key (which can itself be a modifier key) is logically pressed when the specified modifier keys are logically down, and no other modifier keys are logically down.

- Either the `grab_window` is an ancestor of (or is) the focus window, or the `grab_window` is a descendant of the focus window and contains the pointer.

- A passive grab on the same key combination does not exist on any ancestor of `grab_window`.

The active grab is terminated automatically when the logical state of the keyboard has the specified key released (independent of the logical state of the modifier keys).

Note that the logical state of a device (as seen by client applications) may lag the physical state if device event processing is frozen.

A `modifiers` argument of `AnyModifier` is equivalent to issuing the request for all possible modifier combinations (including the combination of no modifiers). It is not required that all modifiers specified have currently assigned `KeyCodes`. A `keycode` argument of `AnyKey` is equivalent to issuing the request for all possible `KeyCodes`. Otherwise, the specified key-

Xt Functions and Macros

code must be in the range specified by `min_keycode` and `max_keycode` in the connection setup, or a `BadValue` error results.

If some other client has issued a `XGrabKey()` with the same key combination on the same window, a `BadAccess` error results. When using `AnyModifier` or `AnyKey`, the request fails completely, and a `BadAccess` error results (no grabs are established) if there is a conflicting grab for any combination.

`XGrabKey()` can generate `BadAccess`, `BadValue`, and `BadWindow` errors.

See Also

XtAddGrab(1), *XtGrabButton*(1), *XtGrabKeyboard*(1), *XtGrabPointer*(1), *XtRegisterGrabAction*(1), *XtSetKeyboardFocus*(1), *XtUngrabButton*(1), *XtUngrabKey*(1), *XtUngrabKeyboard*(1), *XtUngrabPointer*(1).

XtGrabKeyboard

Name

XtGrabKeyboard – actively grab the keyboard.

Synopsis

```
int XtGrabKeyboard(widget, owner_events, pointer_mode, keyboard_mode, time)
    Widget widget;
    Boolean owner_events;
    int pointer_mode, keyboard_mode;
    Time time;
```

Inputs

widget
    Specifies the widget for whose window the keyboard is to be grabbed. Must be of class Core or any subclass thereof.

owner_events
    Specifies whether the pointer events are to be reported normally within this application (pass True) or only to the grab window (pass False).

pointer_mode
    Controls processing of pointer events during the grab. Either GrabMode-Sync or GrabModeAsync.

keyboard_mode
    Controls processing of keyboard events during the grab. Either GrabMode-Sync or GrabModeAsync.

time
    Specifies the time when the grab should take place. Pass either a timestamp (from an event) or the constant CurrentTime.

Description

If the specified widget is realized XtGrabKeyboard() calls XGrabKeyboard() specifying the widget's window as the *grab_window*, passing its remaining argument unmodified, and returning whatever XGrabKeyboard() returns. If the widget is not realized, XGrabKeyboard() immediately returns GrabNotViewable. No future automatic ungrab is implied by XtGrabKeyboard().

See the "Background" section below for a description of the arguments and an explanation of event processing during an active keyboard grab.

Usage

When the keyboard is grabbed, all key events are delivered to the widget you specify or to your application, regardless of the location of the pointer. There are not many occasions when this is a reasonable thing to do, because it locks out input to other applications. *xterm* grabs the keyboard to implement secure mode.

Most applications will never need to issue a grab. XtAddGrab() (called by XtPopup()) can be used to implement modal popups inside an application, and XtSetKeyboard-Focus() can be used to redirect keyboard focus within an application. Neither function actually issues a grab, and so does not interrupt event processing by other clients.

Xt Functions and Macros

To cancel an active keyboard grab, use `XtUngrabKeyboard()`.

Background

The `XGrabKeyboard()` function actively grabs control of the keyboard and generates `FocusIn` and `FocusOut` events. Further key events are reported only to the grabbing client. `XGrabKeyboard()` overrides any active keyboard grab by this client. If *owner_events* is `False`, all generated key events are reported with respect to *grab_window*. If *owner_events* is `True` and if a generated key event would normally be reported to this client, it is reported normally; otherwise, the event is reported with respect to the *grab_window*. Both `KeyPress` and `KeyRelease` events are always reported, independent of any event selection made by the client.

If the *keyboard_mode* argument is `GrabModeAsync`, keyboard event processing continues as usual. If the keyboard is currently frozen by this client, then processing of keyboard events is resumed. If the *keyboard_mode* argument is `GrabModeSync`, the state of the keyboard (as seen by client applications) appears to freeze, and the X server generates no further keyboard events until the grabbing client issues a releasing `XAllowEvents()` call or until the keyboard grab is released. Actual keyboard changes are not lost while the keyboard is frozen; they are simply queued in the server for later processing.

If *pointer_mode* is `GrabModeAsync`, pointer event processing is unaffected by activation of the grab. If *pointer_mode* is `GrabModeSync`, the state of the pointer (as seen by client applications) appears to freeze, and the X server generates no further pointer events until the grabbing client issues a releasing `XAllowEvents()` call or until the keyboard grab is released. Actual pointer changes are not lost while the pointer is frozen; they are simply queued in the server for later processing.

If the keyboard is actively grabbed by some other client, `XGrabKeyboard()` fails and returns `AlreadyGrabbed`. If *grab_window* is not viewable, it fails and returns `GrabNotViewable`. If the keyboard is frozen by an active grab of another client, it fails and returns `GrabFrozen`. If the specified time is earlier than the last-keyboard-grab time or later than the current X server time, it fails and returns `GrabInvalidTime`. Otherwise, the last-keyboard-grab time is set to the specified time (`CurrentTime` is replaced by the current X server time).

`XGrabKeyboard()` can generate `BadValue` and `BadWindow` errors.

See Also

XtAddGrab(1), *XtGrabButton*(1), *XtGrabKey*(1), *XtGrabPointer*(1), *XtRegisterGrabAction*(1), *XtUngrabButton*(1), *XtUngrabKey*(1), *XtUngrabKeyboard*(1), *XtUngrabPointer*(1).

Name

XtGrabPointer – actively grab the pointer.

Synopsis

```
int XtGrabPointer(widget, owner_events, event_mask, pointer_mode, key-
      board_mode,
      confine_to, cursor, time)
   Widget widget;
   Boolean owner_events;
   unsigned int event_mask;
   int pointer_mode, keyboard_mode;
   Window confine_to;
   Cursor cursor;
   Time time;
```

Inputs

widget   Specifies the widget for whose window the pointer is to be grabbed. Must be of class Core or any subclass thereof.

owner_events
             Specifies whether the pointer events are to be reported normally within this application (pass True) or only to the grab window (pass False).

event_mask   Specifies the event mask to take effect during the grab.

pointer_mode
             Controls processing of pointer events during the grab. Either GrabMode-Sync or GrabModeAsync.

keyboard_mode
             Controls processing of keyboard events during the grab. Either GrabMode-Sync or GrabModeAsync.

confine_to   Specifies the ID of the window to confine the pointer, or None.

cursor   Specifies the cursor to be displayed during the grab, or None.

time   Specifies the time when the grab request took place. Pass either a timestamp (from an event), or the constant CurrentTime.

Returns

GrabSuccess or one of the error values described below.

Description

If the specified widget is realized, XtGrabPointer() establishes an active pointer grab by calling XGrabPointer() with the widget's window as the grab window and passing the remaining arguments unmodified. It returns the value returned by XGrabPointer(). If the widget is not realized, XGrabPointer() immediately returns GrabNotViewable. No future automatic ungrab is implied by XtGrabPointer().

See the "Background" section below for a description of the arguments and an explanation of event processing during an active pointer grab.

Usage

When the pointer is grabbed, all pointer events will be delivered to the widget you specify or to the rest of your application, regardless of the location of the pointer. Pointer grabs can be used by applications like *xmag* and window managers which need to use the pointer to indicate a point on or a region of the screen, regardless of the applications that are under the pointer.

Most applications never need to grab the pointer. Note that XtAddGrab() does not actually grab anything.

To cancel an active pointer grab, use XtUngrabPointer().

Background

XGrabPointer() actively grabs control of the pointer and returns GrabSuccess if the grab was successful. Further pointer events are reported only to the grabbing client. XGrab-Pointer() overrides any active pointer grab by this client. If *owner_events* is False, all generated pointer events are reported with respect to *grab_window* and are reported only if selected by *event_mask*. If *owner_events* is True and if a generated pointer event would normally be reported to this client, it is reported as usual. Otherwise, the event is reported with respect to the *grab_window* and is reported only if selected by *event_mask*. For either value of *owner_events*, unreported events are discarded.

If the *pointer_mode* is GrabModeAsync, pointer event processing continues as usual. If the pointer is currently frozen by this client, the processing of events for the pointer is resumed. If the *pointer_mode* is GrabModeSync, the state of the pointer, as seen by client applications, appears to freeze, and the X server generates no further pointer events until the grabbing client calls XAllowEvents() or until the pointer grab is released. Actual pointer changes are not lost while the pointer is frozen; they are simply queued in the server for later processing.

If the *keyboard_mode* is GrabModeAsync, keyboard event processing is unaffected by activation of the grab. If the *keyboard_mode* is GrabModeSync, the state of the keyboard, as seen by client applications, appears to freeze, and the X server generates no further keyboard events until the grabbing client calls XAllowEvents() or until the pointer grab is released. Actual keyboard changes are not lost while the pointer is frozen; they are simply queued in the server for later processing.

If *cursor* is specified, it is displayed regardless of what window the pointer is in. If None is specified, the normal cursor for that window is displayed when the pointer is in *grab_window* or one of its subwindows; otherwise, the cursor for *grab_window* is displayed.

If a *confine_to* window is specified, the pointer is restricted to stay contained in that window. The *confine_to* window need have no relationship to the *grab_window*. If the pointer is not initially in the *confine_to* window, it is warped automatically to the closest edge just before the grab activates and enter/leave events are generated as usual. If the *confine_to* window is subsequently reconfigured, the pointer is warped automatically, as necessary, to keep it contained in the window.

The *time* argument allows you to avoid certain circumstances that come up if applications take a long time to respond or if there are long network delays. Consider a situation where you have two applications, both of which normally grab the pointer when clicked on. If both applications specify the timestamp from the event, the second application may wake up faster and successfully grab the pointer before the first application. The first application then will get an indication that the other application grabbed the pointer before its request was processed.

XGrabPointer() generates EnterNotify and LeaveNotify events.

Either if *grab_window* or *confine_to* window is not viewable or if the *confine_to* window lies completely outside the boundaries of the root window, XGrabPointer() fails and returns GrabNotViewable. If the pointer is actively grabbed by some other client, it fails and returns AlreadyGrabbed. If the pointer is frozen by an active grab of another client, it fails and returns GrabFrozen. If the specified time is earlier than the last-pointer-grab time or later than the current X server time, it fails and returns GrabInvalidTime. Otherwise, the last-pointer-grab time is set to the specified time (CurrentTime is replaced by the current X server time).

XGrabPointer() can generate BadCursor, BadValue, and BadWindow errors.

Structures

Each of the event types listed in the table below set a single bit in an event mask. The *event_mask* argument is formed by combining these symbols with the bitwise OR operator (|). Note that the nonmaskable event types do not appear in this table and cannot be requested in an event mask.

NoEventMask	Button1MotionMask	StructureNotifyMask
KeyPressMask	Button2MotionMask	ResizeRedirectMask
KeyReleaseMask	Button3MotionMask	SubstructureNotifyMask
ButtonPressMask	Button4MotionMask	SubstructureRedirectMask
ButtonReleaseMask	Button5MotionMask	FocusChangeMask
EnterWindowMask	ButtonMotionMask	PropertyChangeMask
LeaveWindowMask	KeymapStateMask	ColormapChangeMask
PointerMotionMask	ExposureMask	OwnerGrabButtonMask
PointerMotionHintMask	VisibilityChangeMask	

See Also

XtAddGrab(1), *XtGrabButton*(1), *XtGrabKey*(1), *XtGrabKeyboard*(1), *XtRegisterGrabAction*(1), *XtUngrabButton*(1), *XtUngrabKey*(1), *XtUngrabKeyboard*(1), *XtUngrabPointer*(1).

XtHasCallbacks

Name

XtHasCallbacks – determine the status of a widget's callback list.

Synopsis

```
XtCallbackStatus XtHasCallbacks(object, callback_name)
    Widget object;
    String callback_name;
```

Inputs

object   Specifies the object; may be of class Object or any subclass thereof.

callback_name   Specifies the callback list to be checked.

Returns

An XtCallbackStatus value.

Description

XtHasCallbacks() checks the widget for a resource named *callback_name*. If the resource does not exist or is not of type XtRCallback, XtHasCallbacks() returns Xt-CallbackNoList. If the callback list exists but is empty, it returns XtCallbackHas-None. If the callback list contains at least one callback procedure, it returns XtCallback-HasSome.

Structures

```
typedef enum {
    XtCallbackNoList,
    XtCallbackHasNone,
    XtCallbackHasSome
} XtCallbackStatus;
```

See Also

XtAddCallbacks(1), *XtCallCallbacks*(1), *XtCallCallbackList*(1).

XtInitialize

Name

XtInitialize – initialize toolkit and display.

Synopsis

```
Widget XtInitialize(shell_name, application_class, options, num_options,
        argc, argv)
    String shell_name;       /* unused */
    String application_class;
    XrmOptionDescRec options[];
    Cardinal num_options;
    Cardinal *argc;
    char *argv[];
```

Inputs

shell_name   This parameter is ignored; you can specify NULL.

application_class

Specifies the class name of this application.

options   Specifies how to parse the command line for any application-specific resources. The options argument is passed as a parameter to XtDisplayInitialize().

num_options   Specifies the number of entries in options list.

argc   Specifies a pointer to the number of command line parameters.

argv   Specifies the command line parameters.

Outputs

argc   Returns the number of command line arguments remaining after the command line is parsed with XtDisplayInitialize()

argv   Returns the command line as modified by XtDisplayInitialize().

Returns

A toplevel applicationShell widget.

Availability

XtInitialize() has been superseded by XtAppInitialize().

Description

XtInitialize() is a convenience function for initializing an Xt application. It calls XtToolkitInitialize() to initialize the toolkit internals, creates a default application context for use by other superseded functions, calls XtOpenDisplay() with *display_string* NULL and *application_name* NULL, and finally calls XtAppCreateShell() with *application_name* NULL and returns the created shell. The semantics of calling XtInitialize() more than once are undefined.

Xt Functions and Macros (side tab)

Usage

XtInitialize() has been superseded in Release 4 by XtAppInitialize(), which is a more general initialization function which supports multiple application contexts and fallback resources, among other things. There are a number of Xt functions that have been superseded by "XtApp" versions that take an application context as an argument. If you want to use these superseded functions, you must initialize your application with XtInitialize() which creates the default application context that these functions all use.

If you do not want to use multiple application contexts, multiple displays, or fallback resources, you can continue to use XtInitialize(). We recommend, however, that you use XtApp-Initialize() and the other XtApp*() application context specific functions.

See XtAppInitialize() for more information.

See Also

XtAppCreateShell(1), *XtAppInitialize*(1), *XtOpenDisplay*(1), *XtToolkitInitialize*(1).

XtInitializeWidgetClass

Name

XtInitializeWidgetClass – initialize a widget class without creating any widgets.

Synopsis

```
void XtInitializeWidgetClass(object_class)
    WidgetClass object_class;
```

Inputs

object_class   Specifies the object class to initialize; may be of class objectClass or any subclass thereof.

Availability

Release 4 and later.

Description

XtInitializeWidgetClass() initializes a widget class in the same way that XtCreate-Widget does, but without creating any widgets. It checks the class_inited field of the specified class and all its superclasses, in superclass-to-subclass order, and if that field is False for any class, it calls the class_initialize() and class_part_initial-ize() methods for the class and all of its superclasses. Finally, the class_inited field of the specified class is set to nonzero.

If the specified widget class is already initialized, XtInitializeWidgetClass() returns immediately.

Usage

A widget class is automatically initialized when the first instance of a widget is created; few applications will need to use this function.

If a class initialization procedure registers type converters, those type converters are not available until the first object of the class or subclass is created or until XtInitializeWidget-Class() is called. This function was added in Release 4 so that the XtVaTypedArg feature of XtVaCreateWidget() can be used to convert a resource value while creating the first instance of a particular widget class.

See Also

XtVaCreateWidget(1).

XtInsertEventHandler

Name

XtInsertEventHandler – register an event handler procedure that receives events before or after all previously registered event handlers.

Synopsis

```
void XtInsertEventHandler(w, event_mask, nonmaskable, proc, client_data,
        position)
    Widget w;
    EventMask event_mask;
    Boolean nonmaskable;
    XtEventHandler proc;
    XtPointer client_data;
    XtListPosition position;
```

Inputs

w	Specifies the widget for which this event handler is being registered. Must be of class core or any subclass thereof.
event_mask	Specifies the event mask for which to call this procedure.
nonmaskable	Specifies whether this procedure should be called on nonmaskable events
proc	Specifies the procedure that is to be called.
client_data	Specifies additional data to be passed to the client's event handler.
position	Specifies when the event handler is to be called relative to other previously registered handlers.

Availability

Release 4 and later.

Description

XtInsertEventHandler() registers the procedure *proc* and the data *client_data* with the Intrinsics event dispatching mechanism. When an event of one of the types set in *event_mask* occurs on the window of the widget *w*, *proc* will be invoked and *client_data* passed as one of its arguments.

The argument *position* specifies where in the list of event handlers *proc* should be inserted. If it is XtListHead, *proc* will be inserted at the beginning of the list and will be called before all previously registered handlers. If it is XtListTail, *proc* will be inserted at the end of the list and will be called after all previously registered handlers.

If the procedure is already registered with the same *client_data*, the specified *event_mask* augments the existing mask, and the procedure is repositioned in the list according to *position*.

XtInsertEventHandler() is identical to XtAddEventHandler() with the additional *position* argument. See XtAddEventHandler() for more information.

See XtEventHandler(2) for an explanation of how to write an event handler procedure.

Usage

Neither applications nor widgets often need to use event handlers. Using action procedures and translation tables provides a more flexible way to respond to input events.

Structures

The `XtListPosition` type is as follows.

```
typedef enum {
    XtListHead,
    XtListTail
} XtListPosition;
```

See `XtAddEventHandler()` for a list of bits that can be set in the *event_mask* argument.

See Also

XtAddEventHandler(1), *XtAddRawEventHandler*(1), *XtInsertRawEventHandler*(1), *XtRemoveEvent-Handler*(1), *XtRemoveRawEventHandler*(1).

XtInsertRawEventHandler

Name

XtInsertRawEventHandler – register an event handler procedure that receives events before or after all previously registered event handlers, without selecting for the events.

Synopsis

```
void XtInsertRawEventHandler(w, event_mask, nonmaskable, proc, client_data,
        position)
    Widget w;
    EventMask event_mask;
    Boolean nonmaskable;
    XtEventHandler proc;
    XtPointer client_data;
    XtListPosition position;
```

Inputs

w
Specifies the widget for which this event handler is being registered. Must be of class Core or any subclass thereof.

event_mask
Specifies the event mask for which to call this procedure.

nonmaskable
Specifies a Boolean value that indicates whether this procedure should be called on nonmaskable events

proc
Specifies the procedure that is to be registered.

client_data
Specifies additional data to be passed to the client's event handler.

position
Specifies when the event handler is to be called relative to other previously registered handlers.

Availability

Release 4 and later.

Description

XtInsertRawEventHandler() registers the procedure *proc* and the data *client_data* with the Intrinsics event dispatching mechanism. When an event of one of the types set in *event_mask* occurs on the window of the widget *w*, *proc* will be invoked and *client_data* passed as one of its arguments. XtInsertRawEventHandler() never calls XSelectInput() to request to receive the events in *event_mask*.

The argument *position* specifies where in the list of event handlers *proc* should be inserted. If it is XtListHead, *proc* will be inserted at the beginning of the list and will be called before all previously registered handlers. If it is XtListTail, *proc* will be inserted at the end of the list and will be called after all previously registered handlers.

If the procedure is already registered with the same *client_data*, the specified *event_mask* augments the existing mask, and the procedure is repositioned in the list according to *position*.

XtInsertRawEventHandler() is identical to XtAddRawEventHandler() with the additional *position* argument. See XtAddRawEventHandler() for more information.

See XtEventHandler(2) for an explanation of how to write an event handler procedure.

Usage

Neither applications nor widgets often need to use event handlers. Using action procedures and translation tables provides a more flexible way to respond to input events.

Structures

The XtListPosition type is as follows.

```
typedef enum {
    XtListHead,
    XtListTail
} XtListPosition;
```

See XtAddEventHandler() for a list of bits that can be set in the *event_mask* argument.

See Also

XtAddEventHandler(1), *XtAddRawEventHandler*(1), *XtBuildEventMask*(1), *XtInsertEventHandler*(1), *XtRemoveEventHandler*(1), *XtRemoveRawEventHandler*(1).

Xt Functions and Macros

Name

XtInstallAccelerators – install a widget's accelerators on another widget.

Synopsis

```
void XtInstallAccelerators(destination, source)
    Widget destination;
    Widget source;
```

Inputs

destination Specifies the widget in which events specified in the accelerator table will be detected. Must be of class Core or any subclass thereof.

source Specifies the widget whose actions will be invoked when events occur in *destination*. Must be of class Core or any subclass thereof.

Description

XtInstallAccelerators() merges the accelerator table of *source* into the translation table of destination. After this call, events in the *destination* widget will trigger actions in the *source* widget.

If the display_accelerator() method of *source* is non-NULL, XtInstall-Accelerators() calls it with *source* and a canonical representation of the accelerator table that was installed. This method is a hook that is intended to allow a widget to dynamically modify its appearance (a menu button might display the key sequence that will invoke it, for example) when an accelerator is installed.

Usage

It is often convenient to be able to bind events in one widget to actions in another. In particular, it is often useful to be able to invoke menu actions from the keyboard. The Intrinsics provide a facility, called accelerators, that let you accomplish this. An accelerator table is a translation table that binds events in the destination widget to actions in the source widget. The accelerator table can be installed on one or more destination widgets. When an event sequence in *destination* would cause an accelerator action to be invoked, and if the source widget is sensitive, the actions are executed as though triggered by the same event sequence in *source*. The event is passed to the action procedure without modification. The action procedures used within accelerators must assume neither that the source widget is realized, nor that any fields of the event are in reference to the source widget's window if the widget is realized.

Every widget includes an XtNaccelerators resource, which is defined by the Core widget class. The actual value of this resource can be hardcoded by the application or set in a resource file, just like any other resource.

In order for the XtNaccelerators resource to actually be used, however, the application must call XtInstallAccelerators() (or XtInstallAllAccelerators()). This call takes two arguments. The *destination* widget is the widget whose translation table will be augmented with the accelerator table from the *source* widget.

It is difficult to remember which of the two widgets in this call is which. If you want to install a keyboard accelerator so that a keystroke in a text widget invokes an action in a menu button, then the menu button is the source, and the text widget is the destination. You must set the accelerator table in the `XtNaccelerators` resource of the menu button, and then install those accelerators on the text widget.

If you are programming with the Motif widget set, you will generally not be able to use accelerators as described here. Motif provides a different (and incompatible) style of accelerators for use with menus; see Volume 6, *Motif Programming Manual* for more information.

Example

Assume an application whose top-level shell widget is named `topLevel`, and which contains a Command widget instance named `quit`. Further assume that the `quit` widget has the following `XtNaccelerators` resource defined for it:

```
*quit.accelerators: \n\
    <KeyPress>q: notify()
```

The call:

```
XtInstallAccelerators (topLevel, quit);
```

would allow a "q" typed in the application's top-level window to invoke the `quit` widget's `notify` action. The `notify` action invokes the callback list of the button, and assuming that a quit callback was registered, causes the application to terminate.

See Also

XtInstallAllAccelerators(1),
display_accelerator(4).

Name

XtInstallAllAccelerators – install all accelerators from a widget and its descendants onto a destination widget.

Synopsis

```
void XtInstallAllAccelerators(destination, source)
    Widget destination;
    Widget source;
```

Inputs

destination Specifies the widget in which events specified in the accelerator tables will be detected. Must be of class Core or any subclass thereof.

source Specifies the root widget of the widget tree from which the actions of any descendant widget can be invoked when events occur in *destination*. Must be of class Core or any subclass thereof.

Description

XtInstallAllAccelerators() is a convenience function for installing all accelerators from a widget and all its descendants onto a single destination widget. It recursively traverses the widget tree rooted at *source* and installs the accelerator resource values of each widget onto *destination*. It also calls the display_accelerator() method of each widget in the *source* tree that has one.

Usage

A common use for XtInstallAllAccelerators() is to install the accelerators for all the buttons of a menu or an entire menu bar onto a single destination widget. The Xt-Naccelerator resource of each button would be specified when the button was created or would come from the resource database, and the single call to XtInstallAll-Accelerators() would make all those accelerators available in a widget.

Note that if you want to provide keyboard shortcuts for a menu system from within two different text widgets, you will have to call XtInstallAllAccelerators() twice.

Also note that if a widget is not interested in events of a certain type, then those events will propagate up the widget hierarchy to the first ancestor widget that is interested. If your interface contains a composite widget that contains only button and other widgets that are not interested in keyboard input, then you can install a set of keyboard accelerators on the composite widget, and they will be invoked when keyboard events occur anywhere within that widget.

See Also

XtInstallAccelerators(1),
display_accelerator(4).

XtIsApplicationShell

Name

XtIsApplicationShell – test whether a widget is a subclass of the ApplicationShell widget class.

Synopsis

```
Boolean XtIsApplicationShell(object)
    Widget object;
```

Inputs

object   Specifies the object whose class is to be checked; may be of class Object or any subclass thereof.

Returns

True if *object* is of class applicationShell or a subclass thereof; False otherwise.

Description

XtIsApplicationShell() tests whether *object* is a subclass of the ApplicationShell widget class. It may be defined as a macro or a function, and is equivalent to, but may be faster than, calling XtIsSubclass() for this class.

See Also

XtIsSubclass(1).

XtIsComposite

Name

XtIsComposite – test whether a widget is a subclass of the Composite widget class.

Synopsis

```
Boolean XtIsComposite(object)
    Widget object;
```

Inputs

object   Specifies the widget whose class is to be tested; may be of class Object or any subclass thereof.

Returns

True if *object* is of class Composite or a subclass thereof; False otherwise.

Description

XtIsComposite() tests whether *object* is a subclass of the Composite widget class. It may be defined as a macro or a function, and is equivalent to, but may be faster than, calling XtIsSubclass() for this class.

See Also

XtIsSubclass(1).

XtIsConstraint

Name

XtIsConstraint – test whether a widget is a subclass of the Constraint widget class.

Synopsis

```
Boolean XtIsConstraint(object)
    Widget object;
```

Inputs

object   Specifies the widget whose class is to be tested; may be of class Object or any subclass thereof.

Returns

True if *object* is of class Constraint or a subclass thereof; False otherwise.

Description

XtIsConstraint() tests whether *object* is a subclass of the Constraint widget class. It may be defined as a macro or a function, and is equivalent to, but may be faster than, calling XtIsSubclass() for this class.

See Also

XtIsSubclass(1).

Name

XtIsManaged – determine whether a widget is managed by its parent.

Synopsis

```
Boolean XtIsManaged(object)
    Widget object;
```

Inputs

object   Specifies the object whose state is to be tested; may be of class Object or any subclass thereof.

Returns

True if *object* is managed, False otherwise.

Description

XtIsManaged() returns True if the specified object is of class RectObj and is currently managed or False if it is not.

See Also

XtManageChild(1), *XtManageChildren*(1), *XtUnManageChild*(1), *XtUnmanageChildren*(1).

XtIsObject

Name

XtIsObject – test whether a widget is a subclass of the Object widget class.

Synopsis

```
Boolean XtIsObject(object)
    Widget object;
```

Inputs

object   Specifies the object whose class is to be checked; may be of Object Class or any subclass thereof.

Returns

True if object is of class Object or a subclass thereof; False otherwise.

Description

XtIsObject() tests whether object is a subclass of the Object widget class. It may be defined as a macro or a function, and is equivalent to, but may be faster than, calling XtIs-Subclass() for this class.

See Also

XtIsSubclass(1).

Name

XtIsOverrideShell – test whether a widget is a subclass of the OverrideShell widget class.

Synopsis

```
Boolean XtIsOverrideShell(object)
    Widget object;
```

Inputs

object   Specifies the object whose class is to be checked; may be of class Object or any subclass thereof.

Returns

True if *object* is of class OverrideShell or a subclass thereof; False otherwise.

Description

XtIsOverrideShell() tests whether *object* is a subclass of the OverrideShell widget class. It may be defined as a macro or a function, and is equivalent to, but may be faster than, calling XtIsSubclass() for this class.

See Also

XtIsSubclass(1).

XtIsRealized

Name

XtIsRealized – determine whether a widget has been realized.

Synopsis

```
Boolean XtIsRealized(object)
    Widget object;
```

Inputs

object   Specifies the object whose state is to be tested; may be of class Object or any subclass thereof.

Returns

`True` if *object* is realized; `False` otherwise.

Description

`XtIsRealized()` returns `True` if the specified object (or its nearest widget ancestor) has been realized, and `False` otherwise. A widget is realized if it has a nonzero X window ID.

Usage

`XtIsRealized()` is implemented as a function when called from application code, but is replaced by a more efficient macro when called from widget code that includes the file *<X11/IntrinsicP.h>*.

Some widget methods (for example, `set_values()`) might wish to operate differently depending on whether the widget has been realized. In particular, no Xlib calls can refer to a widget's window until the widget is realized.

See Also

XtWindow(1).

Xt Functions and Macros

Name

XtIsRectObj – test whether a widget is a subclass of the RectObj widget class.

Synopsis

```
Boolean XtIsRectObj(object)
    Widget object;
```

Inputs

object   Specifies the object whose class is to be checked; may be of class Object or any subclass thereof.

Returns

`True` if *object* is of class RectObj or a subclass thereof; `False` otherwise.

Description

`XtIsRectObj()` tests whether *object* is a subclass of the RectObj widget class. It may be defined as a macro or a function, and is equivalent to, but may be faster than, calling `XtIs-Subclass()` for this class.

See Also

XtIsSubclass(1).

XtIsSensitive

Name

XtIsSensitive – check the current sensitivity state of a widget.

Synopsis

```
Boolean XtIsSensitive(object)
    Widget object;
```

Inputs

object   Specifies the object whose state is to be tested; may be of class Object or any subclass thereof.

Returns

True if the widget is sensitive; False otherwise.

Description

XtIsSensitive() returns True if *object* is a subclass of RectObj and both its sensitive and ancestor_sensitive fields are True. Otherwise, it returns False.

Usage

An insensitive widget will not have user events dispatched to it, and may display itself specially (grayed out, for example) to indicate this condition.

A widget's sensitivity is often checked by its parent. For example the parent may wish to determine whether it should should pass the keyboard focus to the child, or it may choose to make itself insensitive if all of its children become insensitive.

See Also

XtSetSensitive(1).

XtIsShell

Name

XtIsShell – test whether a widget is a subclass of the Shell widget class.

Synopsis

```
Boolean XtIsShell(object)
    Widget object;
```

Inputs

object   Specifies the object whose class is to be tested; may be of class Object or any subclass thereof.

Returns

True if *object* is of class Shell or a subclass thereof; False otherwise.

Description

XtIsShell() tests whether *object* is a subclass of the Shell widget class. It may be defined as a macro or a function, and is equivalent to, but may be faster than, calling XtIs-Subclass() for this class.

See Also

XtIsSubclass(1).

XtIsSubclass

Name

XtIsSubclass – determine whether a widget is a subclass of a class.

Synopsis

```
Boolean XtIsSubclass(object, object_class)
    Widget object;
    WidgetClass object_class;
```

Inputs

object   Specifies the object instance whose class is to be checked; may be of class Object or any subclass thereof.

object_class Specifies the widget class to test against; may be objectClass or any subclass.

Returns

True if *object* is of class *object_class* or any subclass of it; False otherwise.

Description

XtIsSubclass() returns True if the specified object is of the specified class, or is a subclass (any number of classes removed) of it. Otherwise it returns False.

Usage

Composite widgets that restrict the type of widgets they will accept as children can use XtIsSubclass() to find out whether a widget belongs to the desired widget class.

Public routines that require a widget of a particular class can use XtIsSubclass() to verify that the object they are passed is of the correct type. XtCheckSubclass() does the same thing, but is a macro that is only compiled when the symbol DEBUG is defined by the compiler.

To test whether a given widget is a subclass of an Intrinsics-defined class, the Intrinsics define convenience functions equivalent to XtIsSubclass() for each of the built-in classes. These functions are shown in the table below:

XtIsObject()	XtIsOverrideShell()
XtIsRectObj()	XtIsWMShell()
XtIsWidget()	XtIsVendorShell()
XtIsComposite()	XtIsTransientShell()
XtIsConstraint()	XtIsTopLevelShell()
XtIsShell()	XtIsApplicationShell()

These functions may be defined as macros, and may be faster than calling XtIsSubclass() directly for the built-in classes.

See Also

XtCheckSubclass(1), *XtClass*(1), *XtIs**(1), *XtSuperclass*(1).

Xt Functions and Macros

Name

XtIsTopLevelShell – test whether a widget is a subclass of the TopLevelShell widget class.

Synopsis

```
Boolean XtIsTopLevelShell(object)
    Widget object;
```

Inputs

object   Specifies the object whose class is to be checked; may be of class Object or any subclass thereof.

Returns

True if *object* is of class TopLevelShell or a subclass thereof; False otherwise.

Description

XtIsTopLevelShell() tests whether *object* is a subclass of the TopLevelShell widget class. It may be defined as a macro or a function, and is equivalent to, but may be faster than, calling XtIsSubclass() for this class.

See Also

XtIsSubclass(1).

XtIsTransientShell

Name

XtIsTransientShell – test whether a widget is a subclass of the TransientShell widget class.

Synopsis

```
Boolean XtIsTransientShell(object)
    Widget object;
```

Inputs

object   Specifies the object whose class is to be checked; may be of Object class or any subclass thereof.

Returns

True if *object* is of class TransientShell or a subclass thereof; False otherwise.

Description

XtIsTransientShell() tests whether *object* is a subclass of the TransientShell widget class. It may be defined as a macro or a function, and is equivalent to, but may be faster than, calling XtIsSubclass() for this class.

See Also

XtIsSubclass(1).

Name

XtIsVendorShell – test whether a widget is a subclass of the VendorShell widget class.

Synopsis

```
Boolean XtIsVendorShell(object)
    Widget object;
```

Inputs

object   Specifies the object whose class is to be checked; may be of class Object or any subclass thereof.

Returns

True if *object* is of class VendorShell or a subclass thereof; False otherwise.

Description

XtIsVendorShell() tests whether *object* is a subclass of the VendorShell widget class. It may be defined as a macro or a function, and is equivalent to, but may be faster than, calling XtIsSubclass() for this class.

See Also

XtIsSubclass(1).

Name

XtIsWMShell – test whether a widget is a subclass of the WMShell widget class.

Synopsis

```
Boolean XtIsWMShell(object)
    Widget object;
```

Inputs

object   Specifies the object whose class is to be checked; may be of class Object or any subclass thereof.

Returns

True if *object* is of class WMShell or a subclass thereof; False otherwise.

Description

XtIsWMShell() tests whether *object* is a subclass of the WMShell widget class. It may be defined as a macro or a function, and is equivalent to, but may be faster than, calling XtIs-Subclass() for this class.

See Also

XtIsSubclass(1).

XtIsWidget

Name

XtIsWidget – test whether a widget is a subclass of the Core widget class.

Synopsis

```
Boolean XtIsWidget(object)
    Widget object;
```

Inputs

object   Specifies the object whose class is to be checked; may be of class Object or any subclass thereof.

Returns

True if *object* is of class Core or a subclass thereof; False otherwise.

Description

XtIsWidget() tests whether *object* is a subclass of the Core widget class. It may be defined as a macro or a function, and is equivalent to, but may be faster than, calling XtIs-Subclass() for this class.

See Also

XtIsSubclass(1).

XtKeysymToKeycodeList

Name

XtKeysymToKeycodeList – return the list of keycodes that map to a particular keysym in the keyboard mapping table maintained by the Intrinsics.

Synopsis

```
void XtKeysymToKeycodeList(display, keysym, keycodes_return,
        keycount_return)
    Display *display;
    KeySym keysym;
    KeyCode **keycodes_return;
    Cardinal *keycount_return;
```

Inputs

display　　　　　Specifies the display whose table is required.

keysym　　　　　Specifies the keysym for which to search.

Outputs

keycodes_return

Returns a list of keycodes that have keysyms associated with them or NULL if *keycount_return* is 0.

keycount_return

Returns the number of keycodes in the keycodes list.

Availability

Release 4 and later.

Description

XtKeysymToKeycodeList() returns all the keycodes that have the requested keysym in their entry in the keyboard mapping table associated with *display*. If no keycodes map to the specified keysym, **keycount_return* is 0 and **keycodes_return* is NULL.

The caller should free the storage pointed to by *keycodes_return* using XtFree() when it is no longer useful.

Usage

The Translation Manager automatically converts between keycodes and keysyms. Most applications will never have to use this function or its related functions.

If you needs to examine the keycode-to-keysym table for a particular keycode, you can obtain the current table with XtGetKeysymTable().

See Also

XtConvertCase(1), *XtGetKeysymTable*(1), *XtRegisterCaseConverter*(1), *XtSetKeyTranslator*(1), *XtTranslateKeycode*(1).

Name

XtLastTimestampProcessed – retrieve the timestamp from the most recent event handled by XtDispatchEvent() that contains a timestamp.

Synopsis

```
Time XtLastTimestampProcessed(display)
    Display *display;
```

Inputs

display   Specifies an open display connection.

Returns

The timestamp of the most recently processed event that contains an event, or zero.

Availability

Release 4 and later.

Description

XtLastTimestampProcessed() returns the timestamp of the most recently processed event that contains a timestamp. If no KeyPress, KeyRelease, ButtonPress, ButtonRelease, MotionNotify, EnterNotify, LeaveNotify, PropertyNotify or SelectionClear event has yet been passed to XtDispatchEvent() for the specified display, XtLastTimestampProcessed() returns zero.

Usage

The Intrinsics selection handling routines take arguments of type Time. For ICCCM compliance, these arguments must be the timestamp of the event that triggered the request—the special value CurrentTime is not acceptable. XtLastTimestampProcessed() is a convenience function added in Release 4 to make it easy to obtain an appropriate timestamp, even from within a callback which is not passed an event. The function XtGetSelectionRequest() serves a similar purpose for XtSelectionCallback procedures.

See Also

XtDispatchEvent(1), *XtGetSelectionRequest*(1), *XtGetSelectionValue*(1), *XtOwnSelection*(1).

XtMainLoop

Name

XtMainLoop – continuously process events.

Synopsis

```
void XtMainLoop()
```

Inputs

Returns

`XtMainLoop()` enters an infinite loop and never returns.

Availability

`XtMainLoop()` has been superseded by `XtAppMainLoop()`.

Description

`XtMainLoop()` enters an infinite loop which calls `XtNextEvent()` to wait for events on all displays in *app_context* and `XtDispatchEvent()` to dispatch events.

Usage

`XtMainLoop()` has been superseded by `XtAppMainLoop()`, which performs the same function on a per-application context basis. `XtMainLoop()` now calls `XtAppMainLoop()` passing the default application context created by `XtInitialize()`. Very few programs need multiple application contexts, and you can continue to use `XtMainLoop()` if you initialize your application with `XtInitialize()`. We recommend, however, that you use `Xt-AppInitialize()`, `XtAppMainLoop()`, and the other `XtApp*()` application context specific functions.

See `XtAppMainLoop()` for more information.

See Also

XtAppMainLoop(1), *XtAppNextEvent*(1), *XtDispatchEvent*(1).

Xt Functions and Macros

Name

XtMakeGeometryRequest – request parent to change child's geometry.

Synopsis

```
XtGeometryResult XtMakeGeometryRequest(w, request, compromise_return)
    Widget w;
    XtWidgetGeometry *request;
    XtWidgetGeometry *compromise_return;
```

Inputs

w   Specifies the child widget that is making the request. Must be of class Rect-Obj or any subclass thereof.

request   Specifies the desired widget geometry (size, position, border width, and stacking order).

Outputs

compromise_return

Returns a compromise geometry when the function returns XtGeometry-Almost. May be NULL if the requesting widget is not interested in handling XtGeometryAlmost.

Returns

A response to the request: XtGeometryYes, XtGeometryNo or XtGeometryAlmost.

Description

XtMakeGeometryRequest() requests the parent of *w* to change *w*'s geometry to that specified in *request*. The request_mode field of *request* specifies which elements of its geometry the object is asking to have changed, and the remaining fields of this structure specify the values for each of those elements. If a bit is not set in *request_mode*, then Xt-MakeGeometryRequest() may change that element of the geometry in its effort to satisfy the requested changes.

There are three possible return values from this function, with the following meanings:

XtGeometryYes

The request was granted and has been performed (unless request_mode contained the XtCWQueryOnly bit). The object's internal core geometry fields have been updated and, if it is realized, the window has been correctly configured for the new geometry. The contents of *compromise_return* are undefined. *w*'s resize() method may or may not have been called. XtMakeGeometryRequest() does not call that method, but some parent widgets will call it in the process of satisfying the geometry request. The object should assume that it has not been called and perform any necessary resize calculations.

XtGeometryNo

The request was denied. The contents of *compromise_return* are undefined.

XtGeometryAlmost

> The request could not be satisfied exactly, but the object's parent has proposed a compromise geometry in *compromise_return*. If these compromise values are immediately used in another call to XtMakeGeometryRequest() the request is guaranteed to succeed.

See the "Background" section below for a detailed listing of the steps followed by XtMakeGeometryRequest().

Usage

XtMakeGeometryRequest() should only be used in widget code by widgets which would like to change their own size. This is the only way that a widget is allowed to change its own size.

Applications that want to set a widget size should use XtSetValues() on the various geometry resources of a widget.

A widget that wants to change the geometry of one of its children should use XtConfigure-Widget(), XtMoveWidget() or XtResizeWidget().

Background

XtMakeGeometryRequest() performs the following tasks:

- If the widget is unmanaged or the widget's parent is not realized, it makes the changes to the widget's preferred geometry and returns XtGeometryYes.

- If the parent is not a subclass of compositeWidgetClass or the parent's geometry_manager() method (the function pointed to by the geometry_manager() field in the widget class record) is NULL, it issues an error.

- If the widget's being_destroyed field is True, it returns XtGeometryNo.

- If the widget x, y, width, height, and border_width fields are already equal to the requested values, it returns XtGeometryYes; otherwise, it calls the parent's geometry_manager() method with the given parameters.

- If the parent's geometry manager returns XtGeometryYes, if XtCWQueryOnly is not set in request_mode (see Structures below for details), and if the widget is realized, then XtMakeGeometryRequest() calls the Xlib XConfigureWindow() function to adjust the widget's window (setting its size, location, and stacking order as appropriate).

- If the geometry manager returns XtGeometryDone, the change has been approved and actually has been done. In this case, XtMakeGeometryRequest() does no configuring and returns XtGeometryYes. XtMakeGeometryRequest() never returns Xt-GeometryDone.

- Otherwise, XtMakeGeometryRequest() returns the resulting value from the parent's geometry manager.

Children of non-Composite widgets are always unmanaged; thus, XtMakeGeometry-Request() always returns XtGeometryYes when called by a child of a non-Composite widget.

*Xt Functions
and Macros*

Structures

The return codes from geometry managers are:

```
typedef enum _XtGeometryResult {
    XtGeometryYes,    /* Request accepted */
    XtGeometryNo,     /* Request denied */
    XtGeometryAlmost,/* Request denied but willing to take reply */
    XtGeometryDone    /* never returned by XtMakeGeometryRequest() */
} XtGeometryResult;
```

The `XtWidgetGeometry` structure is similar to but not identical to the corresponding Xlib structure:

```
typedef unsigned long XtGeometryMask;

typedef struct {
    XtGeometryMask request_mode;
    Position x, y;
    Dimension width, height;
    Dimension border_width;
    Widget sibling;
    int stack_mode;
} XtWidgetGeometry;
```

`XtMakeGeometryRequest()`, like the Xlib `XConfigureWindow()` function, uses `request_mode` to determine which fields in the `XtWidgetGeometry` structure you want to specify. The `request_mode` definitions are from *<X11/X.h>*:

```
#define    CWX              (1<<0)
#define    CWY              (1<<1)
#define    CWWidth          (1<<2)
#define    CWHeight         (1<<3)
#define    CWBorderWidth    (1<<4)
#define    CWSibling        (1<<5)
#define    CWStackMode      (1<<6)
```

The Xt Intrinsics also support the following value:

```
#define XtCWQueryOnly    (1<<7)
```

`XtCWQueryOnly` indicates that the corresponding geometry request is only a query as to what would happen if this geometry request were made and that no widgets should actually be changed.

The `stack_mode` definitions are from *<X11/X.h>*:

```
#define    Above        0
#define    Below        1
#define    TopIf        2
#define    BottomIf     3
#define    Opposite     4
```

The Intrinsics also support the following value:

```
#define    XtSMDontChange    5
```

XtSMDontChange indicates that the widget wants its current stacking order preserved. For precise definitions of Above, Below, TopIf, BottomIf, and Opposite, see the reference page for XConfigureWindow() in Volume Two, *Xlib Reference Manual*.

See Also

XtConfigureWidget(1), *XtMakeResizeRequest*(1), *XtMoveWidget*(1), *XtResizeWidget*(1), *geometry_manager*(4).

Name

XtMakeResizeRequest – request parent to change child's size.

Synopsis

```
XtGeometryResult XtMakeResizeRequest(w, width, height, width_return,
        height_return)
    Widget w;
    Dimension width, height;
    Dimension *width_return, *height_return;
```

Inputs

w　　　　　　　　Specifies the child widget making the request.

width, *height*　Specify the desired widget width and height.

Outputs

width_return, *height_return*

　　　　　　　　Return a compromise size when the function returns XtGeometry-Almost. May be NULL if the widget is not interested in compromises.

Returns

A response to the request: XtGeometryYes, XtGeometryNo or XtGeometryAlmost.

Description

XtMakeResizeRequest() is a simplified version of XtMakeGeometryRequest() that a child can use to ask its parent to change its size. It creates an XtWidgetGeometry structure, specifies *width*, and *height*, sets request_mode to (CWWidth |CWHeight), and passes it to XtMakeGeometryRequest(). Note that the geometry manager is free to modify any of the other window attributes (position or stacking order) to satisfy the resize request.

The return values are as for XtMakeGeometryRequest(). If the return value is Xt-GeometryAlmost, *width_return* and *height_return* contain a compromise width and height. If these are acceptable, the widget should immediately make another XtMake-ResizeRequest() and request that the compromise width and height be applied.

See XtMakeGeometryRequest() for more information.

Usage

XtMakeResizeRequest() should only be used in widget code by widgets which would like to change their own size. Applications that want to set a widget size should use XtSet-Values() on the XtNwidth and XtNheight resources of the widget. A widget that wants to change the size of one of its children should use XtResizeWidget().

See Also

XtConfigureWidget(1), *XtMakeGeometryRequest*(1), *XtMoveWidget*(1), *XtResizeWidget*(1),
geometry_manager(4).

XtMalloc

Name

XtMalloc – allocate memory.

Synopsis

```
char *XtMalloc(size);
    Cardinalsize;
```

Inputs

size   Specifies the number of bytes of memory to allocate.

Returns

A pointer to allocated memory.

Description

XtMalloc() allocates and returns a block of *size* bytes of memory. If there is insufficient memory to allocate the new block, XtMalloc() terminates by calling XtErrorMsg().

XtMalloc() makes no guarantee about the contents of the memory when it is allocated.

Usage

In most cases, you will have to cast the return value of XtMalloc() to an appropriate pointer type.

XtNew() and XtNewString() provide slightly higher-level approaches to memory allocation.

Memory allocated with XtMalloc() must be deallocated with XtFree(). The function XtMalloc() is implemented by the Toolkit independently of the particular environment, so programs ported to a system not supporting malloc will still work.

See Also

XtCalloc(1), *XtErrorMsg*(1), *XtFree*(1), *XtNew*(1), *XtNewString*(1), *XtRealloc*(1).

Xt Functions and Macros

XtManageChild

Name

XtManageChild – bring a widget under its parent's geometry management.

Synopsis

```
void XtManageChild(w)
    Widget w;
```

Inputs

w   Specifies the child widget to be managed; Must be of class RectObj or any subclass thereof.

Description

XtManageChild() brings a child widget under the geometry management of its parent. All widgets (except shell widgets) must be managed in order to be visible. Managing a widget will generally make it visible, unless its XtNmappedWhenManaged resource is False.

XtManageChild() constructs a WidgetList of length one and calls XtManage-Children(). See XtManageChildren() for more information.

Usage

Calls to XtCreateWidget() and XtManageChild() can be combined into a single call to XtCreateManagedChild() or XtVaCreateManagedChild().

If you are going to manage multiple children of the same managed and realized parent, it is more efficient to place those children widget into an array and call XtManageChildren() just once, as this results in only a single call to the parent's change_managed() method. If you are creating widgets before the widget tree has been realized, however, managing them one at a time is fine.

A widget can be unmanaged by calling XtUnmanageChild().

See Also

XtCreateManagedWidget(1), *XtIsManaged*(1), *XtManageChildren*(1), *XtSetMappedWhenManaged*(1), *XtUnmanageChild*(1), *XtUnmanageChildren*(1).

XtManageChildren

Name

XtManageChildren – bring an array of widgets under their parent's geometry management.

Synopsis

```
void XtManageChildren(children, num_children)
    WidgetList children;
    Cardinal num_children;
```

Inputs

children   Specifies an array of child widgets. The widgets must all be siblings and must be of class RectObj or any subclass thereof.

num_children Specifies the number of children in the array.

Description

XtManageChildren() brings a list of widgets created with XtCreateWidget() under the geometry management of their parent. All widgets (except shell widgets) must be managed in order to be visible. Managing a widget will generally make it visible, unless its XtNmappedWhenManaged resource is False.

The "Algorithm" section below details the procedure followed by XtManageChildren().

Usage

To manage a single widget, you can use XtManageChild(). To unmanage widgets, use XtUnmanageChild() and XtUnmanageChildren().

If you are going to manage multiple children of the same managed and realized parent, it is more efficient to place those children widget into an array and call XtManageChildren() just once than it is to manage them individually. The former technique results in only a single call to the parent's change_managed() method. If you are creating widgets before the widget tree has been realized, however, managing them one at a time is fine.

Algorithm

XtManageChildren() performs the following:

- Issues an error if the children do not all have the same parent or if the parent is not a subclass of compositeWidgetClass.

- Returns immediately if the common parent is being destroyed; otherwise, for each unique child on the list, XtManageChildren() ignores the child if it already is managed or is being destroyed, and marks it otherwise.

- If the parent is realized XtManageChildren() does the following:

  - Calls the change_managed() method of the widgets' parent.

  - Calls XtRealizeWidget() on each marked child that is unrealized.

  - Maps each marked child that has its XtNmappedWhenManaged resource True.

Xt Functions and Macros

The management of children is independent of the creation and ordering of the children. There is no special list of managed children; the layout routine of the parent should loop through the list of all children and simply ignore those that are not managed (see `XtIsManaged()`).

Structures

```
typedef Widget *WidgetList;
```

See Also

XtCreateManagedWidget(1), *XtIsManaged*(1), *XtManageChild*(1), *XtMoveWidget*(1), *XtRealize-Widget*(1), *XtSetMappedWhenManaged*(1), *XtUnmanageChild*(1), *XtUnmanageChildren*(1).

XtMapWidget

Name

XtMapWidget – map a widget to its display.

Synopsis

```
XtMapWidget(w)
    Widget w;
```

Inputs

w   Specifies the widget to be mapped. Must be of class Core or any subclass thereof.

Description

XtMapWidget() explicitly maps a widget's window, causing it to become visible. A widget must be realized before it can be mapped.

Usage

A widget should be managed before it is mapped; otherwise the window may not appear at the correct location or size.

If a widget's Core XtNmappedWhenManaged resource is set to True, the widget is automatically mapped when it is managed. This is the case for most widgets. Widgets with this resource False must be mapped explicitly with XtMapWidget().

To explicitly unmap a widget without unmanaging it, use XtUnmapWidget().

The XtNmappedWhenManaged resource can also be set (and the widget mapped and unmapped) with XtSetMappedWhenManaged().

See Also

XtSetMappedWhenManaged(1), *XtUnmapWidget*(1).

XtMenuPopdown

Name

XtMenuPopdown – built-in action for popping down a widget.

Synopsis (Translation Table)

```
<Event sequence>: XtMenuPopdown([shell])
```

Inputs

shell   An optional argument which specifies the name of the shell to pop down.

Availability

This action is named `MenuPopdown` prior to Release 4.

Description

`XtMenuPopdown` is a predefined action procedure which does not have a corresponding public C routine. It can only be invoked from a translation table. If passed an argument, that argument is interpreted as a shell name, and `XtMenuPopdown` tries to find the named shell by looking up the widget tree starting at the parent of the widget in which it is invoked. If it finds a shell with the specified name in the popup children of that parent, it pops down the shell by calling `XtPopdown()`; otherwise, it moves up the parent chain as needed. If `XtMenu-Popdown` gets to the application top-level shell widget and cannot find a matching shell, it generates a warning and returns immediately. If `XtMenuPopdown` is called with no argument, it calls `XtPopdown()` on the widget for which the translation is specified.

Usage

Note that `XtMenuPopdown` is an action procedure; you cannot call it from C code.

The action name `MenuPopdown` is a synonym for `XtMenuPopdown`. Either action can be used to pop down menus or other popup shells.

Popup shells can also be popped down by calling `XtPopdown()` explicitly, or by using the predefined callback procedure `XtCallbackPopdown()`.

The action `XtMenuPopup` can be used to pop up a spring-loaded popup from a translation table.

See Also

XtCallbackPopdown(1), *XtMenuPopup*(1), *XtPopDown*(1), *XtPopup*(1), *XtPopupSpringLoaded*(1).

XtMenuPopup

Name

XtMenuPopup – built-in action for popping up a widget.

Synopsis (Translation Table)

`<Event sequence>`: XtMenuPopup(`shell_name`)

Inputs

`shell_name`   Specifies the name of the widget shell to pop up.

Availability

This action is named MenuPopup prior to Release 4.

Description

XtMenuPopdown is a predefined action procedure which does not have a corresponding public C routine. It can only be invoked from a translation table.

XtMenuPopup tries to find the named shell by searching the widget tree starting at the widget in which it is invoked. If it finds a shell with the specified name in the popup children of that widget, it pops up the shell with the appropriate parameters. Otherwise, it moves up the parent chain to find a popup child with the specified name. If XtMenuPopup gets to the application top-level shell widget and has not found a matching shell, it generates a warning and returns immediately.

If XtMenuPopup is invoked on ButtonPress, it calls XtPopupSpringLoaded() on the specified shell widget. If XtMenuPopup is invoked on KeyPress or EnterWindow, it calls XtPopup() on the specified shell widget with *grab_kind* set to XtGrab-Nonexclusive. Otherwise, the translation manager generates a warning message and ignores the action.

XtMenuPopup is specially registered with the translation manager as an action that will invoke a grab. This registration is done by calling XtRegisterGrabAction() specifying *owner_events* True, *event_mask* ButtonPressMask | ButtonReleaseMask, and *pointer_mode* and *keyboard_mode* GrabModeAsync.

Usage

Note that XtMenuPopup is an action procedure; you cannot call it from C code.

MenuPopup is a synonym for XtMenuPopup.

Popup shells can also be popped up explicitly using XtPopup(), XtPopupSpring-Loaded() or one of the predefined popup callback procedures (see XtCallback-Exclusive()).

The action XtMenuPopdown can be used to pop down a shell widget from a translation table.

See Also

XtMenuPopdown(1), *XtPopDown*(1), *XtPopup*(1), *XtPopupSpringLoaded*(1), *XtRegisterGrabAction*(1).

XtMergeArgLists

Name

XtMergeArgLists – merge two `ArgList` arrays.

Synopsis

```
ArgList XtMergeArgLists(args1, num_args1, args2, num_args2)
    ArgList args1;
    Cardinal num_args1;
    ArgList args2;
    Cardinal num_args2;
```

Inputs

args1   Specifies the first `ArgList`.

num_args1   Specifies the number of arguments in the first argument list.

args2   Specifies the second `ArgList`.

num_args2   Specifies the number of arguments in the second argument list.

Returns

An allocated `ArgList` that contains both *args1* and *args2*.

Description

`XtMergeArgLists()` allocates a new `ArgList` large enough to hold *args1* and *args2* and copies both into it. It does not check for duplicate entries.

When the new `ArgList` is no longer needed, the application program should free it with `Xt-Free()`.

Structures

`Arg` is defined as follows:

```
typedef struct {
    String name;
    XtArgVal value;
} Arg, *ArgList;
```

See Also

XtFree(1), *XtSetArg*(1).

Name

XtMoveWidget – move a widget within its parent.

Synopsis

```
void XtMoveWidget(w, x, y)
    Widget w;
    Position x;
    Position y;
```

Inputs

w   Specifies the widget to be moved; must be of class RectObj or any subclass thereof.

x, y   Specify the new widget x and y coordinates.

Description

XtMoveWidget() returns immediately if the specified geometry fields for the widget are the same as the current values. Otherwise, XtMoveWidget() writes the new x and y values into the widget and, if the widget is realized, issues an Xlib XMoveWindow() call on the widget's window.

Usage

XtMoveWidget() should only be used in widget code when a parent widget wants to move one of its children. If an application wants to move a widget, it should set the XtNx and XtNy resources on the widget. If a widget wants to move itself, it must request that change of its parent by calling XtMakeGeometryRequest().

To move and resize a child widget, use XtConfigureWidget(). To simply resize a child widget, use XtResizeWidget().

See Also

XtConfigureWidget(1), *XtMakeGeometryRequest*(1), *XtResizeWidget*(1).

Xt Functions and Macros

Name

XtName – return a pointer to the instance name of the specified object.

Synopsis

```
String XtName(object)
     Widget object;
```

Inputs

object   Specifies the object whose name is desired; may be of class Object or any subclass thereof.

Returns

The resource name of *object*.

Description

XtName() returns a pointer to the instance name of the specified object. The storage is owned by the Intrinsics and must not be modified or freed. The name is not qualified by the names of any of the object's ancestors.

See Also

XtNameToWidget(1).

Name

XtNameToWidget – find a named widget.

Synopsis

```
Widget XtNameToWidget(reference, names);
    Widget reference;
    String names;
```

Inputs

reference   Specifies the widget from which the search is to start. Must be of class Core or any subclass.

names   Specifies the partially qualified name of the desired widget.

Returns

A child of *reference* that matches *names*.

Description

XtNameToWidget() returns a descendant of the *reference* widget whose name matches the specified *names*. The *names* argument specifies a simple object name or a series of simple object name components separated by periods or asterisks. Asterisks have the same meaning to this function as they do in a resource file.

The "Algorithm" section below explains the procedure XtNameToWidget() uses to find the named child.

Usage

If you want to look up an immediate child of a widget, simply pass the widget and the child's unqualified name. If you need to lookup a descendant, you can provide a fully qualified name to that descendant, or if you don't know the full name, or if you don't even know how many levels removed that descendant is, you can use an asterisk before the name.

Note that if there is more than one child with the specified name, it is undefined which will be returned.

You can use XtNameToWidget() to hide the details of a user interface and for modular programming. If module A creates an interface which contains a text widget, and module B need to get the contents of the text widget, module A could export the text widget in a global variable, or instead, it could simply define the name of the text widget as part of the module definition. Then module B, or any other module could look up that widget with XtNameToWidget() when it is needed. Because XtNameToWidget() supports wildcarding, module A can freely change the details of the widget hierarchy it creates as long as the name of the text widget remains unique.

Algorithm

`XtNameToWidget()` returns the descendant with the shortest name that matches the specification according to the following rules (where child is either a popup child or a normal child if the widget is a subclass of Composite):

- Enumerate the object subtree rooted at *reference* widget in breadth-first order, qualifying the name of each object with the names of all its ancestors up to but not including *reference*. The ordering between children of a common parent is not defined.

- Return the first object in the enumeration that matches the specified names, where each component of *names* matches exactly the corresponding component of the qualified object name and an asterisk matches any series of components, including none.

- If no match is found, return `NULL`.

Since breadth-first traversal is specified, the descendant with the shortest matching name (i.e., the fewest number of components), if any, will always be returned. However, since the order of enumeration of children is undefined and since the Intrinsics do not require that all children of a widget have unique names, `XtNameToWidget()` may return any child that matches if there are multiple objects in the subtree with the same name(s). Consecutive separators (periods or asterisks) that contain at least one asterisk are treated as a single asterisk. Consecutive periods are treated as a single period.

See Also

XtCreateWidget(1), *XtName*(1).

Name

XtNew – allocate storage for one instance of a data type.

Synopsis

```
type *XtNew(type)
```

Inputs

`type`   Specifies a data type. Note that this is not a variable.

Returns

A pointer to sufficient allocated memory to store a variable of type `type`.

Description

`XtNew()` is a macro used to allocate storage for one instance of the data type `type`. It is called with the datatype (a type, not a variable) and returns a pointer to enough allocated memory to hold that type. The return value is correctly cast to `type *`.

If there is insufficient memory, `XtNew()` calls `XtErrorMsg()` to display an error message and terminate the application.

Usage

Memory allocated with `XtNew()` must be deallocated with `XtFree()`.

To allocate memory and copy an a string, use `XtNewString()`.

Example

`XtNew()` can be used as follows:

```
typedef struct _node {
    int value;
    struct _node next;
} Node;

Node *n = XtNew(Node);
```

Background

`XtNew()` is simply the following macro:

```
#define XtNew(type) ((type *) XtMalloc((unsigned) sizeof(type)))
```

See Also

XtMalloc(1), *XtNewString*(1).

XtNewString

Name

XtNewString – copy an instance of a string.

Synopsis

```
String XtNewString(string)
    String string;
```

Inputs

string   Specifies a NULL-terminated string.

Returns

A copy of *string* in allocated memory.

Description

XtNewString() allocates enough memory to hold a copy of the specified string and copies the string into that memory. If there is insufficient memory to allocate the new block, XtNew-String() prints an error message and terminates the application by calling XtError-Msg().

Usage

Memory allocated with XtNewString() must be deallocated with XtFree().

To simply allocate a specified amount of memory, use XtMalloc(). To allocate enough memory for one instance of a specified type, use XtNew().

Example

You might use XtNewString() in a situation like this:

```
String name = XtNewString(XtName(w));
```

XtName() returns a string that may not be modified. If you copy it, however, you can do anything you like with it, as long as you remember to free it when you are done with it.

Background

XtNewString() is defined as the following macro:

```
#define XtNewString(str) \
#define XtNewString(str) \
    ((str) != NULL ? (strcpy(XtMalloc((unsigned)strlen(str) + 1),
    str)) : NULL)
```

See Also

XtMalloc(1), *XtFree*(1), *XtNew*(1).

XtNextEvent

Name

XtNextEvent – return next event from input queue.

Synopsis

```
void XtNextEvent(event_return)
    XEvent *event_return;
```

Inputs

None.

Outputs

event_return   Returns the dequeued event structure.

Availability

XtNextEvent() has been superseded by XtAppNextEvent().

Description

XtNextEvent() returns the next event on the input queue. If no events are pending, it flushes the output buffer and blocks. It also dispatches timer and alternate input callbacks and calls any work procedures that have been registered with XtAddWorkProc().

Usage

XtNextEvent() has been superseded by XtAppNextEvent(), which performs the same function on a per-application context basis. XtNextEvent() now calls XtAppNext-Event() passing the default application context created by XtInitialize(). Very few programs need multiple application contexts, and you can continue to use XtNextEvent() if you initialize your application with XtInitialize(). We recommend, however, that you use XtAppInitialize(), XtAppNextEvent(), and the other XtApp*() application context specific functions.

See XtAppNextEvent() for more information.

See Also

XtAppNextEvent(1).

XtNumber

Name

XtNumber – determine the number of elements in a fixed-size array.

Synopsis

```
Cardinal XtNumber(array)
```

Inputs

array   Specifies a fixed-size array of arbitrary type.

Returns

The number of elements in array.

Description

XtNumber() returns the number of elements in the specified argument list, resource list, or other fixed-size array. It works only for objects which have been statically initialized or declared with a fixed number of elements, i.e., arrays whose total size is known at compile time.

Usage

You should use XtNumber() whenever you are passing a static array to a function or storing an static array in a structure that also expects the number of elements in the array. This way, if you change the number of element in the array, the correct number of elements will automatically be compiled in.

Background

XtNumber() is a macro defined as follows:

```
#define XtNumber(arr)   ((Cardinal) (sizeof(arr) / sizeof(arr[0])))
```

See Also

XtOffset(1), *XtOffsetOf*(1), *XtSetArg*(1).

XtOffset

Name

XtOffset – determine the byte offset of a field within a structure pointer type.

Synopsis

```
Cardinal XtOffset(pointer_type, field_name)
```

Inputs

pointer_type Specifies a type that is declared as a pointer to the structure.

field_name Specifies the name of the field in the structure pointed to by *pointer_type*.

Returns

The offset in bytes of the named field from the beginning of the structure type pointed to by *pointer_type*.

Description

XtOffset() is a macro that computes the offset of a named field in a structure, given the field name and a type which points to the structure.

Usage

XtOffset() has been superseded by XtOffsetOf() which takes the structure type itself rather than a pointer to the structure, and is defined in a more portable way.

XtOffset() is usually used to determine the location of an variable within a structure when initializing a resource list. It is used by widget writers, and anyone who needs to fetch application resources with XtGetApplicationResources(). Resource fields are defined in terms of offsets from a base address from the beginning of a widget. Thus, a resource value can be kept up to date by the Resource Manager without any knowledge of the instance structure of the widget; it uses just a relative byte offset.

Background

XtOffset() is a macro defined as follows for most architectures:

```
#define XtOffset(p_type,field) \
    ((Cardinal) (((char *) (&(((p_type)NULL)->field))) - ((char *) NULL)))
```

See Also

XtOffsetOf(1).

XtOffsetOf

Name
XtOffsetOf – determine the byte offset of a field within a structure type.

Synopsis
`Cardinal XtOffsetOf(`*structure_type*`, `*field_name*`)`

Inputs
structure_type
> Specifies a type that is declared as a structure.

field_name Specifies the name of a field of the structure.

Returns
The offset in bytes of the specified field from the beginning of the specified structure.

Availability
Release 4 and later.

Description
`XtOffsetOf()` is a macro that expands to a constant expression that gives the offset in bytes to the specified structure member from the beginning of the structure.

Usage
`XtOffset()` is usually used to determine the location of an variable within a structure when initializing a resource list. It is used by widget writers, and anyone who needs to fetch application resources with `XtGetApplicationResources()`. Resource fields are defined in terms of offsets from a base address from the beginning of a widget. Thus, a resource value can be kept up to date by the Resource Manager without any knowledge of the instance structure of the widget; it uses just a relative byte offset.

`XtOffsetOf()` is slightly more portable than `XtOffset()` which performs the same function but takes a pointer type rather than a structure type.

Example
`XtOffsetOf()` is used to declare a resource list for the Athena Label widget:

```
#define offset(field) XtOffsetOf(LabelRec, field)
static XtResource resources[] = {
    {XtNforeground, XtCForeground, XtRPixel, sizeof(Pixel),
        offset(label.foreground), XtRString, XtDefaultForeground},
    {XtNfont,  XtCFont, XtRFontStruct, sizeof(XFontStruct *),
        offset(label.font),XtRString, XtDefaultFont},
        .
        .
```

Background

XtOffsetOf() is defined in terms of XtOffset() on many systems:

```
#ifdef offsetof
#define XtOffsetOf(s_type,field) offsetof(s_type,field)
#else
#define XtOffsetOf(s_type,field) XtOffset(s_type*,field)
#endif
```

See Also

XtOffset(1).

XtOpenDisplay

Name

XtOpenDisplay – open, initialize, and add a display to an application context.

Synopsis

```
Display *XtOpenDisplay(app_context, display_name, application_name, appli-
        cation_class, options, num_options, argc, argv)
    XtAppContext app_context;
    String display_name;
    String application_name;
    String application_class;
    XrmOptionDescRec *options;
    Cardinal num_options;
    int *argc;            /* was Cardinal * in Release 4 */
    String *argv;
```

Inputs

app_context Specifies the application context.

display_name

Specifies the name of the display to be opened and initialized, or NULL.

application_name

Specifies the name of the application instance, or NULL.

application_class

Specifies the class name of this application, which is usually the generic name for all instances of this application.

options Specifies how to parse the command line for any application-specific resources.

num_options Specifies the number of entries in the options array.

argc Specifies a pointer to the number of command line parameters. In Release 4 and previously, this argument was of type Cardinal *. In Release 5 it is an int *.

argv Specifies the command line parameters.

Outputs

argc Returns the number of command line arguments remaining after the command line is parsed.

argv Returns a modified command line containing only the application name and any arguments that were not recognized as standard Xt options or options specified in *options*.

Returns

A pointer to the opened and initialized Display structure.

Description

XtOpenDisplay() opens and initializes a display, and adds it to the specified application context. Note that a display can be in at most one application context.

XtOpenDisplay() calls XOpenDisplay() with the name of the display to open. If *display_name* is NULL, XtOpenDisplay() uses the current value of the *–display* option specified in *argv* or if no display is specified in *argv*, it uses the user's default display (on POSIX-based systems, this is the value of the DISPLAY environment variable).

If the display is successfully opened, XtOpenDisplay() parses the command line, builds the resource database and does other per-display initialization by calling XtDisplay-Initialize() and passing it the application context, the opened display, the application name, and the remaining arguments. The application name is the value of the *–name* option if it is specified in *argv*, or the value of the *application_name* argument, if it is non-NULL, or the value of the RESOURCE_NAME environment variable if it is set, or the name used to invoke the program. On implementations that conform to ANSI-C Hosted Environment support, this is *argv*[0] less any directory and file type components; that is, the final component of *argv*[0], if specified. If *argv*[0] does not exist or is the empty string, the application name is "main". See XtDisplayInitialize() and XtAppInitialize() for more information on initializing the display. In particular, see XtAppInitialize() for an explanation of how to initialize and array of XrmOptionDescRec in order to specify command line options to be parsed.

XtOpenDisplay() returns the newly opened display or NULL if it failed.

Usage

Most applications open only one display. For these applications, it is easiest to simply call Xt-AppInitialize() which will automatically open and initialize a display. Applications that want to use additional displays will usually open and initialize them with XtOpen-Display(). If a display is already open, it can be initialized and added to an application context, thereby making it known to the Intrinsics, by calling XtDisplayInitialize().

In Release 4, the *argc* argument is of type Cardinal *, and in Release 5, this argument is of type int *. This is a minor incompatibility that may result warnings from ANSI-C compilers when porting from one release to another.

After XtDisplayInitialize() has been called, *argc* and *argv* contain only those arguments that were not in the standard option table or in the table specified by the *options* argument. If the modified *argc* is not zero, most applications simply print out the modified *argv* along with a message listing the allowable options.

Structures

The XrmOptionDescRec structure is as follows. See XtAppInitialize() for information on how it is used.

```
typedef enum {
                            /* Value is ... */
    XrmoptionNoArg,         /* specified in OptionDescRec.value */
    XrmoptionIsArg,         /* the option string itself */
    XrmoptionStickyArg,     /* characters immediately following option */
    XrmoptionSepArg,        /* next argument in argv */
    XrmoptionResArg,        /* next argument is input to XrmPutLineResource */
                            /* Ignore this option and ... */
```

```
    XrmoptionSkipArg,       /* the next argument in argv */
    XrmoptionSkipNArgs,     /* Ignore this option and ... */
                            /* the next value arguments in argv */
    XrmoptionSkipLine       /* the rest of argv */
} XrmOptionKind;

typedef struct {
    char *option;           /* Option name in argv */
    char *specifier;        /* Resource name (without application name) */
    XrmOptionKind argKind;  /* Which style of option it is */
    caddr_t value;          /* Value to provide if XrmoptionNoArg */
} XrmOptionDescRec, *XrmOptionDescList;
```

See Also

XtAppInitialize(1), *XtDisplayInitialize*(1).

XtOverrideTranslations

Name

XtOverrideTranslations – merge new translations, overriding a widget's existing ones.

Synopsis

```
void XtOverrideTranslations(w, translations)
    Widget w;
    XtTranslations translations;
```

Inputs

w   Specifies the widget into which the new translations are to be merged. Must be of class Core or any subclass thereof.

translations   Specifies the compiled translation table to merge in.

Description

XtOverrideTranslations() merges a compiled translation table *translations* into a widget's internal compiled translation table, replacing any existing translations that conflict with the new translations. The table *translations* is not altered by this process. Any "#replace", "#augment", or "#override" directives in *translations* are ignored by this function.

Usage

Use XtParseTranslationTable() to convert a string representation of a translation table to the XtTranslations compiled form.

To merge translations into a widget without overriding existing translations where there are conflicts, use XtAugmentTranslations(). To completely replace a widget's translation table, use XtSetValues() to set a compiled translation table on the widget's XtNtranslations resource. To remove all of a widget's translations, use XtUninstall-Translations().

Translation tables can also be specified in string from a resource file. By default, specifying a value for the translations resource will completely replace the existing translations. If the string form of the translation table begins with the directives "#augment" or "#override", however, then the specified translations will be merged with the widget's existing translations, and new translations that conflict with existing translations will be ignored or will override the existing translations, respectively.

See Also

XtAugmentTranslations(1), *XtParseTranslationTable*(1), *XtUninstallTranslations*(1).

Xt Functions and Macros (side tab)

XtOwnSelection

Name

XtOwnSelection – make selection data available to other clients.

Synopsis

```
Boolean XtOwnSelection(w, selection, time, convert_proc, lose_proc,
        done_proc)
    Widget w;
    Atom selection;
    Time time;
    XtConvertSelectionProc convert_proc;
    XtLoseSelectionProc lose_proc;
    XtSelectionDoneProc done_proc;
```

Inputs

w Specifies the widget that wishes to become the owner.

selection Specifies an atom that describes the type of the selection (usually XA_ PRI-MARY, or XA_SECONDARY).

time Specifies the time when selection ownership should commence. This should be the timestamp of the event that triggered ownership. The value CurrentTime is not acceptable.

convert_proc
Specifies the procedure to call whenever someone requests the current value of the selection.

lose_proc Specifies the procedure to call when the widget loses selection ownership, or NULL if the owner is not interested in being called back.

done_proc Specifies the procedure to call after a transfer completes, or NULL if the owner is not interested in being called back.

Returns

True if the widget successfully became the selection owner; False otherwise.

Description

XtOwnSelection() tells the Intrinsics that as of time *time* widget *w* has data it would like to make available to other clients through the selection named by *selection*. It registers three procedures with the Intrinsics atomic data transfer mechanism: *convert_proc* will be called when a client requests the selection; it must convert the selection data to the requested type. *lose_proc*, if non-NULL, will be called when another widget or another client asserts ownership of the selection. (It will not be called if the widget relinquishes ownership by calling XtDisownSelection() or if the widget fails to gain ownership in the first place.) *done_proc*, if non-NULL will be called after the requesting client has received the data converted by *convert_proc*.

XtOwnSelection() returns True if the widget has successfully become the owner and False otherwise. The widget may fail to become the owner if some other widget has asserted ownership after this widget, as indicated by *time*. Widgets can lose selection ownership either because another client more recently asserted ownership of the selection, or because the widget voluntarily gave up ownership of the selection with `XtDisownSelection()`.

If *done_proc* is NULL, then `convert_proc` must allocate memory for the transfer with one of the Intrinsics memory allocation routines, so that the Intrinsics can automatically free it. If a non-NULL *done_proc* is specified, it is the responsibility of this procedure to free any memory allocated by the *convert_proc*.

See `XtConvertSelectionProc`(2), `XtLoseSelectionProc`(2), and `XtSelection-DoneProc`(2), for information on how to write the procedures that are passed to this function.

Usage

Note that `XtOwnSelection()` simply informs the Intrinsics that a widget would like to own the selection. It is *convert_proc* that must do the real work of transferring the selected data.

Selection ownership is not restricted to widgets; an application can export data as well. The widget argument to `XtOwnSelection()` serves mainly as a handle to be passed to the various procedures. You can use any widget, but it will make the most sense to use the widget that contains the data you will be exporting.

`XA_PRIMARY` and `XA_SECONDARY` are symbolic names for predefined atoms. They are defined in *<X11/Xatom.h>*. You can export data over a custom selection, but if you do, only clients that know the selection name will be able to request the data.

`XtLastTimestampProcessed()` is a convenient way to obtain a timestamp suitable for use as the *time* argument.

See Also

XtDisownSelection(1), *XtGetSelectionValue*(1),
XtConvertSelectionProc(2), *XtLoseSelectionProc*(2), *XtSelectionDoneProc*(2).

Name

XtOwnSelectionIncremental – make selection data available to other clients using the incremental transfer interface.

Synopsis

```
Boolean XtOwnSelectionIncremental(w, selection, time, convert_callback,
        lose_callback, done_callback, cancel_callback, client_data)
    Widget w;
    Atom selection;
    Time time;
    XtConvertSelectionIncrProc convert_callback;
    XtLoseSelectionIncrProc lose_callback;
    XtSelectionDoneIncrProc done_callback;
    XtCancelConvertSelectionProc cancel_callback;
    XtPointer client_data;
```

Inputs

w   Specifies the widget that wishes to become the owner.

selection   Specifies an atom that names the selection (usually, XA_PRIMARY or XA_SECONDARY).

time   Specifies the timestamp that indicates when the selection ownership should commence. This should be the timestamp of the event that triggered ownership; the value CurrentTime is not acceptable.

convert_callback
                Specifies the procedure that is to be called whenever the current value of the selection is requested.

lose_callback Specifies the procedure that is to be called when the widget loses selection ownership or NULL if the owner is not interested in being notified.

done_callback Specifies the procedure that is called after the requestor has received the entire selection or NULL if the owner is not interested in being notified.

cancel_callback
                Specifies the procedure that is to be called when a selection request aborts because a timeout expires, or NULL if the owner is not interested in being notified.

client_data   Specifies the argument that is to be passed to each of the callback procedures when they are called.

Returns

True if the widget successfully became the selection owner; False otherwise.

Availability

Release 4 and later.

Description

XtOwnSelection() tells the Intrinsics that as of time *time* widget *w* has data it would like to make available to other clients through the selection named by *selection*. It registers four procedures with the Intrinsics incremental data transfer mechanism and *client_data* to be passed to each of these procedures.

convert_callback will be called when a client requests the value of the selection. It will be called repeatedly to obtain segments of the selected value until it returns a non-NULL value of zero length. Note that this callback must be able to handle multiple transfer requests at various stages of completion. See XtConvertSelectionIncrProc(2) for more information.

lose_callback will be called, if non-NULL, when another widget or another client asserts ownership of the selection. (It will not be called if the widget relinquishes ownership by calling XtDisownSelection() or if the widget fails to gain ownership in the first place.) See XtLoseSelectionIncrProc(2) for more information.

done_callback will be called, if non-NULL, when all segments of a selection have been transferred. See XtSelectionDoneIncrProc(2) for more information.

cancel_callback will be called, if non-NULL, if a selection request is aborted because a timeout expires. See XtCancelConvertSelctionProc(2) for more information.

XtOwnSelectionIncremental() returns True if the specified widget successfully becomes the selection owner or False otherwise. The widget may fail to become the owner if some other widget has asserted ownership after this widget, as indicated by *time*.

If *done_callback* is NULL, then convert_callback must allocate memory for the transfer with one of the Intrinsics memory allocation routines, so that the Intrinsics can automatically free it. If a non-NULL *done_callback* is specified, it is the responsibility of this procedure or the *cancel_callback* to free any memory allocated by the *convert_callback*. After a selection transfer has started, only one of the *done_callback* or *cancel_callback* procedures will be invoked to indicate completion or termination of the transfer.

The *lose_callback* does not indicate completion of any in-progress transfers; it will be invoked at the time a SelectionClear event is dispatched regardless of any active transfers, which are still expected to continue.

A widget that becomes the selection owner using XtOwnSelectionIncremental() may use XtDisownSelection() to relinquish selection ownership.

Usage

Note that XtOwnSelection() simply informs the Intrinsics that a widget would like to own the selection. It is *convert_proc* that must do the real work of transferring the selected data.

Most selection data can be transferred using the Intrinsics simpler atomic transfer mechanism; see XtOwnSelection(). For some widgets, however, an incremental transfer may be more convenient. A text widget that supports disjoint selections of text, for example, may prefer to export each contiguous segment individually rather than copying them all into one large block.

Note that the Intrinsics will automatically break up and reassemble blocks of data if they are too big for transfer using the underlying X protocol; large data size is therefore not necessarily a reason for using incremental transfers.

Selection ownership is not restricted to widgets; an application can export data as well. The widget argument to `XtOwnSelectionIncremental()` serves mainly as a handle to be passed to the various procedures. You can use any widget, but it will make the most sense to use the widget that contains the data you will be exporting.

`XA_PRIMARY` and `XA_SECONDARY` are symbolic names for predefined atoms. They are defined in *<X11/Xatom.h>*. You can export data over a custom selection, but if you do, only clients that know the selection name will be able to request the data.

`XtLastTimestampProcessed()` is a convenient way to obtain a timestamp suitable for use as the *time* argument.

See Also

XtAppGetSelectionTimeout(1), *XtAppSetSelectionTimeout*(1), *XtDisownSelection*(1), *XtGetSelection-Value*(1), *XtOwnSelection*(1),
XtCancelConvertSelectionProc(2), *XtConvertSelectionIncrProc*(2), *XtLoseSelectionIncrProc*(2), *Xt-SelectionDoneIncrProc*(2).

Name

XtParent – return the parent of the specified widget.

Synopsis

```
Widget XtParent(w)
    Widget w;
```

Inputs

w   Specifies the widget whose parent is to be returned. May be of class Object or any subclass thereof.

Returns

The parent of *w*.

Description

XtParent() returns the parent widget of the specified object.

Usage

XtParent() is implemented as a function when called from application code, but is replaced by a more efficient macro when called from widget code including the file *<X11/IntrinsicP.h>*.

If XtParent() is called on a toplevel shell widget which has no parent (such as those created by XtAppInitialize() or XtAppCreateShell(), for example) it returns NULL.

**Xt Functions
and Macros**

Name

XtParseAcceleratorTable – compile an accelerator table into its internal representation.

Synopsis

```
XtAccelerators XtParseAcceleratorTable(table)
    String table;
```

Inputs

table   Specifies the accelerator table to compile.

Returns

The compiled form of `table`.

Description

`XtParseAcceleratorTable()` compiles the accelerator table into its opaque internal representation. This compiled table can be used to set the `XtNaccelerators` resource of a widget.

The syntax of the string form of an accelerator table is the same as that of a translation table, and is described in Appendix F. The interpretation of the `#augment` and `#override` directives is different in accelerator tables than in translation tables, however. This directive, if specified, applies to what will happen when the accelerator is installed; that is, whether or not the accelerator translations will override the translations in the destination widget. The default is `#augment`, which means that the accelerator translations have lower priority than the destination translations. The `#replace` directive is ignored for accelerator tables.

Usage

An accelerator binds an event sequence in one widget to actions in another. Accelerators are set as a resource of a widget but do not take effect until they are "installed" on a destination widget. See `XtInstallAccelerators()`.

When an accelerator table is specified in a resource file, it is automatically parsed by one of Xt's converters, and `XtParseAcceleratorTable()` is not used.

Another way to parse an accelerator table is to use the `XtVaTypedArg` feature at `XtVaCreateWidget()` or `XtVaSetValues()` and specify the string form directly. This will invoke the appropriate resource converter to compile the table.

See Also

XtInstallAccelerators(1), *XtInstallAllAccelerators*(1).

XtParseTranslationTable

Name

XtParseTranslationTable – compile a translation table into its internal representation.

Synopsis

```
XtTranslations XtParseTranslationTable(table)
    String table;
```

Inputs

table   Specifies the translation table to compile.

Returns

The compiled form of `table`.

Description

XtParseTranslationTable() compiles `table` into its opaque internal representation of type XtTranslations. This compiled form can then be set as the value of a widget's XtNtranslations resource, or merged with a widget's existing translation table with Xt-AugmentTranslations() or XtOverrideTranslations().

The syntax of the string representation of a translation table is documented in Appendix F.

If an empty translation table is required for any purpose, one can be obtained by calling Xt-ParseTranslationTable() and passing an empty string.

Usage

This function is generally only needed by application writers. When writing a widget, you specify a default translation table as a string, which the Intrinsics automatically parse.

You only need to use this function when you want to set translation values from C code; translation tables specified in resource files are automatically compiled by a resource converter.

It is also possible to set a translation table with the XtVaTypedArg feature of XtVa-CreateWidget() and XtVaSetValues(). This allows you to specify the translation table in string form, and have the appropriate resource converter automatically invoked to compile it.

See Also

XtAugmentTranslations(1), *XtOverrideTranslations*(1), *XtUninstallTranslations*(1).

XtPeekEvent

Name

XtPeekEvent – return, but do not remove the event at the head of an application's input queue.

Synopsis

```
Boolean XtPeekEvent(event_return)
    XEvent *event_return;
```

Inputs

event_return   Returns the event information from the head event structure in the queue.

Returns

True if the event at the head of the queue is an X event; False if it is a timer event or an alternate input source event.

Availability

XtPeekEvent() has been superseded by XtAppPeekEvent().

Description

XtPeekEvent() returns a copy of the X event at the head of the input queue, without removing it from the queue. If there is an X event, it returns True. If there are no X events pending, but there are timer or alternate events, XtPeekEvent() returns False. If there are no events pending, XtPeekEvent() blocks.

Usage

XtPeekEvent() has been superseded by XtAppPeekEvent(), which performs the same function on a per-application context basis. XtPeekEvent() now calls XtAppPeek-Event() passing the default application context created by XtInitialize(). Very few programs need multiple application contexts, and you can continue to use XtPeekEvent() if you initialize your application with XtInitialize(). We recommend, however, that you use XtAppInitialize(), XtAppPeekEvent(), and the other XtApp*() application context specific functions.

See XtAppPeekEvent() for more information.

Programs rarely need this much control over the event dispatching mechanism. Most programs use XtAppMainLoop().

See Also

XtAppMainLoop(1), *XtAppPeekEvent*(1), *XtAppPending*(1).

XtPending

Name

XtPending – determine if there are any events in an application's input queue.

Synopsis

```
XtInputMask XtPending()
```

Inputs

None.

Returns

An `XtInputMask` which indicates what kind of events, if any, are pending on *app_context*.

Availability

`XtPending()` has been superseded by `XtAppPending()`.

Description

`XtAppPending()` returns a nonzero value if there are pending events from the X server, timer, or other input sources.

The return value is a bit mask that is the OR of `XtIMXEvent` (an X event), `XtIMTimer` (a timer event—see `XtAppAddTimeOut()`), and `XtIMAlternateInput` (an alternate input event—see `XtAppAddInput()`).

Usage

`XtPending()` has been superseded by `XtAppPending()`, which performs the same function on a per-application context basis. `XtPending()` now calls `XtAppPending()` passing the default application context created by `XtInitialize()`. Very few programs need multiple application contexts, and you can continue to use `XtPending()` if you initialize your application with `XtInitialize()`. We recommend, however, that you use `XtAppInitialize()`, `XtAppPending()`, and the other `XtApp*()` application context specific functions.

See `XtAppPending()` for more information.

Programs rarely need this much control over the event dispatching mechanism. Most programs use `XtAppMainLoop()`.

See Also

XtAppMainLoop(1), *XtAppPeekEvent*(1), *XtAppPending*(1).

Name

XtPopdown – unmap a popup shell.

Synopsis

```
void XtPopdown(popup_shell)
    Widget popup_shell;
```

Inputs

popup_shell Specifies the widget shell to pop down.

Description

XtPopdown() pops down a popup shell and calls the functions registered on the shell's XtNpopdownCallback list. The "Algorithm" section below explains the details of this process.

Usage

The Intrinsics also provide other convenience routines to pop down a popup shell. To perform a pop down from a callback list, register the function XtCallbackPopdown(). To do so from a translation table, use the action XtMenuPopdown.

Popup shell widgets can be created with XtCreatePopupShell(), and can be popped up with XtPopup() or XtPopupSpringLoaded(), or with one of the built-in callback functions (XtCallbackExclusive(), XtCallbackNonexclusive(), or XtCallback-None()), or with the built-in action XtMenuPopup.

Algorithm

XtPopdown() performs the following:

- Calls XtCheckSubclass() to ensure *popup_shell*'s class is a subclass of shell-WidgetClass.

- Checks that the popped_up field of *popup_shell* is True; otherwise, it returns immediately.

- Unmaps *popup_shell*'s window and, if override_redirect is False, sends a synthetic UnmapNotify event as specified by the *Inter-Client Communications Conventions Manual*.

- If *popup_shell*'s grab_kind is either XtGrabNonexclusive or XtGrab-Exclusive, it calls XtRemoveGrab().

- Sets *popup_shell*'s popped_up field to False.

- Calls the callback procedures on the shell's popdown_callback list, specifying a pointer to the value of the shell's grab_kind field as the *call_data* argument.

See Also

XtCallbackPopdown(1), *XtCreatePopupShell*(1), *XtMenuPopdown*(1), *XtPopup*(1), *XtPopupSpring-Loaded*(1), *XtRemoveGrab*(1).

Name
XtPopup – map a popup shell.

Synopsis
```
void XtPopup(popup_shell, grab_kind)
    Widget popup_shell;
    XtGrabKind grab_kind;
```

Inputs
popup_shell Specifies a shell widget returned by XtCreatePopupShell().

grab_kind Specifies how user events should be constrained. (Can be one of XtGrab-
None, XtGrabNonexclusive, XtGrabExclusive.)

Description
XtPopup() calls the functions registered on the shell's XtNpopupCallback list and pops
up the shell widget (and its managed child). The "Algorithm" section below explains this process in more detail.

If *grab_kind* is XtGrabNone, the resulting popup is "modeless", and does not lock out
input events to the rest of the application. If it is XtGrabNonexclusive, then the resulting
popup is "modal" and locks out input to the main application window, but not to other modal
popups that are currently popped up. If it is XtGrabExclusive, then the resulting popup is
modal and locks out input to the main application window and all previous popup windows.
For more details on XtGrabNonexclusive and XtGrabExclusive, see XtAddGrab().

Usage
By default, XtPopup() maps its window to the upper-left corner of the display. You will gen-
erally want to position the shell by setting its XtNx and XtNy resources before calling Xt-
Popup().

The Intrinsics also provide convenience routines to popup a shell. To perform a pop up from a
callback list, register one of the functions XtCallbackNone(), XtCallback-
Nonexclusive(), or XtCallbackExclusive(). To do so from a translation table, use
the XtMenuPopup action.

Widgets can be popped down with XtPopdown(), the XtCallbackPopdown() callback
function, or the XtMenuPopdown action.

If you are using the Motif widget set, you will generally never need to call XtPopup() or
XtPopdown(). The Motif XmDialogShell widget automatically pops up when its child is
managed, and pops down when its child is unmanaged.

Algorithm
The XtPopup() function performs the following:

- Calls XtCheckSubclass() to ensure *popup_shell*'s class is a subclass of shell-
WidgetClass.

- Raises the window and returns if the shell's `popped_up` field is already `True`.

- Calls the callback procedures on the shell's `XtNpopupCallback` list, specifying a pointer to the value of *grab_kind* as the `call_data` argument.

- Sets the shell `popped_up` field to `True`, the shell `spring_loaded` field to `False`, and the shell `grab_kind` field from *grab_kind*.

- If the shell's `XtNcreatePopupChildProc` resource is non-NULL, `XtPopup()` calls the specified procedure with *popup_shell* as the parameter.

- If *grab_kind* is either `XtGrabNonexclusive` or `XtGrabExclusive`, it calls:

  `XtAddGrab(popup_shell, (grab_kind == XtGrabExclusive), False)`

- Calls `XtRealizeWidget()` with *popup_shell* specified.

- Calls `XMapRaised()` with the window of *popup_shell*.

Structures

The `XtGrabKind` type is defined as follows:

```
typedef enum {XtGrabNone, XtGrabNonexclusive, XtGrabExclusive} XtGrabKind;
```

See Also

XtAddGrab(1), *XtCallbackExclusive*(1), *XtCallbackNone*(1), *XtCallbackNonexclusive*(1), *XtCallback-Popdown*(1), *XtCreatePopupShell*(1), *XtMenuPopdown*(1), *XtMenuPopup*(1), *XtPopdown*(1), *XtPopup-SpringLoaded*(1).

XtPopupSpringLoaded

Name

XtPopupSpringLoaded – map a spring-loaded popup from within an application.

Synopsis

```
void XtPopupSpringLoaded(popup_shell)
    Widget popup_shell;
```

Inputs

popup_shell Specifies the shell widget to be popped up.

Availability

Release 4 and later.

Description

XtPopupSpringLoaded() calls the functions registered on the specified shell's XtNpopupCallback callback list and pops the shell up, making it a spring-loaded shell. A spring-loaded shell is one that is popped up in response to a button press and will pop down when the button is released. Spring-loaded shells have events dispatched to them specially to ensure that they receive the button up event, even if it occurs in another window. See XtAdd-Grab() for more details.

XtPopupSpringLoaded() performs exactly like XtPopup(), except that XtPopup-SpringLoaded() does the following:

- Sets the shell *spring_loaded* field to True.

- Always calls XtAddGrab() with *exclusive* set to True and *spring_loaded* set to True.

See XtPopup() for details.

Usage

You can also pop up spring loaded shells by using the XtMenuPopup action in a translation table. This predefined action calls XtPopupSpringLoaded().

Any pop up shell can be popped down with XtPopdown(), the XtCallbackPopdown() callback function, or with the XtMenuPopdown action.

XtPopupSpringLoaded() was added in Release 4, and prior to this release, the only way to pop up a spring loaded shell was to use the MenuPopup action (which has now been renamed XtMenuPopup).

See Also

XtAddGrab(1), *XtCreatePopupShell*(1), *XtMenuPopdown*(1), *XtMenuPopup*(1), *XtPopdown*(1), *Xt-Popup*(1).

XtProcessEvent

Name

XtProcessEvent – get and process one input event of a specified type.

Synopsis

```
void XtProcessEvent(mask)
    XtInputMask mask;
```

Inputs

mask   Specifies what types of events to process.

Availability

XtProcessEvent() has been superseded by XtAppProcessEvent().

Description

XtProcessEvent() processes one X event, alternate input source event or timer event. The mask argument specifies which types of events are to be processed; it is the bitwise inclusive OR (|) of any of the values XtIMXEvent, XtIMTimer, or XtIMAlternateInput, or the value XtIMAll which specifies all three event types. XtProcessEvent() calls any registered background work procedures if there are no events available, and blocks if there are no events and no work procedures.

Usage

XtProcessEvent() has been superseded by XtAppProcessEvent(), which performs the same function on a per-application context basis. XtProcessEvent() now calls XtAppProcessEvent() passing the default application context created by XtInitialize(). Very few programs need multiple application contexts, and you can continue to use XtProcessEvent() if you initialize your application with XtInitialize(). We recommend, however, that you use XtAppInitialize(), Xt-AppProcessEvent(), and the other XtApp*() application context specific functions.

See XtAppProcessEvent() for more information.

Programs rarely need this much control over the event dispatching mechanism. Most programs use XtAppMainLoop().

See Also

XtAppMainLoop(1), *XtAppPeekEvent*(1), *XtAppPending*(1), *XtAppProcessEvent*(1).

XtQueryGeometry

Name

XtQueryGeometry – query a child widget's preferred geometry.

Synopsis

```
XtGeometryResult XtQueryGeometry(w, intended, preferred_return)
    Widget w;
    XtWidgetGeometry *intended;
    XtWidgetGeometry *preferred_return;
```

Inputs

w   Specifies the widget whose geometry preferences are being queried.

intended   Specifies any changes the parent plans to make to the child's geometry, or NULL.

preferred_return
                 Returns the child widget's preferred geometry.

Returns

A response to the request: XtGeometryYes, XtGeometryNo, or XtGeometryAlmost.

Description

XtQueryGeometry() invokes a widget's query_geometry() method to determine its preferred (or at least its current) geometry. Some parents may want to ask their children what their ideal geometry would be if they were not constrained at all. Others, when about to set some aspect of the geometry (such as width), may query the child to determine what its preferred geometry would be given this new constraint. For example, a label widget that supported word-wrapping might want a larger height if its width was being made smaller.

The *intended* structure specifies the geometry values that the parent plans to set. The *geometry_return* structure returns the child's preferred geometry. Each argument has a flags field in which bits are set to indicate which of the geometry fields the respective widgets have set. The return value of the function may be one of the following values:

XtGeometryYes
    The proposed change is acceptable to the child without modifications. This means that the proposed changes are exactly what the child would prefer.

XtGeometryAlmost
    The child does not agree entirely with the proposed change. At least one field in *preferred_return* with a bit set in *preferred_return->request_mode* is different from the corresponding field in *request*, or a bit was set in *preferred_return->request_mode* that was not set in the request. The parent can use or ignore the returned values in *preferred_return*.

XtGeometryNo
    The child would prefer that no changes were made to its current geometry. The parent can respect or ignore this response.

If the child widget does not have a `query_geometry()` method, `XtQueryGeometry()` fills `preferred_return` with the widget's current geometry, sets *preferred_return->request_mode* to zero, and returns `XtGeometryYes`.

If the *intended* argument is NULL, `XtQueryGeometry()` replaces it with a pointer to an `XtWidgetGeometry` structure with a `request_mode` field of zero before calling the `query_geometry()` method.

After calling a child's `query_geometry()` method, `XtQueryGeometry()` sets all fields in *preferred_return* that do not have bits set in *preferred_return->request_mode* to the widget's current geometry values. `XtQueryGeometry()` clears all bits in *preferred_return->request_mode* before calling the `query_geometry()` method, and does not modify the bits set by the child.

See the "Background" section below for more information. See `query_geometry()`(4) for more information on how a widget's `query_geometry()` method should behave.

Usage

Only widgets should ever need to use `XtQueryGeometry()`, and then should only call it for their children. It is usually used when a composite widget is trying to layout its children, for example, when the `changed_managed()` method is called.

Many widgets can simply examine their children's `core.width` and `core.height` fields and use those while calculating layout. Widgets are supposed to set these fields to their desired geometry within their `initialize()` and `set_values()` methods. Since these are the only geometry fields that many parents care about, this technique is often sufficient. If a widget is re-laying out its children from its `resize()` method, however, it may make more sense to use `XtQueryGeometry()`. If a widget has been given a size that is too small, then its children may also be smaller than they prefer. In this case, the children's current sizes are not their preferred sizes, and they must be asked how large they would like to be.

Note that on return from `XtQueryGeometry()`, `preferred_return` always contains the preferred or current geometry (which the widget sets to its preferred geometry when it initializes itself) of the widget. This means that a parent that is willing to respect its child's layout wishes can call `XtQueryGeometry()` and use the contents of *preferred_return* whatever the return value of the function is. If a parent wants to query a preferred size without proposing any particular changes, it can pass NULL for *intended*.

If a parent is not willing to respond to return values of either `XtGeometryAlmost` or `XtGeometryNo` need not bother to call `XtQueryGeometry()`; it can just make the geometry changes that it plans to make.

The cases described in the above two paragraphs are widgets that always respect or never respect their children's preferences. Neither case takes advantage of the full power of this geometry querying scheme. The most common interesting use of `XtQueryGeometry()`, is when a parent wants to constrain the width or height of a child, and would like to know the child's preferred size in the other dimension. A menubar laid out in a Form widget, for example, will probably be laid out across the top and have its width constrained to be equal to the width of the form. If the form becomes too small to display all the items in the menu bar, the menubar might want to wrap onto a second line. In this case, the parent would set the width in *intended*, and use the height returned in *preferred_return*, regardless of the return value of the function. Note that in this case the parent is ignoring any return values of Xt-GeometryNo—it must constrain the width of the menubar even if the child would prefer that the width not be constrained. Many widgets are not as sophisticated as this hypothetical menu bar widget, and cannot to adjust their layout when they find that only one dimension is constrained. Even these children will return a preferred size however, and the form can use the preferred height and ignore the preferred width. The Athena Box widget is an example of a widget that modifies its layout when it finds that it is constrained in one dimension.

Note that if XtQueryGeometry() returns XtGeometryYes, the parent can simply proceed with the geometry changes it indicated in intended without examining the contents of preferred_return. In practice, however, this return value is uncommon, and it may not be worth writing special case code to handle it. In the examples given above, the parent never even needs to check the return value of the function.

Example

Only three widgets in the Athena widget set call XtQueryGeometry(), and none of the Intrinsics widgets call it. The following code is from the Athena Viewport widget.

```
if (!w->viewport.allowvert) {
    intended->height = *clip_height;
    intended->request_mode = CWHeight;
}
if (!w->viewport.allowhoriz) {
    intended->width = *clip_width;
    intended->request_mode = CWWidth;
}

if ( query ) {
    if ( (w->viewport.allowvert || w->viewport.allowhoriz) ) {
        XtQueryGeometry( child, intended, &preferred );

        if ( !(intended->request_mode & CWWidth) )
            if ( preferred.request_mode & CWWidth )
                intended->width = preferred.width;
            else
                intended->width = child->core.width;

        if ( !(intended->request_mode & CWHeight) )
            if ( preferred.request_mode & CWHeight )
                intended->height = preferred.height;
            else
                intended->height = child->core.height;
    }
}
```

Background

If XtQueryGeometry() is called from within a geometry_manager() procedure for the widget that issued XtMakeGeometryRequest() or XtMakeResizeRequest(), the results are not guaranteed to be consistent with the requested changes. The change request passed to the geometry manager takes precedence over the preferred geometry.

The query_geometry() procedure may assume that no XtMakeResizeRequest() or XtMakeGeometryRequest() is in progress for the specified widget; that is, it is not required to construct a reply consistent with the requested geometry if such a request were actually outstanding.

Structures

The possible return values of XtQueryGeometry() are defined as follows:

```
typedef enum {
    XtGeometryYes,    /* Request accepted */
    XtGeometryNo,     /* Request denied */
    XtGeometryAlmost,/* Request denied but willing to take reply */
    XtGeometryDone    /* never returned by XtQueryGeometry() */
} XtGeometryResult;
```

The XtWidgetGeometry structure is similar to but not identical to the corresponding Xlib structure:

```
typedef unsigned long XtGeometryMask;

typedef struct {
    XtGeometryMask request_mode;
    Position x, y;
    Dimension width, height;
    Dimension border_width;
    Widget sibling;
    int stack_mode;
} XtWidgetGeometry;
```

XtQueryGeometry(), like the Xlib XConfigureWindow() function, uses request_mode to determine which fields in the XtWidgetGeometry structure you that the parent and the child have set. The request_mode definitions are from *<X11/X.h>*:

```
#define    CWX              (1<<0)
#define    CWY              (1<<1)
#define    CWWidth          (1<<2)
#define    CWHeight         (1<<3)
#define    CWBorderWidth    (1<<4)
#define    CWSibling        (1<<5)
#define    CWStackMode      (1<<6)
```

The stack_mode definitions are from *<X11/X.h>*:

```
#define    Above            0
#define    Below            1
#define    TopIf            2
```

```
#define   BottomIf        3
#define   Opposite        4
```

The Intrinsics also support the following value:

```
#define   XtSMDontChange    5
```

For precise definitions of `Above`, `Below`, `TopIf`, `BottomIf`, and `Opposite`, see the reference page for `XConfigureWindow()` in Volume Two, *Xlib Reference Manual*. `XtSMDontChange` indicates that the widget wants its current stacking order preserved.

See Also

XtMakeGeometryRequest(1),
query_geometry(4).

*Xt Functions
and Macros*

XtRealizeWidget

Name

XtRealizeWidget – realize a widget instance.

Synopsis

```
void XtRealizeWidget(w)
    Widget w;
```

Inputs

w   Specifies the widget to be realized. Must be of class Core or any subclass thereof.

Description

XtRealizeWidget() creates windows for the specified widget and all of its descendants. If the specified widget is already realized, XtRealizeWidget() simply returns. When a widget is first created, no X window is created along with it. Realizing a widget is the term for creating this window, and no widget can appear on the screen until it is realized. The reason widget creation and window creation are handled separately is one of efficiency: when an interface is first created, there is an initial process of negotiating geometry and assigning a layout to each widget. If the widgets had windows at this point, the geometry negotiation would require many XConfigureWindow() calls to the X server, which would significantly slow down application startup time.

The "Algorithm" section below describes the procedure followed by XtRealizeWidget().

Usage

Most applications will call XtRealizeWidget() once just prior to calling XtAppMainLoop() to process events. The argument to XtRealizeWidget() is usually the top-level widget returned from XtAppInitialize(). If more widgets are subsequently created, they do not need to be realized because when a widget is created as the child of a realized widget, it is automatically realized. Popup shells are also automatically realized, if necessary, when they are popped up.

You can test whether a widget is realized with XtIsRealized(). Until a widget is realized, certain functions will not operate as expected. XtWindow(), for example will not return a valid window if called with an unrealized widget.

You can unrealize a widget (destroy its window) but leave the widget structure intact with XtUnrealizeWidget().

Algorithm

If the widget is already realized, XtRealizeWidget() simply returns. Otherwise it performs the following:

- Binds all action names in the widget's translation table to procedures.

- Makes a postorder traversal of the widget tree rooted at the specified widget and calls each non-NULL change_managed() method of all composite widgets that have one or more managed children.

- Constructs an `XSetWindowAttributes` structure filled in with information derived from the Core widget fields and calls the `realize()` method for the widget, which adds any widget-specific attributes and creates the X window.

- If the widget is not a subclass of compositeWidgetClass, `XtRealizeWidget()` returns; otherwise it continues and performs the following:

  - Descends recursively to each of the widget's managed children and calls the `realize()` methods. Primitive widgets that instantiate children are responsible for realizing those children themselves.

  - Maps all of the managed children windows that have `mapped_when_managed` `True`. If a widget is managed but `mapped_when_managed` is `False`, the widget is allocated visual space but is not displayed.

If the widget is a top-level shell widget (that is, it has no parent), and `mapped_when_managed` is `True`, `XtRealizeWidget()` maps the widget window.

`XtCreateWidget()`, `XtVaCreateWidget()`, `XtRealizeWidget()`, `XtManage-Children()`, `XtUnmanageChildren()`, `XtUnrealizeWidget()`, `XtSetMapped-WhenManaged()`, and `XtDestroyWidget()` maintain the following invariants:

- If a composite widget is realized, then all its managed children are realized.

- If a composite widget is realized, then all its managed children that have `mapped_when_managed` `True` are mapped.

All Intrinsics functions and all widget routines should accept either realized or unrealized widgets. When calling the `realize()` or `change_managed()` methods for children of a composite widget, `XtRealizeWidget()` calls the procedures in reverse order of appearance in the CompositePart `children` list. By default, this ordering of the realize procedures will result in the stacking order of any newly created subwindows being top-to-bottom in the order of appearance on the list, and the most recently created child will be at the bottom.

See Also
XtIsRealized(1), *XtUnrealizeWidget*(1),
realize(4).

XtRealloc

Name

XtRealloc – change the size of an allocated block of storage.

Synopsis

```
char *XtRealloc(ptr, num);
    char *ptr;
    Cardinal num;
```

Inputs

ptr   Specifies a pointer to memory allocated with `XtMalloc()`, `XtCalloc()`, or `XtRealloc()`, or `NULL`.

num   Specifies the new number of bytes of memory desired in the block.

Returns

A pointer to allocated memory.

Description

`XtRealloc()` changes the size of the block of allocated memory pointed to by *ptr* to be at least *num* bytes large. In order to make this size change, it may have to allocate a new block of memory and copy the contents of the old block (or as much as will fit) into the new block. If it allocates a new block of memory, it frees the old block. In either case, it returns a pointer to a block of memory which is of the requested size. If there is insufficient memory to allocate the new block, `XtRealloc()` terminates by calling `XtErrorMsg()`.

If *ptr* is `NULL`, `XtRealloc()` simply calls `XtMalloc()` to allocate a block of memory of the requested size.

Usage

Note that `XtRealloc()` may move the contents of your allocated memory to a new location; the return value may or may not be the same as *ptr*. Not all memory can be safely reallocated. If there are multiple pointers to a block of memory scattered through out an application (such as pointers to a widget record), then reallocating that memory is not safe, because all pointers to it cannot be updated. Other memory (such as the array of children maintained privately by the Composite widget class) can be safely updated because there should be only one pointer to it in the application (in this case the pointer is the `composite.children` field of the widget). These cautions are no different than those required with the standard `realloc()` function.

In most cases, you will have to cast the return value of `XtRealloc()` to an appropriate pointer type.

Note that because `XtRealloc()` behaves like `XtMalloc()` when passed a `NULL` pointer, (something that `realloc()` does not do), you don't have to write special case code to allocate the first chunk of memory with `XtMalloc()` and subsequent chunks with `Xt-Realloc()`; you can simply use `XtRealloc()` everywhere.

Memory allocated with `XtRealloc()` must be deallocated with `XtFree()`. The function `XtRealloc()` is implemented by the Toolkit independently of the particular environment, so programs ported to a system not supporting `malloc` will still work.

See Also

XtCalloc(1), *XtFree*(1), *XtMalloc*(1), *XtNew*(1), *XtNewString*(1).

XtRegisterCaseConverter

Name

XtRegisterCaseConverter – register a case converter.

Synopsis

```
void XtRegisterCaseConverter(display, proc, start, stop)
    Display *display;
    XtCaseProc proc;
    KeySym start;
    KeySym stop;
```

Inputs

display	Specifies the display from which the key events are to come.
proc	Specifies the XtCaseProc that is to do the conversions.
start	Specifies the first keysym for which this converter is valid.
stop	Specifies the last keysym for which this converter is valid.

Description

XtRegisterCaseConverter() registers *proc* with the Intrinsics as a procedure to be called in order to determine the correct uppercase and lowercase versions of any keysyms between *start* and *stop* inclusive. The registered converter overrides any previous converters registered in that range.

See XtCaseProc(2) for a description of how to write a case converter procedure.

Usage

The Translation Manager uses case converters as part of its keycode-to-keysym translation process. The default converter understands case conversion for all keysyms defined in the X11 protocol. You will probably never need to register a case converter unless you are working with non-standard keysyms.

The only way to remove a converter is to register a new one, perhaps an "identity" converter which performs no conversion at all.

The registered case converters are invoked by the translation manager, and can also be explicitly called with the function XtConvertCase().

Structures

```
typedef XID KeySym;
```

See Also

XtConvertCase(1), *XtGetKeysymTable*(1), *XtKeysymToKeycodeList*(1), *XtSetKeyTranslator*(1), *XtTranslateKeycode*(1),
XtCaseProc(2), *XtKeyProc*(2).

Name

XtRegisterGrabAction – register an action procedure as one that needs a passive grab to function properly.

Synopsis

```
void XtRegisterGrabAction(action_proc, owner_events, event_mask,
        pointer_mode, keyboard_mode)
    XtActionProc action_proc;
    Boolean owner_events;
    unsigned int event_mask;
    int pointer_mode, keyboard_mode;
```

Inputs

action_proc Specifies the action procedure that requires a passive grab.

owner_events

Specifies whether pointer events generated during the grab are reported normally within the application (`True`) or only to the widget that invokes the action (`False`).

event_mask Specifies the event mask to take effect during the grab.

pointer_mode

Controls processing of pointer events during the grab. Either `GrabMode-Sync` or `GrabModeAsync`.

keyboard_mode

Controls processing of keyboard events during the grab. Either `GrabMode-Sync` or `GrabModeAsync`.

Availability

Release 4 and later.

Description

XtRegisterGrabAction() registers *action_proc* as an action procedure that needs to have a passive grab in order for it to work properly. When this action appears in a translation table, the Intrinsics will automatically perform the appropriate passive key or button grab, depending on the event sequence that invokes the action. The *owner_events*, *event_mask*, *pointer_mode*, and *keyboard_mode* arguments are passed to XtGrab-Key() or XtGrabButton() when the passive grab is made.

See the "Background" section below for full details. See XtGrabKey() and XtGrab-Button() for more information about passive grabs.

Usage

When you passively grab a button/modifiers or key/modifiers combination, all events that occur when that button or key and those modifiers are down will be delivered to the widget you specify or to your application, regardless of the location of the pointer.

Very few action procedures need a grab to function properly. Note that a button grab is always automatically invoked between a button down and the corresponding button up event, so that a text widget, for example, that wanted to scroll its text when the user dragged the mouse out of the window could do so without registering the action procedure with this function.

Grabs are required by some kinds of popup menus, and `XtRegisterGrabAction()` is used by the predefined action `XtMenuPopup`.

Background

`XtRegisterGrabAction()` adds the specified *action_proc* to a list known to the translation manager. When a widget is realized, or when the translations of a realized widget or the accelerators installed on a realized widget are modified, its translation table and any installed accelerators are scanned for action procs on this list.

If any are invoked on `ButtonPress` or `KeyPress` events as the only or final event in a sequence, the Intrinsics will call `XtGrabButton()` or `XtGrabKey()` for the widget with every button or keycode that maps to the event detail field, passing the specified *owner_events*, *event_mask*, *pointer_mode*, and *keyboard_mode*.

- For `ButtonPress` events, the modifiers specified in the grab are determined directly from the translation specification, and *confine_to* and *cursor* are specified as `None`.

- For `KeyPress` events:

    + If the translation table entry specifies colon (:) in the modifier list, the modifiers are determined by calling the key translator procedure registered for the display and by calling `XtGrabKey()` for every combination of standard modifiers that map the key-code to the specified event detail keysym, and ORing any modifiers specified in the translation table entry, and *event_mask* is ignored.

    + If the translation table entry does not specify colon in the modifier list, the modifiers specified in the grab are those specified in the translation table entry only.

For both `ButtonPress` and `KeyPress` events, "don't care modifiers" are ignored unless the translation entry explicitly specifies "Any" in the modifiers field.

If the specified *action_proc* is already registered for the calling process, the new values replace the previously specified values for any widgets that are realized following the call, but existing grabs are not altered on currently-realized widgets.

When translations or installed accelerators are modified for a realized widget, any previous key or button grabs that were registered as a result of the old bindings are released, provided that the old bindings do not appear in the new bindings and are not explicitly grabbed by the client with `XtGrabKey()` or `XtGrabButton()`.

See Also

XtAddActions(1), *XtAppAddActionHook*(1), *XtAppAddActions*(1), *XtCallActionProc*(1), *XtGetAction-Keysym*(1), *XtRemoveActionHook*(1).

Name

XtReleaseGC – deallocate a shared GC when it is no longer needed.

Synopsis

```
void XtReleaseGC(object, gc)
    Widget object;
    GC gc;
```

Inputs

object   Specifies any object on the display for which the GC was created; may be of class Object or any subclass thereof.

gc   Specifies the GC to be deallocated.

Description

XtReleaseGC() deallocates a shared GC allocated with XtGetGC() or XtAllocate-GC(). The Intrinsics maintain a reference count on all shared GCs and call XFreeGC() when the last user of a GC releases it.

See Also

XtAllocateGC(1), *XtGetGC*(1).

Name

XtRemoveActionHook – unregister an action hook procedure.

Synopsis

```
void XtRemoveActionHook(id)
     XtActionHookId id;
```

Inputs

id   Identifies the action hook to be removed.

Availability

Release 4 and later.

Description

XtRemoveActionHook() removes the specified action hook procedure from the list in which it was registered. The *id* argument is the value returned by XtAppAddAction-Hook() when the action hook procedure was registered.

Structures

XtActionHookId is an opaque type.

See Also

XtAppAddActionHook(1),
XtActionHookProc(2).

Name

XtRemoveAllCallbacks – delete all procedures from a callback list.

Synopsis

```
void XtRemoveAllCallbacks(object, callback_name)
    Widget object;
    String callback_name;
```

Inputs

object   Specifies the object whose callbacks are to be deleted; may be of class Object or any subclass thereof.

callback_name Specifies the name of the callback list from which procedures are to be removed.

Description

`XtRemoveAllCallbacks()` removes all callback procedures registered on the callback list named by *callback_name* in the object *object*. It also frees all memory allocated by the Intrinsics for that callback list.

Usage

This is a dangerous function to call, because callbacks that you are unaware of may have been registered on any list of your object. Simply creating a widget may cause special resource converter destructor procedures to be registered on the widget's destroy callback, for example. If you use a convenience routine that creates both a dialog shell and the dialog child widget, as a further example, that convenience routine may register a destroy callback on the child so that the shell will be automatically destroyed if the child is destroyed.

In general, you should use `XtRemoveCallback()` to remove specified procedure/data pairs that you have registered on a list. You can also use `XtRemoveCallbacks()` to remove an array of procedure/data pairs.

See Also

XtAddCallback(1), *XtAddCallbacks*(1), *XtCallCallbacks*(1), *XtRemoveCallback*(1), *XtRemoveCallbacks*(1).

Xt Functions and Macros

XtRemoveCallback

Name
XtRemoveCallback – remove a callback from a callback list.

Synopsis
```
void XtRemoveCallback(object, callback_name, callback, client_data)
    Widget object;
    String callback_name;
    XtCallbackProc callback;
    XtPointer client_data;
```

Inputs
object Specifies the object; may be of class Object or any subclass thereof.

callback_name
Specifies the name of the callback list from which the callback is to be removed.

callback Specifies the callback procedure which is to be removed.

client_data Specifies the data which was registered with the specified procedure.

Description
XtRemoveCallback() removes the *callback*/*client_data* pair from the callback list named by *callback_name* of the object *object*. If there is no entry in the specified callback list that matches both *callback* and *client_data*, XtRemoveCallback() returns without generating a warning message.

Usage
Note that there is no way to remove all calls to a specified procedure from a callback list. To remove a procedure from a callback list, you must specify the *client_data* it was registered with.

If you want to remove several procedure/data pairs from a callback list at the same time, use XtRemoveCallbacks().

See Also
XtAddCallback(1), *XtAddCallbacks*(1), *XtCallCallbacks*(1), *XtRemoveAllCallbacks*(1), *XtRemove-Callbacks*(1).

XtRemoveCallbacks

Name

XtRemoveCallbacks – remove a list of callbacks from a callback list.

Synopsis

```
void XtRemoveCallbacks(object, callback_name, callbacks)
    Widget object;
    String callback_name;
    XtCallbackList callbacks;
```

Inputs

object   Specifies the object; may be of class Object or any subclass thereof.

callback_name
                    Specifies the callback list from which the callbacks are to be removed.

callbacks   Specifies a NULL-terminated array of procedure/data pairs to be removed from the callback list.

Description

XtRemoveCallbacks() removes each of the procedure/data pairs in *callbacks* from the callback list named by *callback_name* of object *object*.

Each callback is removed only if it exactly matches a procedure/data pair registered on the callback list. If a procedure/data pair in the *callbacks* array does not match a pair on the callback list, XtRemoveCallbacks() does nothing with that array element and does not generate a warning message.

Because there is not an argument that specifies the number of elements in the *callbacks* array, the last element of this array should be a XtCallbackRec structure with NULL in both fields.

Usage

Because XtRemoveCallbacks() requires the caller to allocate and initialize an array of procedure/data pairs, it may often be easier to simply call XtRemoveCallback() repeatedly. The exception is when a statically initialized array is used to both add and remove callbacks.

Structures

```
typedef struct _XtCallbackRec {
    XtCallbackProc  callback;
    XtPointer       closure;
} XtCallbackRec, *XtCallbackList;
```

See Also

XtAddCallback(1), *XtAddCallbacks*(1), *XtCallCallbacks*(1), *XtRemoveAllCallbacks*(1), *XtRemoveCallback*(1).

Name

XtRemoveEventHandler – remove an event handler, or change the conditions under which it is called.

Synopsis

```
void XtRemoveEventHandler(w, event_mask, nonmaskable, proc, client_data)
    Widget w;
    EventMask event_mask;
    Boolean nonmaskable;
    XtEventHandler proc;
    XtPointer client_data;
```

Inputs

w   Specifies the widget for which this handler is registered. Must be of class Core or any subclass thereof.

event_mask   Specifies the events for which to unregister this handler.

nonmaskable   Specifies whether this handler should be unregistered for nonmaskable events.

proc   Specifies the handler procedure.

client_data   Specifies the client data with which the procedure was registered.

Description

XtRemoveEventHandler() stops the *proc/client_data* event handler pair registered with XtAddEventHandler() or XtInsertEventHandler() from being called from widget *w* in response to the events specified in *event_mask*. In addition, if *nonmaskable* is True, then the handler will no longer be called in response to the nonmaskable events: GraphicsExpose, NoExpose, SelectionClear, SelectionRequest, SelectionNotify, ClientMessage, and MappingNotify.

A handler is removed only if both the procedure *proc* and *client_data* match a previously registered handler/data pair. If a handler to be removed fails to match a procedure, or if it has been registered with a different value of *client_data*, XtRemoveEventHandler() returns without reporting an error.

XtRemoveEventHandler() accepts the special value XtAllEvents in the *event_handler* argument as a signal that the event handler should no longer be called in response to any maskable events. This value should not be combined with other event mask bits, and should not be used to select events in other functions.

If the widget is realized, and no other handler requires events of any of the specified types, Xt-RemoveEventHandler() calls XSelectInput(), as necessary to prevent the widget from receiving further events of those types.

Usage

Note that XtRemoveEventHandler() does not necessarily *remove* an event handler; rather, it modifies the conditions for which it is called. To prevent an event handler from being called at all, call XtRemoveEventHandler() with an *event_mask* of XtAllEvents and with *nonmaskable* True.

To remove or change the event mask for a "raw" event handler registered with XtAddRaw-EventHandler() or XtInsertRawEventHandler(), use XtRemoveRawEvent-Handler().

Structures

Each of the event types listed in the table below set a single bit in an event mask. The *event_mask* argument is formed by combining these symbols with the bitwise OR operator (|). Note that the nonmaskable event types do not appear in this table and cannot be requested in an event mask.

NoEventMask	Button1MotionMask	StructureNotifyMask
KeyPressMask	Button2MotionMask	ResizeRedirectMask
KeyReleaseMask	Button3MotionMask	SubstructureNotifyMask
ButtonPressMask	Button4MotionMask	SubstructureRedirectMask
ButtonReleaseMask	Button5MotionMask	FocusChangeMask
EnterWindowMask	ButtonMotionMask	PropertyChangeMask
LeaveWindowMask	KeymapStateMask	ColormapChangeMask
PointerMotionMask	ExposureMask	OwnerGrabButtonMask
PointerMotionHintMask	VisibilityChangeMask	

See Appendix C, *Event Reference*, for more information on event types and masks.

In addition to these standard X event masks, the Intrinsics define a special value for use by this function:

```
/* XtAllEvents is valid only for XtRemoveEventHandler and
 * XtRemoveRawEventHandler; don't use it to select events!
 */
#define XtAllEvents ((EventMask) -1L)
```

See Also

XtAddEventHandler(1), *XtInsertEventHandler*(1), *XtRemoveRawEventHandler*(1), *XtEventHandler*(2).

XtRemoveGrab

Name

XtRemoveGrab – redirect user input from modal widget back to normal destination.

Synopsis

```
void XtRemoveGrab(w)
    Widget w;
```

Inputs

w   Specifies the widget to remove from the modal cascade.

Description

XtRemoveGrab() removes the specified widget from the modal cascade, along with any widgets which were more recently added to the cascade. It issues a warning if the specified widget is not in the modal cascade.

See XtAddGrab() for more information about the modal cascade, and how events are dispatched to it.

Usage

The modal cascade is the set of modal widgets currently popped up. If there is a modal cascade, XtDispatchEvent() does not deliver events to the rest of the application; instead it ignores those events or delivers them to a widget in the modal cascade.

To add a widget to the modal cascade, use XtAddGrab(). Note that this function does not actually issue a grab; it simulates one by changing the way events are dispatched.

Most applications will never need to call XtAddGrab() or XtRemoveGrab(). The functions XtPopup(), XtPopupSpringLoaded(), and XtPopdown() do so automatically.

See Also

XtAddGrab(1), *XtDispatchEvent*(1), *XtPopdown*(1), *XtPopup*(1), *XtPopupSpringLoaded*(1).

          X Toolkit Intrinsics Reference Manual

XtRemoveInput

Name

XtRemoveInput – unregister an alternate input source callback.

Synopsis

```
void XtRemoveInput(id)
    XtInputId id;
```

Inputs

id   Identifies the input source and callback procedure.

Description

XtRemoveInput() causes the Intrinsics to stop calling a callback procedure registered with XtAppAddInput(). The id argument is a handle returned by the call to XtAppAdd-Input() which registered the input callback. If there are not any other callbacks registered for the same input source, the Intrinsics stop monitoring that source.

Usage

Alternate input events (on POSIX systems) usually signal that there is data available to be read on a file descriptor, which is often a pipe or socket. See XtAppAddInput() for more information.

Structures

The XtInputId type is defined as follows:

```
typedef unsigned long XtInputId;
```

See Also

XtAppAddInput(1),
XtInputCallbackProc(2).

XtRemoveRawEventHandler

Name

XtRemoveRawEventHandler – remove a raw event handler, or change the conditions under which it is called.

Synopsis

```
void XtRemoveRawEventHandler(w, event_mask, nonmaskable, proc, client_data)
    Widget w;
    EventMask event_mask;
    Boolean nonmaskable;
    XtEventHandler proc;
    XtPointer client_data;
```

Inputs

w   Specifies the widget for which this handler is registered. Must be of class Core or any subclass thereof.

event_mask   Specifies the events for which to unregister this handler.

nonmaskable Specifies whether this handler should be unregistered for nonmaskable events.

proc   Specifies the handler procedure.

client_data Specifies the client data with which the procedure was registered.

Description

XtRemoveRawEventHandler() stops the *proc/client_data* event handler pair registered with XtAddRawEventHandler() or XtInsertRawEventHandler() from being called from widget *w* in response to the events specified in *event_mask*. In addition, if *nonmaskable* is True, then the handler will no longer be called in response to the nonmaskable events: GraphicsExpose, NoExpose, SelectionClear, SelectionRequest, SelectionNotify, ClientMessage, and MappingNotify.

A handler is removed only if both the procedure *proc* and *client_data* match a previously registered handler/data pair. If a handler to be removed fails to match a procedure, or if it has been registered with a different value of *client_data*, XtRemoveRawEventHandler() returns without reporting an error.

XtRemoveRawEventHandler() accepts the special value XtAllEvents in the *event_handler* argument as a signal that the event handler should no longer be called in response to any maskable events. This value should not be combined with other event mask bits, and should not be used to select events in other functions.

Because the procedure is a raw event handler, this function does not affect the widget's event mask and never calls XSelectInput().

Usage

Note that XtRemoveRawEventHandler() does not necessarily *remove* an event handler; rather, it modifies the conditions for which it is called. To prevent an event handler from being called at all, call XtRemoveRawEventHandler() with an *event_mask* of XtAllEvents and with *nonmaskable* True.

To remove or change the event mask for a event handler registered with `XtAddEvent-Handler()` or `XtInsertEventHandler()`, use `XtRemoveEventHandler()`.

Structures

Each of the event types listed in the table below set a single bit in an event mask. The *event_mask* argument is formed by combining these symbols with the bitwise OR operator (|). Note that the nonmaskable event types do not appear in this table and cannot be requested in an event mask.

NoEventMask	Button1MotionMask	StructureNotifyMask
KeyPressMask	Button2MotionMask	ResizeRedirectMask
KeyReleaseMask	Button3MotionMask	SubstructureNotifyMask
ButtonPressMask	Button4MotionMask	SubstructureRedirectMask
ButtonReleaseMask	Button5MotionMask	FocusChangeMask
EnterWindowMask	ButtonMotionMask	PropertyChangeMask
LeaveWindowMask	KeymapStateMask	ColormapChangeMask
PointerMotionMask	ExposureMask	OwnerGrabButtonMask
PointerMotionHintMask	VisibilityChangeMask	

See Appendix C, *Event Reference*, for more information on event types and masks.

In addition to these standard X event masks, the Intrinsics define a special value for use by this function:

```
/* XtAllEvents is valid only for XtRemoveEventHandler and
 * XtRemoveRawEventHandler; don't use it to select events!
 */
#define XtAllEvents ((EventMask) -1L)
```

See Also

XtAddRawEventHandler(1), *XtInsertRawEventHandler*(1), *XtRemoveEventHandler*(1), *XtEventHandler*(2).

XtRemoveTimeOut

Name

XtRemoveTimeOut – unregister a timeout procedure.

Synopsis

```
void XtRemoveTimeOut(id)
    XtIntervalId id;
```

Inputs

id   Identifies the timeout interval and the timeout callback to be removed.

Description

XtRemoveTimeOut() unregisters the timeout callback identified by *id*. *id* is the handle returned by the call to XtAppAddTimeOut() that registered the timeout interval and the procedure.

Usage

Note that timeouts are automatically removed once they expire and the callback has been called; therefore, you often do not need to call XtRemoveTimeOut(). On the other hand, if you need user input within a specified amount of time, for example, then you should register a timeout callback, and if the input arrives before the timeout callback is called, then you should remove the timeout callback so that it isn't called when the application is not expecting it.

Structures

The XtIntervalId structure is defined as follows:

```
typedef unsigned long XtIntervalId;
```

See Also

XtAppAddTimeOut(1),
XtTimerCallbackProc(2).

Name

XtRemoveWorkProc – unregister a work procedure.

Synopsis

```
void XtRemoveWorkProc(id)
    XtWorkProcId id;
```

Inputs

id   Identifies the work procedure to unregister.

Description

XtRemoveWorkProc() explicitly removes the specified background work procedure. The *id* argument is the handle returned by XtAppAddWorkProc() when the procedure was registered.

Usage

Note that a work procedure is removed automatically if it returns True. In many cases, therefore, you do not have to call XtRemoveWorkProc().

Structures

The XtWorkProcId type is defined as follows:

```
typedef unsigned long XtWorkProcId;
```

See Also

XtAppAddWorkProc(1),
XtWorkProc(2).

Xt Functions and Macros

XtResizeWidget

Name
XtResizeWidget – resize a child widget.

Synopsis
```
void XtResizeWidget(w, width, height, border_width)
    Widget w;
    Dimension width;
    Dimension height;
    Dimension border_width;
```

Inputs
w
Specifies the widget to be resized. Must be of class RectObj or any subclass thereof.

width, height, border_width
Specify the new widget size and border width.

Description
XtResizeWidget() changes the width, height, and border width of w as specified. It stores the new values into the widget record, and if the widget is realized, calls XConfigure-Window() to change the size of the widget's window. Whether or not the widget is realized, XtResizeWidget() calls the widget's resize() method to notify it of the size changes.

If the specified size is equal to the current size, XtResizeWidget() returns immediately without calling XConfigureWindow() or the resize() method.

See resize()(4) for information about the responsibilities of the resize() method.

Usage
XtResizeWidget() should only be used by a parent widget to change the size of its children. If an application wishes to change the size of a widget, it should set the XtNwidth and XtNheight (and possibly the XtNborderWidth) resources of the widget. If a widget would like to resize itself, it must *request* a new size with XtMakeGeometryRequest() or XtMakeResizeRequest().

To move a child widget, use XtMoveWidget(). To move and resize a widget in the same call, use XtConfigureWidget().

See Also
XtConfigureWidget(1), *XtMakeGeometryRequest*(1), *XtMakeResizeRequest*(1), *XtMoveWidget*(1), *XtResizeWindow*(1),
resize(4).

Name

XtResizeWindow – resize a widget's window.

Synopsis

```
void XtResizeWindow(w)
    Widget w;
```

Inputs

w   Specifies the widget. Must be of class Core or any subclass thereof.

Description

XtResizeWindow() calls the Xlib function XConfigureWindow() to make the window of the specified widget match its Core width, height, and border_width fields. XtResizeWindow() does not call the widget's resize() method.

The call to XConfigureWindow() is done unconditionally because there is no way to tell (without a server query) whether the widget's window already has the specified size.

Usage

You should rarely need to call XtResizeWindow(), and should only call it from widget code. Usually, a widget will call XtResizeWidget() to set size values in the widget's fields and call XConfigureWindow().

You only need to use XtResizeWindow() when a widget's core size fields have gotten out of sync with the window's actual size (this will not happen if you follow standard geometry management procedures) and want to force the widget's window to match the size specified in the widget's fields. In this case, XtResizeWindow() will not work, because it assumes that the widget's fields and the window size are in sync and would decide that XConfigureWindow() does not need to be called.

See Also

XtResizeWidget(1).

XtResolvePathname

Name

XtResolvePathname – search for a file using standard substitutions in a path list.

Synopsis

```
String XtResolvePathname(display, type, filename, suffix, path,
        substitutions, num_substitutions, predicate)
    Display *display;
    String type, filename, suffix, path;
    Substitution substitutions;
    Cardinal num_substitutions;
    XtFilePredicate predicate;
```

Inputs

display Specifies the display.

type Specifies the type of the file to find, or NULL; substituted for %T.

filename Specifies the base name of the file to find, or NULL; substituted for %N.

suffix Specifies the suffix of the file to find, or NULL; substituted for %S.

path Specifies the list of file specifications to test, or NULL.

substitutions
Specifies a list of additional substitutions to make into the path, or NULL.

num_substitutions
Specifies the number of entries in *substitutions*.

predicate Specifies a procedure called to test each potential file name, or NULL.

Returns

A filename, or NULL if no appropriate file was found.

Availability

Release 4 and later.

Description

XtResolvePathname() is used to find a file (often a resource file) which has a name, and is installed in a directory, that depends on the language in use by the application, the type of the file, the class name of the application, and, in Release 5, the value of the customization resource.

XtResolvePathname() performs a number of standard substitutions, and any extra substitutions specified in *substitutions*, on each colon-separated element of *path* in turn, and passes the resulting string to *predicate*. If *predicate* returns True, XtResolve-Pathname() returns the string. If *predicate* does not return True for any of the elements in *path*, XtResolvePathname() returns NULL.

It is the responsibility of the caller to free the returned string using XtFree() when it is no longer needed.

If *predicate* is NULL, then an internal predicate is used that returns True if the string is the name of a readable file (and is not a directory), and returns False otherwise. See XtFile-Predicate(2) for more details on how to write a customized file predicate procedure.

If any element in *path* contains a percent sign followed by one of the standard characters N, T, S, C, L, l, t, or c, then that two-character sequence is replaced with one of the standard substitutions described below. If a percent sign is followed by a substitution character specified in *substitutions*, then that non-standard substitution will be performed. See the "Background" section below for more information on non-standard substitutions. The standard substitutions are as follows:

%T The value of the *type* argument. This is the general category of file, such as "app-defaults," "bitmap," or "help." If *type* is NULL, the empty string is used.

%N The value of the *filename* argument, or the application's class name if *filename* is NULL. (The application's class name is passed to XtAppInitialize() or Xt-DisplayInitialize() and is associated with the display).

%S The value of the *suffix* argument. For app-defaults file, this should be NULL. For bitmap files, however, it might be ".bm". If *suffix* is NULL, the empty string is used.

%C The value of the customization resource in the database associated with *display*. The user may set this resource to a value such as "–color" to indicate that files (resource files, bitmaps, etc.) appropriate for a color screen should be found, or to "–mono" if they are using a monochrome screen. If this resource is not specified, the empty string is used for the substitution. This substitution is performed only in Release 5 and later releases.

%L The value of the language string associated with the display. This is the value of the xnlLanguage resource in Release 4, and in Release 5 and later, it is the value of this resource or the value returned by the language procedure, if any is registered. (See Xt-SetLanguageProc() and XtDisplayInitialize() for more information.) In Release 5, if the xnlLanguage resource is not set, the language procedure will usually return the value of the LANG environment variable.

%l The "language part" of the language string of the display.

%t The "territory part" of the language string of the display.

%c The "codeset part" of the language string of the display.

These substitutions are performed on the elements of *path*, or if *path* is NULL, on the path specified in the XFILESEARCHPATH environment variable. If this variable is not defined, a default path is used.

See the "Background" section below for an explanation of the default path, the various parts of the language string, and of non-standard substitutions.

Usage

The Intrinsics use XtResolvePathname() to find an application's app-defaults file (see XtAppInitialize()). If your application reads other files which contain bitmaps, help text, or other information that may need to be customized depending on the user's customization resource or preferred language, you should use XtResolvePathname() to find the file. This greatly aids the portability and customizability of your application.

A disadvantage of this approach is that it requires your files to be installed in locations removed from the application itself. Still, files have to be installed somewhere, and XtResolve-Pathname() provides some standardization for this installation process.

Note that you can pass NULL for many of the arguments to this function. The return value of the function is a filename, not an opened file.

If you are not interested in any of the standard substitutions, or the default path, you can use XtFindFile() to search for a file. This is a lower-level function than most applications will want to use. XtResolvePathname() calls XtFindFile() itself.

Example

To find the app-defaults file for an application, you can simply use XtResolvePathname as follows:

```
filename = XtResolvePathname(dpy, "app-defaults", NULL, NULL, NULL,
                            NULL, 0, NULL);
```

If your application needs to read a help file which you plan to install in */usr/lib/X11/help* (*/usr/lib/X11/* will be part of the default path on most implementations) with the same name as the application class, and with the suffix, ".txt", you could use XtResolvePathname() as follows:

```
filename = XtResolvePathname(dpy, "help", NULL, ".txt", NULL,
                            NULL, 0, NULL);
```

If your application needs to read a number of bitmap files, you should probably not install them directly in */usr/lib/X11/bitmaps* because their names may conflict with bitmaps used by other applications. You could find them from a subdirectory of this directory as follows:

```
sprintf(basename, "%s/%s", application_class, bitmap_name);
bitmap_file = XtResolvePathname(dpy, "bitmaps", basename, ".bm",
                               NULL, NULL, 0, NULL);
```

Background

This section explains the default path used by XtResolvePathname(), the various parts of the language string, and how to specify non-standard substitutions.

The Default Path

If the *path* argument is NULL, the value of the XFILESEARCHPATH environment variable will be used. If XFILESEARCHPATH is not defined, an implementation-specific default path will be used which contains at least 6 entries. These entries must contain the following substitutions:

1. %C, %N, %S, %T, %L or %C, %N, %S, %T, %l, %t, %c

2. %C, %N, %S, %T, %l

3. %C, %N, %S, %T

4. %N, %S, %T, %L or %N, %S, %T, %l, %t, %c

5. %N, %S, %T, %l

6. %N, %S, %T

The order of these six entries within the path must be as given above. The order and use of substitutions within a given entry is implementation dependent. If the path begins with a colon, it will be preceded by %N%S. If the path includes two adjacent colons, %N%S will be inserted between them.

A suggested value for the default path on POSIX-based systems is:

*/usr/lib/X11/%L/%T/%N%C%S:/usr/lib/X11/%l/%T/%N%C%S:\
/usr/lib/X11/%T/%N%C%S:/usr/lib/X11/%L/%T/%N%S:\
/usr/lib/X11/%l/%T/%N%S:/usr/lib/X11/%T/%N%S*

Using this example, if the user has specified a language, it will be used as a subdirectory of /usr/lib/X11 that will be searched for other files. If the desired file is not found there, the lookup will be tried again using just the language part of the specification. If the file is not there, it will be looked for in /usr/lib/X11. The *type* parameter is used as a subdirectory of the language directory or of /usr/lib/X11, and *suffix* is appended to the file name.

The Language String

In Release 4, the language string was of the following form:

> *language* [*_territory*] [*.codeset*]

In Release 5, the format of the language string is specified to be implementation defined, and it may have a "language part" a "territory" part and a "codeset part". In practice, the Release 4 format is still a common one, with a language string like "en_GB.iso8859-1" meaning English, as spoken in Great Britain, encoded in the ISO8859-1 encoding (Latin-1).

Non-standard Substitutions

You can have XtResolvePathname() introduce additional substitutions into the specified path by passing an array of SubstitutionRec structures. Each element in *substitutions* is a structure that contains a character and a string. If any element in *path* contains a percent sign followed by a character that appears in *substitutions*, then that two character sequence will be replaced by the corresponding string in *substitutions*.

There are two substitution sequences that are treated specially:

- The character sequence %: (percent colon) specifies an embedded colon that is not a delimiter; the sequence is replaced by a single colon.

- The character sequence %% (percent percent) specifies a percent character that does not introduce a substitution; the sequence is replaced by a single percent character.

A substitution string entry of NULL is equivalent to a pointer to an empty string.

If the operating system does not interpret multiple embedded name separators in the path (i.e., "/" in POSIX) the same way as a single separator, XtResolvePathname() will collapse multiple separators into a single one after performing all string substitutions. Except for collapsing embedded separators, the contents of the string substitutions are not interpreted by

`XtResolvePathname()` and may therefore contain any operating-system-dependent characters, including additional name separators.

Structures

The `Substitution` type is defined as follows:

```
typedef struct {
    char match;
    String substitution;
} SubstitutionRec, *Substitution;
```

See Also

XtAppInitialize(1), *XtDisplayInitialize*(1), *XtFindFile*(1), *XtSetLanguageString*(1), *XtFilePredicate*(2).

Name

XtScreen – return the screen pointer for the specified widget.

Synopsis

```
Screen *XtScreen(w)
    Widget w;
```

Inputs

w   Specifies the widget; must be of class Core or any subclass thereof.

Returns

The screen pointer for *w*.

Description

XtScreen() returns a pointer to the Screen structure of the screen the specified widget is on.

Usage

XtScreen() is implemented as a function when called from application code, but is replaced by a more efficient macro when called from widget code including the file *<X11/IntrinsicP.h>*.

Use XtScreenOfObject() to return the display of a widget or the nearest widget ancestor of a non-widget object.

See Also

XtDisplay(1), *XtScreenOfObject*(1), *XtWindow*(1).

Xt Functions and Macros

XtScreenDatabase

Name

XtScreenDatabase – obtain the resource database for a screen.

Synopsis

```
XrmDatabase XtScreenDatabase(screen)
    Screen *screen;
```

Inputs

screen   Specifies the screen for which the database should be obtained.

Returns

The resource database of *screen*.

Availability

Release 5 and later.

Description

XtScreenDatabase() returns the fully merged resource database for the specified screen. If that database has not already been built (by XtDisplayInitialize(), for example), XtScreenDatabase() builds it. If the specified screen does not belong to a display initialized by XtDisplayInitialize(), the results are undefined.

See XtDisplayInitialize() for a description of how a resource database is built for a screen.

Usage

XtDatabase() returns the database associated with the default screen of a display. Prior to Release 5, this database was used for all screens of a display.

You should rarely need to use the database of a screen or display directly. XtGetApplicationResources() and related functions provide a more manageable approach to obtaining resource values.

Structures

XrmDatabase is an opaque data type.

See Also

XtAppInitialize(1), *XtDatabase*(1), *XtDisplayInitialize*(1), *XtGetApplicationResources*(1).

XtScreenOfObject

Name

XtScreenOfObject – return the screen pointer of a non-widget object.

Synopsis

```
Screen *XtScreenOfObject(object)
     Widget object;
```

Inputs

object   Specifies the object; may be of class Object or any subclass thereof.

Returns

The screen of *object*, or if its nearest widget ancestor.

Availability

Release 4 and later.

Description

XtScreenOfObject() is identical in function to XtScreen() if the object is a widget; otherwise XtScreenOfObject() returns the screen pointer for the nearest ancestor of object that is of class Core.

Usage

If you are working with windowed objects, use XtScreen() rather than XtScreen-OfObject(). XtScreen() may be implemented as an efficient macro for widget code that includes the file *<X11/IntrinsicP.h>*.

See Also

XtDisplayOfObject(1), *XtScreen*(1), *XtWindowOfObject*(1).

Name

XtSetArg – set a resource name and value in an argument list.

Synopsis

```
void XtSetArg(arg, resource_name, value)
    Arg arg;
    String resource_name;
    XtArgVal value;
```

Inputs

arg   Specifies the Arg structure to set.

resource_name
            Specifies the name of the resource.

value   Specifies the value of the resource, or its address.

Description

XtSetArg() sets *arg*.name to *resource_name*, and sets *arg*.value to *value*. If the size of the resource is less than or equal to the size of an XtArgVal, the resource value is stored directly in *value*; otherwise, a pointer to it is stored in *value*.

XtSetArg() is implemented as the following macro:

```
#define XtSetArg(arg, n, d) \
    ((void)( (arg).name = (n), (arg).value = (XtArgVal)(d) ))
```

Because this macro evaluates *arg* twice, you must not use an expression with autoincrement, autodecrement or other side effects for this argument.

Usage

Many Intrinsics functions need to be passed pairs of resource names and values in an ArgList to set or override resource values. XtSetArg() is used to set or dynamically change values in an Arg structure or ArgList array.

Note that in Release 4, a number of functions beginning with the prefix XtVa were added to the Intrinsics. These functions accept a NULL-terminated variable-length argument list instead of a single ArgList array. Often these forms of the functions are easier to use.

Example

XtSetArg() is usually used in a highly stylized manner to minimize the probability of making a mistake; for example:

```
Arg args[20];
int n;

n = 0;
XtSetArg(args[n], XtNheight, 100);      n++;
XtSetArg(args[n], XtNwidth, 200);       n++;
XtSetValues(widget, args, n);
```

Incrementing the array index on the same line means that resource settings can be easily read, inserted, deleted or commented out on a line-by-line basis. If you use this approach, be careful when using `XtSetArg()` inside an `if` statement—don't forget to use curly braces to include the increment statement.

Alternatively, an application can statically declare the argument list:

```
static Args args[] = {
        {XtNheight, (XtArgVal) 100},
        {XtNwidth, (XtArgVal) 200},
};
XtSetValues(Widget, args, XtNumber(args));
```

Structures

The `Arg` and `ArgList` types are defined as follows:

```
typedef struct {
    String name;
    XtArgVal value;
} Arg, *ArgList;
```

The definition of `XtArgVal` differs depending on architecture—its purpose is precisely to make code portable between architectures with different word sizes.

See Also

XtMergeArgLists(1), *XtNumber*(1).

Xt Functions and Macros

XtSetErrorHandler

Name

XtSetErrorHandler – set the low-level error handler procedure.

Synopsis

```
void XtSetErrorHandler(handler)
    XtErrorHandler handler;
```

Inputs

handler   Specifies the new low-level fatal error procedure, which should not return.

Availability

XtSetErrorHandler() has been superseded by XtAppSetErrorHandler().

Description

XtSetErrorHandler() registers the procedure *handler* as the procedure to be invoked by XtError(). It should display the string it is passed and then must terminate the application; if it returns the subsequent behavior of the Intrinsics is undefined.

Usage

XtSetErrorHandler() has been superseded by XtAppSetErrorHandler(), which performs the same function on a per-application context basis. XtSetErrorHandler() now calls XtAppSetErrorHandler() passing the default application context created by XtInitialize(). Very few programs need multiple application contexts, and you can continue to use XtSetErrorHandler() if you initialize your application with Xt-Initialize(). We recommend, however, that you use XtAppInitialize(), XtApp-SetErrorHandler(), and the other XtApp*() application context specific functions.

See XtAppSetErrorHandler() for more information.

See Also

XtAppSetErrorHandler(1), *XtAppSetErrorMsgHandler*(1), *XtAppSetWarningHandler*(1), *XtErrorHandler*(2).

XtSetErrorMsgHandler

Name

XtSetErrorMsgHandler – set the high-level error handler procedure.

Synopsis

```
void XtSetErrorMsgHandler(msg_handler)
    XtErrorMsgHandler msg_handler;
```

Inputs

`msg_handler`   Specifies the new high-level fatal error procedure, which should not return.

Availability

`XtSetErrorMsgHandler()` has been superseded by `XtAppSetErrorMsgHandler()`.

Description

`XtSetErrorMsgHandler()` registers the procedure `msg_handler` as the procedure to be invoked by `XtErrorMsg()`.

Usage

`XtSetErrorMsgHandler()` has been superseded by `XtAppSetErrorMsgHandler()`, which performs the same function on a per-application context basis. `XtSetErrorMsgHandler()` now calls `XtAppSetErrorMsgHandler()` passing the default application context created by `XtInitialize()`. Very few programs need multiple application contexts, and you can continue to use `XtSetErrorMsgHandler()` if you initialize your application with `XtInitialize()`. We recommend, however, that you use `XtAppInitialize()`, `XtAppSetErrorMsgHandler()`, and the other `XtApp*()` application context specific functions.

See `XtAppSetErrorMsgHandler()` for more information.

See Also

XtAppSetErrorHandler(1), *XtAppSetErrorMsgHandler*(1), *XtAppSetWarningMsgHandler*(1), *XtErrorMsgHandler*(2).

Xt Functions and Macros

Name

XtSetKeyTranslator – register a key translator.

Synopsis

```
void XtSetKeyTranslator(display, proc)
    Display *display;
    XtKeyProc proc;
```

Inputs

display   Specifies the display from which to translate the events.

proc   Specifies the procedure that is to perform key translations.

Description

XtSetKeyTranslator() registers the specified procedure as the current key translator. The default translator is XtTranslateKey(), an XtKeyProc that uses the Shift, Lock, and group modifiers with the interpretations defined by the X11 protocol. XtTranslateKey() is provided so that new translators can call it to get default keycode-to-keysym translations and so that the default translator can be reinstalled.

See XtKeyProc(2) for an explanation of the responsibilities of a key translator procedure.

Usage

The key translator procedure is called by the Translation Manager to convert incoming keycodes and modifier bits to keysyms. The only reason you would have to write and install your own key translator procedure is if you were working with non-standard keysyms.

The only way to remove a translator is to register a new one. For example, the default key translator (XtTranslateKey()) can be explicitly reinstalled.

See Also

XtConvertCase(1), *XtGetKeysymTable*(1), *XtKeysymToKeycodeList*(1), *XtRegisterCaseConverter*(1), *Xt-TranslateKeycode*(1), *XtTranslateKey*(1),
XtKeyProc(2).

XtSetKeyboardFocus

Name

XtSetKeyboardFocus – redirect keyboard input to a widget.

Synopsis

```
void XtSetKeyboardFocus(subtree, descendant)
    Widget subtree, descendant;
```

Inputs

subtree Specifies the widget to be considered the root of the subtree for which the keyboard focus is to be set. Must be of class Core or any subclass thereof.

descendant Specifies a normal (non-popup) descendant of *subtree* to which keyboard events are to be redirected, or None. May be of class Object or any subclass thereof.

Description

XtSetKeyboardFocus() causes XtDispatchEvent() to remap keyboard events that occur within the widget hierarchy rooted at *subtree* and to dispatch them to *descendant*. If *descendant* is not a subclass of Core, it is replaced by its closest windowed ancestor. If *descendant* is None, keyboard events within *subtree* will be dispatched normally.

When *subtree* or one of its descendants acquires the X keyboard focus, or the pointer moves into the subtree such that keyboard events would now be delivered to *subtree*, a FocusIn event is generated for *descendant* if FocusChange events have been selected by *descendant*. Similarly, when *subtree* loses the X keyboard focus or the keyboard focus for one of its ancestors, a FocusOut event is generated for *descendant* if FocusChange events have been selected by *descendant*.

For more details on how events are dispatched after a call to XtSetKeyboardFocus(), see XtDispatchEvent().

Usage

XtSetKeyboardFocus() does not call the Xlib function XSetInputFocus(); it simply causes the Intrinsics to dispatch events differently. For most applications, this approach is preferred over the more heavy-handed Xlib function.

Example

If a dialog box contains a Label widget, some Button widgets, and a single Text widget for input, it is good style to allow the user to enter text into the dialog when the mouse is anywhere over the dialog, not only when the mouse is over the Text widget itself. This can be arranged with code like the following:

```
Widget shell, box, text, prompt, ok_button, cancel_button;

XtPopup(shell, XtGrabExclusive);
XtSetKeyboardFocus(box, text);
```

After this call to XtSetKeyboardFocus(), whenever the dialog box gets the X input focus (for example, when the mouse moves into it) all keyboard events will be redirected at the text widget.

See Also

XtAddGrab(1), *XtDispatchEvent*(1).

XtSetLanguageProc

Name

XtSetLanguageProc – register the language procedure called to set the locale.

Synopsis

```
XtLanguageProc XtSetLanguageProc(app_context, proc, client_data)
      XtAppContext app_context;
      XtLanguageProc proc;
      XtPointer client_data;
```

Inputs

app_context Specifies the application context in which the language procedure is to be used, or NULL.

proc Specifies the language procedure.

client_data Specifies additional data to be passed to the language procedure when it is called.

Returns

The previously registered language procedure.

Availability

Release 5 and later.

Description

XtSetLanguageProc() registers *proc* as the language procedure that will be called (with *client_data*) from XtDisplayInitialize() for all subsequent displays initialized in the application context *app_context*. The language procedure is called by XtDisplay-Initialize() (in Release 5) in order to determine the language string and perform whatever localization is required by an internationalized application.

If *app_context* is NULL, the specified language procedure is registered in all application contexts created by the calling process, including any future application contexts that may be created. If *proc* is NULL a default language procedure is registered.

XtSetLanguageProc() returns the previously registered language procedure. If a language procedure has not yet been registered, the return value is unspecified but if it is used in a subsequent call to XtSetLanguageProc(), it will cause the default language procedure to be registered.

Note that the "default" language procedure is not registered by default; you must call XtSet-LanguageProc() with a *proc* of NULL to register this default procedure. If XtSet-LanguageProc() is never called, XtDisplayInitialize() determines the language string by the same procedure it used prior to Release 5. See XtDisplayInitialize() for more information.

See the "Background" section below for a description of the default language procedure. See XtLanguageProc(2) for an explanation of how to write a language procedure.

Xt Functions and Macros

Usage

Most internationalized applications should call `XtSetLanguageProc()` directly before calling `XtAppInitialize()`. The default language procedure should be adequate for applications that use only the internationalization facilities provided by ANSI-C and Xlib.

Example

A client wishing to use this default procedure to establish locale can do so as in following example:

```
Widget top;
XtSetLanguageProc(NULL, NULL, NULL);
top = XtAppInitialize( ... );
```

Background

The default language procedure does the following:

- Sets the locale according to the environment. On ANSI C-based systems this is done by calling `setlocale(LC_ALL, `*`language`*`)`. If an error is encountered a warning message is issued with `XtWarning()`.

- Calls `XSupportsLocale()` to verify that the current locale is supported. If the locale is not supported, a warning message is issued with `XtWarning()` and the locale is set to "C."

- Calls `XSetLocaleModifiers()` specifying the empty string.

- Returns the value of the current locale. On ANSI-C-based systems this is the return value from a final call to `setlocale(LC_ALL, NULL)`.

See Also

XtDisplayInitialize(1),
XtLanguageProc(2).

XtSetMappedWhenManaged

Name

XtSetMappedWhenManaged – set the value of a widget's XtNmappedWhenManaged resource and map or unmap the window.

Synopsis

```
void XtSetMappedWhenManaged(w, map_when_managed)
    Widget w;
    Boolean map_when_managed;
```

Inputs

w   Specifies the widget. Must be of class Core or any subclass thereof.

map_when_managed
                  Specifies the new value of the map_when_managed field.

Description

If *w* is realized and managed and if *map_when_managed* is set to True, XtSetMapped-WhenManaged() maps the widget's window. If the widget is realized and managed and if the new value of *map_when_managed* is set to False, XtSetMappedWhenManaged() unmaps the widget's window. In both cases, XtSetMappedWhenManaged() sets the value of the widget's XtNmappedWhenManaged resource as specified by the *map_when_managed* argument.

XtSetMappedWhenManaged() is a convenience function that is equivalent to (but slightly faster than) calling XtSetValues() to set the new value for the XtNmappedWhenManaged resource, and then mapping or unmapping the widget as appropriate.

Usage

A widget is normally mapped when it is managed, which is usually the desired behavior. This behavior can be overridden by setting the XtNmappedWhenManaged resource for the widget to False, and then calling XtSetMappedWhenManaged() to map and unmap the widget or by calling XtMapWidget() and XtUnmapWidget() explicitly.

A widget that is managed but unmapped will have screen space allocated for it, but will not appear in that space. A widget that is unmanaged will not have screen space allocated for it, and if mapped will likely appear in an undesirable place.

See Also

XtManageChild(1), *XtMapWidget*(1), *XtUnmapWidget*(1).

XtSetMultiClickTime

Name

XtSetMultiClickTime – set the multi-click time.

Synopsis

```
void XtSetMultiClickTime(display, time)
      Display *display;
      int time;
```

Inputs

display   Specifies the display connection.

time   Specifies the multi-click time in milliseconds.

Availability

Release 4 and later.

Description

XtSetMultiClickTime() sets the time interval used by the translation manager to determine when multiple events are interpreted as a repeated event. When a repeat count is specified in a translation entry the time interval between arrival of each pair of repeated events (e.g., between two ButtonPress events) must be less than the multi-click time in order for the translation actions to be taken.

Usage

The value of the multi-click time must remain completely under the user's control. An application should not set it except when directed to by the user. It is acceptable to set this value when the user specifies the new time in a "Preferences" configuration dialog box created by the application, for example, and it is also acceptable to set the multi-click time from a value saved in a user preferences file.

The initial multi-click time value can be specified as an application resource with name multiClickTime and class MultiClickTime. The multi-click time is unique for each Display and is retrieved from the resource database by XtDisplayInitialize(). If no value is specified, the default initial value is 200 milliseconds.

See Also

XtGetMultiClickTime(1).

Name

XtSetSelectionTimeout – set the Intrinsics selection timeout value.

Synopsis

```
void XtSetSelectionTimeout(timeout)
    unsigned long timeout;
```

Inputs

timeout   Specifies the selection timeout in milliseconds.

Availability

XtSetSelectionTimeout() has been superseded by XtAppSetSelection-
Timeout().

Description

XtSetSelectionTimeout() sets the Intrinsics selection timeout value. The selection timeout is the time within which two communicating applications must respond to one another. The initial timeout value is set by the selectionTimeout application resource, which has a default value of 5000 milliseconds (5 seconds).

Usage

XtSetSelectionTimeout() has been superseded by XtAppSetSelection-
Timeout(), which performs the same function on a per-application context basis. XtSet-
SelectionTimeout() now calls XtAppSetSelectionTimeout() passing the default application context created by XtInitialize(). Very few programs need multiple application contexts, and you can continue to use XtSetSelectionTimeout() if you initialize your application with XtInitialize(). We recommend, however, that you use XtApp-
Initialize(), XtAppSetSelectionTimeout(), and the other XtApp*() application context specific functions.

See XtAppSetSelectionTimeout() for more information.

See Also

XtAppGetSelectionTimeout(1), *XtAppSetSelectionTimeout*(1).

Name

XtSetSensitive – set the sensitivity state of a widget.

Synopsis

```
void XtSetSensitive(w, sensitive)
    Widget w;
    Boolean sensitive;
```

Inputs

w	Specifies the widget.
sensitive	Specifies whether the widget should receive keyboard, pointer, and focus events.

Description

XtSetSensitive() sets the sensitivity state of *w*. If *sensitive* is False, then *w* and all of its descendants will become insensitive and will not have any KeyPress, KeyRelease, ButtonPress, ButtonRelease, MotionNotify, EnterNotify, LeaveNotify, FocusIn, or FocusOut events dispatched to them. If *sensitive* is True, and if *w*'s XtNancestorSensitive resource is also True, then *w* and its children will be made sensitive again, except for any children that have explicitly been made insensitive by calling Xt-SetSensitive() or by setting their XtNsensitive resource.

See the "Background" section below for more details on the algorithm followed by XtSet-Sensitive() and on how the sensitivity of a widget affects the sensitivity of its descendants.

Usage

Many widgets will display themselves differently when they are insensitive. A common approach is to draw themselves through a stipple mask so that they appear grayed-out. Xt-SetSensitive() uses XtSetValues() when it sets the XtNsensitive and Xt-NancestorSensitive resources, so widget's can check for changes to these resources in their set_values() method and take the appropriate action.

In an application, it is good style to make any widget insensitive if it does not currently make sense for the user to select it. A menu item labeled "Delete Selected Items", for example, should be insensitive if there are not any currently selected items. A button that pops up a modal dialog box should be made insensitive while that dialog box is popped up, so that the user cannot attempt to pop it up again.

You can test the sensitivity state of a widget by calling XtIsSensitive().

Note that you can also set the sensitivity of a widget by setting the XtNsensitive resource directly. It is better to use XtSetSensitive because this handles composite widgets correctly. If you want a non-composite widget to be insensitive when it is created, you can specify False for XtNsensitive from a resource file or an argument list. You can query the value of the XtNancestorSensitive resource, but you should never set it.

Popup shells will have their XtNancestorSensitive resource set to False if their parent was insensitive when they were created. Since XtSetSensitive() on the parent will not modify the resource in the popup child, you should either be sure that you only create popup shells as children of sensitive widgets, or that you include a line like the following in your app-defaults file:

```
*TransientShell.ancestorSensitive: True
```

Background

Widget sensitivity is controlled by the `sensitive` and `ancestor_sensitive` fields in the Core instance record. `XtNsensitive` and `XtNancestorSensitive` are the resource names for these fields. A widget can be insensitive because its `sensitive` field is `False` or because one of its ancestors is insensitive. A widget can, but does not need to, distinguish these two cases visually.

`XtSetSensitive()` first calls `XtSetValues()` on the current widget to set the `XtNsensitive` resource to the value specified by *sensitive*. If *sensitive* is `False` and the widget is a subclass of Composite, `XtSetSensitive()` recursively propagates the new value down the children tree by calling `XtSetValues()` on each child to set `ancestor_sensitive` to `False`. If *sensitive* is `True` and the widget is a subclass of Composite and the widget's `ancestor_sensitive` field is `True`, then `XtSetSensitive()` sets the `ancestor_sensitive` of each child to `True` and then recursively calls `XtSetValues()` on each normal descendant that is now sensitive to set `ancestor_sensitive` to `True`.

`XtSetSensitive()` ensures that if a parent has either `sensitive` or `ancestor_sensitive` set to `False`, then all children have `ancestor_sensitive` set to `False`.

See Also

XtGetValues(1), *XtIsSensitive*(1), *XtSetValues*(1).

XtSetSubvalues

Name

XtSetSubvalues – copy resource settings from an `ArgList` to a subpart resource structure.

Synopsis

```
void XtSetSubvalues(base, resources, num_resources, args, num_args)
    XtPointer base;
    XtResourceList resources;
    Cardinal num_resources;
    ArgList args;
    Cardinal num_args;
```

Inputs

base   Specifies the base address of the subpart data structure into which the resources should be written.

resources   Specifies the subpart resource list.

num_resources
    Specifies the number of resources in the resource list.

args   Specifies an argument list of name/value pairs that contain the resource settings to be copied into the subpart data structure.

num_args   Specifies the number of arguments in the argument list.

Description

`XtSetSubvalues()` copies the values of named resources from *args* into the structure pointed to by *base*. The resource list *resources* specifies the size of each resource in this structure, and its offset from *base*. The name of each resource in *args* is looked up in this resource list, and the resource's specified size and offset are used to copy the resource value into the subpart structure. If the name of a resource in *args* does not match any of the resources described by *resources*, then that resource name/value pair in *args* is silently ignored.

See `XtGetApplicationResources()` for a description of the various fields of a `Xt-Resource` structure and an example of initializing an `XtResourceList`.

Usage

If a widget has subpart resources, it can fetch initial values for those resources from the resource database by calling `XtGetSubresources()` from its `initialize()` method and passing the user's argument list to override values from the database. In the resource file, the subpart will have a name, and the subpart resources will be specified under that name in the resource hierarchy. Most widgets will want to allow the user to set the values of subpart resources from application code as well. One way to do this is to call `XtSetSubvalues()` from within the widget's `set_values()` method, passing the subpart resource list and the user's argument list. (Prior to Release 4, you had to use the `set_values_hook()` method for this purpose.) With this approach, subpart resources seem just like normal widget resources to the user; both types of resources can be set by calling `XtSetValues()`. Another approach is to provide a special function (which will use `XtSetSubvalues()`) to set values of your subpart. This approach emphasizes that the subpart is a distinct component of the widget.

Note that a more flexible alternative to subparts is to use non-widget objects which the user can create as children of your widget. This way the user has a handle on the "subparts" and can manipulate them directly.

To get the values of named resources from a subpart, use `XtGetSubvalues()`.

To set resource values in a subpart structure using a NULL-terminated variable-length argument list instead of an `ArgList`, use `XtVaSetSubvalues()`.

Structures

`XtResource` is defined as follows:

```
typedef struct _XtResource {
    String     resource_name;   /* Resource name */
    String     resource_class;  /* Resource class */
    String     resource_type;   /* Representation type desired */
    Cardinal   resource_size;   /* Size in bytes of representation */
    Cardinal   resource_offset;/* Offset from base to put resource value */
    String     default_type;    /* Representation type of specified default */
    XtPointer default_addr;     /* Address of resource default value */
} XtResource, *XtResourceList;
```

See `XtGetApplicationResources()` for an explanation of the fields of this structure.

`Arg` are defined as follows:

```
typedef struct {
    String name;
    XtArgVal value;
} Arg, *ArgList;
```

See Also

XtGetApplicationResources(1), *XtGetSubresources*(1), *XtGetSubvalues*(1), *set_values*(4).

XtSetTypeConverter

Name

XtSetTypeConverter – register a "new-style" type converter for all application contexts in a process.

Synopsis

```
void XtSetTypeConverter(from_type, to_type, converter, convert_args,
        num_args, cache_type, destructor)
    String from_type, to_type;
    XtTypeConverter converter;
    XtConvertArgList convert_args;
    Cardinal num_args;
    XtCacheType cache_type;
    XtDestructor destructor;
```

Inputs

from_type Specifies the source type.

to_type Specifies the destination type.

converter Specifies the resource type converter procedure.

convert_args

 Specifies additional conversion arguments, or NULL.

num_args Specifies the count of additional conversion arguments, or zero.

cache_type Specifies whether or not resources produced by this converter are sharable or display-specific and when they should be freed.

destructor Specifies a destroy procedure for resources produced by this conversion, or NULL if no additional action is required to deallocate resources produced by converter.

Description

XtSetTypeConverter() registers *converter* in all application contexts as a "new-style" resource converter to convert data of resource type *from_type* to resource type *to_type*. The *convert_args* array describes a list of additional arguments that will be computed and passed to the converter when it is invoked. *cache_type* specifies how converted values should be cached, and *destructor* optionally specifies a procedure to be called to free up resources when a cached value is no longer needed.

XtSetTypeConverter() is identical to XtAppSetTypeConverter() except that it registers the converter in all current application contexts, and all future application contexts. (In particular, note that XtAppSetTypeConverter() does not supersede XtSetType-Converter() as is the case with many other XtApp functions.) For more information about the arguments and usage of this function, see XtAppSetTypeConverter().

Structures

The XtConvertArgRec structure is defined as follows:

```
typedef enum {
        /* address mode              parameter representation */
        XtAddress,                 /* address */
        XtBaseOffset,              /* offset */
        XtImmediate,               /* constant */
        XtResourceString,          /* resource name string */
        XtResourceQuark,           /* resource name quark */
        XtWidgetBaseOffset,        /* offset */
        XtProcedureArg             /* procedure to call */
} XtAddressMode;

typedef struct {
        XtAddressMode address_mode;
        XtPointer address_id;
        Cardinal size;
} XtConvertArgRec, *XtConvertArgList;
```

The XtCacheType and its legal values are defined as follows:

```
typedef int XtCacheType;

#define             XtCacheNone          0x001
#define             XtCacheAll           0x002
#define             XtCacheByDisplay     0x003
#define             XtCacheRefCount      0x100
```

See XtAppSetTypeConverter() for an explanation of each of the fields and values of these types.

See Also

XtAppSetTypeConverter(1), *XtCallConverter*(1), *XtConvertAndStore*(1),
XtDestructor(2), *XtTypeConverter*(2).

*Xt Functions
and Macros*

Name

XtSetValues – set widget resources from an argument list.

Synopsis

```
void XtSetValues(object, args, num_args)
    Widget object;
    ArgList args;
    Cardinal num_args;
```

Inputs

object   Specifies the object whose resources are to be modified; may be of class Object or any subclass thereof.

args   Specifies an array of name/value pairs that name the resources to be set and specify their new values.

num_args   Specifies the number of elements in *args*.

Description

XtSetValues() sets the resources of *object* named in *args* to the values specified in *args*. Once these values are copied from *args* into the widget, the widget's set_values() methods are called which gives the widget an opportunity to check the new values for consistency, update private widget fields to reflect the new state of the resources, or even to undo some of the changes. The "Background" section below explains the details of this process.

Usage

XtSetValues() is the primary way for a user to modify widget resources of a widget once that widget has been created. See XtSetArg() for information on setting resource names and values into an ArgList.

To set resources specified in a NULL-terminated variable-length argument list rather than an ArgList, use XtVaSetValues(). This is often a more convenient function to use because it does not require you to initialize an ArgList array.

Note that not all widget resources may be set with XtSetValues(). Some may only be set when a widget is created, and others should be treated as read-only resources. The documentation for the particular widget should indicate which resources are not settable with XtSetValues().

To query the values of named resources, use XtGetValues() or XtVaGetValues().

Example

You can use XtSetValues() as follows to set widget resources:

```
Arg args[10];
int i;
XFontStruct *bold_font;
Pixel bright_red;

/*
```

```
 * set up an argument list, assuming we've already obtained
 * the font and the color from somewhere else.
 */
i = 0;
XtSetArg(args[i], XtNlabel, "Quit"); i++;
XtSetArg(args[i], XtNfont, bold_font); i++;
XtSetArg(args[i], XtNforeground, bright_red); i++;

/* set the values */
XtSetValues(s, args, i);
```

Background

XtSetValues() starts with the resources specified for the Object class fields and proceeds down the subclass chain to the object. At each stage, it replaces the *object* resource fields with any values specified in the argument list. XtSetValues() then calls the set_values() methods for the object in superclass-to-subclass order. If the object has any non-NULL set_values_hook() methods, these are called immediately after the corresponding set_values() method. This procedure permits subclasses to set subpart data via XtSetValues(). (Note, though, that as of Release 4, this can be done directly from the set_values() method.)

If the class of the object's parent is a subclass of constraintWidgetClass, XtSetValues() also updates the object's constraints. It starts with the constraint resources specified for constraintWidgetClass and proceeds down the subclass chain to the parent's class. At each stage, it replaces the constraint resource fields with any values specified in the argument list. It then calls the constraint set_values() methods from constraintWidgetClass down to the parent's class. The constraint set_values() methods are called with widget arguments, as for all set_values() methods, not just the constraint records, so that they can make adjustments to the desired values based on full information about the widget. Any arguments specified that do not match a resource list entry are silently ignored.

If the object is of a subclass of RectObj, XtSetValues() determines if a geometry request is needed by comparing the old object to the new object. If any geometry changes are required, XtSetValues() restores the original geometry and makes the request on behalf of the widget. If the geometry manager returns XtGeometryYes, XtSetValues() calls the object's resize() method. If the geometry manager returns XtGeometryDone, XtSetValues() continues, as the object's resize procedure should have been called by the geometry manager. If the geometry manager returns XtGeometryNo, XtSetValues() ignores the geometry request and continues. If the geometry manager returns XtGeometryAlmost, XtSetValues() calls the set_values_almost() method, which determines what should be done. XtSetValues() then repeats this process, deciding once more whether the geometry manager should be called.

Finally, if any of the set_values() methods returned True, and the widget is realized, XtSetValues() causes the widget's expose procedure to be invoked by calling XClearArea() on the widget's window.

Structures

`Arg` is defined as follows:

```
typedef struct {
    String name;
    XtArgVal value;
} Arg, *ArgList;
```

See Also

XtGetValues(1), *XtSetArg*(1), *XtVaGetValues*(1), *XtVaSetValues*(1),
set_values(4), *set_values_almost*(4), *set_values_hook*(4).

XtSetWMColormapWindows

Name

XtSetWMColormapWindows – set WM_COLORMAP_WINDOWS property to inform window manager of custom colormaps.

Synopsis

```
void XtSetWMColormapWindows(widget, list, count)
    Widget widget;
    Widget* list;
    Cardinal count;
```

Inputs

widget   Specifies the widget on whose window the WM_COLORMAP_WINDOWS property will be stored. Must be of class Core or any subclass thereof.

list   Specifies a list of widgets whose windows are to be listed in the WM_COLORMAP_WINDOWS property.

count   Specifies the number of widgets in list.

Availability

Release 4 and later.

Description

XtSetWMColormapWindows() returns immediately if *widget* is not realized or if *count* is 0. Otherwise, XtSetWMColormapWindows() constructs an ordered list of windows by examining each widget in the list in turn and:

- Ignoring the widget if it is not realized or

- Adding the widget's window to the window list if the widget is realized and if its colormap resource differs from the colormap resources of all widgets whose windows are already on the window list.

Finally, XtSetWMColormapWindows() stores the resulting window list in the WM_COLORMAP_WINDOWS property on the specified widget's window. This tells the window manager which windows have a custom colormap, so that the window manager can install these colormaps at the appropriate time.

See section 4.1.8 of the *Inter-Client Communications Conventions Manual* for details on the meaning of the WM_COLORMAP_WINDOWS property.

Usage

Only applications that make sophisticated use of color and use multiple colormaps will ever need to call this function.

Xt Functions and Macros

Name

XtSetWarningHandler – set the low-level warning handler procedure.

Synopsis

```
void XtSetWarningHandler(handler)
    XtErrorHandler handler;
```

Inputs

handler   Specifies the new low-level warning procedure.

Availability

XtSetWarningHandler() has been superseded by XtAppSetWarningHandler().

Description

XtSetWarningHandler() registers the procedure *handler* as the procedure to be invoked by XtWarning(). It should display the string it is passed and return.

Usage

XtSetWarningHandler() has been superseded by XtAppSetWarningHandler(), which performs the same function on a per-application context basis. XtSetWarning-Handler() now calls XtAppSetWarningHandler() passing the default application context created by XtInitialize(). Very few programs need multiple application contexts, and you can continue to use XtSetWarningHandler() if you initialize your application with XtInitialize(). We recommend, however, that you use XtApp-Initialize(), XtAppSetWarningHandler(), and the other XtApp*() application context specific functions.

See XtAppSetWarningHandler() for more information.

See Also

XtAppSetErrorHandler(1), *XtAppSetErrorMsgHandler*(1), *XtAppSetWarningMsgHandler*(1), *XtApp-Warning*(1),
XtErrorHandler(2), *XtErrorMsgHandler*(2).

XtSetWarningMsgHandler

Name

XtSetWarningMsgHandler – set the high-level warning handler procedure.

Synopsis

```
void XtSetWarningMsgHandler(msg_handler)
    XtErrorMsgHandler msg_handler;
```

Inputs

`msg_handler` Specifies the new high-level nonfatal error procedure.

Availability

`XtSetWarningMsgHandler()` has been superseded by `XtAppSetWarningMsg-Handler()`.

Description

`XtSetWarningMsgHandler()` registers the procedure `msg_handler` as the procedure to be invoked by `XtWarningMsg()`.

Usage

`XtSetWarningMsgHandler()` has been superseded by `XtAppSetWarningMsg-Handler()`, which performs the same function on a per-application context basis. `XtSet-WarningMsgHandler()` now calls `XtAppSetWarningMsgHandler()` passing the default application context created by `XtInitialize()`. Very few programs need multiple application contexts, and you can continue to use `XtSetWarningMsgHandler()` if you initialize your application with `XtInitialize()`. We recommend, however, that you use `XtAppInitialize()`, `XtAppSetWarningMsgHandler()`, and the other `XtApp*()` application context specific functions.

See `XtAppSetWarningMsgHandler()` for more information.

See Also

XtAppSetErrorHandler(1), *XtAppSetErrorMsgHandler*(1), *XtAppSetWarningHandler*(1), *XtAppWarning-Msg*(1),
XtErrorMsgHandler(2).

XtStringConversionWarning

Name

XtStringConversionWarning – emit boilerplate string conversion error message.

Synopsis

```
void XtStringConversionWarning(src, dst_type)
    String src, dst_type;
```

Inputs

src   Specifies the string that could not be converted.

dst_type   Specifies the name of the type to which the string could not be converted.

Description

`XtStringConversionWarning()` is a convenience routine for use in old-style resource converters that convert from strings. It issues a warning message with the name `conversionError`, type `string`, class `XtToolkitError`, and default message string:

`"Cannot convert src to type dst_type"`

It can be used by a conversion routine to announce a nonfatal conversion error.

Usage

New-style resource converters should call `XtDisplayStringConversionWarning()` instead of `XtStringConversionWarning()` to display their conversion warning messages. These functions display similar messages and differ only in that `XtDisplayStringConversionWarning()` is passed a display pointer as its first argument.

Old-style converters are not passed a display pointer, and so must use the old function `XtStringConversionWarning()` which does not require one.

See Also

XtDisplayStringConversionWarning(1).

XtSuperclass

Name

XtSuperclass – obtain a widget's superclass.

Synopsis

```
WidgetClass XtSuperclass(object)
    Widget object;
```

Inputs

object Specifies the object whose superclass is to be returned; may be of class Object or any subclass thereof.

Returns

The superclass of *object*.

Description

XtSuperclass() returns a pointer to the class structure of the widget's superclass.

Usage

XtSuperclass() is implemented as a function when called from application code, but is replaced by a more efficient macro when called from widget code that includes the file *<X11/IntrinsicP.h>*.

See Also

XtCheckSubclass(1), *XtClass*(1), *XtIsSubclass*(1).

Xt Functions
and Macros

XtToolkitInitialize

Name

XtToolkitInitialize – initialize the X Toolkit internals.

Synopsis

```
void XtToolkitInitialize()
```

Description

XtToolkitInitialize() initializes internal Toolkit data structures. It does not set up an application context or open a display.

XtAppInitialize() calls XtToolkitInitialize() in the course of its initialization. Programs too sophisticated to use XtAppInitialize() (such as those that create multiple application contexts) may want to call XtToolkitInitialize() explicitly.

The semantics of calling XtToolkitInitialize() more than once are undefined.

See Also

XtAppInitialize(1).

Name

XtTranslateCoords – translate an x-y coordinate pair from widget coordinates to root coordinates.

Synopsis

```
void XtTranslateCoords(w, x, y, root_x_return, root_y_return)
    Widget w;
    Position x, y;
    Position *root_x_return, *root_y_return;
```

Inputs

w   Specifies the widget.

x, y   Specify x and y coordinates, relative to w.

Outputs

root_x_return, root_y_return

Return the same x and y coordinates, relative to the root window.

Description

XtTranslateCoords() transforms the widget-relative coordinates x and y into coordinates relative to the root window, and returns these transformed coordinates in root_x_return and root_y_return.

XtTranslateCoords() is similar to the Xlib XTranslateCoordinates() function, which also translates window-relative coordinates to display-relative coordinates. But XtTranslateCoords() does not usually generate a server request because most of the time the required information is already in the widget's data structures.

Usage

XtTranslateCoords() is useful in popping up a popup shell, since it must be explicitly moved from its default location at the upper-left corner of the screen. A typical approach is to pop up dialogs centered over the main application window.

See Also

Core(3).

XtTranslateKey

Name

XtTranslateKey – the default keycode-to-keysym translator.

Synopsis

```
void XtTranslateKey(display, keycode, modifiers,
        modifiers_return, keysym_return)
    Display *display;
    KeyCode keycode;
    Modifiers modifiers;
    Modifiers *modifiers_return;
    KeySym *keysym_return;
```

Inputs

display   Specifies the display that the keycode is from.

keycode   Specifies the keycode to translate.

modifiers   Specifies the modifiers to be applied to the keycode.

Outputs

modifiers_return

        Returns the modifiers examined by the key translator.

keysym_return

        Returns the resulting keysym.

Description

XtTranslateKey() is the default XtKeyProc used by the Translation Manager. It takes a keycode and returns the corresponding keysym, recognizing Shift, Lock, and group modifiers. It handles all the keysyms defined by the X Protocol.

XtTranslateKey() is provided for two main reasons: so that new translators with expanded functionality can call it to get default keycode-to-keysym translations in addition to whatever they add, and so that the default translator can be reinstalled.

See XtKeyProc(2) for more information on the behavior of this and all key translator procedures.

Usage

The Translation Manager invokes the currently registered key translator procedure to convert incoming keycodes to keysyms. Only clients that need to work with non-standard keysyms should need to register alternate key translator procedures.

XtTranslateKey() can be invoked directly, or the currently registered key translator can be invoked by calling XtTranslateKeycode(). A new translator can be registered by calling XtSetKeyTranslator(). There is no way to remove a translator; to reinstall the default behavior, call XtSetKeyTranslator() with XtTranslateKey() as the *proc* argument.

Structures

The `KeyCode` and `KeySym` types are defined as follows:

```
typedef unsigned char KeyCode;
typedef XID KeySym;
```

The `Modifiers` type and its legal values are defined as follows:

```
typedef unsigned int Modifiers;
#define ShiftMask(1<<0)
#define LockMask(1<<1)
#define ControlMask(1<<2)
#define Mod1Mask(1<<3)
#define Mod2Mask(1<<4)
#define Mod3Mask(1<<5)
#define Mod4Mask(1<<6)
#define Mod5Mask(1<<7)
```

See Also

XtRegisterCaseConverter(1), *XtSetKeyTranslator*(1), *XtTranslateKeycode*(1),
XtKeyProc(2).

XtTranslateKeycode

Name

XtTranslateKeycode – invoke the currently registered keycode-to-keysym translator.

Synopsis

```
void XtTranslateKeycode(display, keycode, modifiers, modifiers_return,
        keysym_return)
    Display *display;
    KeyCode keycode;
    Modifiers modifiers;
    Modifiers *modifiers_return;
    KeySym *keysym_return;
```

Inputs

display   Specifies the display that the keycode is from.

keycode   Specifies the keycode to translate.

modifiers   Specifies the modifiers to be applied to the keycode.

Outputs

modifiers_return

Returns a mask that indicates the modifiers actually used to generate the keysym.

keysym_return

Returns the resulting keysym.

Description

XtTranslateKeycode() converts a keycode plus modifiers into a keysym. It invokes the currently registered keycode-to-keysym translator (XtTranslateKey() by default) and passes its arguments directly to that converter.

See XtTranslateKey() for a description of the default translator. See XtKeyProc(2) for more details on the operation of a keycode-to-keysym translator procedure.

Usage

The Translation Manager invokes the currently registered key translator procedure to convert incoming keycodes to keysyms. Only clients that need to work with non-standard keysyms should need to register alternate key translator procedures.

The default key translator, XtTranslateKey(), can also be invoked directly. A new translator can be registered by calling XtSetKeyTranslator().

Structures

The KeyCode and KeySym types are defined as follows:

```
typedef unsigned char KeyCode;
typedef XID KeySym;
```

The Modifiers type and its legal values are defined as follows:

```
typedef unsigned int Modifiers;
```

```
#define ShiftMask(1<<0)
#define LockMask(1<<1)
#define ControlMask(1<<2)
#define Mod1Mask(1<<3)
#define Mod2Mask(1<<4)
#define Mod3Mask(1<<5)
#define Mod4Mask(1<<6)
#define Mod5Mask(1<<7)
```

See Also

XtRegisterCaseConverter(1), *XtSetKeyTranslator*(1), *XtTranslateKey*(1), *XtKeyProc*(2).

XtUngrabButton

Name

XtUngrabButton – cancel a passive button grab.

Synopsis

```
void XtUngrabButton(widget, button, modifiers)
    Widget widget;
    unsigned int button;
    Modifiers modifiers;
```

Inputs

widget Specifies the widget in whose window the button was grabbed.

button Specifies the mouse button to be ungrabbed.

modifiers Specifies the modifier keys to be ungrabbed.

Availability

Release 4 and later.

Description

XtUngrabButton() cancels a passive grab of the specified button/modifiers combination. If *w* is realized, XtUngrabButton() calls XUngrabButton() specifying the widget's window as the ungrab window, and passing the remaining arguments unmodified. If the widget is not realized, XtUngrabButton() removes the deferred XtGrabButton() request, if any, for the specified widget, button, and modifiers.

The *button* argument is one of Button1, Button2, Button3, Button4, Button5, or the constant AnyButton, which is equivalent to issuing the ungrab request for all possible buttons.

The *modifiers* argument is a bitwise OR of one or more of the following symbols: Shift-Mask, LockMask, ControlMask, Mod1Mask, Mod2Mask, Mod3Mask, Mod4Mask, Mod5Mask. The special value AnyModifier is also allowed; using it is equivalent to issuing the ungrab button request for all possible modifier combinations (including no modifiers).

XtUngrabButton() has no effect on an active grab.

See XtGrabButton() for more information on passive button grabs.

Usage

You should rarely need to use passive button grabs. An automatic grab takes place between a ButtonPress event and the corresponding ButtonRelease event, so an explicit grab is not necessary in some of the most common situations. It may be necessary for some styles of menus, however.

Note that XtAddGrab() and spring-loaded popups can be used in place of passive grabs in many circumstances. These do not actually issue any X server grabs.

Structures

The `Modifiers` type is defined as follows:

```
typedef unsigned int Modifiers;
```

See Also

XtAddGrab(1), *XtGrabButton*(1), *XtGrabKey*(1), *XtGrabKeyboard*(1), *XtGrabPointer*(1), *XtUngrabKey*(1), *XtUngrabKeyboard*(1), *XtUngrabPointer*(1).

XtUngrabKey

Name

XtUngrabKey – cancel a passive key grab.

Synopsis

```
void XtUngrabKey(widget, keycode, modifiers)
        Widget widget;
        KeyCode keycode;
        Modifiers modifiers;
```

Inputs

widget Specifies the widget in whose window the key was grabbed.

keycode Specifies the keycode to be ungrabbed.

modifiers Specifies the modifiers to be ungrabbed.

Availability

Release 4 and later.

Description

XtUngrabKey() cancels a passive grab on the specified keycode/modifiers combination for widget *w*. If *w* is realized, XtUngrabKey() calls XUngrabKey() specifying the widget's window as the ungrab window and passing the remaining argument unmodified. If the widget is not realized XtUngrabKey() removes the deferred XtGrabKey() request, if any, for the specified widget, keycode and modifiers.

The *keycode* argument is the keycode of the key you want to ungrab, or the special value AnyKey which is equivalent to issuing the request for all possible nonmodifier key codes.

The *modifiers* argument is a bitwise OR of one or more of the following symbols: Shift-Mask, LockMask, ControlMask, Mod1Mask, Mod2Mask, Mod3Mask, Mod4Mask, Mod5Mask. The special value AnyModifier is also allowed; using it is equivalent to issuing the ungrab button request for all possible modifier combinations (including no modifiers).

XtUngrabKey() has no effect on an active grab.

See XtGrabKey() for more details on passive key grabs.

Usage

Most applications will never need to issue a passive grab. XtAddGrab() (called by Xt-Popup()) can be used to implement modal popups inside an application, and XtSet-KeyboardFocus() can be used to redirect keyboard focus within an application. Neither function actually issues a grab, and so does not interrupt event processing by other clients.

Structures

The Modifiers and KeyCode types are defined as follows:

```
typedef unsigned int Modifiers;
typedef unsigned char KeyCode;
```

See Also

XtAddGrab(1), *XtGrabButton*(1), *XtGrabKey*(1), *XtGrabKeyboard*(1), *XtGrabPointer*(1), *XtSet-KeyboardFocus*(1), *XtUngrabButton*(1), *XtUngrabKeyboard*(1), *XtUngrabPointer*(1).

XtUngrabKeyboard

Name

XtUngrabKeyboard – release an active keyboard grab.

Synopsis

```
void XtUngrabKeyboard(widget, time)
      Widget widget;
      Time time;
```

Inputs

widget   Specifies the widget which has the active keyboard grab.

time   Specifies the time when the grab should end. `CurrentTime` is acceptable.

Availability

Release 4 and later.

Description

XtUngrabKeyboard() releases an active keyboard grab by calling XUngrab-Keyboard(), passing the display of *widget* and *time*.

The *time* argument may be a timestamp or the constant `CurrentTime`. If the specified time is earlier than the last-keyboard-grab time or later than the current server time the keyboard will not be ungrabbed.

See XtGrabKeyboard() for more information about grabbing the keyboard.

Usage

Most applications will never need to issue a grab. XtAddGrab() (called by XtPopup()) can be used to implement modal popups inside an application, and XtSetKeyboard-Focus() can be used to redirect keyboard focus within an application. Neither function actually issues a grab, and so does not interrupt event processing by other clients.

See Also

XtAddGrab(1), *XtGrabButton*(1), *XtGrabKey*(1), *XtGrabKeyboard*(1), *XtGrabPointer*(1), *XtSet-KeyboardFocus*(1), *XtUngrabButton*(1), *XtUngrabKey*(1), *XtUngrabPointer*(1).

Name

XtUngrabPointer – release an active pointer grab.

Synopsis

```
void XtUngrabPointer(widget, time)
    Widget widget;
    Time time;
```

Inputs

widget   Specifies the widget which has the active pointer grab.

time   Specifies the time at which the grab should end. CurrentTime is acceptable.

Availability

Release 4 and later.

Description

XtUngrabPointer() releases an active pointer grab by calling XUngrabPointer() with the display of *w* and *time*.

The *time* argument may be a timestamp or the constant CurrentTime. If this time is earlier than the last-keyboard-grab time or later than the current server time the keyboard will not be ungrabbed.

See XtGrabPointer() for more information on active pointer grabs.

Usage

Most applications will never have to issue a pointer grab. Note that the pointer is automatically grabbed between every button down event and the corresponding button up event; this covers the case for which pointer grabs are most commonly needed.

See Also

XtGrabButton(1), *XtGrabKey*(1), *XtGrabKeyboard*(1), *XtGrabPointer*(1), *XtSetKeyboardFocus*(1), *XtUngrabButton*(1), *XtUngrabKey*(1), *XtUngrabKeyboard*(1).

XtUninstallTranslations

Name

XtUninstallTranslations – remove all existing translations from a widget.

Synopsis

```
void XtUninstallTranslations(w)
    Widget w;
```

Inputs

w   Specifies the widget from which the translations are to be removed.

Description

XtUninstallTranslations() removes a widget's translation table.

Usage

Many widgets will not function correctly without their translations. A widget without translations will not respond to keyboard or mouse events, unless it explicitly registers an event handler for these events.

You can completely replace a widget's translations by setting a new translation table on the
XtNtranslations resource of the widget. You can merge new translations with existing
translations with XtAugmentTranslations() and XtOverrideTranslations().

See Also

XtAugmentTranslations(1), *XtOverrideTranslations*(1), *XtParseTranslationTable*(1).

XtUnmanageChild

Name

XtUnmanageChild – remove a widget from its parent's managed list.

Synopsis

```
void XtUnmanageChild(w)
    Widget w;
```

Inputs

w   Specifies the child widget to be unmanaged; must be of class RectObj or any subclass thereof.

Description

XtUnmanageChild() unmaps the specified widget and removes it from its parent's geometry management. The widget will disappear from the screen, and (depending on its parent) may no longer have screen space allocated for it.

XtUnmanageChild() simply calls XtUnmanageChildren(). See that function for more information about the procedure for unmanaging a widget.

Usage

Unmanaging a widget is the usual method for temporarily making it invisible. It can be re-managed with XtManageChild().

You can unmap a widget, but leave it under geometry management by calling XtUnmap-Widget(). You can destroy a widget's window without destroying the widget by calling Xt-UnrealizeWidget(). You can destroy a widget completely with XtDestroyWidget().

If you will be unmanaging several sibling widgets, it is more efficient to call XtUnmanage-Children() because this only generates a single call to the parent's change_managed() method. It is often more convenient to simply call XtUnmanageChild() several times, however.

See Also

XtIsManaged(1), *XtManageChild*(1), *XtManageChildren*(1), *XtUnmanageChildren*(1).

Xt Functions and Macros

XtUnmanageChildren

Name

XtUnmanageChildren – remove a list of children from a parent widget's managed list.

Synopsis

```
void XtUnmanageChildren(children, num_children)
    WidgetList children;
    Cardinal num_children;
```

Inputs

children   Specifies an array of child widgets. Each child must be of class RectObj or any subclass thereof.

num_children Specifies the number of elements in `children`.

Description

`XtUnmanageChildren()` unmaps the specified widgets and removes them from their parent's geometry management. The widgets will disappear from the screen, and (depending on its parent) may no longer have screen space allocated for them.

Each of the widgets in the `children` array must have the same parent.

See the "Algorithm" section below for full details of the widget unmanagement procedure.

Usage

Unmanaging widgets is the usual method for temporarily making them invisible. They can be re-managed with `XtManageChildren()`.

You can unmap a widget, but leave it under geometry management by calling `XtUnmapWidget()`. You can destroy a widget's window without destroying the widget by calling `XtUnrealizeWidget()`. You can destroy a widget completely with `XtDestroyWidget()`.

If you are only going to unmanage a single widget, it is more convenient to call `XtUnmanageChild()`. It is often more convenient to call `XtUnmanageChild()` several times than it is to declare and initialize an array of widgets to pass to `XtUnmanageChildren()`. Calling `XtUnmanageChildren()` is more efficient, however, because it only calls the parent's `change_managed()` method once.

Algorithm

`XtUnmanageChildren()` performs the following:

- Issues an error if the children do not all have the same parent or if the parent is not a subclass of `compositeWidgetClass`.

- Returns immediately if the common parent is being destroyed; otherwise, for each unique child on the list, `XtUnmanageChildren()` performs the following:

  - Ignores the child if it already is unmanaged or is being destroyed.

  - Otherwise, if the child is realized, it makes it nonvisible by unmapping it.

- Calls the `change_managed()` method of the widgets' parent if the parent is realized.

Structures

The `WidgetList` type is simply an array of widgets:

```
typedef Widget *WidgetList;
```

See Also

XtDestroyWidget(1), *XtIsManaged*(1), *XtManageChild*(1), *XtManageChildren*(1), *XtUnmanageChild*(1).

XtUnmapWidget

Name

XtUnmapWidget – unmap a widget explicitly.

Synopsis

```
XtUnmapWidget(w)
    Widget w;
```

Inputs

w   Specifies the widget to be unmapped; must be of class core or any subclass thereof.

Description

XtUnmapWidget() unmaps a widget's window from its display, causing it to become invisible. The widget remains under the geometry management of its parent, and will continue to have screen space allocated for it.

Usage

Most widgets are automatically mapped when they are managed, as controlled by the XtNmappedWhenManaged resource. Widgets that are not mapped automatically can be mapped and unmapped explicitly with XtMapWidget() and XtUnmapWidget().

Unmanaging a widget, rather than unmapping it, is the usual method for temporarily removing a widget from the display.

See Also

XtMapWidget(1), *XtSetMappedWhenManaged*(1), *XtUnmanageChild*(1).

XtUnrealizeWidget

Name

XtUnrealizeWidget – destroy the windows associated with a widget and its descendants.

Synopsis

```
void XtUnrealizeWidget(w)
    Widget w;
```

Inputs

w   Specifies the widget. Must be of class Core or any subclass thereof.

Description

XtUnrealizeWidget() unmanages the specified widget and destroys the windows associated with the widget and all of its non-popup descendants.

The "Algorithm" section below explains the details of this process.

Usage

Note that this call simply destroys the windows associated with the widgets. The widget instances themselves remain intact. To recreate the windows at a later time, call XtRealizeWidget() again. Compare this to XtDestroyWidget(), which destroys the widgets themselves.

Unmanaging a widget is the usual method for temporarily removing it from the screen. Unrealizing a widget frees up resources on the X server, and may be a better choice for widgets that are only infrequently visible.

Algorithm

If the widget is currently unrealized, XtUnrealizeWidget() simply returns; otherwise, it performs the following:

- Unmanages the widget if the widget is managed.

- Makes a post-order (child to parent) traversal of the widget tree rooted at the specified widget and, for each widget that has declared a callback list named unrealizeCallback, executes the procedures on the XtNunrealizeCallback list.

- Destroys the widget's window and any subwindows by calling XDestroyWindow() on the specified widget's window.

Any events that are either in the queue or that arrive following a call to XtUnrealizeWidget() will be dispatched as if the window(s) of the unrealized widget(s) had never existed.

See Also

XtDestroyWidget(1), *XtRealizeWidget*(1), *XtUnmanageWidget*(1).

XtVaAppCreateShell

Name

XtVaAppCreateShell – create a top-level widget that is the root of a widget tree, using varargs argument style.

Synopsis

```
Widget XtVaAppCreateShell(application_name, application_class,
        widget_class, display, ..., NULL)
    String application_name;
    String application_class;
    WidgetClass widget_class;
    Display *display;
```

Inputs

application_name
> Specifies the resource name of the shell widget.

application_class
> Specifies the class name of this application.

widget_class
> Specifies the widget class for the top-level widget.

display   Specifies the display.

..., NULL   A NULL-terminated variable-length list of resource name/value pairs to override any other resource specifications.

Returns

A toplevel shell widget of the specified class.

Availability

Release 4 and later.

Description

XtVaAppCreateShell() creates a top-level shell widget that is the root of a widget tree and a resource name hierarchy (i.e. a widget that has no parent). It is identical to XtApp-CreateShell() except that the *args* array of resource names and values and the *num_args* argument of that function are replaced with a NULL-terminated variable-length argument list.

See XtAppCreateShell() for more information on this function. See XtVaSet-Values() for more information on using variable-length argument lists to specify resources.

Usage

Most applications create secondary top-level shells with XtCreatePopupShell() which creates a widget in the same resource hierarchy as the rest of the application. Most applications can use XtAppInitialize() or XtVaAppInitialize() to initialize the toolkit and create their first shell.

See Also

XtAppCreateShell(1), *XtAppInitialize*(1), *XtCreatePopupShell*(1), *XtVaAppInitialize*(1), *XtVaSetValues*(1).

XtVaAppInitialize

Name

XtVaAppInitialize – initialize the X Toolkit internals, using varargs argument style.

Synopsis

```
Widget XtVaAppInitialize(app_context_return, application_class, options,
        num_options, argc_in_out, argv_in_out, fallback_resources, ...,
        NULL)
    XtAppContext *app_context_return;
    String application_class;
    XrmOptionDescList options;
    Cardinal num_options;
    int *argc_in_out;        /* was type Cardinal * in Release 4 */
    String *argv_in_out;
    String *fallback_resources;
```

Inputs

application_class   Specifies the class name of the application.

options   Specifies the command line options table.

num_options   Specifies the number of entries in options.

argc_in_out   Specifies a pointer to the number of command line arguments. This argument was a `Cardinal *` in Release 4, and is an `int *` in Release 5.

argv_in_out   Specifies the command line arguments array.

fallback_resources

Specifies resource values to be used if the application class resource file cannot be opened, or NULL.

..., NULL   A NULL-terminated variable-length list of resource name/value pairs to override any other resource specifications for the created shell.

Outputs

app_context_return

Returns the application context, if non-NULL.

Returns

A toplevel shell widget of class `applicationShellWidgetClass`.

Availability

Release 4 and later.

Description

XtVaAppInitialize() initializes the Toolkit internals, creates an application context, opens and initializes a display, and creates the initial application shell. It is identical to Xt-AppInitialize() except that the *args* array of resource names and values and the *num_args* argument of that function are replaced with a NULL-terminated variable-length argument list.

See `XtAppInitialize()` for more information on this function. See `XtVaSetValues()` for more information on using variable-length argument lists to specify resources.

See Also

XtAppInitialize(1), *XtVaSetValues*(1).

Name

XtVaCreateArgsList – create a varargs list for use with the XtVaNestedList symbol.

Synopsis

```
XtVarArgsList XtVaCreateArgsList(unused, ..., NULL)
     XtPointer unused;
```

Inputs

unused   This argument is not currently used and must be specified as NULL.

..., NULL   A NULL-terminated variable-length list of resource name/value pairs.

Returns

An XtVarArgsList which can be used in future calls to other XtVa functions.

Availability

Release 4 and later.

Description

XtVaCreateArgsList() allocates, copies its arguments into, and returns a pointer to a structure that can be used in future calls to XtVa functions using the special symbol XtVa-NestedList. When this symbol appears in place of a resource name in a variable-length argument list, the next value is interpreted not as a resource value itself, but as a nested argument list of resource name/resource value pairs.

When an XtVarArgsList is created, any entries in the list of type XtVaTypedArg are copied as specified without applying conversions; they will be converted when the list is actually used. Pointer types (including strings) passed to XtVaCreateArgsList() are not copied; the caller must ensure that the data remains valid for the lifetime of the created Xt-VarArgsList.

When no longer needed, the returned list should be freed using XtFree().

See XtVaSetValues() for full details on the use of variable length argument lists.

Usage

Nested lists can be useful with the XtVa functions in the same circumstances that statically initialized ArgLists are useful to the non-XtVa functions: when there are a set of resources that will be applied to more than one widget. The example below presents one such case.

Example

You might want to use nested argument lists to define a set of related resources that will be applied to multiple widgets:

```
XFontStruct *normal_font, *bold_font;
XtVarArgsList caution_resources;
Widget box, commit, abort;

caution_resources = XtVaCreateArgsList(NULL,
                    XtNFont, bold_font,
                    XtVaTypedArg, XtNforeground, XtRString, "red", 4,
```

```
                          XtNborderWidth, 4,
                          NULL);

commit = XtVaCreateWidget("commit", buttonWidgetClass, box,
                          XtNlabel, "Commit All Changes",
                          XtVaNestedList, caution_resources,
                          NULL);

abort = XtVaCreateWidget("abort", buttonWidgetClass, box,
                          XtNlabel, "Abort Transaction",
                          XtVaNestedList, caution_resources,
                          NULL);

/* free the list since I'm not going to use it again */
XtFree(caution_resources);
```

Structures

The `XtVarArgsList` type is defined as follows:

```
typedef XtPointer XtVarArgsList;
```

See Also

XtVaSetValues(1).

XtVaCreateManagedWidget

Name

XtVaCreateManagedWidget – create and manage a widget, specifying resources with a varargs list.

Synopsis

```
Widget XtVaCreateManagedWidget(name, widget_class, parent, ..., NULL)
    String name;
    WidgetClass widget_class;
    Widget parent;
```

Inputs

name   Specifies the resource name for the created widget.

widget_class
                    Specifies the widget class pointer for the created widget. Must be rectObj-
                    Class or any subclass.

parent   Specifies the parent widget. Must be of class Composite or any subclass
                    thereof.

..., NULL   A NULL-terminated variable-length list of resource name/value pairs to over-
                    ride any other resource specifications.

Returns

The created and managed widget.

Availability

Release 4 and later.

Description

XtVaCreateManagedWidget() creates a widget or object named *name*, of class
widget_class, as a child of *parent*, and with resource values as specified in the remaining
arguments. It is identical to XtCreateManagedWidget() except that the *args* array of
resource names and values and the *num_args* argument of that function are replaced with a
NULL-terminated variable-length argument list.

See XtCreateManagedWidget() for more information on this function. See XtVaSet-
Values() for more information on using variable-length argument lists to specify resources.

See Also

XtCreateWidget(1), *XtCreateManagedWidget*(1), *XtManageChild*(1), *XtVaCreateWidget*(1), *XtVaSet-
Values*(1).

XtVaCreatePopupShell

Name

XtVaCreatePopupShell – create a popup shell, specifying resources with a varargs list.

Synopsis

```
Widget XtVaCreatePopupShell(name, widget_class, parent, ..., NULL)
    String name;
    WidgetClass widget_class;
    Widget parent;
```

Inputs

name   Specifies the resource name for the created shell widget.

widget_class

        Specifies the widget class pointer for the created shell widget.

parent   Specifies the parent widget. Must be of class Core or any subclass thereof.

..., NULL   A NULL-terminated variable-length list of resource name/value pairs to override any other resource specifications.

Returns

A shell widget of the specified class.

Availability

Release 4 and later.

Description

XtVaCreatePopupShell() creates and returns a shell widget of class *widget_class* and named *name*, as a popup child of *parent*. It is identical to XtCreatePopupShell() except that the *args* array of resource names and values and the *num_args* argument of that function are replaced with a NULL-terminated variable-length argument list.

See XtCreatePopupShell() for more information on this function. See XtVaSetValues() for more information on using variable-length argument lists to specify resources.

See Also

XtCreatePopupShell(1), *XtVaSetValues*(1).

Name

XtVaCreateWidget – create a widget, specifying resources with a varargs list.

Synopsis

```
Widget XtVaCreateWidget(name, object_class, parent, ..., NULL)
    String name;
    WidgetClass object_class;
    Widget parent;
```

Inputs

name   Specifies the resource name for the created widget.

object_class
                        Specifies the widget class pointer for the created object; may be objectClass
                        or any subclass.

parent   Specifies the parent widget. May be of class Object or any subclass thereof.

..., NULL   A NULL-terminated variable-length list of resource name/value pairs to over-
                        ride any other resource specifications.

Returns

A widget of the specified class.

Availability

Release 4 and later.

Description

XtVaCreateWidget() creates and returns a widget or object of class *widget_class*
with name *name*, as a child of *parent*. It is identical to XtCreateWidget() except that
the *args* array of resource names and values and the *num_args* argument of that function are
replaced with a NULL-terminated variable-length argument list.

See XtCreateWidget() for more information on this function. See XtVaSetValues()
for more information on using variable-length argument lists to specify resources.

See Also

XtCreateManagedWidget(1), *XtCreateWidget*(1), *XtVaCreateManagedWidget*(1), *XtVaSetValues*(1).

Name

XtVaGetApplicationResources – retrieve resources for the overall application using varargs argument style.

Synopsis

```
void XtVaGetApplicationResources(object, base, resources, num_resources,
        ..., NULL)
    Widget object;
    XtPointer base;
    XtResourceList resources;
    Cardinal num_resources;
```

Inputs

object   Specifies the object that identifies the resource database to search (the database is that associated with the display for this object); may be of class Object or any subclass thereof.

base   Specifies the address of structure into which the resources will be written.

resources Specifies the resource list for the subpart.

num_resources
     Specifies the number of resources in the resource list.

..., NULL A NULL-terminated variable-length list of resource name/value pairs to override any other resource specifications.

Availability

Release 4 and later.

Description

XtVaGetApplicationResources() obtains values for the resources described by *resources*, from the variable-length argument list, the resource database, or from the default values associated with each resource, and stores these values into the structure pointed to by base. It is identical to XtGetApplicationResources() except that the *args* array of resource names and values and the *num_args* argument of that function are replaced with a NULL-terminated variable-length argument list.

See XtGetApplicationResources() for more information on this function. See XtVaSetValues() for more information on using variable-length argument lists to specify resources.

See Also

XtGetApplicationResources(1), *XtVaGetSubresources*(1), *XtVaSetValues*(1).

Name

XtVaGetSubresources – fetch resources for widget subparts, using varargs argument style.

Synopsis

```
void XtVaGetSubresources(object, base, name, class, resources,
        num_resources, ..., NULL)
    Widget object;
    XtPointer base;
    String name;
    String class;
    XtResourceList resources;
    Cardinal num_resources;
```

Inputs

object   Specifies the object used to qualify the subpart resource name and class; may be of class Object or any subclass thereof.

base   Specifies the base address of the subpart data structure into which the resources will be written.

name   Specifies the name of the subpart.

class   Specifies the class of the subpart.

resources   Specifies the resource list for the subpart.

num_resources
      Specifies the number of resources in the resource list.

..., NULL   A NULL-terminated variable-length list of resource name/value pairs to override any other resource specifications.

Availability

Release 4 and later.

Description

XtVaGetSubresources() gets values for each of the resources described in *resources* from the variable length argument list, the resource database, or the default values associated with each resource, and stores these values into the structure pointed to by base. It is identical to XtGetSubresources() except that the *args* array of resource names and values and the *num_args* argument of that function are replaced with a NULL-terminated variable-length argument list.

See XtGetSubresources() for more information on this function. See XtVaSet-Values() for more information on using variable-length argument lists to specify resources. See XtGetApplicationResources() for a description of how to declare an Xt-ResourceList.

See Also

XtGetApplicationResources(1), *XtGetSubresources*(1), *XtVaSetValues*(1).

XtVaGetSubvalues

Name

XtVaGetSubvalues – retrieve the current values of subpart resources, using varargs argument style.

Synopsis

```
void XtVaGetSubvalues(base, resources, num_resources, ..., NULL)
    XtPointer base;
    XtResourceList resources;
    Cardinal num_resources;
```

Inputs

base   Specifies the base address of the subpart data structure for which the resources should be retrieved.

resources   Specifies the subpart resource list.

num_resources
                 Specifies the number of resources in the resource list.

..., NULL   A NULL-terminated variable-length list of resource names and the addresses at which the values of those resources are to be stored.

Availability

Release 4 and later.

Description

XtVaGetSubvalues() obtains the values of the resources named in the variable-length argument list (and described in the resource list *resources*) from the subpart structure pointed to by *base*, and stores those values at the addresses specified in the variable length argument list. Note that the special symbol XtVaTypedArg is not supported by XtVaGet-Subvalues(). If XtVaTypedArg is specified in the list, a warning message is issued and the entry is then ignored.

XtVaGetSubvalues() is identical to XtGetSubvalues() except that the *args* array of resource names and values and the *num_args* argument of that function are replaced with a NULL-terminated variable-length argument list.

See XtGetSubvalues() for more information on this function. See XtVaSetValues() for more information on using variable-length argument lists to specify resources. See Xt-GetApplicationResources() for information on how to declare an XtResource-List.

See Also

XtGetApplicationResources(1), *XtGetSubvalues*(1), *XtVaSetValues*(1).

Name

XtVaGetValues – retrieve the current values of widget resources, using varargs argument style.

Synopsis

```
void XtVaGetValues(object, ..., NULL)
      Widget object;
```

Inputs

object   Specifies the object whose resource values are to be returned; may be of class Object or any subclass thereof.

..., NULL   A NULL-terminated variable-length list of resource names and the addresses at which the values of those resources are to be stored.

Availability

Release 4 and later.

Description

XtVaGetValues() gets the values of the resources named in the variable length argument list from the specified widget or object and stores those values at the addresses specified in the argument list. It is the caller's responsibility to ensure that sufficient storage is allocated. If XtVaTypedArg is specified, the following type argument field specifies the representation desired by the caller and the following size argument specifies the number of bytes allocated to store the result of the conversion. If the size is insufficient, a warning message is issued and the list entry is skipped.

XtVaGetValues() is identical to XtGetValues() except that the *args* array of resource names and values and the *num_args* argument of that function are replaced with a NULL-terminated
variable-length argument list.

See XtGetValues() for more information on this function. See XtVaSetValues() for more information on using variable-length argument lists to specify resources.

Example

You can use XtVaGetValues() as follows:

```
Pixel color;
XFontStruct *font;
String label;
Widget w;

XtVaGetValues(w,
            XtNforeground, &color,
            XtNfont, &font,
            XtNlabel &label,
            NULL);
```

See Also
>   *XtGetValues*(1), *XtSetValues*(1), *XtVaSetValues*(1).

XtVaSetSubvalues

Name

XtVaSetSubvalues – set the current values of subpart resources, using varargs argument style.

Synopsis

```
void XtVaSetSubvalues(base, resources, num_resources, ..., NULL)
        XtPointer base;
        XtResourceList resources;
        Cardinal num_resources;
```

Inputs

base   Specifies the base address of the subpart data structure into which the resources should be written.

resources   Specifies the subpart resource list.

num_resources

                Specifies the number of resources in the resource list.

..., NULL   A NULL-terminated variable-length list of resource name/value pairs to override any other resource specifications.

Availability

Release 4 and later.

Description

XtVaSetSubvalues() sets the resources named in the variable length argument list to the values specified in the same list. The values are copied into the structure pointed to by *base* at the offset specified by the resource descriptions in *resources*. Note that the special resource name XtVaTypedArg is not supported by XtVaSetSubvalues(). If XtVaTypedArg is specified in the list, a warning message is issued and the entry is then ignored.

XtVaSetSubvalues() is identical to XtSetSubvalues() except that the *args* array of resource names and values and the *num_args* argument of that function are replaced with a NULL-terminated variable-length argument list.

See XtSetSubvalues() for more information on this function. See XtVaSetValues() for more information on using variable-length argument lists to specify resources. See XtGetApplicationResources() for a description of how to declare an XtResourceList.

See Also

XtGetApplicationResources(1), *XtSetSubvalues*(1), *XtVaSetValues*(1).

XtVaSetValues

Name

XtVaSetValues – set resource values for a widget, using varargs argument style.

Synopsis

```
void XtVaSetValues(object, ..., NULL)
      Widget object;
```

Inputs

object   Specifies the object whose resources are to be modified; may be of class Object or any subclass thereof.

..., NULL   A NULL-terminated variable-length list of resource name/value pairs to override any other resource specifications.

Availability

Release 4 and later.

Description

XtVaSetValues() sets the resources of *object* named in the variable-length argument list to the values specified in the same list. It is identical to XtSetValues() except that the *args* array of resource names and values and the *num_args* argument of that function are replaced with a NULL-terminated variable-length argument list.

The "Background" section below explains how to specify resource names and values in a variable-length argument list. See XtSetValues() for more information on setting widget resources.

Usage

Using variable-length argument lists is usually much more convenient than passing an ArgList which must be declared and initialized. Note that the varargs interface is less efficient than the ArgList interface, because each varargs function converts its argument list into an ArgList and calls the corresponding ArgList function. Unless you are setting or querying resources repeatedly, however, this overhead is not generally significant.

Variable-length argument lists cannot be type-checked by the compiler, and so using XtVaSetValues() and other varargs functions can be a source of bugs. Be sure to end all of your argument lists with NULL, and be sure that the type of each argument is as expected. If you specify only a single name/value pair per line, it will be easy to delete or comment out resources, and to insert new resources at an acceptable place.

Example

You can use XtVaSetValues() as in the following example:

```
XtVaSetValues(w,
            XtNlabel, "Enter a value:",
            XtNjustify, XtJustifyRight,
            XLVaTypedArg, XtNforeground, XtRString, "red", 4,
            NULL);
```

Background

This function and the other `XtVa` functions have resource names and values specified in a NULL-terminated variable-length argument list, rather than an `ArgList` array. Generally, the argument list to these functions will consist of resource names (of type `String`) followed by resource values (these are of type `XtArgVal`, but because varargs lists cannot be type-checked, you do not have to cast your values). There are two special symbols which can be used in place of a resource name, however. Each symbol modifies the interpretation of the following arguments.

`XtVaNestedList`

> If you specify a resource name of `XtVaNestedList`, the following argument will be interpreted as an `XtVarArgsList` value, as returned by `XtVaCreateArgsList()`. The resource names and values on this nested list will be treated exactly as if they were specified at the current point in the original list. Nested lists may contain other nested lists, to any depth of nesting.

`XtVaTypedArg`

> If you specify a resource name of `XtVaTypedArg`, then the following four arguments will be interpreted specially as instructions to invoke a resource converter and set a resource to the result of the conversion. The first following argument is the name of the resource to be set, and must be of type `String`. The second following argument is also a `String`, the resource type of the following value. This type, plus the type of the named resource identify the resource converter to be invoked. This argument is usually `Xt-RString`, or one of the other `XtR` types predefined by the Intrinsics. The third following argument is the value to be converted. It is of the type specified by the previous argument, usually a `String`. If the type is not `XtRString`, then if the value fits in an `XtArgVal`, it is passed directly in the argument list, otherwise a pointer to the value is passed. Finally, the forth following argument is the size in bytes of the type. If the type is `XtRString`, however, then type should be the length of the string plus one, not `sizeof(String)`.

The example above show a use of the `XtVaTypedArg` value. See `XtVaCreateArgs-List()` for an example of `XtVaNestedList`.

See Also

XtSetValues(1), *XtVaCreateArgsList*(1).

XtWarning

Name

XtWarning – call the low-level warning handler.

Synopsis

```
void XtWarning(message)
    String message;
```

Inputs

message   Specifies the nonfatal error message to be reported.

Availability

`XtWarning()` has been superseded by `XtAppWarning()`.

Description

`XtWarning()` passes its argument to the installed low-level warning handler. On POSIX systems, the default handler is `_XtDefaultWarning()`. It prints the message to the stderr stream and returns.

Usage

`XtWarning()` has been superseded by `XtAppWarning()`, which performs the same function on a per-application context basis. `XtWarning()` now calls `XtAppWarning()` passing the default application context created by `XtInitialize()`. Very few programs need multiple application contexts, and you can continue to use `XtWarning()` if you initialize your application with `XtInitialize()`. We recommend, however, that you use `XtApp-Initialize()`, `XtAppWarning()`, and the other `XtApp*()` application context specific functions.

See `XtAppWarning()` for more information.

`XtWarning()` calls the "low-level" warning handler. It is better to use `XtAppWarning-Msg()` which calls the "high-level" warning handler. The high-level handler looks up the warning message in a resource database and so allows for customization and internationalization of error messages.

See Also

XtAppWarning(1), *XtAppWarningMsg*(1).

Name

XtWarningMsg – call the high-level warning handler.

Synopsis

```
void XtWarningMsg(name, type, class, default, params, num_params)
    String name;
    String type;
    String class;
    String default;
    String *params;
    Cardinal *num_params;
```

Inputs

name	Specifies the general kind of error.
type	Specifies the detailed name of the error.
class	Specifies the resource class of the error.
default	Specifies the default message to use if no message is found in the database.
params	Specifies an array of values to be inserted into the message.
num_params	Specifies the number of elements in *params*.

Availability

XtWarningMsg() has been superseded by XtAppWarningMsg().

Description

XtWarningMsg() passes all of its arguments to the installed high-level warning handler. The default high-level warning handler is _XtDefaultWarningMsg(). It calls XtApp-GetErrorDatabaseText() to lookup an error message of the specified *name*, *type*, and *class* in the error database. If no such message is found, XtAppGetErrorDatabase-Text() returns the specified *default* message. In either case, _XtDefaultWarning-Msg() does a printf-style substitution of *params* into the message, and passes the resulting text to the low-level warning handler by calling XtWarning().

Usage

XtWarningMsg() has been superseded by XtAppWarningMsg(), which performs the same function on a per-application context basis. XtWarningMsg() now calls XtApp-WarningMsg() passing the default application context created by XtInitialize(). Very few programs need multiple application contexts, and you can continue to use Xt-WarningMsg() if you initialize your application with XtInitialize(). We recommend, however, that you use XtAppInitialize(), XtAppWarningMsg(), and the other Xt-App*() application context specific functions.

See XtAppWarningMsg() for more information.

See Also

XtAppErrorMsg(1), *XtAppWarningMsg*(1).

XtWidgetToApplicationContext

Name

XtWidgetToApplicationContext – get the application context for a given widget.

Synopsis

```
XtAppContext XtWidgetToApplicationContext(object)
    Widget object;
```

Inputs

object   Specifies the object for which you want the application context; may be of class Object or any subclass thereof.

Returns

The application context of *object*.

Description

XtWidgetToApplicationContext() returns the application context in which the specified widget or object was created.

Usage

This function is useful when an application context argument is required in widget code.

See Also

XtCreateApplicationContext(1).

Xt Functions and Macros

XtWindow

Name

XtWindow – return the window of the specified widget.

Synopsis

```
Window XtWindow(w)
    Widget w;
```

Inputs

w   Specifies the widget. Must be of class Core or any subclass thereof.

Returns

The window of w.

Description

XtWindow() returns the window of the specified widget. Note that the window is obtained from the Core window field, which may be NULL if the widget has not yet been realized.

Usage

XtWindow() is implemented as a function when called from application code, but is replaced by a more efficient macro when called from widget code that includes the file *<X11/Intrinsic-P.h>*.

Use XtWindowOfObject() to return the window of a widget or the nearest widget ancestor of a non-widget object.

See Also

XtDisplay(1), *XtScreen*(1), *XtWindowOfObject*(1), *XtWindowToWidget*(1).

XtWindowOfObject

Name

XtWindowOfObject – return the window for the nearest ancestor of object that is of class Core.

Synopsis

```
Window XtWindowOfObject(object)
      Widget object;
```

Inputs

object   Specifies the object; may be of class Object or any subclass thereof.

Returns

The window of *object* or of its nearest widget ancestor.

Availability

Release 4 and later.

Description

XtWindowOfObject·() is identical in function to XtWindow() if *object* is a widget; otherwise XtWindowOfObject() returns the window for the nearest ancestor of *object* that is of class Core or any subclass thereof.

Usage

If you are working with windowed objects, use XtWindow() rather than XtWindow-OfObject(). XtWindow() may be implemented as an efficient macro for widget code that includes the file *<X11/IntrinsicP.h>*.

See Also

XtDisplayOfObject(1), *XtScreenOfObject*(1), *XtWindow*(1).

XtWindowToWidget

Name

XtWindowToWidget – translate a window and display pointer into a widget ID.

Synopsis

```
Widget XtWindowToWidget(display, window)
    Display *display;
    Window window;
```

Inputs

display   Specifies the display on which the window is defined.

window   Specifies the window for which you want the widget.

Returns

The widget that created *window* on *display*, or NULL.

Description

XtWindowToWidget() takes a display pointer and a window and returns the associated widget ID. The widget must be within the same application as the caller.

If the specified display and window do not match any widget created by the application, Xt-WindowToWidget() returns NULL.

Usage

This function can be useful to convert the window of an XEvent structure into the corresponding widget. If you use the standard Intrinsics event dispatching mechanisms, however, this should not ever be necessary.

See Also

XtNameToWidget(1), *XtWindow*(1).

Section 2

Prototype Procedures

This section contains alphabetically-organized reference pages for each of the procedure types defined by the Intrinsics and used by Xt programs and widgets as callbacks, handlers, methods, and so on. In C parlance these are sometimes called prototype procedures.

The first reference page, Introduction, *explains the format and contents of each of the following pages.*

In This Section:

Introduction

This page describes the format and contents of each reference page in Section 2, which covers all of the procedure types used by the Intrinsics for callback procedures, handler procedures, widget methods, and so on.

Name

Function type — a brief description of the purpose of the function type.

Synopsis

This section shows the signature of the function: the names and types of the arguments, and the type of the return value. Each prototype procedure has a typedef which defines a name for its particular signature.

Inputs

This subsection describes each of the function arguments that pass information to the function.

Outputs

This subsection describes any of the function arguments that are used to return information from the function. These arguments are always of some pointer type, any you must remember to dereference them correctly in your function, and must store the appropriate information at the address they specify. The names of these arguments are usually suffixed with _return to indicate that values are returned in them. Some arguments both supply and return a value; they will be listed in this section and in the "Inputs" section above. Finally, note that because the list of function arguments is broken into "Input" and "Output" sections, they do not always appear in the same order that they are passed to the function. See the function signature for the actual calling order.

Returns

This subsection explains what, if anything, the function should return.

Availability

This section appears for prototype procedures that were added in Release 4 or Release 5, and also function types that are now superseded by other, preferred, function types.

Description

This section explains what the function should do, how it is registered, and what its arguments and return value are. If you've written functions of this type before and are just looking for a refresher, this section and the synopsis above should be all you need.

Usage

This section appears for most of the function types and provides less formal information about the function: hints on how to write it, things to watch out for, and related functions that you might want to consider.

Example

This section shows an example function for most of the prototype procedures. The example is usually derived from the X11R5 source code for the Xaw widget set or one of the standard MIT clients.

Structures

This section shows the definition of any structures, enumerated types, typedefs, or symbolic constants used by the function type.

See Also

This section refers you to related functions, prototype procedures, Intrinsics widget classes, or widget methods. The numbers in parenthesis following each reference refer to the sections of this book in which they are found.

XtAcceptFocusProc

Name

XtAcceptFocusProc – interface definition for the `accept_focus()` method.

Synopsis

```
typedef Boolean (*XtAcceptFocusProc)(Widget, Time*);
    Widget widget;
    Time *time;
```

Inputs

w   Specifies the widget to take the focus.

time   Specifies the time of the event that causes the parent to offer focus to the child.

Returns

`True` if the widget took the focus, `False` otherwise.

Description

`XtAcceptFocusProc` is the type of the Core `accept_focus()` method. See `accept_focus`(4) for more information.

See Also

accept_focus(4).

XtActionHookProc

Name

XtActionHookProc – interface definition for action hook procedure.

Synopsis

```
typedef void (*XtActionHookProc)(Widget, XtPointer, String, XEvent*,
        String*, Cardinal*);
    Widget w;
    XtPointer client_data;
    String action_name;
    XEvent* event;
    String* params;
    Cardinal* num_params;
```

Inputs

w Specifies the widget whose action is about to be dispatched.

client_data Specifies data that was registered with this procedure in a call to XtApp-AddActionHook().

action_name Specifies the name of the action to be dispatched.

event Specifies the event argument that will be passed to the action routine.

params Specifies the action parameters that will be passed to the action routine.

num_params Specifies the number of elements in *params*.

Availability

Release 4 and later.

Description

An XtActionHookProc registered with XtAppAddActionHook() will be called just before any action procedure is invoked by the Translation Manager. *client_data* is whatever data was registered with the action hook procedure in the call to XtAppAddAction-Hook(). *action_name* is the name of the action procedure that is about to be invoked. It is the name the action procedure was registered with, and can be used in a call to XtCall-ActionProc(). The *w*, *event*, *params*, and *num_params* arguments are the arguments that will be passed directly to the action procedure.

Action hooks should not modify any of the data pointed to by the arguments other than the *client_data* argument.

Usage

One use of an XtActionHookProc is to record the arguments passed to each action so that user actions are recorded for later playback using XtCallActionProc(). This is one way to implement keyboard macros.

See Also

XtAppAddActionHook(1), *XtCallActionProc*(1), *XtRemoveActionHook*(1),
XtActionProc(2).

XtActionProc

Name

XtActionProc – interface definition for action procedure.

Synopsis

```
typedef void (*XtActionProc)(Widget, XEvent *, String *, Cardinal *);
    Widget w;
    XEvent *event;
  . String *params;
    Cardinal *num_params;
```

Inputs

w	Specifies the widget in which the event occurred that caused the action to be called.
event	Specifies the event that caused the action to be called. If the action is called after a sequence of events, then the last event in the sequence is used.
params	Specifies an array of strings that were specified in the translation table as comma-separated arguments to the action.
num_params	Specifies the number of strings in *params*.

Description

An XtActionProc is an action procedure. Action procedures are given names in an Xt-ActionList and that array of name/procedure pairs is then registered with the Translation Manager either through a call to XtAppAddActions() or by statically initializing the actions field of the Core widget record. The translation table of a widget binds event sequences into a sequence of action procedures, and the Translation Manager automatically invokes the action procedures when the specified event sequences occur.

The *params* argument is an array of strings that the action may use. These strings are the comma-separated arguments specified in the translation table. An action procedure may use or ignore them, and may invoke a resource converter to convert strings to convert each of the strings to some other desired type.

Action procedures should not assume that the widget in which they are invoked is realized; an accelerator can cause an action procedure to be called for a widget that does not yet have a window.

Usage

As an application programmer, you can often customize the behavior of a widget either by adding callback functions to one of the lists defined by the widget, or by writing and registering custom action procedures and invoking them from the widget's translation table. Callbacks are the simpler approach and are usually sufficient. Action procedures are usually used when you need to directly bind particular user events to particular actions–for example, when the widget does not provide a callback that is invoked in response to the event type that you are interested in. If you wanted to pop up a menu when the mouse entered a widget, or draw a box when the user clicked and dragged the mouse, for example, you would probably use action procedures. Note that action procedures are not registered with a *client_data* argument as callbacks

Prototype Procedures

are, and so application-level action procedures may have to depend on global data. Widget-level action procedures can usually get all the data they need from their widget argument.

Note that it is usually a widget's action procedures that invoke the functions registered on that widget's callback lists.

Many action routines are intentionally written not to depend on the detailed information inside any particular type of event, so that the user may use the translation table to invoke the action in response to different types of events. For example, it is useful for an action routine normally triggered by a pointer click to work when called in response to a key instead. Such an action should not depend on the event structure fields unique to button events. If your action does depend on the details of a particular event type, you must cast the *event* argument to a pointer to an event structure of the appropriate type.

When you write a widget or an application, you should document each of the action procedures that users may invoke from a translation table, and document any arguments each action expects, and also the event types that the action can be safely called on. Also, if an action procedure invokes the procedures on a callback list without checking that the widget is realized, the callback documentation must note that the widget may not yet be realized.

In many action procedures, the last two arguments are unused. When you don't use the last two arguments, be sure to place the *lint* comment /*ARGSUSED*/ just before the action procedure definition. To conform to ANSI-C standards, all four arguments of an action should be declared, even if the trailing arguments are not used.

The Intrinsics reserve all action names and parameters starting with the characters "Xt" for future standard enhancements. Users, applications, and widgets should not declare action names or pass parameters starting with these characters except to invoke specified built-in Intrinsics functions.

Example

The following two action procedures are from the Xaw Command widget:

```
static void
Highlight(w,event,params,num_params)
Widget w;
XEvent *event;
String *params;
Cardinal *num_params;
{
  CommandWidget cbw = (CommandWidget)w;

  if ( *num_params == (Cardinal) 0)
    cbw->command.highlighted = HighlightWhenUnset;
  else {
    if ( *num_params != (Cardinal) 1)
      XtWarning("Too many parameters passed to highlight action table.");
    switch (params[0][0]) {
    case 'A':
    case 'a':
      cbw->command.highlighted = HighlightAlways;
```

```
        break;
      default:
        cbw->command.highlighted = HighlightWhenUnset;
        break;
      }
    }

    if (XtIsRealized(w))
      PaintCommandWidget(w, HighlightRegion(cbw), TRUE);
}

/* ARGSUSED */
static void
Notify(w,event,params,num_params)
Widget w;
XEvent *event;
String *params;          /* unused */
Cardinal *num_params;    /* unused */
{
  CommandWidget cbw = (CommandWidget)w;

  /* check to be sure state is still Set so that user can cancel
     the action (e.g., by moving outside the window, in the default
     bindings.
  */
  if (cbw->command.set)
    XtCallCallbackList(w, cbw->command.callbacks, NULL);
}
```

Structures

The `XtActionsRec` structure and the `XtActionList` type are defined as follows:

```
typedef struct _XtActionsRec{
    String string;
    XtActionProc proc;
} XtActionsRec;

typedef struct _XtActionsRec *XtActionList;
```

See Also

XtAppAddActions(1).

Prototype
Procedures

XtAlmostProc

Name

XtAlmostProc – interface definition for the `set_values_almost()` method.

Synopsis

```
typedef void (*XtAlmostProc)(Widget, Widget, XtWidgetGeometry *,
        XtWidgetGeometry *);
    Widget old;
    Widget set;
    XtWidgetGeometry *request;
    XtWidgetGeometry *reply;
```

Inputs

old   Specifies a copy of the object as it was before the `XtSetValues()` call.

set   Specifies the object instance record as modified by the various `set_values()` methods.

request   Specifies the original geometry request that was sent to the geometry manager that returned `XtGeometryAlmost`.

reply   Specifies the compromise geometry that was returned by the geometry manager that returned `XtGeometryAlmost`.

Description

`XtAlmostProc` is the type of the core `set_values_almost()` method. See `set_values_almost`(4) for more information.

See Also

set_values_almost(4).

Name

XtArgsFunc – interface definition for the `set_values_hook()` method.

Synopsis

```
typedef Boolean (*XtArgsFunc)(Widget, ArgList, Cardinal *);
    Widget widget;
    ArgList args;
    Cardinal *num_args;
```

Inputs

widget	Specifies the widget which is having its resources set.
args	Specifies the argument list passed to `XtSetValues()`.
num_args	Specifies a pointer to the number of elements in *args*.

Returns

`True` if the widget should be drawn; `False` otherwise.

Availability

Obsolete in Release 4 and later.

Description

XtArgsFunc is the type of the Core `set_values_hook()` method. It is obsolete in Release 4 and later because the *args* and *num_args* arguments are now passed directly to the `set_value()` method. See `set_values_hook(4)` for more information.

See Also

set_values_hook(4).

XtArgsProc

Name

XtArgsProc – interface definition for the `initialize_hook()` and `get_values_hook()` methods.

Synopsis

```
typedef void (*XtArgsProc)(Widget, ArgList, Cardinal *);
    Widget widget;
    ArgList args;
    Cardinal *num_args;
```

Inputs

widget   Specifies the widget that is being initialized or passed to `XtGetValues()`.

args   Specifies the argument list that was passed to `XtCreateWidget()` or `XtGetValues()`.

num_args   Specifies a pointer to the number of elements in *args*.

Description

`XtArgsProc` is the type of the Core `initialize_hook()` method and the Core and Constraint `get_values_hook()` methods. The `initialize_hook()` method is obsolete in Release 4 and later because the *args* and *num_args* arguments are now passed directly to the `initialize()` method. See the reference pages for these methods in Section 4 for more information.

See Also

get_values_hook(4), *Constraint get_values_hook*(4), *initialize_hook*(4).

Name

XtCallbackProc – interface definition for callback procedure.

Synopsis

```
typedef void (*XtCallbackProc)(Widget, XtPointer, XtPointer);
    Widget w;
    XtPointer client_data;
    XtPointer call_data;
```

Inputs

w   Specifies the widget for which the callback is registered.

client_data Specifies the data that was registered with this callback.

call_data   Specifies data passed by the widget; its type is defined by the particular callback list of the particular widget class.

Description

XtCallbackProc is the type of all procedures registered on callback lists with XtAddCallback() or XtAddCallbacks(). A callback procedure is called when a widget calls XtCallCallbacks() or XtCallCallbackList() to invoke all the procedures that have been registered on one of its callback lists. Most callback lists are invoked from an action procedure in response to an event or series of events, as when an Xaw Command widget is clicked on, or when an Xaw Scrollbar widget is scrolled.

An XtCallbackProc takes three arguments:

- The first argument is the widget that triggered the callback: the widget for which the callback procedure was registered. You would use the value of this argument in your callback function if you registered the same function as a callback for two different widgets, and if you wanted to distinguish in the callback which widget called it, or you would use it if the purpose of the callback were to perform some operation on the widget itself.

- The second argument, *client_data*, is whatever value was passed as the last argument of XtAddCallback(). *client_data* provides a way for the client registering the callback also to register data that the callback procedure will need. This may be data of any type, cast to an XtPointer when registered, and cast back to the desired type within the callback procedure. Generally, callback procedures should be passed whatever data they are to operate on as their *client_data*; if this is not done, the callback procedure will have to rely on global variables.

- The third argument, *call_data*, is data supplied by the widget. The argument is of type XtPointer, but the actual type of the data depends on the particular widget class, and the callback list of that widget. Some widgets pass no data in this argument, others pass a single scalar type, and others pass a pointer to a structure of some type. The Xaw Command widget doesn't provide any *call_data*, but the Xaw Scroll widget, for example, passes back the current position of the scrollbar. The documentation for the widget will specify the contents of this argument if it is used. The *call_data* argument may not contain all the relevant information that a callback procedure might need. Callback procedures can also use `XtGetValues()` or other functions to obtain more information about the state of the widget.

See the "Background" section below for more information about registering callback procedures and about callback lists.

Usage

Almost every application will define and register a number of callback procedures. Once you have created the widgets that make up your application's interface and called `XtAppMain-Loop()`, it is the callback procedures that you have registered that do all the processing for your application.

Action procedures and event handlers are other ways of having a procedure invoked when certain events occur, but are both lower level and far less commonly used than callback procedures. See `XtAppAddActions()` and `XtAddEventHandler()`.

You can also register procedures to be called when the application is idle, when a timeout expires, or when there is input available from a source other than the X server. This is done with `XtAppAddWorkProc()`, `XtAppAddTimeOut()`, and `XtAppAddInput()`. The procedures registered are similar in concept to callback procedures, but are not of type `Xt-CallbackProc`.

Note that not all callbacks are called in response to user events. The `XtNdestroyCallback` list of all widgets and objects is invoked when an object is destoyed, for example, and the `Xt-NpopupCallback` list of Shell widgets is called just before the shell widget is popped up, whether or not a user event directly triggered the popup.

If any of the arguments are unused in your callback procedure, use the `/* ARGSUSED */` comment to avoid warnings from *lint*. For ANSI-C type checking, you should declare your callbacks with all three arguments even if some are unused. Note that you can use procedures that are not of type `XtCallbackProc` (such as `XtUnmanageChild()`, for example) if you cast those procedures to type `XtCallbackProc` when you register them.

Example

The following callback procedure is from the *editres* client:

```
/* ARGSUSED */
void
PannerCallback(w, closure, report_ptr)
Widget w;
XtPointer closure, report_ptr;
{
    Arg args[2];
    XawPannerReport *report = (XawPannerReport *) report_ptr;

    if (global_tree_info == NULL)
        return;

    XtSetArg (args[0], XtNx, -report->slider_x);
    XtSetArg (args[1], XtNy, -report->slider_y);
```

```
    XtSetValues(global_tree_info->tree_widget, args, TWO);
}
```

It is registered by *editres* on the `XtNreportCallback` list of the widget `panner`, and is registered with another widget, `porthole` as `client_data`.

```
XtAddCallback(panner, XtNreportCallback, PannerCallback, (XtPointer) porthole);
```

Background

Whenever a client wants to pass a callback list as an argument in an `XtCreateWidget()`, `XtSetValues()`, or `XtGetValues()` call, it should specify the address of a NULL-terminated array of type `XtCallbackList`.

When a callback procedure, or list of callback procedures, is passed as a resource argument, Xt constructs an internal data structure for the callback list. Subsequently, callback lists cannot be queried. Because Xt doesn't support a string-to-callback resource converter, callbacks cannot be specified in resource files. The internal form can only be accessed by the Intrinsics functions `XtAddCallback()`, `XtAddCallbacks()`, `XtRemoveCallback()`, `XtRemove-Callbacks()`, `XtCallCallbacks()`, `XtCallCallbackList()`, and `XtHas-Callbacks()`. Furthermore, since callback lists are handled specially by the Intrinsics, widget procedures should not allocate memory for callback lists passed as resources. Unlike other resources, a widget's `initialize()` method should not attempt to make copies of resources of type `XtRCallback`.

For the Intrinsics to find and correctly handle callback lists, they must be declared with a resource type of `XtRCallback`. The internal representation of a callback list is implementation-dependent; widgets may make no assumptions about the value stored in this resource if it is non-NULL. Except to compare the value to NULL (which is equivalent to `XtCallback-HasNone` returned by `XtHasCallbacks()`), access to callback list resources must be made through other Intrinsics procedures.

Structures

The `XtCallbackRec` structure and the `XtCallbackList` types are defined as follows:

```
typedef struct _XtCallbackRec {
    XtCallbackProc  callback;
    XtPointer       closure;
} XtCallbackRec, *XtCallbackList;
```

See Also

XtAddCallback(1), *XtAddCallbacks*(1), *XtCallCallbacks*(1), *XtHasCallbacks*(1), *XtRemoveCallback*(1), *XtRemoveCallbacks*(1).

XtCancelConvertSelectionProc

Name

XtCancelConvertSelectionProc – interface definition for procedure to cancel incremental selection transfer.

Synopsis

```
typedef void (*XtCancelConvertSelectionProc)(Widget, Atom*, Atom*,
        XtRequestId*, XtPointer);
    Widget w;
    Atom *selection;
    Atom *target;
    XtRequestId *request_id;
    XtPointer client_data;
```

Inputs

w	Specifies the widget that owns the selection.
selection	Specifies the atom that names the selection being transferred.
target	Specifies the target type to which the conversion was done.
request_id	Specifies an opaque identification for a specific request.
client_data	Specifies the value passed in by the widget when it took ownership of the selection.

Availability

Release 4 and later.

Description

This procedure is registered in a call to XtOwnSelectionIncremental(), and is called by the Intrinsics to abort an incremental transfer when (as determined by the selection timeout or other mechanism) any remaining segments of the selection no longer need to be transferred. Upon receiving this callback, the selection request is considered complete and the owner should free the memory and any other resources that have been allocated for the transfer.

The w, selection, and client_data arguments are those passed in the call to XtOwnSelectionIncremental(). The target and request_id arguments are the selection target type specified by the selection requestor, and the unique ID assigned to this transfer by the Intrinsics. Both will have been passed to a previous call to the XtConvertSelectionIncrProc also registered with XtOwnSelectionIncremental().

See Also

XtGetSelectionValueIncremental(1), *XtGetSelectionValuesIncremental*(1), *XtGetSelectionTimeout*(1), *XtOwnSelectionIncremental*(1), *XtSetSelectionTimeout*(1), *XtConvertSelectionIncrProc*(2), *XtLoseSelectionIncrProc*(2), *XtSelectionDoneIncrProc*(2).

Name

XtCaseProc – interface definition for procedure to convert the case of keysyms.

Synopsis

```
typedef void (*XtCaseProc) (Display*, KeySym, KeySym *, KeySym *);
    Display *display
    KeySym  keysym;
    KeySym  *lower_return;
    KeySym  *upper_return;
```

Inputs

display   Provides the display connection for which the conversion is required.

keysym   Specifies the keysym to convert.

Outputs

lower_return Returns the lowercase equivalent for *keysym*.

upper_return Returns the uppercase equivalent for *keysym*.

Description

An XtCaseProc is a case converter procedure registered with XtRegisterCase-Converter(), and invoked by XtConvertCase() and by the Translation Manager in order to obtain the uppercase and lowercase versions of a keysym. It should store the upper and lower case versions of keysym at the addresses specified by *lower_return* and *upper_return*. If there is no case distinction, it should store keysym at both locations.

Usage

You should only need to write a case converter procedure if you are working with non-standard keysyms.

Example

The default case converter from the R4 Intrinsics is as follows:

```
/* ARGSUSED */
void _XtConvertCase(dpy, sym, lower, upper)
    Display *dpy;
    KeySym sym;
    KeySym *lower;
    KeySym *upper;
{
    *lower = sym;
    *upper = sym;
    switch(sym >> 8) {
        case 0:
            if ((sym >= XK_A) && (sym <= XK_Z))
                *lower += (XK_a - XK_A);
            else if ((sym >= XK_a) && (sym <= XK_z))
                *upper -= (XK_a - XK_A);
            else if ((sym >= XK_Agrave) && (sym <= XK_Odiaeresis))
```

```
            *lower += (XK_agrave - XK_Agrave);
        else if ((sym >= XK_agrave) && (sym <= XK_odiaeresis))
            *upper -= (XK_agrave - XK_Agrave);
        else if ((sym >= XK_Ooblique) && (sym <= XK_Thorn))
            *lower += (XK_oslash - XK_Ooblique);
        else if ((sym >= XK_oslash) && (sym <= XK_thorn))
            *upper -= (XK_oslash - XK_Ooblique);
        break;
    default:
        /* XXX do all other sets */
        break;
    }
}
```

See Also

XtConvertCase(1), *XtGetKeysymTable*(1), *XtKeysymToKeycodeList*(1), *XtRegisterCaseConverter*(1), *XtSetKeyTranslator*(1), *XtTranslateKeycode*(1).

XtConvertArgProc

Name

XtConvertArgProc – interface definition for procedure to obtain an argument for a resource converter.

Synopsis

```
typedef void (*XtConvertArgProc)(Widget, Cardinal *, XrmValue *);
    Widget object;
    Cardinal *size;
    XrmValue *value_return;
```

Inputs

object   Specifies the object for which the resource is being converted, or NULL if the converter was invoked by XtCallConverter() or XtDirect-Convert(). May be of class Object or any subclass thereof.

size   Specifies a pointer to the size field from the XtConvertArgRec structure.

Outputs

value_return Returns the address and size of the argument.

Availability

Release 4 and later.

Description

A procedure of type XtConvertArgProc gets an argument needed when calling a resource converter. It is registered in the address_id field of an XtConvertArgRec structure with the address_mode field XtProcedureArg. This XtConvertArgRec structure must be part of an XtConvertArgList array which is registered with a converter procedure with XtAppSetTypeConverter(), XtSetTypeConverter(), or XtAppAdd-Converter().

When invoked, the XtConvertArgProc procedure must derive its argument value (generally from the specified *object*) and store the address and size of the value in the XrmValue structure pointed to by its *value_return* argument. The *size* argument is not assigned any meaning by the Intrinsics, and can be used like *client_data* to a callback procedure, if desired.

To permit re-entry, XtConvertArgProc should return the address of storage whose lifetime is no shorter than the lifetime of *object*. If *object* is NULL, the lifetime of the conversion argument must be no shorter than the lifetime of the resource with which the conversion argument is associated. The Intrinsics do not guarantee to copy this storage, but they do guarantee not to reference it if the resource is removed from the conversion cache.

If the XtConvertArgProc modifies the resource database, the changes affect any in-progress widget creation or XtGetApplicationResources() or XtGetSubresources() calls in an implementation-defined manner. Insertion of new entries into the database and modification of existing entries is allowed, however, and will not directly cause an error.

Prototype Procedures

See `XtAppSetTypeConverter()` for an explanation of how to declare an `XtConvert-ArgList` which will invoke an `XtConvertArgProc`.

Example

The `XtConvertArgProc` used by the Intrinsics String-to-Cursor converter is shown below, along with the `XtConvertArgList` that registers it. It looks up the `Display *` of the specified widget, and places its address (a `Display **`) in *value->addr*. (Note that `DisplayOfScreen()` is a macro, so the ampersand before it is legal.)

```
/*ARGSUSED*/
static void FetchDisplayArg(widget, size, value)
    Widget widget;
    Cardinal *size;
    XrmValue* value;
{

    if (widget == NULL)
        XtErrorMsg("missingWidget", "fetchDisplayArg", XtCXtToolkitError,
                    "FetchDisplayArg called without a widget to reference",
                    (String*)NULL, (Cardinal*)NULL);
        /* can't return any useful Display and caller will de-ref NULL,
            so aborting is the only useful option */

    value->size = sizeof(Display*);
    value->addr = (XPointer)&DisplayOfScreen(XtScreenOfObject(widget));
}

static XtConvertArgRec Const displayConvertArg[] = {
    {XtProcedureArg, (XtPointer)FetchDisplayArg, 0},
};
```

The String-to-Cursor converter could now be registered with a call like the following. Given the `displayConvertArg` array defined above, that converter would be invoked with `args[0].addr`, the address of the Display pointer that the converter should use.

```
XtSetTypeConverter(XtQString,  XtQCursor, CvtStringToCursor,
                    displayConvertArg, XtNumber(displayConvertArg),
                    XtCacheByDisplay, FreeCursor);
```

See Also

XtAppSetTypeConverter(1), *XtAppAddConverter*(1), *XtSetTypeConverter*(1), *XtTypeConverter*(2).

XtConvertSelectionIncrProc

Name

XtConvertSelectionIncrProc – interface definition for a procedure to return selection data incrementally.

Synopsis

```
typedef Boolean (*XtConvertSelectionIncrProc)(Widget, Atom*, Atom*, Atom*,
      XtPointer*, unsigned long*, int*, unsigned long*, XtPointer,
      XtRequestId*);
    Widget w;
    Atom *selection;
    Atom *target;
    Atom *type_return;
    XtPointer *value_return;
    unsigned long *length_return;
    int *format_return;
    unsigned long *max_length;
    XtPointer client_data;
    XtRequestId *request_id;
```

Inputs

w	Specifies the widget which currently owns this selection.
selection	Specifies the atom that names the selection requested (usually XA_PRIMARY or XA_SECONDARY).
target	Specifies the type of information requested about selection (FILENAME, TEXT, or XA_WINDOW, for example).
max_length	Specifies the maximum number of bytes which may be transferred at any one time.
client_data	Specifies the data registered with this procedure in the call to XtOwnSelectionIncremental().
request_id	Identifies the transfer request (multiple concurrent requests are possible) for which data is to be returned.

Outputs

type_return	Returns the property type of the converted value of the selection. (Both FILENAME and TEXT might have property type XA_STRING, for example.)
value_return	Returns the address of the converted value of the selection. The selection owner is responsible for allocating this storage.
length_return	Returns the length of the value in value_return, in units as specified by format_return.
format_return	Returns the size in bits of each of the length_return elements of value_return. Must be 8, 16, or 32; this information allows the X server to byte-swap the data if necessary.

Returns

True if the conversion is successful; False otherwise.

Availability

Release 4 and later.

Description

An XtConvertSelectionIncrProc is registered in a call to XtOwnSelection-Incremental(). This procedure is called repeatedly by the Intrinsics selection mechanism to get pieces of the selection value.

On the first call with a particular *request_id*, an XtConvertSelectionIncrProc should determine whether it will be able to convert the selection to the requested target type. If not, it should return False immediately. Otherwise, it should allocate memory (of not more than *max_length* bytes) and place the first "chunk" or increment of the converted selection value in it. Then it should set *value_return* to the address of this allocated memory, and set *type_return*, *length_return*, and *format_return* as appropriate and return True.

On subsequent calls with the same *request_id*, an XtConvertSelectionIncrProc() should return the converted subsequent chunks of the selection value, again setting all the return arguments and returning True. It may reuse the previously allocated block of memory.

When an XtConvertSelectionIncrProc is called after it has transferred the last of the selection data, it should store a non-NULL value in *value_return* and zero in *length_return* to indicate that the entire selection has been delivered. After returning this final segment, the *request_id* may be re-used by the Intrinsics to begin a new transfer.

If an XtSelectionDoneIncrProc proc was registered with the XtConvert-SelectionIncrProc, then that procedure is responsible for freeing any memory allocated for a transfer when that transfer completes. If no XtSelectionDoneIncrProc is registered, the Intrinsics will automatically call XtFree() on the final value returned. If an incremental transfer is aborted before it completes, the XtCancelConvertSelectionProc is responsible for freeing any memory allocated for that transfer.

Each XtConvertSelectionProc should respond to target value TARGETS by returning a value containing the list of the targets they are prepared to convert their selection into. The list of targets should be an array of interned Atoms, and return_type should be XA_ATOM.

An XtConvertSelectionIncrProc will not be called with a *target* of MULTIPLE or TIMESTAMP (see Section 2.6.2 of the *Inter-Client Communications Conventions Manual*, Appendix L in Volume Zero). The Intrinsics automatically break a MULTIPLE request into a series of calls to the procedure, and automatically respond to a TIMESTAMP request using the time passed to XtOwnSelectionIncremental().

See XtConvertSelectionProc(2) for more information on handling requests for the selection value.

Usage

An `XtConvertSelectionIncrProc` must be prepared to handle multiple concurrent transfer requests; i.e., it cannot assume that it will be called repeatedly with a single *request_id* until that transfer is complete, and then be called with a new *request_id*. For this reason, it must remember how far along in each transfer it is for each *request_id*. The Xlib Context Manager (see `XSaveContext()`) can be useful for this purpose.

See Also

XtGetSelectionValueIncremental(1), *XtGetSelectionValuesIncremental*(1), *XtOwnSelectionIncremental*(1), *XtCancelConvertSelectionProc*(2), *XtConvertSelectionProc*(2), *XtLoseSelectionIncrProc*(2), *XtSelectionDoneIncrProc*(2).

Name

XtConvertSelectionProc – interface definition for a procedure to return requested selection
data.

Synopsis

```
typedef Boolean (*XtConvertSelectionProc)(Widget, Atom *, Atom *, Atom *,
        XtPointer *, unsigned long *, int *);
    Widget w;
    Atom *selection;
    Atom *target;
    Atom *type_return;
    XtPointer *value_return;
    unsigned long *length_return;
    int *format_return;
```

Inputs

w   Specifies the widget that currently owns the selection.

selection   Specifies the atom that describes the selection requested (usually
XA_PRIMARY or XA_SECONDARY).

target   Specifies the type of information requested about the selection
(FILENAME, TEXT, or XA_WINDOW, for example).

Outputs

type_return   Returns the property type of the converted value of the selection. (Both
FILENAME and TEXT might have property type XA_STRING, for example.)

value_return Returns the address of the converted value of the selection. The selection
owner is responsible for allocating this storage.

length_return Returns the length of the value in value_return, in units as specified
by format_return.

format_return Returns the size in bits of each of the length_return elements of
value_return. Must be 8, 16, or 32; this information allows the X
server to byte-swap the data if necessary.

Returns

True if the conversion is successful; False otherwise.

Description

An XtConvertSelectionProc is registered in a call to XtOwnSelection() when a
client requests to become the owner of a selection. It is called when the value of the selection
is requested.

If an XtConvertSelectionProc cannot convert the selection data to the requested target type, it should return False. Otherwise, it should convert the value, allocating memory
for it if necessary. It should store the type of the converted data (which is generally not the
same as target) in type_return, store the address of the converted value in

value_return, store the number of blocks of converted data in *length_return*, store the size of each of those blocks of converted data in *format_return*, and return True.

If an XtSelectionDoneProc was registered with the XtConvertSelectionProc, then this procedure will be called when the requestor has copied the converted data, and should free any memory allocated for that data. If no XtSelectionDoneProc was registered, then the Intrinsics will automatically free the returned value by calling XtFree().

Each XtConvertSelectionProc should respond to target value TARGETS by returning a value containing the list of the targets they are prepared to convert their selection into. The list of targets should be an array of interned Atoms, and *type_return* should be XA_ATOM.

An XtConvertSelectionProc will not be called with a *target* of MULTIPLE or TIME STAMP (see Section 2.6.2 of the *Inter-Client Communications Conventions Manual*, Appendix L in Volume Zero). The Intrinsics automatically break a MULTIPLE request into a series of calls to the procedure, and automatically respond to a TIMESTAMP request using the time passed to XtOwnSelection().

Usage

Most widgets that display data of any sort should make that data selectable by the user, and should call XtOwnSelection() with an XtConvertSelectionProc when data is selected by the user.

Although it is usually widgets that handle selections, there are times when an application might want to export selected data. A calculator program might have a menu item labeled "Cut", for example, which would call XtOwnSelection() to make the currently displayed value available for pasting. (It would probably also have a "Paste" command that would call Xt-GetSelectionValue() to obtain the currently selected value and use it, if it is a number.)

An XtConvertSelectionProc transfers the selection value in a single block, and relies on the Intrinsics to break that block up and reassemble it as necessary if it is larger than the maximum size for a single transfer to the X server. This procedure and the XtOwn-Selection() function that registers it are part of the Intrinsics atomic selection transfer mechanism. In Release 4 and later, the Intrinsics also support an incremental transfer mechanism which allows the selection owner to return the selection value a piece at a time. If there is a large amount of selected data, the incremental interface means that it does not have to be copied all at once—on systems with limited memory, this can be important. Also, some selections, such as disjoint pieces of text in a text widget, are more naturally transferred in separate pieces. See XtOwnSelectionIncremental(1) and XtConvertSelectionIncr-Proc(2) for more information.

The Xmu function XmuConvertStandardSelection() converts the selection to the following standard targets: CLASS, CLIENT_WINDOW, DECNET_ADDRESS, HOSTNAME, IP_ADDRESS, NAME, OWNER_OS, TARGETS, TIMESTAMP, and USER. It is used in the example shown below. See Section 2.6.5 of the *Inter-Client Communications Conventions Manual* for the meaning of these standard targets. See XmuConvertStandard-Selection(6) for more information.

When working with selections, you will have to work with Atoms. Many standard Atoms are defined in *<X11/Xatom.h>*. Those that are not (for example, TARGETS) may be interned explicitly as Atoms by calling the Xlib function XInternAtom(). The Xmu library provides an alternate function, XmuInternAtom(), which caches Atoms on the client side. Additionally, the header *<Xmu/Atoms.h>* defines a number of macros, such as XA_TARGETS(dpy), which call XmuInternAtom() and take a Display pointer as their single argument.

Example

The example XtConvertSelectionProc below is from the client *xclipboard*. It can be easily adapted for use by most widgets and applications. Note the use of predefined Atoms and the Xmu Atom macros. XmuConvertStandardSelection() is used to convert to the standard target types, and also (when the target is TARGETS) to return a list of those standard types that it supports. This list is then augmented with the types supported explicitly by the procedure.

```
#include <X11/Xatom.h>
#include <X11/Xmu/Atoms.h>
#include <X11/Xmu/StdSel.h>

static Boolean ConvertSelection(w, selection, target,
                                type, value, length, format)
    Widget w;
    Atom *selection, *target, *type;
    XtPointer *value;
    unsigned long *length;
    int *format;
{
    Display* d = XtDisplay(w);
    XSelectionRequestEvent* req =
        XtGetSelectionRequest(w, *selection, (XtRequestId)NULL);

    if (*target == XA_TARGETS(d)) {
        Atom* targetP;
        Atom* std_targets;
        unsigned long std_length;
        XmuConvertStandardSelection(w, req->time, selection, target, type,
                                (caddr_t*)&std_targets, &std_length, format);
        *value = XtMalloc(sizeof(Atom)*(std_length + 5));
        targetP = *(Atom**)value;
        *targetP++ = XA_STRING;
        *targetP++ = XA_TEXT(d);
        *targetP++ = XA_LENGTH(d);
        *targetP++ = XA_LIST_LENGTH(d);
        *targetP++ = XA_CHARACTER_POSITION(d);
        *length = std_length + (targetP - (*(Atom **) value));
        bcopy((char*)std_targets, (char*)targetP, sizeof(Atom)*std_length);
        XtFree((char*)std_targets);
        *type = XA_ATOM;
        *format = 32;
        return True;
```

```
    }

    if (*target == XA_LIST_LENGTH(d) ||
        *target == XA_LENGTH(d))
    {
        long * temp;

        temp = (long *) XtMalloc(sizeof(long));
        if (*target == XA_LIST_LENGTH(d))
          *temp = 1L;
        else                        /* *target == XA_LENGTH(d) */
          *temp = (long) TextLength (text);

        *value = (caddr_t) temp;
        *type = XA_INTEGER;
        *length = 1L;
        *format = 32;
        return True;
    }

    if (*target == XA_CHARACTER_POSITION(d))
    {
        long * temp;

        temp = (long *) XtMalloc(2 * sizeof(long));
        temp[0] = (long) 0;
        temp[1] = TextLength (text);
        *value = (caddr_t) temp;
        *type = XA_SPAN(d);
        *length = 2L;
        *format = 32;
        return True;
    }

    if (*target == XA_STRING ||
      *target == XA_TEXT(d) ||
      *target == XA_COMPOUND_TEXT(d))
    {
        extern char *_XawTextGetSTRING();
        if (*target == XA_COMPOUND_TEXT(d))
            *type = *target;
        else
            *type = XA_STRING;
        *length = TextLength (text);
        *value = _XawTextGetSTRING((TextWidget) text, 0, *length);
        *format = 8;
        return True;
    }
```

```
        if (XmuConvertStandardSelection(w, req->time, selection, target, type,
                                        (caddr_t *)value, length, format))
            return True;

        return False;
    }
```

See Also

XtGetSelectionValue(1), *XtOwnSelection*(1),
XtConvertSelectionIncrProc(2), *XtSelectionDoneProc*(2),
XmuConvertStandardSelection(6).

XtConverter

Name

XtConverter – interface definition for old-style resource converter.

Synopsis

```
typedef void (*XtConverter)(XrmValue *, Cardinal *, XrmValue *,
        XrmValue *);
    XrmValue *args;
    Cardinal *num_args;
    XrmValue *from;
    XrmValue *to_return;
```

Inputs

args   Specifies an array of additional XrmValue arguments to the converter if
             additional context is needed to perform the conversion, or NULL.

num_args   Specifies the number of arguments in args.

from   Specifies the address and size of the value to convert.

Outputs

to_return   Returns the address and size of the converted value.

Description

An XtConverter is an old-style resource converter, registered with XtAppAdd-
Converter(), and invoked automatically by the Intrinsics to convert resources of the appropriate type, or invoked directly with XtConvertAndStore() or XtDirectConvert().

An XtConverter should perform the following actions:

• Check to see that the number of arguments passed is correct.

• Attempt the type conversion.

• If successful, return the address and size of the converted value in the to_return argument, otherwise, call XtWarningMsg() or XtStringConversionWarning() and
  return without modifying to_return.

Most type converters just take the data described by the specified from argument and return
data by writing into the to_return argument. A few need other information, such as a display or screen pointer. These converters can be registered with an XtConvertArgList
which will cause the Intrinsics to compute an argument list for the converter before invoking it.
See XtAppSetTypeConverter() for information on declaring XtConvertArgList
arrays.

Note that the address written in to_return->addr cannot be that of a local variable of the
converter because this is not valid after the converter returns. It should be the address of a
static variable.

Usage

An XtConverter is an "old-style" resource converter. In Release 4, the "new-style"
resource converter XtTypeConverter was defined. There are still existing old-style conver-

ters in use, but if you are going to write a new converter, you should write an XtType-
Converter instead of an XtConverter. See XtTypeConverter(2) for more information.

Note that the *num_args* argument is a pointer to the number of elements in *args*, and not the
number of arguments itself. Be sure to dereference this argument correctly before using it.

Example

The following procedure is a modified version of the String-to-Justification converter from the
Xmu library:

```
/* ARGSUSED */
void
XmuCvtStringToJustify(args, num_args, fromVal, toVal)
    XrmValuePtr args;          /* unused */
    Cardinal   *num_args;      /* unused */
    XrmValuePtr fromVal;
    XrmValuePtr toVal;
{
    static XtJustify    e;
    static XrmQuark     XrmQEleft;
    static XrmQuark     XrmQEcenter;
    static XrmQuark     XrmQEright;
    static int          haveQuarks = 0;
    XrmQuark    q;
    char        *s = (char *) fromVal->addr;
    char        lowerName[1000];

    if (s == NULL) return;
    if (!haveQuarks) {
        XrmQEleft   = XrmPermStringToQuark(XtEleft);
        XrmQEcenter = XrmPermStringToQuark(XtEcenter);
        XrmQEright  = XrmPermStringToQuark(XtEright);
        haveQuarks = 1;
    }
    XmuCopyISOLatin1Lowered(lowerName, s);
    q = XrmStringToQuark(lowerName);

    if (q == XrmQEleft)        e = XtJustifyLeft;
    else if (q == XrmQEcenter) e = XtJustifyCenter;
    else if (q == XrmQEright)  e = XtJustifyRight;
    else {
        XtStringConversionWarning(s, XtRJustify);
        return;
    }

    toVal->size = sizeof(XtJustify);
    toVal->addr = (caddr_t) &e;
}
```

Structures

The `XrmValue` structure is defined as follows:

```
typedef struct {
    unsigned int    size;
    XPointer        addr;
} XrmValue, *XrmValuePtr;
```

See Also

XtAppAddConverter(1), *XtAppSetTypeConverter*(1), *XtConvert*(1), *XtDirectConvert*(1), *XtSetType-Converter*(1), *XtStringConversionWarning*(1), *XtTypeConverter*(2).

Name

XtCreatePopupChildProc – interface definition for an `XtNcreatePopupChildProc` procedure.

Synopsis

```
typedef void (*XtCreatePopupChildProc)(Widget);
    Widget shell;
```

Inputs

shell   Specifies the shell which is being popped up.

Description

An `XtCreatePopupChildProc` is registered as the value of the `XtNcreatePopup-ChildProc` resource of a shell widget. It will be called by `XtPopup()` just before the shell is popped up, and is intended to provide an opportunity for the application to create the popup child of the shell. See `XtPopup(1)` and `Shell(3)` for more information.

Usage

None of the standard MIT clients make use of the `XtNcreatePopupChildProc` resource, and most applications will probably find it simpler to either create both popup shell and popup child in advance, or to delay creation of both until just before `XtPopup()` is called. Note that `XtPopup()` also calls the procedures on a shell's `XtNpopupCallback` list, and a callback on this list can be used for the same purpose as an `XtNcreatePopupChildProc`.

Note that an `XtNcreatePopupChildProc` procedure is not a widget class method. It could be considered an "instance method" rather than a "class method." In this way it is similar to the `XtNinsertPosition` procedure of the Composite widget class.

See Also

XtPopup(1),
Shell(3).

XtDestructor

Name

XtDestructor – interface definition for procedure to destroy cached resource data returned by a new-style resource converter.

Synopsis

```
typedef void (*XtDestructor) (XtAppContext, XrmValue *, XtPointer,
    XrmValue *, Cardinal *);
  XtAppContext app;
  XrmValue *to;
  XtPointer converter_data;
  XrmValue *args;
  Cardinal *num_args;
```

Inputs

app   Specifies in application context in which the resource is being freed.

to   Specifies the address and size of the cached resource value produced by the type converter.

converter_data
                   Specifies the *converter_data* returned by the type converter.

args   Specifies the additional converter arguments as passed to the type converter when the conversion was performed.

num_args   Specifies the number of additional converter arguments.

Availability

Release 4 and later.

Description

An XtDestructor is optionally registered with an XtTypeConverter new-style resource converter in a call to XtAppSetTypeConverter() or XtSetTypeConverter(). It is called when a resource returned by that converter is freed from the cache. The Intrinsics automatically free the memory occupied by the resource value (i.e., the memory pointed to by *to*->addr), so the destructor should not do this but must deallocate the resource itself if it is a shared resource (such as an open file, or a Pixmap owned by the X server) and free any associated memory (if the resource value is a pointer type, for example, the Intrinsics will only free the memory that holds the pointer, not the structure pointed to by the pointer).

The *converter_data* argument is data returned by the type converter in its *converter_data* argument. This data may be of any type, cast to an XtPointer by the converter, and cast back to the original type by the destructor procedure. It serves a similar purpose to *client_data* arguments to callback and other procedures, and can be used to identify other memory that must be freed, X resources that must be deallocated, and so on.

The *args* and *num_args* arguments are the additional arguments passed to the resource converter when the conversion was performed. These values are also part of the resource cache, and can be used by the destructor to figure out what must be freed. The destructor should not free the *args* array; the Intrinsics will free it automatically.

*Prototype
Procedures*

See XtAppSetTypeConverter(1) for more information on resource conversion and caching. See XtTypeConverter(2) for more information on the responsibilities of a resource converter procedure.

Example

The following procedure is the XtDestructor registered with the Intrinsics String-to-Pixel converter. It deallocates the Pixel, which is an X server resource. Note that it does not free the memory that the cursor is stored in. The *converter_data* argument (called closure here) is used to indicate whether this Pixel should be freed, or whether it is permanently allocated. See XtTypeConverter(2) for the converter procedure which accompanies this destructor.

```
/* ARGSUSED */
static void FreePixel(app, toVal, closure, args, num_args)
    XtAppContext app;
    XrmValuePtr toVal;
    XtPointer   closure;
    XrmValuePtr args;
    Cardinal    *num_args;
{
    Screen          *screen;
    Colormap        colormap;

    if (*num_args != 2) {
        XtAppWarningMsg(app, XtNwrongParameters,"freePixel",XtCXtToolkitError,
                    "Freeing a pixel requires screen and colormap arguments",
                    (String *)NULL, (Cardinal *)NULL);
        return;
    }

    screen = *((Screen **) args[0].addr);
    colormap = *((Colormap *) args[1].addr);

    if (closure) {
        XFreeColors( DisplayOfScreen(screen), colormap,
                    (unsigned long*)toVal->addr, 1, (unsigned long)0);
    }
}
```

Structures

The XrmValue structure is defined as follows:

```
typedef struct {
    unsigned int    size;
    XPointer        addr;
} XrmValue, *XrmValuePtr;
```

See Also

XtAppSetTypeConverter(1), *XtSetTypeConverter*(1),
XtTypeConverter(2).

Name

XtErrorHandler – interface definition for low-level error and warning handler procedures.

Synopsis

```
typedef void (*XtErrorHandler)(String);
    String message;
```

Inputs

message   Specifies the error message.

Description

An `XtErrorHandler` is registered as an error or warning handler with `XtAppSetError-Handler()` or `XtAppSetWarningHandler()`. It is invoked by `XtAppError()` or `Xt-AppError()`. The error handler should display the specified string in some appropriate fashion. Some applications may wish to log errors to a file as well. Error handlers should exit; warning handlers should return.

See `XtErrorMsgHandler`(2) for a description of the high-level error and warning handler procedure.

Example

The Intrinsics default error and warning handlers are shown below. The `XTERROR_PREFIX` and `XTWARNING_PREFIX` symbols are by default the empty string in the MIT implementation, but may be configured when the Intrinsics are compiled.

```
void _XtDefaultError(message)
    String message;
{
    extern void exit();

    (void)fprintf(stderr, "%sError: %s\n", XTERROR_PREFIX, message);
    exit(1);
}

void _XtDefaultWarning(message)
    String message;
{
    if (message && *message)
        (void)fprintf(stderr, "%sWarning: %s\n", XTWARNING_PREFIX, message);
    return;
}
```

See Also

XtAppError(1), *XtAppSetErrorHandler*(1), *XtAppSetWarningHandler*(1), *XtAppWarning*(1), *XtErrorMsgHandler*(1).

XtErrorMsgHandler

Name

XtErrorMsgHandler – interface definition for high-level error and warning handler procedures.

Synopsis

```
typedef void (*XtErrorMsgHandler)(String, String, String, String, String *,
        Cardinal *);
    String name;
    String type;
    String class;
    String defaultp;
    String *params;
    Cardinal *num_params;
```

Inputs

name   Specifies the name that is concatenated with the specified type to form the resource name of the error message.

type   Specifies the type that is concatenated with the name to form the resource name of the error message.

class   Specifies the resource class of the error message.

defaultp   Specifies the default message to use if no error database entry is found.

params   Specifies a pointer to a list of values to be substituted in the message.

num_params Specifies the number of values in the parameter list.

Description

An XtErrorMsgHandler is registered as a high-level error or warning handler with Xt-AppSetErrorMsgHandler() or XtAppSetWarningMsgHandler(). It is invoked by XtAppErrorMsg() or XtAppWarningMsg().

An XtErrorMsgHandler should look up an error message of the specified *name*, *type*, and *class* in an error database of some sort, and display the message it finds, or use the supplied default *defaultp*. Whether a message is found in a database or the default message is used, the specified *params* should be substituted into the message using standard printf() substitutions before it is displayed.

Usage

A custom high-level error or warning handler may find it useful to use XtAppGetError-Database() or XtAppGetErrorDatabaseText(). This latter function looks up an error message in a standard X resource database by concatenating the *name* and *type* arguments into the resource name of the message and using class as the resource class of the message. See XtAppGetErrorDatabaseText(1) for more details.

A high-level error or warning handler should generally display the message it builds by calling the corresponding low-level handler with XtAppError() or XtAppWarning(). This allows customization at two independent levels of abstraction.

Usually, the *name* argument will describe the general kind of error, such as `invalid-Parameters` or `invalidWindow`, and the *type* argument provides extra information about the error, such as the name of the function in which the error was detected.

Note that application-context-specific error handling is not implemented in MIT release, though the `XtApp` version of all the error handling routines are present. Most implementation will support only a single set of error handlers for all application contexts, and if a new handler is registered in one app context, it will take effect in all contexts.

Example

The example below shows the Intrinsics default error message handler:

```
void _XtDefaultErrorMsg (name,type,class,defaultp,params,num_params)
    String name,type,class,defaultp;
    String* params;
    Cardinal* num_params;
{
    char buffer[1000], message[1000];
    XtGetErrorDatabaseText(name,type,class,defaultp, buffer, 1000);

    /*need better solution here, perhaps use lower level printf primitives? */
    if (params == NULL || num_params == NULL || *num_params == 0)
        XtError(buffer);
    else {
        int i = *num_params;
        String par[10];
        if (i > 10) i = 10;
        bcopy( (char*)params, (char*)par, i * sizeof(String) );
        bzero( &par[i], (10-i) * sizeof(String) );
        (void) sprintf(message, buffer, par[0], par[1], par[2], par[3],
                    par[4], par[5], par[6], par[7], par[8], par[9]);
        XtError(message);
        if (i != *num_params)
            XtWarning( "some arguments in previous message were lost" );
    }
}
```

See Also

XtAppErrorMsg(1), *XtAppSetErrorMsgHandler*(1), *XtAppSetWarningMsgHandler*(1), *XtAppWarning-Msg*(1),
XtErrorHandler(2).

Prototype
Procedures

Name

XtEventHandler – interface definition for event handler procedure.

Synopsis

```
typedef void (*XtEventHandler)(Widget, XtPointer, XEvent *, Boolean *);
    Widget w;
    XtPointer client_data;
    XEvent *event;
    Boolean *continue_to_dispatch_return
```

Inputs

w	Specifies the widget for which the handler was registered.
client_data	Specifies data registered with this event handler.
event	Specifies the event that triggered this call.

Outputs

continue_to_dispatch_return

Returns a Boolean indicating whether to call the remaining event handlers that are registered for the current event.

Description

An XtEventHandler is registered with XtAddEventHandler(), XtAddRawEvent-Handler(), XtInsertEventHandler(), or XtInsertRawEventHandler(). It is called when one of the events that it was registered to handle occurs on the widget it was registered for.

An XtEventHandler should do whatever processing is necessary for the widget or application to handle the event *event* that occurred on widget *w*. The *client_data* argument can be arbitrary data registered with the event handler procedure. It is cast to an XtPointer when registered and should be cast back to the appropriate type within the event handler.

The *continue_to_dispatch_return* is the address of a Boolean variable which is intialized to True by the Intrinsics before the event handler is called. If a handler sets this variable to False, then no more handlers will be dispatched for the event. Doing this may lead to portability problems because implementations of the Intrinsics are allowed to add event handlers for any widget at any time. If you prevent these potential "invisible" event handlers from receiving events, the Intrinsics are not guaranteed to behave as expected.

Usage

Most widgets and applications do not need to use event handlers explicitly. Instead they can use translation tables and action procedures.

Example

The procedure below is an event handler from the *xmag* client. It is a special handler that follows the location of the mouse while it is dragged with the button down and a pointer grab is in effect. When the button is released, it magnifies a new area of the screen, releases the pointer grab, and calls XtRemoveEventHandler() on itself.

```
/*
 * ResizeEH() -- Event Handler for resize of selection box.
 */
static void
ResizeEH(w, closure, event, continue_to_dispatch)        /* ARGSUSED */
     Widget w; XtPointer closure; XEvent *event; Boolean *continue_to_dispatch;
{
  hlPtr data = (hlPtr)closure;
  switch (event->type) {
  case MotionNotify:
    data->x = event->xmotion.x_root;
    data->y = event->xmotion.y_root;
    break;
  case ButtonRelease:
    GetImageAndAttributes(FindWindow(event->xmotion.x_root,
                     event->xmotion.y_root),
            min(data->homeX,event->xbutton.x_root),
            min(data->homeY,event->xbutton.y_root),
            abs(data->homeX - event->xbutton.x_root),
            abs(data->homeY - event->xbutton.y_root),
            data);
    if (data->newScale)
      PopupNewScale(data);
    else
      SWSetImage(data->scaleInstance, data->image);
    XtUngrabPointer(w, CurrentTime);
    XtRemoveEventHandler(w, PointerMotionMask|ButtonReleaseMask,
                     True, ResizeEH, (XtPointer)data);
    data->selectMode = done;
    break;
  }
}
```

This event handler is registered with the following code, invoked when the user presses mouse
button 2.

```
XtAddEventHandler(w, PointerMotionMask|ButtonReleaseMask,
               True, ResizeEH, (XtPointer)data);
```

See Also

XtAddEventHandler(1), *XtAddRawEventHandler*(1), *XtAppAddActions*(1), *XtRemoveEventHandler*(1),
XtRemoveRawEventHandler(1).

Name

XtExposeProc – interface definition for the Core expose() method.

Synopsis

```
typedef void (*XtExposeProc)(Widget, XEvent *, Region);
    Widget widget;
    XEvent *event;
    Region region;
```

Inputs

w   Specifies the widget instance requiring redisplay.

event   Specifies the exposure event, which specifies the rectangle that requires redisplay.

region   Specifies the union of all rectangles in this exposure sequence.

Description

XtExposeProc is the type of the Core (and RectObj) expose() method. See expose(4) for more information.

See Also

expose(4).

Name

XtFilePredicate – interface definition for a filename evaluation procedure.

Synopsis

```
typedef Boolean (*XtFilePredicate)(String);
    String filename;
```

Inputs

filename   Specifies a potential filename.

Returns

True if *filename* is acceptable; False otherwise.

Description

An XtFilePredicate is specified in calls to XtResolvePathname() and XtFind-File(), and is called to judge filenames found by those procedures. If the string is appropriate for the intended use (if it names a readable file, for example) then the XtFilePredicate should return True; otherwise it should return False.

Example

The default predicate used by XtResolvePathname() and XtFindFile() simply tests that the specified filename exists, is readable, and is not a directory. This default procedure is shown below. Note that it attempts to handle some operating system dependencies.

```
static Boolean TestFile(path)
    String path;
{
#ifdef VMS
    return TRUE;           /* Who knows what to do here? */
#else
    struct stat status;

    return (access(path, R_OK) == 0 &&       /* exists and is readable */
            stat(path, &status) == 0 &&       /* get the status */
#ifndef X_NOT_POSIX
            S_ISDIR(status.st_mode) == 0);    /* not a directory */
#else
            (status.st_mode & S_IFDIR) == 0); /* not a directory */
#endif /* X_NOT_POSIX else */
#endif /* VMS */
}
```

See Also

XtFindFile(1), *XtResolvePathname*(1).

Name

XtGeometryHandler – interface definition for `geometry_manager()`,
`query_geometry()`, and `root_geometry_manager()`
methods.

Synopsis

```
typedef XtGeometryResult (*XtGeometryHandler)(Widget, XtWidgetGeometry *,
    XtWidgetGeometry *);
    Widget w;
    XtWidgetGeometry *request;
    XtWidgetGeometry *geometry_return;
```

Inputs

`w`	Specifies the widget.
`request`	Specifies the requested geometry.

Outputs

`geometry_return`
Specifies the reply geometry.

Returns

A response to the request: `XtGeometryYes`, `XtGeometryNo` or `XtGeometryAlmost`.

Description

`XtGeometryHandler()` is the type of the Composite `geometry_manager()` method,
the Core and RectObj `query_geometry()` method, and the Shell `root_geometry_man-
ager()` method. See the reference pages for those methods in Section 4 for more information.

See Also

geometry_manager(4), *query_geometry*(4), *root_geometry_manager*(4).

Name

XtInitProc – interface definition for the `initialize()` methods.

Synopsis

```
typedef void (*XtInitProc)(Widget, Widget, ArgList, Cardinal *);
    Widget request;
    Widget init;
    ArgList args;
    Cardinal *num_args;
```

Inputs

request   Specifies the widget with resource values as requested by the argument list, the resource database, and the widget defaults, before any initialization.

init   Specifies a widget with resource and nonresource values modified by calls to the widget's superclasses' `initialize()` methods.

args   Specifies the argument list passed to `XtCreateWidget()`.

num_args   Specifies the number of arguments in *args*.

Description

`XtInitProc` is the type of the Core and Object `initialize()` method and the Constraint `initialize()` method. See the `initialize()` reference pages in Section 4.

See Also

initialize(4), *Constraint initialize*(4).

XtInputCallbackProc

Name

XtInputCallbackProc – interface definition for procedure to handle file, pipe, or socket activity.

Synopsis

```
typedef void (*XtInputCallbackProc)(XtPointer, int *, XtInputId *);
    XtPointer client_data;
    int *source;
    XtInputId *id;
```

Inputs

client_data   Specifies the data that was registered with this procedure in `XtAppAdd-Input()`.

source   Specifies the file descriptor (on POSIX systems) that generated the event.

id   Specifies the ID that was returned when this procedure was registered with `XtAppAddInput()` call.

Description

An `XtInputCallbackProc` is registered with `XtAppAddInput()`. It is called when there is activity of the specified type (read, write, or error) on a specified file descriptor (which can be a file, pipe, or socket).

An `XtInputCallbackProc` should do whatever is necessary to handle the activity on the alternate event source. If EOF is read on the descriptor, the procedure can un-register itself by passing its *id* argument to `XtRemoveInput()`.

Usage

An `XtInputCallbackProc` is inherently operating-system-dependent and will have to be ported when the widget or application is ported to a new operating system. On non-POSIX systems, the *source* argument is some OS-dependent identifier of an input source.

Example

The procedure below is an `XtInputCallbackProc` from the `xconsole` client (which is new in X11R5). Note that it reads input with the POSIX `read()` system call, and that it closes the file descriptor and removes the input source if it reaches EOF or gets an error on the input source.

```
static void inputReady (w, source, id)
    XtPointer    w;
    int          *source;
    XtInputId     *id;
{
    char    buffer[1025];
    int     n;

    n = read (*source, buffer, sizeof (buffer) - 1);
    if (n <= 0)
    {
        fclose (input);
```

```
        XtRemoveInput (*id);
    }
    Notify ();
    buffer[n] = ' ';
    if (app_resources.stripNonprint)
    {
        stripNonprint (buffer);
        n = strlen (buffer);
    }
    TextAppend ((Widget) text, buffer, n);
}
```

This procedure is registered with the following call:

```
input_id = XtAddInput (fileno (input), (XtPointer) XtInputReadMask,
                       inputReady, (XtPointer) text);
```

See Also
XtAppAddInput(1), *XtRemoveInput*(1).

Prototype Procedures

Name

XtKeyProc – interface definition for keycode-to-keysym translation procedure.

Synopsis

```
typedef void (*XtKeyProc)(Display *, KeyCode, Modifiers, Modifiers *,
            KeySym *);
    Display *display;
    KeyCode keycode;
    Modifiers modifiers;
    Modifiers *modifiers_return;
    KeySym *keysym_return;
```

Inputs

display   Specifies the display that the keycode is from.

keycode   Specifies the keycode that is to be translated.

modifiers   Specifies the mask that indicates what modifier keys (Shift, Meta, Control, etc.) are pressed.

Outputs

modifiers_return

Returns a mask that specifies the modifier keys that the function examined in making the conversion.

keysym_return

Returns the resulting keysym.

Description

An XtKeyProc is registered in a call to XtSetKeyTranslator() and is invoked explicitly by a call to XtTranslateKeycode() and automatically by the Translation Manager in order to convert incoming keycodes to keysyms.

An XtKeyProc must convert the *keycode* and *modifiers* into a keysym and return that keysym in *keysym_return*. It should return the modifiers that it considers in its translation in *modifiers_return*. The value returned in this argument will be a constant for any given XtKeyProc.

An XtKeyProc must be implemented so that multiple calls with the same *display*, *keycode*, and *modifiers* arguments will return the same result until either a new case converter (an XtCaseProc) is registered or a MappingNotify event is received.

Usage

XtTranslateKey() is the default XtKeyProc. It should be sufficient for all applications except those that use non-standard keysyms.

When writing an XtKeyProc, you will probably need to call XtConvertCase(), and Xt-GetKeysymTable(). You may also want to invoke XtTranslateKey() directly to translate the standard keysyms.

See Also

XtConvertCase(1), *XtGetKeysymTable*(1), *XtKeysymToKeycodeList*(1), *XtRegisterCaseConverter*(1), *Xt-SetKeyTranslator*(1), *XtTranslateKey*(1), *XtTranslateKeycode*(1).

XtLanguageProc

Name

XtLanguageProc – interface definition for a procedure to set the locale and return the language string.

Synopsis

```
typedef String (*XtLanguageProc)(Display*, String, XtPointer);
      Display *display;
      String language;
      XtPointer client_data;
```

Inputs

display   Specifies the connection to the X server.

language   Specifies the initial language string obtained from the command line or server per-display resources, or NULL if no language specification is found.

client_data Specifies data registered with this function in the call to XtSetLanguageProc().

Returns

The language string for the display.

Availability

Release 5 and later.

Description

An XtLanguageProc and its *client_data* argument are registered with a call to XtSetLanguageProc(). It is invoked by XtDisplayInitialize() with the initial value of the language string or NULL.

A language procedure is passed the language string, if any, from the application command line or per-display resources, and should use that string to localize the application appropriately. Setting the locale usually involves calling setlocale(), XSupportsLocale(), and XSetLocaleModifiers(), but applications that use other localization schemes may need to do different or additional initialization in this procedure.

An XtLanguageProc returns a string which will be set as the language string of the display by XtDisplayInitialize(), and will be used in future calls to XtResolvePathname() to find localized files. The returned string may be different than the *language* argument. If *language* is NULL, for example, a language procedure might determine the locale from an environment variable and return that value. If the language procedure calls setlocale(), then the return value of this function is an appropriate return value for the function. The Intrinsics will make a private copy of this string.

Usage

All internationalized programs should call XtSetLanguageProc() before calling XtAppInitialize(), but most can simply use the default language procedure (pass NULL for the *proc* argument). The default procedure should be sufficient for all applications that use only ANSI-C and X-based internationalization schemes.

Example

The following is the Intrinsics default language procedure:

```
/*ARGSUSED*/
static String _XtDefaultLanguageProc(dpy, xnl, closure)
    Display   *dpy;      /* unused */
    String    xnl;
    XtPointer  closure; /* unused */
{
    if (! setlocale(LC_ALL, xnl))
        XtWarning("locale not supported by C library, locale unchanged");

    if (! XSupportsLocale()) {
        XtWarning("locale not supported by Xlib, locale set to C");
        setlocale(LC_ALL, "C");
    }
    if (! XSetLocaleModifiers(""))
        XtWarning("X locale modifiers not supported, using default");

    return setlocale(LC_ALL, NULL); /* re-query in case overwritten */
}
```

See Also

XtDisplayInitialize(1), *XtSetLanguageProc*(1).

Prototype Procedures

Name

XtLoseSelectionIncrProc – interface definition for a procedure called when the selection owner loses ownership.

Synopsis

```
typedef void (*XtLoseSelectionIncrProc)(Widget, Atom*, XtPointer);
    Widget w;
    Atom *selection;
    XtPointer client_data;
```

Inputs

w	Specifies the widget that has lost the selection ownership.
selection	Specifies the atom that names the selection.
client_data	Specifies the value passed in by the widget when it took ownership of the selection.

Availability

Release 4 and later.

Description

An XtLoseSelectionIncrProc is optionally registered in a call to XtOwnSelection-Incremental(), and is called by the Intrinsics to inform the selection owner that the selection has been claimed by another widget or another client. This procedure is not called if the selection owner relinquishes selection ownership by calling XtDisownSelection(). It should do whatever is appropriate for the widget or application upon losing the ownership of the selection.

Note that this procedure is not a request to the widget to relinquish selection ownership; it is called after the widget has already lost the selection.

Usage

Most selection owners will want to display selected data specially highlighted, and so will need to be informed when they lose the selection so that they can unhighlight that data.

An XtLoseSelectionIncrProc is used in the Intrinsics incremental selection transfer mechanism. An XtLoseSelectionProc is a similar procedure used by the more convenient atomic transfer mechanism. An XtLoseSelectionProc does not have a *client_data* argument.

See Also

XtGetSelectionValueIncremental(1), *XtGetSelectionValuesIncremental*(1), *XtOwnSelectionIncremental*(1), *XtCancelConvertSelectionProc*(2), *XtConvertSelectionIncrProc*(2), *XtLoseSelectionProc*(2), *XtSelectionDoneIncrProc*(2).

Name

XtLoseSelectionProc – interface definition for procedure to notify the selection owner it has lost selection ownership.

Synopsis

```
typedef void (*XtLoseSelectionProc)(Widget, Atom *);
    Widget w;
    Atom *selection;
```

Inputs

w   Specifies the widget that has lost selection ownership.

selection   Specifies the atom that names the selection.

Description

An XtLoseSelectionProc is optionally registered in a call to XtOwnSelection() and is called by the Intrinsics when the widget it was registered with loses the selection because another widget or client has claimed the selection. It is not called when the selection owner relinquishes selection ownership with XtDisownSelection(). This procedure should take whatever action is appropriate for the widget or application when it loses selection ownership.

Note that this procedure is not a request to the widget to relinquish selection ownership; it is called after the widget has already lost the selection.

Usage

Most selection owners (widgets or applications) will want to display selected data highlighted in some way, and so will need to be informed when they lose the selection so that they can unhighlight that data.

An XtLoseSelectionIncrProc is a similar procedure type used by the Intrinsics incremental selection transfer mechanism. It takes an additional *client_data* argument.

Example

The XtLoseSelectionProc below is from the *xcalc* client. It simply unhighlights the value currently shown in the calculator display.

```
/*
 * called when xcalc loses ownership of the selection.
 */
/*ARGSUSED*/
void lose(w, selection)
    Widget      w;
    Atom        *selection;
{
    XawToggleUnsetCurrent(LCD);
}
```

Prototype Procedures

See Also

XtDisownSelection(1), *XtGetSelectionValue*(1), *XtGetSelectionValueIncremental*(1), *XtOwnSelection*(1), *XtLoseSelectionIncrProc*(2).

Name

XtOrderProc – interface definition for an `XtNinsertPosition` procedure.

Synopsis

```
typedef Cardinal (*XtOrderProc)(Widget);
    Widget w;
```

Inputs

w   Specifies the widget.

Description

An `XtOrderProc` is registered as the value of the `XtNinsertPosition` resource of a composite widget, and is called by some subclasses of Composite to determine the position in the Composite `children` array at which a newly created child should be inserted.

An `XtOrderProc` should return the position in the array at which *w* should be inserted. A return value of zero means that it should be the first widget in the array, a return value of one means that there should be one widget before it in the array, and so on. A return value equal to the `XtNnumChildren` resource indicates that the widget should be placed at the end of the array, which is the default if no `XtOrderProc` is registered.

Usage

Note that for many composite widgets, the position of a child in the `children` array has nothing to do with its position on the screen. The `XtNinsertPosition` resource will only be interesting if the widget does not provide any other method of positioning its children.

The Composite class `insert_child()` method calls the `XtOrderProc`, if any, registered on the `XtNinsertPosition` resource. Most composite subclasses inherit or call this procedure explicitly and will therefore do the same.

Note that the `XtNinsertPosition` procedure is not a method of the widget class. It could be considered an "instance method" rather than a "class method." In this way it is similar to the procedure that can be registered on the `XtNcreatePopupChildProc` resource of a shell widget.

Example

None of the standard MIT clients make use of the `XtNinsertPosition` resource. An example of where an `XtOrderProc` might be useful is an application that dynamically creates a number of button widgets (to represent mail folders or newsgroups, perhaps) and places them in a simple Xaw Box widget. Since these buttons will differ from user to user, and can be inserted and deleted during a session, it would be logical to place them in alphabetical order. An `XtOrderProc` could do this by using `XtGetValues()` to get the current list of widget children, and then comparing the name (using `XtName()`) of the specified widget against the names of all the existing widgets.

See Also

Composite(3),
delete_child(4), *insert_child*(4).

XtProc

Name

XtProc – interface definition for the `class_initialize()` method.

Synopsis

```
typedef void (*XtProc)(void);
```

Description

`XtProc` is the type of the Core, RectObj, and Object `class_initialize()` method. See `class_initialize`(4) for more information.

See Also

class_initialize(4).

Name

XtRealizeProc – interface definition for the `realize()` method.

Synopsis

```
typedef void (*XtRealizeProc)(Widget, XtValueMask, XSetWindowAttributes *);
    Widget w;
    XtValueMask value_mask;
    XSetWindowAttributes *attributes;
```

Inputs

`w`	Specifies the widget.
`value_mask`	Specifies which fields in the `attributes` structure to use.
`attributes`	Specifies the window attributes to use in the `XCreateWindow()` call.

Description

`XtRealizeProc` is the type of the Core `realize()` method. See `realize(4)` for more information.

See Also

realize(4).

XtResourceDefaultProc

Name

XtResourceDefaultProc – interface definition for procedure called to obtain a resource default value.

Synopsis

```
typedef void (*XtResourceDefaultProc)(Widget, int, XrmValue *)
    Widget w;
    int offset;
    XrmValue *value_return;
```

Inputs

w   Specifies the widget whose resource is to be obtained.

offset   Specifies the offset of the field in the widget record.

Outputs

value_return
    Returns the address of the default resource value.

Description

An `XtResourceDefaultProc` is registered in an `XtResource` structure of an `XtResourceList` array by specifying the special value `XtRCallProc` for the `default_type` field, and specifying the procedure in the `default_addr` field. It is called by the Intrinsics when the default value of that resource is required.

An `XtResourceDefaultProc` should determine the default value of the resource, convert it to the correct type if necessary, and store the address of the value at `value_return`->addr. It need not store the size of this value because the resource manager already knows the size of the resource.

See `XtGetApplicationResources`(1) for more information on the fields of the `XtResource` structure and an example of how to declare one.

Usage

An `XtResourceDefaultProc` is passed the offset of the resource field in the widget or object w as its `offset` argument. It should not use this argument to set the resource value directly in the object. It can use it to identify which resource value is desired, if the same procedure is used to obtain default values for more than one resource. It can also be used to obtain the same resource value from some other already initialized widget of the same class, as is shown in the example below.

Example

The default value for the `XtNdepth` resource of the Core widget class should be whatever value the widget's parent has. To implement this, the `XtNdepth` resource is declared with an `XtResourceDefaultProc` as follows:

```
{XtNdepth, XtCDepth, XtRInt,sizeof(int),
     XtOffsetOf(CoreRec,core.depth),
     XtRCallProc, (XtPointer)_XtCopyFromParent},
```

The _XtCopyFromParent() XtResourceDefaultProc is defined by the Intrinsics as follows. Note how the resource value is returned and how the *offset* argument is used.

```
void _XtCopyFromParent(widget, offset, value)
    Widget      widget;
    int         offset;
    XrmValue    *value;
{
    if (widget->core.parent == NULL) {
        XtAppWarningMsg(XtWidgetToApplicationContext(widget),
                        "invalidParent","xtCopyFromParent",
                        XtCXtToolkitError,
                        "CopyFromParent must have non-NULL parent",
                        (String *)NULL, (Cardinal *)NULL);
        value->addr = NULL;
        return;
    }
    value->addr = (XPointer)(((char *)widget->core.parent) + offset);
}
```

See Also

XtGetApplicationResources(1), *XtGetSubresources*(1).

Name

XtSelectionCallbackProc – interface definition for procedure called when requested selection data is ready.

Synopsis

```
typedef void (*XtSelectionCallbackProc)(Widget, XtPointer, Atom *, Atom *,
        XtPointer, unsigned long *, int *);
    Widget w;
    XtPointer client_data;
    Atom *selection;
    Atom *type;
    XtPointer value;
    unsigned long *length;
    int *format;
```

Inputs

w	Specifies the widget that requested the selection value.
client_data	Specifies data registered with this procedure when the selection value was requested.
selection	Specifies the selection that was requested (usually XA_PRIMARY or XA_SECONDARY).
type	Specifies the representation type of the selection value (for example, XA_STRING).
value	Specifies a pointer to the selection value.
length	Specifies the number of elements in value.
format	Specifies the size in bits of the data elements of value.

Description

An XtSelectionCallbackProc is registered in a call to XtGetSelectionValue(), XtGetSelectionValues(), XtGetSelectionValueIncremental(), or XtGetSelectionValuesIncremental(). Because interclient communication is asynchronous, these functions cannot return the selection value directly, and instead register an XtSelectionCallbackProc to be called when the selection owner has converted and transferred the requested data.

The w, client_data, and selection arguments are the same as those passed when the selection value was requested. The type argument is a pointer to an Atom that identifies the type of the returned data. This is generally not the same as the Atom that was passed as the requested target type. If the target was the Atom FILENAME, for example, the type of the returned value will probably be XA_STRING. If the selection owner does not respond within the Intrinsics timeout interval, the Intrinsics call this callback with the special value XT_CONVERT_FAIL in type. Note that XT_CONVERT_FAIL is not actually an Atom, and does not need to be interned. An XtSelectionCallbackProc should test its type argument to verify that the type of the data is as expected, or is at least something it can handle.

The *value* argument is a pointer to the selection value. It is an array of *length* elements, each element *format* bits long, and should be interpreted as indicated by the *type* argument. *format* will be one of 8, 16, or 32. The requesting client owns the storage allocated for the selection value and is responsible for freeing it by calling XtFree() when it is done with it. If there is no owner for the specified selection, or that owner cannot convert the selected data to the requested type, then this callback is called with *value* NULL and *length* zero.

If an XtSelectionCallbackProc is registered with XtGetSelectionValue(), then it will only be called once, with the complete selection value converted to the single requested target type. If it is registered with XtGetSelectionValues(), it will be called once for each target type that is specified in that call. Each call will pass the entire selected values. These two functions are part of the Intrinsics atomic selection transfer mechanism, and will only call their XtSelectionCallbackProc once to deliver a selection value. If the selection value is larger than will fit in a single X protocol request, the Intrinsics transparently handle breaking up the value and reassembling it after transfer.

If an XtSelectionCallbackProc is registered with XtGetSelectionValue-Incremental() or XtGetSelectionValuesIncremental(), then it will be called at least twice for each selection value it delivers. These two functions are part of the Intrinsics incremental selection transfer mechanism, and call their XtSelectionCallbackProc to deliver the selection value piece by piece. When the last chunk of a selection value has been transferred, the callback is called a final time with *length* zero, and a non-NULL *value*, which is a special signal that the transfer is complete. The callback must free this non-NULL value, even though the *length* argument is zero.

Usage

Note that the *selection*, *type*, *length*, and *format* arguments to this callback are pointers to their values rather than the values themselves. This is unusual in a procedure of this type, and you should be sure to dereference them correctly. Note that you should not modify the values pointed to by these arguments.

An XtSelectionCallbackProc can generally simply test *type* to see if it is one of the possible values that it knows how to handle. If *type* is XT_CONVERT_FAIL, or some unrecognized type, the callback can just return silently, or may notify the user that the selection failed by calling XBell(), for example. It should do the same if called with zero *length* and a NULL *value*.

When working with selections, you will have to work with Atoms. Many standard Atoms are predefined in *<X11/Xatom.h>*, and have symbolic names beginning with XA_. Atoms that are not defined in this file (TARGETS, for example) may be interned explicitly as Atoms by calling the Xlib function XInternAtom(). The Xmu library provides an alternate function, Xmu-InternAtom() which caches Atoms on the client side. Additionally, the header *<Xmu/Atoms.h>* defines a number of macros, such as XA_TARGETS(dpy), which call Xmu-InternAtom() and take a Display pointer as their single argument.

Example

The following XtSelectionCallbackProc is modified from the X11R5 *bitmap* client.

```
/* ARGSUSED */
void SelectionCallback(w, cldat, selection, type, value, length, format)
    Widget w;
    XtPointer cldat;
    Atom *selection, *type;
    XtPointer value;
    unsigned long *length;
    int *format;
{
    BitmapWidget BW = (BitmapWidget) w;
    Pixmap *pixmap;

    if ((*length != 0) && (value != NULL)) {
        switch (*type) {
        case XA_BITMAP:
        case XA_PIXMAP:
            DestroyBitmapImage(&BW->bitmap.storage);
            pixmap = (Pixmap *) value;
            BW->bitmap.storage = GetImage(BW, *pixmap);
            XFree((char *)pixmap);
            break;
        }
    }

    BW->bitmap.selection.limbo = FALSE;
}
```

This `XtSelectionCallbackProc` procedure is registered by the procedure below, also modified from the X11R5 *bitmap* client. Note that this procedure will optionally enter a local event loop so that it appears to block. If called with *wait* True, then it will not return until the selection value has been transferred.

```
void BWRequestSelection(w, btime, wait)
    Widget w;
    Time btime;
    Boolean wait;
{
    BitmapWidget BW = (BitmapWidget) w;

    XtGetSelectionValue(w, XA_PRIMARY, XA_PIXMAP,
                    SelectionCallback, NULL, btime);

    BW->bitmap.selection.limbo = TRUE;
    if (wait)
      while (BW->bitmap.selection.limbo) {
        XEvent event;
        XtNextEvent(&event);
        XtDispatchEvent(&event);
      }
}
```

See Also

XtDisownSelection(1), *XtGetSelectionValue*(1), *XtGetSelectionValueIncremental*(1), *XtGetSelection-Values*(1), *XtGetSelectionValuesIncremental*(1), *XtOwnSelection*(1), *XtOwnSelectionIncremental*(1).

Name

XtSelectionDoneIncrProc – interface definition for procedure called when an incremental selection transfer completes.

Synopsis

```
typedef void (*XtSelectionDoneIncrProc)(Widget, Atom *, Atom *,
        XtRequestId *, XtPointer);
    Widget w;
    Atom *selection;
    Atom *target;
    XtRequestId *request_id;
    XtPointer client_data;
```

Inputs

w	Specifies the widget that owns the selection.
selection	Specifies the atom that names the selection being transferred.
target	Specifies the target type to which the conversion was done.
request_id	Identifies the specific conversion request that completed.
client_data	Specifies data registered with this procedure when the widget took ownership of the selection.

Availability

Release 4 and later.

Description

An XtSelectionDoneIncrProc is optionally registered in a call to XtOwnSelection-Incremental(), and is called by the Intrinsics after the requestor has retrieved the final (zero-length) segment of the incremental transfer to indicate that the entire transfer is complete. The *w*, *selection*, and *client_data* arguments are those passed to XtOwnSelection-Incremental(). The *target* and *request_id* arguments are those that were passed to the XtConvertSelectionIncrProc registered with this procedure.

An XtSelectionDoneIncrProc should free any memory that was allocated for the transfer of the selection value. If no procedure is specified, the Intrinsics will automatically free (using XtFree()) the last value returned by the XtConvertSelectionIncrProc. If a single buffer is used to transfer all the chunks of the selection, this automatic freeing by the Intrinsics should be sufficient. If separate buffers are used or other memory or resources are allocated to transfer the selection value, an XtSelectionDoneIncrProc should be provided to free them.

Usage

It is usually more convenient to use the Intrinsics atomic selection transfer mechanism which transfers the selection value in a single chunk. See XtOwnSelection(1) and Xt-SelectionDoneProc for more information.

See Also

XtGetSelectionValueIncremental(1), *XtGetSelectionValuesIncremental*(1), *XtOwnSelection*(1), *XtOwn-SelectionIncremental*(1),
XtCancelConvertSelectionProc(2), *XtConvertSelectionIncrProc*(2), *XtLoseSelectionIncrProc*(2), *Xt-SelectionDoneProc*(2).

Name

XtSelectionDoneProc – interface definition for procedure called after selection transfer is completed.

Synopsis

```
typedef void (*XtSelectionDoneProc)(Widget, Atom *, Atom *);
    Widget w;
    Atom *selection;
    Atom *target;
```

Inputs

w	Specifies the widget that owns the converted selection.
selection	Specifies the atom that names the selection that was transferred.
target	Specifies the target type to which the conversion was done.

Description

An XtSelectionDoneProc is optionally registered in a call to XtOwnSelection(), and is called by the Intrinsics after the corresponding XtConvertSelectionProc has been called and the data it returns is transferred to the requestor.

An XtSelectionDoneProc should free the memory returned by the XtConvert-SelectionProc and any other memory or resources allocated by that procedure to convert the selection value. If no XtSelectionDoneProc is registered with XtOwn-Selection(), then the Intrinsics will automatically free the memory returned by the Xt-ConvertSelectionProc by calling XtFree().

Usage

Most XtConvertSelectionProc procedures will allocate a single block of memory with XtMalloc() and can simply rely on the Intrinsics to free that block with XtFree(). In this case, there is no need for an XtSelectionDoneProc.

Note that an XtSelectionDoneProc is not passed a *client_data* argument, nor is it passed a pointer to the memory that was returned by the XtConvertSelectionProc. In a widget, the widget structure can point to the memory that must be freed, but in an application, you will probably have to rely on a global variable, as in the example below.

The XtSelectionDoneProc and XtOwnSelection() are part of the Intrinsics atomic selection transfer mechanism. For some selection values, it may be more convenient to transfer the selection value in pieces. This can be done with the incremental transfer mechanism; see XtOwnSelectionIncremental(1).

Example

The *xcalc* client uses a static character string to store the selection value. Because this is not allocated memory, it should not be freed, so *xcalc* provides a XtSelectionDoneProc which simply sets the static buffer to contain the empty string:

```
static char selstr[LCD_STR_LEN]; /* storage for selections from the LCD */

/*ARGSUSED*/
void done(w, selection, target)
    Widget      w;
    Atom        *selection;
    Atom        *target;
{
    selstr[0] = ' ';
}
```

This XtSelectionDoneProc is registered with this call:

```
XtOwnSelection(LCD, XA_PRIMARY, time, convert, lose, done);
```

See Also

XtDisownSelection(1), *XtGetSelectionValue*(1), *XtGetSelectionValues*(1), *XtOwnSelection*(1), *XtOwnSelectionIncremental*(1),
XtConvertSelectionProc(2).

XtSetValuesFunc

Name

XtSetValuesFunc – interface definition for the set_values() methods.

Synopsis

```
typedef Boolean (*XtSetValuesFunc)(Widget, Widget, Widget, ArgList,
        Cardinal *);
    Widget current;
    Widget request;
    Widget set;
    ArgList args;
    Cardinal *num-args;
```

Inputs

current	Specifies a copy of the widget as it was before the XtSetValues() call.
request	Specifies a copy of the widget with all values changed as asked for by the XtSetValues() call before any class set_values() procedures have been called.
set	Specifies the widget as modified by all previous called set_values() procedures.
args	Specifies the argument list passed to XtSetValues().
num_args	Specifies the number of arguments in the argument list.

Returns

True if the widget should be redrawn, False otherwise.

Description

XtSetValuesFunc is the type of the Object, RectObj, and Core set_values() method, and of the Constraint set_values() method. See those reference pages in Section 4 for more information.

See Also

set_values(4), *Constraint set_values*(4).

Name

XtStringProc – interface definition for the `display_accelerator()` method.

Synopsis

```
typedef void (*XtStringProc)(Widget, String)
    Widget w;
    String string;
```

Inputs

w	Specifies the source widget that supplied the accelerators.
string	Provides the string representation of the accelerators currently registered for the widget.

Description

XtStringProc is the type of the Core `display_accelerator()` method. See `display_accelerator(4)` for more information.

See Also

display_accelerator(4).

Name

XtTimerCallbackProc – interface definition for procedure invoked when timeouts expire.

Synopsis

```
typedef void (*XtTimerCallbackProc)(XtPointer, XtIntervalId *);
    XtPointer client_data;
    XtIntervalId *id;
```

Inputs

client_data   Specifies the data that was registered with this procedure.

id   Specifies the ID returned when this procedure was registered.

Description

An XtTimerCallbackProc is registered in a call to XtAppAddTimeOut(), and is invoked when the specified number of milliseconds elapse. The *client_data* argument is data registered with the procedure in the call to XtAppAddTimeOut(), and the *id* argument is the value returned by that function.

A timer callback is called once, and then is automatically removed. If you want a callback to be called repeatedly, re-register the callback each time it is called,

Example

The following XtTimerCallbackProc is from the *xmh* program. It re-registers itself so that it will be called repeatedly. Note that it uses its *client_data* argument to supply the application context so that it can re-register itself.

```
/*ARGSUSED*/
static void NeedToCheckScans(client_data, id)
    XtPointer client_data;
    XtIntervalId *id;            /* unused */
{
    int i;
    if (!subProcessRunning) {
        DEBUG("[magic toc check ...")
        for (i = 0; i < numScrns; i++) {
            if (scrnList[i]->toc)
                TocRecheckValidity(scrnList[i]->toc);
            if (scrnList[i]->msg)
                TocRecheckValidity(MsgGetToc(scrnList[i]->msg));
        }
        DEBUG(" done]\n")
    }
    (void) XtAppAddTimeOut((XtAppContext)client_data,
                        (unsigned long) app_resources.rescan_interval,
                        NeedToCheckScans, client_data);
}
```

This procedure is initiallly registered with the following code:

```
if (app_resources.rescan_interval > 0) {
    app_resources.rescan_interval *= 60000;
    (void) XtAppAddTimeOut(appCtx,
            (unsigned long) app_resources.rescan_interval,
            NeedToCheckScans, (XtPointer)appCtx);
}
```

See Also

XtAppAddTimeOut(1), *XtRemoveTimeOut*(1).

XtTypeConverter

Name

XtTypeConverter – interface definition for a new-style resource converter.

Synopsis

```
typedef Boolean (*XtTypeConverter)(Display *, XrmValue *, Cardinal *,
        XrmValue *, XrmValue *, XtPointer *);
    Display *display;
    XrmValue *args;
    Cardinal *num_args;
    XrmValue *from;
    XrmValue *to;
    XtPointer *converter_data;
```

Inputs

display   Specifies the Display connection with which this conversion is associated.

args   Specifies a list of additional XrmValue arguments to the converter, or NULL.

num_args   Specifies the number of arguments in *args*.

from   Specifies the address and size of the value to convert.

to_in_out   Specifies the address at which the converted value is to be stored, or NULL, and the number of bytes allocated for the value at that address.

Outputs

to_in_out   Returns the address at which the converted value was stored, and the actual number of bytes occupied by that value.

converter_data

Returns arbitrary data which will be passed to the destructor procedure, if any, associated with this converter when the converted resource is freed from the resource cache.

Returns

True if the conversion was successful; False otherwise.

Availability

Release 4 and later.

Description

An XtTypeConverter is a "new-style" resource converter registered with XtAppSet-TypeConverter() or XtSetTypeConverter(). It is invoked by the Intrinsics to convert resource values between the types for which it is registered, or can be invoked explicitly with XtConvertAndStore() or XtCallConverter().

An XtTypeConverter should convert the value pointed to by *from*->addr (which is *from*->size bytes long) into the appropriate type and store the converted value at *to_in_out*->addr. If this pointer is NULL, the converter should store the converted value in its own storage and place the size and address of this storage into *to_in_out*. This memory remains under the ownership of the converter and must not be modified by the caller. The type converter is permitted to use static storage for this purpose and therefore the caller must immediately copy the data upon return from the converter.

If `to_in_out->addr` is not NULL, the converter must check the `size` field to insure that sufficient space has been allocated before storing the converted value.

- If insufficient space is specified, the converter should update the `size` field to indicate number of bytes required and should return `False` without modifying the data pointed to by the `addr` field.

- If sufficient space was allocated by the caller, the converter should store the converted value at the location pointed to by the `addr` field and set the `size` field to the number of bytes actually occupied by the converted value.

For converted values of type `XtRString`, the size should include the NULL-terminating byte, if any.

The converter may return any value it wishes in *converter_data*; this data is similar to the *client_data* argument to a callback and will be passed to the destructor, if any, associated with this converter when the resource value is freed by the Intrinsics. See `XtDestructor`(2) for more information.

The *args* argument is an array of values (such as a Screen pointer or Colormap ID) that the converter may need to perform the conversion. The contents and interpretation of this array are determined by the `XtConvertArgList` array supplied when the converter is registered. The Intrinsics use the `XtConvertArgList` to compute an array of `XrmValue` to pass to the converter each time it is invoked. An `XtTypeConverter` that expects values in its `args` argument must be registered with a suitable `XtConvertArgList` or it will not work correctly. See `XtAppSetTypeConverter()` for information on declaring `XtConvertArgList` arrays.

The *display* argument to an `XtTypeConverter` may be used by some converters in the conversion process, and is also needed to obtain the application context (with the function `XtDisplayToApplicationContext()`) in order to report warning messages. Note that one of the primary differences between "new-style" and "old-style" converters is that new-style converters have this *display* argument.

An `XtTypeConverter` should return `True` if the conversion was successful and return `False` otherwise. If the conversion cannot be performed due to an improper source value, a warning message should be issued with `XtAppWarningMsg()` or `XtDisplayStringConversionWarning()`.

Usage

Note that the *num_args* argument is a pointer to the number of elements in *args*, and not the number of arguments itself. Be sure to dereference this argument correctly before using it.

An `XtTypeConverter` must check both the `addr` and `size` fields of its *to_in_out* argument, and be prepared to return the converted value in different ways depending on the values in these fields. To encapsulate all the requirements for returning a converted value, the standard converters defined by the Intrinsics all call a macro named `done()` which is passed the converted value and returns it in the correct way depending on the *to_in_out* argument. This `done()` macro is shown in the example below.

All type converters should define some set of values for which they are guaranteed to succeed, so that these values can be used as widget and application resource defaults. For some string converters, this may mean defining a string value which will be handled specially by the converter. It is useful if you give this string a symbolic name. The special constants `Xt-DefaultFont`, `XtDefaultForeground`, and `XtDefaultBackground` are strings of this type which are specially recognized by their converters.

If you write a widget that has a resource which is of some enumerated type, you should write a converter routine which will convert between the symbolic names of each value and the values themselves. This converter should then be registered in your widget's `class_initialize()` method.

If you are writing a programming library or an application that defines non-standard types, it may be useful to provide string converters for those types. This allows resources of that type to be specified from a resource file. An application that supported user-configurable popup menus, for example, might include a String-to-Menu converter.

If your converter needs additional arguments to perform the conversion, you should declare and export the `XtConvertArgList` array to be registered with the converter, or at least document the array that must be registered. Since the wrong arguments will likely cause your converter to dump core, you should consider defining the argument list part of the process of writing the converter. Note that there are also two `XtConvertArgLists` predefined by the Intrinsics: `screenConvertArg` passes the widget's `screen` field to the converter in `args[0]`, and `colorConvertArgs` passes the widget's `screen` field to the converter in `args[0]` and the widget's `colormap` field in `args[1]`.

A type converter may invoke other converters to aid with its conversion. When converting complex types, this is a good idea because it allows differing source types that convert into a common intermediate type to make maximum use of the type converter cache.

The Intrinsics define a number of standard converters which do not need to be registered. See `XtConvertAndStore()` for a list of these predefined converters. There are also a number of other useful converters defined in the Xmu library which do need to be registered explicitly. See `XmuCvtStringToMisc`(6).

Example

The `done()` macro below is from the X11R5 Intrinsics. It is used to return a converted resource value correctly depending on the *to_in_out* argument (which is here given the name `toVal`). Note that the *type* argument is used to declare a static variable to store the value in when *to_in_out* (or `toVal`) does not provide a location to store it.

```
#define done(type, value) \
        {                                                          \
            if (toVal->addr != NULL) {                             \
                if (toVal->size < sizeof(type)) {                  \
                    toVal->size = sizeof(type);                    \
```

```
                    return False;                                    \
                }                                                    \
                *(type*)(toVal->addr) = (value);                     \
            }                                                        \
            else {                                                   \
                static type static_val;                              \
                static_val = (value);                                \
                toVal->addr = (XPointer)&static_val;                 \
            }                                                        \
            toVal->size = sizeof(type);                              \
            return True;                                             \
        }
```

An `XtTypeConverter` from the X11R5 Intrinsics to convert between a string and a `Pixel` is shown below, along with the `XtConvertArgList` that it must be registered with. Note how it checks *num_args* and then determines the screen and colormap from its *args* argument. Also note that it tests for two special values: the strings with symbolic names `Xt-DefaultForeground` and `XtDefaultBackground`. It is guaranteed to successfully convert these values. The `pd` variable is an Intrinsics internal structure, and `pd->rv` indicates whether or not the `reverseVideo` application resource is specified in the resource database.

This converter returns a `Boolean` in its *converter_data* argument (called `clo-sure_ret` here) which indicates to the resource destructor whether or not it should deallocate the color. The pixels associated with `XtDefaultForeground` and `XtDefaultBackground` are never deallocated. See `XtDestructor`(2) for the destructor procedure that accompanies this converter.

Finally, note that this converter uses the `done` macro five times, which is inefficient because it expands to a large macro. With some simple reorganization, it need only be called once.

```
XtConvertArgRec Const colorConvertArgs[] = {
    {XtWidgetBaseOffset, (XtPointer)XtOffsetOf(WidgetRec, core.screen),
     sizeof(Screen *)},
    {XtWidgetBaseOffset, (XtPointer)XtOffsetOf(WidgetRec, core.colormap),
     sizeof(Colormap)}
};

Boolean XtCvtStringToPixel(dpy, args, num_args, fromVal, toVal, closure_ret)
    Display*    dpy;
    XrmValuePtr args;
    Cardinal    *num_args;
    XrmValuePtr fromVal;
    XrmValuePtr toVal;
    XtPointer   *closure_ret;
{
    String       str = (String)fromVal->addr;
    XColor       screenColor;
    XColor       exactColor;
    Screen       *screen;
    XtPerDisplay pd = _XtGetPerDisplay(dpy);
    Colormap     colormap;
```

```
    Status          status;
    String          params[1];
    Cardinal        num_params=1;

if (*num_args != 2) {
    XtAppWarningMsg(pd->appContext, XtNwrongParameters, "cvtStringToPixel",
                    XtCXtToolkitError,
        "String to pixel conversion needs screen and colormap arguments",
                    (String *)NULL, (Cardinal *)NULL);
    return False;
}

screen = *((Screen **) args[0].addr);
colormap = *((Colormap *) args[1].addr);

if (CompareISOLatin1(str, XtDefaultBackground) == 0) {
    *closure_ret = False;
    if (pd->rv) done(Pixel, BlackPixelOfScreen(screen))
    else        done(Pixel, WhitePixelOfScreen(screen));
}
if (CompareISOLatin1(str, XtDefaultForeground) == 0) {
    *closure_ret = False;
    if (pd->rv) done(Pixel, WhitePixelOfScreen(screen))
    else        done(Pixel, BlackPixelOfScreen(screen));
}

status = XAllocNamedColor(DisplayOfScreen(screen), colormap,
                         (char*)str, &screenColor, &exactColor);
if (status == 0) {
    String msg, type;
    params[0] = str;
    /* Server returns a specific error code but Xlib discards it.  Ugh */
    if (XLookupColor(DisplayOfScreen(screen), colormap, (char*)str,
                    &exactColor, &screenColor)) {
        type = "noColormap";
        msg = "Cannot allocate colormap entry for
    }
    else {
        type = "badValue";
        msg = "Color name
    }

    XtAppWarningMsg(pd->appContext, type, "cvtStringToPixel",
                    XtCXtToolkitError, msg, params, &num_params);
    *closure_ret = False;
    return False;
} else {
    *closure_ret = (char*)True;
    done(Pixel, screenColor.pixel);
}
}
```

Structures

The `XrmValue` structure is defined as follows:

```
typedef struct {
    unsigned int    size;
    XPointer        addr;
} XrmValue, *XrmValuePtr;
```

See Also

XtAppSetTypeConverter(1), *XtCallConverter*(1), *XtConvertAndStore*(1), *XtDisplayStringConversion-Warning*(1), *XtSetTypeConverter*(1),
XmuCvtStringToMisc(6).

XtWidgetClassProc

Name

XtWidgetClassProc – interface definition for the `class_part_initialize()` method.

Synopsis

```
typedef void (*XtWidgetClassProc)(WidgetClass);
    WidgetClass class;
```

Inputs

`class`   Specifies a pointer to the widget class structure.

Description

XtWidgetClassProc is the type of the Object, RectObj, and Core `class_part_ini-tialize()` method. See `class_part_initialize(4)` for more information.

See Also

class_part_initialize(4).

XtWidgetProc

Name

XtWidgetProc – interface definition for many common widget methods.

Synopsis

```
typedef void (*XtWidgetProc)(Widget);
    Widget w;
```

Inputs

w   Specifies the widget.

Description

XtWidgetProc is the type of the Object, RectObj, and Core destroy() method, the Constraint destroy() method, the RectObj and Core resize() method, and the Composite change_managed(), insert_child(), and delete_child() methods. See the reference pages in Section 4 for more information.

See Also

change_managed(4), *delete_child*(4), *destroy*(4), *Constraint destroy*(4), *insert_child*(4), *resize*(4).

Prototype Procedures

Name

XtWorkProc – interface definition for procedure called when the event loop is idle.

Synopsis

```
typedef Boolean (*XtWorkProc)(XtPointer);
    XtPointer client_data;
```

Inputs

client_data   Specifies data registered with this procedure.

Returns

`True` if the procedure should not be called again; `False` otherwise.

Description

An `XtWorkProc` is registered with `XtAppAddWorkProc()` and is called by `XtAppMain-Loop()` and `XtAppProcessEvent()` if there are no events pending and the application would otherwise block.

The `client_data` argument is data of any type registered in the call to `XtAppAddWork-Proc()`. It is generally cast to an `XtPointer` when registered and cast back to the appropriate type within the `XtWorkProc`. An `XtWorkProc` must get all of its context from this argument or from global variables.

An `XtWorkProc` should perform a single short task and return. If it does not return quickly then events that arrive while it is running will not be handled immediately, and the response time seen by the user will suffer. If a work procedure has a lot of processing to do, it should perform a piece of it, save its state in static variables, and return `False`. When an `XtWork-Proc` returns `False`, the Intrinsics will call it again the next time the event loop is idle, and it can resume its processing where it left off. When it completes all of its processing, it should return `True`, and the Intrinsics will automatically un-register it, so that it will not be called again.

Usage

One possible use of work procedures is to create the widgets in dialog boxes which are not needed immediately when an application starts up. This will save start up time for the main application window, and will probably also mean that the dialog boxes will be fully created by the time the user requests that one is popped up.

You can register multiple work procedures, and they will be performed one at a time. The most recent work procedure added has the highest priority. Therefore, for example, if you want to create ten popup widgets during idle time, you might add ten work procedures. The pop up that you expect to need first should be created by the last work procedure registered. See the example below for an alternate approach, however.

You can explicitly remove a work procedure with `XtRemoveWorkProc()`.

Example

The first procedure below is an `XtWorkProc` that creates several dialog widgets. Note that it returns after creating each dialog. If the dialogs are needed before they are created by this procedure, they will have to be created explicitly as shown in the second procedure below. The only standard client in X11R5 that uses work procedures is *xfontsel* which performs sophisticated scheduling of all the background work of parsing the names of all the fonts available from the server.

```
Widget file_dialog = NULL;
Widget print_dialog = NULL;
Widget confirm_dialog = NULL;

Boolean CreateDialogsInBackground(client_data)
XtPointer client_data;
{
    Widget toplevel = (Widget) client_data;
    static int num = 0;

    num++;

    switch(num) {
    case 1:
        if (file_dialog == NULL)
            file_dialog = CreateFileDialog(toplevel);
        return False;
    case 2:
        if (print_dialog == NULL)
            print_dialog = CreatePrintDialog(toplevel);
        return False;
    case 3:
        if (confirm_dialog == NULL)
           confirm_dialog = CreateConfirmDialog(toplevel);
        return True;
    }
    return True;
}

void DoFileDialog(toplevel)
Widget toplevel;
{
    if (file_dialog == NULL)
        file_dialog = CreateFileDialog(toplevel);
    XtPopup(file_dialog, XtGrabExclusive);
}
```

This work procedure could be registered with a call like the following:

```
    toplevel = XtAppInitialize(...);
    BuildInterface(toplevel);
    XtRealizeWidget(toplevel);

    XtAppAddWorkProcedure(app_context, CreateDialogsInBackground,
                          (XtPointer) toplevel);

    XtAppMainLoop(app_context);
```

See Also

XtAppAddWorkProc(1), *XtRemoveWorkProc*(1).

Section 3

Intrinsics Classes

This section contains alphabetically-organized reference pages for each of the widget classes defined by the Xt Intrinsics. Each page describes the resources and the class and instance structures for the widget class. The resource information will be useful to programmers working with subclasses of these widget classes, but the class and instance structures sections should only be of interest to widget writers who are writing subclasses of these widgets.

The first reference page, Introduction, explains the format and contents of each of the following pages.

In This Section:

This page describes the format and contents of each reference page in Section 3, which covers the each of the Intrinsics widget types.

Name

Widget – a brief description of the widget.

Synopsis

Public Headers:	The files to include when you use this widget.
Private Header:	The files to include when you subclass this widget.
Class Name:	The name of the widget class; used as the resource class for each instance of the widget.
Class Hierarchy:	The superclasses of this widget, listed in superclass-to-subclass order. The arrow symbol ($\rightarrow$) indicates a subclass.
Class Pointer:	The global variable that points to the widget class structure. This is the value used when creating a widget.
Instantiation:	C code that instantiates the widget, for widgets that can be instantiated.
Functions/Macros:	Functions and/or macros specific to this widget class.

Availability

This section appears for widget classes that were added in Release 4. None were added in Release 5.

Description

This section gives an overview of the widget class and the functionality it provides.

New Resources

This section lists, in tabular form, the name, class, type, and default for each new resorurce defined by this widget, and also provides a paragraph describing each new resource. The table in this section also has a fifth column, labeled "Access," which explains when the resource can be set and queried. If the letter C appears in this column, the resource can be set when the widget is created. If the letter S appears in the column, the resource may be set with `XtSet-Values()`. If the letter G appears, the resource value may be queried with `XtGet-Values()`.

Inherited Resources

This section lists, in tabular form, each of the resoruces inherited by this widget class, along with the superclass from which they are inherited.

Class Structure

This section shows the class part structure and class structure for the widget class, and provides a paragraph describing each field of the class part structure and how it should be initialized.

Extension Structure

This section, if present, shows any extension structures that have been defined for the widget class, and explains how the fields of the structure should be initialized.

Instance Structure

This section shows the widget instance structure for the widget class. The Xt specification does not require that the fields be in the order shown, and it allows implementations to add other fields to the instance structure.

See Also

This section refers you to related functions, prototype procedures, Intrinsics widget classes, or widget methods. The numbers in parenthesis following each reference refer to the sections of this book in which they are found.

ApplicationShell

Name

ApplicationShell widget class – main shell for an application.

Synopsis

Public Headers: *<X11/StringDefs.h>*
                         <X11/Shell.h>

Private Header: *<X11/ShellP.h>*

Class Name: ApplicationShell

Class Hierarchy: Core → Composite → Shell → WMShell → VendorShell → TopLevel-
Shell → ApplicationShell

Class Pointer: `applicationShellWidgetClass`

Instantiation: *widget* = `XtAppInitialize(...)`
                or
                widget = `XtAppCreateShell(`*app_name*, *app_class*,
                                        `applicationShellWidgetClass, ...)`

Functions/Macros: `XtAppCreateShell()`, `XtVaAppCreateShell()`,
                `XtIsApplicationShell()`

Description

An ApplicationShell is the normal top-level window for an application. It does not have a parent and is at the root of the widget tree. An application should have only one Application-Shell, unless the application is implemented as multiple logical applications. Normally, an application will use TopLevelShell widgets for other top-level windows. An ApplicationShell is returned by the call to `XtVaAppInitialize()`. It can also be created explicitly with a call to `XtVaAppCreateShell()`.

New Resources

ApplicationShell defines the following resources:

Name	Class	Type	Default	Access
XtNargc	XtCArgc	int	0	CSG
XtNargv	XtCArgv	String *	NULL	CSG

XtNargc
> Number of arguments in `XtNargv`.

XtNargv
> List of command-line arguments used to start the application. This is the standard C argv, passed in the call to `XtAppInitialize()`. It is used to set the WM_COMMAND property for this window.

Intrinsics
Classes

Inherited Resources

ApplicationShell inherits the following resources. The resources are listed alphabetically, along with the superclass that defines them.

Resource	Inherited From	Resource	Inherited From
XtNaccelerators	Core	XtNmaxAspectX	WMShell
XtNallowShellResize	Shell	XtNmaxAspectY	WMShell
XtNancestorSensitive	Core	XtNmaxHeight	WMShell
XtNbackground	Core	XtNmaxWidth	WMShell
XtNbackgroundPixmap	Core	XtNminAspectX	WMShell
XtNbaseHeight	WMShell	XtNminAspectY	WMShell
XtNbaseWidth	WMShell	XtNminHeight	WMShell
XtNborderColor	Core	XtNminWidth	WMShell
XtNborderPixmap	Core	XtNmwmDecorations	VendorShell
XtNborderWidth	Core	XtNmwmFunctions	VendorShell
XtNchildren	Composite	XtNmwmInputMode	VendorShell
XtNcolormap	Core	XtNmwmMenu	VendorShell
XtNcreatePopupChild- Proc	Shell	XtNnumChildren	Composite
XtNdefaultFontList	VendorShell	XtNoverrideRedirect	Shell
XtNdeleteResponse	VendorShell	XtNpopdownCallback	Shell
XtNdepth	Core	XtNpopupCallback	Shell
XtNdestroyCallback	Core	XtNsaveUnder	Shell
XtNgeometry	Shell	XtNscreen	Core
XtNheight	Core	XtNsensitive	Core
XtNheightInc	WMShell	XtNshellUnitType	VendorShell
XtNiconic	TopLevelShell	XtNtitle	WMShell
XtNiconMask	WMShell	XtNtitleEncoding	WMShell
XtNiconName	TopLevelShell	XtNtransient	WMShell
XtNiconNameEncoding	TopLevelShell	XtNtranslations	Core
XtNiconPixmap	WMShell	XtNuseAsyncGeometry	VendorShell
XtNiconWindow	WMShell	XtNvisual	Shell
XtNiconX	WMShell	XtNwaitForWm	WMShell
XtNiconY	WMShell	XtNwidth	Core
XtNinitialResources- Persistent	Core	XtNwidthInc	WMShell
XtNinitialState	WMShell	XtNwindowGroup	WMShell
XtNinput	WMShell	XtNwinGravity	WMShell
XtNinsertPosition	Composite	XtNwmTimeout	WMShell
XtNkeyboardFocusPolicy	VendorShell	XtNx	Core
XtNmappedWhenManaged	Core	XtNy	Core

Class Structure

The ApplicationShell class structure contains only an extension field. Its declaration is similar to those of the other shells:

```
typedef struct {
    XtPointer extension;            /* pointer to extension record */
} ApplicationShellClassPart;

typedef struct _ApplicationShellClassRec {
    CoreClassPart core_class;
    CompositeClassPart composite_class;
    ShellClassPart shell_class;
    WMShellClassPart wm_shell_class;
    VendorShellClassPart vendor_shell_class;
    TopLevelShellClassPart top_level_shell_class;
    ApplicationShellClassPart application_shell_class;
} ApplicationShellClassRec;
```

There are no extensions currently defined for this class, and the `extension` field should be NULL.

Instance Structure

The ApplicationShell instance structure contains at least the following fields (which need not be in this order):

```
typedef struct {
    char *class;
    XrmClass xrm_class;
    int argc;
    char **argv;
} ApplicationShellPart;

typedef  struct {
    CorePart  core;
    CompositePart  composite;
    ShellPart  shell;
    WMShellPart wm;
    VendorShellPart vendor;
    TopLevelShellPart topLevel;
    ApplicationShellPart application;
} ApplicationShellRec, *ApplicationShellWidget;
```

See Also

Shell(3), *TopLevelShell*(3).

Composite

Name

Composite widget class – fundamental widget with children.

Synopsis

Public Headers: *<X11/StringDefs.h>*
                          <X11/Composite.h>

Private Header: *<X11/CompositeP.h>*

Class Name: Composite

Class Hierarchy: Core → Composite

Class Pointer: `compositeWidgetClass`

Instantiation: Composite is an Intrinsics meta-class, and is not normally instantiated.

Functions/Macros: `XtIsComposite()`

Description

Composite is the superclass of all classes that can have children. It defines methods for geometry management of those children.

New Resources

Composite defines the following resources:

Name	Class	Type	Default	Access
XtNchildren	XtCReadOnly	WidgetList	NULL	G
XtNinsertPosition	XtCInsertPosition	(*)()	NULL	CSG
XtNnumChildren	XtCReadOnly	Cardinal	0	G

`XtNchildren`
> List of widget's children.

`XtNinsertPosition`
> Points to an `XtOrderProc()` function which is to be called to determine the position at which each child should be inserted into the `XtNchildren` array.

`XtNnumChildren`
> Length of the array in `XtNchildren`.

Inherited Resources

Composite inherits the following resources. The resources are listed alphabetically, along with the superclass that defines them.

Resource	Inherited From	Resource	Inherited From
XtNaccelerators	Core	XtNheight	Core
XtNancestor-Sensitive	Core	XtNinitialResources-Persistent	Core

Resource	Inherited From	Resource	Inherited From
XtNbackground	Core	XtNmappedWhen- Managed	Core
XtNbackground- Pixmap	Core	XtNscreen	Core
XtNborderColor	Core	XtNsensitive	Core
XtNborderPixmap	Core	XtNtranslations	Core
XtNborderWidth	Core	XtNwidth	Core
XtNcolormap	Core	XtNx	Core
XtNdepth	Core	XtNy	Core
XtNdestroyCallback	Core		

Class Structure

The composite class structure is defined as follows:

```
typedef struct {
    XtGeometryHandler geometry_manager;/* geometry manager for children */
    XtWidgetProc change_managed;      /* change managed state of child */
    XtWidgetProc insert_child;        /* physically add child to parent */
    XtWidgetProc delete_child;        /* physically remove child */
    XPointer extension;               /* pointer to extension record */
} CompositeClassPart;

typedef struct {
    CoreClassPart                     core_class;
    CompositeClassPart                composite_class;
} CompositeClassRec, *CompositeWidgetClass;
```

The fields of this class structure have the following meanings:

geometry_manager()
> The geometry_manager() method called when a child widget requests a new size or location. See the reference page in Section 4. Use XtInheritGeometryManager to inherit the geometry_manager() method of the superclass.

change_managed()
> The change_managed() method called when a child or children become managed or unmanaged. See the reference page in Section 4. Use XtInheritChangeManaged to inherit the change_managed() method of the superclass.

insert_child()
> The insert_child() method called to add a child to the widgets children instance array. See the reference page in Section 4. Use XtInheritInsertChild to inherit the insert_child() method of the superclass.

delete_child()
> The delete_child() method called to add a child to the widgets children instance array. See the reference page in Section 4. Use XtInheritDeleteChild to inherit the delete_child() method of the superclass.

*Intrinsics
Classes*

extension
> A linked list of extension records, or NULL. There is currently one extension defined for Composite which allows the class to specify whether it accepts non-widget children. See below.

Extension Structure

There is one extension defined for the Composite class. The extension structure is shown below; the record_type field should be NULLQUARK, and the version field should be XtCompositeExtensionVersion. The accepts_objects field should be True if the class should accept non-widget objects as children, or False if it should not accept them.

```
typedef struct {
    XtPointer next_extension;    /* next record is linked list, or NULL */
    XrmQuark record_type;        /* NULLQUARK */
    long version;                /* XtCompositeExtensionVersion */
    Cardinal record_size;        /* use sizeof() */
    Boolean accepts_objects;
} CompositeClassExtensionRec, *CompositeClassExtension;
```

Instance Structure

The composite instance structure contains at least the following fields (which need not be in this order):

```
typedef struct {
    WidgetList  children;        /* array of ALL widget children */
    Cardinal    num_children;    /* total number of widget children */
    Cardinal    num_slots;       /* number of slots in children array */
    XtOrderProc insert_position; /* compute position of new child */
} CompositePart;

typedef struct {
    CorePart                     core;
    CompositePart                composite;
} CompositeRec, *CompositeWidget;
```

See Also

XtManageChildren(1),
XtOrderProc(2),
Core(3),
change_managed(4), *delete_child*(4), *geometry_manager*(4), *insert_child*(4).

Name
Constraint widget class – a widget that provides constraint resources for its children.

Synopsis

Public Headers:	*<X11/StringDefs.h>*
	<X11/Constraint.h>
Private Header:	*<X11/ConstraintP.h>*
Class Name:	Constraint
Class Hierarchy:	Core → Composite → Constraint
Class Pointer:	`constraintWidgetClass`
Instantiation:	Constraint is an Intrinsics meta-class, and is not normally instantiated.
Functions/Macros:	`XtIsConstraint()`

Description

Constraint widgets are a subclass of `compositeWidgetClass`. Their name is derived from the fact that they may manage the geometry of their children based on constraints associated with each child. These constraints can be as simple as the maximum width and height the parent will allow the child to occupy or as complicated as how other children should change if this child is moved or resized. Constraint widgets let a parent define resources that are supplied for their children. For example, if the Constraint parent defines the maximum sizes for its children, these new size resources are retrieved for each child as if they were resources that were defined by the child widget. Accordingly, constraint resources may be included in the argument list or resource file just like any other resource for the child.

Constraint widgets have all the responsibilities of normal composite widgets and, in addition, must process and act upon the constraint information associated with each of their children.

To make it easy for widgets and the Intrinsics to keep track of the constraints associated with a child, every widget has a `constraints` field, which is the address of a parent-specific structure that contains constraint information about the child. If a child's parent is not a subclass of `constraintWidgetClass`, then the child's `constraints` field is NULL.

Note that the constraint data structures are transparent to the child; that is, when a child is managed by a parent that is a subclass of a constraint widget, there is no difference, as far as the child is concerned, from being managed by a normal composite widget.

See the "Background" section below for more information on Constraint and constraint resources.

New Resources
Constraint defines no new resources.

Inherited Resources
Constraint inherits the following resources. The resources are listed alphabetically, along with the superclass that defines them.

Resource	Inherited From	Resource	Inherited From
XtNaccelerators	Core	XtNheight	Core
XtNancestorSensitive	Core	XtNinitialResources- Persistent	Core
XtNbackground	Core	XtNinsertPosition	Composite
XtNbackgroundPixmap	Core	XtNmappedWhen- Managed	Core
XtNborderColor	Core	XtNnumChildren	Composite
XtNborderPixmap	Core	XtNscreen	Core
XtNborderWidth	Core	XtNsensitive	Core
XtNchildren	Composite	XtNtranslations	Core
XtNcolormap	Core	XtNwidth	Core
XtNdepth	Core	XtNx	Core
XtNdestroyCallback	Core	XtNy	Core

Class Structure

The Constraint class record is defined as follows:

```
typedef struct {
    XtResourceList resources;      /* constraint resource list */
    Cardinal num_resources;        /* number of constraints in list */
    Cardinal constraint_size;      /* size of constraint record */
    XtInitProc initialize;         /* constraint initialization */
    XtWidgetProc destroy;          /* constraint destroy proc */
    XtSetValuesFunc set_values;    /* constraint set_values proc */
    XtPointer extension;           /* pointer to extension record */
} ConstraintClassPart;

typedef struct {
    CoreClassPart              core_class;
    CompositeClassPart         composite_class;
    ConstraintClassPart        constraint_class;
} ConstraintClassRec, *ConstraintWidgetClass;
```

The fields of the Constraint class part have the following meanings:

resources
> An array of XtResource, each of which defines a single constraint resource for the widget class. See XtGetApplicationResources() for an explanation of how to define resources and declare an XtResourceList.

num_resources
> The number of element in the resources array.

constraint_size
> The size of the constraint instance record for this widget class. A block this size will be automatically allocated for each child of an instance of this widget class, and will be pointed to by that child's Core constraints instance field. Use sizeof to initialize this field.

initialize()

The constraint initialize() method, called to initialize the part of constraint instance record added by this widget class. See the reference page in Section 4. This is a chained method and cannot be inherited. Use NULL if the constraint part defined by this class does not need any initialization.

destroy()

The constraint destroy() method, called to deallocate any memory or other resources associated with the part of the constraint instance record added by this widget class when a child widget is destroyed. See the reference page in Section 4. This is a chained method and cannot be inherited. Use NULL if the constraint part defined by this class does not need any special deallocation.

set_values()

The constraint set_values() method, called when XtSetValues() is called on a child widget. See the reference page in Section 4. This is a chained method and cannot be inherited. Use NULL if the constraint part defined by this class does not have any resources.

extension

A linked list of extension records, or NULL. There is currently one extension defined for Constraint which adds a get_values_hook() method; see below.

Extension Structure

The Intrinsics define one extension to Constraint:

```
typedef struct {
    XtPointer next_extension;        /* next record is linked list, or NULL */
    XrmQuark record_type;            /* NULLQUARK */
    long version;                    /* XtConstraintExtensionVersion */
    Cardinal record_size;            /* use sizeof() */
    XtArgsProc get_values_hook;
} ConstraintClassExtensionRec, *ConstraintClassExtension;
```

The record_type field should be NULLQUARK, the version field should be Xt-ConstraintExtensionVersion, and the get_values_hook() field should be the get_values_hook() method for the constraint resources. See Constraint get_values_hook(4).

Instance Structure

The Constraint instance structure defines no new fields:

```
typedef struct _ConstraintPart {
    XtPointer dummy;                 /* No new fields, keep C compiler happy */
} ConstraintPart;
```

```
typedef struct {
    CorePart                        core;
    CompositePart                   composite;
    ConstraintPart                  constraint;
} ConstraintRec, *ConstraintWidget;
```

Background

Constraints are allocated, initialized, deallocated and otherwise maintained insofar as possible by the Intrinsics. The constraint class record part has several entries that facilitate this. All entries in `ConstraintClassPart` are information and procedures that are defined and implemented by the parent, but they are called whenever actions are performed on the parent's children.

The `XtCreateWidget()` function uses the `constraint_size` field to allocate a constraint record when a child is created. The `constraint_size` field gives the number of bytes occupied by a constraint record. `XtCreateWidget()` also uses the constraint resources to fill in resource fields in the constraint record associated with a child. It then calls the constraint `initialize()` methods so that the parent can compute constraint fields that are derived from constraint resources and can possibly move or resize the child to conform to the given constraints.

The `XtGetValues()` and `XtSetValues()` functions use the constraint resources to get the values or set the values of constraint associated with a child. `XtSetValues()` then calls the constraint `set_values()` methods so that a parent can recompute derived constraint fields and move or resize the child as appropriate.

If the Constraint widget or any of its superclasses have declared a `ConstraintClass-Extension` record in the constraint class part extension fields with a record type of `NULLQUARK`, and if the `get_values_hook()` field in the extension record is non-NULL, then `XtGetValues()` calls the `get_values_hook()` method(s) to allow the parent to return derived constraint fields.

The `XtDestroyWidget()` function calls the constraint destroy method to deallocate any dynamic storage associated with a constraint record. The constraint record itself must not be deallocated by the constraint destroy method; `XtDestroyWidget()` does this automatically.

See Also

Core(3), *Composite*(3),
Constraint destroy(4), *Constraint get_values_hook*(4), *Constraint initialize*(4), *Constraint set_values*(4).

Name

Core widget class – fundamental object class with a window.

Synopsis

Public Headers:	*<X11/StringDefs.h>*
	<X11/Core.h>
Private Header:	*<X11/CoreP.h>*
Class Name:	Core
Class Hierarchy:	Object → RectObj → *unnamed* → Core
Class Pointer:	`widgetClass` or `coreWidgetClass`
Instantiation:	Core is an Intrinsics meta-class, and is not normally instantiated.
Functions/Macros:	`XtIsWidget()`

Description

Core is the fundamental class for windowed widgets. All widgets with windows are subclasses of Core. Core is sometimes instantiated for use as a basic drawing area.

New Resources

Core has the following resources (some of which are actually defined by the Object and Rect-Obj classes):

Name	Class	Type	Default	Access
XtNaccelerators	XtCAccelerators	XtAccelerators	NULL	CSG
XtNancestor- Sensitive	XtCSensitive	Boolean	dynamic	G
XtNbackground	XtCBackground	Pixel	dynamic	CSG
XtNbackground- Pixmap	XtCPixmap	Pixmap	XmUNSPECIFIED_ PIXMAP	CSG
XtNborderColor	XtCBorderColor	Pixel	XtDefault- Foreground	CSG
XtNborderPixmap	XtCPixmap	Pixmap	XmUNSPECIFIED_ PIXMAP	CSG
XtNborderWidth	XtCBorderWidth	Dimension	1	CSG
XtNcolormap	XtCColormap	Colormap	dynamic	CG
XtNdepth	XtCDepth	int	dynamic	CG
XtNheight	XtCHeight	Dimension	dynamic	CSG
XtNinitial- Resources- Persistent	XtCInitial- Resources- Persistent	Boolean	True	CG
XtNmappedWhen- Managed	XtCMappedWhen- Managed	Boolean	True	CSG
XtNscreen	XtCScreen	Screen *	dynamic	CG
XtNsensitive	XtCSensitive	Boolean	True	CSG
XtNtranslations	XtCTranslations	XtTranslations	NULL	CSG

*Intrinsics
Classes*

Name	Class	Type	Default	Access
XtNwidth	XtCWidth	Dimension	dynamic	CSG
XtNx	XtCPosition	Position	0	CSG
XtNy	XtCPosition	Position	0	CSG

XtNaccelerators
> A translation table bound with its actions for a widget. A destination widget can be set up to use this accelerator table. See XtInstallAccelerators(1).

XtNancestorSensitive
> Specifies whether the object has an insensitive ancestor. Default value is (a) True (if the widget is a top-level shell), (b) copied from the XtNancestorSensitive resource of its parent (if the widget is a popup shell), or (c) the bitwise AND of the XtNsensitive and XtNancestorSensitive resources of the parent (for other widgets). See Xt-SetSensitive(1).

XtNbackground
> Widget's background color.

XtNbackgroundPixmap
> Pixmap with which to tile the background, beginning at the upper-left corner.

XtNborderColor
> Pixel value that defines the color of the border.

XtNborderPixmap
> Pixmap with which to tile the border, beginning at the upper-left corner of the border.

XtNborderWidth
> Width (in pixels) of the window's border.

XtNcolormap
> Colormap used in converting to pixel values. Previously created pixel values are unaffected. The default value is the screen's default colormap (for top-level shells) or is copied from the parent (for other widgets).

XtNdepth
> Number of bits allowed for each pixel. The Xt Intrinsics set this resource when the widget is created. As with the XtNcolormap resource, the default value comes from the screen's default or is copied from the parent.

XtNdestroyCallback
> List of callbacks invoked when the widget is destroyed.

XtNheight
> Window height (in pixels), excluding the border.

XtNinitialResourcesPersistent
> Specifies whether resources should be reference counted. If True (default), it is assumed that the widget won't be destroyed while the application is running, and thus the widget's resources are not reference counted. Set this resource to False if your

application might destroy the widget and will need to deallocate the resources. See Xt-ConvertAndStore(1).

XtNmappedWhenManaged

If True (default), the widget becomes visible (is mapped) as soon as it is both realized and managed. If False, the application performs the mapping and unmapping of the widget. If changed to False after the widget is realized and managed, the widget is unmapped. See XtSetMappedWhenManaged(1).

XtNscreen

Screen of the widget.

XtNsensitive

Specifies whether a widget receives input (is sensitive). XtSetSensitive() can be used to change a widget's sensitivity and to guarantee that if a parent has its Xt-Nsensitive resource set to False, then its children will have their XtNancestor-Sensitive resource set to False. See XtSetSensitive(1).

XtNtranslations

Points to a translation table; must be compiled with XtParseTranslation-Table(). See XtOverrideTranslations(1) and XtAugment-Translations(1).

XtNwidth

Window width (in pixels), excluding the border.

XtNx

The x-coordinate of the widget's upper-left outer corner, relative to the upper-left inner corner of its parent.

XtNy

The y-coordinate of the widget's upper-left outer corner, relative to the upper-left inner corner of its parent.

Class Structure

The Core class structure is defined as follows:

```
typedef struct _CoreClassPart {
    WidgetClass superclass;          /* pointer to superclass ClassRec */
    String class_name;               /* widget resource class name */
    Cardinal widget_size;            /* size in bytes of widget record */
    XtProc class_initialize;         /* class initialization proc */
    XtWidgetClassProc class_part_initialize;/* dynamic initialization */
    XtEnum class_inited;             /* has class been initialized? */
    XtInitProc initialize;           /* initialize subclass fields */
    XtArgsProc initialize_hook;      /* notify that initialize called */
    XtRealizeProc realize;           /* XCreateWindow for widget */
    XtActionList actions;            /* widget semantics name to proc map */
    Cardinal num_actions;            /* number of entries in actions */
    XtResourceList resources;        /* resources for subclass fields */
    Cardinal num_resources;          /* number of entries in resources */
```

```
    XrmClass xrm_class;             /* resource class quarkified */
    Boolean compress_motion;        /* compress MotionNotify for widget */
    XtEnum compress_exposure;       /* compress Expose events for widget*/
    Boolean compress_enterleave;    /* compress enter and leave events */
    Boolean visible_interest;       /* select for VisibilityNotify */
    XtWidgetProc destroy;           /* free data for subclass pointers */
    XtWidgetProc resize;            /* geom manager changed widget size */
    XtExposeProc expose;            /* redisplay window */
    XtSetValuesFunc set_values;     /* set subclass resource values */
    XtArgsFunc set_values_hook;     /* notify that set_values called */
    XtAlmostProc set_values_almost;/* set_values got "Almost" geo reply */
    XtArgsProc get_values_hook;     /* notify that get_values called */
    XtAcceptFocusProc accept_focus;/* assign input focus to widget */
    XtVersionType version;          /* version of Intrinsics used */
    XtPointer callback_private;     /* list of callback offsets */
    String tm_table;                /* default translation table */
    XtGeometryHandler query_geometry;/* return preferred geometry */
    XtStringProc display_accelerator;/* display your accelerator */
    XtPointer extension;            /* pointer to extension record */
  } CoreClassPart;

typedef struct {
      CoreClassPart core_class;
} WidgetClassRec, *WidgetClass, CoreClassRec, *CoreWidgetClass;
```

The meanings of each of the fields in the Core class structure are as follows:

superclass

> A pointer to the class record of this widget's superclass. That class record is declared in the superclass' private header file.

class_name

> A constant string that names the class.

widget_size

> The size of the *instance* structure for this widget. Use sizeof.

class_initialize()

> The class_initialize() method called to perform one-time initialization for this class. See the reference page in Section 4. This is a chained method which cannot be inherited. Set to NULL if no special initialization is needed for the class.

class_part_initialize()

> The class_part_initialize() method called to perform initialization for the class part structure. See the reference page in Section 4. This is a chained method which cannot be inherited. Set to NULL if no special initialization is needed for your class part.

class_inited

> Whether the class structure has been initialized yet. Always initialize to False.

initialize()

> The initialize() method called to initialize the instance structure. See the reference page in Section 4. This is a chained method which cannot be inherited. Set to NULL if no special initialization of the widget instance structure is needed.

initialize_hook()

> The (obsolete) initialize_hook() method. See the reference page in Section 4. This is a chained method which cannot be inherited. Set to NULL if no special initialization is needed.

realize()

> The realize() method called to create a window for the widget. See the reference page in Section 4. Use XtInheritRealize to inherit the realize() method of the superclass.

actions

> The action name to action procedure mapping which will be used by this widget when binding translation tables to actions. These are automatically registered with the Intrinsics when the Core class_part_initialize() method is performed. The array must be permanently allocated, and the Intrinsics may overwrite it with an internal compiled form of the action table. The action names must be permanently allocated strings.

num_actions

> The number of elements in the actions array.

resources

> An array of XtResource, each element of which defines a single resource for the widget. See XtGetApplicationResources(1) for an explanation of how to define resources.

num_resources

> The number of elements in the resources array.

xrm_class

> This field is private to the Resource Manager. Initialize it to NULLQUARK.

compress_motion

> If True, the Intrinsics will only report the last of a sequence of pointer motion events.

compress_exposure

> Specifies how Expose and GraphicsExpose events should be delivered to the widget. If False or XtExposeNoCompress, all exposure events will be delivered. There are a number of other possibilities; see expose(4) for full details.

compress_enterleave

> If True, the Intrinsics will discard pairs of enter and leave events from the input queue that have no intervening events between them.

**Intrinsics
Classes**

visible_interest

> If `True`, the Intrinsics will request `VisibilityNotify` events for the Widget and update the `visible` field of the Core *instance* structure as they arrive. The `visible` field is guaranteed to be `True` by the time an exposure event is processed (i.e., by the time the `expose()` method is called) if any part of the widget is visible, but is `False` if the widget is fully obscured. If `visible_interest` is `False`, then the `visible` instance field is always `True`.

destroy()

> The `destroy()` method called when a widget of this class is destroyed. See the reference page in Section 4. This is a chained method and cannot be inherited. Initialize it to `NULL` if no special processing needs to be done when an instance of this widget class is destroyed.

resize()

> The `resize()` method called when a widget of this class is resized by its parent. See the reference page in Section 4. Use `XtInheritResize` to inherit the `resize()` method of the superclass.

expose()

> The `expose()` method called when exposure events arrive for this widget. See the reference page in Section 4. Use `XtInheritExpose` to inherit the `expose()` method of the superclass.

set_values()

> The `set_values()` method called when an application sets resource values in the instance record with `XtSetValues()`. See the reference page in Section 4. This is a chained method and cannot be inherited. Specify `NULL` if the widget class has no resources.

set_values_hook()

> The (obsolete) `set_values_hook()` method. See the reference page in Section 4. This method is chained and cannot be inherited.

set_values_almost()

> The `set_values_almost()` method called when a geometry request in an `XtSetValues()` call cannot be completely satisfied. See the reference page in Section 4. Use `XtInheritSetValuesAlmost` to inherit the `set_values_almost()` method of the superclass.

get_values_hook()

> The `get_values_hook()` method called in response to `XtGetValues()`. See the reference page in Section 4. This is a chained method and cannot be inherited.

accept_focus()

> The `accept_focus()` method called by a parent to offer keyboard focus to a child. See the reference page in Section 4. Use `XtInheritAcceptFocus` to inherit the `accept_focus()` method of the superclass.

version

> The *version* field indicates the toolkit implementation version number and is used for runtime consistency checking of the toolkit and widgets in an application. Widget writers must set it to the implementation-defined symbolic value XtVersion in the widget class structure initialization. Those widget writers who believe that their widget binaries are compatible with other implementations of the Intrinsics can put the special value XtVersionDontCheck in the *version* field to disable version checking for those widgets. If a widget needs to compile alternative code for different revisions of the Intrinsics interface definition, it may use the symbol XtSpecificationRelease. Use of XtVersion allows the Intrinsics implementation to recognize widget binaries that were compiled with older implementations.

callback_private

> This field is private to callback handling; initialize to NULL.

tm_table

> The default translation table for widgets of this class. It may be overridden by clients that set the XtNtranslations resource of the widget instance. This field should specify a translation table in string form (see Appendix F for the syntax); the Intrinsics will automatically compile it into an internal form. Use XtInheritTranslations to inherit the translation table of the superclass.

query_geometry()

> The query_geometry() method, called by a parent widget to discover the preferred geometry of a child. See the reference page in Section 4. Use XtInheritQuery-Geometry to inherit the query_geometry() method of the superclass.

display_accelerator()

> The display_accelerator() method, called when a widget's accelerators have been installed on a destination widget. See the reference page in Section 4. Use Xt-InheritDisplayAccelerator to inherit the display_accelerator() method of the superclass.

extension

> A linked list of extension records. There are currently no extensions defined for the Core widget class, so this field should be initialized to NULL.

Instance Structure

The Core instance record contains at least the following fields. The fields need not be in the order shown, but because the Object and RectObj superclasses were defined after Core was standardized, Core duplicates the instance records of those classes, and the duplicate fields must be in the same position in the Object, RectObj, and Core instance structures.

```
typedef struct {
  Widget self;                        /* pointer to widget itself */
  WidgetClass widget_class;           /* pointer to widget's ClassRec */
  Widget parent;                      /* parent widget */
  Boolean being_destroyed;            /* marked for destroy */
  XtCallbackList destroy_callbacks;   /* called when widget destroyed */
```

```
    XtPointer constraints;              /* constraint record */
    Position x, y;                      /* window position */
    Dimension width, height;            /* window dimensions */
    Dimension border_width;             /* window border width */
    Boolean managed;                    /* is widget geometry managed? */
    Boolean sensitive;                  /* is widget sensitive to user events */
    Boolean ancestor_sensitive;         /* are all ancestors sensitive? */
    XtTranslations accelerators;        /* accelerator translations */
    Pixel border_pixel;                 /* window border pixel */
    Pixmap border_pixmap;               /* window border pixmap or NULL */
    WidgetList popup_list;              /* list of pop ups */
    Cardinal num_popups;                /* how many pop ups */
    String name;                        /* widget resource name */
    Screen *screen;                     /* window's screen */
    Colormap colormap;                  /* colormap */
    Window window;                      /* window ID */
    Cardinal depth;                     /* number of planes in window */
    Pixel background_pixel;             /* window background pixel */
    Pixmap background_pixmap;           /* window background pixmap or NULL */
    Boolean visible;                    /* is window mapped and not occluded? */
    Boolean mapped_when_managed;        /* map window if it is managed? */
} CorePart;

typedef struct {
  CorePart core;
} WidgetRec, *Widget, CoreRec, *CoreWidget;
```

See Also

Core(3), *Object*(3), *RectObj*(3),
class_initialize(4), *class_part_initialize*(4), *destroy*(4), *display_accelerator*(4), *expose*(4),
get_values_hook(4), *initialize*(4), *initialize_hook*(4), *query_geometry*(4), *realize*(4), *resize*(4),
set_values(4), *set_values_almost*(4), *set_values_hook*(4).

Object

Name
Object widget class – fundamental object class.

Synopsis
Public Headers:	*<X11/StringDefs.h>*
	<X11/Object.h>
Private Header:	*<X11/ObjectP.h>*
Class Name:	Object
Class Hierarchy:	Object
Class Pointer:	`objectClass`
Instantiation:	Object is an Intrinsics meta-class, and is not normally instantiated.
Functions/Macros:	`XtIsObject()`

Availability
Release 4 and later.

Description
Object is the root of the class hierarchy; it does not have a superclass. All objects and widgets are subclasses of Object. Object encapsulates the mechanisms for resource management and is never instantiated.

Prior to Release 4, Core was the root of the class hierarchy. The Object class was made public in Release 4 to enable programmers to use the Intrinsics classing and resource handling mechanisms for things besides widgets. Objects make many common uses of subresources obsolete. See the "Background" section below for more information on using non-widget objects.

New Resources
Object defines the following resources:

Name	Class	Type	Default	Access
XtNdestroyCallback	XtCCallback	XtCallbackList	NULL	C

XtNdestroyCallback
> List of callbacks invoked when the Object is destroyed.

Class Structure
The Object class structure is shown below. Because the Object class was defined after Core was already standardized, the fields of these two class structures must match. Therefore, the fields named obj*n* below exist only to pad out the structure. The use of each of the remaining fields is exactly as for the Core class.

```
typedef struct _ObjectClassPart {
    WidgetClass superclass;
```

Intrinsics Classes

```
    String class_name;
    Cardinal widget_size;
    XtProc class_initialize;
    XtWidgetClassProc class_part_initialize;
    XtEnum class_inited;
    XtInitProc initialize;
    XtArgsProc initialize_hook;
    XtProc obj1;
    XtPointer obj2;
    Cardinal obj3;
    XtResourceList resources;
    Cardinal num_resources;
    XrmClass xrm_class;
    Boolean obj4;
    XtEnum obj5;
    Boolean obj6;
    Boolean obj7;
    XtWidgetProc destroy;
    XtProc obj8;
    XtProc obj9;
    XtSetValuesFunc set_values;
    XtArgsFunc set_values_hook;
    XtProc obj10;
    XtArgsProc get_values_hook;
    XtProc obj11;
    XtVersionType version;
    XtPointer callback_private;
    String obj12;
    XtProc obj13;
    XtProc obj14;
    XtPointer extension;
} ObjectClassPart;

typedef struct _ObjectClassRec {
    ObjectClassPart object_class;
} ObjectClassRec, *ObjectClass;
```

There is no extension defined for the Object class, and the `extension` field should be `NULL`.

Instance Structure

The Object instance structure contains at least the fields shown below. The fields need not be in the order shown, but because the Object class was defined after Core was standardized, the position of each of these fields must be the same for both classes.

```
typedef struct _ObjectPart {
    Widget self;
    WidgetClass widget_class;
    Widget parent;
    XrmName xrm_name;
    Boolean being_destroyed;
    XtCallbackList destroy_callbacks;
```

```
    XtPointer constraints;
} ObjectPart;

typedef struct _ObjectRec {
    ObjectPart object;
} ObjectRec, *Object;
```

Background

Composite widget classes that wish to accept non-widget children must set the `accepts_objects` field in the `CompositeClassExtension` structure to `True`. `Xt-CreateWidget()` will otherwise generate an error message on an attempt to create a non-widget child.

Of the classes defined by the Intrinsics, only ApplicationShell accepts non-widget children, and the class of any non-widget child must not be `rectObjClass` or any subclass. The intent of allowing Object children of ApplicationShell is to provide clients a simple mechanism for establishing the resource naming root of an object hierarchy.

Starting in Release 4, the WidgetClass arguments to the following procedures may be `objectClass` or any subclass:

- `XtInitializeWidgetClass()`, `XtCreateWidget()`, `XtVaCreateWidget()`

- `XtIsSubclass()`, `XtCheckSubclass()`

- `XtGetResourceList()`, `XtGetConstraintResourceList()`

The Widget arguments to the following procedures may be of class Object or any subclass:

- `XtCreateWidget()`, `XtVaCreateWidget()`

- `XtAddCallback()`, `XtAddCallbacks()`, `XtRemoveCallback()`, `XtRemove-Callbacks`, `XtRemoveAllCallbacks()`, `XtCallCallbacks()`, `XtHas-Callbacks()`, `XtCallCallbackList()`

- `XtClass()`, `XtSuperclass()`, `XtIsSubclass()`, `XtCheckSubclass()`, `Xt-IsObject()`, `XtIsRectObj()`, `XtIsWidget()`, `XtIsComposite()`, `XtIs-Constraint()`, `XtIsShell()`, `XtIsOverrideShell()`, `XtIsWMShell()`, `Xt-IsVendorShell()`, `XtIsTransientShell()`, `XtIsToplevelShell`, `XtIs-ApplicationShell()`.

- `XtIsManaged()`, `XtIsSensitive()`
  (both will return `False` if argument is not a subclass of `RectObj`)

- `XtIsRealized()`
  (returns the state of the nearest windowed ancestor if argument is not of a subclass of `Core`)

- `XtWidgetToApplicationContext()`

- `XtDestroyWidget()`

Intrinsics Classes

- `XtDisplayOfObject()`, `XtScreenOfObject()`, `XtWindowOfObject()`
- `XtSetKeyboardFocus()` (descendant)
- `XtGetGC()`, `XtReleaseGC()`
- `XtName()`
- `XtSetValues()`, `XtGetValues()`, `XtVaSetValues()`, `XtVaGetValues()`,
- `XtGetSubresources()`, `XtGetApplicationResources()`, `XtVaGetSub-resources`, `XtVaGetApplicationResources()`
- `XtConvert()`, `XtConvertAndStore()`

The return value of the following procedures will be of class Object or a subclass:

- `XtCreateWidget()`, `XtVaCreateWidget()`
- `XtParent()`
- `XtNameToWidget()`

The return value of the following procedures will be `objectClass` or a subclass:

- `XtClass()`, `XtSuperclass()`

See Also

Core(3).

OverrideShell

Name

OverrideShell widget class – popup shell that bypasses window management.

Synopsis

Public Headers:	*<X11/StringDefs.h>*
	<X11/Shell.h>
Private Header:	*<X11/ShellP.h>*
Class Name:	OverrideShell
Class Hierarchy:	Core → Composite → Shell → OverrideShell
Class Pointer:	`overrideShellWidgetClass`
Instantiation:	*widget* = `XtCreatePopupShell(`*name*`,`
	`overrideShellWidgetClass, ...)`
Functions/Macros:	`XtIsOverrideShell()`

Description

OverrideShell is a direct subclass of Shell that performs no interaction with window managers. It is used for widgets (such as popup menus) that should bypass the window manager.

New Resources

OverrideShell defines no new resources, but it redefines the default values of both `Xt-NoverrideRedirect` and `XtNsaveUnder` to `True`.

Inherited Resources

OverrideShell inherits the following resources. The resources are listed alphabetically, along with the superclass that defines them.

Resource	Inherited From	Resource	Inherited From
XtNaccelerators	Core	XtNinitialResources- Persistent	Core
XtNallowShellResize	Shell	XtNinsertPosition	Composite
XtNancestorSensitive	Core	XtNmappedWhenManaged	Core
XtNbackground	Core	XtNnumChildren	Composite
XtNbackgroundPixmap	Core	XtNoverrideRedirect	Shell
XtNborderColor	Core	XtNpopdownCallback	Shell
XtNborderPixmap	Core	XtNpopupCallback	Shell
XtNborderWidth	Core	XtNsaveUnder	Shell
XtNchildren	Composite	XtNscreen	Core
XtNcolormap	Core	XtNsensitive	Core
XtNcreatePopupChild- Proc	Shell	XtNtranslations	Core
XtNdepth	Core	XtNvisual	Shell

Intrinsics Classes

Resource	Inherited From		Resource	Inherited From
XtNdestroyCallback	Core		XtNwidth	Core
XtNgeometry	Shell		XtNx	Core
XtNheight	Core		XtNy	Core

Class Structure

The OverrideShell class structure contains only an extension field. Its declaration is similar to those of the other shells:

```
typedef struct {
    XtPointer extension;          /* pointer to extension record */
} OverrideShellClassPart;

typedef struct _OverrideShellClassRec {
    CoreClassPart core_class;
    CompositeClassPart composite_class;
    ShellClassPart shell_class;
    OverrideShellClassPart override_shell_class;
} OverrideShellClassRec;
```

There are no extensions currently defined for this class, and the `extension` field should be NULL.

Instance Structure

The OverrideShell instance structure contains no new fields:

```
typedef struct { int empty; } OverrideShellPart;

typedef struct {
    CorePart core;
    CompositePart composite;
    ShellPart shell;
    OverrideShellPart override;
} OverrideShellRec, *OverrideShellWidget;
```

See Also

Shell(3).

RectObj

Name

RectObj widget class – fundamental object class with geometry.

Synopsis

Public Headers:	*<X11/StringDefs.h>*
	<X11/RectObj.h>
Private Header:	*<X11/RectObjP.h>*
Class Name:	RectObj
Class Hierarchy:	Object → RectObj
Class Pointer:	`rectObjClass`
Instantiation:	RectObj is an Intrinsics meta-class, and is not normally instantiated.
Functions/Macros:	`XtIsRectObj()`

Availability

Release 4 and later.

Description

RectObj is a direct subclass of Object. It does not have a window, but does have a width, height, and location, and encapsulates the mechanisms for geometry management.

RectObj can be subclassed to provide widget-like objects (sometimes called "gadgets") that do not use windows and that do not have features often unused in simple widgets. This can save memory resources both in the server and in applications.

See the "Background" section below for more information on using RectObj objects.

New Resources

RectObj defines the following resources:

Name	Class	Type	Default	Access
XtNancestorSensitive	XtCSensitive	Boolean	dynamic	G
XtNborderWidth	XtCBorderWidth	Dimension	1	CSG
XtNheight	XtCHeight	Dimension	dynamic	CSG
XtNsensitive	XtCSensitive	Boolean	True	CSG
XtNwidth	XtCWidth	Dimension	dynamic	CSG
XtNx	XtCPosition	Position	0	CSG
XtNy	XtCPosition	Position	0	CSG

`XtNancestorSensitive`
> Specifies whether the object has an insensitive ancestor. Default value is the bitwise AND of the `XtNsensitive` and `XtNancestorSensitive` resources of the parent. See `XtSetSensitive`(1).

XtNborderWidth
>   Width (in pixels) of the window's border.

XtNheight
>   Window height (in pixels), excluding the border.

XtNsensitive
>   Specifies whether a gadget receives input (is sensitive). `XtSetSensitive()` can be used to change a widget's sensitivity and to guarantee that if a parent has its `Xt-Nsensitive` resource set to `False`, then its children will have their `XtNancestor-Sensitive` resource set to `False`. See `XtSetSensitive`(1).

XtNwidth
>   Window width (in pixels), excluding the border.

XtNx
>   The x-coordinate of the widget's upper-left outer corner, relative to the upper-left inner corner of its parent.

XtNy
>   The y-coordinate of the widget's upper-left outer corner, relative to the upper-left inner corner of its parent.

Inherited Resources

RectObj inherits the following resource.

Resource	Inherited From
XtNdestroyCallback	Object

Class Structure

The RectObj class structure is shown below. Because the RectObj class was defined after Core was already standardized, the fields of these two class structures must match. Therefore, the fields named `rectn` below exist only to pad out the structure. The use of each of the remaining fields is exactly as for the Core class.

```
typedef struct _RectObjClassPart {
    WidgetClass superclass;
    String class_name;
    Cardinal widget_size;
    XtProc class_initialize;
    XtWidgetClassProc class_part_initialize;
    XtEnum class_inited;
    XtInitProc initialize;
    XtArgsProc initialize_hook;
    XtProc rect1;
    XtPointer rect2;
    Cardinal rect3;
    XtResourceList resources;
    Cardinal num_resources;
```

```
    XrmClass xrm_class;
    Boolean rect4;
    XtEnum rect5;
    Boolean rect6;
    Boolean rect7;
    XtWidgetProc destroy;
    XtWidgetProc resize;
    XtExposeProc expose;
    XtSetValuesFunc set_values;
    XtArgsFunc set_values_hook;
    XtAlmostProc set_values_almost;
    XtArgsProc get_values_hook;
    XtProc rect9;
    XtVersionType version;
    XtPointer callback_private;
    String rect10;
    XtGeometryHandler query_geometry;
    XtProc rect11;
    XtPointer extension ;
} RectObjClassPart;

typedef struct _RectObjClassRec {
    RectObjClassPart rect_class;
} RectObjClassRec, *RectObjClass;
```

There is no extension defined for this class, and the `extension` field in the class part structure should be NULL.

Instance Structure

The RectObj instance structure contains at least the fields shown below. The fields need not be in the order shown, but because the RectObj class was defined after Core was standardized, the position of each of these fields must be the same for both classes.

```
typedef struct _RectObjPart {
    Position x, y;
    Dimension width, height;
    Dimension border_width;
    Boolean managed;
    Boolean sensitive;
    Boolean ancestor_sensitive;
} RectObjPart;

typedef struct _RectObjRec {
    ObjectPart object;
    RectObjPart rectangle;
} RectObjRec;
```

Background

In the following discussion, "RectObj" refers only to objects that are a subclass of RectObj and that are not a subclass of Core.

Composite widget classes that wish to accept RectObj children must set the `accepts_objects` field in the `CompositeClassExtension` extension structure to `True`. `XtCreateWidget()` will otherwise generate an error if called to create a non-widget child.

If gadgets are defined in an object set, the parent is responsible for much more than the parent of a widget. The parent must request and handle input events that occur for the gadget. The parent is also responsible for making sure that when it receives an expose event, the gadget children get drawn correctly. Subclasses of RectObj have expose procedures, but the parent is free to ignore them, instead drawing the contents of the child itself. This can potentially save graphics context switching. The precise contents of the `Expose` event and `Region` arguments to the RectObj expose procedure are not specified by the Intrinsics; a particular rectangle object is free to define not only the coordinate system origin (self-relative or parent-relative) but also whether the rectangle, the Region, or both are assumed to have been intersected by the visible region of the object.

Normally, a composite widget that accepts non-widget children documents those children it can handle, since a gadget, unlike a widget, cannot be viewed as a completely self-contained entity. Since a particular composite widget class is usually designed to handle gadgets of only a limited set of classes, it should check the classes of newly added children in its `insert_child()` method to make sure that it can deal with them.

The Intrinsics will clear areas of a parent window obscured by RectObj children, causing `Expose` events, under the following circumstances:

- A RectObj child is managed or unmanaged.

- In a call to `XtSetValues()` on a RectObj child, one or more of the `set_values()` methods returns `True`.

- In a call to `XtConfigureWidget()` on a RectObj child, areas will be cleared corresponding to both the old and the new child geometries, including the border, if the geometry changes.

- In a call to `XtMoveWidget()` on a RectObj child, areas will be cleared corresponding to both the old and the new child geometries, including the border, if the geometry changes.

- In a call to `XtResizeWidget()` on a RectObj child, an single rectangle will be cleared corresponding to the larger of the old and the new child geometries, if they are different.

- In a call to `XtMakeGeometryRequest()` (or `XtMakeResizeRequest()`) on a RectObj, if the manager returns `XtGeometryYes`, two rectangles will be cleared corresponding to both the old and the new child geometries.

Stacking order is not supported for RectObjs. If the child geometries overlap, Composite widgets with RectObj children can define any semantics desired, including making this an error.

When a RectObj is playing the role of a widget, developers must be reminded to avoid making assumptions about the object passed in the `Widget` argument to a callback procedure.

The `WidgetClass` arguments to the following functions may be `rectObjClass` or any subclass:

- `XtCreateManagedWidget()`, `XtVaCreateManagedWidget()`

The `Widget` arguments to the following functions may be of class RectObj or any subclass:

- `XtConfigureWidget()`, `XtMoveWidget()`, `XtResizeWidget()`
- `XtMakeGeometryRequest()`, `XtMakeResizeRequest()`
- `XtManageChildren()`, `XtManageChild()`, `XtUnmanageChildren()`, `XtUnmanageChild()`
- `XtQueryGeometry()`
- `XtSetSensitive()`
- `XtTranslateCoords()`

The return value of the following functions will be of class RectObj or a subclass:

- `XtCreateManagedWidget()`, `XtVaCreateManagedWidget()`

See Also
Core(3), *Object*(3).

Name

Shell widget class – fundamental widget class that controls the interaction between top-level windows and the window manager.

Synopsis

Public Headers:	*<X11/StringDefs.h>*
	<X11/Shell.h>
Private Header:	*<X11/ShellP.h>*
Class Name:	Shell
Class Hierarchy:	Core → Composite → Shell
Class Pointer:	`shellWidgetClass`
Instantiation	Shell is an Intrinsics meta-class, and is not normally instantiated.
Functions/Macros:	`XtIsShell()`

Description

Shell is a subclass of Composite that handles interactions with the window manager for its single allowed child widget.

Widgets negotiate their size and position with their parent widget (i.e., the widget that directly contains them). Widgets at the top of the hierarchy do not have parent widgets. Instead, they must deal with the outside world. To provide for this, each top-level widget is created as a child of a special widget, called a Shell.

Shells have been designed to be as nearly invisible as possible. Clients have to create them (the top-level widget returned by a call to `XtAppInitialize()` or `XtCreate-ApplicationContext()` is a Shell widget, as is a popup widget created with `Xt-Popup()`), but they should never have to worry about their sizes.

If a shell widget is resized from the outside (typically by a window manager), the shell widget also resizes its child widget automatically. Similarly, if the shell's child widget needs to change size, it can make a geometry request to the shell, and the shell negotiates the size change with the outer environment. Clients should never attempt to change the size of their shells directly.

There are seven different types of shells. Only four of these are public (i.e., should be instantiated by applications):

OverrideShell

Used for shell windows that completely bypass the window manager (for example, popup menu shells).

TransientShell

Used for shell windows that can be manipulated by the window manager but are not allowed to be iconified separately (for example, Dialog boxes that make no sense without their associated application). They are iconified by the window manager only if the main application shell is iconified.

TopLevelShell
> Used for normal top-level windows (for example, any additional top-level widgets an application needs).

ApplicationShell
> Used by the window manager to define a separate application instance, which is the main top-level window of the application.

Three classes of shells are internal and should not be instantiated or subclassed:

Shell Provides the base class for shell widgets and the fields needed for all types of shells. Shell is a direct subclass of Composite.

WMShell
> Contains fields needed by the common window manager protocol.

VendorShell
> Contains fields used to communicate with vendor-specific window managers.

Figure 1 shows the class hierarchy for Shell widgets.

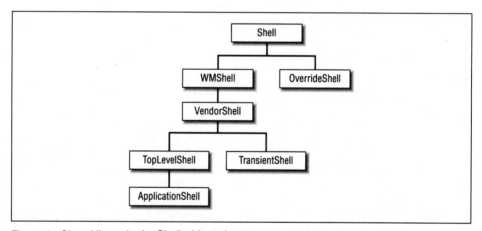

Figure 1. Class Hierarchy for Shell widget classes

New Resources

Shell defines the following resources:

Name	Class	Type	Default	Access
XtNallowShell- Resize	XtCAllowShell- Resize	Boolean	False	CG
XtNcreatePopup- ChildProc	XtCCreatePopup- ChildProc	(*)()	NULL	CSG
XtNgeometry	XtCGeometry	String	NULL	CSG
XtNoverride- Redirect	XtCOverride- Redirect	Boolean	False	CSG
XtNpopdownCallback	XtCCallback	XtCallbackList	NULL	C
XtNpopupCallback	XtCCallback	XtCallbackList	NULL	C
XtNsaveUnder	XtCSaveUnder	Boolean	False	CSG
XtNvisual	XtCVisual	Visual *	CopyFromParent	CSG

XtNallowShellResize

> If `False` (default), the Shell widget refuses geometry requests from its children (by returning `XtGeometryNo`). If `True`, the shell will attempt to satisfy the geometry request by interacting with the window manager.

XtNcreatePopupChildProc

> A pointer to a procedure that creates a child widget—but only when the shell is popped up, not when the application is started. This is useful in menus, for example, since you don't need to create the menu until it is popped up. This procedure is called after those specified in the `XtNpopupCallback` resource.

XtNgeometry

> Specifies the size and position of the window in the standard X geometry string format. This string is parsed with the Xlib function `XWMGeometry()` using the `XtNx`, `XtNy`, `XtNwidth`, and `XtNheight` resources from the Core part, and the `XtNwidthInc` and `XtNheightInc` and other size and position resources from the WMShell part as defaults. If the geometry specifies an x or y position, then `USPosition` is set. If the geometry specifies a width or height, then `USSize` is set. Any fields in the geometry specification override the corresponding values in the Core *x*, *y*, *width*, and *height* fields. If *geometry* is NULL or contains only a partial specification, then the Core *x*, *y*, *width*, and *height* fields are used and `PPosition` and `PSize` are set as appropriate. The geometry string is not copied by any of the Intrinsics Shell classes; a client specifying the string in an arglist or varargs list must ensure that the value remains valid until the shell widget is realized.

XtNoverrideRedirect

> If `True`, the window manager will not intercede when this window is popped up. Popup menus usually have this resource `True`.

popdownCallback

> A list of procedures to be called immediately before the shell is popped up with `Xt-Popup()`.

popupCallback
> A list of procedures to be called immediately after the shell is popped down with Xt-Popdown().

XtNsaveUnder
> If True, the X server is requested to save the screen contents that are obscured when this widget is mapped, thereby avoiding the overhead of sending expose events after the widget is unmapped. This is useful for popup menus.

XtNvisual
> The Visual that is used when creating the widget.

Inherited Resources

Shell inherits the following resources. The resources are listed alphabetically, along with the superclass that defines them.

Resource	Inherited From	Resource	Inherited From
XtNaccelerators	Core	XtNheight	Core
XtNancestor-Sensitive	Core	XtNinitial-Resources-Persistent	Core
XtNbackground	Core	XtNinsertPosition	Composite
XtNbackground-Pixmap	Core	XtNmappedWhen-Managed	Core
XtNborderColor	Core	XtNnumChildren	Composite
XtNborderPixmap	Core	XtNscreen	Core
XtNborderWidth	Core	XtNsensitive	Core
XtNchildren	Composite	XtNtranslations	Core
XtNcolormap	Core	XtNwidth	Core
XtNdepth	Core	XtNx	Core
XtNdestroy-Callback	Core	XtNy	Core

Class Structure

The Shell class structure contains only an extension field:

```
typedef struct {
    XtPointer extension;    /* pointer to extension record */
} ShellClassPart;

typedef struct _ShellClassRec {
    CoreClassPart            core_class;
    CompositeClassPart       composite_class;
    ShellClassPart           shell_class;
} ShellClassRec;
```

Extension Structure

There is one extension defined for the Shell · class which provides a root_geometry_manager() method. The extension structure is shown below; the record_type field should be NULLQUARK, and the version field should be XtShell-ExtensionVersion. The root_geometry_manager field is the procedure which negotiates geometry with the window manager. See root_geometry_manager(4).

```
typedef struct {
    XtPointer next_extension;
    XrmQuark record_type;
    long version;
    Cardinal record_size;
    XtGeometryHandler root_geometry_manager;
} ShellClassExtensionRec, *ShellClassExtension;
```

If there is no ShellClassPart extension record is declared with record_type equal to NULLQUARK, then the root_geometry_manager() method is inherited from the shell's superclass.

Instance Structure

The Shell instance structure contains at least the following fields (which need not be in this order):

```
typedef struct {
        String geometry;
        XtCreatePopupChildProc create_popup_child_proc;
        XtGrabKind grab_kind;
        Boolean spring_loaded;
        Boolean popped_up;
        Boolean allow_shell_resize;
        Boolean client_specified;
        Boolean save_under;
        Boolean override_redirect;
        XtCallbackList popup_callback;
        XtCallbackList popdown_callback;
} ShellPart;
```

```
typedef struct {
        CorePart            core;
        CompositePart       composite;
        ShellPart           shell;
} ShellRec, *ShellWidget;
```

See Also

ApplicationShell(3), *OverrideShell*(3), *TopLevelShell*(3), *TransientShell*(3), *VendorShell*(3), *WMShell*(3).

Name

TopLevelShell widget class – additional top-level shells for an application.

Synopsis

Public Headers:	*<X11/StringDefs.h>*
	<X11/Shell.h>
Private Header:	*<X11/ShellP.h>*
Class Name:	TopLevelShell
Class Hierarchy:	Core → Composite → Shell → WMShell → VendorShell → TopLevel-Shell
Class Pointer:	`topLevelShellWidgetClass`
Instantiation:	*widget* = XtCreatePopupShell(*name*,
	topLevelShellWidgetClass, ...)
Functions/Macros:	`XtIsTopLevelShell()`

Description

The TopLevelShell widget class is a subclass of VendorShell that is used for additional shells in applications having more than one top-level window (one of which serves as the root of a widget instance tree).

New Resources

TopLevelShell defines the following resources:

Name	Class	Type	Default	Access
XtNiconic	XtCIconic	Boolean	False	CSG
XtNiconName	XtCIconName	String	NULL	CSG
XtNiconNameEncoding	XtCIconNameEncoding	Atom	XA_STRING	CSG

`XtNiconic`

If `True`, the widget is realized as an icon, regardless of the value of the `XtNinitial-State` resource. When the value of this resource is set for a running application, the TopLevelShell will iconify or de-iconify the window appropriately, following the conventions defined by the *Inter-Client Communications Conventions Manual*. When TopLevelShell de-iconifies a window, it calls `XtPopup` with the *grab_kind* argument set to `XtGrabNone`.

`XtNiconName`

The icon name for the application. Stored in the WM_ICON_NAME property of the shell's window. Most window managers will interpret this property and display the name.

XtNiconNameEncoding

> The property type of the encoding of the XtNiconName resource. Stored in the WM_ICON_NAME property of the shell's window.

Inherited Resources

TopLevelShell inherits the following resources. The resources are listed alphabetically, along with the superclass that defines them.

Resource	Inherited From	Resource	Inherited From
XtNaccelerators	Core	XtNmaxHeight	WMShell
XtNallowShellResize	Shell	XtNmaxWidth	WMShell
XtNancestorSensitive	Core	XtNminAspectX	WMShell
XtNbackground	Core	XtNminAspectY	WMShell
XtNbackgroundPixmap	Core	XtNminHeight	WMShell
XtNbaseHeight	WMShell	XtNminWidth	WMShell
XtNbaseWidth	WMShell	XtNmwmDecorations	VendorShell
XtNborderColor	Core	XtNmwmFunctions	VendorShell
XtNborderPixmap	Core	XtNmwmInputMode	VendorShell
XtNborderWidth	Core	XtNmwmMenu	VendorShell
XtNchildren	Composite	XtNnumChildren	Composite
XtNcolormap	Core	XtNoverrideRedirect	Shell
XtNcreatePopupChild- Proc	Shell	XtNpopdownCallback	Shell
XtNdefaultFontList	VendorShell	XtNpopupCallback	Shell
XtNdeleteResponse	VendorShell	XtNsaveUnder	Shell
XtNdepth	Core	XtNscreen	Core
XtNdestroyCallback	Core	XtNsensitive	Core
XtNgeometry	Shell	XtNshellUnitType	VendorShell
XtNheight	Core	XtNtitle	WMShell
XtNheightInc	WMShell	XtNtitleEncoding	WMShell
XtNiconMask	WMShell	XtNtransient	WMShell
XtNiconPixmap	WMShell	XtNtranslations	Core
XtNiconWindow	WMShell	XtNuseAsyncGeometry	VendorShell
XtNiconX	WMShell	XtNvisual	Shell
XtNiconY	WMShell	XtNwaitForWm	WMShell
XtNinitialResources- Persistent	Core	XtNwidth	Core
XtNinitialState	WMShell	XtNwidthInc	WMShell
XtNinput	WMShell	XtNwindowGroup	WMShell
XtNinsertPosition	Composite	XtNwinGravity	WMShell
XtNkeyboardFocusPolicy	VendorShell	XtNwmTimeout	WMShell
XtNmappedWhenManaged	Core	XtNx	Core
XtNmaxAspectX	WMShell	XtNy	Core
XtNmaxAspectY	WMShell		

Class Structure

The TopLevelShell class structure contains only an extension field:

```
typedef struct {
    XtPointer extension;    /* pointer to extension record */
} TopLevelShellClassPart;

typedef struct _TopLevelShellClassRec {
    CoreClassPart core_class;
    CompositeClassPart composite_class;
    ShellClassPart shell_class;
    WMShellClassPart wm_shell_class;
    VendorShellClassPart vendor_shell_class;
    TopLevelShellClassPart top_level_shell_class;
} TopLevelShellClassRec;
```

There is no extension defined for TopLevelShell, and the `extension` field should be NULL.

Instance Structure

The TopLevelShell instance structure contains at least the following fields (which need not be in this order):

```
typedef struct {
    String icon_name;
    Boolean iconic;
    Atom icon_name_encoding;
} TopLevelShellPart;

typedef struct {
    CorePart core;
    CompositePart composite;
    ShellPart shell;
    WMShellPart wm;
    VendorShellPart vendor;
    TopLevelShellPart topLevel;
} TopLevelShellRec, *TopLevelShellWidget;
```

See Also

Shell(3), *WMShell*(3).

Intrinsics
Classes

TransientShell

Name

TransientShell widget class – popup shell that interacts with the window manager.

Synopsis

Public Headers:	*<X11/StringDefs.h>*
	<X11/Shell.h>
Private Header:	*<X11/ShellP.h>*
Class Name:	TransientShell
Class Hierarchy:	Core → Composite → Shell → WMShell → VendorShell → Transient-Shell
Class Pointer:	`transientShellWidgetClass`
Instantiation:	*widget* = XtCreatePopupShell(*name*, transientShellWidgetClass, ...)
Functions/Macros:	`XtIsTransientShell()`

Description

TransientShell is a subclass of VendorShell that is used for popup shell widgets, such as dialog boxes, that don't bypass window management. Most window managers will not allow the user to iconify a TransientShell window on its own, and may iconify it automatically if the window that it is transient for is iconified. If you want a shell that can be iconified, use TopLevelShell. If you want a shell independent of the window manager, use OverrideShell.

New Resources

TransientShell defines the following resources:

Name	Class	Type	Default	Access
XtNtransientFor	XtCTransientFor	Widget	NULL	CSG

XtNtransientFor

> The widget from which the TransientShell will pop up or some other widget that the TransientShell is logically "transient for." The window of this widget will be stored in the WM_TRANSIENT_FOR property on the TransientShell window, where it can be used by ICCCM-compliant window managers. If the value of this resource is NULL or identifies an unrealized widget, then TransientShell uses the value of the WMShell resource XtNwindowGroup.

Inherited Resources

TransientShell inherits the following resources. The resources are listed alphabetically, along with the superclass that defines them. TransientShell sets the resources XtNtransient and XtNsaveUnder to True.

Resource	Inherited From	Resource	Inherited From
XtNaccelerators	Core	XtNmaxHeight	WMShell
XtNallowShellResize	Shell	XtNmaxWidth	WMShell
XtNancestorSensitive	Core	XtNminAspectX	WMShell
XtNbackground	Core	XtNminAspectY	WMShell
XtNbackgroundPixmap	Core	XtNminHeight	WMShell
XtNbaseHeight	WMShell	XtNminWidth	WMShell
XtNbaseWidth	WMShell	XtNmwmDecorations	VendorShell
XtNborderColor	Core	XtNmwmFunctions	VendorShell
XtNborderPixmap	Core	XtNmwmInputMode	VendorShell
XtNborderWidth	Core	XtNmwmMenu	VendorShell
XtNchildren	Composite	XtNnumChildren	Composite
XtNcolormap	Core	XtNoverrideRedirect	Shell
XtNcreatePopupChild- Proc	Shell	XtNpopdownCallback	Shell
XtNdefaultFontList	VendorShell	XtNpopupCallback	Shell
XtNdeleteResponse	VendorShell	XtNsaveUnder	Shell
XtNdepth	Core	XtNscreen	Core
XtNdestroyCallback	Core	XtNsensitive	Core
XtNgeometry	Shell	XtNshellUnitType	VendorShell
XtNheight	Core	XtNtitle	WMShell
XtNheightInc	WMShell	XtNtitleEncoding	WMShell
XtNiconMask	WMShell	XtNtransient	WMShell
XtNiconPixmap	WMShell	XtNtranslations	Core
XtNiconWindow	WMShell	XtNuseAsyncGeometry	VendorShell
XtNiconX	WMShell	XtNvisual	Shell
XtNiconY	WMShell	XtNwaitForWm	WMShell
XtNinitialResources- Persistent	Core	XtNwidth	Core
XtNinitialState	WMShell	XtNwidthInc	WMShell
XtNinput	WMShell	XtNwindowGroup	WMShell
XtNinsertPosition	Composite	XtNwinGravity	WMShell
XtNkeyboardFocusPolicy	VendorShell	XtNwmTimeout	WMShell
XtNmappedWhenManaged	Core	XtNx	Core
XtNmaxAspectX	WMShell	XtNy	Core
XtNmaxAspectY	WMShell		

Class Structure

The TransientShell class structure contains only an extension field:

```
typedef struct {
    XtPointer extension;    /* pointer to extension record */
} TransientShellClassPart;

typedef struct _TransientShellClassRec {
    CoreClassPart core_class;
```

```
      CompositeClassPart composite_class;
      ShellClassPart shell_class;
      WMShellClassPart wm_shell_class;
      VendorShellClassPart vendor_shell_class;
      TransientShellClassPart transient_shell_class;
} TransientShellClassRec;
```

There is no extension defined for TransientShell, and the `extension` field should be NULL.

Instance Structure

The TransientShell instance structure contains at least the following fields (which need not be in this order):

```
typedef struct {
      Widget transient_for;
} TransientShellPart;

typedef struct {
      CorePart core;
      CompositePart composite;
      ShellPart shell;
      WMShellPart wm;
      VendorShellPart vendor;
      TransientShellPart transient;
} TransientShellRec, *TransientShellWidget;
```

See Also

Shell(3) *TopLevelShell*(3), *WMShell*(3).

VendorShell

Name

VendorShell widget class – shell widget class for vendor-specific hooks for interaction with custom window managers.

Synopsis

Public Headers:	*<X11/StringDefs.h>*
	<X11/Vendor.h>
Private Header:	*<X11/VendorP.h>*
Class Name:	VendorShell
Class Hierarchy:	Core → Composite → Shell → WMShell → VendorShell
Class Pointer:	`vendorShellWidgetClass`
Instantiation:	VendorShell is an Intrinsics meta-class, and is not normally instantiated.
Functions/Macros:	`XmIsVendorShell()`

Description

VendorShell is a subclass of WMShell that allows software vendors to provide hooks (class methods, resources, etc.) to support their custom window managers. As shipped by MIT, VendorShell defines no new class or instance fields, nor any resources. Vendors may implement a different VendorShell and ship that. Applications linked with this custom Vendor-Shell will be able to interact specially with the custom window manager.

The Motif widget set contains a custom VendorShell which provides a number of resources not documented here. See Volume 6B, *Motif Reference Manual* for more information on that VendorShell widget.

New Resources

VendorShell defines no new resources.

Inherited Resources

VendorShell inherits the following resources. The resources are listed alphabetically, along with the superclass that defines them.

Resource	Inherited From	Resource	Inherited From
XtNaccelerators	Core	XtNmaxAspectX	WMShell
XtNallowShellResize	Shell	XtNmaxAspectY	WMShell
XtNancestorSensitive	Core	XtNmaxHeight	WMShell
XtNbackground	Core	XtNmaxWidth	WMShell
XtNbackgroundPixmap	Core	XtNminAspectX	WMShell
XtNbaseHeight	WMShell	XtNminAspectY	WMShell
XtNbaseWidth	WMShell	XtNminHeight	WMShell
XtNborderColor	Core	XtNminWidth	WMShell
XtNborderPixmap	Core	XtNnumChildren	Composite
XtNborderWidth	Core	XtNoverrideRedirect	Shell
XtNchildren	Composite	XtNpopdownCallback	Shell

Resource	Inherited From	Resource	Inherited From
XtNcolormap	Core	XtNpopupCallback	Shell
XtNcreatePopupChild- Proc	Shell	XtNsaveUnder	Shell
XtNdepth	Core	XtNscreen	Core
XtNdestroyCallback	Core	XtNsensitive	Core
XtNgeometry	Shell	XtNtitle	WMShell
XtNheight	Core	XtNtitleEncoding	WMShell
XtNheightInc	WMShell	XtNtransient	WMShell
XtNiconMask	WMShell	XtNtranslations	Core
XtNiconPixmap	WMShell	XtNvisual	Shell
XtNiconWindow	WMShell	XtNwaitForWm	WMShell
XtNiconX	WMShell	XtNwidth	Core
XtNiconY	WMShell	XtNwidthInc	WMShell
XtNinitialResources- Persistent	Core	XtNwindowGroup	WMShell
XtNinitialState	WMShell	XtNwinGravity	WMShell
XtNinput	WMShell	XtNwmTimeout	WMShell
XtNinsertPosition	Composite	XtNx	Core
XtNmappedWhenManaged	Core	XtNy	Core

Class Structure

The VendorShell class structure contains only an extension field:

```
typedef struct {
    XtPointer extension;    /* pointer to extension record */
} VendorShellClassPart;

typedef struct _VendorShellClassRec {
    CoreClassPart core_class;
    CompositeClassPart composite_class;
    ShellClassPart shell_class;
    WMShellClassPart wm_shell_class;
    VendorShellClassPart vendor_shell_class;
} VendorShellClassRec;
```

There is not an extension defined for VendorShell (as shipped by MIT) and the `extension` field should be NULL.

Instance Structure

The VendorShell instance structure (as shipped by MIT) is defined as follows:

```
typedef struct {
    int vendor_specific;
} VendorShellPart;.

typedef struct {
    CorePart core;
```

```
        CompositePart composite;
        ShellPart shell;
        WMShellPart wm;
        VendorShellPart vendor;
} VendorShellRec, *VendorShellWidget;
```

See Also

Shell(3).

Name

WMShell widget class – fundamental shell widget class that interacts with an ICCCM-compliant window manager.

Synopsis

Public Headers:	*<X11/StringDefs.h>* *<X11/Shell.h>*
Private Header:	*<X11/ShellP.h>*
Class Name:	WMShell
Class Hierarchy:	Core → Composite → Shell → WMShell
Class Pointer:	wmShellWidgetClass
Instantiation:	WMShell is an Intrinsics meta-class, and is not normally instantiated.
Functions/Macros:	XtIsWMShell()

Description

WMShell is a direct subclass of Shell that provides basic window manager interaction. It should not be instantiated itself; its subclasses TransientShell, TopLevelShell, and Application-Shell provide additional functionality suitable for particular types of top-level windows.

New Resources

WMShell defines the following resources:

Name	Class	Type	Default	Access
XtNbaseHeight	XtCBaseHeight	int	XtUnspecifiedShellInt	CSG
XtNbaseWidth	XtCBaseWidth	int	XtUnspecifiedShellInt	CSG
XtNheightInc	XtCHeightInc	int	XtUnspecifiedShellInt	CSG
XtNiconMask	XtCIconMask	Pixmap	NULL	CSG
XtNiconPixmap	XtCIconPixmap	Pixmap	NULL	CSG
XtNiconWindow	XtCIconWindow	Window	NULL	CSG
XtNiconX	XtCIconX	int	−1	CSG
XtNiconY	XtCIconY	int	−1	CSG
XtNinitialState	XtCInitialState	int	NormalState	CSG
XtNinput	XtCInput	Boolean	False	CSG
XtNmaxAspectX	XtCMaxAspectX	int	XtUnspecifiedShellInt	CSG
XtNmaxAspectY	XtCMaxAspectY	int	XtUnspecifiedShellInt	CSG
XtNmaxHeight	XtCMaxHeight	int	XtUnspecifiedShellInt	CSG
XtNmaxWidth	XtCMaxWidth	int	XtUnspecifiedShellInt	CSG
XtNminAspectX	XtCMinAspectX	int	XtUnspecifiedShellInt	CSG
XtNminAspectY	XtCMinAspectY	int	XtUnspecifiedShellInt	CSG
XtNminHeight	XtCMinHeight	int	XtUnspecifiedShellInt	CSG
XtNminWidth	XtCMinWidth	int	XtUnspecifiedShellInt	CSG
XtNtitle	XtCTitle	String	dynamic	CSG
XtNtitleEncoding	XtCTitleEncoding	Atom	XA_STRING	CSG

Name	Class	Type	Default	Access
XtNtransient	XtCTransient	Boolean	False	CSG
XtNwaitForWm	XtCWaitForWm	Boolean	True	CSG
XtNwidthInc	XtCWidthInc	int	XtUnspecifiedShellInt	CSG
XtNwindowGroup	XtCWindowGroup	Window	dynamic	CSG
XtNwinGravity	XtCWinGravity	int	dynamic	CSG
XtNwmTimeout	XtCWmTimeout	int	5000 ms	CSG

Many of these resources are hints to the window manager which can be set with the Xlib function `XSetWMProperties()`. The default value for these resources is `Xt-UnspecifiedShellInt` for integer resources, or `None` for the pixmaps and windows. If any of these resources is not changed from its default value, then WMShell will not set the corresponding flag bit in the hints structure when it sets the appropriate properties, and that particular hint will be unspecified. See the Shell `XtNgeometry` resource for more information on size hints for a shell widget. See `XSetWMProperties()` and the ICCCM for more information on the window properties that are used to convey hints to window managers.

`XtNbaseHeight`
`XtNbaseWidth`

The base dimensions from which the preferred height and width can be stepped up or down (as specified by `XtNheightInc` or `XtNwidthInc`).

`XtNheightInc`

The step size by which the widget's height may be adjusted. An application that displays lines of text might set this to the font height, so that it can always display a whole number of lines. The base height is `XtNbaseHeight`, and the height can decrement to the value of `XtNminHeight` or increment to the value of `XtNmaxHeight`. See also `Xt-NwidthInc`.

`XtNiconMask`

A bitmap that the window manager can use in order to clip the application's icon into a nonrectangular shape.

`XtNiconPixmap`

A pixmap that the window manager is requested to display as the application's icon.

`XtNiconWindow`

The ID of a window that the window manager is requested to use as the application's icon. The application is responsible for drawing in this window and handling Expose events on it.

`XtNiconX`
`XtNiconY`

Window manager hints for the initial root window coordinates of the application's icon.

XtNinitialState

> The initial appearance of the widget instance. Possible values are defined in *<X11/Xutil.h>*:

```
NormalState    /* application starts as a window */
IconicState    /* application starts as an icon */
```

XtNinput

> A Boolean that, in conjunction with the WM_TAKE_FOCUS atom in the WM_PROTOCOLS property, determines the application's keyboard focus model. The result is determined by the value of XtNinput and the existence of the atom, as described below:

Value of XtNinput Resource	WM_TAKE_FOCUS Atom	Keyboard Focus Model
False	Does not exist.	No input allowed.
True	Does not exist.	Passive.
True	Exists.	Locally active.
False	Exists.	Globally active.

See the *Inter-Client Communications Conventions Manual*, Section 4.1.17 (in Appendix L of Volume Zero), for more information on these models of keyboard focus.

XtNmaxAspectX
XtNmaxAspectY

> The numerator and denominator, respectively, of the maximum aspect ratio requested for this widget.

XtNmaxHeight
XtNmaxWidth

> The maximum dimensions for the widget's preferred height or width.

XtNminAspectX
XtNminAspectY

> The numerator and denominator, respectively, of the minimum aspect ratio requested for this widget.

XtNminHeight
XtNminWidth

> The minimum dimensions for the widget's preferred height or width.

XtNtitle

> The string that the window manager displays as the application's name. The default is the icon name, or if that isn't specified, the name of the application.

XtNtitleEncoding

> An Atom which specifies the encoding of the XtNtitle resource.

XtNtransient

If `True`, this indicates a popup window or some other transient widget which should have its WM_TRANSIENT_FOR property set (see the `XtNwindowGroup` resource below, and also the `XtNtransientFor` resource of the TransientShell class). Different window managers will interpret this property differently, and may provide fewer decorations (no iconify button, for example) than they would for a non-transient window.

XtNwaitForWm

If `True` (default), the shell waits for a response from the window manager before changing the size of a widget. The timeout interval is specified by the `XtNwmTimeout` resource. If the window manager does not respond within this time, this resource will be set to `False`, though it may be reset to its original value later. When this resource is `False`, the shell relies on asynchronous notification from the window manager and does not wait for a response.

XtNwidthInc

The step size by which the widget's width may be adjusted. The base width is `Xt-NbaseWidth`, and the width can decrement to the value of `XtNminWidth` or increment to the value of `XtNmaxWidth`. See also `XtNheightInc`.

XtNwindowGroup

This is a hint to the window manager that this shell is associated with the main window or "group leader" window specified by this resource. Some window managers may allow groups of related windows to be manipulated together. If the shell widget is not the root of the widget hierarchy, then WMShell sets the default value of this resource to the window ID of the root widget if that widget is realized. This resource can be set to the special value `XtUnspecifiedWindowGroup` to indicate that the window group hint should not be set. If `XtNtransient` is `True`, and if the shell is not a subclass of `TransientShell`, and if this resource is not `XtUnspecifiedWindowGroup`, then it will be set as the value of the WM_TRANSIENT_FOR property. See also the `Xt-NtransientFor` resource of the TransientShell class.

XtNwinGravity

The window gravity used in positioning the widget. Unless an initial value is given, this resource will be set when the widget is realized. The default value is `NorthWest-Gravity` (if the Shell resource `XtNgeometry` is NULL); otherwise, `XtNwin-Gravity` assumes the value returned by the `XWMGeometry()` routine.

XtNwmTimeout

The number of milliseconds that the X Toolkit waits for a response from the window manager. This resource is meaningful when the `XtNwaitForWm` resource is set to `True`. If the window manager does not respond to a geometry request within this time, the shell assumes that the window manager is not functioning properly and sets `Xt-NwaitForWm` to `False`.

Inherited Resources

WMShell inherits the following resources. The resources are listed alphabetically, along with the superclass that defines them.

Resource	Inherited From	Resource	Inherited From
XtNaccelerators	Core	XtNinitialResources- Persistent	Core
XtNallowShellResize	Shell	XtNinsertPosition	Composite
XtNancestorSensitive	Core	XtNmappedWhenManaged	Core
XtNbackground	Core	XtNnumChildren	Composite
XtNbackgroundPixmap	Core	XtNoverrideRedirect	Shell
XtNborderColor	Core	XtNpopdownCallback	Shell
XtNborderPixmap	Core	XtNpopupCallback	Shell
XtNborderWidth	Core	XtNsaveUnder	Shell
XtNchildren	Composite	XtNscreen	Core
XtNcolormap	Core	XtNsensitive	Core
XtNcreatePopupChild- Proc	Shell	XtNtranslations	Core
XtNdepth	Core	XtNvisual	Shell
XtNdestroyCallback	Core	XtNwidth	Core
XtNgeometry	Shell	XtNx	Core
XtNheight	Core	XtNy	Core

Class Structure

The WMShell class structure contains only an extension field:

```
typedef struct {
    XtPointer extension;   /* pointer to extension record */
} WMShellClassPart;

typedef struct {
    CorePart core;
    CompositePart composite;
    ShellPart shell;
    WMShellPart wm;
} WMShellRec, *WMShellWidget;
```

Instance Structure

The WMShell instance structure contains at least the following fields (which need not be in this order):

```
typedef struct {
        String title;
        int wm_timeout;
        Boolean wait_for_wm;
        Boolean transient;
        struct _OldXSizeHints {
```

```
            long flags;
            int x, y;
            int width, height;
            int min_width, min_height;
            int max_width, max_height;
            int width_inc, height_inc;
            struct {
                    int x;
                    int y;
            } min_aspect, max_aspect;
      } size_hints;
      XWMHints wm_hints;
      int base_width, base_height, win_gravity;
      Atom title_encoding;
} WMShellPart;

typedef struct {
      CorePart core;
      CompositePart composite;
      ShellPart shell;
      WMShellPart wm;
} WMShellRec, *WMShellWidget;
```

The XWMHints type is defined (in *<X11/Xutil.h>*) as follows:

```
typedef struct {
      long flags;              /* marks which fields in this structure are
                                  defined */
      Bool input;              /* does this application rely on the window
                                  manager to get keyboard input? */
      int initial_state;       /* see below */
      Pixmap icon_pixmap;      /* pixmap to be used as icon */
      Window icon_window;      /* window to be used as icon */
      int icon_x, icon_y;      /* initial position of icon */
      Pixmap icon_mask;        /* icon mask bitmap */
      XID window_group;        /* id of related window group */
      /* this structure may be extended in the future */
} XWMHints;
```

See Also

Shell(3).

Section 4

Intrinsics Methods

This section contains reference pages for the methods defined by the Intrinsics widget classes. Methods are the functions that contain the basic code for every widget, and so these reference pages will only be of interest to widget writers. Every method is registered on a field of the widget class structure. The reference pages in this section are named after these class structure fields. Since the Core and Constraint widget classes have four field names in common, the Constraint version of these methods have the word Constraint in their page headers. These Constraint methods are alphabetized together with the corresponding Core methods, not under the letter C.

The first reference page, Introduction, *explains the format and contents of each of the following pages.*

In This Section:

This page describes the format and contents of each reference page in Section 4, which covers the widget class methods for all the Intrinsics widget classes.

Name

Method – a brief description of the purpose of the method.

Synopsis

This section shows the signature of the method: the names and types of the arguments, and the type of the return value. Each method is of one of the function types documented in Section 2 of this book.

Inputs

This subsection describes each of the arguments that pass information to the method.

Outputs

This subsection describes any of the arguments that are used to return information from the method. These arguments are always of some pointer type, so you must remember to dereference them correctly in your function, and must store the appropriate information at the address they specify. The names of these arguments are usually suffixed with _return to indicate that values are returned in them. Some arguments both supply and return a value; they will be listed in this section and in the "Inputs" section above. Finally, note that because the list of function arguments is broken into "Input" and "Output" sections, they do not always appear in the same order that they are passed to the function. See the function signature for the actual calling order.

Returns

This subsection explains the return value of the method, if any.

Availability

This section appears for methods that were added in Release 4 or Release 5, and also for methods that are now obsolete.

Description

This section explains how this method is registered in an widget class structure, what the method should do, and the method's arguments and return value. It also explains how to inherit the method from a superclass, if it is an inheritable method, or how the method is chained, if it is a chained method.

Usage

This section appears for most methods and provides less formal information about the method: typical tasks for the method, tips on implementation, things to watch out for, and related methods that you might want to look into.

Example

This section provides an example of most of the widget methods. Important features of each example are noted. These examples are generally taken from the Xaw widget set.

Background

This section presents detailed technical material related to the method. It is usually derived directly from the Xt specification, and is therefore definitive. You should not often have to refer to this section, but the material here is necessary for a complete understanding of the workings of the Intrinsics.

Structures

This section shows the definition of any structures, enumerated types, typedefs, or symbolic constants used by the method.

See Also

This section refers you to related functions, prototype procedures, Intrinsics widget classes, or widget methods. The numbers in parenthesis following each reference refer to the sections of this book in which they are found.

Name

accept_focus – Core class method for accepting or rejecting the keyboard focus.

Synopsis

```
typedef Boolean (*XtAcceptFocusProc)(Widget, Time *);
    Widget w;
    Time *time;
```

Inputs

w   Specifies the widget.

time   Specifies the X time of the event causing the parent to offer focus to the child.

Returns

True if the child actually took the focus; False otherwise.

Description

The accept_focus() method is registered on the accept_focus field of the Core class part structure and is invoked by XtCallAcceptFocus() when a parent widget wants to offer keyboard focus to a widget. If the widget wants the keyboard focus, it should take it with the Xlib function XSetInputFocus() and return True. If the widget does not currently want the focus, it should return False.

The ICCCM requires that a widget use Parent for the *revert_to* argument to XSet-InputFocus().

The accept_focus() method is not chained. If a widget class does not define an accept_focus() method, it can use XtInheritAcceptFocus to inherit the method from its superclass. If the widget never wants the focus, it should have an accept_focus field of NULL.

Usage

Note that this method is an invitation to take the focus, not notification that focus has changed, and not a command to take the focus.

A widget that needs to know when it loses the focus can specify translations or event handlers for FocusIn and FocusOut events.

None of the Intrinsics or Xaw widget classes define an accept_focus() method, and none of them ever call XtCallAcceptFocus().

An application that wants to direct keyboard events to a particular widget should use XtSet-KeyboardFocus().

See Also

XtCallAcceptFocus(1), *XtSetKeyboardFocus*(1).

Name

change_managed – Composite class method to respond to a change in a list of managed
          widgets.

Synopsis

```
typedef void (*XtWidgetProc)(Widget);
    Widget w;
```

Inputs

w   Specifies the widget that has had children managed or unmanaged.

Description

The change_managed() method is registered on the change_managed field of the Composite class part structure, and is invoked when a child or children are managed or unmanaged
with XtManageChild(), XtManageChildren(), XtUnmanageChild(), or Xt-
UnmanageChildren().

When a child is managed or unmananged, it generally means that the layout of all the children
of the widget should be redone. Note that this method does not have an argument which specifies which children have had their managed state changed. change_managed() should loop
through all of the children in its children array, using XtIsManaged() to determine
which are managed and should therefore be included in the layout calculations.

The change_managed() method is not chained. A widget class that does not define a
change_managed() method can inherit this method from its superclass by specifying Xt-
InheritChangeManaged in its Composite change_managed() class field.

Usage

Many change_managed() methods simply call a general layout routine which may also be
called from other places in the widget such as the resize() method.

Example

The following procedure is the change_managed() method for the Xaw Form widget. Note
how it loops through all of its children, setting constraint fields for those that are managed, and
then calls a layout routine (which is a class method of the Form widget in this case) to recalculate the layout of all children. It makes no attempt to determine which children have been managed or unmanaged.

```
static void ChangeManaged(w)
    Widget w;
{
  FormWidget fw = (FormWidget)w;
  FormConstraints form;
  WidgetList children, childP;
  int num_children = fw->composite.num_children;
  Widget child;

  /*
   * Reset virtual width and height for all children.
```

```
        */

    for (children = childP = fw->composite.children ;
         childP - children < num_children; childP++) {
      child = *childP;
      if (XtIsManaged(child)) {
        form = (FormConstraints)child->core.constraints;

/*
 * If the size is one (1) then we must not change the virtual sizes, as
 * they contain useful information.  If someone actually wants a widget
 * of width or height one (1) in a form widget he will lose, can't win
 * them all.
 *
 * Chris D. Peterson 2/9/89.
 */

        if ( child->core.width != 1)
          form->form.virtual_width = (int) child->core.width;
        if ( child->core.height != 1)
          form->form.virtual_height = (int) child->core.height;
      }
    }
    (*((FormWidgetClass)w->core.widget_class)->form_class.layout)
                                   ((FormWidget) w, w->core.width,
                                    w->core.height, TRUE);

}
```

See Also

Composite(3), *Constraint*(3).

Name

class_initialize – Object class method for one-time class initialization.

Synopsis

```
typedef void (*XtProc)(void);
```

Description

The `class_initialize()` method is registered on the `class_initialize` field of the Object, RectObj, or Core class structures, and is called exactly once by the Intrinsics before any instances of the class are created.

The `class_initialize()` method takes no arguments and returns no value. It performs initialization that should be done once for this class and all its subclasses, such as registering type converters and interning atoms and quarks. Compare this with the `class_part_initialize()` method which is called once for its class and also for every subclass, and is responsible for initializing fields in the class part structure.

The `class_initialize()` method is chained in superclass-to-subclass order, and cannot be inherited. If a class does not need to do any one-time initialization, it should specify NULL in its `class_initialize` field.

See the "Background" section below for more information on when this method is called.

Usage

The `class_initialize()` method performs initialization for the class. It is the `initialize()` method that performs initialization for the instance structure of a widget.

Example

The following procedure is the `class_initialize()` method of the Xaw Form widget. Note that it registers two resource converters, and interns quarks (in global variables) for use by the String-to-EdgeType converter.

```
static void ClassInitialize()
{
    static XtConvertArgRec parentCvtArgs[] = {
        {XtBaseOffset, (XtPointer)XtOffsetOf(WidgetRec, core.parent),
            sizeof(Widget)}
    };
    XawInitializeWidgetSet();
    XtQChainLeft   = XrmPermStringToQuark("chainleft");
    XtQChainRight  = XrmPermStringToQuark("chainright");
    XtQChainTop    = XrmPermStringToQuark("chaintop");
    XtQChainBottom = XrmPermStringToQuark("chainbottom");
    XtQRubber      = XrmPermStringToQuark("rubber");

    XtAddConverter( XtRString, XtREdgeType, _CvtStringToEdgeType, NULL, 0 );
    XtSetTypeConverter (XtRString, XtRWidget, XmuNewCvtStringToWidget,
                        parentCvtArgs, XtNumber(parentCvtArgs), XtCacheNone,
                        NULL);
}
```

Background

All widget classes, whether they have a `class_initialize()` method or not, must start with their `class_inited` field `False`.

The first time a widget of a class is created, `XtCreateWidget()` ensures that the widget class and all superclasses are initialized, in superclass-to-subclass order, by checking each `class_inited` field. If this field is `False`, `XtCreateWidget()` calls the `class_initialize()` and the `class_part_initialize()` methods for the class and all its superclasses. The Intrinsics then set the `class_inited` field to a nonzero value. After the one-time initialization, a class structure is constant. This initialization process can also be performed explicitly, without creating a widget, by calling `XtInitializeWidgetClass()`.

See Also

XtInitializeWidgetClass(1),
Core(3),
class_part_initialize(4), *initialize*(4).

Name

class_part_initialize – Object class method to initialize class part structure fields.

Synopsis

```
typedef void (*XtWidgetClassProc)(WidgetClass);
    WidgetClass subclass;
```

Inputs

subclass Specifies the pointer to a widget class structure. It is the class that registered this method or a subclass thereof.

Description

The `class_part_initialize()` method is registered on the `class_part_initialize` field of the Object, RectObj, or Core class structure, and is called to dynamically initialize any fields in the class part structure of its widget class for the class itself, and also for any subclasses of the widget class.

During class initialization, the `class_part_initialize()` method for the class and for all its superclasses is called in superclass-to-subclass order on the class record. These procedures do any dynamic initializations necessary to their class's part of the record, including resolution of any inherited methods defined in the class. For example, if a widget class *C* has superclasses Core, Composite, *A*, and *B*, then the class record for *C* is passed first to Core's `class_part_initialize()` method. This resolves any inherited Core methods and compiles the textual representations of the resource list and action table that are defined in the Core class part. Next, the Composite's `class_part_initialize()` is called to initialize the Composite part of *C*'s class record. Finally, the `class_part_initialize()` procedures for *A*, *B*, and *C* (in order) are called. All these methods will be called again if subclass *D* of class *C* is initialized, this time to initialize the various parts of *D*'s class structure.

The `class_part_initialize()` method is chained in superclass-to-subclass order and cannot be inherited. Classes that do not define any new class fields or that need no extra processing for them can set their `class_part_initialize` field to be NULL.

See the "Background" section below for more details on when class initialization is performed.

Usage

The `subclass` argument to a `class_part_initialize()` procedure may be the widget class itself, or any subclass of it. You should cast it to a pointer to your widget class and use that pointer to access the fields of the class part structure that your class defines. If you need to access the superclass, use the `superclass` field in the Object, RectObj, or Core class part. This is shown in the example below.

The most common usage of the `class_part_initialize()` method is to handle inheritance of class methods and other fields. If you define a class with a method or other field that can be inherited, you should define a special value that the writer of the subclass can use to inherit the field (use the constant `_XtInherit` cast to the appropriate type, as shown in the example below) and provide a `class_part_initialize()` method which checks the inheritable field for this special value and overwrites it with the contents of the superclass's field.

Example

The following procedure is the `class_part_initialize()` method for the Xaw Form widget class. Note how it determines the immediate superclass and handles the inheritance of the Form `layout()` class method.

Note that it does not initialize the Core, Composite, or Constraint class part fields, nor does it make any assumptions about its `WidgetClass` argument except that it is a subclass of Form. Also note that when this method is called for the Form widget class itself, the variable `super` will be set to the superclass of Form, which cannot correctly be cast to `FormWidgetClass`. This is a bug, but will never cause problems, because the Form class itself will never have to inherit any fields.

Note that the identifier `class` is a reserved word in C++, and your code will be more portable if you avoid using it as an argument name in C code.

```
static void ClassPartInitialize(class)
    WidgetClass class;
{
    register FormWidgetClass c = (FormWidgetClass)class;
    register FormWidgetClass super = (FormWidgetClass)
        c->core_class.superclass;

    if (c->form_class.layout == XtInheritLayout)
        c->form_class.layout = super->form_class.layout;
}
```

The constant `XtInheritLayout` is defined as follows (in *<X11/Xaw/FormP.h>*):

```
#define XtInheritLayout ((Boolean (*)())_XtInherit)
```

Background

All widget classes, whether or not they have class and class part initialization procedures, must start with their `class_inited` field `False`.

The first time a widget of a class is created, `XtCreateWidget()` ensures that the widget class and all superclasses are initialized, in superclass-to-subclass order, by checking each `class_inited` field. If this field is `False`, `XtCreateWidget()` calls the `class_initialize()` and the `class_part_initialize()` methods for the class and all its superclasses. The Intrinsics then set the `class_inited` field to a nonzero value. After the one-time initialization, a class structure is constant. This initialization can also be performed explicitly, without creating a widget, by calling `XtInitializeWidgetClass()`.

See Also

XtInitializeWidgetClass(1),
Core(3),
class_initialize(4), *initialize*(4).

Name

delete_child – Composite class method called when a child is destroyed.

Synopsis

```
typedef void (*XtWidgetProc)(Widget);
    Widget w;
```

Inputs

w   Specifies the child that is to be removed from its parent's `children` array.

Description

The `delete_child()` method is registered on the `delete_child` field of the Composite class part structure. It is called by `XtDestroyWidget()` to remove a child from its parent's `children` array.

Note that the argument to the `delete_child()` method is the child widget, not the composite widget that defines the method. This method must remove the specified child from its parent's `children` array, and free up any other memory that the class uses to keep track of the child.

The `delete_child()` method is not chained. If a class does not define a `delete_child()` method, it should inherit the method from its superclass by specifying `XtInheritDeleteChild` in the `delete_child` field of its Composite class part structure. This field should not be set to NULL.

Usage

Most widgets simply inherit the `delete_child()` method from their superclass. Some widget classes, though, create companion widgets for each of their children (the Xaw Paned widget creates the Grip widgets that separate the panes, for example) or maintain information about each child that must be freed up when the child is destroyed. These classes must provide their own `delete_child()` procedures. These procedures commonly "envelop" their superclass's method by providing a procedure that does class-specific processing and explicitly invokes the superclass method. This technique allows a kind of non-automatic inheritance, and is shown in the example below.

Note that the Composite `insert_child()` and `delete_child()` methods exploit internal common data structures, so you should inherit or envelop both or neither. If you do not inherit or envelop these methods, then your methods are responsible for adding and removing the child widget from the `children` array.

Example

The following procedure is the `delete_child()` method of the Xaw Paned widget class. Note how it destroys the Grip widget that was automatically created as a sibling of the child, and then explicitly invokes its superclass's `delete_child()` method to remove the child from the Composite `children` array. See `insert_child(4)` for the corresponding `insert_child()` procedure.

```
static void DeleteChild(w)
Widget w;
{
    /* remove the subwidget info and destroy the grip */
    if ( IsPane(w) && HasGrip(w) ) XtDestroyWidget(PaneInfo(w)->grip);

    /* delete the child widget in the composite children list with the */
    /* superclass delete_child routine.                                */
    (*SuperClass->composite_class.delete_child) (w);

} /* DeleteChild */
```

In this example, `SuperClass` is a symbolic name for the superclass of the Paned widget class. Note that this method does *not* determine the superclass as follows:

```
XtSuperclass(XtParent(w))
```

The parent of *w* may be a subclass of `Paned`, and therefore its superclass pointer will not always be the class whose method should be invoked.

See Also

Composite(3),
insert_child(4).

Name

destroy – Object class method called when a widget is destroyed.

Synopsis

```
typedef void (*XtWidgetProc)(Widget);
    Widget w;
```

Inputs

w   Specifies the widget that is being destroyed.

Description

The destroy() method is registered on the destroy field of the Object, RectObj, or Core class part structures. It is invoked by XtDestroyWidget() as part of the destruction process when any widget or object is destroyed, and should deallocate any memory or resources associated with the part of the widget instance structure specific to this class. It does not free the widget instance structure itself.

The destroy() methods of a widget class and all its superclasses are called in subclass-to-superclass order. (Note that this is the reverse of the usual superclass-to-subclass chaining sequence.) The destroy() method of a widget class should deallocate memory or other resources that were explicitly allocated by this class. Any resource that was obtained from the resource database or passed in an argument list was not created by the widget and therefore should not be destroyed by it (unless the widget allocated memory to copy the resource value, in which case the memory must be freed).

To reclaim memory, at least the following deallocations should be performed:

- Call XtFree() on dynamic storage allocated with XtCalloc(), XtMalloc(), etc.
- Call XFreePixmap() on pixmaps created with direct Xlib calls.
- Call XtReleaseGC() on GCs allocated with XtGetGC().
- Call XFreeGC() on GCs allocated with direct Xlib calls.
- Call XtRemoveEventHandler() on event handlers added with XtAddEvent-Handler().
- Call XtRemoveTimeOut() on timers created with XtAppAddTimeOut().
- Call XtDestroyWidget() for each child if the widget has children and is not a subclass of compositeWidgetClass.

The destroy() method is chained, so it cannot be inherited. If a widget does not need to deallocate any storage, the destroy field in its widget class record should be NULL.

See XtDestroyWidget(1) for details on the process of widget destruction.

Usage

In general, a destroy() method will deallocate any resources allocated in the initialize() and set_values() methods. This often includes GCs, pixmaps, and any copies that were made of string resources.

Example

The following procedure is the `destroy()` method of the Xaw Label widget. It frees the copy it made of its label string resource, deallocates two shared GCs, and frees the stipple pixmap it used to draw itself in insensitive mode.

```
static void Destroy(w)
    Widget w;
{
    LabelWidget lw = (LabelWidget)w;

    XtFree( lw->label.label );
    XtReleaseGC( w, lw->label.normal_GC );
    XtReleaseGC( w, lw->label.gray_GC);
    XmuReleaseStippledPixmap( XtScreen(w), lw->label.stipple );
}
```

See Also

XtDestroyWidget(1),
Core(3),
Constraint destroy(4), *initialize*(4), *set_values*(4).

Name

Constraint destroy – Constraint class method for freeing resources associated with a child's constraint record.

Synopsis

```
typedef void (*XtWidgetProc)(Widget);
    Widget w;
```

Inputs

w   Specifies the widget being destroyed.

Description

The Constraint destroy() method is registered on the destroy field of the Constraint class part structure (which is not the same as the destroy field of the Object or Core class part structure). It is called by XtDestroyWidget() when the child of a constraint widget is destroyed, and should deallocate any memory or resources associated with the part of the constraint record of w that is owned by the class. It should not deallocate the constraint record itself.

This method is similar to the Object destroy() method. The Constraint destroy() methods of a widget class and its superclasses are called in subclass-to-superclass order, starting at the class of the parent of w, and ending at the Constraint class. Therefore, the Constraint destroy() method should deallocate only memory and resources associated with the part of the constraint record specific to its class, and not the memory or resources allocated by any of its superclasses.

The Constraint destroy() method is chained, and so cannot be inherited. If a constraint widget does not need to deallocate any memory or resources associated with its constraint part structure, the destroy field in its Constraint class part record can be NULL.

See destroy(4) for more information about what should be freed and what should not. See XtDestroyWidget(1) for details on the widget and object destruction process.

Example

The following procedure is the Constraint destroy() method of the Xaw Tree widget. Note that it uses a macro (defined below) to cast the specified widget's constraint field appropriately, and calls XtParent() on the specified widget to obtain the Tree widget itself.

This procedure is a somewhat unusual example, because it does not directly call XtFree(), XtReleaseGC(), or similar functions on fields of the constraint record. The constraint records of the Tree class are linked in a tree structure, and this procedure is used to remove a node from that tree. This might have been more appropriate in the delete_child() method instead.

```
static void ConstraintDestroy (w)
    Widget w;
{
    TreeConstraints tc = TREE_CONSTRAINT(w);
    TreeWidget tw = (TreeWidget) XtParent(w);
```

```
    int i;

    /*
     * Remove the widget from its parent's sub-nodes list and
     * make all this widget's sub-nodes sub-nodes of the parent.
     */

    if (tw->tree.tree_root == w) {
       if (tc->tree.n_children > 0)
         tw->tree.tree_root = tc->tree.children[0];
       else
         tw->tree.tree_root = NULL;
    }

    delete_node (tc->tree.parent, (Widget) w);
    for (i = 0; i< tc->tree.n_children; i++)
      insert_node (tc->tree.parent, tc->tree.children[i]);

    layout_tree ((TreeWidget) (w->core.parent), FALSE);
}
```

The useful TREE_CONSTRAINTS macro is defined as follows:

```
#define TREE_CONSTRAINT(w) ((TreeConstraints)((w)->core.constraints))
```

See Also

XtDestroyWidget(1),
Constraint(3), *Core*(3).

display_accelerator

Name

display_accelerator – Core method to display current accelerators.

Synopsis

```
typedef void (*XtStringProc)(Widget, String);
    Widget w;
    String string;
```

Inputs

w   Specifies the source widget that supplied the accelerators.

string   Provides the string representation of the accelerators that were installed.

Description

The Core `display_accelerator()` method is registered on the `display_accelera-tor` field of the Core class part structure, and is called when the application installs a widget's accelerators with `XtInstallAccelerators()` or `XtInstallAllAccelerators()`.

The argument *w* is the widget instance that has had its accelerators installed, and *string* is a string representation of the widget's accelerator table. Some widget classes will want to display themselves differently when accelerators are installed so that the user is aware that they are available. (Menu buttons that display their keyboard equivalents are a good example.)

The method is passed a string version of the current accelerator table, in canonical form. This form may differ from the original source of the accelerator table itself.

The `display_accelerator()` method is not chained. A widget class can inherit its super-class's `display_accelerator()` method by specifying `XtInheritDisplay-Accelerator` in its Core `display_accelerator` field. A widget that does not wish to display any accelerators may set this field to NULL.

Usage

The translation table syntax is not particularly easy for a user to read or particularly easy for a widget to convert into a simpler form, so a widget class may prefer to define a resource which is the string that should be displayed when the accelerator is installed. That way the application programmer can specify both the accelerator and the representation of the accelerator that the user will see.

None of the Intrinsics or Xaw widget classes define a `display_accelerator()` method.

See Also

XtInstallAccelerators(1).

Name

expose – Core class method that draws a widget's graphics.

Synopsis

```
typedef void (*XtExposeProc)(Widget, XEvent *, Region);
    Widget w;
    XEvent *event;
    Region region;
```

Inputs

w	Specifies the widget instance requiring redisplay.
event	Specifies the exposure event giving the rectangle requiring redisplay.
region	Specifies the union of all rectangles in this exposure sequence.

Description

The expose() method is installed on the expose field of the Core class part structure, and is called to draw or redraw the widget's window when exposure events arrive for that window. An expose() method may also be registered on the expose field of the RectObj class part structure, but because RectObj widgets do not have windows, this method will not be called by the Intrinsics. (Although some composite widgets may call the expose() methods of their non-widget children.)

The *w* argument is the widget for which exposure events have arrived. *event* is the exposure event, or the latest in a series of exposure events, if the widget uses exposure compression. It contains a bounding box of the exposed area. *region* is NULL if there is no exposure compression, or specifies the union of all exposure events in the compressed sequence. The expose() method must redraw at least the graphics within the bounding box of the event. Simple widgets may simply redraw their entire window; more complicated widgets may attempt to minimize the amount of redraw required by using the *region* argument. Exposure compression is specified with the compress_exposure field in the Core class part structure. See the "Background" section below for details.

A widget need not redisplay itself if it is not visible. A widget can obtain a hint about whether it is currently visible by checking the visible field in the Core instance structure. If visible_interest in the Core class structure is True, then the visible field is usually False if no part of the widget is currently visible. See the "Background" section for details.

The expose() method is not chained. A widget class can inherit the expose() method of its superclass by specifying XtInheritExpose on the expose field of its RectObj or Core class part structure. A widget that does not display any graphics (such as many composite widgets) can set this field to NULL.

The long "Usage" section below explains some common strategies to handling expose events on a widget.

Usage

The expose() method is responsible for initially drawing into a widget's window and for redrawing the window every time a part of the window becomes exposed. This redrawing is necessary because the X server does not normally maintain the contents of windows when they are obscured. When a window becomes visible again, it must be redrawn.

Most widgets keep track of what they draw in some form of arrays or display lists. This could be an array of lines of text to be drawn, for example, or an array of lines which can be drawn with a single call to `XDrawLines()`. When a widget of this sort needs to redisplay itself, it simply calls the procedure that draws the widget based on the saved data.

The graphic contents of a widget often change in response to user events handled with action procedures or event handlers. These procedures usually draw into the widget directly, but must also store the appropriate data so that the current state of the widget can be regenerated, if necessary.

An `expose()` method can be made more efficient if as much data as possible is pre-computed. A label widget that draws its text centered in its window, for example, should pre-compute the x and y coordinates at which the text will be drawn. If it does not, the expose method will have to compute the position based on the height of the font, the width of the string (which is time consuming to compute), and the size of the window. These pre-computed positions should only need to be updated in the `resize()` and `set_values()` methods.

Simple widgets may just redisplay their entire window when the expose event is called. More complicated widgets may redisplay everything within the bounding box of the event (which will be the same as the bounding box of the specified Region if it is non-`NULL`). For widgets that are very time-consuming for the client or server to redraw, you might want to use this region in a more sophisticated way. You can use this region as a clip mask in your GC (see `XSetRegion()`) to clip output to the exposed region, and possibly calculate which drawing primitives affect this area. Xlib also provides region mathematics routines (such as `XRectIn-Region()`) so that you can compare the regions in which your widget needs to draw graphics with the region that was exposed. If certain areas do not require redrawing, you can skip the code that redraws them. If you plan to write a sophisticated `expose()` method, bear in mind that the calculations required to optimize the redisplay are time consuming, too, and too much clipping and testing of rectangles may slow down your widget. The cost/benefit ratio should be examined.

Some widgets do not bother to remember how to redraw themselves. Instead they draw their graphics into a pixmap and copy the contents of the pixmap into their window as needed. For some widgets this approach is much simpler than retaining the state needed to redraw from scratch. If the widget is very large, however, the pixmap will take up a lot of memory in the X server.

A widget that is insensitive (see `XtSetSensitive`(1)) may wish to indicate this to the user by drawing itself in a different way. A common approach is to draw with a GC with a stipple to so that everything appears "grayed-out."

A composite widget that accepts non-widget children which are subclasses of RectObj ("gadgets") will have to display the graphics of those children in its own window. It may narrowly define the types of children it will accept to be the type of children that it knows how to draw. Or instead it may require that its RectObj children have their own `expose()` methods and call those methods when it detects that the region of the window occupied by a child needs to be redrawn.

If a widget has no display semantics, it can specify NULL for the expose() field. Many composite widgets serve only as containers for their children and have no expose() method. If the expose() method is NULL, XtRealizeWidget() fills in a default bit gravity of NorthWestGravity before it calls the widget's realize() method.

Example

The following procedure is the expose() method of the Xaw Label widget with code for handling the left bitmap and multi-line string removed. Note that it first tests that the exposed region intersects the region that the label string or pixmap occupies. It also has commented-out code that sets the region as the clipmask of the GC. For such a simple redisplay, doing the clipping may have taken more time than simply drawing the text of pixmap. This method does not test the visible field, and the widget class has its visible_interest field set to False. Finally, note that if the widget is insensitive, it uses a special GC to draw itself "grayed-out."

```
/* ARGSUSED */
static void Redisplay(w, event, region)
    Widget w;
    XEvent *event;
    Region region;
{
    LabelWidget lw = (LabelWidget) w;
    GC gc;

    if (region != NULL) {
        int x = lw->label.label_x;
        unsigned int width = lw->label.label_width;
        if (lw->label.lbm_width) {
            if (lw->label.label_x > (x = lw->label.internal_width))
                width += lw->label.label_x - x;
        }
        if (XRectInRegion(region, x, lw->label.label_y,
                        width, lw->label.label_height) == RectangleOut)
            return;
    }

    gc = XtIsSensitive((Widget)lw) ? lw->label.normal_GC : lw->label.gray_GC;
#ifdef notdef
    if (region != NULL) XSetRegion(XtDisplay(w), gc, region);
#endif /*notdef*/
    if (lw->label.pixmap == None) {
        int len = lw->label.label_len;
        char *label = lw->label.label;
        Position y = lw->label.label_y + lw->label.font->max_bounds.ascent;

        if (len) {
            if (lw->label.encoding)
                XDrawString16(XtDisplay(w), XtWindow(w), gc,
                            lw->label.label_x, y, (TXT16*)label, len/2);
```

```
            else
                XDrawString(XtDisplay(w), XtWindow(w), gc,
                            lw->label.label_x, y, label, len);
        }
    } else if (lw->label.label_len == 1) { /* depth */
        XCopyPlane(XtDisplay(w), lw->label.pixmap, XtWindow(w), gc,
                        0, 0, lw->label.label_width, lw->label.label_height,
                        lw->label.label_x, lw->label.label_y, 1L);
    } else {
        XCopyArea(XtDisplay(w), lw->label.pixmap, XtWindow(w), gc,
                        0, 0, lw->label.label_width, lw->label.label_height,
                        lw->label.label_x, lw->label.label_y);
    }
#ifdef notdef
    if (region != NULL) XSetClipMask(XtDisplay(w), gc, (Pixmap)None);
#endif /* notdef */
}
```

Background

Many widgets prefer to process a series of exposure events as a single expose region rather than as individual rectangles. Widgets with complex displays might use the expose region as a clip list in a graphics context, and widgets with simple displays might ignore the region entirely and redisplay their whole window or might get the bounding box from the region and redisplay only that rectangle.

In either case, these widgets want some kind of exposure compression. The com-press_exposure field in the widget class structure specifies the type and number of exposure events that will be dispatched to the widget's expose procedure. This field must be set to XtExposeNoCompress, XtExposeCompressSeries, XtExposeCompress-Multiple, or XtExposeCompressMaximal, optionally ORed with any combination of the XtExposeGraphicsExpose, XtExposeGraphicsExposeMerged, and Xt-ExposeNoExpose flags. (Specifying False for the compress_exposure field is equivalent to XtExposeNoCompress with no flags and specifying True is equivalent to Xt-ExposeCompressSeries with no flags.)

If the *compress_exposure* field in the widget class structure does not specify XtExpose-NoCompress, the event manager calls the widget's expose procedure only once for a series of exposure events. In this case, all Expose or GraphicsExpose events are accumulated into a region. When the final event is received, the event manager replaces the rectangle in the event with the bounding box for the region and calls the widget's expose() method, passing the modified exposure event and the region.

The different types of exposure compression are as follows:

XtExposeNoCompress
> No exposure compression is performed; every selected event is individually dispatched to the expose procedure with a *region* argument of NULL.

XtExposeCompressSeries

Each series of exposure events is coalesced into a single event, which is dispatched when an exposure event with count equal to zero is reached.

XtExposeCompressMultiple

Consecutive series of exposure events are coalesced into a single event, which is dispatched when an exposure event with count equal to zero is reached and either the event queue is empty or the next event is not an exposure event for the same widget.

XtExposeCompressMaximal

All expose series currently in the queue for the widget are coalesced into a single event without regard to intervening non-exposure events. If a partial series is in the end of the queue, the Intrinsics will block until the end of the series is received.

The optional flags have the following meanings:

XtExposeGraphicsExpose

Specifies that GraphicsExpose events are also to be dispatched to the expose procedure. GraphicsExpose events will be compressed, if specified, in the same manner as Expose events.

XtExposeGraphicsExposeMerged

Specifies in the case of XtExposeCompressMultiple and XtExposeCompress-Maximal that a series of GraphicsExpose and Expose events are to be compressed together, with the final event type determining the type of the event passed to the expose procedure. If this flag is not set, then only series of the same event type as the event at the head of the queue are coalesced. This flag also implies XtExposeGraphics-Expose.

XtExposeNoExpose

Specifies that NoExpose events are also to be dispatched to the expose procedure. No-Expose events are never coalesced with other exposure events or with each other.

Some widgets use substantial computing resources to display data. However, this effort is wasted if the widget is not actually visible on the screen (e.g., when the widget is obscured by another application or is iconified). The visible field in the Core widget instance structure provides the widget with a hint that it need not display data. If any part of the widget is visible, the visible field is guaranteed to be True by the time an Expose event is processed; if the widget is not visible, this field is usually False.

Widgets can either use or ignore the visible hint. If they ignore it, the visible_inter-est field in their widget class record should be set to False. In this case, the visible field is initialized to True and never changes. If visible_interest is True, however, the event manager asks for VisibilityNotify events for the widget and updates the visi-ble field accordingly.

Structures

`Region` is an opaque type defined by Xlib.

See Also

Core(3).

Name

geometry_manager – Composite class method called when a child requests a new geometry.

Synopsis

```
typedef XtGeometryResult (*XtGeometryHandler)(Widget, XtWidgetGeometry *,
        XtWidgetGeometry *);
    Widget w;
    XtWidgetGeometry *request;
    XtWidgetGeometry *geometry_return;
```

Inputs

w   Specifies the child widget making the request.

request   Specifies the requested geometry.

Outputs

geometry_return
     Specifies the reply geometry.

Returns

The parent's reply: XtGeometryYes, XtGeometryNo, XtGeometryAlmost, or Xt-GeometryDone.

Description

The geometry_manager() method is registered on the geometry_manager() Composite class part field, and is called when a child widget requests a new geometry or size with Xt-MakeGeometryRequest() or XtMakeResizeRequest(). The geometry_manager field must respond to the request by approving it, rejecting it, or proposing a compromise.

The geometry_manager() method should examine the contents of the *request* structure (see the "Structures" section below) and determine if it can grant the request. request->request_mode contains flags which specify which of the remaining fields of the structure the child cares about.

If the widget can satisfy all the changes requested, it should return XtGeometryYes. If the XtCWQueryOnly flag is not specified, then it should update the specified widget's x, y, width, height, and border_width fields appropriately before it returns. The Intrinsics will take these new values and actually call XtConfigureWidget() to change the widget's window as appropriate. Some composite widgets may find it more convenient to call their internal layout procedure (if XtCWQueryOnly is not specified) from their geometry_manager() method and actually configure the child themselves. In this case, they should return XtGeometryDone instead of XtGeometryYes. See the warning about this approach, however, in the "Background" section below. If the geometry_manager() method returns Xt-GeometryYes or XtGeometryDone, it does not need to return any values in the *geometry_return* argument.

If the geometry_manager() cannot grant the request (because it asks for a position change when only size changes are allowed, for example) it can return XtGeometryNo and the child will remain at its current size. It may also return XtGeometryNo if the requested geometry is identical to the current geometry. When it returns `XtGeometryNo`, it does not need to return any values in the `geometry_return` argument.

If the `geometry_manager()` cannot satisfy the request exactly, but can come close (for example, if it can change the height but not the width, or can make the height larger but not as large as requested) it can return `XtGeometryAlmost`, and set the compromise geometry in `geometry_return`. By returning `XtGeometryAlmost`, it is guaranteeing that it will return `XtGeometryYes` and make the change if the child requests the compromise geometry immediately.

The `geometry_manager()` method is not chained. If a class does not define its own `geometry_manager()` method, it can use `XtInheritGeometryManager` to inherit the method from its superclass. The `geometry_manager` field of a widget should not be NULL unless the widget class is sure that none of its children will ever issue geometry requests.

See the "Background" section below for full details on this process. See `XtMakeGeometry-Request`(1) for the child widget's perspective on geometry negotiation.

Usage

A child will usually initiate a geometry request in response to a change in one of its resources. When a Label widget gets a new string, for example, it may need to grow to accommodate that label. If its parent refuses to grant the resize request, the label may be truncated. Note that the `geometry_manager()` method is not involved in the geometry negotiations that percolate down from above when a window is resized or when a widget is first managed.

In order to determine whether it can grant a geometry request, some widgets will have to make a geometry request of their own to their parent, and the request may percolate up the chain. With `XtCWQueryOnly` requests and `XtGeometryAlmost` replies, the geometry negotiation process can become quite complicated. In practice, however, most widgets do not perform geometry management nearly so sophisticated (and confusing) as the mechanism allows.

Some composite widgets will have a resource that controls whether they will allow any child to resize itself. If this resource disallows geometry changes, the geometry manager will always return `XtGeometryNo`. Constraint widgets can use constraint resources to provide this functionality on a child-by-child basis. Some widgets (the Xaw Label, for example) have a resource that controls whether they will ever make a resize request to their parent. All these mechanisms simplify the task of the geometry manager procedure.

Some composite widgets will have a liberal policy towards geometry requests. The Xaw Tree widget, for example, will allow any child's resize request without actually testing whether it will have to become larger and whether its parent will allow that. If the child's resize request causes the Tree to request a resize, and the Tree is not allowed to resize, then some of the children of the Tree will probably not be displayed correctly. The philosophy here is that the application developer can take whatever steps are required to ensure that this situation never arises.

The best approach to geometry management is probably to make do with the simplest `geometry_manager()` method possible. The geometry management mechanism provided by the Intrinsics is so general (and so poorly understood) that there are various incompatible styles of geometry management that are supported. A geometry manager can be almost as complicated as you choose to make it, but most of the sophisticated situations it is designed to handle will rarely occur in practice. Keep in mind that many children widgets will not respond in any sophisticated way to XtGeometryAlmost replies, and that the grandparent widget may also not be sophisticated enough to provide useful return values to a complex geometry manager.

Example

The procedure below is the geometry_manager() method Xaw Tree widget. It is a permissive geometry manager which will allow resize requests, but never position requests. It never returns XtGeometryAlmost. This method may be a little too restrictive: if a programmer requests a size and position change for a child in a single call to XtSetValues(), XtSetValues() will call XtMakeGeometryRequest() for the child, but the Tree widget will deny the size change request because it is accompanied by the position change request.

The geometry manager for the Xaw Form widget is not shown here, but it is worth looking at. It checks a constraint resource for each child to determine if it is resizable. It also disallows position requests and never returns XtGeometryAlmost.

The geometry manager for the Xaw Paned widget may also be worth some study. It is a more sophisticated manager that does return XtGeometryAlmost sometimes. This is a more complex method because the Paned widget constrains its children's widths to all be the same size.

```
/* ARGSUSED */
static XtGeometryResult GeometryManager (w, request, reply)
    Widget w;
    XtWidgetGeometry *request;
    XtWidgetGeometry *reply;
{
    TreeWidget tw = (TreeWidget) w->core.parent;

    /*
     * No position changes allowed!.
     */
    if ((request->request_mode & CWX && request->x!=w->core.x)
        ||(request->request_mode & CWY && request->y!=w->core.y))
      return (XtGeometryNo);

    /*
     * Allow all resize requests.
     */
    if (request->request_mode & CWWidth)
      w->core.width = request->width;
    if (request->request_mode & CWHeight)
      w->core.height = request->height;
    if (request->request_mode & CWBorderWidth)
      w->core.border_width = request->border_width;

    if (tw->tree.auto_reconfigure) layout_tree (tw, FALSE);
    return (XtGeometryYes);
}
```

Background

A bit set to zero in the *request* request_mode field means that the child widget does not care about the value of the corresponding field. Then, the geometry manager can change it as it wishes. A bit set to 1 means that the child wants that geometry element changed to the value in the corresponding field.

If the geometry manager can satisfy all changes requested, and if XtCWQueryOnly is not specified, it updates the widget's x, y, width, height, and border_width values appropriately. Then, it returns XtGeometryYes, and the value of the *geometry_return* argument is undefined. The widget's window is moved and resized automatically by XtMake-GeometryRequest().

Homogeneous Composite widgets often find it convenient to treat the widget making the request the same as any other widget, possibly reconfiguring it using XtConfigure-Widget() or XtResizeWidget() as part of its layout process, unless XtCWQueryOnly is specified. If it does this, it should return XtGeometryDone to inform XtMake-GeometryRequest() that it does not need to do the configuration itself.

To remain compatible with layout techniques used in older widgets (before XtGeometry-Done was added to the Intrinsics), a geometry manager should avoid using XtResize-Widget() or XtConfigureWidget() on the child making the request because the layout process of the child may be in an intermediate state in which it is not prepared to handle a call to its resize procedure. A self-contained widget set may choose this alternative geometry management scheme, however, provided that it clearly warns widget developers of the compatibility consequences.

Although XtMakeGeometryRequest() resizes the widget's window (if the geometry manager returns XtGeometryYes), it does not call the widget class's resize procedure. The requesting widget must perform whatever resizing calculations are needed explicitly.

If the geometry manager chooses to disallow the request, the widget cannot change its geometry. The value of the *geometry_return* argument is undefined, and the geometry manager returns XtGeometryNo.

Sometimes the geometry manager cannot satisfy the request exactly, but it may be able to satisfy a similar request. That is, it could satisfy only a subset of the requests (for example, size but not position) or a lesser request (for example, it cannot make the child as big as the request but it can make the child bigger than its current size). In such cases, the geometry manager fills in *geometry_return* with the actual changes it is willing to make, including an appropriate mask, and returns XtGeometryAlmost.

If a bit in geometry_return->request_mode is 0, the geometry manager does not change the corresponding value if the *geometry_return* argument is used immediately in a new request. If a bit is 1, the geometry manager does change that element to the corresponding value in *geometry_return*. More bits may be set in *geometry_return*->request_mode than in the original request if the geometry manager intends to change other fields should the child accept the compromise.

When `XtGeometryAlmost` is returned, the widget must decide if the compromise suggested in *geometry_return* is acceptable. If it is, the widget must not change its geometry directly; rather, it must make another call to `XtMakeGeometryRequest()`.

If the next geometry request from this child uses the *geometry_return* box filled in by an `XtGeometryAlmost` return, and if there have been no intervening geometry requests on either its parent or any of its other children, the geometry manager must grant the request, if possible. That is, if the child asks immediately with the returned geometry, it should get an answer of `XtGeometryYes`. However, the user's window manager may affect the final outcome.

To return an `XtGeometryYes`, the geometry manager frequently rearranges the position of other managed children by calling `XtMoveWidget()`. However, a few geometry managers may sometimes change the size of other managed children by calling `XtResizeWidget()` or `XtConfigureWidget()`. If `XtCWQueryOnly` is specified, the geometry manager must return how it would react to this geometry request without actually moving or resizing any widgets.

Geometry managers must not assume that the *request* and *geometry_return* arguments point to independent storage. The caller is permitted to use the same field for both, and the geometry manager must allocate its own temporary storage, if necessary.

Sometimes a geometry manager cannot respond to a geometry request from a child without first making a geometry request to the widget's own parent (the original requestor's grandparent). If the request to the grandparent would allow the parent to satisfy the original request, the geometry manager can make the intermediate geometry request as if it were the originator. On the other hand, if the geometry manager already has determined that the original request cannot be completely satisfied (for example, if it always denies position changes), it needs to tell the grandparent to respond to the intermediate request without actually changing the geometry because it does not know if the child will accept the compromise. To accomplish this, the geometry manager uses `XtCWQueryOnly` in the intermediate request.

When `XtCWQueryOnly` is used, the geometry manager needs to cache enough information to exactly reconstruct the intermediate request. If the grandparent's response to the intermediate query was `XtGeometryAlmost`, the geometry manager needs to cache the entire reply geometry in the event the child accepts the parent's compromise.

If the grandparent's response was `XtGeometryAlmost`, it may also be necessary to cache the entire reply geometry from the grandparent when `XtCWQueryOnly` is not used. If the geometry manager is still able to satisfy the original request, it may immediately accept the grandparent's compromise and then act on the child's request. If the grandparent's compromise geometry is insufficient to allow the child's request and if the geometry manager is willing to offer a different compromise to the child, the grandparent's compromise should not be accepted until the child has accepted the new compromise.

Note that a compromise geometry returned with `XtGeometryAlmost` is guaranteed only for the next call to the same widget; therefore, a cache of size 1 is sufficient.

Structures

The return codes from geometry managers are:

```
typedef enum _XtGeometryResult {
    XtGeometryYes,    /* Request accepted */
    XtGeometryNo,     /* Request denied */
    XtGeometryAlmost,/* Request denied but willing to take reply */
    XtGeometryDone    /* Request accepted and performed */
} XtGeometryResult;
```

The XtWidgetGeometry structure is similar to but not identical to the corresponding Xlib structure:

```
typedef unsigned long XtGeometryMask;

typedef struct {
    XtGeometryMask request_mode;
    Position x, y;
    Dimension width, height;
    Dimension border_width;
    Widget sibling;
    int stack_mode;
} XtWidgetGeometry;
```

XtMakeGeometryRequest(), like the Xlib XConfigureWindow() function, uses request_mode to determine which fields in the XtWidgetGeometry structure you want to specify. The request_mode definitions are from <*X11/X.h*>:

```
#define   CWX               (1<<0)
#define   CWY               (1<<1)
#define   CWWidth           (1<<2)
#define   CWHeight          (1<<3)
#define   CWBorderWidth     (1<<4)
#define   CWSibling         (1<<5)
#define   CWStackMode       (1<<6)
```

The Xt Intrinsics also support the following value:

```
#define XtCWQueryOnly    (1<<7)
```

XtCWQueryOnly indicates that the corresponding geometry request is only a query as to what would happen if this geometry request were made and that no widgets should actually be changed.

The stack_mode definitions are from <*X11/X.h*>:

```
#define   Above             0
#define   Below             1
#define   TopIf             2
#define   BottomIf          3
#define   Opposite          4
```

The Intrinsics also support the following value:

```
#define   XtSMDontChange    5
```

XtSMDontChange indicates that the widget wants its current stacking order preserved. For precise definitions of Above, Below, TopIf, BottomIf, and Opposite, see the reference page for XConfigureWindow() in Volume Two, *Xlib Reference Manual*.

See Also

XtConfigureWidget(1), *XtMakeResizeRequest*(1), *XtMoveWidget*(1), *XtResizeWidget*(1), *Composite*(3), *Constraint*(3).

Name

get_values_hook – Object class method for obtaining values of resources that do not appear in the resource list.

Synopsis

```
typedef void (*XtArgsProc)(Widget, ArgList, Cardinal *);
    Widget w;
    ArgList args;
    Cardinal *num_args;
```

Inputs

w	Specifies the widget or object that is having its resources queried.
args	Specifies the argument list that was passed to XtGetValues().
num_args	Specifies the number of arguments in the argument list.

Description

The get_values_hook() method is registered on the get_values_hook() field of the Object, RectObj, or Core class part structure, and is called by XtGetValues() to give the widget a chance to supply the value of any resources that do not appear in the widget's resource list (by calling XtGetSubvalues() on a subpart, for example) or to modify any of the returned values.

The get_values_hook() method is chained in superclass-to-subclass order, and cannot be inherited. Classes that do not need a get_value_hook() method should specify NULL in the get_values_hook() field of their class structure.

See XtGetValues(1) for more information on when this method is invoked.

Usage

If a widget or object has subparts with resources that do not appear in the resource list of the object itself, it can use the get_values_hook() method to call XtGetSubvalues() passing a pointer to the subpart, the subpart resource list, and the args and num_args argument list. Using this technique, the application programmer will be able to query the value of subpart resources as if they were normal widget resources.

Note that since the Object class was added in Release 4, it is often easier to use objects rather than subparts, because objects get more automatic resource handling by the Intrinsics than subparts do. A get_values_hook() procedure is not limited to calling XtGet-Subvalues(); it can call XtGetValues() on a widget or object, as shown in the examples below. When using objects rather than subparts, it is also possible to give the application programmer direct control over creating those objects. If the programmer keeps a pointer to the created object, then she can directly set and query the resource values of the object, and no get_values_hook() is necessary in the parent.

The get_values_hook() method can also be used to modify the resource values in args that would otherwise be returned to the user. A widget that displays a string, for example, might want to return a copy of that string to the programmer rather than the string itself, so that if the programmer modifies the string, the widget will not be affected. Widgets that use the `get_values_hook()` method in this way should be sure to document which resources are copied in this way and must be freed by the user. (None of the Intrinsics widgets nor the Xaw widgets do this.)

Note that the `get_values_hook()` method is not obsolete as are the other hook methods, `initialize_hook()` and `set_values_hook()`.

Example

The two procedures below are the `get_values_hook()` methods of the Xaw Dialog and Xaw Text widget classes. Note that both use `XtGetValues()` to obtain resources of a child widget or object, which they "export" as one of their own resources.

The Dialog method checks the incoming argument list for a resource named `XtNvalue`, and only queries the child for that single resource. The Text method simply passes the entire argument list in `XtGetValues()` calls to two different child objects. This method assumes that the Text widget and its two children objects do not have any resources by the same name, so there is not potential for name conflicts. The Text widget controls the types of its subobjects, so this is a reasonable assumption. Since all objects have an `XtNdestroyCallback` resource, however, if you were to query the value of this resource for the Text widget, you would get the callback list for one of its internal objects instead. (This is not a practical problem because the callback list is in an internal compiled form and should not be queried anyway.)

```
static void
GetValuesHook(w, args, num_args)
Widget w;
ArgList args;
Cardinal * num_args;
{
  Arg a[1];
  String s;
  DialogWidget src = (DialogWidget) w;
  register int i;

  for (i=0; i < *num_args; i++)
    if (streq(args[i].name, XtNvalue)) {
      XtSetArg(a[0], XtNstring, &s);
      XtGetValues(src->dialog.valueW, a, 1);
      *((char **) args[i].value) = s;
    }
}

static void
GetValuesHook(w, args, num_args)
Widget w;
ArgList args;
Cardinal * num_args;
{
  XtGetValues( ((TextWidget) w)->text.source, args, *num_args );
  XtGetValues( ((TextWidget) w)->text.sink, args, *num_args );
}
```

See Also

    XtGetSubvalues(1), *XtGetValues*(1),
    Core(3).

Constraint get_values_hook

Name

Constraint get_values_hook – Constraint class method for obtaining values of constraint resources that do not appear in the Constraint resource list.

Synopsis

```
typedef void (*XtArgsProc)(Widget, ArgList, Cardinal *);
    Widget w;
    ArgList args;
    Cardinal *num_args;
```

Inputs

w   Specifies the widget or object that is having its resources queried.

args   Specifies the argument list that was passed to XtGetValues().

num_args   Specifies the number of arguments in the argument list.

Availability

Release 4 and later.

Description

The Constraint get_values_hook() method is registered on the get_values_hook field of a ConstraintClassExtensionRec with record_type NULLQUARK, which is itself registered on the extension field of the Constraint class part structure. If such an extension exists, then this method is called when XtGetValues() is called for a child of the constraint widget, and gives the constraint widget the opportunity to set values for resources that do not appear in the Constraint resource list, or to modify any of the resource values that are to be returned.

The Constraint get_values_hook() method is chained in superclass-to-subclass order, and cannot be inherited. Classes that do not need a get_value_hook() method can set NULL in the Constraint extension record, or can simply omit the extension record.

See XtGetValues(1) for more information on when this method is invoked.

Usage

The usage of this method is similar to the normal get_values_hook() method: the widget can use XtGetSubvalues() or XtGetValues() to obtain the values of constraint resources that do not appear on its Constraint resource list, so that it can export them as if they did appear on that list. This method can also be used to modify the returned values in any way, by making a copy of string resource values, for example. See get_values_hook(4) for more information.

None of the Intrinsics widgets nor any of the Xaw widgets define a Constraint get_values_hook() method.

See Also

XtGetSubvalues(1), *XtGetValues*(1),
Core(3),
get_values_hook(4).

Name

initialize – Object class method for initializing a widget or object instance structure.

Synopsis

```
typedef void (*XtInitProc)(Widget, Widget, ArgList, Cardinal *);
    Widget request;
    Widget init;
    ArgList args;
    Cardinal *num_args;
```

Inputs

request   Specifies the widget or object instance with resource values set as requested by the argument list, the resource database, and the widget defaults.

init   Specifies the same widget or object with values, both resource and non-resource, as modified by superclass initialize() methods.

args   Specifies the argument list that was passed to XtCreateWidget().

num_args   Specifies the number of entries in the argument list.

Description

The initialize() method is registered on the initialize field of the Object, RectObj, or Core class part structure, and is called by XtCreateWidget() to initialize the instance structure of a newly created widget.

The *init* argument widget becomes the actual widget instance record once all initialize procedures are called; the *request* argument is simply a copy made after resources are fetched for the widget, but before any of the initialize() methods are called. Therefore, the initialize() method should change only the *init* widget, and if the method needs to call any routines that operate on a widget, it should specify *init* as the widget instance. The *request* argument is provided so that an initialize() method can distinguish initialization done by a superclass from resource values requested by a user. In some cases, this may require the method to examine *args*, the actual argument list passed to XtCreate-Widget(). See the "Background" section below for more details.

The args argument allows a widget to initialize the values of subpart resources (by calling XtSetSubvalues()) or any other resources that do not appear on the widget class resource list. A widget that automatically creates child widgets may use args and num_args in a call to XtCreateWidget().

At a minimum, the initialize() method must compute values for Core width and height, if they have not been computed by a superclass. Note that a widget may only directly assign its own width and height within the initialize(), initialize_hook(), set_values(), and set_values_hook() methods.

The *args* and *num_args* arguments were added to this method in Release 4. Prior to Release 4, any initialization that requires these arguments must be done in the initialize_hook() method.

The `initialize()` method is chained in superclass-to-subclass order and it cannot be inherited. If a widget class does not need to perform any initialization, it should specify NULL for the `initialize` field of the class record.

See `XtCreateWidget`(1) for full details on the initialization process for a newly created widget.

Usage

The `initialize()` method usually does the following:

- Allocates space for and copies any resources that are referenced by address. For example, if a widget has a resource that is a `String`, it cannot depend on the characters at that address remaining constant but must dynamically allocate space for the string and copy it to the new space. (Note though, that you should neither allocate space for nor copy callback lists; the Intrinsics handles these specially.)

- Computes values for resources that were unspecified. Most resources will have a useful default value, but others will require special handling if they are unspecified. For example, if `width` and `height` are zero, the widget might compute an appropriate width and height based on its resources, `num_rows` and `num_columns`. A label widget, as another example, might use its resource name if its label string resource is unspecified, and use the width and height of the string if its `width` and `height` fields are left unspecified.

- Computes values for fields that are derived from resources. For example, graphics contexts (GCs) that the widget uses are derived from resources such as `background`, `foreground`, and `font`.

- Checks certain fields for internal consistency. For example, it makes no sense to specify a colormap and a visual together when the colormap was not created with the given visual. A widget may also check some resources for reasonable values: a label widget that only supports single line labels might issue a warning message if given a string to display that contains newline characters.

- Overrides superclass resource default values or values initialized by a superclass. In particular, the size calculations of a superclass are often incorrect for a subclass, and the subclass must modify or recalculate fields declared and computed by its superclass. Note that if the programmer explicitly requested a value for a superclass resource, a subclass shouldn't override that value. The *request* argument can be used to determine whether a value was explicitly requested or simply initialized by the superclass. If a class wants to override the default value of a superclass resource, it may need to check `args` to determine whether the resource was unspecified, or explicitly specified to be the same as the default. See the "Background" section below for more information.

- Uses `args` and `num_args` to initialize the values of any resources that do not appear on the class resource list. These may be subpart resources initialized with `XtSetSubvalues()`, or resources of objects or widgets that are explicitly created by the `initialize()` procedure.

Example

The following procedure is the `initialize()` method, slightly modified from the Xaw Label widget. Note that it makes a copy of its `String` resource, calls procedures to allocate GCs, and sets its initial size if that size is not explicitly set. An `initialize()` method will often call other functions to allocate GCs and other resources, so that these functions can be reused in the `set_values()` method. If the foreground color was changed in `set_values()`, for example, the GC would have to be freed and reallocated.

This procedure explicitly invokes the widget's `resize()` method. Label's resize procedure will pre-compute the location at which the label will be displayed, based on the size of the window, the size of the label, and the setting of the `XtNjustify` resource. This must be done every time the widget changes size, and by calling the `resize()` method, the `initialize()` method avoids having to duplicate these calculations itself.

Note that this procedure (and most other `initialize()` procedures in existence) has named its *init* argument new. "new" is a reserved word in C++, and your programs will be more portable if you avoid using it in your C code.

```
/* ARGSUSED */
static void Initialize(request, new, args, num_args)
 Widget request, new;
 ArgList args;
 Cardinal *num_args;
{
    LabelWidget lw = (LabelWidget) new;

    if (lw->label.label == NULL)
        lw->label.label = XtNewString(lw->core.name);
    else {
        lw->label.label = XtNewString(lw->label.label);
    }

    GetnormalGC(lw);
    GetgrayGC(lw);

    SetTextWidthAndHeight(lw);

    if (lw->core.height == 0)
        lw->core.height = lw->label.label_height + 2*lw->label.internal_height;

    set_bitmap_info (lw);                 /* need core.height */

    if (lw->core.width == 0)              /* need label.lbm_width */
        lw->core.width = (lw->label.label_width + 2 * lw->label.internal_width
                        + LEFT_OFFSET(lw));

    lw->label.label_x = lw->label.label_y = 0;
    (*XtClass(new)->core_class.resize) ((Widget)lw);

} /* Initialize */
```

Background

Sometimes a subclass may want to overwrite values filled in by its superclass. In particular, size calculations of a superclass are often incorrect for a subclass and in this case, the subclass must modify or recalculate fields declared and computed by its superclass.

As an example, a subclass can visually surround its superclass display. In this case, the width and height calculated by the superclass's `initialize()` method are too small and need to be incremented by the size of the surround. The subclass needs to know whether its super-class's size was calculated by the superclass or specified explicitly. All widgets must place themselves into whatever size is explicitly given, but they should compute a reasonable size if no size is requested.

The *request*, *init*, and *args* arguments provide the necessary information for a subclass to determine the difference between a specified resource value and a resource value computed by a superclass. The *request* widget is the widget as originally requested. The *init* widget starts with the values in the request, but it has been updated by all the superclass's `initialize()` methods called so far. If a field differs in the *request* and *init* widgets, then it has been initialized or modified by a superclass. If the field in *request* differs from the default value of that resource, then the user of the widget requested an explicit value for that resource, and the subclass should not modify it. If the value in *request* is the same as the resource default, then the user did not specify a value for that widget, or specified a value that was the same as the default. The `initialize()` method can check *args* to determine if the default value was in fact explicitly requested from an argument list. There is no way to determine, however, if the default value was explicitly requested from a resource file. Probably the best approach to this problem is to specify an unreasonable default value for the resource. A default width and height of zero are a good example. Then if *request* shows the default value, the resource was either unspecified or the user requested an unreasonable value. In either case, the `initialize()` method should set it to some other value (possibly the "real," documented default value of the resource).

In the case above of a subclass that wants to place some sort of border around its superclass, the subclass can see if the width and height in the *request* widget are zero. If so, it may add its border size to the `width` and `height` fields that the superclass set in the *init* widget. If not, it means that the application programmer explicitly requested a size for the widget, and it must make do with that size.

See Also

XtCreateWidget(1),
Core(3).

Constraint initialize

Name

Constraint initialize – Constraint class method to initialize a child object or widget's constraint record.

Synopsis

```
typedef void (*XtInitProc)(Widget, Widget, ArgList, Cardinal *);
    Widget request;
    Widget init;
    ArgList args;
    Cardinal *num_args;
```

Inputs

request   Specifies the newly created child widget or object instance with its constraint record resource values set as requested by the argument list, the resource database, and the constraint defaults.

init   Specifies the same widget or object with its constraint record fields as modified by any superclass Constraint initialize() methods.

args   Specifies the argument list that was passed to XtCreateWidget().

num_args   Specifies the number of entries in the argument list.

Description

The Constraint initialize() method is registered on the initialize field of the Constraint class part structure, and is called by XtCreateWidget() when a child of the constraint widget is created. The Constraint initialize() method performs the same sort of initializations on the constraint record of a widget that the normal (Object, RectObj, or Core) initialize() method performs on the widget instance structure.

The request and *init* arguments specify the child widget that is being created. The constraints field of the *request* widget points to a copy of the constraint record as it was after all of the constraint resources were initialized from the argument list, the resource database, or the resource list defaults. The constraints field of the *init* widget points to the actual constraints record of the widget, and has been further initialized by the Constraint initialize() method of any Constraint superclasses of the parent widget. All modifications should be made to the *init* constraints record; the *request* argument exists so that the widget class can determine which field of the constraints record have been modified by superclass Constraint initialize() methods.

The Constraint initialize() method is chained in superclass-to-subclass order, and cannot be inherited. If nothing in the constraint structure needs initialization, the Constraint class part initialize field should be NULL.

The *args* and *num_args* arguments were added to this method in Release 4.

See initialize(4) for an explanation of the things that an initialize procedure should do. See XtCreateWidget(1) for full details of the widget creation process.

Example

The following procedure is the Constraint `initialize()` method, slightly modified, of the Athena Form widget class. Note how it obtains the constraint record and the parent form widget from the supplied child widget. Note also that it provides "dynamic defaults" for two of its constraint resources: if dx or dy is equal to some default value (i.e., if it was not explicitly specified), then it will be replaced by the value of the `XtNdefaultSpacing` resource from the Form widget itself.

Note that this procedure (and most other `initialize()` procedures in existence) has named its *init* argument new. "new" is a reserved word in C++, and your programs will be more portable if you avoid using it in your C code.

```
/* ARGSUSED */
static void ConstraintInitialize(request, new, args, num_args)
    Widget request, new;
    ArgList args;
    Cardinal *num_args;
{
    FormConstraints form = (FormConstraints)new->core.constraints;
    FormWidget fw = (FormWidget)new->core.parent;

    form->form.virtual_width = (int) new->core.width;
    form->form.virtual_height = (int) new->core.height;

    if (form->form.dx == default_value)
        form->form.dx = fw->form.default_spacing;

    if (form->form.dy == default_value)
        form->form.dy = fw->form.default_spacing;

    form->form.deferred_resize = False;
}
```

See Also

XtCreateWidget(1),
Constraint(3), *Core*(3),
Constraint *destroy*(4), *initialize*(4), Constraint *set_values*(4).

initialize_hook

Name

initialize_hook – obsolete Object method for initializing subpart data.

Synopsis

```
typedef void (*XtArgsProc)(Widget, ArgList, Cardinal *);
    Widget w;
    ArgList args;
    Cardinal *num_args;
```

Inputs

w   Specifies the newly created widget.

args   Specifies the argument list that was passed to XtCreateWidget().

num_args   Specifies the number of arguments in the argument list.

Availability

Obsolete in Release 4 and later.

Description

The initialize_hook() method is registered on the initialize_hook field of the Object, RectObj, or Core class part structure, and is called by XtCreateWidget().

As of Release 4, the initialize_hook() method is obsolete because all of its arguments are now passed to the initialize() method. Its purpose had been to allow the widget class to use the argument list to initialize fields that did not appear in the class resource list, by calling XtSetSubvalues(), for example.

The initialize_hook() method is chained in superclass-to-subclass order and is called for compatibility with older widgets. It cannot be inherited and new widgets should set their initialize_hook field to NULL. See XtCreateWidget(1) for details on when it is called. See initialize(4) for more information on initializing subparts or other fields that do not appear in the class resource list.

See Also

XtCreateWidget(1), *XtSetSubvalues*(1),
Core(3),
get_values_hook(4), *set_values_hook*(4), *initialize*(4).

Name

insert_child – Composite class method called when a child is created.

Synopsis

```
typedef void (*XtWidgetProc)(Widget);
    Widget w;
```

Inputs

w   Specifies the widget which has been created and is to be added to its parent's `children` array.

Description

The `insert_child()` method is registered on the `insert_child` field of the Composite class part structure. It is called by `XtCreateWidget()` to insert a newly created child into its parent's `children` array.

Note that the argument to the `insert_child()` method is the child widget, not the composite widget that defines the method. This method must add the specified child to its parent's `children` array, and do anything else that the particular class uses to keep track of its children.

The `insert_child()` method is not chained. If a class does not define an `insert_child()` method, it should inherit the method from its superclass by specifying `XtInheritInsertChild` in the `insert_child` field of its Composite class part structure. This field should never be NULL.

Usage

Most composite widgets inherit this method from their superclass. Some composite widget classes define their own `insert_child()` method so that they can order their children in some convenient way, create companion widgets for each child, or limit the number or class of their children. These classes commonly "envelop" their superclass's method by providing a procedure that does class-specific processing and explicitly invokes the superclass method. This technique allows a kind of non-automatic inheritance, and is shown in the example below.

Note that the Composite `insert_child()` and `delete_child()` methods exploit internal common data structures, so you should inherit or envelop both or neither. If you do not inherit or envelop these methods, then your methods are responsible for adding and removing the child widget from the `children` array. The "Background" section below explains what the `insert_child()` method of the Composite class itself does.

Example

The following procedure is the `insert_child()` method of the Xaw Paned widget class. Note that it first calls the `insert_child()` method of its superclass, and then creates a Grip widget for the new child. (Unless the child has constraint resource `XtNshowGrip` False.) See `delete_child`(4) for the corresponding `delete_child()` method.

```
static void InsertChild(w)
register Widget w;
```

```
{
    Pane pane = PaneInfo(w);

    /* insert the child widget in the composite children list with the */
    /* superclass insert_child routine.                                */
    (*SuperClass->composite_class.insert_child)(w);

    if (!IsPane(w)) return;

    /* ||| Panes will be added in the order they are created, temporarily */

    if ( pane->show_grip == TRUE ) {
        CreateGrip(w);
        if (pane->min == PANED_GRIP_SIZE)
            pane->min = PaneSize(pane->grip, IsVert((PanedWidget) XtParent(w)));
    }
    else {
        if (pane->min == PANED_GRIP_SIZE)
            pane->min = 1;
        pane->grip = NULL;
    }

    pane->size = 0;
    pane->paned_adjusted_me = FALSE;

} /* InsertChild */
```

In this example, `SuperClass` is a symbolic name for the superclass of the Paned widget class. Note that this method does *not* determine the superclass as follows:

```
XtSuperclass(XtParent(w))
```

The parent of *w* may be a subclass of `Paned`, and therefore its superclass pointer will not always be the class whose method should be invoked.

Background

The `insert_child()` method of the Composite class itself is commonly inherited by sub-classes or explicitly invoked by them. It performs the following:

- Calls the `XtOrderProc` registered on the `XtNinsertPosition` resource of the composite widget to determine the position in the children array at which the child should be inserted. If there is no procedure specified for this resource, it inserts the child at the end of the array.

- Inserts the child at the appropriate position in the array, moving other children if necessary. If there is not enough room to insert a new child in the children array (that is, num_children = num_slots), it reallocates the array and updates num_slots.

- Increments num_children.

If a composite widget class does not have an `CompositeClassExtension` record or if the `accepts_objects` field of that record is `False`, the Intrinsics will not allow non-widget children of that widget. Therefore, the `insert_child()` method of a widget class that does not accept object children is guaranteed never to be passed a non-widget child.

See Also

XtCreateWidget(1),
Composite(3), *Constraint*(3),
delete_child(4).

query_geometry

Name

query_geometry – RectObj method called to request a widget's preferred size and position.

Synopsis

```
typedef XtGeometryResult (*XtGeometryHandler)(Widget, XtWidgetGeometry *,
        XtWidgetGeometry *);
    Widget w;
    XtWidgetGeometry *request;
    XtWidgetGeometry *preferred_return
```

Inputs

w   Specifies the widget or object that is being queried.

request   Specifies the geometry changes that the parent plans to make.

Outputs

preferred_return

Returns the widget or object's preferred geometry.

Returns

The widget's reply: XtGeometryYes, XtGeometryNo, or XtGeometryAlmost.

Description

The query_geometry() method is registered on the query_geometry field of the Rect-Obj or Core class part structure. It is invoked by XtQueryGeometry() when the widget's parent wants to determine the widget's preferred geometry. The parent may call this function when it want to know the widget's ideal size in the absence of any constraints, or it may call it before changing some of the widget's geometry fields in order to find out the widget's preference for the other fields.

The *request* argument indicates the geometry changes the parent plans to make. *request*->request_mode contains flags that indicate which of the remaining fields are significant. (See the "Structures" section below for a description of the structure and a list of the flags.) The query_geometry() method should examine this proposed change, set its preferred geometry in *preferred_return*, setting *preferred_return*-> request_mode to indicate which geometry field it cares about, and return one of the following values:

XtGeometryYes

The widget agrees to the change; the parent should make exactly the change it proposed. When query_geometry() returns this value, the contents of *preferred_return* should be identical to the contents of *request*, for each flag bit set in *preferred_return*. This means that the parent's proposed geometry is exactly the widget's preferred geometry (or that the widget has a flexible notion of "preferred" and feels that the proposal is good enough).

XtGeometryNo

This return value means that the widget's current geometry *is* its preferred geometry, and it would rather not be changed. When this value is returned, query_geometry() doesn't have to fill in *preferred_return*, because XtQueryGeometry() will fill in any unspecified fields with their current values, which in this case are the preferred values. It is of course up to the parent widget whether or not to honor this request not to change.

XtGeometryAlmost

This return value means that the widget would like a geometry change, but that its preferred geometry differs from the proposed geometry. query_geometry() should return this value if at least one bit is set in the return flags that was not set in the proposed flags, or if any of the returned values (that have their flag bit set) differ from the corresponding proposed values.

Note that query_geometry() need only return its preferences for the fields it cares about (generally width and height). XtQueryGeometry() will fill in any unspecified fields with the widget's current value. Also, query_geometry() can ignore flag bits set in *request* for fields that it does not care about. If a widget doesn't care about its location, for example, and its parent proposes to change its location without changing its size, it should still place its preferred size in *preferred_return*, and follow the rules above to determine which value to return.

It is up to the parent widget to decide what to do with the return value from this function (which it gets from XtQueryGeometry()). Some parents will respect the widget's requests, but many will ignore them. Generally, if a parent sets a flag in request, it will change that field, regardless of the widget's return value. The power of the query_geometry() method lies in the fact that the widget can propose additional geometry changes with the Xt-GeometryAlmost return value. A parent that constrains the width of a widget may call Xt-QueryGeometry() to determine how high the widget would like to be, given its new width. A label widget that supported word wrapping, for example, might request a larger height if its width were made smaller. A cooperating parent would make its change to the width, but also change the height as the child requested.

The query_geometry() method is not chained. Widget classes that do not define a query_geometry() method can inherit the method from their superclass by specifying Xt-InheritQueryGeometry on the query_geometry field of the RectObj or Core class part structure. Widgets that have no preference about their geometry can set this field to NULL.

See the "Background" section below for more details on the query_geometry() method. See XtQueryGeometry(1) for the parent widget's perspective on this geometry negotiation process.

Usage

Like the geometry_manager() method, the query_geometry() method can be confusing, and can become almost arbitrarily complex. The query_geometry() mechanism allows much more flexibility than most widgets need and more than most parents support. The fact that there are three possible return values which do not have very clearly defined meanings (at least not well defined in practice) to the child or to the parent makes the situation all the more confusing. There are some factors that can simplify the query_geometry() method, however.

Most widgets do not care about anything other than their width and height, and their `query_geometry()` methods never need to return preferred information about position, border width, or stacking order. Most parents won't bother to query these fields anyway.

Most widgets treat their width and height independently, and do not try to increase their height if their width shrinks, for example. These widgets can use a simple method like the example shown below.

Some widgets do not even have a preference about their size. A label widget's preferred size is whatever it takes to display the string or pixmap, and a composite widget's preferred size may be whatever it takes to lay out its children. A scrollbar, however, can make do with whatever size it is given, and can simply inherit the `query_geometry()` method of its parent.

Example

The following procedure is the `query_geometry()` method from the Xaw Label widget. Most of the Xaw widgets that have a `query_geometry()` method use almost identical procedures. The first thing it does is set its preferred width and height, which are the width and height of the label plus internal margins. Then it checks to see if the parent's requested geometry had both width and height flags set (note that it masks out any other bits for fields that it does not care about), and if so, and if the parent's request matches the preferred size, it returns `XtGeometryYes`. Otherwise, if the preferred size matches the widget's current size, it returns `XtGeometryNo`, and otherwise it returns `XtGeometryAlmost`.

Note that this procedure does not attempt to do anything special if only its width or only its height are constrained. The `query_geometry()` method of the Xaw Box widget does handle this case, and may be worth study if you will be writing a similar widget.

```
static XtGeometryResult QueryGeometry(w, intended, preferred)
    Widget w;
    XtWidgetGeometry *intended, *preferred;
{
    register LabelWidget lw = (LabelWidget)w;

    preferred->request_mode = CWWidth | CWHeight;
    preferred->width = (lw->label.label_width + 2 * lw->label.internal_width +
                    LEFT_OFFSET(lw));
    preferred->height = lw->label.label_height + 2*lw->label.internal_height;

    if (  ((intended->request_mode & (CWWidth | CWHeight))
               == (CWWidth | CWHeight)) &&
          intended->width == preferred->width &&
          intended->height == preferred->height)
        return XtGeometryYes;
    else if (preferred->width == w->core.width &&
            preferred->height == w->core.height)
        return XtGeometryNo;
    else
        return XtGeometryAlmost;
}
```

Background

The `query_geometry()` method is expected to examine the bits set in *request*->request_mode, evaluate the proposed geometry for the widget, and store the result in *preferred_return* (setting the bits in preferred_return->request_mode corresponding to those geometry fields that it cares about). If the proposed geometry change is acceptable without modification, the `query_geometry()` method should return XtGeometryYes. If at least one field in *preferred_return* is different from the corresponding field in *request* or if a bit was set in *preferred_return* that was not set in *request*, the `query_geometry()` method should return XtGeometryAlmost. If the preferred geometry is identical to the current geometry, the `query_geometry()` method should return XtGeometryNo.

Note that the `query_geometry()` method may assume that no XtMakeResize-Request() or XtMakeGeometryRequest() is in progress for the specified widget; that is, it is not required to construct a reply consistent with the requested geometry if such a request were actually outstanding.

After calling the `query_geometry()` method or if the `query_geometry()` field is NULL, XtQueryGeometry() examines all the unset bits in *preferred_return*->request_mode and sets the corresponding fields in *preferred_return* to the current values from the widget instance. If CWStackMode is not set, the stack_mode field is set to XtSMDontChange. XtQueryGeometry() returns either the value returned by the `query_geometry()` method or XtGeometryYes if the `query_geometry()` field is NULL.

Therefore, the caller can interpret a return of XtGeometryYes as not needing to evaluate the contents of the reply and, more importantly, not needing to modify its layout plans. A return of XtGeometryAlmost means either that both the parent and the child expressed interest in at least one common field and the child's preference does not match the parent's intentions or that the child expressed interest in a field that the parent might need to consider. A return value of XtGeometryNo means that both the parent and the child expressed interest in a field and that the child suggests that the field's current value is its preferred value. In addition, whether or not the caller ignores the return value or the reply mask, it is guaranteed that the *preferred_return* structure contains complete geometry information for the child.

Parents are expected to call XtQueryGeometry() in their layout routine and wherever other information is significant after change_managed() has been called. The change_managed() method may assume that the child's current geometry is its preferred geometry. Thus, the child is still responsible for storing values into its own geometry during its initialize() method.

Structures

The possible return values of a `query_geometry()` method are defined as follows:

```
typedef enum {
    XtGeometryYes,    /* Request accepted */
    XtGeometryNo,     /* Request rejected */
    XtGeometryAlmost, /* Compromise proposed */
```

```
    XtGeometryDone    /* never returned by query_geometry */
} XtGeometryResult;
```

The XtWidgetGeometry structure is similar to but not identical to the corresponding Xlib structure:

```
typedef unsigned long XtGeometryMask;
```

```
typedef struct {
    XtGeometryMask request_mode;
    Position x, y;
    Dimension width, height;
    Dimension border_width;
    Widget sibling;
    int stack_mode;
} XtWidgetGeometry;
```

XtQueryGeometry(), like the Xlib XConfigureWindow() function, uses request_mode to determine which fields in the XtWidgetGeometry structure the parent and the child have set. The request_mode definitions are from *<X11/X.h>*:

```
#define    CWX                  (1<<0)
#define    CWY                  (1<<1)
#define    CWWidth              (1<<2)
#define    CWHeight             (1<<3)
#define    CWBorderWidth        (1<<4)
#define    CWSibling            (1<<5)
#define    CWStackMode          (1<<6)
```

The stack_mode definitions are from *<X11/X.h>*:

```
#define    Above                0
#define    Below                1
#define    TopIf                2
#define    BottomIf             3
#define    Opposite             4
```

The Intrinsics also support the following value:

```
#define    XtSMDontChange    5
```

For precise definitions of Above, Below, TopIf, BottomIf, and Opposite, see the reference page for XConfigureWindow() in Volume Two, *Xlib Reference Manual*. Xt-SMDontChange indicates that the widget wants its current stacking order preserved.

See Also

XtQueryGeometry(1),
Core(3).

Name

realize – Core class method to create a widget's window.

Synopsis

```
typedef void (*XtRealizeProc)(Widget, XtValueMask *,
        XSetWindowAttributes *);
    Widget w;
    XtValueMask *value_mask;
    XSetWindowAttributes *attributes;
```

Inputs

w   Specifies the widget that is to have its window created.

value_mask   Specifies which fields in the *attributes* structure are set.

attributes   Specifies the window attributes derived from the widget instance structure.

Description

The realize() method is registered on the realize field of the Core class part structure. It is called when a widget is realized (generally because an ancestor was realized with Xt-RealizeWidget()) and is responsible for creating an X window for the widget.

The *attributes* argument points to an XSetWindowAttributes structure that has been initialized by the Intrinsics, and *value_mask* points to a set of flags that specify which fields have been initialized. The XSetWindowAttributes structure is shown in the "Structures" section below. The fields are initialized as follows:

- background_pixmap is set to the value of the widget's XtNbackgroundPixmap resource, or if this resource is unspecified, the background_pixel field is set to the value of the widget's XtNbackground resource.

- border_pixmap is set to the value of the widget's XtNborderPixmap resource, or, if this resource is unspecified, the border_pixel field is set to the value of the Xt-NborderColor resource.

- colormap is set to the value of the XtNcolormap resource of the widget.

- event_mask is set based on the event handlers registered for the widget, the translations that are specified for the widget, whether the widget has an expose() method, and whether the widget's visible_interest field is True.

- bit_gravity is set to NorthWestGravity if the widget does not have an expose() method.

The realize() method may set any other field in *attributes* as appropriate for the particular widget class (and its superclasses), and then should create the widget's window by calling XtCreateWindow(). This is a convenient procedure that automatically uses the correct parent, position, size, etc., from the widget's instance record, and sets the created window in the widget's window field. See XtCreateWindow(1) for more information.

The realize() method is not chained. A widget class that does not need any special window attributes set should inherit the realize method from its superclass by specifying

`XtInheritRealize` on the `realize` field of the Core class part structure. No widget should have a `NULL realize()` method.

Usage

Note that the *value_mask* argument to this method is a pointer to the value mask, not the value mask itself. This is unusual, and you should be careful to correctly de-reference this argument when using it.

The `realize()` method defined for Core calls `XtCreateWindow()` with the passed *value_mask* and *attributes* and with the *windowClass* and *visual* arguments set to `CopyFromParent`. This is sufficient for most widgets; both Composite and Constraint inherit it, and most new widget subclasses can do the same.

A common reason to write a custom `realize()` method is to set the `bit_gravity` window attribute to something other than its default value. A label widget might set bit gravity depending on the justification of the label, for example, and thereby avoid some expose events when the widget was resized. If a widget uses the Shape extension to obtain a non-rectangular window, the window should be re-shaped in the `realize()` method. (The Xaw Command widget does this.) A composite widget can control the stacking order of its children by explicitly realizing them in the desired order from within its own `realize()` method. Also, a non-composite widget that creates its own private children widgets must explicitly realize them from the `realize()` method.

Custom `realize()` methods usually explicitly call the `realize()` method of their superclass. The superclass's method may have inherited the Core `realize()` method and create the window, or it may set its own fields in *attributes* and invoke the method of *its* superclass. Eventually a method will be called that actually creates the window and returns. "Enveloping" the `realize()` method in this way creates a kind of subclass-to-superclass chaining. When you envelop a method of your superclass, use the superclass pointer directly, do *not* use `XtSuperclass()` to obtain the superclass of the supplied widget instance. If *B* is a subclass of *A*, for example, then the widget passed to *B*'s `realize()` method may be of class *B*, or may be of some subclass *C* of *B*. If you call `XtSuperclass()` on this widget, you will get class *B* rather than class *A*, and the `realize()` method will recursively call itself and loop until it runs out of stack space and crashes.

Example

The following procedures are the `realize()` methods from the X11R5 Xaw Command and Panner widgets. The first simply calls its superclass's method to create the window, and then uses the Shape extension to change the window's shape. The second procedure sets a background pixmap for the window, even if the core `XtNbackgroundPixmap` resource is unspecified, and then calls its superclass's method.

Note that the first procedure finds its superclass's method by going through its own class pointer directly. The second procedure envelops the superclass method incorrectly, using the instance pointer. A subclass of this widget that inherited this method would crash when realized, as described in the section above.

```
static void Realize(w, valueMask, attributes)
    Widget w;
    Mask *valueMask;
    XSetWindowAttributes *attributes;
{
    (*commandWidgetClass->core_class.superclass->core_class.realize)
        (w, valueMask, attributes);

    ShapeButton( (CommandWidget) w, FALSE);
}

static void Realize (gw, valuemaskp, attr)
    Widget gw;
    XtValueMask *valuemaskp;
    XSetWindowAttributes *attr;
{
    PannerWidget pw = (PannerWidget) gw;
    Pixmap pm = XtUnspecifiedPixmap;
    Boolean gotpm = FALSE;

    if (pw->core.background_pixmap == XtUnspecifiedPixmap) {
        if (pw->panner.stipple_name) pm = BACKGROUND_STIPPLE (pw);

        if (PIXMAP_OKAY(pm)) {
            attr->background_pixmap = pm;
            *valuemaskp |= CWBackPixmap;
            *valuemaskp &= ~CWBackPixel;
            gotpm = TRUE;
        }
    }
    (*gw->core.widget_class->core_class.superclass->core_class.realize)
      (gw, valuemaskp, attr);

    if (gotpm) XFreePixmap (XtDisplay(gw), pm);
}
```

Structures

The XSetWindowAttributes structure, the XtValueMask type, and the flags that can be set in this type are defined as follows:

```
typedef struct {
    Pixmap background_pixmap;        /* background or None or ParentRelative * /
    unsigned long background_pixel;  /* background pixel */
    Pixmap border_pixmap;            /* border of the window */
    unsigned long border_pixel;      /* border pixel value */
    int bit_gravity;                 /* one of bit gravity values */
    int win_gravity;                 /* one of the window gravity values */
    int backing_store;               /* NotUseful, WhenMapped, Always */
    unsigned long backing_planes;    /* planes to be preserved if possible */
    unsigned long backing_pixel;     /* value to use in restoring planes */
    Bool save_under;                 /* should bits under be saved (popups) */
    long event_mask;                 /* set of events that should be saved */
```

```
        long do_not_propagate_mask;     /* set of events that shouldn't propagate */
        Bool override_redirect;         /* boolean value for override-redirect */
        Colormap colormap;              /* colormap to be associated with window */
        Cursor cursor;                  /* cursor to be displayed (or None) */
} XSetWindowAttributes;

typedef unsigned long    XtValueMask;

#define CWBackPixmap            (1L<<0)
#define CWBackPixel             (1L<<1)
#define CWBorderPixmap          (1L<<2)
#define CWBorderPixel           (1L<<3)
#define CWBitGravity            (1L<<4)
#define CWWinGravity            (1L<<5)
#define CWBackingStore          (1L<<6)
#define CWBackingPlanes         (1L<<7)
#define CWBackingPixel          (1L<<8)
#define CWOverrideRedirect      (1L<<9)
#define CWSaveUnder             (1L<<10)
#define CWEventMask             (1L<<11)
#define CWDontPropagate         (1L<<12)
#define CWColormap              (1L<<13)
#define CWCursor                (1L<<14)
```

See Also

XtCreateWindow(1), *XtRealizeWidget*(1),
Core(3).

Name

resize – RectObj class method called when a widget is resized.

Synopsis

```
typedef void (*XtWidgetProc)(Widget);
    Widget w;
```

Inputs

w   Specifies the widget that has been resized.

Description

The `resize()` method is registered on the `resize` field of the RectObj or Core class part structure. It is called when a widget is resized through a call to `XtResizeWidget()` or `XtConfigureWidget()`, and is responsible for doing any layout of children or recalculating any cached values necessary for the widget to draw itself at its new size.

The `resize()` method is called whether or not the widget is realized. The `width`, `height`, and `border_width` fields of the widget contain the new size of the widget. Note that this method is not responsible for drawing the widget at its new size. Unless the widget's window has bit gravity set (which is not the default) then when the window is resized, an `Expose` event will be generated, and the `expose()` method will be called by the Intrinsics. If the `resize()` method does call the `expose()` method, then the widget will be redrawn twice.

The widget must treat `resize()` as a command, not as a request. A widget must neither change its own size from within the `resize()` method, nor appeal the size change by calling `XtMakeGeometryRequest()` or `XtMakeResizeRequest()`.

Note that the `resize()` method is not invoked by `XtMakeResizeRequest()` or `XtMakeGeometryRequest()`, but it may be called if the parent explicitly resizes the widget while granting the resize request. Because the widget does not know whether its `resize()` method was called, it should be prepared to perform the necessary layout or calculation after making a geometry request, and may choose to do this simply by calling its resize procedure directly. Resize procedures should be written so that they can safely be called more than once in a row.

The `resize()` method is not chained. A widget class can inherit the `resize()` method of its superclass by specifying `XtInheritResize` in the `resize` field of the RectObj or Core class part structure. A widget that needs do no computation when resized can set this field to NULL.

Usage

Very simple widgets may check their size and compute how to draw themselves every time their `expose()` procedure is called. A widget that does this does not need a `resize()` method and can specify NULL. Most widgets however, do some pre-computation so that they can more efficiently redraw themselves. The Xaw Label widget, for example, computes the starting position of the text it draws based on the size of the window, the size of the text, the margins, and the value of the `XtNjustify` resource. This pre-computed value is valid until the window size, the label, the font, the margins, or the justification changes. Label's `resize()` method calls an internal procedure to perform these calculations. This procedure is also called from the `set_values()` method.

Many composite widgets must recompute the layout of their children when they are resized. This may involve moving or resizing the children widgets. Composite widgets will often call an internal layout procedure from their `resize()` method, and will call the same procedure from their `change_managed()` method and perhaps also their `geometry_manager()` method.

Example

The following procedures are the `resize()` methods of the Xaw Clock and Porthole widgets. The first pre-computes a number of values used to draw the clock at a given size, and the second ensures that the child of the Porthole is at least as large as the Porthole itself. Note that the Clock `resize()` method is optimized only to do the resize calculations if the widget is realized. In order to do this, though, it must call this procedure from its `realize()` method. The Xaw Mailbox widget, which simply displays a pixmap, is so simple that it does not need a `resize()` method. The Xaw Form and Box widgets are examples of composite widgets that must perform some sophisticated layout computations when they are resized.

```
static void Resize (gw)
    Widget gw;
{
    ClockWidget w = (ClockWidget) gw;
    /* don't do this computation if window hasn't been realized yet. */
    if (XtIsRealized(gw) && w->clock.analog) {
        /* need signed value since Dimension is unsigned */
        int radius = ((int) min(w->core.width, w->core.height) -
            (int) (2 * w->clock.padding)) / 2;
        w->clock.radius = (Dimension) max (radius, 1);

        w->clock.second_hand_length =
            (int)(SECOND_HAND_FRACT * w->clock.radius) / 100;
        w->clock.minute_hand_length =
            (int)(MINUTE_HAND_FRACT * w->clock.radius) / 100;
        w->clock.hour_hand_length =
            (int)(HOUR_HAND_FRACT * w->clock.radius) / 100;
        w->clock.hand_width =
            (int)(HAND_WIDTH_FRACT * w->clock.radius) / 100;
        w->clock.second_hand_width =
            (int)(SECOND_WIDTH_FRACT * w->clock.radius) / 100;

        w->clock.centerX = w->core.width / 2;
        w->clock.centerY = w->core.height / 2;
    }
}

static void Resize (gw)
    Widget gw;
{
    PortholeWidget pw = (PortholeWidget) gw;
```

```
        Widget child = find_child (pw);

        /*
         * If we have a child, we need to make sure that it is
         * at least as big as we are and in the right place.
         */
        if (child) {
            Position x, y;
            Dimension width, height;

            layout_child (pw, child, NULL, &x, &y, &width, &height);
            XtConfigureWidget (child, x, y, width, height, (Dimension) 0);
        }

        SendReport (pw, (unsigned int) (XawPRCanvasWidth|XawPRCanvasHeight));
    }
```

See Also

XtConfigureWidget(1), *XtResizeWidget*(1),
Core(3).

Name

root_geometry_manager – Shell class method called to negotiate shell geometry requests with a window manager.

Synopsis

```
typedef XtGeometryResult (*XtGeometryHandler)(Widget, XtWidgetGeometry *,
        XtWidgetGeometry *);
    Widget w;
    XtWidgetGeometry *request;
    XtWidgetGeometry *geometry_return;
```

Inputs

w   Specifies the shell widget making the request.

request   Specifies the requested geometry.

Outputs

geometry_return
             Specifies the reply geometry.

Returns

The window manager's reply: XtGeometryYes, XtGeometryNo, XtGeometryAlmost, or XtGeometryDone.

Availability

Release 4 and later.

Description

The root_geometry_manager() method is registered on the root_geometry_manager field of a ShellClassExtensionRec structure with record_type NULLQUARK, which is itself registered on the extension field of the Shell class part structure. The root_geometry_manager() method will be called when a shell widget calls XtMakeGeometryRequest() or XtMakeResizeRequest(), and should negotiate the requested size with the window manager.

The arguments to this method are the same as those passed to the geometry_manager() method. The root_geometry_manager() method should pass the geometry request on to the window manager. If the window manager permits the new geometry, the root_geometry_manager() should return XtGeometryYes; if the window manager denies the geometry request or it does not change the window geometry within some timeout interval (the XtNwmTimeout resource for WMShell, for example), the root_geometry_manager() should return XtGeometryNo. If the window manager makes some alternative geometry change, the root_geometry_manager() method may either return XtGeometryNo and handle the new geometry as a resize, or may return XtGeometryAlmost in anticipation that the shell will accept the compromise. If the compromise is not accepted, the new size must then be handled as a resize.

Communication with a window manager is an asynchronous process, but the `root_geome-try_manager()` procedure must return its answer synchronously. It will have to issue its request and then block until the reply arrives.

The `root_geometry_manager()` method is not chained. It can be inherited by specifying `XtInheritRootGeometryManager` in the Shell extension record. If there is no Shell extension record with `record_type` equal to `NULLQUARK`, then the Intrinsics will behave as if an extension was specified with `XtInheritRootGeometryManager`.

See the *Inter-Client Communications Conventions Manual* for information on communicating with window managers. See `geometry_manager`(4) for a description of the structures and the possible return values of this method.

Usage

The `root_geometry_manager()` method of the Shell class itself handles communication with ICCCM-compliant window managers. It sets the appropriate properties to make the geometry request, then uses `XCheckIfEvent()` to block until an `ConfigureNotify` event arrives in reply. This method also uses private functions internal to the Intrinsics in order to correctly handle the events. Because of the complexity and implementation-specific nature of this method, classes that want to define a custom `root_geometry_manager()` method should make their requests to the window manager, and then call their superclass's method to make additional requests, block, and get the response.

See Also

XtMakeGeometryRequest(1), *XtMakeResizeRequest*(1),
Shell(3),
geometry_manager(4).

Name

set_values – Object class method for handling resource changes.

Synopsis

```
typedef Boolean (*XtSetValuesFunc)(Widget, Widget, Widget, ArgList,
        Cardinal *);
    Widget current;
    Widget request;
    Widget set;
    ArgList args;
    Cardinal *num_args;
```

Inputs

current   Specifies a copy of the widget made by XtSetValues() before any resources are changed or any set_values() methods are called.

request   Specifies a copy of the widget made by XtSetValues() after the resources are changed as requested, but before any set_values() methods are called.

set   Specifies the actual widget with resources set and as modified by any super-class methods that have been called by XtSetValues().

args   Specifies the argument list passed to XtSetValues().

num_args   Specifies the number of arguments in the *args*.

Returns

True if the resource changes require the widget to be redrawn; False otherwise.

Description

The set_values() method is registered on the set_values field of the Object, RectObj, or Core class part structure. It is called by XtSetValues() to do any processing necessary when the values of widget resources are changed. This method is chained in superclass-to-sub-class order.

The *set* argument is the widget that has had its resources set, and has been passed to the super-class set_values() methods. Any changes to resource or non-resource fields should be made to this widget.

The *current* argument is a copy of the widget that was made by XtSetValues() before any of the resource values were changed as requested in the argument list. The set_values() method can compare the resource fields of *set* and *current* to determine which resources have been changed.

The *request* argument is a copy of the widget made after the resource values were set, but before XtSetValues() called any set_values() methods. A set_values() method can compare fields in *request*, *set*, and *current* to determine whether a field was set from the argument list (i.e., at the request of the programmer) or whether it was modified by a super-class set_values() method. A set_values() method may override values set by a superclass, but shouldn't change values that are explicitly requested in a call to XtSet-Values(). See the "Background" section below for more information.

The *args* and *num_args* arguments are the argument list that was passed to XtSet-Values() (or the variable-length argument list passed to XtVaSetValues() transformed into an ArgList). They can be used to set subpart resources with XtSetSubvalues(), to set values on privately created children widgets, or to set any other resources that do not appear on the resource list of the widget class. The *args* and *num_args* arguments were added to this method in Release 4. Prior to Release 4, subpart and other resources had to be set in the set_values_hook() method, which is now obsolete.

The set_values() method returns True if the widget needs to be redrawn in response to the resources changes, and False otherwise. It should not do any redisplay itself; if any of the set_values() methods returns True, XtSetValues() will generate an Expose event for the window by calling XClearArea(), and the widget's expose() method will be called.

A programmer may call XtSetValues() to set a widget's geometry fields directly. A set_values() method may also set these fields in response to other resource changes (if a label widget's label changes, for example, it may change its width). Note that this is one of the few times that a widget is allowed to directly set its own geometry fields. The other times are in the initialize() and (obsolete) initialize_hook() methods, and the (also obsolete) set_values_hook() method. A set_value() method may directly set its geometry fields, but should not do any processing based on those new values; the widget's parent must approve them first. If any of a widget's geometry fields have changed after all the set_values() methods have been called, XtSetValues() will call XtMakeGeometry-Request() to actually request the geometry change from the widget's parent. If the request is denied, XtSetValues() will reset the geometry fields to their original values. If the request is successful and the widget's size has changed, it will invoke the widget's resize() method. Most widgets will receive an Expose event after they are resized, and so a change to geometry fields alone is not reason enough for set_values() to return True.

The set_values() method must not assume that the widget is realized.

The set_values() method is chained in superclass-to-subclass order and cannot be inherited. If a widget has no resources, or needs to do no recalculation when those resources change, it does not need a set_values() method and can specify NULL for the set_values field of the class part structure.

See XtSetValues(1) for full details on the resource-setting process. See Constraint set_values(4) for information about handling changes to Constraint resources. See the "Background" section below for information about overriding values set by a superclass.

Usage

A typical set_values() method will compare the fields of *set* and *current* for most resources defined by the class. If a resource value has changed, it will take whatever actions are appropriate. Some common tasks of the set_values() method are:

- Copies resources that are passed by reference. If a resource that was copied in the `initialize()` method has changed, the old value must be freed, and the new value copied. String resources are typically copied by a widget so that the programmer may modify or free them after setting them in the widget. If this freeing and copying are done in separate procedures, the procedure to free the value can usually be shared with the `destroy()` method and the procedure to copy the value can usually be shared with the `initialize()` method.

- Recomputes derived fields when the resources they are derived from have changed. If the `XtNforeground` or `XtNfont` resource of a widget has changed, for example, it will probably have to free its current shared GC and allocate a new one. Note that resources may be derived from other resources. If a widget's width can be specified through either the `XtNwidth` or the `XtNcolumns` resource, then a change to either of these resources should cause a change to the other (and if both are changed, one should take clearly defined and documented precedence). If the code to calculate the values of derived fields is placed in separate procedures (code to allocate GCs, for example) those procedures can usually be shared with the `initialize()` method.

- Checks modified resources for consistency and reasonableness. If inconsistent or unreasonable resources are found, their values should be set to something valid, and a warning message should be issued.

- Restores the value of resource that are not allowed to be changed. Some widgets do not allow changes to some of their resources. If these values are changed in the `set_values()` method, they should be reset (i.e., the *set* field restored from the *current* field) and a warning message should be issued.

- Overrides derived fields calculated by superclasses, if necessary. If the `XtNcolumns` resource of a widget has changed, for example, a superclass may have one way of deriving `XtNwidth` from it, and a subclass may have a different way (the subclass may have different margins, for example). See the "Background" section below, for further discussion about overriding values set by a superclass.

- Uses *args* and *num_args* to set the value of resources that do not appear in the class resource list. These may be subpart resources (set with `XtSetSubvalues()`) or resources of children objects or widgets (set with `XtSetValues()`) which the widget wants to export as its own. (See `get_values_hook(4)` for a discussion and examples of widgets that export resources of child widgets or subparts.)

- Checks for changes to the sensitivity state of the widget. `XtSetSensitive()` uses `XtSetValues()` to set the `sensitive` and `ancestor_sensitive` fields of a widget. A widget class that displays itself differently when insensitive should check for sensitivity changes in its `set_values()` method. See `XtSetSensitive(1)` for more information on widget sensitivity.

- Keeps track of whether the widget needs to be redrawn. A common technique in `set_values()` methods is to initialize a `needs_redraw` variable to `False`, and then set it to `True` if any resources are changed that would require the widget to be redrawn. This value then becomes the return value of the method. A widget will commonly need to be redrawn if colors, fonts, or other GC components have changed; if its sensitivity state has changed; or if a resource that specifies data to be displayed (the `XtNlabel` resource of the Label widget, for example) has changed.

Example

The following procedure is the `set_values()` method, slightly edited, from the Xaw List widget. Note that it frees and reallocates its GCs if the foreground, background, or font have changed. If any of a large number of resources have changed that would affect the layout or size of the list, it calls an internal procedure that will calculate internal layout information and set new values for the widget's geometry fields. Finally, it checks whether it has been made insensitive and if so, turns off its highlighting.

Note that this procedure (and most existing `set_values()` methods) names the *set* argument new. "new" is a reserved word in C++, and your code will be more portable if you avoid using it in C.

```
/* ARGSUSED */
static Boolean SetValues(current, request, new, args, num_args)
Widget current, request, new;
ArgList args;
Cardinal *num_args;
{
    ListWidget cl = (ListWidget) current;
    ListWidget rl = (ListWidget) request;
    ListWidget nl = (ListWidget) new;
    Boolean redraw = FALSE;

    if ((cl->list.foreground != rl->list.foreground) ||
        (cl->core.background_pixel != rl->core.background_pixel) ||
        (cl->list.font != rl->list.font) ) {
        XGCValues values;
        XGetGCValues(XtDisplay(current), cl->list.graygc, GCTile, &values);
        XmuReleaseStippledPixmap(XtScreen(current), values.tile);
        XtReleaseGC(current, cl->list.graygc);
        XtReleaseGC(current, cl->list.revgc);
        XtReleaseGC(current, cl->list.normgc);
        GetGCs(new);
        redraw = TRUE;
    }

    /* Reset row height. */
    if ((cl->list.row_space != rl->list.row_space) ||
        (cl->list.font != rl->list.font))
        nl->list.row_height = nl->list.font->max_bounds.ascent
                            + nl->list.font->max_bounds.descent
                            + nl->list.row_space;

    if ((cl->core.width != rl->core.width)                          ||
        (cl->core.height != rl->core.height)                        ||
        (cl->list.internal_width != rl->list.internal_width)    ||
        (cl->list.internal_height != rl->list.internal_height)  ||
```

**Intrinsics
Methods**

```
            (cl->list.column_space != rl->list.column_space)      ||
            (cl->list.row_space != rl->list.row_space)            ||
            (cl->list.default_cols != rl->list.default_cols)      ||
            (  (cl->list.force_cols != rl->list.force_cols) &&
               (rl->list.force_cols != rl->list.ncols) )          ||
            (cl->list.vertical_cols != rl->list.vertical_cols)    ||
            (cl->list.longest != rl->list.longest)                ||
            (cl->list.nitems != rl->list.nitems)                  ||
            (cl->list.font != rl->list.font)                      ||
            (cl->list.list != rl->list.list)                        ) {

        ResetList(new, TRUE, TRUE);
        redraw = TRUE;
    }

    if (cl->list.list != rl->list.list)
        nl->list.is_highlighted = nl->list.highlight = NO_HIGHLIGHT;

    if ((cl->core.sensitive != rl->core.sensitive) ||
        (cl->core.ancestor_sensitive != rl->core.ancestor_sensitive)) {
        nl->list.highlight = NO_HIGHLIGHT;
        redraw = TRUE;
    }

    if (!XtIsRealized(current))
        return(FALSE);

    return(redraw);
}
```

Background

Like the `initialize()` method, `set_values()` mostly deals only with the fields defined in the subclass, but it has to resolve conflicts with its superclass, especially conflicts over width and height.

Sometimes a subclass may want to overwrite values filled in by its superclass. In particular, size calculations of a superclass are often incorrect for a subclass and, in this case, the subclass must modify or recalculate fields declared and computed by its superclass.

As an example, a subclass can visually surround its superclass display. In this case, the width and height calculated by the superclass `set_values()` method are too small and need to be incremented by the size of the surround. The subclass needs to know if its superclass's size was calculated by the superclass or was specified explicitly. All widgets must place themselves into whatever size is explicitly given, but they should compute a reasonable size if no size is requested. How does a subclass know the difference between a specified size and a size computed by a superclass?

The *request* and *set* parameters provide the necessary information. The *request* widget is a copy of the widget, updated as originally requested. The *set* widget starts with the values in the request, but it has additionally been updated by all superclass `set_values()` methods called so far. A subclass `set_values()` method can compare these two to resolve any potential conflicts. The `set_values()` method need not refer to the *request* widget unless it must resolve conflicts between the *current* and *set* widgets. Any changes the widget needs to make, including geometry changes, should be made in the *set* widget.

In the above example, the subclass with the visual surround can see if the `width` and `height` in the *request* widget differ from the `width` and `height` in the *set* widget. If so, it means that a superclass has modified these fields (which means that the programmer did not request them specifically) and the subclass can add its surround size to the *width* and *height* fields in the *set* widget. If the fields are the same, the subclass must make do with the specified size.

There is a twist, however, on this problem of not overriding resources explicitly requested by the user. If the programmer sets a new label on a Label widget, for example, the widget is allowed to change its size as needed to accommodate the label. If the programmer sets a new label and a new width at the same time, however, the new width should take precedence, regardless of the size of the label. The difficulty arises in the case that the programmer requests a particular width which happens to be the current width. He is expecting to get exactly that width, but the `set_values()` method may not detect that that resource has changed, and will resize the widget as required for the new label. The only general way out of this situation is to check each element of *args* to see if the any of the resources that are being set are named `Xt-Nwidth`.

See Also

XtSetValues(1),
Core(3),
Constraint set_values(4), *set_values_almost*(4), *set_values_hook*(4).

Constraint set_values

Name

Constraint set_values – Constraint class method called to handle changes to constraint resources.

Synopsis

```
typedef Boolean (*XtSetValuesFunc)(Widget, Widget, Widget, ArgList,
        Cardinal *);
    Widget current;
    Widget request;
    Widget set;
    ArgList args;
    Cardinal *num-args;
```

Inputs

current   Specifies a copy of the child widget (and that widget's constraint record) made by XtSetValues() before any resources are changed or any class methods are called.

request   Specifies a copy of the child widget (and that widget's constraint record) made by XtSetValues() after the constraint and normal resources are changed as requested, but before any class set_values() methods are called.

set   Specifies the child widget with constraint and normal resources set and as modified by any superclass methods that have been called by XtSet-Values().

args   Specifies the argument list passed to XtSetValues().

num_args   Specifies the number of arguments in the *args*.

Returns

True if the resource changes require the child widget to be redrawn; False otherwise.

Description

The Constraint set_values() method is registered on the set_value field of the Constraint class part structure. It is invoked when XtSetValues() is called on a child of the constraint widget to do any processing necessary to handle resource changes in the child's constraint record.

The arguments to the Constraint set_values() method are the same as those passed to the child's Object, RectObj, or Core set_values() method. The constraints field of each of the widget arguments points to a copy of the child's constraints procedure made at the appropriate point by XtSetValues(). The Constraint set_values() procedure must perform the same sort of processing on this record as the normal set_values() method performs on the widget instance record itself.

The Constraint set_values() method will deal primarily with the fields of the constraint record, but may also modify widget instance fields as necessary. If the constraint for the maximum height of a child is changed to a value that is less than the current height of the child, for example, the Constraint set_values() method may change the height instance field of the child widget. If the parent needs to change the geometry of the child, it needn't call `Xt-ConfigureWidget()` directly; if any child geometry fields are changed by this or other `set_values()` methods, `XtSetValues()` will call `XtMakeGeometryRequest()`, which will invoke the parent's `geometry_manager()` method, which can do any necessary processing.

As with the Object `set_values()` method, the Constraint `set_values()` method should return `True` if the widget should be redrawn. Unless this method actually modifies fields in the widget instance structure itself, however, a redraw will never be useful because the child's `expose()` method cannot take constraint fields into account.

The Constraint `set_values()` method should not assume that the child widget is realized.

The `args` and `num_args` arguments were added in Release 4.

The Constraint `set_values()` method is chained in superclass-to-subclass order, and cannot be inherited. If none of the resources in a class's constraint record need special processing when their values are changed, this method may be `NULL`.

See `set_values`(4) for information on the arguments to this function, and a discussion of the typical tasks of a `set_values()` method. See `XtSetValues`(1) for full details on the widget creation process.

Example

The following procedure is the Constraint `set_values()` method, lightly edited, of the Xaw Paned widget class. Note that it obtains the constraint records of the *current* and *set* arguments (which are named `old` and `new` here) and compares their fields to determine what has changed. Note also that "new" is a reserved word in C++, and your C code will be more portable if you avoid using it as an argument name.

```
#define PaneInfo(w)      ((Pane)(w)->core.constraints)

/* ARGSUSED */
static Boolean
PaneSetValues(old, request, new, args, num_args)
Widget old, request, new;
ArgList args;
Cardinal *num_args;
{
    Pane old_pane = PaneInfo(old);
    Pane new_pane = PaneInfo(new);

    /* Check for new min and max. */

    if (old_pane->min != new_pane->min || old_pane->max != new_pane->max)
        XawPanedSetMinMax(new, (int)new_pane->min, (int)new_pane->max);

    /* Check for change in XtNshowGrip. */

    if (old_pane->show_grip != new_pane->show_grip)
        if (new_pane->show_grip == TRUE) {
            CreateGrip(new);
            if (XtIsRealized(XtParent(new))) {
```

```
                    if (XtIsManaged(new)) /* if paned is unrealized this will
                                   happen automatically at realize time.*/
                        XtManageChild(PaneInfo(new)->grip); /* manage the grip. */
                    CommitNewLocations( (PanedWidget) XtParent(new) );
                }
            }
            else if ( HasGrip(old) ) {
                XtDestroyWidget( old_pane->grip );
                new_pane->grip = NULL;
            }

        return(False);
    }
```

See Also

XtSetValues(1),
Constraint(3), *Core*(3),
set_values(4).

Name

set_values_almost – RectObj class method to negotiate compromise geometries.

Synopsis

```
typedef void (*XtAlmostProc)(Widget, Widget, XtWidgetGeometry *,
        XtWidgetGeometry *);
    Widget current;
    Widget set;
    XtWidgetGeometry *request_in_out;
    XtWidgetGeometry *reply;
```

Inputs

current   Specifies a copy of the object made by XtSetValues() before any
             resources were set or set_values() methods were called.

set   Specifies the object. It has had its resources set and fields modified by
             set_values(), set_value_hook(), and Constraint set_values()
             methods.

request_in_out
             Specifies the geometry request that was sent to the geometry manager.

reply   Specifies the compromise geometry that was returned by the geometry man-
             ager.

Outputs

request_in_out
             Returns the desired geometry; can be empty, the compromise geometry, or
             some new geometry to try.

Description

The set_values_almost() method is registered on the set_values_almost field of
the RectObj or Core class part structure. It is invoked by XtSetValues() when a widget's
geometry fields have changed, but the widget's parent's geometry_manager() will not
allow the requested geometry and returns XtGeometryNo or XtGeometryAlmost.

When a widget's geometry fields have been changed from the argument list, or by one of the
set_values() methods, Constraint set_values(), or set_values_hook() methods
that were called to handle the resource changes, XtSetValues() restores the original values, and calls XtMakeGeometryRequest() to actually request the new values from the
widget's parent. If the return value of the request is XtGeometryNo or XtGeometry-
Almost, XtSetValues() calls the widget's set_values_almost() method to determine whether the geometry should be left as is, the proposed compromise geometry accepted,
or some other geometry tried.

The *current* and *set* arguments are the same as the arguments by the same name that are
passed to the set_values() method, except that the geometry fields of *set* (x, y, width,
height, and border_width) contain the original values of the widget geometry, not the
requested values.

The *request_in_out* argument is the geometry request made by XtSetValues(); it contains the new values of the geometry fields that changed, and *request_in_out*->request_mode contains flags that indicate which of those fields are set. If the geometry request returned XtGeometryAlmost, then *reply* contains the proposed compromise geometry. If the request returned XtGeometryNo, then *reply*->request_mode will be zero.

The set_values_almost() method should do one of the following:

- Set *request_in_out*->request_mode to zero to terminate geometry negotiation and retain the original geometry.

- Copy the contents of *reply* into *request_in_out* to accept the compromise geometry. The parent is guaranteed to accept the compromise.

- Set some other geometry proposal into request_in_out. If the parent does not accept this geometry, the *set_values_almost ()* method will be called again.

Note that the set_values_almost() method is not chained as are the set_values(), set_values_hook(), and Constraint set_values() methods. A widget class can inherit the set_values_almost() method of its superclass by specifying XtInherit-SetValuesAlmost on the set_values_almost field of the RectObj or Core class part structure. It is not specified what will happen if the set_values_almost field is NULL (though some of the Xaw widgets have this method NULL).

The Intrinsics specification says in one place that set_value_almost() will be called on a result of XtGeometryNo, and says in another that it will not. Until the specification is clarified, set_values_almost() methods should be prepared to handle this case, but widget must not rely on these methods to detect it.

See set_values(4) for more information on the current and set arguments. See Xt-SetValues(1) for a full description of the resource setting algorithm. See XtMake-GeometryRequest(1) and geometry_manager(4) for details on geometry management.

Usage

Most classes will inherit this method from their superclass. The RectObj set_values_almost() method always accepts the compromise geometry; it is shown in the example below.

Example

The following procedure is the RectObj set_values_almost() method. It simply copies the contents of *reply* into *request_in_out* in order to accept the compromise geometry.

```
/*ARGSUSED*/
static void RectSetValuesAlmost(old, new, request, reply)
    Widget              old;
    Widget              new;
    XtWidgetGeometry    *request;
    XtWidgetGeometry    *reply;
```

```
{
    *request = *reply;
}
```

Structures

The `XtWidgetGeometry` structure is similar, but not identical, to the corresponding Xlib structure:

```
typedef unsigned long XtGeometryMask;

typedef struct {
    XtGeometryMask request_mode;
    Position x, y;
    Dimension width, height;
    Dimension border_width;
    Widget sibling;
    int stack_mode;
} XtWidgetGeometry;
```

The `request_mode` definitions are from *<X11/X.h>*:

```
#define    CWX               (1<<0)
#define    CWY               (1<<1)
#define    CWWidth           (1<<2)
#define    CWHeight          (1<<3)
#define    CWBorderWidth     (1<<4)
#define    CWSibling         (1<<5)
#define    CWStackMode       (1<<6)
```

The `stack_mode` definitions are from *<X11/X.h>*:

```
#define    Above             0
#define    Below             1
#define    TopIf             2
#define    BottomIf          3
#define    Opposite          4
```

The Intrinsics also support the following value:

```
#define    XtSMDontChange    5
```

For precise definitions of `Above`, `Below`, `TopIf`, `BottomIf`, and `Opposite`, see the reference page for `ConfigureWindow()` in Volume Two, *Xlib Reference Manual*. `XtSMDont-Change` indicates that the widget wants its current stacking order preserved.

See Also

XtMakeGeometryRequest(1), *XtSetValues*(1),
Core(3),
geometry_manager(4), *set_values*(4).

set_values_hook

Name

set_values_hook – obsolete Object method for handling changes to subpart resources.

Synopsis

```
typedef Boolean (*XtArgsFunc)(Widget, ArgList, Cardinal *);
    Widget w;
    ArgList args;
    Cardinal *num_args;
```

Inputs

w   Specifies the widget whose nonwidget resource values are to be changed.

args   Specifies the argument list that was passed to XtSetValues().

num_args   Specifies the number of arguments in the argument list.

Returns

True if the widget should be redrawn; False otherwise.

Availability

Obsolete in Release 4 and later.

Description

The set_values_hook() method is registered on the set_values_hook field of the Object, RectObj, or Core class part structure. It is called by XtSetValues() after the class's set_values() method has been called.

As of Release 4, the set_values_hook() method is obsolete, because the *args* and *num_args* arguments are now passed to the set_values() method. Its purpose had been to allow the value of subpart resources to be set from the argument list, by calling XtSet-Subvalues() for example.

The arguments to the set_values_hook() method are the widget and the argument list that were passed to XtSetValues(). The widget will have been modified by any superclass methods that have already been called. It should return True if the change to subpart resources will require the widget to be redraw, and False otherwise.

The set_values_hook() method is chained in superclass-to-subclass order and is called for compatibility with older widgets. It cannot be inherited, and any new widget classes should set their set_values_hook field to NULL. See XtSetValues(1) for details on when this method is called. See set_values(4) for a discussion of setting the values of subpart resources, and other resources that do not appear on the class resource list.

See Also

XtSetSubvalues(1), *XtSetValues*(1),
Core(3),
set_values(4).

Section 5

Athena Classes

This section contains alphabetically-organized reference pages for the Athena widgets. The Xaw library is part of the core MIT X distribution, but is not part of the Intrinsics, and is not a standard of the X Consortium. Application writers who are not using one of the commercial widget sets will find them very useful.

The first reference page, Introduction, *explains the format and contents of each of the following pages.*

In This Section:

Introduction

This page describes the format and contents of each reference page in Section 5, covering the Athena Widget Classes.

Name

Name – brief description of the widget class.

Synopsis

The Synopsis section presents the required include files, Class name, and the widget class pointer to be specified in calls to `XtCreateWidget()`. For example:

Public Headers:	*<X11/StringDefs.h> <X11/Xaw/Box.h>*
Private Header:	*<X11/Xaw/BoxP.h>*
Class Name:	Box
Class Pointer:	`boxWidgetClass`
Instantiation:	*widget* = `XtCreateWidget(`*name*`, boxWidgetClass, ...)`

Class Hierarchy

This section shows the hierarchy from which this widget inherits functionality and resources.

Availability

The Availability section specifies that a given function is only available in Release 5 and later releases. If there is no Availability section, the function is available in Release 4 and Release 5, and later releases.

Description

The Description section describes what the widget does. It also contains miscellaneous information such as examples of usage, special notes, and pointers to related information in this manual.

Resources

The Resources section provides a table listing all resources defined by this widget and all its superclasses, along with their types, default values, and a brief description. If the resource is new in Release 5, the first column will begin with (R5). The description column may begin with the following code letters denoting special restrictions placed upon individual resources:

(A)   This resource may be automatically adjusted when another resource is changed.

(C)   This resource is only settable at widget creation time, and may not be modified with `XtSetValues()`.

(D)   Do not modify this resource. While setting this resource will work, it can cause unexpected behavior. When this symbol appears, there is another preferred interface provided by the Intrinsics.

(R)   This resource is READ-ONLY, and may not be modified.

After the table is a detailed description of each new resource defined by this widget (but not those defined by superclasses). To see the detailed description of superclass resources, see the reference page for the superclass.

Constraint Resources

For subclasses of Constraint, this section describes any Constraint Resources that can be set on children but that are interpreted by this widget.

Layout Semantics

For subclasses of Composite and Constraint, this section describes any aspects of layout policy not covered in the sections on Resources or Constraint Resources.

Translations and Actions

The Translations and Actions section lists and describes the actions defined by this widget, and shows the default translation table. You can use this information to modify or replace the translation table for an instance of this widget.

Callback Structures

The Callback Structures section shows the structures the widget uses to pass data to client-supplied callback functions.

Public Functions

The Public Functions section describes all public functions defined by the widget. These normally provide interfaces for getting information from or putting information into the widget.

See Also

The See Also section lists widgets related to Name.

Box

Name

Box widget – geometry-managing box widget.

Synopsis

Public Headers: *<X11/StringDefs.h> <X11/Xaw/Box.h>*

Private Header: *<X11/Xaw/BoxP.h>*

Class Name: Box

Class Pointer: `boxWidgetClass`

Instantiation: *widget* = XtCreateWidget(*name*, boxWidgetClass, ...)

Class Hierarchy

Core → Composite → Box

Description

The Box widget provides geometry management of arbitrary widgets in a box of a specified dimension. Box moves but does not resize its children. The children are rearranged when the Box is resized, when its children are resized, or when children are managed or unmanaged. The Box widget always attempts to pack its children as closely as possible within the geometry allowed by its parent.

Box widgets are commonly used to manage a related set of Command widgets and are frequently called ButtonBox widgets, but the children are not limited to buttons.

The children are arranged on a background that has its own specified dimensions and color.

Resources

When creating a Box widget instance, the following resources are retrieved from the argument list or from the resource database:

Name (XtN...)	Type	Default	Description
XtNaccelerators	AcceleratorTable	NULL	List of event-to-action bindings to be executed by this widget, even though the event occurred in another widget.
XtNancestor-Sensitive	Boolean	True	(D) Sensitivity state of the ancestors of this widget: a widget is insensitive if either it or any of its ancestors is insensitive.
XtNbackground	Pixel	XtDefault-Background	Window background color.
XtNbackground-Pixmap	Pixmap	XtUnspecified-Pixmap	Window background pixmap.
XtNborderColor	Pixel	XtDefault-Foreground	Window border color.

Name (XtN . . .)	Type	Default	Description
XtNborderPixmap	Pixmap	XtUnspecified-Pixmap	Window border pixmap.
XtNborderWidth	Dimension	1	Border width on button box.
XtNchildren	WidgetList	NULL	(R) List of all this composite widget's current children.
XtNcolormap	Colormap	Parent's colormap.	Colormap that this widget will use.
XtNdepth	int	Parent's depth.	(C) Depth of this widget's window.
XtNdestroy-Callback	XtCallbackList	NULL	Callbacks for XtDestroy-Widget().
XtNheight	Dimension	See below.	(A) Viewing height of inner window.
XtNhSpace	Dimension	4	Pixel distance left and right of children.
XtNmappedWhen-Managed	Boolean	TRUE	Whether XtMapWidget() is automatic.
XtNnumChildren	Cardinal	0	(R) Number of children in this composite widget.
XtNorientation	Orientation	XtOrientVertical	See below.
XtNscreen	Screen	Parent's screen.	(R) Screen on which this widget is displayed.
XtNsensitive	Boolean	TRUE	Whether widget receives input.
XtNtranslations	TranslationTable	NULL	Event-to-action translations.
XtNvSpace	Dimension	4	Pixel distance top and bottom of children.
XtNwidth	Dimension	See below.	(A) Viewing width of inner window.
XtNx	Position	0	x coordinate in pixels.
XtNy	Position	0	y coordinate in pixels.

The Box widget positions its children in rows with XtNhSpace pixels to the left and right of each child and XtNvSpace pixels between rows. If the Box width is not specified, the Box widget uses the width of the widest child. Each time a child is managed or unmanaged, the Box widget attempts to reposition the remaining children to compact the box. Children are positioned in order, from left to right and from top to bottom. The packing algorithm used depends on the value of XtNorientation, which is described below. After positioning all children, the Box widget attempts to shrink its own size to the minimum dimensions required for the layout.

The XtNorientation resource specifies whether the preferred shape of the box (i.e., the result returned by the query_geometry() class method) is tall and narrow (XawOrient-Vertical) or short and wide (XawOrientHorizontal). When the Box is a child of a parent which enforces width constraints, it is usually better to specify `XawOrientVertical` (the default). When the parent enforces height constraints, it is usually better to specify `XawOrientHorizontal`.

The packing algorithm used by the Box widget depends on the value of `XtNorientation`. The two possibilities are:

`XawOrientVertical`

> When the next child does not fit on the current row, a new row is started. If a child is wider than the width of the box, the box will request a larger width from its parent and will begin the layout process from the beginning if a new width is granted.

`XawOrientHorizontal`

> When the next child does not fit in the current column, a new column is started. If a child is taller than the height of the box, the box will request a larger height from its parent and will begin the layout process from the beginning if a new height is granted.

See Also

Composite(3), *Core*(3),
Command(5).

Command

Name

Command widget – command button activated by pointer click.

Synopsis

Public Headers:	*<X11/StringDefs.h> <X11/Xaw/Command.h>*
Private Header:	*<X11/Xaw/CommandP.h>*
Class Name:	Command
Class Pointer:	`commandWidgetClass`
Instantiation:	*widget* = `XtCreateWidget(`*name*`, commandWidgetClass, ...)`

Class Hierarchy

Core → Simple → Label → Command

Description

The Command widget is an area, often rectangular, that contains a text or pixmap label. This selectable area is sometimes referred to as a "button". When the pointer cursor is on the button, the button border is highlighted to indicate that the button is ready for selection. When pointer button 1 is pressed, the command widget indicates that it has been selected by reversing its foreground and background colors. When the pointer button is released, the Command widget's `notify` action is invoked, calling all functions on its callback list.

Resources

When creating a Command widget instance, the following resources are retrieved from the argument list or from the resource database:

Name (XtN...)	Type	Default	Description
XtNaccelerators	AcceleratorTable	NULL	List of event-to-action bindings to be executed by this widget, even though the event occurred in another widget.
XtNancestor-Sensitive	Boolean	True	(D) Sensitivity state of the ancestors of this widget: a widget is insensitive if either it or any of its ancestors is insensitive.
XtNbackground	Pixel	XtDefault-Background	Window background color.
XtNbackground-Pixmap	Pixmap	XtUnspecified-Pixmap	Window background pixmap.
XtNbitmap	Pixmap	None	Pixmap to display in place of the label.
XtNborderColor	Pixel	XtDefault-Foreground	Window border color.

Name (XtN...)	Type	Default	Description
XtNborderPixmap	Pixmap	XtUnspecified-Pixmap	Window border pixmap.
XtNborderWidth	Dimension	1	Width of button border.
XtNcallback	XtCallbackList	NULL	Callback for button select.
XtNcolormap	Colormap	Parent's colormap.	Colormap that this widget will use.
XtNcornerRound-Percent	Dimension	25	See below.
XtNcursor	Cursor	None	Pointer cursor.
XtNdepth	int	Parent's depth.	(C)Depth of this widget's window.
XtNdestroy-Callback	XtCallbackList	NULL	Callbacks for Xt-DestroyWidget().
XtNencoding	unsigned char	XawTextEncoding8bit	For I18N.
XtNfont	XFontStruct*	XtDefaultFont	Label font.
XtNforeground	Pixel	XtDefault-Foreground	Foreground color.
XtNheight	Dimension	font height + 2 * XtNinternalHeight	(A) Button height.
XtNhighlight-Thickness	Dimension	2	(A) Width of border to be highlighted.
XtNinsensitive-Border	Pixmap	Gray pixmap.	Border when not sensitive.
XtNinternal-Height	Dimension	2	Internal border height for highlighting.
XtNinternalWidth	Dimension	4	Internal border width for highlighting.
XtNjustify	XtJustify	XtJustifyCenter	Type of text alignment.
XtNlabel	String	Name of widget.	Button label.
(R5) XtNleftBitmap	Bitmap	None	Pixmap before label.
XtNmappedWhen-Managed	Boolean	TRUE	Whether XtMapWidget() is automatic.
XtNresize	Boolean	TRUE	Whether to auto-resize in SetValues.
XtNscreen	Screen	Parent's screen.	(R) Screen on which this widget is displayed: this is not a settable resource.
XtNsensitive	Boolean	TRUE	Whether widget receives input.
XtNshapeStyle	ShapeStyle	Rectangle	See below.
XtNtranslations	Translation-Table	See below.	Event-to-action translations.
XtNwidth	Dimension	XtNlabel width + 2 * XtNinternalWidth	(A) Button width.

Name (XtN...)	Type	Default	Description
XtNx	Position	0	x coordinate in pixels.
XtNy	Position	0	y coordinate in pixels.

Note that the Command widget supports two callback lists: `XtNdestroyCallback` and `XtNcallback`. The `notify` action executes the callbacks on the `XtNcallback` list. The `call_data` argument is unused.

The new resources (not inherited from superclasses) associated with the Command widget are:

`XtNcallback`
  The callback list executed by the `notify` action.

`XtNhighlightThickness`
  The thickness of the line drawn by the `highlight` action.

`XtNshapeStyle`
  Nonrectangular buttons may be created using this resource. Nonrectangular buttons are supported only on a server that supports the `Shape Extension`. If nonrectangular buttons are specified for a server lacking this extension, the shape is ignored and the widgets will be rectangular. The following shapes are currently supported: `XmuShapeRectangle`, `XmuShapeOval`, `XmuShapeEllipse`, and `XmuShapeRoundedRectangle`.

`XtNcornerRoundPercent`
  When a `ShapeStyle` of `roundedRectangle` is used, this resource controls the radius of the rounded corner. The radius of the rounded corners is specified as a percentage of the length of the shortest side of the widget.

Translations and Actions

The following are the default translation bindings that are used by the Command widget:

```
<EnterWindow>:highlight( )
<LeaveWindow>:reset( )
<Btn1Down>:set( )
<Btn1Up>:notify( ) unset( )
```

With these bindings, the user can cancel the action before releasing the button by moving the pointer out of the Command widget.

The Command widget supports the following actions:

• Switching the button between the foreground and background colors with `set` and `unset`.

• Processing application callbacks with `notify`.

• Switching the internal border between highlighted and unhighlighted states with `highlight` and `unhighlight`.

The full list of actions supported by Command is as follows:

highlight ()   Displays the internal highlight border in the color (XtNforeground or XtNbackground) that contrasts with the interior color of the Command widget. The conditions WhenUnset and Always are understood by this action procedure. If no argument is passed, WhenUnset is assumed.

unhighlight () Displays the internal highlight border in the color (XtNforeground or XtNbackground) that matches the interior color of the Command widget.

set ()   Enters the set state, in which notify is possible and displays the interior of the button, including the highlight border, in the foreground color. The label is displayed in the background color.

unset ()   Cancels the set state and displays the interior of the button, including the highlight border, in the background color. The label is displayed in the foreground color.

reset ()   Cancels any set or highlight and displays the interior of the button in the background color, with the label displayed in the foreground color.

notify ()   Executes the callback list specified by XtNcallback, if executed in the set state. The value of the *call_data* argument is undefined.

See Also

Box(5), *Label*(5), *MenuButton*(5).

Dialog

Name

Dialog widget – dialog box widget.

Synopsis

Public Headers:	*<X11/StringDefs.h> <X11/Xaw/Dialog.h>*
Private Header:	*<X11/Xaw/DialogP.h>*
Class Name:	Dialog
Class Pointer:	`dialogWidgetClass`
Instantiation:	*widget* = XtCreateWidget(*name*, dialogWidgetClass, ...)

Class Hierarchy

Core → Composite → Constraint → Form → Dialog

Description

The Dialog widget implements a commonly used interaction semantic to prompt for auxiliary input from a user. For example, you can use a Dialog widget when an application requires a small piece of information, such as a filename, from the user. A Dialog widget is simply a special case of the Form widget that provides a convenient way to create a *preconfigured form.*

The typical Dialog widget contains three areas. The first line contains a description of the function of the Dialog widget, for example, the string *Filename:*. The second line contains an area into which the user types input. The third line can contain buttons that let the user confirm or cancel the Dialog input. Any of these areas may be omitted by the application.

Resources

When creating a Dialog widget instance, the following resources are retrieved from the argument list or from the resource database:

Name (XtN...)	Type	Default	Description
XtNaccelerators	AcceleratorTable	NULL	List of event-to-action bindings to be executed by this widget, even though the event occurred in another widget.
XtNancestor-Sensitive	Boolean	True	(D) Sensitivity state of the ancestors of this widget: a widget is insensitive if either it or any of its ancestors is insensitive.
XtNbackground	Pixel	XtDefault-Background	Window background color.
XtNbackground-Pixmap	Pixmap	XtUnspecified-Pixmap	Window background pixmap.
XtNborderColor	Pixel	XtDefault-Foreground	Window border color.
XtNborderPixmap	Pixmap	XtUnspecified-Pixmap	Window border pixmap.
XtNborderWidth	Dimension	1	Width of border in pixels.

Name (XtN...)	Type	Default	Description
XtNchildren	WidgetList	NULL	(R) List of all this composite widget's current children.
XtNcolormap	Colormap	Parent's colormap.	Colormap that this widget will use.
XtNdefault-Distance	int	4	Default value for XtNhoriz-Distance and XtNvert-Distance.
XtNdepth	int	Parent's depth.	(C) Depth of this widget's window.
XtNdestroy-Callback	XtCallbackList	NULL	Callbacks for XtDestroy-Widget().
XtNheight	Dimension	Computed at realize.	(A) Height of dialog.
XtNicon	Pixmap	None	See below.
XtNlabel	String	"label"	See below.
XtNmappedWhen-Managed	Boolean	TRUE	Whether XtMapWidget() is automatic.
XtNnumChildren	Cardinal	0	(R) Number of children in this composite widget.
XtNscreen	Screen	Parent's screen.	(R) Screen on which this widget is displayed.
XtNsensitive	Boolean	TRUE	Whether widget receives input.
XtNtranslations	TranslationTable	NULL	Event-to-action translations.
XtNvalue	char*	NULL	Pointer to default string.
XtNwidth	Dimension	Computed at realize.	(A) Width of dialog.
XtNx	Position	0	x coordinate in pixels.
XtNy	Position	0	y coordinate in pixels.

The instance name of the label widget within the Dialog widget is *label*, and the instance name of the Dialog value widget is *value*.

The new resources (not inherited from superclasses) associated with the Dialog widget are:

XtNicon
> A pixmap image to be displayed immediately to the left of the Dialog widget's label.

XtNlabel
> A Latin1 string to be displayed at the top of the Dialog widget.

XtNvalue
> An initial value for the string field into which the user will enter text. By default, no text entry field is available to the user. Specifying an initial value for value activates the text entry field. If string input is desired but no initial value is to be specified, then set this resource to " " (empty string).

Public Functions

- To add a child button to the Dialog box, use `XtCreateWidget()` and specify the widget ID of the previously created Dialog box as the parent of each child. When creating buttons, you do not have to specify form constraints. The Dialog widget will automatically add the constraints.

- To return the character string in the text field, use:

```
char *XawDialogGetValueString(w)
Widget w;
```

where *w* specifies the widget ID of the Dialog box.

If a string was specified in the `XtNvalue` resource, the Dialog widget will store the input directly into the string.

- To add a new button to the Dialog widget use:

XawDialogAddButton.
```
void XawDialogAddButton(w, name, func,
client_data)
        Widget w;
        String name;
        XtCallbackProc func;
        XtPointer client_data;
```

w	Specifies the Dialog widget.
name	Specifies the name of the new Command button to be added to the Dialog.
func	Specifies a callback function to be called when this button is activated. If NULL is specified then no callback is added.
client_data	Specifies the client_data to be passed to the *func*.

See Also

Command(5), *Form*(5), *Text*(5).

Form

Name
Form widget – geometry-managing widget implementing constraints on children.

Synopsis
Public Headers: *<X11/StringDefs.h> <X11/Xaw/Form.h>*

Private Header: *<X11/Xaw/FormP.h>*

Class Name: Form

Class Pointer: `formWidgetClass`

Instantiation: *widget* = XtCreateWidget(*name*, formWidgetClass, ...)

Class Hierarchy
Core → Composite → Constraint → Form

Description
The Form widget can contain an arbitrary number of children of any class. The Form provides geometry management for its children, including individual control of the position of each child. The initial positions of the children may be computed relative to the positions of previously created children. When the Form is resized, it computes new positions and sizes for its children. This computation is based upon information provided as constraints when each child is added to the Form.

Resources
When creating a Form widget instance, the following resources are retrieved from the argument list or from the resource database:

Name (XtN...)	Type	Default	Description
XtNaccelerators	AcceleratorTable	NULL	List of event-to-action bindings to be executed by this widget, even though the event occurred in another widget.
XtNancestor-Sensitive	Boolean	True	(D) Sensitivity state of the ancestors of this widget: a widget is insensitive if either it or any of its ancestors is insensitive.
XtNbackground	Pixel	XtDefault-Background	Window background color.
XtNbackground-Pixmap	Pixmap	XtUnspecified-Pixmap	Window background pixmap.
XtNborderColor	Pixel	XtDefault-Foreground	Window border color.
XtNborderPixmap	Pixmap	XtUnspecified-Pixmap	Window border pixmap.
XtNborderWidth	Dimension	1	Width of border in pixels.
XtNchildren	WidgetList	NULL	(R) List of all this composite widget's current children.

Name (XtN...)	Type	Default	Description
XtNcolormap	Colormap	Parent's colormap.	Colormap that this widget will use.
XtNdefault-Distance	int	4	Default value for XtNhoriz-Distance and XtNvert-Distance.
XtNdepth .	int	Parent's depth.	(C) Depth of this widget's window.
XtNdestroy-Callback	XtCallbackList	NULL	Callbacks for XtDestroy-Widget().
XtNheight	Dimension	Computed at realize.	(A) Height of form.
XtNmappedWhen-Managed	Boolean	TRUE	Whether XtMapWidget() is automatic.
XtNnumChildren	Cardinal	0	(R) Number of children in this composite widget.
XtNscreen	Screen	Parent's screen	(R) Screen on which this widget is displayed.
XtNsensitive	Boolean	TRUE	Whether widget receives input.
XtNtranslations	TranslationTable	NULL	Event-to-action translations.
XtNwidth	Dimension	Computed at realize.	(A) Width of form.
XtNx	Position	0	x coordinate in pixels.
XtNy	Position	0	y coordinate in pixels.

Constraints

When creating children to be added to a Form, the following additional resources are retrieved from the argument list or from the resource database. Note that these resources are maintained by the Form widget, even though they are stored in the child.

Name (XtN...)	Type	Default	Description
XtNbottom	XtEdgeType	XtRubber	See text.
XtNfromHoriz	Widget	NULL	See text.
XtNfromVert	Widget	NULL	See text.
XtNhorizDistance	int	XtdefaultDistance	See text.
XtNleft	XtEdgeType	XtRubber	See text.
XtNresizable	Boolean	FALSE	TRUE if children allowed to resize themselves.
XtNright	XtEdgeType	XtRubber	See text.
XtNtop	XtEdgeType	XtRubber	See text.
XtNvertDistance	int	XtdefaultDistance	See text.

These resources are called constraints, and can be specified to the Form to indicate where the child should be positioned within the Form.

The resources XtNhorizDistance and XtNfromHoriz let the widget position itself a specified number of pixels horizontally away from another widget in the form. As an example,

XtNhorizDistance could equal 10 and XtNfromHoriz could be the widget ID of another widget in the Form. The new widget will be placed 10 pixels to the right of the widget defined in XtNfromHoriz. If XtNfromHoriz equals NULL, then XtNhorizDistance is measured from the left edge of the Form.

Similarly, the resources XtNvertDistance and XtNfromVert let the widget position itself a specified number of pixels vertically away from another widget in the Form. If Xt-NfromVert equals NULL, then XtNvertDistance is measured from the top of the Form. Form provides a cvtStringToWidget conversion procedure. Using this procedure, the resource database may be used to specify the XtNfromHoriz and XtNfromVert resources by widget name rather than widget ID. The string value must be the name of a child of the same Form widget parent.

The XtNtop, XtNbottom, XtNleft, and XtNright resources tell the Form where to position the child when the Form is resized. XtEdgeType is defined in *<X11/Xaw/Form.h>* and is one of XtChainTop, XtChainBottom, XtChainLeft, XtChainRight, or XtRubber.

The values XtChainTop, XtChainBottom, XtChainLeft, and XtChainRight specify that a constant distance is to be maintained from an edge of the child to the top, bottom, left, and right edges, respectively, of the Form. The value XtRubber specifies that a proportional distance from the edge of the child to the left or top edge of the Form is to be maintained when the form is resized. The proportion is determined from the initial position of the child and the initial size of the Form. Form provides an XtRString to XtREdgeType resource converter to allow the resize constraints to be specified easily in a resource file.

The default width of the Form is the minimum width needed to enclose the children after computing their initial layout, with a margin of XtNdefaultDistance at the right and bottom edges. If a width and height is assigned to the Form that is too small for the layout, the children will be clipped by the right and bottom edges of the Form.

Public Functions

When a new child becomes managed or an old child unmanaged, the Form widget will recalculate the positions of its children according to the values of the XtNhorizDistance, Xt-NfromHoriz, XtNvertDistance, and XtNfromVert constraints at the time the change is made. No re-layout is performed when a child makes a geometry request.

• To force or defer a re-layout of the Form widget, use XawFormDoLayout():

```
void XawFormDoLayout(w, do_layout)
    Widget w;
    Boolean do_layout;
```

where:

w   Specifies the Form widget.

do_layout Enables (if True) or disables (if False) layout of the Form widget.

When making several changes to the children of a Form widget after the Form has been realized, it is a good idea to disable re-layout until all changes have been made, then allow

Athena Classes

the layout. The Form widget increments an internal count each time `XtFormDoLayout` is called with *do_layout* set to `False`; the Form widget decrements the count when *do_layout* is `True`. When the count reaches 0, the Form widget performs a re-layout.

Grip

Name

Grip widget – attachment point for dragging other widgets.

Synopsis

Public Headers: *<X11/StringDefs.h> <X11/Xaw/Grip.h>*

Private Header: *<X11/Xaw/GripP.h>*

Class Name: Grip

Class Pointer: `gripWidgetClass`

Instantiation: *widget* = XtCreateWidget(*name*, gripWidgetClass, ...)

Class Hierarchy

Core → Simple → Grip

Description

The Grip widget provides a small region in which user input events (such as `ButtonPress` or `ButtonRelease`) may be handled. The most common use for the Grip widget is as an attachment point for visually repositioning an object, such as the pane border in a Paned widget.

Resources

When creating a Grip widget instance, the following resources are retrieved from the argument list or from the resource database:

Name (XtN...)	Type	Default	Description
XtNaccelerators	AcceleratorTable	NULL	List of event-to-action bindings to be executed by this widget, even though the event occurred in another widget.
XtNancestorSensitive	Boolean	True	(D) Sensitivity state of the ancestors of this widget: a widget is insensitive if either it or any of its ancestors is insensitive.
XtNbackground	Pixel	XtDefault-Background	Window background color.
XtNbackgroundPixmap	Pixmap	XtUnspecified-Pixmap	Window background pixmap.
XtNborderColor	Pixel	XtDefault-Foreground	Window border color.
XtNborderPixmap	Pixmap	XtUnspecified-Pixmap	Window border pixmap.
XtNborderWidth	Dimension	0	Width of the border in pixels.
XtNcallback	XtCallbackList	NULL	Action routine.
XtNcolormap	Colormap	Parent's colormap.	Colormap that this widget will use.
XtNcursor	Cursor	None	Cursor for the grip.

Name (XtN...)	Type	Default	Description
XtNdepth	int	Parent's depth.	(C) Depth of this widget's window.
XtNdestroyCallback	XtCallbackList	NULL	Callback for XtDestroy-Widget().
XtNforeground	Pixel	XtDefault-Foreground	Window background color.
XtNheight	Dimension	8	Height of the widget.
XtNinsensitiveBorder	Pixmap	Gray pixmap	Pixmap will be tiled into the widget's border if the widget becomes insensitive.
XtNmappedWhenManaged	Boolean	TRUE	Whether XtMapWidget() is automatic.
XtNscreen	Screen	Parent's screen.	(R) Screen on which this widget is displayed.
XtNsensitive	Boolean	TRUE	Whether widget should receive input.
XtNtranslations	TranslationTable	NULL	Event-to-action translations.
XtNwidth	Dimension	8	Width of the widget.
XtNx	Position	0	x coordinate in pixels.
XtNy	Position	0	y coordinate in pixels.

Note that the Grip widget displays its region with the foreground pixel only.

Translations and Actions

The Grip widget does not declare any default event translation bindings, but it does declare a single action routine named GripAction in its action table. The client specifies an arbitrary event translation table, giving parameters to the GripAction routine.

The GripAction action executes the callbacks on the XtNcallback list, passing as *call_data* a pointer to a XawGripCallData structure, defined in *<X11/Xaw/Grip.h>*:

```
typedef struct _GripCallData {
    XEvent *event;
    String *params;
    Cardinal num_params;
} XawGripCallDataRec, *XawGripCallData,
GripCallDataRec, *GripCallData;  /* for R4 compatibility */
```

In this structure, *event* is a pointer to the input event that triggered the action, and *params* and *num_params* give the string parameters specified in the translation table for the particular event binding.

The following is an example of a GripAction translation table:

```
<Btn1Down>:GripAction(press)
<Btn1Motion>:GripAction(move)
<Btn1Up>:GripAction(release)
```

See Also

Paned(5).

Label

Name
Label widget – widget to display a non-editable string.

Synopsis
Public Headers: *<X11/StringDefs.h> <X11/Xaw/Label.h>*

Private Header: *<X11/Xaw/LabelP.h>*

Class Name: Label

Class Pointer: `labelWidgetClass`

Instantiation: *widget* `= XtCreateWidget(`*name*`, labelWidgetClass, ...)`

Class Hierarchy
Core → Simple → Label

Description
A Label is a non-editable text string or pixmap that is displayed within a window. The string may contain multiple lines of Latin1 characters. It can be aligned to the left, right, or center of its window. A Label can be neither selected nor directly edited by the user.

Resources
When creating a Label widget instance, the following resources are retrieved from the argument list or from the resource database:

Name (XtN...)	Type	Default	Description
XtNaccelerators	AcceleratorTable	NULL	List of event-to-action bindings to be executed by this widget, even though the event occurred in another widget.
XtNancestor-Sensitive	Boolean	True	(D) Sensitivity state of the ancestors of this widget: a widget is insensitive if either it or any of its ancestors is insensitive.
XtNbackground	Pixel	XtDefault-Background	Window background color.
XtNbackground-Pixmap	Pixmap	XtUnspecified-Pixmap	Window background pixmap.
XtNbitmap	Pixmap	None	Pixmap to display in place of the label.
XtNborderColor	Pixel	XtDefault-Foreground	Window border color.
XtNborderPixmap	Pixmap	XtUnspecified-Pixmap	Window border pixmap.
XtNborderWidth	Dimension	1	Border width in pixels.

Name (XtN...)	Type	Default	Description
XtNcolormap	Colormap	Parent's colormap.	Colormap that this widget will use.
XtNcursor	Cursor	None	Pointer cursor.
XtNdepth	int	Parent's depth.	(C) Depth of this widget's window.
XtNdestroy-Callback	XtCallbackList	NULL	Callbacks for XtDestroy-Widget().
(R5) XtNencoding	unsigned char	XawTextEncoding8bit	For I18N.
XtNfont	XFontStruct*	XtDefaultFont	Label font.
XtNforeground	Pixel	XtDefault-Foreground	Foreground color.
XtNheight	Dimension	Font height + 2 * XtNinternalHeight	(A) Height of widget.
XtNinsensitive-Border	Pixmap	Gray pixmap.	Border when not sensitive.
XtNinternal-Height	Dimension	2	See note.
XtNinternalWidth	Dimension	4	See note.
XtNjustify	XtJustify	XtJustifyCenter	Type of text alignment.
XtNlabel	String	Name of widget.	String to be displayed.
(R5) XtNleftBitmap	Bitmap	None	Pixmap before label.
XtNmappedWhen-Managed	Boolean	TRUE	Whether XtMapWidget() is automatic.
XtNresize	Boolean	TRUE	Whether to auto-resize in SetValues.
XtNscreen	Screen	Parent's screen.	(R) Screen on which this widget is displayed: this is not a settable resource.
XtNsensitive	Boolean	TRUE	Whether widget receives input.
XtNtranslations	Translation-Table	See below.	Event-to-action translations.
XtNwidth	Dimension	XtNlabel width +2 * XtNinternalWidth	(A) Width of widget.
XtNx	Position	0	x coordinate in pixels.
XtNy	Position	0	y coordinate in pixels.

Note that the Label widget supports only the XtNdestroyCallback callback list.

The new resources associated with Label are:

XtNbitmap

> Specifies a bitmap to display in place of the text label. The bitmap can be specified as a string in the resource database. The StringToPixmap converter will interpret the string as the name of a file in the bitmap utility format that is to be loaded into a pixmap. The string can be an absolute or a relative filename. If a relative filename is used, the

directory specified by the resource name `bitmapFilePath` or the resource class `BitmapFilePath` is added to the beginning of the specified filename. If the `bitmapFilePath` resource is not defined, the default directory on a POSIX-based system is */usr/include/X11/bitmaps*.

`XtNencoding`

Specifies whether the widget uses 8-bit or 16-bit text functions. New in R5.

`XtNinternalHeight`

Represents the distance in pixels between the top and bottom of the label text or bitmap and the horizontal edges of the Label widget.

`XtNinternalWidth`

Represents the distance in pixels between the ends of the label text or bitmap and the vertical edges of the Label widget.

`XtNjustify`

Specifies left, center, or right alignment of the label string within the Label widget. If it is specified within an `ArgList`, one of the values `XtJustifyLeft`, `XtJustify-Center`, or `XtJustifyRight` can be specified. In a resource of type `string`, one of the values `left`, `center`, or `right` can be specified.

`XtNlabel`

Specifies the text string that is to be displayed in the button if no bitmap is specified. The default is the widget name of the Label widget.

`XtNleftBitmap`

Specifies a name of a bitmap to display in the left margin of the Label. All 1's in the bitmap are rendered in the foreground color, and all 0's will be drawn in the background color. New in R5.

`XtNresize`

Specifies whether the Label widget should attempt to resize to its preferred dimensions whenever `XtSetValues()` is called for it.

Name

List widget – widget for managing row-column geometry.

Synopsis

Public Headers:	*<X11/StringDefs.h> <X11/Xaw/List.h>*
Private Header:	*<X11/Xaw/ListP.h>*
Class Name:	List
Class Pointer:	`listWidgetClass`
Instantiation:	*widget* = `XtCreateWidget(`*name*`, listWidgetClass, ...)`

Class Hierarchy

Core → Simple → List

Description

The List widget is a rectangle that contains a list of strings formatted into rows and columns. When one of the strings is selected, it is highlighted, and an application callback routine is invoked. Only one string may be selected at a time.

Resources

When creating a List widget instance, the following resources are retrieved from the argument list or from the resource database:

Name (XtN...)	Type	Default	Description
XtNaccelerators	AcceleratorTable	NULL	List of event-to-action bindings to be executed by this widget, even though the event occurred in another widget.
XtNancestor-Sensitive	Boolean	True	(D) Sensitivity state of the ancestors of this widget: a widget is insensitive if either it or any of its ancestors is insensitive.
XtNbackground	Pixel	XtDefault-Background	Window background color.
XtNbackground-Pixmap	Pixmap	XtUnspecified-Pixmap	Window background pixmap.
XtNborderColor	Pixel	XtDefault-Foreground	Window border color.
XtNborderPixmap	Pixmap	XtUnspecified-Pixmap	Window border pixmap.
XtNborderWidth	Dimension	1	Width of border.
XtNcallback	XtCallbackList	NULL	Selection callback function.
XtNcolormap	Colormap	Parent's colormap.	Colormap that this widget will use.

Name (XtN...)	Type	Default	Description
XtNcolumnSpacing	Dimension	6	Space between columns in the list.
XtNcursor	Cursor	left_ptr	Pointer cursor.
XtNdefaultColumns	int	2	Number of columns to use.
XtNdepth	int	Parent's depth.	(C) Depth of this widget's window.
XtNdestroy- Callback	XtCallbackList	NULL	Callbacks for XtDestroy- Widget().
XtNfont	XFontStruct*	XtDefaultFont	Font for list text.
XtNforceColumns	Boolean	FALSE	Force the use of XtNdefault- Columns.
XtNforeground	Pixel	XtDefault- Foreground	Foreground (text) color.
XtNheight	Dimension	Contains list exactly.	(A) Height of widget.
XtNinsensitive- Border	Pixmap	Gray pixmap.	Border when not sensitive.
XtNinternalHeight	Dimension	2	Spacing between list and widget edges.
XtNinternalWidth	Dimension	4	Spacing between list and widget edges.
XtNlist	String *	Name of widget.	An array of strings that is the list.
XtNlongest	int	0	(A) Length of the longest list item in pixels.
XtNmappedWhen- Managed	Boolean	TRUE	Whether XtMapWidget() is automatic.
XtNnumberStrings	int	Number of strings.	(A) Number of items in the list.
XtNpasteBuffer	Boolean	FALSE	Copy the selected item to cut buffer 0.
XtNrowSpacing	Dimension	4	Space between rows in the list.
XtNrowSpacing	Dimension	4	Space between rows in the list.
XtNscreen	Screen	Parent's screen.	(R) Screen on which this widget is displayed.
XtNsensitive	Boolean	TRUE	Whether widget receives input.
XtNtranslations	Translation- Table	NULL	Event-to-action translations.
XtNverticalList	Boolean	FALSE	Specify the layout of list items.
XtNwidth	Dimension	Contains list exactly.	(A) Width of widget.
XtNx	Position	0	x coordinate in pixels.
XtNy	Position	0	y coordinate in pixels.

The new resources associated with the List widget are:

XtNcallback

All functions on this list are called whenever the notify action is invoked.

XtNrowSpacing
XtNcolumnSpacing

Specify the amount of space between each of the rows and columns in the list.

XtNdefaultColumns

Specifies the default number of columns, which is used when neither the width nor the height of the List widget is specified or when XtNforceColumns is True.

XtNforceColumns

Specifies that the default number of columns is to be used no matter what the current size of the List widget is.

XtNfont

Specifies the font to be used to display the list.

XtNforeground

Specifies a pixel value that indexes the widget's colormap in order to derive the color to be used to paint the text of the list elements.

XtNinternalHeight

Represents a margin, in pixels, between the top and bottom of the list and the edges of the List widget.

XtNinternalWidth

Represents a margin, in pixels, between the left and right edges of the list and the edges of the List widget.

XtNlist

Specifies the array of text strings that is to be displayed in the List widget. If the default for XtNnumberStrings is used, the list must be NULL-terminated. If a value is not specified for the list, the number of strings is set to 1, and the name of the widget is used as the list.

XtNlongest

Specifies the length, in pixels, of the longest string in the current list. If the client knows the length, it should specify it; otherwise, the List widget computes a default length by searching through the list. If this resource is incorrectly specified, selection of list items may not work properly.

XtNnumberStrings

Specifies the number of strings in the current list. If a value is not specified, the list must be NULL-terminated.

XtNpasteBuffer

If this is True, then the value of the string selected will be put into X cut buffer 0.

XtNverticalList

If this is True, the elements in the list are arranged vertically; if False, the elements are arranged horizontally.

Translations and Actions

The List widget has three predefined actions: Set, Unset, and Notify. Set and Unset allow switching the foreground and background colors for the current list item. Notify allows processing application callbacks.

The following is the default translation table used by the List widget:

```
<Btn1Down>,<Btn1Up>:Set() Notify()
```

Callback Structures

- The List widget supports two callback lists:

    - XtNdestroyCallback
    - XtNcallback

The notify action executes the callbacks on the XtNcallback list.

The *call_data* argument passed to callbacks on the XtNcallback list is a pointer to an XawListReturnStruct structure, defined in *<X11/Xaw/List.h>*:

```
typedef struct _XawListReturnStruct {
    String string;        /* string shown in the list */
    int list_index;       /* index of the item selected */
} XawListReturnStruct;
```

Public Functions

- To change the list of strings that is displayed, use:

```
void XawListChange(w, list, nitems, longest, resize)
    Widget w;
    String * list;
    int nitems, longest;
    Boolean resize;
```

where:

w	Specifies the widget ID.
list	Specifies the new list for the List widget to display.
nitems	Specifies the number of items in the list. If a value less than 1 is specified, the list must be NULL-terminated, and the List widget calculates the number for you.
longest	Specifies the length of the longest item in the list in pixels. If a value less than 1 is specified, the List widget calculates the value for you.

> *resize* Specifies a Boolean value that indicates whether the List widget should try to resize itself (True) or not (False) after making the change. Note that the constraints of the parent of the List widget are always enforced, regardless of the value specified.

Note that XawListChange() will Unset all list elements that are currently Set before the list is actually changed, and will reset the XtNlongest resource. The list is used in place, and it must remain usable either for the lifetime of the List widget or until the list has been changed again with this function or with XtSetValues().

- To highlight an item in the list, use:

```
void XawListHighlight(w, item);
    Widget w;
    int item;
```

where:

> w Specifies the widget ID.
>
> *item* Specifies the index into the current list that indicates the item to be highlighted.

Only one item can be highlighted at a time. If an item is already highlighted when XawListHighlight() is called, the highlighted item is immediately unhighlighted and the new item is highlighted.

- To unhighlight the currently highlighted item in the list, use:

```
void XawListUnhighlight(w);
    Widget w;
```

where *w* specifies the widget ID.

- To retrieve an item in the list, use:

```
XawListReturnStruct *XtListShowCurrent(w);
    Widget w;
```

where *w* specifies the widget ID.

- The XawListShowCurrent() function returns a pointer to an XawListReturn-Struct structure that contains the currently highlighted item. If the value of the index member is XAW_LIST_NONE, the string member is undefined, which indicates that no item is currently selected.

MenuButton

Name

MenuButton widget – button that pops up a menu.

Synopsis

Public Headers:	*<X11/StringDefs.h> <X11/Xaw/MenuButton.h>*
Private Header:	*<X11/Xaw/MenuButtoP.h>*
Class Name:	MenuButton
Class Pointer:	`menuButtonWidgetClass`
Instantiation:	*widget* = XtCreateWidget(*name*, menuButtonWidgetClass, ...)

Class Hierarchy

Core → Simple → Label → Command → MenuButton

Description

The MenuButton widget is an area, often rectangular, that contains a text or pixmap label. This selectable area is referred to as a button. When the pointer cursor is on the button, the button border is highlighted to indicate that the button is ready for selection. When pointer button 1 is pressed, the MenuButton widget pops up the menu that has been named in the `XtNmenuName` resource.

Resources

When creating a MenuButton widget instance, the following resources are retrieved from the argument list or from the resource database:

Name (XtN...)	Type	Default	Description
XtNaccelerators	AcceleratorTable	NULL	List of event-to-action bindings to be executed by this widget, even though the event occurred in another widget.
XtNancestor-Sensitive	Boolean	True	(D) Sensitivity state of the ancestors of this widget: a widget is insensitive if either it or any of its ancestors is insensitive.
XtNbackground	Pixel	XtDefault-Background	Window background color.
XtNbackground-Pixmap	Pixmap	XtUnspecified-Pixmap	Window background pixmap.
XtNbitmap	Pixmap	None	Pixmap to display in place of the label.
XtNborderColor	Pixel	XtDefault-Foreground	Window border color.

Name (XtN...)	Type	Default	Description
XtNborderPixmap	Pixmap	XtUnspecified- Pixmap	Window border pixmap.
XtNborderWidth	Dimension	1	Width of button border.
XtNcallback	XtCallbackList	NULL	Callback for button select.
XtNcolormap	Colormap	Parent's colormap.	Colormap that this widget will use.
XtNcornerRound- Percent	Dimension	25	See below.
XtNcursor	Cursor	None	Pointer cursor.
XtNdepth	int	Parent's depth.	(C) Depth of this widget's window.
XtNdestroy- Callback	XtCallbackList	NULL	Callbacks for XtDestroy- Widget().
XtNencoding	unsigned char	XawTextEncoding8bit	For I18N.
XtNfont	XFontStruct	XtDefaultFont	Label font.
XtNforeground	Pixel	XtDefault- Foreground	Foreground color.
XtNheight	Dimension	Font height + 2 * XtNinternalHeight	(A) Button height.
XtNhighlight- Thickness	Dimension	2 (0 if Shaped)	(A) Width of border to be highlighted.
XtNinsensitive- Border	Pixmap	Gray pixmap.	Border when not sensitive.
XtNinternal- Height	Dimension	2	Internal border height for highlighting.
XtNinternalWidth	Dimension	4	Internal border width for highlighting.
XtNjustify	Justify	XtJustifyCenter	Type of text alignment.
XtNlabel	String	Name of widget.	Button label.
(R5) XtNleftBitmap	Bitmap	None	Pixmap before label.
XtNmappedWhen- Managed	Boolean	True	Whether XtMapWidget() is automatic.
XtNmenuName	String	"menu"	Name of menu.
XtNresize	Boolean	True	Whether to auto-resize in SetValues.
XtNscreen	Screen	Parent's screen.	(R) Screen on which this widget is displayed.
XtNsensitive	Boolean	True	Whether widget receives input.
XtNshapeStype	ShapeStyle	Rectangle	Type of nonrectangular button.
XtNtranslations	TranslationTable	See below.	Event-to-action translations.
XtNwidth	Dimension	XtNlabel width + 2 * XtNinternalWidth	(A) Button Width.

Name (XtN...)	Type	Default	Description
XtNx	Position	0	x-coordinate in pixels.
XtNy	Position	0	y-coordinate in pixels.

Note that the MenuButton widget supports two callback lists: `XtNdestroyCallback` and `XtNcallback`. The notify action executes the callbacks on the `XtNcallback` list. The *call_data* argument is unused.

The new resources (not inherited from superclasses) associated with the MenuButton widget are:

XtNmenuName

> The name of a popup shell to pop up as a menu. The MenuButton searches for this name using `XtNameToWidget()`, starting with itself as the reference widget. If unsuccessful, MenuButton continues to search up the widget tree, using each of its ancestors as the reference widget. If still unsuccessful, MenuButton prints a warning message and gives up. When the menu is found, it is popped up with an exclusive Xt grab mode and with a global passive grab of the pointer button that was pressed. The MenuButton widget does not copy the value of this resource into newly allocated memory. The application programmer must pass the resource value in nonvolatile memory.

Translations and Actions

The following default translation bindings are used by the MenuButton widget:

```
<EnterWindow>:highlight()
<LeaveWindow>:reset()
<BtnDown>:reset() PopupMenu()
```

With these bindings, the user can cancel the action before releasing the button by moving the pointer out of the MenuButton widget.

The MenuButton widget supports the following actions:

- Switching the button between the foreground and background colors with `set` and `unset`.

- Processing application callbacks with `notify`.

- Switching the internal border between highlighted and unhighlighted states with `highlight` and `unhighlight`.

- Popping up a menu with `PopupMenu`.

The actions supported by MenuButton are listed below:

highlight(*condition*)

> Displays the internal highlight border in the color (`XtNforeground` or `XtNbackground`) that contrasts with the interior color of the MenuButton widget. The con-

ditions `WhenUnset` and `Always` are understood by this action procedure. If no argument is passed, `WhenUnset` is assumed.

`unhighlight()`

Displays the internal highlight border in the color (`XtNforeground` or `Xt-Nbackground`) that matches the interior color of the MenuButton widget.

`set()`

Enters the set state, in which `notify` is possible, and displays the interior of the button, including the highlight border, in the foreground color. The label or pixmap is displayed in the background color.

`unset()`

Cancels the set state and displays the interior of the button, including the highlight border, in the background color. The label or pixmap is displayed in the foreground color.

`reset()`

Cancels any `set` or `highlight` action and displays the interior of the button in the background color, with the label or pixmap displayed in the foreground color.

`notify()`

Executes the callback list specified by `XtNcallback`, if executed in the set state. The value of the *call_data* argument is undefined.

`PopupMenu()`

Pops up the menu specified by the `XtNmenuName` resource. `PopupMenu` is registered as a grab action. As a result, clients which pop up menus without using `XtMenuPopup()` or `MenuPopup` or `PopupMenu` in translations will fail to have a grab active. They should make a call to `XtRegisterGrabAction()` on the appropriate action in the application initialization routine, or use a different translation.

See Also

Command(5), *Label*(5), *SimpleMenu*(5).

Paned

Name

Paned widget – geometry-managing widget for vertical or horizontal tiles.

Synopsis

Public Headers:	*<X11/StringDefs.h> <X11/Xaw/Paned.h>*
Private Header:	*<X11/Xaw/PanedP.h>*
Class Name:	Paned
Class Pointer:	`panedWidgetClass`
Instantiation:	*widget* = XtCreateWidget(*name*, panedWidgetClass, ...)

Class Hierarchy

Core → Composite → Constraint → Paned

Description

The Paned widget manages children in a vertically or horizontally tiled fashion. The panes may be dynamically resized by the user by using the *grips* that appear near the right or bottom edge of the border between two panes.

When the pointer is positioned on a grip and pressed, an arrow is displayed that indicates the pane that is being resized. While keeping the pointer button down, the user can move the pointer up and down (or left and right). This, in turn, changes the border between the panes, causing one pane to shrink and some other pane (or panes) to grow. The size of the Paned widget will not change.

The choice of alternate pane is a function of the `XtNmin`, `XtNmax`, and `XtNskipAdjust` constraints on the other panes. With the default bindings, button 1 resizes the pane above or to the left of the selected grip, button 3 resizes the pane below or to the right of the selected grip, and button 2 repositions the border between two panes only.

Resources

When creating a Paned widget instance, the following resources are retrieved from the argument list or from the resource database:

Name (XtN...)	Type	Default	Description
XtNaccelerators	AcceleratorTable	NULL	List of event-to-action bindings to be executed by this widget, even though the event occurred in another widget.
XtNancestor-Sensitive	Boolean	True	(D) Sensitivity state of the ancestors of this widget: a widget is insensitive if either it or any of its ancestors is insensitive.
XtNbackground	Pixel	XtDefault-Background	Window background color.

Name (XtN...)	Type	Default	Description
XtNbackground-Pixmap	Pixmap	XtUnspecified-Pixmap	Window background pixmap.
XtNbetweenCursor	Cursor	Depends on orientation.	(A) Cursor for changing the boundary between two panes.
XtNborderColor	Pixel	XtDefault-Foreground	Window border color.
XtNborderPixmap	Pixmap	XtUnspecified-Pixmap	Window border pixmap.
XtNborderWidth	Dimension	1	Border width (pixels).
XtNchildren	WidgetList	NULL	(R) List of all this composite widget's current children.
XtNcolormap	Colormap	Parent's colormap.	Colormap that this widget will use.
XtNcursor	Cursor	None	Image that will be displayed as the pointer cursor whenever it is in this widget, but not in any of its children (children may also inherit this cursor).
XtNdepth	int	Parent's depth.	(C) Depth of this widget's window.
XtNdestroy-Callback	XtCallbackList	NULL	Callbacks for XtDestroy-Widget().
XtNgripCursor	Cursor	Depends on orientation.	(A) Cursor for grip when not active.
XtNgripIndent	Position	10	Offset of grip from margin (pixels).
XtNgrip-Translations	TranslationTable	See below.	Button bindings for grip.
XtNheight	Dimension	Depends on orientation.	(A) Height of Pane.
XtNhorizontal-BetweenCursor	Cursor	sb_up_arrow	Cursor to be used for the grip when changing the boundary between two panes.
XtNhorizontal-GripCursor	Cursor	sb_h_double_arrow	Cursor to be used for the grips when they are not active.
XtNinternal-BorderColor	Pixel	XtDefaultForeground	Internal border color of the widget's window.
XtNinternal-BorderWidth	Dimension	1	Amount of space left between panes.
XtNleftCursor	Cursor	sb_left_arrow	Cursor for resizing the pane to the left of the grip.
XtNlowerCursor	Cursor	sb_down_arrow	Cursor for resizing the pane below the grip.
XtNmappedWhen-Managed	Boolean	TRUE	Whether XtMapWidget() is automatic.

Name (XtN...)	Type	Default	Description
XtNnumChildren	Cardinal	0	(R) The number of children in this composite widget.
XtNorientation	Orientation	XtOrientVertical	Orientation to stack the panes: this value can be either Xt-OrientVertical or Xt-OrientHorizontal.
XtNrefigureMode	Boolean	TRUE	Whether Pane should adjust children.
XtNrightCursor	Cursor	sb_right_arrow	Cursor for resizing the pane to the right of the grip.
XtNscreen	Screen	Parent's screen.	(R) Screen on which this widget is displayed.
XtNsensitive	Boolean	TRUE	Whether widget receives input.
XtNtranslations	TranslationTable	NULL	Event-to-action translations.
XtNupperCursor	Cursor	sb_up_arrow	Cursor for resizing the pane above the grip.
XtNvertical-BetweenCursor	Cursor	sb_left_arrow	Cursor to be used for the grip when changing the boundary between two panes.
XtNvertical-GripCursor	Cursor	sb_v_double_arrow	Cursor to be used for the grips when they are not active.
XtNwidth	Dimension	Depends on orientation.	(A) Width of Pane.
XtNx	Position	0	x coordinate in pixels.
XtNy	Position	0	y coordinate in pixels.

Constraints

During the creation of a child pane, the following resources, by which the Paned widget controls the placement of the child, can be specified in the argument list or retrieved from the resource database:

Name (XtN...)	Type	Default	Description
XtNallowResize	Boolean	FALSE	If FALSE, ignore child resize requests.
XtNmax	Dimension	Unlimited	Maximum height for pane.
XtNmin	Dimension	1	Minimum height for pane.
XtNpreferredPaneSize	Dimension	ask child	Preferred size of pane.
XtNresizeToPreferred	Boolean	False	Specifies whether to resize each pane to its preferred size when the Paned widget is resized.
XtNshowGrip	Boolean	True	Specifies whether to show a grip for this pane.
XtNskipAdjust	Boolean	FALSE	TRUE if the Paned widget should not automatically resize pane.

Layout Semantics

To make effective use of the Paned widget, it is helpful to know the rules it uses to determine which child will be resized in any given situation. Three rules determine which child is resized. Although these rules are always the same, the panes that are searched can change depending upon what caused the relayout.

1. Do not let a pane grow larger than its max or smaller than its min.

2. Do not adjust panes with skipAdjust set.

3. Do not adjust panes away from their preferred size, although moving one closer to its preferred size is fine.

When searching the children, the Paned widget looks for panes that satisfy all three rules; if unsuccessful, the Paned widget eliminates rule 3 and then rule 2. Rule 1 is always enforced.

If the relayout is due to a resize or a change in management, then the panes are searched from bottom to top. If the relayout is due to grip movement, then they are searched from the grip selected in the direction opposite the pane selected.

Resizing Panes from a Grip Action

The pane above (or to the left of) the grip is resized by invoking the GripAction with Up-LeftPane specified. The panes below (or to the right of) the grip are each checked against all rules, then against rules 2 and 1, and finally against rule 1 only. No pane above (or to the left of) the chosen pane will ever be resized.

The pane below (or to the right of) the grip is resized by invoking the GripAction with LowRightPane specified. The panes above (or to the left of) the grip are each checked in this case. No pane below (or to the right of) the chosen pane will ever be resized.

Invoking GripAction with ThisBorderOnly specified just moves the border between the panes. No other panes are ever resized.

Resizing Panes after the Paned Widget is Resized

When the Paned widget is resized, it must determine a new size for each pane. There are two methods of doing this. The Paned widget can either give each pane its preferred size and then resize the panes to fit, or it can use the current sizes and then resize the panes to fit. The resizeToPreferred resource allows the application to tell the Paned widget whether to query the child about its preferred size (subject to the preferredPaneSize) or to use the current size when refiguring the pane locations after the pane has been resized.

There is one special case. All panes assume they should resize to their preferred size until the Paned widget becomes visible to the user.

The Paned widget always resizes its children to their preferred sizes when a new child is managed, or a geometry management request is honored. The Paned widget will first attempt to resize itself to contain its panes exactly. If this is not possible, it will hunt through the children, from bottom to top (right to left), looking for a pane to resize.

Note that when a user resizes a pane with the grips, the Paned widget assumes that this new size is the preferred size of the pane.

Translations and Actions

The Paned widget has no action routines of its own, as all actions are handled through the grips. The grips are each assigned a default Translation table.

```
<Btn1Down>:GripAction(Start, UpLeftPane)
<Btn2Down>:GripAction(Start, ThisBorderOnly)
<Btn3Down>:GripAction(Start, LowRightPane)
<Btn1Motion>:GripAction(Move, UpLeftPane)
<Btn2Motion>:GripAction(Move, ThisBorderOnly)
<Btn3Motion>:GripAction(Move, LowRightPane)
Any<BtnUp>:GripAction(Commit)
```

The Paned widget interprets the `GripAction` as taking two arguments. The first argument may be any of the following:

Start   Sets up the Paned widget for resizing and changes the cursor of the grip. The second argument determines which pane will be resized, and can take on any of the three values shown above (`UpLeftPane`, `ThisBorderOnly`, `Low-RightPane`).

Move   The internal borders are drawn over the current pane locations to animate where the borders would actually be placed if you were to move this border as shown. The second argument must match the second argument that was passed to the `Start` action that began this process. If these arguments are not passed, the behavior is undefined.

Commit   This argument causes the Paned widget to commit the changes selected by the previously started action. The cursor is changed back to the grip's inactive cursor. No second argument is needed in this case.

Public Functions

You add panes after the parent frame is created. Any type of widget can be a pane *except* Grip. Grip widgets have a special meaning for the Paned widget, and adding a Grip as its own pane will confuse the Paned widget.

- To enable or disable a child's request for pane resizing, use `XawPanedAllowResize()`:

```
void XawPanedAllowResize(w, allow_resize)
    Widget w;
    Boolean allow_resize;
```

where:

w   Specifies the widget ID of the child widget pane.

allow_resize   Enables or disables a pane window for resizing requests.

If *allow_resize* is `True`, the Paned widget allows geometry requests from the child to change the pane's height. If *allow_resize* is `False`, the Paned widget ignores geometry requests from the child to change the pane's height. The default state is `True` before the Paned widget is realized and `False` after it is realized. This procedure is equivalent to changing the `XtNallowResize` resource for the child.

- To change the minimum and maximum height settings for a pane, use `XawPanedSet-MinMax()`:

    ```
    void XawPanedSetMinMax(w, min, max)
          Widget w;
          int min, max;
    ```

  where:

`w`	Specifies the widget ID of the child widget pane.
`min`	Specifies the minimum height of the child, in pixels.
`max`	Specifies the maximum height of the child, in pixels.
	This procedure is equivalent to setting the `XtNmin` and `Xt-Nmax` resources for the child.

- To retrieve the minimum and maximum height settings for a pane, use `XawPanedGet-MinMax()`:

    ```
    void XawPanedGetMinMax(w, min_return, max_return)
          Widget w;
          int *min_return, *max_return;   /* RETURNED */
    ```

  where:

`w`	Specifies the widget ID of the Paned widget.
`min_return`	Returns the minimum height of the child, expressed in pixels.
`max_return`	Returns the maximum height of the child, expressed in pixels.
	This procedure is equivalent to getting the `min` and `max` resources for this child.

- To enable or disable automatic recalculation of pane sizes and positions, use `XawPaned-SetRefigureMode()`:

    ```
    void XawPanedSetRefigureMode(w, mode)
          Widget w;
          Boolean mode;
    ```

  where:

`w`	Specifies the widget ID of the Paned widget.
`mode`	Enables or disables refiguration.

  You should set the mode to `False` if you add multiple panes to or remove multiple panes from the parent frame after it has been realized, unless you can arrange to manage all the panes at once using `XtManageChildren()`. After all the panes are added, set the mode to `True`. This avoids unnecessary geometry calculations and "window dancing."

- To retrieve the number of panes in a paned widget, use `XawPanedGetNumSub()`:

```
int XawPanedGetNumSub(w)
      Widget w;
```

where *w* specifies the widget ID of the Paned widget.

This function returns the number of panes in the Paned widget. This is *not* the same as the number of children, since the grips are also children of the Paned widget.

Name

Panner widget – a "scrollbar" for two dimensions.

Synopsis

Public Headers:	*<X11/StringDefs.h> <X11/Xaw/Panner.h>*
Private Header:	*<X11/Xaw/PannerP.h>*
Class Name:	Panner
Class Pointer:	`pannerWidgetClass`
Instantiation:	*widget* = XtCreateWidget(*name*, pannerWidgetClass, ...)

Class Hierarchy

Core → Simple → Panner

Availability

Release 5 and later.

Description

The Panner widget is conceptually a two-dimensional scrollbar. It displays a rectangle within a rectangle—the inner rectangle (the "slider") represents the visible portion of a larger area (the "canvas") represented by the outer rectangle. The size of the inner rectangle represents the size of the visible area relative to the whole, and its position indicates the relative position of the visible area within the whole. The user may drag the inner rectangle with the mouse (or use keyboard arrow keys) to pan through the large diagram or document (or whatever) that is being displayed. The Panner widget is typically used with a Porthole widget to scroll a third widget in two dimensions.

When a Panner is created, it is drawn with the slider in a contrasting color. The slider may be moved around the canvas by pressing, dragging, and then releasing Button1. While scrolling is in progress, the application receives notification through callback procedures which it may use to update any associated widgets. Notification may be done either as the slider is dragged, or only when the slider is released.

Resources

When creating a Panner widget instance, the following resources are retrieved from the argument list or from the resource database:

Name	Type	Default	Description
XtNaccelerators	AcceleratorTable	NULL	Accelerators for this widget.
XtNallowOff	Boolean	False	Whether the slider can go beyond the edges.
XtNancestor-Sensitive	Boolean	True	Sensitivity state of the ancestors of this widget.
XtNbackground	Pixel	XtDefault-Background	Window background color.

Athena
Classes

Name	Type	Default	Description
XtNbackgroundPixmap	Pixmap	XtUnspecified-Pixmap	Window background pixmap.
XtNbackgroundStipple	String	NULL	Background pattern.
XtNbitmap	Pixmap	None	Pixmap to display in place of the label.
XtNborderColor	Pixel	XtDefault-Foreground	Window border color.
XtNborderPixmap	Pixmap	XtUnspecified-Pixmap	Window border pixmap.
XtNborderWidth	Dimension	1	Width of button border.
XtNcanvasHeight	Dimension	0	Height of the canvas to pan.
XtNcanvasWidth	Dimension	0	Width of the canvas to pan.
XtNcolormap	Colormap	Parent's colormap.	Colormap that this widget will use.
XtNcursor	Cursor	None	Pointer cursor.
XtNcursorName	String	NULL	A cursor glyph name.
XtNdefaultScale	Dimension	8	Panner size as % of canvas.
XtNdepth	int	Parent's depth.	Depth of this widget's window.
XtNdestroyCallback	XtCallbackList	NULL	Callbacks for XtDestroy-Widget.
XtNforeground	Pixel	XtDefault-Foreground	Widget foreground color.
XtNheight	Dimension	0	Widget height.
XtNinsensitiveBorder	Pixmap	Gray pixmap.	Border when not sensitive.
XtNinternalSpace	Dimension	4	Margin around slider.
XtNlineWidth	Dimension	0	Width of rubberband lines.
XtNmappedWhen-Managed	Boolean	TRUE	Whether XtMapWidget is automatic.
XtNpointerColor	Pixel	XtDefault-Foreground	Cursor foreground color.
XtNpointerColor-Background	Pixel	XtDefault-Background	Cursor background color.
XtNreportCallback	XtCallbackList	NULL	Callback for panner motion.
XtNresize	Boolean	True	Whether to resize Panner with canvas.
XtNrubberBand	Boolean	False	Whether to do continuous scrolling.
XtNscreen	Screen	Parent's screen.	Screen on which this widget is displayed: this is not a settable resource.
XtNsensitive	Boolean	TRUE	Whether widget receives input.

Name	Type	Default	Description
XtNshadowColor	Pixel	XtDefault-Foreground	Color of thumb shadow.
XtNshadowThickness	Dimension	2	Width of thumb shadow.
XtNsliderX	Position	0	X location of thumb.
XtNsliderY	Position	0	Y location of thumb.
XtNsliderHeight	Dimension	0	Thumb height.
XtNsliderWidth	Dimension	0	Thumb width.
XtNtranslations	Translation-Table	See below.	Event-to-action translations.
XtNwidth	Dimension	0	Widget width.
XtNx	Position	0	x-coordinate in pixels.
XtNy	Position	0	y-coordinate in pixels.

The new resources (not inherited from superclasses) available to the Repeater widget are:

XtNallowOff
>   Whether to allow the edges of the slider to go off the edges of the canvas.

XtNbackgroundStipple
>   The name of a bitmap pattern to be used as the background for the area representing the canvas.

XtNcanvasHeight
>   The height of the canvas.

XtNcanvasWidth
>   The width of the canvas.

XtNdefaultScale
>   The percentage size that the Panner widget should have relative to the size of the canvas.

XtNforeground
>   The slider foreground color.

XtNinternalSpace
>   The width of internal border in pixels between a slider representing the full size of the canvas and the edge of the Panner widget.

XtNlineWidth
>   The width of the lines in the rubberbanding rectangle when rubberbanding is in effect instead of continuous scrolling. The default is 0.

XtNreportCallback
>   All functions on this callback list are called when the slider is moved.

XtNresize
>   Whether or not to resize the panner whenever the canvas size is changed so that the XtNdefaultScale is maintained.

XtNrubberBand

Whether or not scrolling should be discrete (only moving a rubberbanded rectangle until the scrolling is done) or continuous (moving the slider itself). This controls whether or not the move action procedure also invokes the notify action procedure.

XtNshadowColor

The color of the shadow underneath the slider.

XtNshadowThickness

The width of the shadow underneath the slider.

XtNsliderX

The X location of the slider in the coordinates of the canvas.

XtNsliderY

The Y location of the slider in the coordinates of the canvas.

XtNsliderHeight

The height of the slider.

XtNsliderWidth

The width of the slider.

Translations and Actions

The actions supported by the Panner widget are:

start()

This action begins movement of the slider.

stop()

This action ends movement of the slider.

abort()

This action ends movement of the slider and restores it to the position it held when the start action was invoked.

move()

This action moves the outline of the slider (if the XtNrubberBand resource is True) or the slider itself (by invoking the notify action procedure).

page(*xamount*,*yamount*)

This action moves the slider by the specified amounts. The format for the amounts is a signed or unsigned floating-point number (e.g., +1.0 or −.5) followed by either "p" indicating pages (slider sizes), or "c" indicating canvas sizes. A signed number indicates a relative coordinate and an unsigned number indicates an absolute coordinate. Thus, page(+0,+.5p) represents vertical movement down one-half the height of the slider and page(0,0) represents moving to the upper left corner of the canvas. This action causes the callbacks on the XtNreportCallback list to be invoked.

notify()

This action informs the application of the slider's current position by invoking the Xt-NreportCallback functions registered by the application.

set(*what*,*value*)

>   This action changes the behavior of the Panner. The *what* argument must currently be the string "rubberband" and controls the value of the XtNrubberBand resource. The *value* argument may have one of the values "on," "off," or "toggle."

The default bindings for Panner are:

```
<Btn1Down>:start()
<Btn1Motion>:move()
<Btn1Up>:notify() stop()
<Btn2Down>:abort()
<Key>KP_Enter:set(rubberband,toggle)
<Key>space:page(+1p,+1p)
<Key>Delete:page(-1p,-1p)
<Key>BackSpace:page(-1p,-1p)
<Key>Left:page(-.5p,+0)
<Key>Right:page(+.5p,+0)
<Key>Up:page(+0,-.5p)
<Key>Down:page(+0,+.5p)
<Key>Home:page(0,0)
```

Callback Structures

The functions registered on the XtNreportCallback list are invoked by the notify action with a *call_data* argument which is a pointer to a structure of type XawPanner-Report:

```
/*
 * XawPannerReport - this structure is used by the reportCallback of the
 * Panner, Porthole, Viewport, and Scrollbar widgets to report its
 * position.  All fields must be filled in, although the changed field
 * may be used as a hint as to which fields have been altered since the
 * last report.
 */
typedef struct {
    unsigned int changed;/* mask, see below */
    Position slider_x, slider_y;/* location of slider within outer */
    Dimension slider_width, slider_height;  /* size of slider */
    Dimension canvas_width, canvas_height;  /* size of canvas */
} XawPannerReport;

#define XawPRSliderX(1 << 0)
#define XawPRSliderY(1 << 1)
#define XawPRSliderWidth(1 << 2)
#define XawPRSliderHeight(1 << 3)
#define XawPRCanvasWidth(1 << 4)
#define XawPRCanvasHeight(1 << 5)
#define XawPRAll(63)/* union of above */
```

Public Functions

No public functions defined.

See Also

    Porthole(5), *Simple*(5).

Porthole

Name

Porthole widget – a panable view of a larger child widget.

Synopsis

Public Headers:	*<X11/StringDefs.h> <X11/Xaw/Porthole.h>*
Private Header:	*<X11/Xaw/PortholeP.h>*
Class Name:	Porthole
Class Pointer:	`portholeWidgetClass`
Instantiation:	*widget* = XtCreateWidget(*name*, portholeWidgetClass, ...)

Class Hierarchy

Core → Composite → Porthole

Availability

Release 5 and later.

Description

The Porthole widget provides geometry management of a list of arbitrary widgets, only one of which may be managed at any particular time. The managed child widget is reparented within the porthole and is moved around by the application (typically under the control of a Panner widget). The Porthole widget allows its managed child to request any size that is as large or larger than the Porthole itself and any location so long as the child still obscures all of the Porthole.

Resources

When creating a Porthole widget instance, the following resources are retrieved from the argument list or from the resource database:

Name	Type	Default	Description
XtNaccelerators	AcceleratorTable	NULL	Accelerators for this widget.
XtNancestor-Sensitive	Boolean	True	Sensitivity state of the ancestors of this widget.
XtNbackground	Pixel	XtDefault-Background	Window background color.
XtNbackground-Pixmap	Pixmap	XtUnspecified-Pixmap	Window background pixmap.
XtNborderColor	Pixel	XtDefault-Foreground	Window border color.
XtNborderPixmap	Pixmap	XtUnspecified-Pixmap	Window border pixmap.
XtNborderWidth	Dimension	1	Border width on button porthole.

Name	Type	Default	Description
XtNchildren	WidgetList	NULL	List of all this composite widget's current children.
XtNcolormap	Colormap	Parent's colormap.	Colormap that this widget will use.
XtNdepth	int	Parent's depth.	Depth of this widget's window.
XtNdestroy-Callback	XtCallbackList	NULL	Callbacks for XtDestroy-Widget
XtNheight	Dimension	See below.	Viewing height of inner window.
XtNmappedWhen-Managed	Boolean	TRUE	Whether XtMapWidget is automatic.
XtNnumChildren	Cardinal	0	Number of children in this composite widget.
XtNreportCallback	XtCallbackList	NULL	Called when child moves or resizes.
XtNscreen	Screen	Parent's screen.	Screen on which this widget is displayed.
XtNsensitive	Boolean	TRUE	Whether widget receives input.
XtNtranslations	TranslationTable	NULL	Event-to-action translations.
XtNwidth	Dimension	See below.	Viewing width of inner window.
XtNx	Position	0	x-coordinate in pixels.
XtNy	Position	0	y-coordinate in pixels.

There is only one new resource (not inherited from a superclass) associated with the Panner widget:

XtNreportCallback

> A list of functions to invoke whenever the managed child widget changes size or position. The *call_data* argument is of type XawPannerReport *, shown below.

Callback Structures

The functions registered on the XtNreportCallback list are invoked with a call_data argument which is a pointer to a structure of type XawPannerReport:

```
/*
 * XawPannerReport - this structure is used by the reportCallback of the
 * Panner, Porthole, Viewport, and Scrollbar widgets to report its
 * position.  All fields must be filled in, although the changed field
 * may be used as a hint as to which fields have been altered since the
 * last report.
 */
typedef struct {
    unsigned int changed;/* mask, see below */
```

```
      Position slider_x, slider_y;/* location of slider within outer */
      Dimension slider_width, slider_height;  /* size of slider */
      Dimension canvas_width, canvas_height;  /* size of canvas */
} XawPannerReport;

#define XawPRSliderX(1 << 0)
#define XawPRSliderY(1 << 1)
#define XawPRSliderWidth(1 << 2)
#define XawPRSliderHeight(1 << 3)
#define XawPRCanvasWidth(1 << 4)
#define XawPRCanvasHeight(1 << 5)
#define XawPRAll(63)/* union of above */
```

Public Functions

No public functions defined.

See Also

Composite(5), *Panner*(5).

Repeater

Name

Repeater widget – a Command widget with auto-repeat.

Synopsis

Public Headers:	*<X11/StringDefs.h>* *<X11/Xaw/Repeater.h>*
Private Header:	*<X11/Xaw/RepeaterP.h>*
Class Name:	Repeater
Class Pointer:	`repeaterWidgetClass`
Instantiation:	*widget* = `XtCreateWidget(`*name*`,` `repeaterWidgetClass,` `...)`

Class Hierarchy

Core → Simple → Label → Command → Repeater

Availability

Release 5 and later.

Description

The Repeater widget is a version of the Command button that triggers at an increasing rate while it is held down. It is typically used to implement valuators or certain types of scrollbars.

Resources

When creating a Repeater widget instance, the following resources are retrieved from the argument list or from the resource database:

Name	Type	Default	Description
XtNaccelerators	AcceleratorTable	NULL	Accelerators for this widget.
XtNancestor- Sensitive	Boolean	True	Sensitivity state of the ancestors of this widget.
XtNbackground	Pixel	XtDefault- Background	Window background color.
XtNbackground- Pixmap	Pixmap	XtUnspecified- Pixmap	Window background pixmap.
XtNbitmap	Pixmap	None	Pixmap to display in place of the label.
XtNborderColor	Pixel	XtDefault- Foreground	Window border color.
XtNborderPixmap	Pixmap	XtUnspecified- Pixmap	Window border pixmap.
XtNborderWidth	Dimension	1	Width of button border.
XtNcallback	XtCallbackList	NULL	Called for each activation.
XtNcolormap	Colormap	Parent's colormap.	Colormap that this widget will use.

Name	Type	Default	Description
XtNcornerRound-Percent	Dimension	25	Radius of rounded corner.
XtNcursor	Cursor	None	Pointer cursor.
XtNcursorName	String	NULL	A cursor glyph name.
XtNdecay	int	5	See below.
XtNdepth	int	Parent's depth.	Depth of this widget's window.
XtNdestroy-Callback	XtCallbackList	NULL	Callbacks for XtDestroyWidget.
XtNencoding	unsigned char	XawTextEncoding8bit	8 or 16-bit text.
XtNflash	Boolean	False	Whether to flash on auto-repeat.
XtNfont	XFontStruct*	XtDefaultFont	Label font.
XtNforeground	Pixel	XtDefaultForeground	Foreground color
XtNheight	Dimension	font height + 2 * XtNinternalHeight	Button height
XtNhighlight-Thickness	Dimension	2	Width of border to be highlighted.
XtNinitialDelay	int	200	See below.
XtNinsensitive-Border	Pixmap	Gray pixmap.	Border when not sensitive.
XtNinternal-Height	Dimension	2	Internal border height for highlighting.
XtNinternalWidth	Dimension	4	Internal border width for highlighting.
XtNjustify	XtJustify	XtJustifyCenter	Type of text alignment.
XtNlabel	String	Name of widget.	Button label.
XtNleftBitmap	Pixmap	None	A bitmap to display to the left of the label.
XtNmappedWhen-Managed	Boolean	TRUE	Whether XtMapWidget is automatic.
XtNminimumDelay	int	10	See below.
XtNpointerColor	Pixel	XtDefaultForeground	Cursor foreground color.
XtNpointerColor-Background	Pixel	XtDefaultBackground	Cursor background color.
XtNrepeatDelay	int	50	See below.
XtNresize	Boolean	TRUE	Whether to auto-resize in SetValues.
XtNscreen	Screen	Parent's screen.	Screen on which this widget is displayed: this is not a settable resource.
XtNsensitive	Boolean	TRUE	Whether widget receives input.
XtNshapeStyle	ShapeStyle	XmuShapeRectangle	Shape of button.

Name	Type	Default	Description
XtNstartCallback	XtCallbackList	NULL	Called when button pressed.
XtNstopCallback	XtCallbackList	NULL	Called when button released.
XtNtranslations	Translation- Table	See below.	Event-to-action translations.
XtNwidth	Dimension	XtNlabel width + 2* XtNinternalWidth	Button width.
XtNx	Position	0	x-coordinate in pixels.
XtNy	Position	0	y-coordinate in pixels.

The Repeater widget invokes the callbacks on the XtNstartCallback and XtNcallback lists when it receives a ButtonDown event. If the button is held down, it starts a timer for XtNinitialDelay milliseconds. If the button is still down when that time has passed, it invokes the functions on the XtNcallback list again, and begins to repeat. The second repetition occurs after XtNrepeatDelay milliseconds, and subsequent intervals are reduced by XtNdecay milliseconds until they reach a minimum of XtNminimumDelay milliseconds. When the mouse button is released, the callbacks on the XtNstopCallback list are invoked, and all the timers are removed.

The new resources (not inherited from superclasses) associated with the Repeater widget are:

XtNdecay
> The number of milliseconds to subtract from the repeat interval after each repetition. The interval starts at XtNrepeatDelay and decreases to XtNminimumDelay. The default is 5 milliseconds.

XtNflash
> Whether or not to flash the Repeater button whenever the timer goes off. The default is False.

XtNinitialDelay
> The number of milliseconds before the Repeater widget begins to repeat. The default is 200.

XtNminimumDelay
> The minimum time between callbacks in milliseconds. The default is 10.

XtNrepeatDelay
> The number of milliseconds between repetitions, once the XtNinitialDelay has elapsed and the widget has begun to repeat. The actual delay interval will have XtNdecay milliseconds subtracted from it at each repetition until it reaches XtNminimumDelay.

XtNstartCallback
> The list of functions executed from the start action (typically when the Repeater button is first pressed). The call_data parameter is unused.

`XtNstopCallback`

> The list of functions executed from the `stop` action (typically when the Repeater button is released). The *call_data* parameter is unused.

Translations and Actions

The Repeater widget supports the following actions beyond those of the Command button:

`start()`

> This invokes the functions on the `XtNstartCallback` and `XtNcallback` lists and sets a timer to go off in `XtNinitialDelay` milliseconds. The timer will cause the `Xt-Ncallback` functions to be invoked with increasing frequency until the `stop` action occurs.

`stop()`

> This invokes the functions on the `XtNstopCallback` list and prevents any further timers from occurring until the next `start` action.

The following are the default translation bindings used by the Repeater widget:

```
<EnterWindow>:highlight()
<LeaveWindow>:unhighlight()
<Btn1Down>:set() start()
<Btn1Up>:stop() unset()
```

See Also

Command(5).

Scrollbar

Name

Scrollbar widget – widget to control scrolling of viewing area in another widget.

Synopsis

Public Headers: *<X11/StringDefs.h> <X11/Xaw/Scrollbar.h>*

Private Header: *<X11/Xaw/ScrollbarP.h>*

Class Name: Scrollbar

Class Pointer: `scrollbarWidgetClass`

Instantiation: *widget* = `XtCreateWidget(`*name*`,` `scrollbarWidgetClass,` *. . .*`)`

Class Hierarchy

Core → Simple → Scrollbar

Description

The Scrollbar widget is a rectangular area that contains a slide region and a thumb (slide bar). A Scrollbar can be used alone, as a valuator, or within a composite widget (for example, a Viewport). A Scrollbar can be aligned either vertically or horizontally.

When a Scrollbar is created, it is drawn with the thumb in a contrasting color. The thumb is normally used to scroll client data and to give visual feedback on the percentage of the client data that is visible.

Each pointer button invokes a specific scrollbar action. That is, given either a vertical or horizontal alignment, the pointer button actions will scroll or return data as appropriate for that alignment. Pointer buttons 1 and 3 do not perform scrolling operations by default. Instead, they return the pixel position of the cursor on the scroll region. When pointer button 2 is clicked, the thumb moves to the current pointer position. When pointer button 2 is held down and the pointer is moved, the thumb follows the pointer.

The pointer cursor in the scroll region changes, depending on the current action. When no pointer button is pressed, the pointer cursor appears as an arrow that points in the direction(s) in which scrolling can occur. When pointer button 1 or 3 is pressed, the pointer cursor appears as a single-headed arrow that points in the logical direction that the client will move the data. When pointer button 2 is pressed, the pointer cursor appears as an arrow that points to the thumb.

While scrolling is in progress, the application receives notification from callback procedures. For both scrolling actions, the callback returns the Scrollbar widget ID, `client_data`, and the pixel position of the pointer when the button was released. For smooth scrolling, the callback routine returns the scroll bar widget, `client_data`, and the current relative position of the thumb. When the thumb is moved using pointer button 2, the callback procedure is invoked continuously. When either button 1 or button 3 is pressed, the callback procedure is invoked only when the button is released, and the client callback procedure is responsible for moving the thumb.

Resources

When creating a Scrollbar widget instance, the following resources are retrieved from the argument list or from the resource database:

Name (XtN...)	Type	Default	Description
XtNaccelerators	AcceleratorTable	NULL	List of event-to-action bindings to be executed by this widget, even though the event occurred in another widget.
XtNancestor-Sensitive	Boolean	True	(D) Sensitivity state of the ancestors of this widget: a widget is insensitive if either it or any of its ancestors is insensitive.
XtNbackground	Pixel	XtDefault-Background	Window background color.
XtNbackground-Pixmap	Pixmap	XtUnspecified-Pixmap	Window background pixmap.
XtNborderColor	Pixel	XtDefault-Foreground	Window border color.
XtNborderPixmap	Pixmap	XtUnspecified-Pixmap	Window border pixmap.
XtNborderWidth	Dimension	1	Width of button border.
XtNcolormap	Colormap	Parent's colormap.	Colormap that this widget will use.
XtNdepth	int	Parent's depth.	(C) Depth of this widget's window.
XtNdestroy-Callback	XtCallbackList	NULL	Callbacks for XtDestroy-Widget.
XtNforeground	Pixel	XtDefault-Foreground	Thumb color.
XtNheight	Dimension	See below.	(A) Height of scroll bar.
XtNjumpProc	XtCallbackList	NULL	Callback for thumb select.
XtNlength	Dimension	1	Major dimension (height of XtorientVertical).
XtNmappedWhen-Managed	Boolean	TRUE	Whether XtMapWidget() is automatic.
XtNminimumThumb	Dimension	7	Smallest size, in pixels, to which the thumb can shrink.
XtNorientation	XtOrientation	XtorientVertical	Orientation (vertical or horizontal).
XtNscreen	Screen	Parent's screen.	(R) Screen on which this widget is displayed.
XtNscrollDCursor	Cursor	XC_sb_down_arrow	Cursor for scrolling down.
XtNscrollHCursor	Cursor	XC_sb_h_double_arrow	Idle horizontal cursor.

Name (XtN...)	Type	Default	Description
XtNscrollLCursor	Cursor	XC_sb_left_arrow	Cursor for scrolling left.
XtNscrollProc	XtCallbackList	NULL	Callback for the slide region.
XtNscrollRCursor	Cursor	XC_sb_right_arrow	Cursor for scrolling right.
XtNscrollUCursor	Cursor	XC_sb_up_arrow	Cursor for scrolling up.
XtNscrollVCursor	Cursor	XC_sb_v_arrow_	Idle vertical cursor.
XtNsensitive	Boolean	TRUE	Whether widget receives input.
XtNshown	float	0.0	Percentage the thumb covers.
XtNthickness	Dimension	14	Minor dimension (height if XtorientHorizontal).
XtNthumb	Bitmap	Gray pixmap.	Thumb pixmap.
XtNtopOfThumb	float	0.0	Position on scroll bar.
XtNtranslations	Translation-Table	See below.	Event-to-action translations.
XtNwidth	Dimension	Depends on orientation.	(A) Width of scroll bar.
XtNx	Position	NULL	x coordinate in pixels.
XtNy	Position	NULL	y coordinate in pixels.

The new resource defined by this widget are:

XtNforeground

A pixel value which indexes the widget's colormap to derive the color used to draw the thumb.

XtNjumpProc

All functions on this callback list are called when the NotifyThumb action is invoked. See the Scrollbar Actions section for details.

XtNminimumThumb

The smallest size, in pixels, to which the thumb can shrink.

XtNorientation

The orientation is the direction that the thumb will be allowed to move. This value can be either XtorientVertical or XtorientHorizontal.

scrollProc

All functions on this callback list may be called when the NotifyScroll action is invoked.

shown

This is the size of the thumb, expressed as a percentage (0.0 - 1.0) of the length of the scrollbar.

thumb

This pixmap is used to tile (or stipple) the thumb of the scrollbar. If no tiling is desired, then set this resource to None. This resource will accept either a bitmap or a pixmap that is the same depth as the window. The resource converter for this resource constructs bitmaps from the contents of files.

```
topOfThumb
```
   The location of the top of the thumb, as a percentage (0.0 - 1.0) of the length of the scrollbar. This resource was called `top` in previous versions of the Athena widget set. The name collided with the a Form widget constraint resource, and had to be changed.

You can set the dimensions of the Scrollbar two ways. As for all widgets, you can use the `Xt-Nwidth` and `XtNheight` resources. In addition, you can use an alternative method that is independent of the vertical or horizontal orientation:

```
XtNlength
```
   Specifies the height for a vertical Scrollbar and the width for a horizontal Scrollbar.

```
XtNthickness
```
   Specifies the width for a vertical Scrollbar and the height for a horizontal Scrollbar.

The Scrollbar has six cursor resources. The class for all cursor resources is `XtCCursor`.

```
scrollDCursor
```
   This cursor is used when scrolling backward in a vertical scrollbar.

```
scrollHCursor
```
   This cursor is used when a horizontal scrollbar is inactive.

```
scrollLCursor
```
   This cursor is used when scrolling forward in a horizontal scrollbar.

```
scrollRCursor
```
   This cursor is used when scrolling backward in a horizontal scrollbar, or when thumbing a vertical scrollbar.

```
scrollUCursor
```
   This cursor is used when scrolling forward in a vertical scrollbar, or when thumbing a horizontal scrollbar.

```
scrollVCursor
```
   This cursor is used when a vertical scrollbar is inactive.

Translations and Actions

The actions supported by the Scrollbar widget are:

```
StartScroll(value)
```
   The possible values are `Forward`, `Backward`, or `Continuous`. This must be the first action to begin a new movement.

```
NotifyScroll(value)
```
   The possible values are `Proportional` or `FullLength`. If the argument to `StartScroll` was `Forward` or `Backward`, `NotifyScroll` executes the `XtNscrollProc` callbacks and passes either the position of the pointer if its argument is `Proportional` or the full length of the scroll bar if its argument is `FullLength`. If the argument to `Start-Scroll` was `Continuous`, `NotifyScroll` returns without executing any callbacks.

`EndScroll()`   This must be the last action after a movement is complete.

`MoveThumb()`   Repositions the scroll bar thumb to the current pointer location.

`NotifyThumb()`   Calls the `XtNjumpProc` callbacks and passes the relative position of the pointer as a percentage of the scroll bar length.

The default bindings for Scrollbar are:

```
<Btn1Down>:StartScroll(Forward)
<Btn2Down>:StartScroll(Continuous) MoveThumb() NotifyThumb()
<Btn3Down>:StartScroll(Backward)
<Btn2Motion>:MoveThumb() NotifyThumb()
<BtnUp>:NotifyScroll(Proportional) EndScroll()
```

Examples of additional bindings a user might wish to specify in a resource file are:

```
*Scrollbar.Translations: \
  ~Meta<KeyPress>space:StartScroll(Forward) NotifyScroll(FullLength) \
   Meta<KeyPress>space:StartScroll(Backward) NotifyScroll(FullLength) \
EndScroll()
```

Callback Functions

- The `XtNscrollProc` callback is used for incremental scrolling and is called by the `NotifyScroll` action. `XtNscrollProc` looks like this:

```
void ScrollProc(scrollbar, client_data, position)
    Widget scrollbar;
    XtPointer client_data;
    XtPointer position;    /* int */
```

where:

    `scrollbar`   Specifies the ID of the Scrollbar.

    `client_data` Specifies the client data.

    `position`   Returns the pixel position of the thumb in integer form.

`position` is a signed quantity and should be cast to an `int` when used. Using the default button bindings, button 1 returns a positive value and button 3 returns a negative value. In both cases, the magnitude of the value is the distance of the pointer in pixels from the top (or left) of the Scrollbar. The value will never be greater than the length of the Scrollbar.

- The `XtNjumpProc` callback is used for jump scrolling and is called by the `Notify-Thumb` action. The `XtNjumpProc` callback procedure looks like this:

```
void JumpProc(scrollbar, client_data, percent)
    Widget scrollbar;
    XtPointer client_data;
    XtPointer percent_ptr;    /* float* */
```

where:

> *scrollbar*   Specifies the ID of the scroll bar window.
>
> *client_data* Specifies the client data.
>
> *percent_ptr* Specifies the floating point position of the thumb (0.0 – 1.0).

The XtNjumpProc callback is used to implement smooth scrolling and is called by the NotifyThumb action. *percent_ptr* must be cast to a pointer to float before use:

```
float percent = *(float*)percent_ptr;
```

With the default button bindings, button 2 moves the thumb interactively, and the Xt-NjumpProc is called on each new position of the pointer, while the pointer button remains down. The value specified by *percent_ptr* is the current location of the thumb (from the top or left of the Scrollbar) expressed as a percentage of the length of the Scrollbar.

An older interface used XtNthumbProc and passed the percentage by value rather than by reference. This interface is not portable across machine architectures but is still supported as of R5 for those (nonportable) applications that used it.

- To set the position and length of a Scrollbar thumb, use XawScrollbarSetThumb():

```
void XawScrollbarSetThumb(w, top, shown)
    Widget w;
    float top;
    float shown;
```

where:

> *w*   Specifies the Scrollbar widget ID.
>
> *top*   Specifies the position of the top of the thumb as a fraction of the length of the Scrollbar.
>
> *shown*   Specifies the length of the thumb as a fraction of the total length of the Scrollbar.

XawScrollbarThumb moves the visible thumb to position (0.0 – 1.0) and length (0.0 – 1.0). Either *top* or *shown* can be specified as –1.0, in which case the current value is left unchanged. Values greater than 1.0 are truncated to 1.0.

If called from XtNjumpProc, XawScrollbarSetThumb() has no effect.

Setting Float Resources

The XtNshown and XtNtopOfThumb resources are of type float. These resources can be difficult to get into an argument list. The reason is that C performs an automatic cast of the float value to an integer value, usually truncating the important information. The following code fragment is one portable method of getting a float into an argument list.

```
top = 0.5;
if (sizeof(float) > sizeof(XtArgVal)) {
/*
 * If a float is larger than an XtArgVal then pass this
 * resource value by reference.
 */
XtSetArg(args[0], XtNshown, &top);
}
else {
/*
 * Convince C not to perform an automatic conversion, which
 * would truncate 0.5 to 0.
 */
XtArgVal * l_top = (XtArgVal *) &top;
XtSetArg(args[0], XtNshown, *l_top);
}
```

See Also

Viewport(5).

Simple

Name

Simple widget – Core subclass with cursor control and insensitivity indication.

Synopsis

Public Headers:	*<X11/StringDefs.h> <X11/Xaw/Simple.h>*
Private Header:	*<X11/Xaw/SimpleP.h>*
Class Name:	Simple
Class Pointer:	`simpleWidgetClass`
Instantiation:	This widget is not normally instantiated.

Class Hierarchy

Core → Simple

Description

The Simple widget is not very useful by itself, as it has no semantics of its own. Its main purpose is to be used as a common superclass for the other simple (non-composite) Athena widgets. It might also be a good superclass to use for widgets you write. This widget adds five resources to the resource list provided by the Core widget and its superclasses.

Resources

When creating a Simple widget instance, the following resources are retrieved from the argument list or from the resource database:

Name (XtN...)	Type	Default	Description
XtNaccelerators	Accelerator-Table	NULL	List of event-to-action bindings to be executed by this widget, even though the event occurred in another widget.
XtNancestorSensitive	Boolean	True	(D) Sensitivity state of the ancestors of this widget: a widget is insensitive if either it or any of its ancestors is insensitive.
XtNbackground	Pixel	XtDefault-Background	Window background color.
XtNbackgroundPixmap	Pixmap	XtUnspecified-Pixmap	Window background pixmap.
XtNborderColor	Pixel	XtDefault-Foreground	Window border color.
XtNborderPixmap	Pixmap	XtUnspecified-Pixmap	Window border pixmap.
XtNborderWidth	Dimension	1	Border width in pixels.
XtNcolormap	Colormap	Parent's colormap.	Colormap that this widget will use.
XtNcursor	Cursor	None	Pointer cursor.

Name (XtN...)	Type	Default	Description
(R5) XtNcursorName	String	NULL	
XtNdepth	int	Parent's depth.	(C) Depth of this widget's window.
XtNdestroyCallback	XtCallback-List	NULL	Callbacks for XtDestroy-Widget().
XtNheight	Dimension	Font height + 2 * XtNinternalHeight	Height of widget.
XtNinsensitiveBorder	Pixmap	Gray pixmap.	Border when not sensitive.
XtNinternalHeight	Dimension	2	See note.
XtNmappedWhenManaged	Boolean	TRUE	Whether XtMapWidget() is automatic.
(R5) XtNpointerColor	Pixel	XtDefaultForeground	
(R5) XtNpointerColor-Background	Pixel	XtDefaultBackground	
XtNscreen	Screen	Parent's screen.	(R) Screen on which this widget is displayed: this is not a settable resource.
XtNsensitive	Boolean	TRUE	Whether widget receives input.
XtNtranslations	Translation-Table	See below.	Event-to-action translations.
XtNwidth	Dimension	XtNlabel width +2 * XtNinternalWidth	Width of widget.
XtNx	Position	0	x coordinate in pixels.
XtNy	Position	0	y coordinate in pixels.

The new resources associated with Simple are:

XtNcursor

>Specifies a cursor to be used in the widget's window. You must create the cursor before setting this resource in C code.

XtNcursorName

>Specifies a cursor by name to be used in the widget's window. This saves you from having to create a cursor yourself. You supply just a name from the standard cursor font. New in R5.

XtNinsensitiveBorder

>Specifies a pixmap that will be used for the border when the widget is insensitive.

XtNpointerColor

>Specifies a foreground color used when creating the cursor specified in XtNcursorName. If this is changed then a new cursor will be recreated. New in R5.

XtNpointerColorBackground

>Specifies a background color used when creating the cursor specified in XtNcursor-Name. If this is changed then a new cursor will be recreated. New in R5.

SimpleMenu

Name

SimpleMenu widget – menu container widget.

Synopsis

Public Headers: *<X11/StringDefs.h> <X11/Xaw/SimpleMenu.h>*

Private Header: *<X11/Xaw/SimpleMenP.h>*

Class Name: SimpleMenu

Class Pointer: `simpleMenuWidgetClass`

Instantiation: *widget* = `XtCreatePopupShell(`*name*`, simpleMenuWidget-Class,...);`

Class Hierarchy

Core → Composite → Shell → OverrideShell → SimpleMenu

Description

The SimpleMenu widget is a container for menu entries. It is a direct subclass of shell, and is usually created with `XtCreatePopupShell()`. This is the only part of the menu that actually contains a window, since each menu pane is a gadget. SimpleMenu "glues" the individual menu entries together into one menu.

Resources

The resources associated with the SimpleMenu widget control aspects that will affect the entire menu.

Name (XtN...)	Class Type	Default	Description
XtNaccelerators	AcceleratorTable	NULL	List of event-to-action bindings to be executed by this widget, even though the event occurred in another widget.
XtNancestor-Sensitive	Boolean	True	(D) Sensitivity state of the ancestors of this widget. A widget is insensitive if either it or any of its ancestors is insensitive.
XtNallowShellResize	Boolean	True	Whether the menu can be resized.
XtNbackground	Pixel	XtDefault-Background	Window background color.
XtNbackground-Pixmap	Pixmap	XtUnspecified-Pixmap	Window background pixmap.
XtNbackingStore	BackingStore	See below.	See below.
XtNborderColor	Pixel	XtDefault-Foreground	Window border color.

Name (XtN...)	Class Type	Default	Description
XtNborderPixmap	Pixmap	XtUnspecified-Pixmap	Window border pixmap.
XtNborderWidth	Dimension	1	Width of button border.
XtNbottomMargin	Dimension	0	See below.
XtNchildren	WidgetList	NULL	(R) List of all this composite widget's current children.
XtNcreatePopup-ChildProc	Function	NULL	Procedure to call after the menu pops up.
XtNcolormap	Colormap	Parent's colormap.	Colormap that this widget will use.
XtNcursor	Cursor	None	Pointer cursor.
XtNdepth	int	Parent's depth.	(C) Depth of this widget's window.
XtNdestroy-Callback	XtCallbackList	NULL	Callbacks for XtDestroy-Widget().
XtNgeometry	String	NULL	Geometry specification for menu.
XtNheight	Dimension	Enough space for all entries.	Menu height.
XtNlabel	String	Name of widget.	See below.
XtNlabelClass	Pointer	SmeBSBObjectClass	See below.
XtNmappedWhen-Managed	Boolean	True	Whether XtMapWidget() is automatic.
XtNmenuOnScreen	Boolean	True	See below.
XtNnumChildren	Cardinal	0	(R) The number of children in this composite widget.
XtNoverrideRedirect	Boolean	True	See below.
XtNpopdownCallback	Callback	NULL	See below.
XtNpopupCallback	Callback	NULL	See below.
XtNpopupOnEntry	Widget	Label (or first entry)	(A) See below.
XtNrowHeight	Dimension	0	See below.
XtNsaveUnder	Boolean	False	See below.
XtNscreen	Screen	Parent's screen.	(R) Screen on which this widget is displayed.
XtNsensitive	Boolean	True	Whether widget receives input.
XtNtopMargin	Dimension	0	See below.
XtNtranslations	TranslationTable	NULL	Event-to-action translations.
XtNvisual	Visual	CopyFromParent	Visual type.
XtNwidth	Dimension	Width of widest entry.	Menu width.
XtNx	Position	0	x-coordinate in pixels.
XtNy	Position	0	y-coordinate in pixels.

XtNbackingStore

Determines what type of backing store will be used for the menu. Legal values for this resource are NotUseful, WhenMapped, and Always. These values are the backing-store integers defined in *<X11/X.h>*.

If default is specified (the default behavior) the server will use whatever it thinks is appropriate.

XtNbottomMargin
XtNtopMargin

The amount of space between the top or bottom of the menu and the menu entry closest to that edge.

XtNcursor

The shape of the mouse pointer whenever it is in this widget.

XtNgeometry

If this resource is specified, it overrides the x, y, width and height of this widget. The format of this string is [*<width>*x*<height>*][{+ -} *<xoffset>* {+ -}*<yoffset>*].

XtNlabel

This label will be placed at the top of the SimpleMenu and cannot be highlighted. The name of the label object is menuLabel. Using this name, it is possible to modify the label's attributes through the resource database. When the label is created, the Xt-Nlabel is hard-coded to the value of XtNlabel, and XtNjustify is hard-coded as XtJustifyCenter.

XtNlabelClass

Specifies the type of Sme object created as the menu label.

XtNmenuOnScreen

If the menu is automatically positioned under the cursor with the XawPosition-SimpleMenu action, and if this resource is True, then the menu is always fully visible on the screen.

XtNoverrideRedirect

Determines the value of the override_redirect attribute of the SimpleMenu's window. The override_redirect attribute of a window determines whether a window manager may interpose itself between this window and the root window of the display. For more information, see the *Inter-Client Communications Conventions Manual*.

XtNpopdownCallback
XtNpopupCallback

These callback functions are called by the Xt Intrinsics whenever the shell is popped up or down. (See *X Toolkit Intrinsics – C Language Interface* for details.)

XtNpopupOnEntry

The XawPositionSimpleMenu action pops up the SimpleMenu with its label (or first entry) directly under the pointer, by default. To pop up the menu under another entry, set this resource to the menu entry that *should* be under the pointer when the menu is popped up. This allows the application to offer the user a default menu entry that can be selected without moving the pointer.

XtNrowHeight

If this resource is 0 (the default), then each menu entry is given its desired height. If this resource has any other value, then all menu entries are forced to be XtNrowHeight pixels high.

XtNsaveUnder

If this is True, then save unders will be active on the menu's window.

Translations and Actions

The following default translation bindings are used by the SimpleMenu widget:

```
<EnterWindow>:highlight()
<LeaveWindow>:unhighlight()
<BtnMotion>:highlight()
<BtnUp>:MenuPopdown() notify() unhighlight()
```

With these bindings, the user can pop down the menu without activating any of the callback functions, by releasing the pointer button when no menu item is highlighted.

The SimpleMenu widget supports the following actions:

- Switching the entry under the mouse pointer between the foreground and background colors with highlight and unhighlight.

- Processing menu entry callbacks with notify.

The actions supported by SimpleMenu are listed below:

highlight()

Highlights the menu entry that is currently under the pointer. Only an item that is highlighted is notified when the notify action is invoked. The look of a highlighted entry is determined by the menu entry.

unhighlight()

Unhighlights the currently highlighted menu item and returns it to its normal look.

notify()

Notifies the currently highlighted menu entry that it has been selected. It is the responsibility of the menu entry to take the appropriate action.

MenuPopdown(*menu*)

Built-in action to pop down a menu widget.

Positioning the SimpleMenu

If the SimpleMenu widget is to be used as a pulldown menu, then either the MenuButton(5) widget or some other outside means should be used to place the menu when it is popped up.

If popup menus are desired you must add the XawPositionSimpleMenu and XtMenu-Popup() actions to the translation table of the widget that will be popping up the menu. XawPositionSimpleMenu is a global action procedure. It is registered by the

SimpleMenu widget either when the first such action is created or when the convenience routine `XawSimpleMenuAddGlobalActions()` is called.

For example, these are the translations needed to pop up some of *xterm's* menus:

```
!Ctrl<Btn1Down>: XawPositionSimpleMenu(xterm) XtMenuPopup(xterm)
!Ctrl<Btn2Down>: XawPositionSimpleMenu(modes) XtMenuPopup(modes)
```

Note that the ! excludes unspecified modifiers.

`XawPositionSimpleMenu(menu)`

> The `XawPositionSimpleMenu` routine searches for the menu name passed to it using `XtNameToWidget()`, starting with the widget invoking the action as the reference widget. If unsuccessful, this routine continues to search up the widget tree, using each of the invoking widget's ancestors as the reference widget. If still unsuccessful, the routine prints a warning message and gives up. `XawPositionSimpleMenu` positions the menu directly under the pointer. The menu is placed so that the pointer is centered on the entry named by the `popupOnEntry` resource. If the `XtNmenuOn-Screen` resource is `True`, then the menu is always fully visible on the screen.

Public Functions

- The `XawPositionSimpleMenu` action routine can often be invoked before any menus have been created. This can occur when an application uses dynamic menu creation. In these cases an application needs to register this global action routine by calling `Xaw-SimpleMenuAddGlobalActions()`:

```
void XawSimpleMenuAddGlobalActions(app_con)
    XtAppContext app_con;
```

where *app_con* specifies the application context in which this action should be registered.

This function need only be called once per application and must be called before any widget that uses `XawPositionSimpleMenu` action is realized.

- To get the currently highlighted menu entry, use `XawSimpleMenuGetActive-Entry()`:

```
Widget XawSimpleMenuGetActiveEntry(w)
    XtAppContext w;
```

where *w* specifies the SimpleMenu widget.

This function returns either the menu entry that is currently highlighted or `NULL` if no entry is highlighted.

- To clear the SimpleMenu widget's internal information about the currently highlighted menu entry, use `XawSimpleMenuClearActiveEntry()`:

```
Widget XawSimpleMenuClearActiveEntry(w)
    XtAppContext w;
```

where *w* specifies the SimpleMenu widget.

This function unsets all internal references to the currently highlighted menu entry. It does not unhighlight or otherwise alter the appearance of the active entry. This function is primarily for use by implementors of menu entries.

See Also

MenuButton(5), *Sme*(5), *SmeBSB*(5), *SmeLine*(5).

Sme

Name

Sme object – base class for menu entries.

Synopsis

Public Headers: *<X11/StringDefs.h> <X11/Xaw/Sme.h>*

Private Header: *<X11/Xaw/SmeP.h>*

Class Name: Sme

Class Pointer: `smeObjectClass`

Instantiation: *widget* = `XtCreateWidget(`*name*`, smeObjectClass, ...)`

Class Hierarchy

Object → RectObj → Sme

Description

The Sme object is the base class for all menu entries that are children of SimpleMenu. While this object is intended mainly to be subclassed, it may be used in a menu to add blank space between menu entries.

Resources

The resources associated with the Sme object are defined in this section and affect only the single menu entry specified by this object.

Name (XtN...)	Class Type	Default	Description
XtNancestorSensitive	Boolean	True	Sensitivity state of the ancestors of this widget: a widget is insensitive if either it or any of its ancestors is insensitive.
XtNborderWidth	Dimension	1	Width of button border.
XtNcallback	XtCallbackList	NULL	Callback for `notify` action.
XtNdestroyCallback	XtCallbackList	NULL	Callbacks for `XtDestroyWidget()`.
XtNheight	Dimension	0	Object height.
XtNsensitive	Boolean	True	Whether widget receives input.
XtNwidth	Dimension	1	Object width.
XtNx	Position	0	x-coordinate in pixels.
XtNy	Position	0	y-coordinate in pixels.

Keep in mind that the SimpleMenu widget forces all menu items to be the width of the widest entry.

Subclassing the Sme Object

To create a new Sme object, you must define a few class procedures. These procedures allow the SimpleMenu to highlight and unhighlight the menu entry as the pointer cursor moves over it, as well as notifying the entry when the user has selected it.

Three new class methods are defined by the Sme object. All of these methods may be inherited from the Sme object, although the default semantics are not very interesting.

Highlight()   Called to put the menu entry into the highlighted state.

Unhighlight() Called to return the widget to its normal (unhighlighted) state.

Notify()   Called when the user selects this menu entry.

Other than using these specialized class procedures, creating a new object is straightforward. Just subclass Sme and define new redisplay and highlight procedures. Here is some information that can help you avoid some common mistakes.

1. Objects can be 0 pixels high.

2. Objects draw on their parent's window; therefore, the drawing dimensions are different from those of widgets. For instance, y locations vary from y to $y + height$, not from 0 to *height.*

3. XtSetValues() calls may come from the application while the SimpleMenu is in its notify procedure. The SimpleMenu may later call the menu entry's unhighlight procedure. Due to the asynchronous nature of X, the Expose event generated by XtSet-Values() will come *after* this unhighlight.

4. Remember, the menu entry does not own the window. Share the space with other menu entries: never draw outside your own section of the menu.

See Also

MenuButton(5), *SimpleMenu*(5), *SmeBSB*(5), *SmeLine*(5).

Name

SmeBSB object – basic menu entry.

Synopsis

Public Headers:	*<X11/StringDefs.h> <X11/Xaw/SmeBSB.h>*
Private Header:	*<X11/Xaw/SmeBSBP.h>*
Class Name:	SmeBSB
Class Pointer:	smeBSBObjectClass
Instantiation:	*widget* = XtCreateWidget(*name*, smeBSBObjectClass, ...)

Class Hierarchy

Object → RectObj → Sme → SmeBSB

Description

The SmeBSB object is used to create a menu entry that contains a string, and optional bitmaps in its left and right margins. The parent is expected to be SimpleMenu. Since each menu entry is an independent object, the application is able to change the font, color, height, and other attributes of the menu entries, on an entry-by-entry basis.

Resources

The resources associated with the SmeBSB object are defined in this section, and affect only the single menu entry specified by this object.

Name (XtN...)	Class Type	Default	Description
XtNancestor-Sensitive	Boolean	True	(D) Sensitivity state of the ancestors of this widget: a widget is insensitive if either it or any of its ancestors is insensitive.
XtNborderWidth	Dimension	1	Width of button border.
XtNcallback	XtCallbackList	NULL	Callback for notify action.
XtNdestroy-Callback	XtCallbackList	NULL	Callbacks for XtDestroyWidget().
XtNfont	XFontStruct*	XtDefaultFont	Menu entry font.
XtNforeground	Pixel	XtDefault-Foreground	Foreground color.
XtNheight	Dimension	Font height + XtNvertSpace	(A) Menu entry height.
XtNjustify	XtJustify	XtJustifyCenter	Type of text alignment.
XtNlabel	String	Name of widget.	Menu entry text.
XtNleftBitmap	Pixmap	XtUnspecified-Pixmap	See below.
XtNleftMargin	Dimension	4	See below.
XtNrightBitmap	Pixmap	XtUnspecified-Pixmap	See below.
XtNrightMargin	Dimension	4	See below.

Name (XtN...)	Class Type	Default	Description
XtNsensitive	Boolean	True	Whether widget receives input.
vertSpace	int	25	
XtNwidth	Dimension	Text width + margins	(A) Width of menu entry.
XtNx	Position	0	x-coordinate in pixels.
XtNy	Position	0	y-coordinate in pixels.

The new resources (not inherited from superclasses) associated with the SmeBSB object are:

XtNforeground

Specifies a pixel value that indexes the parent's colormap to derive the foreground color of the menu entry's window. This color is also used to render all 1's in XtNleftBitmap and XtNrightBitmap.

XtNjustify

Specifies how the label is to be rendered between the left and right margins when the space is wider than the actual text. This resource may be specified with the values Xt-JustifyLeft, XtJustifyCenter, or XtJustifyRight. When specifying the justification from a resource file, the values left, center, or right may be used.

XtNlabel

Specifies the string to be display in the menu entry. The exact location of this string within the bounds of the menu entry is controlled by the resources XtNleftMargin, Xt-NrightMargin, XtNvertSpace, and XtNjustify.

XtNleftBitmap
XtNrightBitmap

Specifies a name of a bitmap to display in the left or right margin of the menu entry. All 1's in the bitmap are rendered in the foreground color of the SimpleMenu widget, and all 0's will be drawn in the background color of the SimpleMenu widget. The programmer must ensure that the menu entry is tall enough and that the appropriate margin is wide enough to accept the bitmap. If care is not taken, the bitmap might extend into either another menu entry or this entry's label.

XtNleftMargin
XtNrightMargin

Specifies the amount of space (in pixels) to leave between the edge of the menu entry and the label string.

XtNvertSpace

Specifies the amount of vertical padding to place around the label of a menu entry. The label and bitmaps are always centered vertically within the menu. Values for this resource are expressed as a percentage of the font's height. The default value (25) increases the default height to 125% of the font's height.

See Also
MenuButton(5), *SimpleMenu*(5), *Sme*(5), *SmeLine*(5).

*Athena
Classes*

Name
SmeLine object – menu item separator.

Synopsis
Public Headers:	*<X11/StringDefs.h> <X11/Xaw/SmeLine.h>*
Private Header:	*<X11/Xaw/SmeLineP.h>*
Class Name:	SmeLine
Class Pointer:	smeLineObjectClass
Instantiation:	*widget* = XtCreateWidget(*name*, smeLineObjectClass, ...)

Class Hierarchy
Object → RectObj → Sme → SmeLine

Description
The SmeLine object is used to add a horizontal line or menu separator to a SimpleMenu. Since each menu entry is an independent object, the application is able to change the color, height, and other attributes of the menu entries, on an entry-by-entry basis. This entry is not selectable, and does not highlight when the pointer cursor is over it.

Resources
The resources associated with the SmeLine object are defined in this section, and affect only the single menu entry specified by this object.

Name (XtN...)	Class Type	Default	Description
XtNancestor-Sensitive	Boolean	True	Sensitivity state of the ancestors of this widget: a widget is insensitive if either it or any of its ancestors is insensitive.
XtNborderWidth	Dimension	1	Width of button border.
XtNcallback	XtCallbackList	NULL	Callback for notify action.
XtNdestroy-Callback	XtCallbackList	NULL	Callbacks for XtDestroyWidget().
XtNforeground	Pixel	XtDefault-Foreground	Foreground color.
XtNheight	Dimension	0	Object height.
XtNlineWidth	Dimension	1	See below.
XtNsensitive	Boolean	True	Whether widget receives input.
XtNstipple	Pixmap	XtUnspecified-Pixmap	See below.
XtNwidth	Dimension	1	Object width.
XtNx	Position	0	x-coordinate in pixels.
XtNy	Position	0	y-coordinate in pixels.

XtNforeground

A pixel value that indexes the parent's colormap to derive the foreground color of the menu entry's window. This color is also used to render all 1's in XtNleftBitmap and XtNrightBitmap.

XtNlineWidth

The width of the horizontal line to be displayed.

XtNstipple

If a bitmap is specified for this resource, the line will be stippled through it. This allows the menu separator to be rendered as something more exciting than just a line. For instance, if you define a stipple that is a chain link, then your menu separators will look like chains.

See Also

MenuButton(5), *SimpleMenu*(5), *Sme*(5), *SmeBSB*(5).

StripChart

Name

StripChart widget – widget to display a real-time graphic chart.

Synopsis

Public Headers: *<X11/StringDefs.h> <X11/Xaw/StripChart.h>*

Private Header: *<X11/Xaw/StripCharP.h>*

Class Name: StripChart

Class Pointer: `stripChartWidgetClass`

Instantiation: *widget* = XtCreateWidget(*name*, stripChartWidgetClass, ...)

Class Hierarchy

Core → Simple → StripChart

Description

The StripChart widget is used to provide a real-time graphic chart of a single value. This widget is used by *xload* to provide the load graph. It will read data from an application, and update the chart at the `XtNupdate` interval specified.

Resources

When creating a StripChart widget instance, the following resources are retrieved from the argument list or from the resource database:

Name (XtN...)	Class Type	Default	Description
XtNaccelerators	AcceleratorTable	NULL	List of event-to-action bindings to be executed by this widget, even though the event occurred in another widget.
XtNancestor-Sensitive	Boolean	True	(D) Sensitivity state of the ancestors of this widget: a widget is insensitive if either it or any of its ancestors is insensitive.
XtNbackground	Pixel	XtDefault-Background	Window background color.
XtNbackground-Pixmap	Pixmap	XtUnspecified-Pixmap	Window background pixmap.
XtNborderColor	Pixel	XtDefault-Foreground	Window border color.
XtNborderPixmap	Pixmap	XtUnspecified-Pixmap	Window border pixmap.
XtNborderWidth	Dimension	1	Border width in pixels.
XtNcolormap	Colormap	Parent's colormap.	Colormap that this widget will use.
XtNcursor	Cursor	None.	Pointer cursor.
XtNdepth	int	Parent's depth.	(C) Depth of this widget's window.

Name (XtN...)	Class Type	Default	Description
XtNdestroy- Callback	XtCallbackList	NULL	Callbacks for XtDestroy- Widget().
XtNforeground	Pixel	XtDefault- Foreground	Foreground color.
XtNgetValue	Callback	NULL	See below.
XtNheight	Dimension	Font height + 2 * XtNinternal- Height	Height of widget.
XtNhighlight	Pixel	XtDefault- Foreground	See below.
XtNinsensitive- Border	Pixmap	Gray pixmap.	Border when not sensitive.
XtNjumpScroll	int	Half the width of the widget.	(A) See below.
XtNmappedWhen- Managed	Boolean	TRUE	Whether XtMapWidget() is auto- matic.
XtNminScale	int	1	See below.
XtNscreen	Screen	Parent's screen.	(R) Screen on which this widget is displayed.
XtNsensitive	Boolean	TRUE	Whether widget receives input.
XtNtranslations	Translation- Table	See below.	Event-to-action translations.
XtNupdate	int	10	See below.
XtNwidth	Dimension	0	The height and width of this widget in pixels.
XtNx	Position	0	x-coordinate in pixels.
XtNy	Position	0	y-coordinate in pixels.

The new resources (not inherited from superclasses) associated with the StripChart widget are:

XtNgetValue
: This is a list of functions to call every XtNupdate seconds. This function will get the value to be graphed by the StripChart widget. The section below, *Getting the StripChart Value*, describes the calling interface in more detail. This callback list should contain only one function. If this callback list contains more than one function, the behavior is undefined.

XtNhighlight
: A pixel value which indexes the widget's colormap to derive the color that will be used to draw the scale lines on the graph.

XtNjumpScroll
: When the graph reaches the right edge of the window it must be scrolled to the left. This resource specifies the number of pixels it will jump. Smooth scrolling can be achieved by setting this resource to 1.

XtNminScale
: The minimum scale for the graph. The number of divisions on the graph will always be greater than or equal to this value.

XtNupdate   The number of seconds between graph updates. Each update is represented
                   on the graph as a 1 pixel wide line. Every XtNupdate seconds the get-
                   Value procedure will be used to get a new graph point, and this point will
                   be added to the right end of the StripChart.

Getting The StripChart Value

The StripChart widget will call the application routine passed to it as the XtNgetValue callback function every XtNupdate seconds to obtain another point for the StripChart graph.
The calling interface for the XtNgetValue callback is:

```
void (*getValueProc)(w, client_data, value)
    Widget w;
    XtPointer client_data;
    XtPointer value;      /* double * */
```

w   Specifies the StripChart widget.

client_data   Specifies the client data.

value   Returns a pointer to a double. The application should set the address pointed
                   to by this argument to a double containing the value to be graphed on the
                   StripChart.

This function is used by the StripChart to call an application routine. The routine will pass the
value to be graphed back to the StripChart in the value field of this routine.

Template

Name

Template widget – widget to create a custom widget.

Synopsis

Public Headers:	*<X11/StringDefs.h> <X11/Xaw/Template.h>*
Private Header:	*<X11/Xaw/TemplateP.h>*
Class Name:	Template
Class Pointer:	`templateShellWidgetClass`
Instantiation:	This widget in not normally instantiated until you write your own functionality for it.

Description

Although the task of creating a new widget may at first appear a little daunting, there is a basic pattern that all widgets follow. The Athena widget library contains three files that are intended to assist in writing a custom widget: *Template.h*, *TemplateP.h*, and *Template.c*. However, it may be easier to start with a widget that has more real code to copy and modify.

Reasons for wishing to write a custom widget include:

- Convenient access to resource management procedures to obtain fonts, colors, etc., even if user customization is not desired.

- Convenient access to user input dispatch and translation management procedures.

- Access to callback mechanisms for building higher-level application libraries.

- Customizing the interface or behavior of an existing widget to suit a special application need.

- Desire to allow user customization of resources such as fonts, colors, etc., or to allow convenient re-binding of keys and buttons to internal functions.

- Converting a non-Toolkit application to use the Toolkit.

In each of these cases, the operation needed to create a new widget is to "subclass" an existing one. If the desired semantics of the new widget are similar to an existing one, then the implementation of the existing widget should be examined to see how much work would be required to create a subclass that will then be able to share the existing class methods. Much time will be saved in writing the new widget if an existing widget class's `Expose`, `Resize`, and/or `GeometryManager` method can be shared by the subclass.

Note that some trivial uses of a "bare-bones" widget may be achieved simply by creating an instance of the Core widget. The class variable to use when creating a Core widget is `widgetClass`. The geometry of the Core widget is determined entirely by the parent widget.

Often, an application will need a certain set of functions—and many copies of them. For example, when converting an older application to use the Toolkit, it may be desirable to have a "Window widget" class that might have the following semantics:

- Allocate two drawing colors in addition to a background color.

- Allocate a text font.

- Execute an application-supplied function to handle exposure events.

- Execute an application-supplied function to handle user input events.

Of course, a completely general-purpose `WindowWidgetClass` could be constructed to export all class methods as callback lists, but such a widget would be very large and would have to choose some arbitrary number of resources, such as colors, to allocate. An application that used many instances of the general-purpose widget would therefore waste many resources unnecessarily.

This section outlines the procedure to follow to construct a special-purpose widget to address the items listed above. The reader should refer to the appropriate sections of Volume Four, *X Toolkit Intrinsics Programming Manual*, for complete details of the material outlined here.

All Athena widgets have three separate files associated with them:

- A *public* header file containing declarations needed by applications programmers.

- A *private* header file containing additional declarations needed by the widget and any subclasses.

- A source code file containing the implementation of the widget.

This separation of functions into three files is suggested for all widgets, but nothing in the Toolkit actually requires this format. In particular, a private widget created for a single application may easily combine the public and private header files into a single file, or merge the contents into another application header file. Similarly, the widget implementation can be merged into other application code.

In the following example, the public header file *<X11/Xaw/Template.h>*, the private header file *<X11/Xaw/TemplateP.h>*, and the source code file *<X11/Xaw/Template.c>* are modified to produce the Window widget described above. In each case, the files have been designed so that you can make a global string replacement of *Template* and *template* with the name of your new widget, using the appropriate case.

Public Header File

The public header file contains declarations that will be required by any application module that needs to refer to the widget; whether to create an instance of the class, to perform an `Xt-SetValues()` operation, or to call a public routine implemented by the widget class.

The contents of the Template public header file, *<X11/Xaw/Template.h>*, are:

```
#ifndef _Template_h
#define _Template_h

/***************************************************************
 *
 * Template widget
 *
 ***************************************************************/
```

```
/* Resources:

Name                 Class               RepType         Default Value
----                 -----               -------         -------------
background           Background          Pixel           XtDefaultBackground
border               BorderColor         Pixel           XtDefaultForeground
borderWidth          BorderWidth         Dimension       1
destroyCallback      Callback            Pointer         NULL
height               Height              Dimension       0
mappedWhenManaged    MappedWhenManaged   Boolean         TRUE
sensitive            Sensitive           Boolean         TRUE
width                Width               Dimension       0
x                    Position            Position        0
y                    Position            Position        0

*/

/* define any special resource names here *
 * that are not in <X11/StringDefs.h> */

#define XtNtemplateResource          "templateResource"

#define XtCTemplateResource          "TemplateResource"

/* declare specific TemplateWidget class and instance datatypes */

typedef struct _TemplateClassRec*    TemplateWidgetClass;
typedef struct _TemplateRec*         TemplateWidget;

/* declare the class constant */

extern WidgetClass templateWidgetClass;

#endif  _Template_h
```

You will notice that most of this file is documentation. The crucial parts are the last 8 lines, where macros for any private resource names and classes are defined and where the widget class datatypes and class record pointer are declared.

For the Window widget, we want two drawing colors, a callback list for user input and an Xt-NexposeCallback callback list, and we will declare three convenience procedures, so we need to add:

```
/* Resources:
                     . . .
callback             Callback            Callback        NULL
drawingColor1        Color               Pixel           XtDefaultForeground
drawingColor2        Color               Pixel           XtDefaultForeground
exposeCallback       Callback            Callback        NULL
font                 Font                XFontStruct*    XtDefaultFont
                     . . .
*/

#define XtNdrawingColor1    "drawingColor1"
#define XtNdrawingColor2    "drawingColor2"
```

```
#define XtNexposeCallback   "exposeCallback"

extern Pixel WindowColor1(/* Widget */);
extern Pixel WindowColor2(/* Widget */);
extern Font  WindowFont(/* Widget */);
```

Note that we have chosen to call the input callback list by its generic name, XtNcallback, rather than by a specific name. If widgets that define a single user-input action all choose the same resource name, then there is greater possibility for an application to switch between widgets of different types.

Private Header File

The private header file contains the complete declaration of the class and instance structures for the widget and any additional private data that will be required by anticipated subclasses of the widget. Information in the private header file is normally hidden from the application and is designed to be accessed only through other public procedures, such as XtSetValues().

The contents of the Template private header file, *<X11/Xaw/TemplateP.h>*, are:

```
#ifndef _TemplateP_h
#define _TemplateP_h

#include "Template.h"
/* include superclass private header file */
#include <X11/Xaw/CoreP.h>

/* define unique representation types not found in <X11/StringDefs.h> */

#define XtRTemplateResource     "TemplateResource"

typedef struct {
      int empty;
} TemplateClassPart;

typedef struct _TemplateClassRec {
      CoreClassPart core_class;
      TemplateClassParttemplate_class;
} TemplateClassRec;

extern TemplateClassRec templateClassRec;

typedef struct {
      /* resources */
      char* resource;
      /* private state */
} TemplatePart;

typedef struct _TemplateRec {
      CorePart      core;
      TemplatePart  template;
} TemplateRec;

#endif  _TemplateP_h
```

The private header file includes the private header file of its superclass, thereby exposing the entire internal structure of the widget. It may not always be advantageous to do this; your own project development style will dictate the appropriate level of detail to expose in each module.

The Window widget needs to declare two fields in its instance structure to hold the drawing colors—a resource field for the font, and a field for the expose and user input callback lists:

```
typedef struct {
        /* resources */
        Pixel color_1;
        Pixel color_2;
        XFontStruct* font;
        XtCallbackList expose_callback;
        XtCallbackList input_callback;
        /* private state */
        /* (none) */
} WindowPart;
```

Widget Source File

The source code file implements the widget class itself. The unique part of this file is the declaration and initialization of the widget class record structure and the declaration of all resources and action routines added by the widget class.

The contents of the Template implementation file, *<X11/Xaw/Template.c>*, are:

```
#include <X11/IntrinsicP.h>
#include <X11/StringDefs.h>
#include "TemplateP.h"

static XtResource resources[] = {
#define offset(field) XtOffset(TemplateWidget, template.Peeld)
    /* {name, class, type, size, offset, default_type, default_addr}, */
    { XtNtemplateResource, XtCTemplateResource, XtRTemplateResource, \
      sizeof(char*), offset(resource), XtRString, "default" },
#undef offset
};

static void TemplateAction(/* Widget, XEvent*, String*, Cardinal* */);

static XtActionsRec actions[] =
{
    /* {name, procedure}, */
    {"template", TemplateAction},
};

static char translations[] =
"   <Key>: template() 0;
```

```
TemplateClassRec templateClassRec = {
    {   /* core fields */
        /* superclass */                (WidgetClass) &widgetClassRec,
        /* class_name */                "Template",
        /* widget_size */               sizeof(TemplateRec),
        /* class_initialize */          NULL,
        /* class_part_initialize */     NULL,
        /* class_inited */              FALSE,
        /* initialize */                NULL,
        /* initialize_hook */           NULL,
        /* realize */                   XtInheritRealize,
        /* actions */                   actions,
        /* num_actions */               XtNumber(actions),
        /* resources */                 resources,
        /* num_resources */             XtNumber(resources),
        /* xrm_class */                 NULLQUARK,
        /* compress_motion */           TRUE,
        /* compress_exposure */         TRUE,
        /* compress_enterleave */       TRUE,
        /* visible_interest */          FALSE,
        /* destroy */                   NULL,
        /* resize */                    NULL,
        /* expose */                    NULL,
        /* set_values */                NULL,
        /* set_values_hook */           NULL,
        /* set_values_almost */         XtInheritSetValuesAlmost,
        /* get_values_hook */           NULL,
        /* accept_focus */              NULL,
        /* version */                   XtVersion,
        /* callback_private */          NULL,
        /* tm_table */                  translations,
        /* query_geometry */            XtInheritQueryGeometry,
        /* display_accelerator */       XtInheritDisplayAccelerator,
        /* extension */                 NULL
    },
    { /* template fields */
        /* empty */                     0
    }
};

WidgetClass templateWidgetClass = (WidgetClass)&templateClassRec;
```

The resource list for the Window widget might look like the following:

```
static XtResource resources[] = {
#define offset(field) XtOffset(WindowWidget, window.Peeld)
    /* {name, class, type, size, offset, default_type, default_addr}, */
    { XtNdrawingColor1, XtCColor, XtRPixel, sizeof(Pixel),
         offset(color_1), XtRString, XtDefaultForeground },
    { XtNdrawingColor2, XtCColor, XtRPixel, sizeof(Pixel),
         offset(color_2), XtRString, XtDefaultForeground },
```

```
    { XtNfont, XtCFont, XtRFontStruct, sizeof(XFontStruct*),
          offset(font), XtRString, XtDefaultFont },
    { XtNexposeCallback, XtCCallback, XtRCallback, sizeof(XtCallbackList),
          offset(expose_callback), XtRCallback, NULL },
    { XtNcallback, XtCCallback, XtRCallback, sizeof(XtCallbackList),
          offset(input_callback), XtRCallback, NULL },
#undef offset
};
```

The user input callback will be implemented by an action procedure that passes the event pointer as *call_data*. The action procedure is declared as:

```
/* ARGSUSED */
static void InputAction(w, event, params, num_params)
    Widget w;
    XEvent *event;
    String *params;/* unused */
    Cardinal *num_params;/* unused */
{
    XtCallCallbacks(w, XtNcallback, (caddr_t)event);
}

static XtActionsRec actions[] =
{
    /* {name, procedure}, */
    {"input", InputAction},
};
```

and the default input binding will be to execute the input callbacks on `KeyPress` and `ButtonPress`:

```
static char translations[] =
"    <Key>:input() \n\
     <BtnDown>:input() \
";
```

In the class record declaration and initialization, the only field that is different from the Template is the expose procedure:

```
/* ARGSUSED */
static void Redisplay(w, event, region)
    Widget w;
    XEvent *event;    /* unused */
    Region region;
{
    XtCallCallbacks(w, XtNexposeCallback, (caddr_t)region);
}
WindowClassRec windowClassRec = {
    ...
    /* expose */  Redisplay,
```

Athena Classes

The Window widget will also declare three public procedures to return the drawing colors and the font ID, saving the application the effort of constructing an argument list for a call to `Xt-GetValues()`:

```
Pixel WindowColor1(w)
     Widget w;
{
     return ((WindowWidget)w)->window.color_1;
}

Pixel WindowColor2(w)
     Widget w;
{
     return ((WindowWidget)w)->window.color_2;
}

Font WindowFont(w)
     Widget w;
{
     return ((WindowWidget)w)->window.font->fid;
}
```

The Window widget is now complete. The application can retrieve the two drawing colors from the widget instance by calling either the `XtGetValues()` or the `WindowColor` functions. The actual window created for the Window widget is available by calling the `Xt-Window()` function.

Name

Text widget – text-editing widget.

Synopsis

Public Headers: *<X11/StringDefs.h>* *<X11/Xaw/AsciiText.h>* *<X11/Xaw/Text.h>* *<X11/Xaw/TextSrc.h>* *<X11/Xaw/TextSink.h>* *<X11/Xaw/AsciiSrc.h>* *<X11/Xaw/AsciiSink.h>*

Private Header: *<X11/Xaw/TextP.h>* *<X11/Xaw/TextSrcP.h>* *<X11/Xaw/TextSinkP.h>* *<X11/Xaw/AsciiTextP.h>* *<X11/Xaw/AsciiSrcP.h>* *<X11/Xaw/AsciiSink-P.h>*

Class Name: AsciiText

Class Pointer: `asciiTextWidgetClass`

Instantiation: *widget* = `XtCreateWidget(`*name*`, asciiTextWidgetClass, ...)`

Class Hierarchy

Core → Simple → Text → AsciiText

Description

A Text widget is a window that provides a way for an application to display one or more lines of text. The displayed text can reside in a file on disk or in a string in memory. An option also lets an application display a vertical Scrollbar in the Text window, letting the user scroll through the displayed text. Other options allow an application to let the user modify the text in the window or search for a specific string.

The Text widget is divided into three parts:

- Source object
- Sink object
- Text widget

The idea is to separate the storage of the text (source) from the painting of the text (sink). The Text widget proper coordinates the sources and sinks. The AsciiText widget is a subclass of the Text widget that automatically creates the source and sink for the client. By default, the Ascii-Text widget uses a string in memory as the source; setting the `asciiSrc.type` resource to `XawAsciiFile` specifies use of a disk file. The AsciiText's sink is a single-font, single-color ASCII sink. A client can, if it so chooses, explicitly create the source and sink before creating the Text widget.

The source stores and manipulates the text, and determines what editing functions may be performed on the text.

The sink obtains the fonts and the colors in which to paint the text. The sink also computes what text can fit on each line.

If a string in memory is used as the source, the application must allocate the amount of space needed. If a disk source is used, the file will not be updated until a call to `XawAsciiSave()`

is made. When a disk source is being used, the `useStringInPlace` resource is ignored. Three types of edit mode are available:

- Append-only
- Read-only
- Editable

Append-only mode lets the user enter text into the window, while read-only mode does not. Text may be entered only if the insertion point is after the last character in the window. Editable mode lets the user place the cursor anywhere in the text and modify the text at that position. The text cursor position can be modified by using the keystrokes or pointer buttons defined by the event bindings. (See Translations and Actions below.)

Resources

When creating a Text widget instance, the following resources are retrieved from the argument list or from the resource database:

Name (XtN...)	Type	Default	Description
XtNaccelerators	Accelerator-Table	NULL	List of event-to-action bindings to be executed by this widget, even though the event occurred in another widget.
XtNancestor-Sensitive	Boolean	True	(D) Sensitivity state of the ancestors of this widget: a widget is insensitive if either it or any of its ancestors is insensitive.
XtNautoFill	Boolean	False	Specifies whether the Text widget will automatically break a line when the user attempts to type into the right margin.
XtNbackground	Pixel	XtDefault-Background	Window background color.
XtNbackground-Pixmap	Pixmap	None	Window background pixmap.
XtNborderColor	Pixel	XtDefault-Foreground	Window border color.
XtNborderPixmap	Pixmap	None	Window border pixmap.
XtNborderWidth	Dimension	4	Border width in pixels.
XtNbottomMargin	Position	2	Amount of space, in pixels, between the edge of the window and the edge of the text within the window.
AsciiText.XtNcallback	XtCallback-List	NULL	List of callbacks called every time the text buffer changes.
XtNcolormap	Colormap	Parent's colormap.	Colormap that this widget will use.
XtNcursor	Cursor	XC_xterm	Pointer cursor.

Name (XtN...)	Type	Default	Description
XtNdataCompression	Boolean	True	If `True`, the `AsciiSrc` will compress its data to the minimum size required every time the text string is saved, or the value of the string is queried.
XtNdepth	int	Parent's depth.	(C) Depth of this widget's window.
XtNdestroyCallback	XtCallback-List	NULL	Callbacks for `XtDestroyWidget()`.
XtNdisplayCaret	Boolean	True	Whether to display the text caret.
AsciiText.XtNdisplay-Nonprinting	Boolean	True	Whether to display a nonprintable character as the string `^@`: if `False`, it will be printed as a blank.
XtNdisplayPosition	int	0	Character position of first line.
AsciiText.XtNecho	Boolean	True	Whether or not to echo characters to the screen.
AsciiText.XtNedit-Type	XawTextEdit-Type*	XawtextRead	Edit mode.†
AsciiSink.XtNfore-ground	Pixel	Black	Foreground color.
AsciiText.XtNfont	XFontStruct*	Fixed	Fontname.
AsciiText.XtNfore-ground	Pixel	XtDefault-Foreground	Pixel value which indexes the Text widget's colormap to derive the foreground color used by the text sink.
XtNheight	Dimension	Font height.	(A) Height of widget.
XtNinsensitive-Border	Pixmap	Gray pixmap.	Pixmap will be tiled into the widget's border if the widget becomes insensitive.
XtNinsertPosition	int	0	Character position of caret.
XtNleftMargin	Dimension	2	Left margin in pixels.
AsciiText.XtNlength	int	String length.	(A) Size of the string buffer.
XtNmappedWhenManaged	Boolean	TRUE	Whether `XtMapWidget()` is automatic.
AsciiText.XtNpiece-Size	XawText-Position	BUFSIZ	Size of the internal chunks into which the text buffer is broken down for memory management.
XtNresize	XawTextResize-Mode	XawtextResize-Never	Whether the widget should attempt to resize to its preferred dimensions whenever its resources are modified with `XtSetValues()`.

---

†`XawTextEditType` (R5) was `XawEditType` in R4.

Name (XtN...)	Type	Default	Description
XtNrightMargin	Position	2	Amount of space, in pixels, between the edge of the window and the corresponding edge of the text within the window.
XtNscreen	Screen	Parent's screen.	(R) Screen on which this widget is displayed.
XtNscrollHorizontal	XawTextScroll-Mode	XawtextScroll-Never	See XtNscrollVertical.
XtNscrollVertical	XawTextScroll-Mode	XawtextScroll-Never	Control the placement of scrollbars on the left and bottom edge of the text widget: these resources accept the values XawtextScroll-Always, XawtextScrollWhen-Needed, and XawtextScroll-Never.
XtNselectTypes	XawTextSelect-Type*	See below.	Selection units for multi-click.
XtNsensitive	Boolean	TRUE	Whether widget receives input.
AsciiText.XtNstring	String	NULL	String for the text source.
XtNtextSink	Widget	None	See below.
XtNtextSource	Widget	None	See below.
XtNtopMargin	Position	2	Amount of space, in pixels, between the edge of the window and the corresponding edge of the text within the window.
XtNtranslations	Translation-Table	See above.	Event-to-action translations.
XtNtype	AsciiType	XawAsciiString	May be either XawAsciiString or XawAsciiFile.
(R5) XtNunrealize-Callback	XtCallback-List	NULL	Called when unrealized.
XtNuseStringInPlace	Boolean	False	If True, will disable the memory management provided by the Text widget, updating the string resource in place.
XtNwidth	Dimension	100	Width of widget (pixels).

Name (XtN...)	Type	Default	Description
AsciiText.XtNwrap	WrapMode	XawtextWrap-Never	Accepted values are XawtextWrapNever, XawtextWrapLine, and XawtextWrapWord: with XawtextWrapLine, all text that is beyond the right edge of the window will be displayed on the next line; with XawtextWrapWord, the same action occurs but the text is broken at a word boundary if possible. If no wrapping is enabled, then the text will extend off the edge of the window and a small rectangle will be painted in the right margin to alert the user that this line is too long.
XtNx	Position	0	x coordinate in pixels.
XtNy	Position	0	y coordinate in pixels.

The AsciiSrc can be either of two types: XawAsciiFile or XawAsciiString.

AsciiSrc objects of type XawAsciiFile read the text from a file and store it into an internal buffer. This buffer may then be modified, provided the text widget is in the correct edit mode, just as if it were a source of type XawAsciiString. Unlike R3 and earlier versions of the AsciiSrc, it is now possible to specify an editable disk source.

AsciiSrc objects of type XawAsciiString have the text buffer implemented as a string. The string owner is responsible for allocating and managing storage for the string. In the default case for AsciiSrc objects of type XawAsciiString, the resource useStringInPlace is false, and the widget owns the string. The initial value of the string resource, and any update made by the application programmer to the string resource with XtSetValues(), is copied into memory private to the widget, and managed internally by the widget. The application writer does not need to worry about running out of buffer space (subject to the total memory available to the application). The performance does not decay linearly as the buffer grows large, as is necessarily the case when the text buffer is used in place. The application writer must use XtGetValues() to determine the contents of the text buffer, which will return a copy of the widget's text buffer as it existed at the time of the XtGetValues() call. This copy is not affected by subsequent updates to the text buffer, i.e., it is not updated as the user types input into the text buffer. This copy is freed upon the next call to XtGetValues to retrieve the string resource; however, to conserve memory, there is a convenience routine, XawAsciiSrcFreeString, allowing the application programmer to direct the widget to free the copy.

When the resource useStringInPlace is true and the AsciiSrc object is of type XawAsciiString, the application is the string owner. The widget will take the value of the string resource as its own text buffer, and the length resource indicates the buffer size. In this case the buffer contents change as the user types at the widget; it is not necessary to call XtGetValues() on the string resource to determine the contents of the buffer—it will simply return the address of the application's implementation of the text buffer.

Note that:

1. The `XtNeditType` attribute has one of the values `XawtextAppend`, `XawtextEdit`, or `XawtextRead`.

2. The value of the `XtNtype` resource determines whether the `XtNstring` resource contains the name of a file to be opened or a buffer to be displayed by the Text widget. A converter has been registered for this resource and accepts the values `string` and `file`.

Selections

`XtNselectionTypes` is an array of entries of type `XawTextSelectType` and is used for multiclick. As the pointer button is clicked in rapid succession, each click highlights the next "type" described in the array.

`XawselectAll`	Selects the contents of the entire buffer.
`XawselectChar`	Selects text characters as the pointer moves over them.
`XawselectLine`	Selects the entire line.
`XawselectNull`	Indicates the end of the selection array.
`XawselectParagraph`	Selects the entire paragraph (delimited by newline characters).
`XawselectPosition`	Selects the current pointer position.
`XawselectWord`	Selects whole words (delimited by whitespace) as the pointer moves onto them.

The default `selectType` array is:

```
{XawselectPosition, XawselectWord, XawselectLine, XawselectParagraph,
               XawselectAll, XawselectNull}
```

For the default case, two rapid pointer clicks highlight the current word, three clicks highlight the current line, four clicks highlight the current paragraph, and five clicks highlight the entire text. If the timeout value is exceeded, the next pointer click returns to the first entry in the selection array. The selection array is not copied by the Text widget. The client must allocate space for the array and cannot deallocate or change it until the Text widget is destroyed or until a new selection array is set.

To modify the selections, a programmer must construct a `XawTextSelectType` array (called the selection array) containing the selections desired and pass this as the new value for the `XtNselectionTypes` resource. The selection array may also be modified using the `XawTextSetSelectionArray()` function. All selection arrays must end with the value `XawselectNull`. The `selectionTypes` resource has no converter registered and cannot be modified through the resource manager.

The array contains a list of entries that will be called when the user attempts to select text in rapid succession with the `select-start` action (usually by clicking a pointer button). The first entry in the selection array will be used when the `select-start` action is initially called. The next entry will be used when `select-start` is called again, and so on. If a timeout value (1/10 of a second) is exceeded, the next `select-start` action will begin at the top of the selection array. When `XawselectNull` is reached, the array is recycled beginning with the first element.

Translations and Actions

Many standard keyboard editing facilities are supported by the event bindings. The following actions are supported:

Cursor Movement Actions	*Delete Actions*
Forward-character	Delete-next-character
Backward-character	Delete-previous-character
Forward-word	Delete-next-word
Backward-word	Delete-previous-word
Forward-paragraph	Delete-selection
Backward-paragraph	
Beginning-of-line	*Selection Actions*
End-of-line	Insert-selection
Next-line	Select-word
Previous-line	Select-all
Next-page	Select-start
Previous-page	Select-adjust
Beginning-of-file	Select-end
End-of-file	Extend-start
Scroll-one-line-up	Extend-adjust
Scroll-one-line-down	Extend-end

New Line Actions	*Miscellaneous Actions*
Newline-and-indent	Redraw-display
Newline-and-backup	Insert-file
Newline	Insert-char
	Display-caret
	Focus-in
Kill Actions	Focus-out
Kill-word	Search
Backward-kill-word	Multiply
Kill-selection	Form-paragraph
Kill-to-end-of-line	No-op
Kill-paragraph	Transpose-characters
Kill-to-end-of-paragraph	

- A page corresponds to the size of the Text window. For example, if the Text window is 50 lines in length, scrolling forward one page is the same as scrolling forward 50 lines.

- The `delete` action deletes a text item. The `kill` action deletes a text item and puts the item in the kill buffer (X cut buffer 1).

- The `insert-selection` action retrieves the value of a specified X selection or cut buffer, with fall-back to alternative selections or cut buffers.

Cursor Movement Actions

`forward-character( )`
`backward-character( )`

> These actions move the insertion point forward or backward one character in the buffer. If the insertion point is at the end (or beginning) of a line, this action moves the insertion point to the next (or previous) line.

`forward-word( )`
`backward-word( )`

> These actions move the insertion point to the next or previous word boundary. A word boundary is defined as a space, a tab, or a carriage return.

`forward-paragraph( )`
`backward-paragraph( )`

> These actions move the insertion point to the next or previous paragraph boundary. A paragraph boundary is defined as two carriage returns in a row with only spaces or tabs between them.

`beginning-of-line( )`
`end-of-line( )`

> These actions move to the beginning or end of the current line. If the insertion point is already at the end or beginning of the line, no action is taken.

`next-line( )`
`previous-line( )`

> These actions move the insertion point up or down one line. If the insert point is currently n characters from the beginning of the line then it will be n characters from the beginning of the next or previous line. If n is past the end of the line, the insertion point is placed at the end of the line.

`next-page( )`
`previous-page( )`

> These actions move the insertion point up or down one page in the file. One page is defined as the current height of the text widget. These actions always place the insertion point at the first character of the top line.

`beginning-of-file( )`
`end-of-file( )`

> These actions place the insertion point at the beginning or end of the current text buffer. The text widget is then scrolled the minimum amount necessary to make the new insertion point location visible.

`scroll-one-line-up( )`
`scroll-one-line-down( )`

> These actions scroll the current text field up or down by one line. They do not move the insertion point. Other than the scrollbars, this is the only way that the insertion point

may be moved off of the visible text area. The widget will be scrolled so that the insertion point is back on the screen as soon as some other action is executed.

Delete Actions

```
delete-next-character()
delete-previous-character()
```
These actions remove the character immediately after or before the insertion point. If a carriage return is removed, the next line is appended to the end of the current line.

```
delete-next-word()
delete-previous-word()
```
These actions remove all characters between the insertion point location and the next word boundary. A word boundary is defined as a space, a tab or a carriage return.

```
delete-selection()
```
This action removes all characters in the current selection. The selection can be set with the selection actions.

Selections Actions

```
select-word()
```
This action selects the word in which the insertion point is currently located. If the insertion point is between words, it will select the previous word.

```
select-all()
```
This action selects the entire text buffer.

```
select-start()
```
This action sets the insertion point to the current pointer location, where a selection then begins. If many of these selection actions occur quickly in succession then the selection count mechanism will be invoked.

```
select-adjust()
```
This action allows a selection started with the `select-start` action to be modified, as described above.

```
select-end(name[,name, . . .])
```
This action ends a text selection that began with the `select-start` action, and asserts ownership of the selection or selections specified. A *name* can be a selection (e.g., PRIMARY) or a cut buffer (e.g., CUT_BUFFER0). Note that case is important. If no *names* are specified, PRIMARY is asserted.

```
extend-start()
```
This action finds the nearest end of the current selection, and moves it to the current pointer location.

```
extend-adjust()
```
This action allows a selection started with an `extend-start` action to be modified.

```
extend-end(name[,name, . . .])
```
This action ends a text selection that began with the `extend-start` action, and asserts ownership of the selection or selections specified. A *name* can be a selection (e.g.,

PRIMARY) or a cut buffer (e.g., CUT_BUFFER0). Note that case is important. If no *name* is given, PRIMARY is asserted.

`insert-selection(name[,name, . . . ])`

This action retrieves the value of the first (left-most) named selection that exists or the cut buffer that is not empty. This action then inserts it into the Text widget at the current insertion point location. A *name* can be a selection (e.g., PRIMARY) or a cut buffer (e.g., CUT_BUFFER0). Note that case is important.

New Line Actions

`newline-and-indent()`

This action inserts a newline into the text and adds spaces to that line to indent it to match the previous line. (Note: this action still has a few bugs.)

`newline-and-backup()`

This action inserts a newline into the text *after* the insertion point.

`newline()`

This action inserts a newline into the text *before* the insertion point.

Kill Actions

`kill-word()`
`backward-kill-word()`

These actions act exactly like the `delete-next-word` and `delete-previous-word` actions, but they store the word that was killed into the kill buffer (CUT_BUFFER_1).

`kill-selection()`

This action deletes the current selection and stores the deleted text into the kill buffer (CUT_BUFFER_1).

`kill-to-end-of-line()`

This action deletes the entire line to the right of the insertion point, and stores the deleted text into the kill buffer (CUT_BUFFER_1).

`kill-paragraph()`

This action deletes the current paragraph. If the insertion point is between paragraphs, it deletes the paragraph above the insertion point, and stores the deleted text into the kill buffer (CUT_BUFFER_1).

`kill-to-end-of-paragraph()`

This action deletes everything between the current insertion point and the next paragraph boundary, and puts the deleted text into the kill buffer (CUT_BUFFER_1).

Miscellaneous Actions

`redraw-display()`

This action recomputes the location of all the text lines on the display, scrolls the text to center vertically the line containing the insertion point on the screen, clears the entire screen, and then redisplays it.

insert-file([*filename*])

This action activates the insert file popup. The *filename* option specifies the default filename to put in the filename buffer of the popup. If no *filename* is specified the buffer is empty at startup.

insert-char()

This action may be attached only to a key event. It calls XLookupString() to translate the event into a (rebindable) Latin-1 character (sequence) and inserts that sequence into the text at the insertion point.

insert-string(*string*[,*string*, . . .])

This action inserts each *string* into the text at the insertion point location. Any *string* beginning with the characters "0x" and containing only valid hexadecimal digits in the remainder is interpreted as a hexadecimal constant and the corresponding single character is inserted instead.

display-caret(*state*,*when*)

This action allows the insertion point to be turned on and off. The *state* argument specifies the desired state of the insertion point. This value may be any of the string values accepted for Boolean resources (e.g., on, True, off, False, etc.). If no arguments are specified, the default value is True. The *when* argument specifies, for EnterNotify or LeaveNotify events, whether or not the focus field in the event is to be examined. If the second argument is not specified, or specified as something other than always, then if the action is bound to an EnterNotify or LeaveNotify event, the action will be taken only if the focus field is True. An augmented binding that might be useful is:

```
*Text.Translations: #override \
    <FocusIn>:      display-caret(on) \n\
    <FocusOut>:     display-caret(off)
```

focus-in()
focus-out()

These actions do not currently do anything.

search(*direction*,[*string*])

This action activates the search popup. The *direction* must be specified as either forward or backward. The string is optional and is used as an initial value for the "Search for:" string.

multiply(*value*)

The multiply action allows the user to multiply the effects of many of the text actions. Thus the following action sequence:

```
multiply(10) delete-next-word()
```

will delete 10 words. It does not matter whether these actions take place in one event or many events. Using the default translations the key sequence Control-u, Control-d will delete 4 characters. Multiply actions can be chained; thus,

```
multiply(5) multiply(5)
```

is the same as

```
multiply(25)
```

If the string `reset` is passed to the multiply action the effects of all previous multiplies are removed and a beep is sent to the display.

`form-paragraph()`
> This action removes all the carriage returns from the current paragraph and reinserts them so that each line is as long as possible, while still fitting on the current screen. Lines are broken at word boundaries if at all possible. This action currently works only on Text widgets that use ASCII text.

`transpose-characters()`
> This action will switch the positions of the character to the left of the insertion point and the character to the right of the insertion point. The insertion point will then be advanced one character.

`no-op([action])`
> The no-op action makes no change to the text widget, and is used mainly to override translations. This action takes one optional argument. If this argument is `RingBell` then a beep is sent to the display.

Event Bindings

The default event bindings for the Text widget are:

```
char defaultTextTranslations[] = "\
    Ctrl<Key>F:             forward-character() \n\
    Ctrl<Key>B:             backward-character() \n\
    Ctrl<Key>D:             delete-next-character() \n\
    Ctrl<Key>A:             beginning-of-line() \n\
    Ctrl<Key>E:             end-of-line() \n\
    Ctrl<Key>H:             delete-previous-character() \n\
    Ctrl<Key>J:             newline-and-indent() \n\
    Ctrl<Key>K:             kill-to-end-of-line() \n\
    Ctrl<Key>L:             redraw-display() \n\
    Ctrl<Key>M:             newline() \n\
    Ctrl<Key>N:             next-line() \n\
    Ctrl<Key>O:             newline-and-backup() \n\
    Ctrl<Key>P:             previous-line() \n\
    Ctrl<Key>V:             next-page() \n\
    Ctrl<Key>W:             kill-selection() \n\
    Ctrl<Key>Y:             unkill() \n\
    Ctrl<Key>Z:             scroll-one-line-up() \n\
    Meta<Key>F:             forward-word() \n\
    Meta<Key>B:             backward-word() \n\
    Meta<Key>I:             insert-file() \n\
    Meta<Key>K:             kill-to-end-of-paragraph() \n\
    Meta<Key>V:             previous-page() \n\
    Meta<Key>Y:             stuff() \n\
    Meta<Key>Z:             scroll-one-line-down() \n\
    :Meta<Key>d:            delete-next-word() \n\
```

```
:Meta<Key>D:              kill-word() \n\
:Meta<Key>h:              delete-previous-word() \n\
:Meta<Key>H:              backward-kill-word() \n\
:Meta<Key>:               beginning-of-file() \n\
:Meta<Key>:               end-of-file() \n\
:Meta<Key>]:              forward-paragraph() \n\
:Meta<Key>[:              backward-paragraph() \n\
~Shift Meta<Key>Delete:      delete-previous-word() \n\
 Shift Meta<Key>Delete:      backward-kill-word() \n\
~Shift Meta<Key>Backspace:   delete-previous-word() \n\
 Shift Meta<Key>Backspace:   backward-kill-word() \n\
<Key>Right:               forward-character() \n\
<Key>Left:                backward-character() \n\
<Key>Down:                next-line() \n\
<Key>Up:                  previous-line() \n\
<Key>Delete:              delete-previous-character() \n\
<Key>BackSpace:           delete-previous-character() \n\
<Key>Linefeed:            newline-and-indent() \n\
<Key>Return:              newline() \n\
<Key>:                    insert-char() \n\
<FocusIn>:                focus-in() \n\
<FocusOut>:               focus-out() \n\
<Btn1Down>:               select-start() \n\
<Btn1Motion>:             extend-adjust() \n\
<Btn1Up>:                 extend-end(PRIMARY, CUT_BUFFER0) \n\
<Btn2Down>:               insert-selection(PRIMARY, CUT_BUFFER0) \n\
<Btn3Down>:               extend-start() \n\
<Btn3Motion>:             extend-adjust() \n\
<Btn3Up>:                 extend-end(PRIMARY, CUT_BUFFER0)";
```

A user-supplied resource entry can use application-specific bindings, a subset of the supplied default bindings, or both. The following is an example of a user-supplied resource entry that uses a subset of the default bindings:

```
Xmh*Text.Translations: \
     <Key>Right:       forward-character() \n\
     <Key>Left:        backward-character() \n\
     Meta<Key>F:       forward-word() \n\
     Meta<Key>B:       backward-word() \n\
     :Meta<Key>]:      forward-paragraph() \n\
     :Meta<Key>[:      backward-paragraph() \n\
     <Key>:            insert-char()
```

An augmented binding that is useful with the *xclipboard* utility is:

```
*Text.Translations: #override \
     Button1 <Btn2Down>:extend-end(CLIPBOARD)
```

The Text widget fully supports the X selection and cut buffer mechanisms. The following actions can be used to specify button bindings that will cause Text to assert ownership of one or more selections, to store the selected text into a cut buffer, and to retrieve the value of a selection or cut buffer and insert it into the text value.

insert-selection(*name*[,*name*, . . .])
> Retrieves the value of the first (left-most) named selection that exists or the cut buffer that is not empty and inserts it into the input stream. The specified name can be that of any selection (for example, PRIMARY or SECONDARY) or a cut buffer (i.e., CUT_BUFFER0 through CUT_BUFFER7). Note that case matters.

select-start()
> Unselects any previously selected text and begins selecting new text.

select-adjust()
extend-adjust()
> Continues selecting text from the previous start position.

start-extend()
> Begins extending the selection from the farthest (left or right) edge.

select-end(*name*[,*name*, . . .])
extend-end(*name*[,*name*, . . .])
> Ends the text selection, asserts ownership of the specified selection(s), and stores the text in the specified cut buffer(s). The specified name can be that of a selection (for example, PRIMARY or SECONDARY) or a cut buffer (i.e., CUT_BUFFER0 through CUT_BUFFER7). Note that case is significant. If CUT_BUFFER0 is listed, the cut buffers are rotated before storing into buffer 0.

XawWMProtocols([*wm_protocol_name*])
> This action is written specifically for the transient shells instantiated by the Text widget, which are the file insertion and the search and replace dialog boxes. This action is attached to those shells by the Text widget, in order to handle Client-Message events with the WM_PROTOCOLS atom in the detail field. This action supports WM_DELETE_WINDOW on the Text widget popups, and may support other window manager protocols if necessary in the future. The popup will be dismissed if the window manager sends a WM_DELETE_WINDOW request and there are no parameters in the action call, which is the default. The popup will also be dismissed if the parameters include the string "wm_delete_window", and the event is a ClientMessage event requesting dismissal or is not a Client-Message event. This action is not sensitive to the case of the strings passed as parameters.

Public Functions

A Text widget lets both the user and the application take control of the text being displayed. The user takes control with the scroll bar or with key strokes defined by the event bindings.

The scroll bar option places the scroll bar on the left side of the window and can be used with any editing mode. The application takes control with procedure calls to the Text widget to:

- Display text at a specified position.

- Highlight specified text areas.

- Replace specified text areas.

The text that is selected within a Text window may be assigned to an X selection or copied into a cut buffer and can be retrieved by the application with the Intrinsics `XtGetSelection-Value()` or the Xlib `XFetchBytes()` functions, respectively. Several standard selection schemes (e.g., character/word/paragraph with multiclick) are supported through the event bindings.

`AsciiTextWidgetClass` is actually a source and a sink along with a `textWidgetClass`. If you want to create an instance of the class `textWidgetClass` separately, you must provide a source and a sink when the widget is created. The Text widget cannot be instantiated without both.

- To enable an application to select a piece of text, use `XawTextSetSelection()`:

```
void XawTextSetSelection(w, left, right)
    Widget w;
    XawTextPosition left, right;
```

where:

`w`	Specifies the window ID.
`left`	Specifies the character position at which the selection begins.
`right`	Specifies the character position at which the selection ends.

If redisplay is enabled, this function highlights the text and makes it the PRIMARY selection. This function does not have any effect on CUT_BUFFER0. `XawTextPosition` is defined as follows:

```
typedef long XawTextPosition;
```

Character positions in the Text widget begin at 0 and end at $n+1$, where n is the number of characters in the Text source widget.

- To unhighlight previously highlighted text in a window, use `XawTextUnset-Selection()`:

```
void XawTextUnsetSelection(w)
    Widget w;
```

where *w* specifies the window ID.

- To enable the application to get the character positions of the selected text, use `XawText-GetSelectionPos()`:

```
void XawTextGetSelectionPos(w, begin_return, end_return)
    Widget w;
    XawTextPosition *begin_return, *end_return;
```

where:

    w   Specifies the window ID.

    begin_return   Specifies a pointer to the location to which the beginning character position of the selection is returned.

    end_return   Specifies a pointer to the location to which the ending character position of the selection is returned.

If the returned values are equal, there is no current selection.

- To enable an application to replace text, use `XawTextReplace()`:

```
int XawTextReplace(w, start_pos, end_pos, text)
    Widget w;
    XawTextPosition start_pos, end_pos;
    XawTextBlock *text;
```

where:

    w   Specifies the window ID.

    start_pos   Specifies the starting character position of the text replacement.

    end_pos   Specifies the ending character position of the text replacement.

    text   Specifies the text to be inserted into the file. This function cannot replace text in read-only Text widgets, and it can only append text to an append-only Text widget.

The `XawTextReplace()` function deletes text in the specified range (*startPos*, *endPos*) and inserts the new text at *start_pos*. The return value is `XawEditDone` if the replacement is successful, `XawPositionError` if the edit mode is `XawtextAppend` and *start_pos* is not the position of the last character of the source, or `XawEditError` if either the source was read-only or the range to be deleted is larger than the length of the source.

The `XawTextBlock` structure (defined in *<X11/Xaw/Text.h>*) contains:

```
typedef struct {
    int firstPos;
    int length;
    char *ptr;
    Atom format;
} XawTextBlock, *XawTextBlockPtr, *TextBlockPtr;
                                    /* last for R4 compat */
```

The `firstPos` field is the starting point to use within the `ptr` field. The value is usually zero. The `length` field is the number of characters that are transferred from the `ptr` field. The number of characters transferred is usually the number of characters in `ptr`, which is the string to insert into the Text widget. The `format` field is not currently used, but should be specified as `FMT8BIT`. The `XawTextReplace()` arguments *start_pos* and *end_pos* represent the text source character positions for the existing text that is to be replaced by the text in the `XawTextBlock` structure. The characters from *start_pos* up to but not including *end_pos* are deleted, and the characters that are specified by the text block are inserted in their place. If *start_pos* and *end_pos* are equal, no text is deleted and the new text is inserted after *start_pos*.

Only Latin-1 text is currently supported, and only one font can be used for each Text widget.

- To search for a string in the Text widget, use XawTextSearch():

```
XawTextPosition XawTextSearch(w, dir, text)
        Widget w;
        XawTextScanDirection dir;
        XawTextBlock * text;
```

where:

w	Specifies the window ID.
dir	Specifies the direction to search in. Legal values are XawsdLeft and XawsdRight.
text	Specifies a text block structure (see XawTextReplace() for the definition) that contains the text to search for.

The XawTextSearch() function will begin at the insertion point and search in the direction specified for a string that matches the one passed in *text*. If the string is found, the location of the first character in the string is returned. If the string could not be found, then the value Xaw-TextSearchError is returned.

- To redisplay a range of characters, use XawTextInvalidate():

```
void XawTextInvalidate(w, from, to)
        Widget w;
        XawTextPosition from, to;
```

where:

w	Specifies the window ID.
from	Specifies the starting character to be displayed.
to	Specifies the last character to be displayed.

The XawTextInvalidate() function causes the specified range of characters to be redisplayed immediately if redisplay is enabled, or the next time that redisplay is enabled.

- To enable redisplay, use XawTextEnableRedisplay():

```
void XawTextEnableRedisplay(w)
        Widget w;
```

where *w* specifies the window ID. XawTextEnableRedisplay() flushes any changes due to batched updates when XawTextDisableRedisplay() was called and allows future changes to be reflected immediately.

- To disable redisplay while making several changes, use `XawTextDisable-Redisplay()`:

```
void XawTextDisableRedisplay(w)
      Widget w;
```

where *w* specifies the window ID.

The `XawTextDisableRedisplay()` function causes all changes to be batched until `XawTextDisplay()` or `XawTextEnableRedisplay()` is called.

- To display batched updates, use `XawTextDisplay()`:

```
void XawTextDisplay(w)
    Widget w;
```

where *w* specifies the window ID.

The `XawTextDisplay()` function forces any accumulated updates to be displayed.

The following procedures are convenience procedures that replace calls to `XtSetValues()` or `XtGetValues()` when only a single resource is to be modified or retrieved.

- To obtain the character position of the leftmost character on the first line displayed in the widget (that is, the value of `XtNdisplayPosition`), use `XawTextTopPosition()`.

```
XawTextPosition XawTextTopPosition(w)
      Widget w;
```

where *w* specifies the Text widget.

- To assign a new selection array to a text widget use `XawTextSetSelectionArray()`:

```
void XawTextSetSelectionArray(w, sarray)
      Widget w;
      XawTextSelectType * sarray;
```

w	Specifies the Text widget.
sarray	Specifies a selection array.

Calling this function is equivalent to setting the value of the `XtNselectionTypes` resource.

- To move the insertion caret to the specified source position, use `XawTextSet-InsertionPoint()`:

```
void XawTextSetInsertionPoint(w, position)
      Widget w;
      XawTextPosition position;
```

where:

w	Specifies the Text widget.
position	Specifies the position to which to move the insertion caret.

The text will be scrolled vertically, if necessary, to make the line containing the insertion point visible. The result is equivalent to setting the `XtNinsertPosition` resource.

- To obtain the current position of the insertion caret, use `XawTextGetInsertion-Point()`:

```
XawTextPosition XawTextGetInsertionPoint(w)
      Widget w;
```

where *w* specifies the Text widget.

The result is equivalent to retrieving the value of the `XtNinsertPosition` resource.

- To replace the text source in the specified widget, use `XawTextSetSource()`:

```
void XawTextSetSource(w, source, position)
      Widget w;
      Widget source;
      XawTextPosition position;
```

where:

w	Specifies the Text widget.
source	Specifies the source widget.
position	Specifies the location to place the replacement text.

A display update will be performed if redisplay has not been disabled.

- To obtain the current text source for the specified widget, use `XawTextGetSource()`:

```
XawTextSource XawTextGetSource(w)
      Widget w;
```

where *w* specifies the Text widget.

- To enable and disable the insertion point, use `XawTextDisplayCaret()`:

```
void XawTextDisplayCaret(w, visible)
      Widget w;
      Boolean visible;
```

w	Specifies the Text widget.
visible	Specifies whether caret should be displayed.
	If *visible* is `False`, the insertion point will be disabled. The marker can be re-enabled either by setting *visible* to `True`, by calling `XtSetValues()`, or by executing the *display-caret* action routine.

Creating Sources and Sinks

The following functions for creating and destroying text sources and sinks are called automatically by `asciiTextClass`, and it is therefore necessary for the client to use them only when creating an instance of `textWidgetClass`.

- To create a new ASCII text sink, use `XtCreateWidget()` and specify the class variable `asciiSinkObjectClass`. The resources required by the sink are qualified by the name and class of the parent and the sub-part name `XtNtextSink` and class `XtCTextSink`.

- To deallocate an ASCII text sink, use `XtDestroyWidget()` and specify the widget of the AsciiSink widget. The sink must not be in use by any widget or an error will result.

- To create a new text source, use `XtCreateWidget()` and specify the class variable `asciiSourceObjectClass`. The resources required by the source are qualified by the name and class of the parent and the sub-part name `XtNtextSource` and class `XtCTextSource`.

- To deallocate a text disk source, use `XtDestroyWidget()` and specify the widget of the AsciiSource widget. The sink must not be in use by any widget or an error will result.

Name

Toggle widget – button that maintains a Boolean state.

Synopsis

Public Headers: *<X11/StringDefs.h> <X11/Xaw/Toggle.h>*

Private Header: *<X11/Xaw/ToggleP.h>*

Class Name: Toggle

Class Pointer: `toggleWidgetClass`

Instantiation: *widget* `= XtCreateWidget(`*name*`, toggleWidgetClass, ...)`

Class Hierarchy

Core → Simple → Label → Command → Toggle

Description

The Toggle widget is an area, often rectangular, containing a text or pixmap label. This widget maintains a Boolean state (e.g., True/False or On/Off) and changes state whenever it is selected. When the pointer is on the button, the button border is highlighted to indicate that the button is ready for selection. When pointer button 1 is pressed and released, the Toggle widget indicates that it has changed state by reversing its foreground and background colors, and its `notify` action is invoked, calling all functions on its callback list. If the pointer is moved out of the widget before the button is released, the widget reverts to its normal foreground and background colors, and releasing the button has no effect. This behavior allows the user to cancel an action.

Toggle buttons may also be part of a radio group. A radio group is a list of Toggle buttons in which no more than one Toggle may be set at any time. A radio group is identified by the widget ID of any one of its members. The convenience routine `XawToggleGetCurrent()` returns information about the currently set Toggle button in the radio group.

Resources

When creating a Toggle widget instance, the following resources are retrieved from the argument list or from the resource database:

Name (XtN...)	Type	Default	Description
XtNaccelerators	Accelerator-Table	NULL	List of event-to-action bindings to be executed by this widget, even though the event occurred in another widget.
XtNancestor-Sensitive	Boolean	True	(D) Sensitivity state of the ancestors of this widget. A widget is insensitive if either it or any of its ancestors is insensitive.
XtNbackground	Pixel	XtDefault-Background	Window background color.

Name (XtN...)	Type	Default	Description
XtNbackground-Pixmap	Pixmap	XtUnspecified-Pixmap	Window background pixmap.
XtNbitmap	Pixmap	None	Pixmap to display in place of the label.
XtNborderColor	Pixel	XtDefault-Foreground	Window border color.
XtNborderPixmap	Pixmap	XtUnspecified-Pixmap	Window border pixmap.
XtNborderWidth	Dimension	1	Width of button border.
XtNcallback	XtCallback-List	NULL	Callback for button select.
XtNcolormap	Colormap	Parent's colormap.	Colormap that this widget will use.
XtNcornerRound-Percent	Dimension	25	See below.
XtNcursor	Cursor	None	Pointer cursor.
XtNdepth	int	Parent's depth.	(C) Depth of this widget's window.
XtNdestroy-Callback	XtCallbackList	NULL	Callbacks for XtDestroy-Widget().
XtNencoding	unsigned char	XawTextEncoding-8bit	For I18N.
XtNfont	XFontStruct*	XtDefaultFont	Label font.
XtNforeground	Pixel	XtDefault-Foreground	Foreground color.
XtNheight	Dimension	font height + 2 * XtNinternal-Height	(A) Button height.
XtNhighlight-Thickness	Dimension	2 (0 if shaped)	(A) Width of border to be highlighted.
XtNinsensitive-Border	Pixmap	Gray pixmap.	Border when not sensitive.
XtNinternal-Height	Dimension	2	Internal border height for highlighting.
XtNinternalWidth	Dimension	4	Internal border width for highlighting.
XtNjustify	XtJustify	XtJustifyCenter	Type of text alignment.
XtNlabel	String	Name of widget.	Button label.
(R5) XtNleft-Bitmap	Bitmap	None	Pixmap before label.
XtNmappedWhen-Managed	Boolean	TRUE	Whether XtMapWidget() is automatic.
XtNradioData	Pointer	Name of widget.	See below.
XtNradioGroup	Widget	No radio group.	See below.
XtNresize	Boolean	TRUE	Whether to auto-resize in Set-Values.

Name (XtN...)	Type	Default	Description
XtNscreen	Screen	Parent's screen.	(R) Screen on which this widget is displayed.
XtNsensitive	Boolean	TRUE	Whether widget receives input.
XtNshapeStyle	ShapeStyle	Rectangle	Type of nonrectangular button.
XtNstate	Boolean	Off	See below.
XtNtranslations	Translation-Table	See below.	Event-to-action translations.
XtNwidth	Dimension	XtNlabel width+2* XtNinternalWidth	(A) Button width.
XtNx	Position	0	x-coordinate in pixels.
XtNy	Position	0	y-coordinate in pixels.

Note that:

1. The Toggle widget supports two callback lists: XtNdestroyCallback and XtNcallback. The notify action executes the callbacks on the XtNcallback list when the button is toggled. The *call_data* argument is the value of the XtNstate resource.

2. When a bitmap of depth greater that 1 is specified, the set, unset, and reset actions have no effect, since no foreground and background colors are used in a multi-plane pixmap.

The new resources (not inherited from superclasses) associated with the Toggle widget are:

XtNradioData

Specifies the data that is returned by XawToggleGetCurrent() when this is the currently set widget in the radio group. This value is also used to identify the Toggle that is set by a call to XawToggleSetCurrent(). XawToggleGetCurrent() returns NULL if no widget in a radio group is currently set. Programmers must not specify NULL (or 0) as XtNradioData.

XtNradioGroup

Specifies another Toggle widget that is in the radio group to which this Toggle widget should be added. A radio group is a group of Toggle widgets, only one of which may be set at a time. If this value is NULL (the default), then the Toggle is not part of any radio group and can change state without affecting any other Toggle widgets. If the widget specified in this resource is not already in a radio group, then a new radio group is created containing these two Toggle widgets. No Toggle widget can be in multiple radio groups. The behavior of a radio group of one toggle is undefined. A converter is registered which will convert widget names to widgets without caching.

XtNstate

Specifies whether the Toggle widget is set (True) or unset (False).

Translations and Actions

The following default translation bindings are used by the Toggle widget:

```
<EnterWindow>:highlight(Always)
<LeaveWindow>:unhighlight()
<Btn1Down>,<Btn1Up>:toggle() notify()
```

The Toggle widget supports the following actions:

- Switching the button between the foreground and background colors with `set`, `unset` and `toggle`.

- Processing application callbacks with `notify`.

- Switching the internal border between highlighted and unhighlighted states with `highlight` and `unhighlight`.

The actions supported by Toggle are listed below:

highlight(*condition*)

Displays the internal highlight border in the color (`XtNforeground` or `Xt-Nbackground`) that contrasts with the interior color of the Toggle widget. The conditions `WhenUnset` and `Always` are understood by this action procedure. If no argument is passed, `WhenUnset` is assumed.

unhighlight()

Displays the internal highlight border in the color (`XtNforeground` or `Xt-Nbackground`) that matches the interior color of the Toggle widget.

set()

Enters the set state, in which `notify` is possible, and displays the interior of the button in the foreground color. The label or pixmap is displayed in the background color.

unset()

Cancels the set state and displays the interior of the button, including the highlight border, in the background color. The label or pixmap is displayed in the foreground color.

toggle()

Changes the current state of the Toggle widget, setting the widget if it was previously unset, and unsetting it if it was previously set. If the widget is to be set and is in a radio group, then this action procedure may unset another Toggle widget, causing all routines on its callback list to be invoked. The callback routines for the Toggle to be unset are called before those for the Toggle to be set.

reset()

Cancels any `set` or `highlight` action and displays the interior of the button in the background color, with the label displayed in the foreground color.

notify()

When the button is set, this action calls all functions in the callback list named by the `XtNcallback` resource. The value of the *call_data* argument in these callback functions is undefined.

Radio Groups

Two types of radio groups are typically desired by applications. In the first type, the default translations for the Toggle widget implement a "zero, or one of many" radio group. This means that no more than one button can be active, but no buttons need to be active.

The other type of radio group is "one of many" and has the more restricted policy that exactly one radio button will always be active. Toggle widgets can be used to provide this interface by modifying the translation table of each Toggle in the group:

```
<EnterWindow>:highlight(Always)
<LeaveWindow>:unhighlight()
<Btn1Down>,<Btn1Up>:set() notify()
```

This translation table does not allow any Toggle to be unset unless another Toggle has been set. The application programmer must choose an initial state for the radio group by setting the `Xt-Nstate` resource of one of its member widgets to `True`.

Public Functions

The following functions allow easy access to the Toggle widget's radio group functionality.

- To allow an application to either change the Toggle's radio group, add the Toggle to a radio group, or remove the Toggle from a radio group, use `XawToggleChangeRadio-Group()`.

```
void XawToggleChangeRadioGroup(w, radio_group)
    Widget w, radio_group;
```

where:

w	Specifies the widget ID.
radio_group	Specifies the widget ID of Toggle in the new radio group. If `NULL`, then the Toggle is removed from any radio group of which it is a member.

If a Toggle is already set in the new radio group, and if the Toggle to be added is also set, then the previously set Toggle in the radio group is unset and its callback procedures are invoked.

- To find the currently selected Toggle in a radio group of Toggle widgets, use `XawToggle-GetCurrent()`:

```
XtPointer XawToggleGetCurrent(radio_group);
    Widget radio_group;
```

where *radio_group* specifies the widget ID of any Toggle widget in the radio group.

The value returned by this function is the `radioData` of the Toggle in this radio group that is currently set. The default value for `radioData` is the name of that Toggle widget. If no Toggle is set in the radio group specified, then `NULL` is returned.

- To change the Toggle that is currently set in a radio group, use `XawToggleSet-Current()`:

```
void XawToggleSetCurrent(radio_group, radio_data);
    Widget radio_group;
    XtPointer radio_data;
```

where:

     radio_group   Specifies any Toggle widget in the radio group.

     radio_data   Specifies the `radioData` identifying the Toggle that should be set in the radio group specified by the *radio_group* argument.

`XawToggleSetCurrent()` locates the Toggle widget to be set by matching *radio_data* against the `radioData` for each Toggle in the radio group. If none match, `XawToggleSetCurrent()` returns without making any changes. If more than one Toggle matches, `XawToggleSetCurrent()` arbitrarily chooses a Toggle to set. If this changes the state of any Toggle widgets, all routines in their callback lists will be invoked. The callback routines for a Toggle to be unset are called before those for the Toggle to be set.

- To unset all Toggle widgets in a radio group, use `XawToggleUnsetCurrent()`:

```
void XawToggleUnsetCurrent(radio_group);
    Widget radio_group;
```

where *radio_group* specifies any Toggle widget in the radio group.

If this changes the state of a Toggle widget, all routines on its callback list will be invoked.

See Also
Command(5), *Label*(5), *MenuButton*(5).

Tree

Name

Tree widget – a constraint widget that arranges its children in a tree.

Synopsis

Public Headers: *<X11/StringDefs.h>* *<X11/Xaw/Tree.h>*

Private Header: *<X11/Xaw/TreeP.h>*

Class Name: Tree

Class Pointer: `treeWidgetClass`

Instantiation: *widget* = `XtCreateWidget(`*name*`, treeWidgetClass, ...)`

Class Hierarchy

Core → Composite → Constraint → Tree

Availability

Release 5 and later.

Description

The Tree widget provides geometry management of arbitrary widgets arranged in a directed, acyclic graph (i.e., a tree). The hierarchy is constructed by attaching a constraint resource called `XtNtreeParent` to each child indicating which other node in the tree should be treated as the child's superior. The structure of the tree is shown by laying out the nodes in the standard format for tree diagrams with lines drawn to connect each node with its children.

The Tree sizes itself according to the needs of its children and is not intended to be resized by its parent. Instead, it should be placed inside another composite widget (such as the Porthole or Viewport) that can be used to scroll around in the tree.

Resources

When creating a Tree widget instance, the following resources are retrieved from the argument list or from the resource database:

Name	Type	Default	Description
XtNaccelerators	Accelerator-Table	NULL	Accelerators for this widget.
XtNancestor-Sensitive	Boolean	True	Sensitivity state of the ancestors of this widget.
XtNautoReconfigure	Boolean	False	Whether to re-layout the tree when each new child is added.
XtNbackground	Pixel	XtDefault-Background	Window background color.
XtNbackground-Pixmap	Pixmap	XtUnspecified-Pixmap	Window background pixmap.
XtNborderColor	Pixel	XtDefault-Foreground	Window border color.

Name	Type	Default	Description
XtNborderPixmap	Pixmap	XtUnspecified- Pixmap	Window border pixmap.
XtNborderWidth	Dimension	1	Width of border in pixels.
XtNchildren	WidgetList	NULL	List of all this composite widget's current children.
XtNcolormap	Colormap	Parent's colormap.	Colormap that this widget will use.
XtNdepth	int	Parent's depth.	Depth of this widget's window.
XtNdestroy- Callback	XtCallback- List	NULL	Callbacks for XtDestroyWidget().
XtNforeground	Pixel	XtDefault- Foreground	Widget foreground color.
XtNgravity	XtGravity	West	Window gravity of widget.
XtNheight	Dimension	Computed at realize.	Height of tree.
XtNhSpace	Dimension	20	Horizontal space between children.
XtNlineWidth	Dimension	0	Width of tree lines.
XtNmappedWhen- Managed	Boolean	TRUE	Whether XtMapWidget() is automatic.
XtNnumChildren	Cardinal	0	Number of children in this composite widget.
XtNscreen	Screen	Parent's screen.	Screen on which this widget is displayed.
XtNsensitive	Boolean	TRUE	Whether widget receives input.
XtNtranslations	Translation- Table	NULL	Event-to-action translations.
XtNvSpace	Dimension	6	Vertical space between children.
XtNwidth	Dimension	Computed at realize.	Width of tree.
XtNx	Position	0	x-coordinate in pixels.
XtNy	Position	0	y-coordinate in pixels.

XtNautoReconfigure
: Whether or not to lay out the tree every time a node is added or removed.

XtNforeground
: Foreground color for the widget.

XtNgravity
: Specifies the side of the widget from which the tree should grow. Valid values include WestGravity, NorthGravity, EastGravity, and SouthGravity.

XtNhSpace
: Amount of horizontal space, in pixels, to leave between the children. This resource also specifies the amount of space between the outermost children and the edge of the box.

XtNlineWidth
: The width of the lines drawn between nodes that do not have a XtNtreeGC constraint resource and their inferiors in the tree.

XtNvSpace

> The amount of vertical space, in pixels, to leave between the children. This resource also specifies the amount of space left between the outermost children and the edge of the box.

Constraints

> When creating children to be added to a Tree, the following additional resources are retrieved from the argument list or from the resource database. Note that these resources are maintained by the Tree widget even though they are stored in the child.

Name	Type	Default	Description
XtNtreeGC	GC	NULL	GC used to draw lines between the child and its inferiors in the tree.
XtNtreeParent	Widget	NULL	The child's superior node in the tree.

XtNtreeGC

> This specifies the GC to use when drawing lines between this widget and its inferiors in the tree. If this resource is not specified, the Tree's XtNforeground and XtNlineWidth will be used.

XtNtreeParent

> This specifies the superior node in the tree for this widget. The default is for the node to have no superior (and to therefore be at the top of the tree).

The position of each child in the tree hierarchy (as opposed to the widget hierarchy) is determined by the value of the XtNtreeParent constraint resource. Each time a child is managed or unmanaged, the Tree widget will attempt to reposition the remaining children to fix the shape of the tree if the XtNautoReconfigure resource is set. Children at the root of the tree are drawn at the side specified by the XtNgravity resource. After positioning all children, the Tree widget attempts to shrink its own size to the minimum dimensions required for the layout.

Public Functions

- XawTreeForceLayout() forces a Tree widget to re-layout its children. When adding several children to a Tree widget, it is most efficient to set XtNautoReconfigure to False and use this function once all the widgets have been added.

```
void XawTreeForceLayout(w)
    Widget w;
```

w   specifies the Tree widget.

See Also

Constraint(5).

Viewport

Name

Viewport widget – scrollable viewing area widget.

Synopsis

Public Headers:	*<X11/StringDefs.h> <X11/Xaw/Viewport.h>*
Private Header:	*<X11/Xaw/ViewportP.h>*
Class Name:	Viewport
Class Pointer:	`viewportWidgetClass`
Instantiation:	*widget* = `XtCreateWidget(`*name*`,  viewportWidgetClass,` `...)`

Class Hierarchy

Core → Constraint → Form → Viewport

Description

The Viewport widget consists of a frame window, one or two Scrollbars, and an inner window (usually containing a child widget). The size of the frame window is determined by the viewing size of the data that is to be displayed and the dimensions to which the Viewport is created. The inner window is the full size of the data that is to be displayed and is clipped by the frame window. The Viewport widget controls the scrolling of the data directly. No application callbacks are required for scrolling.

When the geometry of the frame window is equal in size to the inner window, or when the data does not require scrolling, the Viewport widget automatically removes any scroll bars. The `forceBars` option causes the Viewport widget to display any scroll bar permanently.

Resources

When creating a Viewport widget instance, the following resources are retrieved from the argument list or from the resource database:

Name (XtN...)	Type	Default	Description
XtNaccelerators	Accelerator-Table	NULL	List of event-to-action bindings to be executed by this widget, even though the event occurred in another widget.
XtNancestor-Sensitive	Boolean	True	(D) Sensitivity state of the ancestors of this widget: a widget is insensitive if either it or any of its ancestors is insensitive.
XtNallowHoriz	Boolean	FALSE	Flag to allow horizontal scroll bars.
XtNallowVert	Boolean	FALSE	Flag to allow vertical scroll bars.
XtNbackground	Pixel	XtDefault-Background	Window background color.
XtNbackground-Pixmap	Pixmap	XtUnspecified-Pixmap	Window background pixmap.

Name (XtN...)	Type	Default	Description
XtNborderColor	Pixel	XtDefault- Foreground	Window border color.
XtNborderPixmap	Pixmap	XtUnspecified- Pixmap	Window border pixmap.
XtNborderWidth	Dimension	1	Width of the border in pixels.
XtNchildren	WidgetList	NULL	(R) List of all current children of this composite widget.
XtNcolormap	Colormap	Parent's colormap.	Colormap that this widget will use.
XtNdepth	int	Parent's depth.	(C) Depth of this widget's window.
XtNdestroy- Callback	XtCallback- List	NULL	Callback for XtDestroyWidget().
XtNforceBars	Boolean	FALSE	Flag to force display of scroll bars.
XtNheight	Dimension	Height of child.	Height of the widget.
XtNmappedWhen- Managed	Boolean	TRUE	Whether XtMapWidget() is automatic.
XtNnumChildren	Cardinal	0	(R) Number of children in this composite widget.
(R5) XtNreport- Callback	XtCallback- List	NULL	Called when viewed area changes.
XtNscreen	Screen	Parent's screen.	(R) Screen on which this widget is displayed.
XtNsensitive	Boolean	TRUE	Whether widget should receive input.
XtNtranslations	Translation- Table	NULL	Event-to-action translations.
XtNuseBottom	Boolean	FALSE	Flag to indicate bottom/top bars.
XtNuseRight	Boolean	FALSE	Flag to indicate right/left bars.
XtNwidth	Dimension	Width of child.	Width of the widget.
XtNx	Position	0	x coordinate in pixels.
XtNy	Position	0	y coordinate in pixels.

The new resource defined by Viewport (not inherited from superclasses) are:

allowHoriz
allowVert   If these resources are **False** then the Viewport will never create a scrollbar in this direction. If it is **True** then the scrollbar will only appear when it is needed, unless **forceBars** is **True**.

forceBars   When **True** the scrollbars that have been *allowed* will always be visible on the screen. If **False** the scrollbars will be visible only when the inner window is larger than the frame. are.IP XtNreport-Callback .5i A list of functions to invoke whenever the managed child widget changes size or position. The *call_data* argument is of type XawPannerReport *, shown on the reference page for the Panner widget. New in R5.

useBottom
useRight By default the scrollbars appear on the left and top of the screen. These resources allow the vertical scrollbar to be placed on the right edge of the Viewport, and the horizontal scrollbar on the bottom edge of the Viewport.

The Viewport widget manages a single child widget. When the size of the child is larger than the size of the Viewport, the user can interactively move the child within the Viewport by repositioning the scroll bars.

The default size of the Viewport before it is realized is the width and/or height of the child. After it is realized, the Viewport will allow its child to grow vertically or horizontally if XtNallowVert or XtNallowHoriz, respectively, were set. If the corresponding vertical or horizontal scrollbar is not enabled, the Viewport will propagate the geometry request to its own parent and the child will be allowed to change size only if the (grand) parent allows it. Regardless of whether or not scrollbars are enabled in the corresponding direction, if the child requests a new size smaller than the Viewport size, the change will be allowed only if the parent of the Viewport allows the Viewport to shrink to the appropriate dimension.

The scrollbar children of the Viewport are named horizontal and vertical. By using these names the programmer can specify resources for the individual scrollbars. XtSet-Values() can be used to modify the resources dynamically once the widget ID has been obtained with XtNameToWidget().

Note that although the Viewport is a subclass of the Form, no resources for the Form may be supplied for any of the children of the Viewport. These constraints are managed internally, and are not meant for public consumption.

Public Functions

To insert a child into a Viewport widget, use XtCreateWidget() and specify as the parent the widget ID of the (previously created) Viewport.

- To remove a child from a Viewport widget, use XtUnmanageChild() or XtDestroy-Widget() and specify the widget ID of the child.

- To delete the inner window, any children, and the frame window, use XtDestroy-Widget() and specify the widget ID of the Viewport widget.

See Also

Scrollbar(5).

Section 6

Miscellaneous Utilities

This section contains alphabetically-organized reference pages for the utility functions from the Xmu library that are most useful to Xt programmers. The remainder of the the Xmu functions are documented in Volume Two, Xlib Reference Manual.

The Xmu library is part of the core MIT distribution, but is not a standard of, nor well supported by the X Consortium. Most of the functions in this section are used by the Xaw library.

The first reference page, Introduction, explains the format and contents of each of the following pages.

In This Section:

This page describes the format and contents of each reference page in Section 6, which covers the functions from the Xmu utilities library that may be useful to Xt programmers. Note that not all vendors supply Xmu with their X Window System software.

Name

Function – a brief description of the function.

Synopsis

This section shows the signature of the function: the names and types of the arguments, and the type of the return value. It also shows the header file that must be included to declare the function. For predefined resource converters and event handlers, this section shows how to register the function, rather than the actual function signature.

Inputs

This subsection describes each of the function arguments that pass information to the function.

Outputs

This subsection describes any of the function arguments that are used to return information from the function. These arguments are always of some pointer type, and you should use the C address-of operator (**&**) to pass the address of the variable in which the function will store the return value. Note that because the list of function arguments is broken into "Input" and "Output" sections, they do not always appear in the same order that they are passed to the function. See the function signature for the actual calling order.

Returns

This subsection explains the return value of the function, if any.

Availability

This section appears for functions that were added in Release 5, and are not available in earlier releases.

Description

This section explains what the function does and describes its arguments and return value. If you've used the function before and are just looking for a refresher, this section and the synopsis above should be all you need.

Usage

This section appears for most functions and provides less formal information about the function: when and how you might want to use it, things to watch out for, and related functions that you might want to consider.

Structures

This section shows the definition of structures, enumerated types, typedefs, or symbolic constants used by the function.

Miscellaneous Utilities

See Also

This section refers you to related functions, prototype procedures, Intrinsics widget classes, or widget methods. The numbers in parentheses following each reference refer to the sections of this book in which they are found.

Name

XmuAddInitializer – register an application context initialization procedure.

Synopsis

```
#include <X11/Xmu/Initer.h>
void XmuAddInitializer(func, data)
    void (*func)();
    caddr_t data;
```

Inputs

func   Specifies the procedure to register.

data   Specifies private data to be passed to the procedure.

Description

XmuAddInitializer() registers a procedure that will be invoked the first time the function XmuCallInitializers() is invoked on a given application context. The procedure will be called with two arguments, the application context and the private data registered with the procedure.

Usage

If a widget needs to do application-context-specific initialization, it can register a function with XmuAddInitializer() in its class_initialize() method, and then call XmuCallInitializers() for the application context of each widget instance in the initialize() method.

See Also

class_initialize(4), *initialize(4)*,
XmuCallInitializers(6).

Name

XmuCallInitializers – call all registered initializer functions for an application context.

Synopsis

```
#include <X11/Xmu/Initer.h>
void XmuCallInitializers(app_context)
    XtAppContext app_context;
```

Inputs

app_context Specifies the application context for which the initializer functions should be called.

Description

If this is the first time it has been called for the given application context, `XmuCall-Initializers()` invokes each of the functions registered with `XmuAddInitializer()`. Each function is called with two arguments, the application context and the private data that was registered with the function. `XmuCallInitializers()` will never call these functions more than once for any application context.

Usage

If a widget needs to do application-context-specific initialization, it can register a function with `XmuAddInitializer()` in its `class_initialize()` method, and then call `XmuCall-Initializers()` for the application context of each widget instance in the `initialize()` method.

See Also

class_initialize(4), *initialize*(4), *XmuAddInitializer*(6).

XmuCompareISOLatin1

Name

XmuCompareISOLatin1 – compare and determine order of two strings, ignoring case.

Synopsis

```
#include <X11/Xmu/CharSet.h>
int XmuCompareISOLatin1(first, second)
    char *first, *second;
```

Inputs

first   Specifies a string to compare.

second   Specifies a string to compare.

Returns

An integer that specifies whether *first* is less than, equal to, or greater than *second*.

Description

XmuCompareISOLatin1() compares two NULL terminated Latin-1 strings, ignoring case differences, and returns an integer greater than, equal to, or less than zero, according to whether first is lexicographically greater than, equal to, or less than second. The two strings are assumed to be encoded using ISO 8859-1 (Latin-1).

Usage

This function is useful in resource converters that convert between strings and enumerated types.

See Also

XmuCopyISOLatin1Lowered(6), *XmuCopyISOLatin1Uppered*(6).

XmuConvertStandardSelection

Name

XmuConvertStandardSelection – convert to standard selection target types.

Synopsis

```
#include <X11/Xmu/StdSel.h>
Boolean XmuConvertStandardSelection(w, time, selection, target, type,
        value, length, format)
    Widget w;
    Time time;
    Atom *selection, *target, *type;
    caddr_t *value;
    unsigned long *length;
    int *format;
```

Inputs

w	Specifies the widget that currently owns the selection.
time	Specifies the time at which the selection was established.
selection	This argument is unused.
target	Specifies the target type for the conversion.

Outputs

type	Returns the property type of the converted value.
value	Returns the converted value.
length	Returns the number of elements in the converted value.
format	Returns the size in bits of the elements of the converted value.

Returns

True if the conversion was successful; False otherwise.

Description

XmuConvertStandardSelection() converts the selection to the following standard targets: CLASS, CLIENT_WINDOW, DECNET_ADDRESS, HOSTNAME, IP_ADDRESS, NAME, OWNER_OS, TARGETS, TIMESTAMP, and USER. It returns True if the conversion was successful, and False if it failed.

XmuConvertStandardSelection() allocates memory for the returned value. The client should free this memory by calling XtFree().

Usage

XmuConvertStandardSelection() converts to the "housekeeping" target types that do not have anything to do with the actual value of the selection. It is particularly useful within an XtConvertSelectionProc registered with a call to XtOwnSelection(). The returned type, value, length, and format can be used directly by that conversion procedure. Note that when this function is used to convert the TARGETS target, it returns only the list of targets that it supports itself. The selection conversion procedure that called it will have to append its own supported targets to this list.

See Also

XtOwnSelection(1),
XtConvertSelectionProc(2).

Miscellaneous Utilities

XmuCopyISOLatin1Lowered

Name

XmuCopyISOLatin1Lowered – copy string, changing uppercase to lowercase.

Synopsis

```
#include <X11/Xmu/CharSet.h>
void XmuCopyISOLatin1Lowered(dst, src)
   char *dst, *src;
```

Inputs

src   Specifies the string to copy.

Outputs

dst   Returns the string copy. Note that this is the first argument to the function, not the second.

Description

XmuCopyISOLatin1Lowered() copies a null-terminated string from *src* to *dst* (including the NULL), changing all Latin-1 uppercase letters to lowercase. The string is assumed to be encoded using ISO 8859-1 (Latin-1).

Usage

This function is useful in resource converters that convert between strings and enumerated types.

See Also

XmuCompareISOLatin1(6), *XmuCopyISOLatin1Uppered*(6).

XmuCopyISOLatin1Uppered

Name

XmuCopyISOLatin1Uppered – copy string, changing lowercase to uppercase.

Synopsis

```
#include <X11/Xmu/CharSet.h>
void XmuCopyISOLatin1Uppered(dst, src)
    char *dst, *src;
```

Inputs

src   Specifies the string to copy.

Outputs

dst   Returns the string copy. Note that this is the first argument to the function, not the second.

Description

XmuCopyISOLatin1Uppered() copies a null-terminated string from *src* to *dst* (including the NULL), changing all Latin-1 lowercase letters to uppercase. The string is assumed to be encoded using ISO 8859-1 (Latin-1).

Usage

This function is useful in resource converters that convert between strings and enumerated types.

See Also

XmuCompareISOLatin1(6), *XmuCopyISOLatin1Lowered*(6).

Miscellaneous Utilities

Name

XmuCreateStippledPixmap – create two pixel by two pixel gray pixmap.

Synopsis

```
#include <X11/Xmu/Drawing.h>
Pixmap XmuCreateStippledPixmap(screen, fore, back, depth)
    Screen *screen;
    Pixel fore, back;
    unsigned int depth;
```

Inputs

screen	Specifies the screen the pixmap is created on.
fore	Specifies the foreground pixel value.
back	Specifies the background pixel value.
depth	Specifies the depth of the pixmap.

Returns

The pixmap.

Description

XmuCreateStippledPixmap() creates a two pixel by two pixel stippled pixmap of specified depth on the specified screen. The pixmap is cached so that multiple requests share the same pixmap. The pixmap should be freed with XmuReleaseStippledPixmap() to maintain correct reference counts.

Usage

This function is useful for widgets that display themselves "grayed" out when they are insensitive.

See Also

XmuReleaseStippledPixmap(6).

XmuCvtFunctionToCallback

Name

XmuCvtFunctionToCallback – convert a function pointer to an XtCallbackList.

Synopsis

```
#include <X11/Xmu/Converters.h>
XtAddConverter(XtRCallProc, XtRCallback, XmuCvtFunctionToCallback,
               NULL, 0);
```

Description

`XmuCvtFunctionToCallback()` is an old-style converter function that converts a function pointer to an `XtCallbackList` containing that function and `NULL` *call_data*.

See Also

XtAddConverter(1), *XtAppAddConverter*(1),
XmuCvtStringToMisc(6), *XmuNewCvtStringToWidget*(6).

XmuCvtStringToMisc

Name

XmuCvtStringToMisc — convert strings to various types.

Synopsis

```
#include <X11/Xmu/Converters.h>

XtAddConverter(XtRString, XtRBackingStore, XmuCvtStringToBackingStore, NULL, 0);
XtAddConverter(XtRString, XtRGravity, XmuCvtStringToGravity, NULL, 0);
XtAddConverter(XtRString, XtRJustify, XmuCvtStringToJustify, NULL, 0);
XtAddConverter(XtRString, XtRLong, XmuCvtStringToLong, NULL, 0);
XtAddConverter(XtRString, XtROrientation, XmuCvtStringToOrientation, NULL, 0);
XtSetTypeConverter(XtRString, XtRShapeStyle,XmuCvtStringToShapeStyle,
                NULL, 0, XtCacheNone, NULL);

static XtConvertArgRec screenConvertArg[] = {
  {XtBaseOffset, (XtPointer)XtOffset(Widget, core.screen), sizeof(Screen *)}
};

XtAddConverter(XtRString, XtRBitmap, XmuCvtStringToBitmap,
            screenConvertArg, XtNumber(screenConvertArg));

static XtConvertArgRec screenConvertArg[] = {
  {XtBaseOffset, (XtPointer)XtOffset(WidgetRec, core.screen), sizeof(Screen *)}
};

XtAddConverter(XtRString, XtRCursor, XmuCvtStringToCursor,
            screenConvertArg, XtNumber(screenConvertArg));

static XtConvertArgRec parentCvtArg[] = {
  {XtBaseOffset, (XtPointer)XtOffset(Widget, core.parent), sizeof(Widget)},
};

XtAddConverter(XtRString, XtRWidget, XmuCvtStringToWidget,
            parentCvtArg, XtNumber(parentCvtArg));

static XtConvertArgRec colorCursorConvertArgs[] = {
  {XtWidgetBaseOffset, (XtPointer) XtOffsetOf(WidgetRec, core.screen),
   sizeof(Screen *)},
  {XtResourceString, (XtPointer) XtNpointerColor,sizeof(Pixel)},
  {XtResourceString, (XtPointer) XtNpointerColorBackground, sizeof(Pixel)},
  {XtWidgetBaseOffset, (XtPointer) XtOffsetOf(WidgetRec,core.colormap),
    sizeof(Colormap)}
};

XtSetTypeConverter(XtRString, XtRColorCursor, XmuCvtStringToColorCursor,
                colorCursorConvertArgs, XtNumber(colorCursorConvertArgs),
                XtCacheByDisplay, NULL);
```

Availability

XmuCvtStringToColorCursor() and XmuCvtStringToGravity() are new in Release 5.

Description

These functions are type converters that convert from strings to various resource types. Some require additional arguments, but most may be registered without any arguments. Two of these functions are X11R4 "new-style" converters registered with `XtSetTypeConverter()`; the rest are "old-style" converters registered with `XtAddConverter()` or `XtAppAdd-Converter()`.

`XmuCvtStringToBackingStore()` converts a string to a backing-store integer as defined in *<X11/X.h>*. The string "notUseful" converts to `NotUseful`, "whenMapped" converts to `WhenMapped`, and "always" converts to `Always`. The string "default" converts to the value `Always + WhenMapped + NotUseful`. The case of the string does not matter.

`XmuCvtStringToGravity()` converts a string to an `XtGravity` enumeration value. The string "forget" or a NULL value convert to `ForgetGravity`, "NorthWestGravity" converts to `NorthWestGravity`, the strings "NorthGravity" and "top" convert to `NorthGravity`, "NorthEastGravity" converts to `NorthEastGravity`, the strings "West" and "left" convert to `WestGravity`, "CenterGravity" converts to `CenterGravity`, "EastGravity" and "right" convert to `EastGravity`, "SouthWestGravity" converts to `SouthWestGravity`, "South-Gravity" and "bottom" convert to `SouthGravity`, "SouthEastGravity" converts to `South-EastGravity`, "StaticGravity" converts to `StaticGravity`, and "UnmapGravity" converts to `UnmapGravity`. The case of the string does not matter.

`XmuCvtStringToJustify()` converts a string to an `XtJustify` enumeration value. The string "left" converts to `XtJustifyLeft`, "center" converts to `XtJustifyCenter`, and "right" converts to `XtJustifyRight`. The case of the string does not matter.

`XmuCvtStringToLong()` converts a string to an integer of type long. It parses the string using `sscanf` with a format of "%ld."

`XmuCvtStringToOrientation()` converts a string to an `XtOrientation` enumeration value. The string "horizontal" converts to `XtorientHorizontal` and "vertical" converts to `XtorientVertical`. The case of the string does not matter.

`XmuCvtStringToShapeStyle()` converts a string to an integer shape style. The string "rectangle" converts to `XmuShapeRectangle`, "oval" converts to `XmuShapeOval`, "ellipse" converts to `XmuShapeEllipse`, and "roundedRectangle" converts to `XmuShape-RoundedRectangle`. The case of the string does not matter.

`XmuCvtStringToBitmap()` creates a bitmap (a Pixmap of depth one) suitable for window manager icons. The string argument is the name of a file in standard bitmap file format. For the possible filename specifications, see the reference page for `XmuLocateBitmapFile()`.

`XmuCvtStringToCursor()` converts a string to a `Cursor`. The string can either be a standard cursor name formed by removing the XC_ prefix from any of the cursor defines listed in Appendix I of Volume Two, a font name and glyph index in decimal of the form "FONT fontname index [[font] index]," or a bitmap filename acceptable to `XmuLocateBitmap-File()`.

`XmuCvtStringToWidget()` converts a string to an immediate child widget of the parent widget passed as an argument. Note that this converter only works for child widgets that have already been created; there is no lazy evaluation. The string is first compared against the names of the normal and popup children, and if a match is found the corresponding child is returned. If no match is found, the string is compared against the classes of the normal and popup children, and if a match is found the corresponding child is returned. The case of the string is significant. The converter XmuNewConvertStringToWidget() performs the same conversion, but allows greater control over the type of caching that will be done on the result of the conversion. Because widget trees are often dynamic in an application, it is usually inappropriate to cache string-to-widget conversion results as is done with XmuCvtStringToWidget().

XmuCvtStringToColorCursor() converts a string to a Cursor with the foreground and background pixels specified by the conversion arguments. The string can either be a standard cursor name formed by removing the XC_ prefix from any of the cursor defines listed in Appendix I of Volume Two, a font name and glyph index (in base 10) of the form "FONT fontname index [[font] index]," or a bitmap filename acceptable to XmuLocateBitmap-File().

See Also

XtAddConverter(1), XtAppAddConverter(1), XtSetTypeConverter(1),
XmuCvtFunctionToCallback(6), XmuNewCvtStringToWidget(6).

XmuGetAtomName

Name

XmuGetAtomName – returns the string corresponding to the specified Atom.

Synopsis

```
#include <X11/Xmu/Atoms.h>
char *XmuGetAtomName(d, atom)
    Display *d;
    Atom atom;
```

Inputs

d   Specifies a connection to an X server; returned from `XOpenDisplay()`.

atom   Specifies the Atom whose name is desired.

Returns

The string that is interned for the specified Atom on the specified display.

Description

`XmuGetAtomName()` returns the string corresponding to the specified Atom. The result is cached, so that subsequent requests do not cause another round trip to the server. If the Atom is zero, `XmuGetAtomName()` returns the string "(BadAtom)".

Usage

Atoms are used when requesting or converting selection values in a widget or an application. This and the related Xmu Atom functions provide client-side caching and help avoid roundtrips to the server. There are also a number of very useful predefined Atom macros in *<X11/Xmu/Atoms.h>*. These macros (`XA_TEXT(d)`, for example) each take a display argument and return the appropriate Atom for that display. They are named to complement the predefined Atoms from *<X11/Xatom.h>*.

See Also

XmuInternAtom(6), *XmuInternStrings*(6), *XmuMakeAtom*(6), *XmuNameofAtom*(6).

Name

XmuInternAtom – obtain an Atom from the server or an `AtomPtr` cache.

Synopsis

```
Atom XmuInternAtom(d, atom_ptr)
      Display *d;
      AtomPtr atom_ptr;
```

Inputs

d   Specifies a connection to an X server; returned from `XOpenDisplay()`.

atom_ptr   Specifies the `AtomPtr`.

Returns

The Atom corresponding to the string in *atom_ptr* for Display *d*.

Description

`XmuInternAtom()` returns an Atom that corresponds to the string initialized in `atom_ptr` for the specified display. If the Atom is not already in the `AtomPtr` cache, `XmuIntern-Atom()` queries the server and caches the result.

Usage

Use `XmuMakeAtom()` to initialize an `AtomPtr` with a string, then use `XmuInternAtom()` to obtain the Atom that corresponds to that string for a particular display. Since a widget may be instantiated on more than one display, widget code should be sure that it is using the correct Atom. In widget code, you can call `XmuMakeAtom()` from your `class_initialize()` procedure, storing the resulting `AtomPtr` in a global variable or class field, and then call `XmuInternAtom()` in your code whenever you need the Atom.

Atoms are used when requesting or converting selection values in a widget or an application. This and the related Xmu Atom functions provide client-side caching and help avoid roundtrips to the server. There are also a number of very useful predefined Atom macros in *<X11/Xmu/Atoms.h>*. These macros (`XA_TEXT(d)`, for example) each take a display argument and return the appropriate Atom for that display. They are named to complement the predefined Atoms from *<X11/Xatom.h>*.

Structures

`AtomPtr` is an opaque type.

See Also

XmuGetAtomName(6), *XmuInternStrings*(6), *XmuMakeAtom*(6), *XmuNameofAtom*(6).

XmuInternStrings

Name

XmuInternAtom – get Atoms for an array of strings.

Synopsis

```
void XmuInternStrings(d, names, count, atoms)
      Display *d;
      String *names;
      Cardinal count;
      Atom *atoms;
```

Inputs

d   Specifies a connection to an X server; returned from `XOpenDisplay()`.

names   Specifies the strings to intern.

count   Specifies the number of strings.

Outputs

atoms

Returns the array of Atoms. This array must be allocated by the caller.

Description

`XmuInternStrings()` converts a list of strings into a list of Atoms, possibly by querying the server. The results are cached, such that subsequent requests do not cause further round trips to the server. The caller is responsible for preallocating the array of Atoms.

Usage

Atoms are used when requesting or converting selection values in a widget or an application. This and the related Xmu Atom functions provide client-side caching and help avoid roundtrips to the server. There are also a number of very useful predefined Atom macros in *<X11/Xmu/Atoms.h>*. These macros (`XA_TEXT(d)`, for example) each take a display argument and return the appropriate Atom for that display. They are named to complement the predefined Atoms from *<X11/Xatom.h>*.

See Also

XmuGetAtomName(6), *XmuInternAtom*(6), *XmuMakeAtom*(6), *XmuNameofAtom*(6).

Name

XmuMakeAtom – create an `AtomPtr` to cache Atom/Display pairs.

Synopsis

```
#include <X11/Xmu/Atoms.h>
AtomPtr XmuMakeAtom(name)
    char* name;
```

Inputs

name   Specifies the Atom name.

Returns

An initialized `AtomPtr` for the string *name*.

Description

`XmuMakeAtom()` creates and initializes an `AtomPtr`, which is an opaque object that contains a string and a list of cached Atoms for that string—one Atom for each display.

Usage

Use `XmuMakeAtom()` to initialize an `AtomPtr` with a string, then use `XmuInternAtom()` to obtain the Atom that corresponds to that string for a particular display. Since a widget may be instantiated on more than one display, widget code should be sure that it is using the correct Atom. In widget code, you can call `XmuMakeAtom()` from your `class_initialize()` procedure, storing the resulting `AtomPtr` in a global variable or class field, and then call `XmuInternAtom()` with that `AtomPtr` and the display in your code whenever you need the Atom.

Atoms are used when requesting or converting selection values in a widget or an application. This and the related Xmu Atom functions provide client-side caching and help avoid roundtrips to the server. There are also a number of very useful predefined Atom macros in *<X11/Xmu/Atoms.h>*. These macros (`XA_TEXT(d)`, for example) each take a display argument and return the appropriate Atom for that display. They are named to complement the predefined Atoms from *<X11/Xatom.h>*.

Structures

`AtomPtr` is an opaque type.

See Also

XmuGetAtomName(6), *XmuInternAtom*(6), *XmuInternStrings*(6), *XmuNameofAtom*(6).

Name

XmuNameOfAtom – return property name string represented by an `AtomPtr`.

Synopsis

```
#include <X11/Xmu/Atoms.h>
char *XmuNameOfAtom(atom_ptr)
    AtomPtr atom_ptr;
```

Inputs

`atom_ptr`   Specifies the `AtomPtr`.

Returns

The string that corresponds to an `AtomPtr`

Description

`XmuNameOfAtom()` returns the string represented by the specified `AtomPtr`.

Usage

Atoms are used when requesting or converting selection values in a widget or an application. This and the related Xmu Atom functions provide client-side caching and help avoid roundtrips to the server. There are also a number of very useful predefined Atom macros in *<X11/Xmu/Atoms.h>*. These macros (`XA_TEXT(d)`, for example) each take a display argument and return the appropriate Atom for that display. They are named to complement the predefined Atoms from *<X11/Xatom.h>*.

See `XmuMakeAtom()` and `XmuInternAtom()` for more information on using `AtomPtr`s.

Structures

`AtomPtr` is an opaque type.

See Also

XmuGetAtomName(6), *XmuInternAtom*(6), *XmuInternStrings*(6), *XmuMakeAtom*(6).

Name

XmuNewCvtStringToWidget – convert string to widget without caching.

Synopsis

```
#include <X11/Xmu/Converters>
static XtConvertArgRec parentCvtArg[] = {
    {XtWidgetBaseOffset, (XtPointer)XtOffsetOf(WidgetRec,core.parent),
     sizeof(Widget)}
};
XtSetTypeConverter(XtRString, XtRWidget, XmuNewCvtStringToWidget,
              parentCvtArg, XtNumber(parentCvtArg), XtCacheNone, NULL);
```

Availability

Release 5 and later.

Description

This converter is identical in functionality to XmuCvtStringToWidget, except that it is a new-style converter, allowing the specification of a cache type at the time of registration. Most widgets will not cache the results of this converter, as the application may dynamically create and destroy widgets, which would cause cached values to become illegal.

See Also

XtSetTypeConverter(1), *XmuCvtFunctionToCallback*(6), *XmuCvtStringToMisc*(6).

Name

XmuReleaseStippledPixmap – release pixmap created with XmuCreateStippled-
Pixmap().

Synopsis

```
#include <X11/Xmu/Drawing.h>
void XmuReleaseStippledPixmap(screen, pixmap)
   Screen *screen;
   Pixmap pixmap;
```

Inputs

screen   Specifies the screen the pixmap was created on.

pixmap   Specifies the pixmap to free.

Description

XmuReleaseStippledPixmap() decrements the reference count on a pixmap created
with XmuCreateStippledPixmap(), and frees the pixmap if it is no longer being referenced.

Usage

This function is useful for widgets that display themselves "grayed" out when they are insensitive.

See Also

XmuCreateStippledPixmap(6).

Miscellaneous Utilities

XmuReshapeWidget

Name

XmuReshapeWidget – change the shape of a widget's Window.

Cynopoio

```
#include <X11/Xmu/Converters.h>
Boolean XmuReshapeWidget(w, shape_style, corner_width, corner_height)
    Widget w;
    int shape_style;
    int corner_width, corner_height;
```

Inputs

w	Specifies the widget to reshape.
shape_style	Specifies the new shape. See Description for allowable values.
corner_width	Specifies the width of the rounded corner for a *shape_style* of XmuShapeRoundedRectangle.
corner_height	Specifies the height of the rounded corner for a *shape_style* of XmuShapeRoundedRectangle.

Returns

False if *shape_style* is invalid; True otherwise.

Availability

Release 4 and later. This function will only work on servers that support the Shape extension.

Description

XmuReshapeWidget() uses the Shape extension to the X protocol to change the shape of the specified widget's window. The shape is specified by the *shape_style* parameter which can have one of the following arguments: XmuShapeRectangle, XmuShapeOval, Xmu-ShapeEllipse, or XmuShapeRoundedRectangle. If the shape is XmuShape-RoundedRectangle, the *corner_width* and *corner_height* parameters specify the bounding box of the rounded part of the corner. These arguments are ignored for any other shape styles. Note that this function does not change the nominal width and height of the widget's window, nor the widget's position within its parent.

XmuReshapeWidget() returns False if it is passed an unsupported value as the *shape_style* argument; otherwise it returns True.

See Also

XmuCvtStringToShapeStyle(6).

XmuWnCountOwnedResources

Name

XmuWnCountOwnedResources — determine the number of resources that a widget class inherits from one of its superclasses.

Synopsis

```
#include <X11/Xmu/WidgetNode.h>
int XmuWnCountOwnedResources(node, owner_node, constraints)
    XmuWidgetNode *node;
    XmuWidgetNode *owner_node;
    Bool constraints;
```

Inputs

node   Specifies the widget class whose resources are being examined.

owner_node   Specifies the superclass of node that is to have its resources counted.

constraints   Specifies whether constraint resources or normal resources should be counted.

Returns

The number of resources of node that are inherited from owner_node.

Availability

Release 5 and later.

Description

This function returns the number of resources of the widget class node which are "contributed" or "owned" by the superclass owner_node. If constraints is False, XmuCountOwnedResources counts normal resources; otherwise it counts constraint resources. node and owner_node must have been passed to XmuWnInitializeNodes() before being used in this function, and node must have been passed to XmuWnFetchResources().

Usage

The XmuWn functions were developed for the specific needs of the *viewres* client, and may not be of general utility.

See Also

XmuWnFetchResources(6), *XmuWnInitializeNodes*(6), *XmuWnNameToNode*(6).

Name

XmuWnFetchResources – get the resource list of a widget class.

Synopsis

```
#include <X11/Xmu/WidgetNode.h>
void XmuWnFetchResources(node, toplevel, top_node)
    XmuWidgetNode *node;
    Widget toplevel;
    XmuWidgetNode *top_node;
```

Inputs

node   Specifies the widget class for that the resource list should be obtained.

toplevel   Specifies a widget that can be used as the parent for a dummy instance of the specified widget class. A top-level shell widget is suitable, for example.

top_node   Specifies the widget class that should be treated as the top of the widget class hierarchy when determining which superclass contributed which resources to the widget class *node*.

Availability

Release 5 and later.

Description

This function obtains a resource list for the normal resources and the constraint resources of a widget class. For each resource it also obtains a pointer to the widget class that "contributed" that resource. XmuWnFetchResources() creates and destroys a dummy widget instance of the specified class. The argument *toplevel* is a widget that may be used as the parent of that dummy widget; a toplevel shell widget is suitable. The *top_node* argument is used to specify the top of the widget hierarchy for the purposes of determining "ownership" of resources. The XmuWidgetNode for the Core class could be used, for example, if the programmer were not interested in considering the Object and RectObj widget classes separately.

XmuWnFetchResources() does not return a value; the resource lists it obtains are stored in its *node* argument, which is of type XmuWidgetNode *. This structure is shown below. The fields *resources* and *constraints* are the normal and constraint resource lists for the widget class, and the fields *nresources*, and *nconstraints* specify the number of elements in each list. Additionally, the fields *resourcewn* and *constraintwn* are arrays of XmuWidgetNode * whose elements point to the widget structure of the widget node class that "owns" the corresponding resource in the resource lists.

The widget nodes passed to XmuWnFetchResources() must first have been initialized in a call to XmuWnInitializeNodes().

Usage

The XmuWn functions were developed for the specific needs of the *viewres* client, and may not be of general utility.

Structures

```
typedef struct _XmuWidgetNode {
    char *label;                                    /* mixed case name */
    WidgetClass *widget_class_ptr;             /* addr of widget class */
    struct _XmuWidgetNode *superclass;     /* superclass of widget_class */
    struct _XmuWidgetNode *children, *siblings;      /* subclass links */
    char *lowered_label;                  /* lowercase version of label */
    char *lowered_classname;         /* lowercase version of class_name */
    Bool have_resources;                 /* resources have been fetched */
    XtResourceList resources;            /* extracted resource database */
    struct _XmuWidgetNode **resourcewn;    /* where resources come from */
    Cardinal nresources;                      /* number of resources */
    XtResourceList constraints;       /* extracted constraint resources */
    struct _XmuWidgetNode **constraintwn; /* where constraints come from */
    Cardinal nconstraints;          /* number of constraint resources */
    XtPointer data;                                    /* extra data */
} XmuWidgetNode;
```

See Also

XmuWnCountOwnedResources(6), _XmuWnInitializeNodes_(6), _XmuWnNameToNode_(6).

Name

XmuWnInitializeNodes – initialize an array of widget nodes.

Synopsis

```
#include <X11/Xmu/WidgetNode.h>
void XmuWnInitializeNodes(node_array, num_nodes)
    XmuWidgeNode *node_array;
    int num_nodes;
```

Inputs

node_array   Specifies an array of widget nodes in alphabetical order.

num_nodes   Specifies the number of nodes in the array.

Availability

Release 5 and later.

Description

XmuWnInitializeNodes() initializes an array of XmuWidgetNode. It must be called before any of the other Xmu widget node functions. The *node_array* argument is typically a statically initialized array of XmuWidgetNode (shown below) in which only the first two fields of each node are specified. XmuWnInitializeNodes() initializes the superclass and subclass links in each XmuWidgetNode structure, and sets the resource fields to NULL. These resource list fields are filled in by the function XmuWnFetchResources(). Note that the array of widget nodes must be in alphabetical order by the value of the *label* field, which needn't be the same as the widget class name.

Usage

The XmuWn functions were developed for the specific needs of the *viewres* client, and may not be of general utility.

Structures

```
typedef struct _XmuWidgetNode {
    char *label;                                    /* mixed case name */
    WidgetClass *widget_class_ptr;                  /* addr of widget class */
    struct _XmuWidgetNode *superclass;        /* superclass of widget_class */
    struct _XmuWidgetNode *children, *siblings;      /* subclass links */
    char *lowered_label;                      /* lowercase version of label */
    char *lowered_classname;           /* lowercase version of class_name */
    Bool have_resources;                    /* resources have been fetched */
    XtResourceList resources;               /* extracted resource database */
    struct _XmuWidgetNode **resourcewn;      /* where resources come from */
    Cardinal nresources;                            /* number of resources */
    XtResourceList constraints;          /* extracted constraint resources */
    struct _XmuWidgetNode **constraintwn; /* where constraints come from */
    Cardinal nconstraints;               /* number of constraint resources */
    XtPointer data;                                 /* extra data */
} XmuWidgetNode;
```

See Also

XmuWnCountOwnedResource(6), *XmuWnFetchResources*(6), *XmuWnNameToNode*(6).

Name

XmuWnNameToNode – look up a widget node by name.

Synopsis

```
#include <X11/Xmu/WidgetNode.h>
XmuWidgetNode *XmuWnNameToNode(node_list, num_nodes, name)
    XmuWidgetNode *node_list;
    int num_nodes;
    char *name;
```

Inputs

node_list   Specifies the array of widget nodes to search.

num_nodes   Specifies the number of nodes in the array.

name   Specifies the name to search for.

Returns

The node that matches *name* or NULL.

Availability

Release 5 and later.

Description

XmuWnNameToNode() searches the specified array of XmuWidgetNode for a node with *label* field or widget class name that matches the specified *name*. It returns the matching node or NULL if none was found. The comparison used is case insensitive.

Usage

The XmuWn functions were developed for the specific needs of the *viewres* client, and may not be of general utility.

See Also

XmuWnCountOwnedResource(6), *XmuWnFetchResources*(6), *XmuWnInitializeNodes*(6).

_XEditResCheckMessages

Name

_XEditResCheckMessages – event handler for the Editres protocol.

Synopsis

```
#include <X11/Xmu/Editres.h>
XtAddEventHandler(shell, (EventMask) 0, True, _XEditResCheckMessages, NULL);
```

Inputs

shell   Specifies the shell widget that is to participate in the Editres protocol.

Availability

Release 5 and later.

Description

_XEditResCheckMessages, though misleadingly named, is a public function in the Xmu library. It is an event handler, which, when registered on a shell widget, allows that shell widget to participate in the Editres protocol. Shell widgets that are subclasses of the Athena VendorShell widget have this event handler registered automatically. When registering this event handler with XtAddEventHandler(), pass an event mask of 0, specify that nonmaskable events should be handled by passing True as the third argument, and pass NULL client data as the last argument.

Miscellaneous Utilities

Appendices

This part of the manual contains handy lists of functions, as well as useful reference information on data types, events, and the like.

In The Appendices:

A
Function Summaries

This quick reference is intended to help you find and use the right function or prototype for a particular task. It organizes the Section 1 and Section 2 reference pages into two lists:

- Listing of functions, macros, and prototype procedures by groups.

- Alphabetical listing of functions, macros, and prototype procedures.

The first column indicates which section to find the routines in. If the name is followed by a (2), the routine can be found in Section 2; otherwise, the routine can be found in Section 1.

Group Listing with Brief Descriptions

Application Contexts

XtCreateApplicationContext()	Create an application context.
XtDestroyApplicationContext()	Destroy an application context and close its displays.
XtDisplayInitialize()	Initialize a display and add it to an application context.
XtGetApplicationNameAndClass()	Return the application name and class as passed to Xt-DisplayInitialize() for a particular Display.
XtOpenDisplay()	Open, initialize, and add a display to an application context.
XtToolkitInitialize()	Initialize the X Toolkit internals.
XtWidgetToApplicationContext()	Get the application context for a given widget.

Argument Lists

XtMergeArgLists()	Merge two ArgList arrays.
XtNumber()	Determine the number of elements in a fixed-size array.
XtOffset()	Determine the byte offset of a field within a structure pointer type.
XtOffsetOf()	Determine the byte offset of a field within a structure type.
XtSetArg()	Set a resource name and value in an argument list.

Callbacks

XtAddCallback()	Add a callback procedure to a named callback list.
XtAddCallbacks()	Add an array of callback procedures to a named callback list.
XtCallbackProc(2)	Interface definition for callback procedure.

`XtCallCallbackList()`	Execute the procedures in a callback list, specifying the callback list by address.
`XtCallCallbacks()`	Execute the procedures on a widget's named callback list.
`XtHasCallbacks()`	Determine the status of a widget's callback list.
`XtRemoveAllCallbacks()`	Delete all procedures from a callback list.
`XtRemoveCallback()`	Remove a callback from a callback list.
`XtRemoveCallbacks()`	Remove a list of callbacks from a callback list.

Error Handling

`XtAppError()`	Call the low-level error handler.
`XtAppErrorMsg()`	Call the high-level fatal error handler.
`XtAppGetErrorDatabase()`	Obtain the default error database.
`XtAppGetErrorDatabaseText()`	Get the text of a named message from the error database.
`XtAppSetErrorHandler()`	Set the low-level error handler procedure.
`XtAppSetErrorMsgHandler()`	Set the high-level error handler.
`XtAppSetWarningHandler()`	Set the low-level warning handler.
`XtAppSetWarningMsgHandler()`	Set the high-level warning handler.
`XtAppWarning()`	Call the low-level warning handler.
`XtAppWarningMsg()`	Call the high-level warning handler.
`XtError()`	Call the low-level fatal error handler.
`XtErrorHandler(2)`	Interface definition for low-level error and warning handler procedures.
`XtErrorMsg()`	Call the high-level fatal error handler.
`XtErrorMsgHandler(2)`	Interface definition for high-level error and warning handler procedures.
`XtGetErrorDatabase()`	Obtain the error database.
`XtGetErrorDatabaseText()`	Get the text of a named message from the error database.
`XtSetErrorHandler()`	Set the low-level error handler procedure.
`XtSetErrorMsgHandler()`	Set the high-level error handler procedure.
`XtSetWarningHandler()`	Set the low-level warning handler procedure.
`XtSetWarningMsgHandler()`	Set the high-level warning handler procedure.
`XtStringConversionWarning()`	Emit boilerplate string conversion error message.
`XtWarning()`	Call the low-level warning handler.
`XtWarningMsg()`	Call the high-level warning handler.

Event Handling

`XtAddEventHandler()`	Register a procedure to be called when specified events occur on a widget.
`XtAddExposureToRegion()`	Merge `Expose` and `GraphicsExpose` events into a region.
`XtAddInput()`	Register a procedure to be called when there is activity on a file descriptor.
`XtAddRawEventHandler()`	Register an event handler without selecting for the event.
`XtAddTimeOut()`	Register a procedure to be called when a specified time elapses.
`XtAddWorkProc()`	Register a procedure to be called when the event loop is idle.
`XtAppAddInput()`	Register a procedure to be called when there is activity on a file descriptor.
`XtAppAddTimeOut()`	Register a procedure to be called when a specified time elapses.
`XtAppAddWorkProc()`	Register a procedure to be called when the event loop is idle.
`XtAppMainLoop()`	Continuously process events.

`XtAppNextEvent()`	Dispatch timer and alternate input event and return the next X event.
`XtAppPeekEvent()`	Return, but do not remove the event at the head of an application's input queue; block if no events are available.
`XtAppPending()`	Determine whether any events are in an application's input queue.
`XtAppProcessEvent()`	Get and process one input event of a specified type.
`XtBuildEventMask()`	Retrieve a widget's event mask.
`XtDispatchEvent()`	Dispatch an event to registered event handlers.
`XtEventHandler(2)`	Interface definition for event handler procedure.
`XtInputCallbackProc(2)`	Interface definition for procedure to handle file, pipe, or socket activity.
`XtInsertEventHandler()`	Register an event handler procedure that receives events before or after all previously registered event handlers.
`XtInsertRawEventHandler()`	Register an event handler procedure that receives events before or after all previously registered event handlers, without selecting for the events.
`XtLastTimestampProcessed()`	Retrieve the timestamp from the most recent event handled by `XtDispatchEvent()` that contains a timestamp.
`XtMainLoop()`	Continuously process events.
`XtNextEvent()`	Return next event from input queue.
`XtPeekEvent()`	Return, but do not remove the event at the head of an application's input queue.
`XtPending()`	Determine if there are any events in an application's input queue.
`XtProcessEvent()`	Get and process one input event of a specified type.
`XtRemoveEventHandler()`	Remove an event handler, or change the conditions under which it is called.
`XtRemoveInput()`	Unregister an alternate input source callback.
`XtRemoveRawEventHandler()`	Remove a raw event handler, or change the conditions under which it is called.
`XtRemoveTimeOut()`	Unregister a timeout procedure.
`XtRemoveWorkProc()`	Unregister a work procedure.
`XtTimerCallbackProc(2)`	Interface definition for procedure invoked when timeouts expire.
`XtWorkProc(2)`	Interface definition for procedure called when the event loop is idle.

File Searching

`XtFindFile()`	Search for a file using substitutions in a path.
`XtResolvePathname()`	Search for a file using standard substitutions in a path list.
`XtFilePredicate(2)`	Interface definition for a filename evaluation procedure.

Geometry Management

`XtConfigureWidget()`	Move and/or resize widget.
`XtMakeGeometryRequest()`	Request parent to change child's geometry.
`XtMakeResizeRequest()`	Request parent to change child's size.
`XtMoveWidget()`	Move a widget within its parent.
`XtOrderProc(2)`	Interface definition for an `XtNinsertPosition` procedure.
`XtQueryGeometry()`	Query a child widget's preferred geometry.
`XtResizeWidget()`	Resize a child widget.

Function Summaries

`XtUnmanageChild()`	Remove a widget from its parent's managed list.
`XtUnmanageChildren()`	Remove a list of children from a parent widget's managed list.

Graphics Context

`XtAllocateGC`	Obtain a sharable GC with modifiable fields.
`XtDestroyGC()`	Release 2 compatible function to free read-only GCs.
`XtGetGC()`	Obtain a read-only, sharable GC.

Initialization

`XtAppCreateShell()`	Create a shell widget at the root of a widget tree.
`XtAppInitialize()`	Initialize the X Toolkit internals, create an application context, open and initialize a display, and create the initial application shell instance.
`XtCloseDisplay()`	Close a display and remove it from an application context.
`XtCreateApplicationShell()`	Create an additional top-level widget.
`XtDisplayToApplicationContext()`	
	Retrieve the application context associated with a Display.
`XtInitialize()`	Initialize toolkit and display.
`XtInitializeWidgetClass()`	Initialize a widget class without creating any widgets.
`XtVaAppCreateShell()`	Create a top-level widget that is the root of a widget tree, using varargs argument style.
`XtVaAppInitialize()`	Initialize the X Toolkit internals, using varargs argument style.

Keyboard Handling

`XtCallAcceptFocus()`	Offer the input focus to a child widget.
`XtCaseProc(2)`	Interface definition for procedure to convert the case of keysyms.
`XtConvertCase()`	Determine uppercase and lowercase versions of a keysym.
`XtGetKeysymTable()`	Return a pointer to the keycode-to-keysym mapping
`XtGrabKey()`	Passively grab a single key of the keyboard.
`XtGrabKeyboard()`	Actively grab the keyboard.
`XtKeyProc(2)`	Interface definition for keycode-to-keysym translation procedure.
`XtKeysymToKeycodeList()`	Return the list of keycodes that map to a particular keysym in the keyboard mapping table maintained by the Intrinsics.
`XtRegisterCaseConverter()`	Register a case converter.
`XtSetKeyboardFocus()`	Redirect keyboard input to a widget.
`XtSetKeyTranslator()`	Register a key translator.
`XtTranslateKey()`	The default keycode-to-keysym translator.
`XtTranslateKeycode()`	Invoke the currently registered keycode-to-keysym translator.
`XtUngrabKey()`	Cancel a passive key grab.
`XtUngrabKeyboard()`	Release an active keyboard grab.

Memory Allocation

`XtCalloc()`	Allocate memory for an array and initialize its bytes to zero.
`XtFree()`	Free allocated memory.
`XtMalloc()`	Allocate memory.
`XtNew()`	Allocate storage for one instance of a data type.

XtNewString()	Copy an instance of a string.
XtRealloc()	Change the size of an allocated block of storage.
XtReleaseGC()	Deallocate a shared GC when it is no longer needed.

Mouse Handling

XtGetMultiClickTime()	Read the multi-click time.
XtGrabButton()	Passively grab a single pointer button.
XtGrabPointer()	Actively grab the pointer.
XtSetMultiClickTime()	Set the multi-click time.
XtUngrabButton()	Cancel a passive button grab.
XtUngrabPointer()	Release an active pointer grab.

Object Information

XtCheckSubclass()	Verify an object's class, if compiled with DEBUG defined.
XtClass()	Obtain a widget's class.
XtDisplay()	Return the X Display pointer for the specified widget.
XtDisplayOfObject()	Return the display pointer for the nearest ancestor of object that is of class Core.
XtIsApplicationShell()	Test whether a widget is a subclass of the ApplicationShell widget class.
XtIsComposite()	Test whether a widget is a subclass of the Composite widget class.
XtIsConstraint()	Test whether a widget is a subclass of the Constraint widget class.
XtIsManaged()	Determine whether a widget is managed by its parent.
XtIsObject()	Test whether a widget is a subclass of the Object widget class.
XtIsOverrideShell()	Test whether a widget is a subclass of the OverrideShell widget class.
XtIsRealized()	Determine whether a widget has been realized.
XtIsRectObj()	Test whether a widget is a subclass of the RectObj widget class.
XtIsSensitive()	Check the current sensitivity state of a widget.
XtIsShell()	Test whether a widget is a subclass of the Shell widget class.
XtIsSubclass()	Determine whether a widget is a subclass of a class.
XtIsTopLevelShell()	Test whether a widget is a subclass of the TopLevelShell widget class.
XtIsTransientShell()	Test whether a widget is a subclass of the TransientShell widget class.
XtIsVendorShell()	Test whether a widget is a subclass of the VendorShell widget class.
XtIsWidget()	Test whether a widget is a subclass of the Core widget class.
XtIsWMShell()	Test whether a widget is a subclass of the WMShell widget class.
XtName()	Return a pointer to the instance name of the specified object.
XtNameToWidget()	Find a named widget.
XtParent()	Return the parent of the specified widget.
XtScreen()	Return the screen pointer for the specified widget.
XtScreenOfObject()	Return the screen pointer of a non-widget object.
XtSuperclass()	Obtain a widget's superclass.
XtWindow()	Return the window of the specified widget.

`XtWindowOfObject()`	Return the window for the nearest ancestor of object that is of class Core.
`XtWindowToWidget()`	Translate a window and display pointer into a widget ID.

Pop Ups

`XtAddGrab()`	Constrain or redirect user input to a modal widget.
`XtCallbackExclusive()`	Callback function to pop up a widget.
`XtCallbackNone()`	Callback function to pop up a widget.
`XtCallbackNonexclusive()`	Callback function to pop up a widget.
`XtCallbackPopdown()`	Callback function to popdown a widget.
`XtCreatePopupChildProc(2)`	Interface definition for an `XtNcreatePopupChildProc` procedure.
`XtCreatePopupShell()`	Create a popup shell widget.
`XtMenuPopdown`	Built-in action for popping down a widget.
`XtMenuPopup`	Built-in action for popping up a widget.
`XtPopdown()`	Unmap a popup shell.
`XtPopup()`	Map a popup shell.
`XtPopupSpringLoaded()`	Map a spring-loaded popup from within an application.
`XtRemoveGrab()`	Redirect user input from modal widget back to normal destination.
`XtVaCreatePopupShell()`	Create a popup shell, specifying resources with a varargs list.

Properties

`XtSetWMColormapWindows()`	Set WM_COLORMAP_WINDOWS property to inform window manager of custom colormaps.

Resource Management

`XtAddConverter()`	Register an "old-style" resource converter.
`XtAppAddConverter()`	Register an "old-style" resource converter.
`XtAppReleaseCacheRefs()`	Decrement the reference counts for cached resources obtained from `XtCallConverter()`.
`XtAppSetFallbackResources()`	Specify a default set of resource values.
`XtAppSetTypeConverter()`	Register a "new-style" type converter in a single application context.
`XtCallbackReleaseCacheRef()`	Callback function to release a cached resource value.
`XtCallbackReleaseCacheRefList()`	
	Callback function to release a list of cached values.
`XtCallConverter()`	Explicitly invoke a "new-style" resource converter and cache result.
`XtConvert()`	Convert resource type.
`XtConvertAndStore()`	Look up and call a resource converter, copying the resulting value.
`XtConvertArgProc(2)`	Interface definition for procedure to obtain an argument for a resource converter.
`XtConverter(2)`	Interface definition for old-style resource converter.
`XtDatabase()`	Obtain the resource database for a display.
`XtDestructor(2)`	Interface definition for procedure to destroy cached resource data returned by a new-style resource converter.
`XtDirectConvert()`	Explicitly invoke an "old-style" resource converter and cache result.

`XtDisplayStringConversionWarning()`	
	Issue a warning message during conversion of string resource values.
`XtGetApplicationResources()`	Set application variables from the resource database.
`XtGetConstraintResourceList()`	Get the constraint resource list structure for a particular widget class.
`XtGetResourceList()`	Get the resource list of a widget class.
`XtGetSubresources()`	Get subpart values from the resource database.
`XtGetSubvalues()`	Copy resource values from a subpart data structure to an argument list.
`XtGetValues()`	Query widget resource values.
`XtResourceDefaultProc(2)`	Interface definition for procedure called to obtain a resource default value.
`XtScreenDatabase()`	Obtain the resource database for a screen.
`XtSetMappedWhenManaged()`	Set the value of a widget's `XtNmappedWhenManaged` resource and map or unmap the window.
`XtSetSensitive()`	Set the sensitivity state of a widget.
`XtSetSubvalues()`	Copy resource settings from an `ArgList` to a subpart resource structure.
`XtSetTypeConverter()`	Register a "new-style" type converter for all application contexts in a process.
`XtSetValues()`	Set widget resources from an argument list.
`XtTypeConverter(2)`	Interface definition for a new-style resource converter.
`XtVaCreateArgsList()`	Create a varargs list for use with the `XtVaNestedList` symbol.
`XtVaGetApplicationResources()`	Retrieve resources for the overall application using varargs argument style.
`XtVaGetSubresources()`	Fetch resources for widget subparts, using varargs argument style.
`XtVaGetSubvalues()`	Retrieve the current values of subpart resources, using varargs argument style.
`XtVaGetValues()`	Retrieve the current values of widget resources, using varargs argument style.
`XtVaSetSubvalues()`	Set the current values of subpart resources, using varargs argument style.
`XtVaSetValues()`	Set resource values for a widget, using varargs argument style.

Selections

`XtAppGetSelectionTimeout()`	Get the current Intrinsics selection timeout value.
`XtAppSetSelectionTimeout()`	Set the Intrinsics selection timeout value.
`XtCancelConvertSelectionProc(2)`	Interface definition for procedure to cancel incremental selection transfer.
`XtConvertSelectionIncrProc(2)`	Interface definition for a procedure to return selection data incrementally.
`XtConvertSelectionProc(2)`	Interface definition for a procedure to return requested selection data.
`XtDisownSelection()`	Indicate that selection data is no longer available.
`XtGetSelectionRequest()`	Retrieve the `SelectionRequest` event that triggered a `XtConvertSelectionProc`.
`XtGetSelectionTimeout()`	Get the current Intrinsics selection timeout value.
`XtGetSelectionValue()`	Request the value of a selection.

`XtGetSelectionValueIncremental()`	
	Obtain the selection value using incremental transfers.
`XtGetSelectionValues()`	Obtain selection data in multiple formats.
`XtGetSelectionValuesIncremental()`	
	Obtain multiple selection values using incremental transfers.
`XtLoseSelectionIncrProc(2)`	Interface definition for a procedure called when the selection owner loses ownership.
`XtLoseSelectionProc(2)`	Interface definition for procedure to notify the selection owner it has lost selection ownership.
`XtOwnSelection()`	Make selection data available to other clients.
`XtOwnSelectionIncremental()`	Make selection data available to other clients using the incremental transfer interface.
`XtSelectionCallbackProc(2)`	Interface definition for procedure called when requested selection data is ready.
`XtSelectionDoneIncrProc(2)`	Interface definition for procedure called when an incremental selection transfer completes.
`XtSelectionDoneProc(2)`	Interface definition for procedure called after selection transfer is completed.
`XtSetSelectionTimeout()`	Set the Intrinsics selection timeout value.

Translations and Actions

`XtActionHookProc(2)`	Interface definition for action hook procedure.
`XtActionProc(2)`	Interface definition for action procedure.
`XtAddActions()`	Register an action table with the Translation Manager.
`XtAppAddActionHook()`	Register a procedure to be called before any action is invoked.
`XtAppAddActions()`	Register an action table with the Translation Manager.
`XtAugmentTranslations()`	Nondestructively merge new translations with widget's existing ones.
`XtCallActionProc()`	Explicitly invoke a named action procedure.
`XtGetActionKeysym()`	Retrieve the keysym and modifiers that matched the final event specification in the translation table entry.
`XtGetActionList`	Get the action table of a widget class.
`XtInstallAccelerators()`	Install a widget's accelerators on another widget.
`XtInstallAllAccelerators()`	Install all accelerators from a widget and its descendants onto a destination widget.
`XtOverrideTranslations()`	Merge new translations, overriding a widget's existing ones.
`XtParseAcceleratorTable()`	Compile an accelerator table into its internal representation.
`XtParseTranslationTable()`	Compile a translation table into its internal representation.
`XtRegisterGrabAction()`	Register an action procedure as one that needs a passive grab to function properly.
`XtRemoveActionHook()`	Unregister an action hook procedure.
`XtUninstallTranslations()`	Remove all existing translations from a widget.

Widget Lifecycle

`XtCreateManagedWidget()`	Create and manage a child widget.
`XtCreateWidget()`	Create an instance of a widget.
`XtDestroyWidget()`	Destroy a widget instance.
`XtManageChild()`	Bring a widget under its parent's geometry management.
`XtManageChildren()`	Bring an array of widgets under their parent's geometry management.

`XtMapWidget()`	Map a widget to its display.
`XtRealizeWidget()`	Realize a widget instance.
`XtUnmapWidget()`	Unmap a widget explicitly.
`XtUnrealizeWidget()`	Destroy the windows associated with a widget and its descendants.
`XtVaCreateManagedWidget()`	Create and manage a widget, specifying resources with a varargs list.
`XtVaCreateWidget()`	Create a widget, specifying resources with a varargs list.

Widget Method Prototypes

`XtAcceptFocusProc(2)`	Interface definition for the `accept_focus()` method.
`XtAlmostProc(2)`	Interface definition for the `set_values_almost()` method.
`XtArgsFunc(2)`	Interface definition for the `set_values_hook()` method.
`XtArgsProc(2)`	Interface definition for the `initialize_hook()` and
`XtExposeProc(2)`	Interface definition for the Core `expose()` method.
`XtGeometryHandler(2)`	Interface definition for `geometry_manager()`, `query_geometry()`, and `root_geometry_manager()` methods.
`XtInitProc(2)`	Interface definition for the `initialize()` methods.
`XtProc(2)`	Interface definition for the `class_initialize()` method.
`XtRealizeProc(2)`	Interface definition for the `realize()` method.
`XtSetValuesFunc(2)`	Interface definition for the `set_values()` methods.
`XtStringProc(2)`	Interface definition for the `display_accelerator()` method.
`XtWidgetClassProc(2)`	Interface definition for the `class_part_initialize()` method.
`XtWidgetProc(2)`	Interface definition for many common widget methods.

Window Manipulation

`XtCreateWindow()`	Create widget's window.
`XtResizeWindow()`	Resize a widget's window.
`XtTranslateCoords()`	Translate an x-y coordinate pair from widget coordinates to root coordinates.

Alphabetical Listing

`XtAcceptFocusProc(2)`	Interface definition for the `accept_focus()` method.
`XtActionHookProc(2)`	Interface definition for action hook procedure.
`XtActionProc(2)`	Interface definition for action procedure.
`XtAddActions()`	Register an action table with the Translation Manager.
`XtAddCallback()`	Add a callback procedure to a named callback list.
`XtAddCallbacks()`	Add an array of callback procedures to a named callback list.
`XtAddConverter()`	Register an "old-style" resource converter.
`XtAddEventHandler()`	Register a procedure to be called when specified events occur on a widget.
`XtAddExposureToRegion()`	Merge `Expose` and `GraphicsExpose` events into a region.
`XtAddGrab()`	Constrain or redirect user input to a modal widget.

XtAddInput()	Register a procedure to be called when there is activity on a file descriptor.
XtAddRawEventHandler()	Register an event handler without selecting for the event.
XtAddTimeOut()	Register a procedure to be called when a specified time elapses.
XtAddWorkProc()	Register a procedure to be called when the event loop is idle.
XtAllocateGC	Obtain a sharable GC with modifiable fields.
XtAlmostProc(2)	Interface definition for the set_values_almost() method.
XtAppAddActionHook()	Register a procedure to be called before any action is invoked.
XtAppAddActions()	Register an action table with the Translation Manager.
XtAppAddConverter()	Register an "old-style" resource converter.
XtAppAddInput()	Register a procedure to be called when there is activity on a file descriptor.
XtAppAddTimeOut()	Register a procedure to be called when a specified time elapses.
XtAppAddWorkProc()	Register a procedure to be called when the event loop is idle.
XtAppCreateShell()	Create a shell widget at the root of a widget tree.
XtAppError()	Call the low-level error handler.
XtAppErrorMsg()	Call the high-level fatal error handler.
XtAppGetErrorDatabase()	Obtain the default error database.
XtAppGetErrorDatabaseText()	Get the text of a named message from the error database.
XtAppGetSelectionTimeout()	Get the current Intrinsics selection timeout value.
XtAppInitialize()	Initialize the X Toolkit internals, create an application context, open and initialize a display, and create the initial application shell instance.
XtAppMainLoop()	Continuously process events.
XtAppNextEvent()	Dispatch timer and alternate input event and return the next X event.
XtAppPeekEvent()	Return, but do not remove the event at the head of an application's input queue; block if no events are available.
XtAppPending()	Determine whether any events are in an application's input queue.
XtAppProcessEvent()	Get and process one input event of a specified type.
XtAppReleaseCacheRefs()	Decrement the reference counts for cached resources obtained from XtCallConverter().
XtAppSetErrorHandler()	Set the low-level error handler procedure.
XtAppSetErrorMsgHandler()	Set the high-level error handler.
XtAppSetFallbackResources()	Specify a default set of resource values.
XtAppSetSelectionTimeout()	Set the Intrinsics selection timeout value.
XtAppSetTypeConverter()	Register a "new-style" type converter in a single application context.
XtAppSetWarningHandler()	Set the low-level warning handler.
XtAppSetWarningMsgHandler()	Set the high-level warning handler.
XtAppWarning()	Call the low-level warning handler.
XtAppWarningMsg()	Call the high-level warning handler.
XtArgsFunc(2)	Interface definition for the set_values_hook() method.

XtArgsProc(2)	Interface definition for the `initialize_hook()` and
XtAugmentTranslations()	Nondestructively merge new translations with widget's existing ones.
XtBuildEventMask()	Retrieve a widget's event mask.
XtCallAcceptFocus()	Offer the input focus to a child widget.
XtCallActionProc()	Explicitly invoke a named action procedure.
XtCallbackExclusive()	Callback function to pop up a widget.
XtCallbackNone()	Callback function to pop up a widget.
XtCallbackNonexclusive()	Callback function to pop up a widget.
XtCallbackPopdown()	Callback function to popdown a widget.
XtCallbackProc(2)	Interface definition for callback procedure.
XtCallbackReleaseCacheRef()	Callback function to release a cached resource value.
XtCallbackReleaseCacheRefList()	Callback function to release a list of cached values.
XtCallCallbackList()	Execute the procedures in a callback list, specifying the callback list by address.
XtCallCallbacks()	Execute the procedures on a widget's named callback list.
XtCallConverter()	Explicitly invoke a "new-style" resource converter and cache result.
XtCalloc()	Allocate memory for an array and initialize its bytes to zero.
XtCancelConvertSelectionProc(2)	Interface definition for procedure to cancel incremental selection transfer.
XtCaseProc(2)	Interface definition for procedure to convert the case of keysyms.
XtCheckSubclass()	Verify an object's class, if compiled with DEBUG defined.
XtClass()	Obtain a widget's class.
XtCloseDisplay()	Close a display and remove it from an application context.
XtConfigureWidget()	Move and/or resize widget.
XtConvert()	Convert resource type.
XtConvertAndStore()	Look up and call a resource converter, copying the resulting value.
XtConvertArgProc(2)	Interface definition for procedure to obtain an argument for a resource converter.
XtConvertCase()	Determine uppercase and lowercase versions of a keysym.
XtConverter(2)	Interface definition for old-style resource converter.
XtConvertSelectionIncrProc(2)	Interface definition for a procedure to return selection data incrementally.
XtConvertSelectionProc(2)	Interface definition for a procedure to return requested selection data.
XtCreateApplicationContext()	Create an application context.
XtCreateApplicationShell()	Create an additional top-level widget.
XtCreateManagedWidget()	Create and manage a child widget.
XtCreatePopupChildProc(2)	Interface definition for an `XtNcreatePopupChildProc` procedure.
XtCreatePopupShell()	Create a popup shell widget.
XtCreateWidget()	Create an instance of a widget.
XtCreateWindow()	Create widget's window.
XtDatabase()	Obtain the resource database for a display.

`XtDestroyApplicationContext()`	Destroy an application context and close its displays.
`XtDestroyGC()`	Release 2 compatible function to free read-only GCs.
`XtDestroyWidget()`	Destroy a widget instance.
`XtDestructor(2)`	Interface definition for procedure to destroy cached resource data returned by a new-style resource converter.
`XtDirectConvert()`	Explicitly invoke an "old-style" resource converter and cache result.
`XtDisownSelection()`	Indicate that selection data is no longer available.
`XtDispatchEvent()`	Dispatch an event to registered event handlers.
`XtDisplay()`	Return the X Display pointer for the specified widget.
`XtDisplayInitialize()`	Initialize a display and add it to an application context.
`XtDisplayOfObject()`	Return the display pointer for the nearest ancestor of object that is of class Core.
`XtDisplayStringConversionWarning()`	
	Issue a warning message during conversion of string resource values.
`XtDisplayToApplicationContext()`	
	Retrieve the application context associated with a Display.
`XtError()`	Call the low-level fatal error handler.
`XtErrorHandler(2)`	Interface definition for low-level error and warning handler procedures.
`XtErrorMsg()`	Call the high-level fatal error handler.
`XtErrorMsgHandler(2)`	Interface definition for high-level error and warning handler procedures.
`XtEventHandler(2)`	Interface definition for event handler procedure.
`XtExposeProc(2)`	Interface definition for the Core `expose()` method.
`XtFilePredicate(2)`	Interface definition for a filename evaluation procedure.
`XtFindFile()`	Search for a file using substitutions in a path.
`XtFree()`	Free allocated memory.
`XtGeometryHandler(2)`	Interface definition for `geometry_manager()`, `query_geometry()`, and `root_geometry_manager()` methods.
`XtGetActionKeysym()`	Retrieve the keysym and modifiers that matched the final event specification in the translation table entry.
`XtGetActionList`	Get the action table of a widget class.
`XtGetApplicationNameAndClass()`	Return the application name and class as passed to `XtDisplayInitialize()` for a particular Display.
`XtGetApplicationResources()`	Set application variables from the resource database.
`XtGetConstraintResourceList()`	Get the constraint resource list structure for a particular widget class.
`XtGetErrorDatabase()`	Obtain the error database.
`XtGetErrorDatabaseText()`	Get the text of a named message from the error database.
`XtGetGC()`	Obtain a read-only, sharable GC.
`XtGetKeysymTable()`	Return a pointer to the keycode-to-keysym mapping
`XtGetMultiClickTime()`	Read the multi-click time.
`XtGetResourceList()`	Get the resource list of a widget class.
`XtGetSelectionRequest()`	Retrieve the `SelectionRequest` event that triggered a `XtConvertSelectionProc`.

XtGetSelectionTimeout()	Get the current Intrinsics selection timeout value.
XtGetSelectionValue()	Request the value of a selection.
XtGetSelectionValueIncremental()	
	Obtain the selection value using incremental transfers.
XtGetSelectionValues()	Obtain selection data in multiple formats.
XtGetSelectionValuesIncremental()	
	Obtain multiple selection values using incremental transfers.
XtGetSubresources()	Get subpart values from the resource database.
XtGetSubvalues()	Copy resource values from a subpart data structure to an argument list.
XtGetValues()	Query widget resource values.
XtGrabButton()	Passively grab a single pointer button.
XtGrabKey()	Passively grab a single key of the keyboard.
XtGrabKeyboard()	Actively grab the keyboard.
XtGrabPointer()	Actively grab the pointer.
XtHasCallbacks()	Determine the status of a widget's callback list.
XtInitialize()	Initialize toolkit and display.
XtInitializeWidgetClass()	Initialize a widget class without creating any widgets.
XtInitProc(2)	Interface definition for the initialize() methods.
XtInputCallbackProc(2)	Interface definition for procedure to handle file, pipe, or socket activity.
XtInsertEventHandler()	Register an event handler procedure that receives events before or after all previously registered event handlers.
XtInsertRawEventHandler()	Register an event handler procedure that receives events before or after all previously registered event handlers, without selecting for the events.
XtInstallAccelerators()	Install a widget's accelerators on another widget.
XtInstallAllAccelerators()	Install all accelerators from a widget and its descendants onto a destination widget.
XtIsApplicationShell()	Test whether a widget is a subclass of the ApplicationShell widget class.
XtIsComposite()	Test whether a widget is a subclass of the Composite widget class.
XtIsConstraint()	Test whether a widget is a subclass of the Constraint widget class.
XtIsManaged()	Determine whether a widget is managed by its parent.
XtIsObject()	Test whether a widget is a subclass of the Object widget class.
XtIsOverrideShell()	Test whether a widget is a subclass of the OverrideShell widget class.
XtIsRealized()	Determine whether a widget has been realized.
XtIsRectObj()	Test whether a widget is a subclass of the RectObj widget class.
XtIsSensitive()	Check the current sensitivity state of a widget.
XtIsShell()	Test whether a widget is a subclass of the Shell widget class.
XtIsSubclass()	Determine whether a widget is a subclass of a class.
XtIsTopLevelShell()	Test whether a widget is a subclass of the TopLevelShell widget class.

Function
Summaries

`XtIsTransientShell()`	Test whether a widget is a subclass of the TransientShell widget class.
`XtIsVendorShell()`	Test whether a widget is a subclass of the VendorShell widget class.
`XtIsWidget()`	Test whether a widget is a subclass of the Core widget class.
`XtIsWMShell()`	Test whether a widget is a subclass of the WMShell widget class.
`XtKeyProc(2)`	Interface definition for keycode to keysym translation procedure.
`XtKeysymToKeycodeList()`	Return the list of keycodes that map to a particular keysym in the keyboard mapping table maintained by the Intrinsics.
`XtLastTimestampProcessed()`	Retrieve the timestamp from the most recent event handled by `XtDispatchEvent()` that contains a timestamp.
`XtLoseSelectionIncrProc(2)`	Interface definition for a procedure called when the selection owner loses ownership.
`XtLoseSelectionProc(2)`	Interface definition for procedure to notify the selection owner it has lost selection ownership.
`XtMainLoop()`	Continuously process events.
`XtMakeGeometryRequest()`	Request parent to change child's geometry.
`XtMakeResizeRequest()`	Request parent to change child's size.
`XtMalloc()`	Allocate memory.
`XtManageChild()`	Bring a widget under its parent's geometry management.
`XtManageChildren()`	Bring an array of widgets under their parent's geometry management.
`XtMapWidget()`	Map a widget to its display.
`XtMenuPopdown`	Built-in action for popping down a widget.
`XtMenuPopup`	Built-in action for popping up a widget.
`XtMergeArgLists()`	Merge two `ArgList` arrays.
`XtMoveWidget()`	Move a widget within its parent.
`XtName()`	Return a pointer to the instance name of the specified object.
`XtNameToWidget()`	Find a named widget.
`XtNew()`	Allocate storage for one instance of a data type.
`XtNewString()`	Copy an instance of a string.
`XtNextEvent()`	Return next event from input queue.
`XtNumber()`	Determine the number of elements in a fixed-size array.
`XtOffset()`	Determine the byte offset of a field within a structure pointer type.
`XtOffsetOf()`	Determine the byte offset of a field within a structure type.
`XtOpenDisplay()`	Open, initialize, and add a display to an application context.
`XtOrderProc(2)`	Interface definition for an `XtNinsertPosition` procedure.
`XtOverrideTranslations()`	Merge new translations, overriding a widget's existing ones.
`XtOwnSelection()`	Make selection data available to other clients.
`XtOwnSelectionIncremental()`	Make selection data available to other clients using the incremental transfer interface.
`XtParent()`	Return the parent of the specified widget.
`XtParseAcceleratorTable()`	Compile an accelerator table into its internal representation.
`XtParseTranslationTable()`	Compile a translation table into its internal representation.

`XtPeekEvent()`	Return, but do not remove the event at the head of an application's input queue.
`XtPending()`	Determine if there are any events in an application's input queue.
`XtPopdown()`	Unmap a popup shell.
`XtPopup()`	Map a popup shell.
`XtPopupSpringLoaded()`	Map a spring-loaded popup from within an application.
`XtProc(2)`	Interface definition for the `class_initialize()` method.
`XtProcessEvent()`	Get and process one input event of a specified type.
`XtQueryGeometry()`	Query a child widget's preferred geometry.
`XtRealizeProc(2)`	Interface definition for the `realize()` method.
`XtRealizeWidget()`	Realize a widget instance.
`XtRealloc()`	Change the size of an allocated block of storage.
`XtRegisterCaseConverter()`	Register a case converter.
`XtRegisterGrabAction()`	Register an action procedure as one that needs a passive grab to function properly.
`XtReleaseGC()`	Deallocate a shared GC when it is no longer needed.
`XtRemoveActionHook()`	Unregister an action hook procedure.
`XtRemoveAllCallbacks()`	Delete all procedures from a callback list.
`XtRemoveCallback()`	Remove a callback from a callback list.
`XtRemoveCallbacks()`	Remove a list of callbacks from a callback list.
`XtRemoveEventHandler()`	Remove an event handler, or change the conditions under which it is called.
`XtRemoveGrab()`	Redirect user input from modal widget back to normal destination.
`XtRemoveInput()`	Unregister an alternate input source callback.
`XtRemoveRawEventHandler()`	Remove a raw event handler, or change the conditions under which it is called.
`XtRemoveTimeOut()`	Unregister a timeout procedure.
`XtRemoveWorkProc()`	Unregister a work procedure.
`XtResizeWidget()`	Resize a child widget.
`XtResizeWindow()`	Resize a widget's window.
`XtResolvePathname()`	Search for a file using standard substitutions in a path list.
`XtResourceDefaultProc(2)`	Interface definition for procedure called to obtain a resource default value.
`XtScreen()`	Return the screen pointer for the specified widget.
`XtScreenDatabase()`	Obtain the resource database for a screen.
`XtScreenOfObject()`	Return the screen pointer of a non-widget object.
`XtSelectionCallbackProc(2)`	Interface definition for procedure called when requested selection data is ready.
`XtSelectionDoneIncrProc(2)`	Interface definition for procedure called when an incremental selection transfer completes.
`XtSelectionDoneProc(2)`	Interface definition for procedure called after selection transfer is completed.
`XtSetArg()`	Set a resource name and value in an argument list.
`XtSetErrorHandler()`	Set the low-level error handler procedure.
`XtSetErrorMsgHandler()`	Set the high-level error handler procedure.
`XtSetKeyboardFocus()`	Redirect keyboard input to a widget.

`XtSetKeyTranslator()`	Register a key translator.
`XtSetMappedWhenManaged()`	Set the value of a widget's `XtNmappedWhenManaged` resource and map or unmap the window.
`XtSetMultiClickTime()`	Set the multi-click time.
`XtSetSelectionTimeout()`	Set the Intrinsics selection timeout value.
`XtSetSensitive()`	Set the sensitivity state of a widget.
`XtSetSubvalues()`	Copy resource settings from an `ArgList` to a subpart resource structure.
`XtSetTypeConverter()`	Register a "new-style" type converter for all application contexts in a process.
`XtSetValues()`	Set widget resources from an argument list.
`XtSetValuesFunc(2)`	Interface definition for the `set_values()` methods.
`XtSetWarningHandler()`	Set the low-level warning handler procedure.
`XtSetWarningMsgHandler()`	Set the high-level warning handler procedure.
`XtSetWMColormapWindows()`	Set WM_COLORMAP_WINDOWS property to inform window manager of custom colormaps.
`XtStringConversionWarning()`	Emit boilerplate string conversion error message.
`XtStringProc(2)`	Interface definition for the `display_accelerator()` method.
`XtSuperclass()`	Obtain a widget's superclass.
`XtTimerCallbackProc(2)`	Interface definition for procedure invoked when timeouts expire.
`XtToolkitInitialize()`	Initialize the X Toolkit internals.
`XtTranslateCoords()`	Translate an x-y coordinate pair from widget coordinates to root coordinates.
`XtTranslateKey()`	The default keycode-to-keysym translator.
`XtTranslateKeycode()`	Invoke the currently registered keycode-to-keysym translator.
`XtTypeConverter(2)`	Interface definition for a new-style resource converter.
`XtUngrabButton()`	Cancel a passive button grab.
`XtUngrabKey()`	Cancel a passive key grab.
`XtUngrabKeyboard()`	Release an active keyboard grab.
`XtUngrabPointer()`	Release an active pointer grab.
`XtUninstallTranslations()`	Remove all existing translations from a widget.
`XtUnmanageChild()`	Remove a widget from its parent's managed list.
`XtUnmanageChildren()`	Remove a list of children from a parent widget's managed list.
`XtUnmapWidget()`	Unmap a widget explicitly.
`XtUnrealizeWidget()`	Destroy the windows associated with a widget and its descendants.
`XtVaAppCreateShell()`	Create a top-level widget that is the root of a widget tree, using varargs argument style.
`XtVaAppInitialize()`	Initialize the X Toolkit internals, using varargs argument style.
`XtVaCreateArgsList()`	Create a varargs list for use with the `XtVaNestedList` symbol.
`XtVaCreateManagedWidget()`	Create and manage a widget, specifying resources with a varargs list.
`XtVaCreatePopupShell()`	Create a popup shell, specifying resources with a varargs list.

`XtVaCreateWidget()`	Create a widget, specifying resources with a varargs list.
`XtVaGetApplicationResources()`	Retrieve resources for the overall application using varargs argument style.
`XtVaGetSubresources()`	Fetch resources for widget subparts, using varargs argument style.
`XtVaGetSubvalues()`	Retrieve the current values of subpart resources, using varargs argument style.
`XtVaGetValues()`	Retrieve the current values of widget resources, using varargs argument style.
`XtVaSetSubvalues()`	Set the current values of subpart resources, using varargs argument style.
`XtVaSetValues()`	Set resource values for a widget, using varargs argument style.
`XtWarning()`	Call the low-level warning handler.
`XtWarningMsg()`	Call the high-level warning handler.
`XtWidgetClassProc(2)`	Interface definition for the `class_part_initialize()` method.
`XtWidgetProc(2)`	Interface definition for many common widget methods.
`XtWidgetToApplicationContext()`	Get the application context for a given widget.
`XtWindow()`	Return the window of the specified widget.
`XtWindowOfObject()`	Return the window for the nearest ancestor of object that is of class Core.
`XtWindowToWidget()`	Translate a window and display pointer into a widget ID.
`XtWorkProc(2)`	Interface definition for procedure called when the event loop is idle.

X Toolkit Data Types

This appendix summarizes the data types used as arguments or return values in Xt Intrinsics functions. Unless otherwise noted, these types are defined in the header file *X11/Intrinsic.h*. Data types (which include simple typedefs as well as structures and enums) are listed alphabetically. Defined symbols (for example, constants used to specify the value of a mask or a field in a structure) or other data types used only to set structure members are listed with the data type in which they are used.

Arg

See `ArgList`.

ArgList

An `ArgList` is used for setting resources in calls to create a widget (`XtCreate-Widget()`, `XtCreateManagedWidget()`, `XtCreatePopupShell()`) as well as in calls to set or get resources (`XtSetValues()`, `XtGetValues()`, `XtSet-Subvalues()`, `XtGetSubvalues()`, `XtSetSubresources()`, `XtGet-Subresources()`). It is defined as follows in *<X11/Intrinsic.h>*:

```
typedef struct {
    String      name;
    XtArgVal    value;
} Arg, *ArgList;
```

The name field is typically a defined constant of the form `XtNresourcename` from either *<X11/Stringdefs.h>* or a widget public header file. It identifies the name of the argument to be set. The `value` field is an `XtArgVal`, a system-dependent typedef chosen to be large enough to hold a pointer to a function. It is often not large enough to hold a `float` or `double`.

Atom

To optimize communication with the server, a property is referenced by string name only once, and subsequently by a unique integer ID called an Atom. Predefined atoms are defined in *<X11/Xatom.h>* using defined symbols beginning with XA_; other atoms can be obtained from the server by calling the Xlib function `XInternAtom()`. The Xmu library supports an atom-caching mechanism to reduce the number of `XIntern-Atom()` calls that may be required. For more information, see *Interclient Communication*, in Volume Four, *X Toolkit Intrinsics Programming Manual*.

Boolean

A typedef from *<X11/Intrinsic.h>* used to indicate `True` (1) or `False` (0). Use either the symbols `TRUE` or `FALSE`, defined in *<X11/Intrinsic.h>* or `True` or `False`, defined in *<X11/Xlib.h>*.

Cardinal

A typedef from *<X11/Intrinsic.h>* used to specify any unsigned integer value.

Cursor

An `XID` (server resource ID) that identifies a cursor resource maintained by the server. A `Cursor` can be returned from any of the Xlib calls `XCreateFontCursor()` (which creates a cursor from the set of standard cursors contained in the cursor font), `XCreateGlyphCursor()` (which creates a cursor from any other font glyph), or `XCreatePixmapCursor()` (which creates a cursor from a bitmap image). In Xt, the only occasion when you specify a `Cursor` is in a call to `XtGrabButton()` or `Xt-GrabPointer()`, as the cursor to be displayed during a grab. The cursor resource must already be allocated by an Xlib call.

Dimension

A typedef from *<X11/Intrinsic.h>* used to specify window sizes. The `Dimension` data type was introduced in R3 to increase portability. R2 applications that specified dimensions as `int` should use `Dimension` instead.

Display

A structure defined in *<X11/Xlib.h>* that contains information about the display the program is running on. `Display` structure fields should not be accessed directly; Xlib provides a number of macros to return essential values. In Xt, a pointer to the current `Display` is returned by a call to `XtDisplay()`. `XtOpenDisplay()` can be used to explicitly open more than one `Display`.

EventMask

A typedef from *<X11/Intrinsic.h>* used to specify which events are selected by an event handler. Specify the value as the bitwise OR of any of the following symbols defined in *<X11/X.h>*:

Event Mask Symbol	Circumstances
`NoEventMask`	No events.
`KeyPressMask`	Keyboard down events.
`KeyReleaseMask`	Keyboard up events.
`ButtonPressMask`	Pointer button down events.
`ButtonReleaseMask`	Pointer button up events.
`EnterWindowMask`	Pointer window entry events.
`LeaveWindowMask`	Pointer window leave events.
`PointerMotionMask`	All pointer motion events.
`PointerMotionHintMask`	Fewer pointer motion events.
`Button1MotionMask`	Pointer motion while button 1 down.
`Button2MotionMask`	Pointer motion while button 2 down.
`Button3MotionMask`	Pointer motion while button 3 down.
`Button4MotionMask`	Pointer motion while button 4 down.
`Button5MotionMask`	Pointer motion while button 5 down.

Event Mask Symbol	Circumstances
ButtonMotionMask	Pointer motion while any button down.
KeymapStateMask	Any keyboard state change on EnterNotify, LeaveNotify, FocusIn, or FocusOut
ExposureMask	Any exposure (except GraphicsExpose and NoExpose).
VisibilityChangeMask	Any change in visibility.
StructureNotifyMask	Any change in window configuration.
ResizeRedirectMask	Redirect resize of this window.
SubstructureNotifyMask	Notify about reconfiguration of children.
SubstructureRedirectMask	Redirect reconfiguration of children.
FocusChangeMask	Any change in keyboard focus.
PropertyChangeMask	Any change in property.
ColormapChangeMask	Any change in colormap.
OwnerGrabButtonMask	Modifies handling of pointer events.

plus the following symbol defined in *<X11/Intrinsic.h>*:

XtAllEvents   All of the above masks: ((EventMask) -1L)

See Appendix C, *Event Reference*, for more information on each of the events selected by these mask values. The XtBuildEventMask() function returns the event mask representing the logical OR of all event masks registered on the widget with XtAddEventHandler(), as well as event masks registered as a result of translations and accelerators installed on the widget.

GC

A Graphics Context. A GC is a pointer to a structure that contains a copy of the settings in a server resource. The server resource, in turn, contains information about how to interpret a graphics primitive. A pointer to a structure of this type is returned by the Xlib call XCreateGC() or the Xt call XtGetGC(). (The latter call does client-side caching of GCs to reduce the number of identical GCs that are created.) GCs are used by all Xlib drawing calls. The members of this structure should not be accessed directly. Values can be changed by passing an XGCValues structure to XtGetGC() or the Xlib XCreateGC() or XChangeGC(). Values can be read with XGetGCValues().

Opaque

As its name implies, a typedef designed for portability, whose contents are not to be used.

Position

A typedef from *<X11/Intrinsic.h>* used to specify x and y coordinates. The Position data type was introduced in R3 to increase portability. R2 applications that specified coordinates as int should use Position instead.

Region

An arbitrary set of pixels on the screen, actually implemented as a linked list of rectangles. Usually, a region is either a rectangular area, several overlapping or adjacent rectangular areas, or a general polygon. A Region is actually a typedef from *<X11/Xutil.h>* pointing to an internal data structure called an _XRegion. There are a number of Xlib functions for creating and manipulating regions; the members of the structure should not be accessed directly. For more information, see Volume Two, *Xlib Reference Manual*. In Xt, the only use is in the call XtAddExposureToRegion().

Screen

A structure that describes the characteristics of a screen (one or more of which make up a display). A pointer to a list of these structures is a member of the Display structure. A pointer to a structure of this type is returned by XtScreen() and XGetWindow-Attributes(). Xlib Macros are provided to access most members of this structure.

```
typedef struct {
    XExtData *ext_data;        /* hook for extension to hang data */
    struct _XDisplay *display;/* back pointer to display structure */
    Window root;               /* root window ID */
    int width, height;         /* width and height of screen */
    int mwidth, mheight;       /* width and height of  in millimeters */
    int ndepths;               /* number of depths possible */
    Depth *depths;             /* list of allowable depths on the screen */
    int root_depth;            /* bits per pixel */
    Visual *root_visual;       /* root visual */
    GC default_gc;             /* GC for the root root visual */
    Colormap cmap;             /* default colormap */
    unsigned long white_pixel;
    unsigned long black_pixel;/* white and black pixel values */
    int max_maps, min_maps;    /* max and min colormaps */
    int backing_store;         /* Never, WhenMapped, Always */
    Bool save_unders;
    long root_input_mask;      /* initial root input mask */
} Screen;
```

The XtScreen() macro can be used in Xt to return the current screen.

String

A typedef for char *.

Substitution

A structure used in XtFindFile() and XtResolvePathname() to specify substitution characters. In the *path* argument to XtFindFile(), each character prefixed by a percent sign (%) is compared to the match member of a Substitution, and if found, is replaced with the string in the substitution member of the same structure. This allows for operating-system-independent filename searches, where substitutions can identify possible pathname separators.

It is defined as follows:

```
typedef struct {
    char match;                /* character to match */
    String substitution;       /* string to substitute */
} SubstitutionRec, *Substitution;
```

SubstitutionRec

See Substitution.

Time

An unsigned long value containing a time value in milliseconds. The constant CurrentTime is interpreted as the time in milliseconds since the server was started.

The `Time` data type is used in event structures and as an argument to `XtAppAddTimeOut()`.

Visual

A structure that defines a way of using color resources on a particular screen.

Widget

A structure returned by calls to create a widget, such as `XtAppInitialize()`, `XtCreateWidget()`, `XtCreateManagedWidget()`, and `XtCreatePopupShell()`. The members of this structure should not be accessed directly from applications; they should regard it as an opaque pointer. Type `Widget` is actually a pointer to a widget instance structure. Widget code accesses instance variables from this structure.

WidgetClass

A pointer to the widget class structure, used to identify the widget class in various Xt calls that create widgets or that return information about widgets. Widget class names have the form *nameWidgetClass*, with the exception of the widget-precursor classes, `Object` and `RectObj`, which have the class pointers `objectClass` and `rectObjClass`, respectively.

WidgetList

A pointer to a list of `Widgets`, used in calls to `XtManageChildren()` and `XtUnManageChildren()`.

Window

A resource maintained by the server, and known on the client side only by an integer ID. In Xt, a widget's window can be returned by the `XtWindow()` macro. Given the window, the corresponding widget can be returned by `XtWindowToWidget()`.

XEvent

A union of all thirty event structures. The first member is always the type, so it is possible to branch on the type, and do event-specific processing in each branch. For more information on the individual event structures, see Appendix C, *Event Reference*.

XGCValues

A structure defined in *<X11/Xlib.h>* that is used to set the values in a Graphics Context using the `XtGetGC()` function, or the Xlib functions `XCreateGC()`, `XChangeGC()`, or `XGetGCValues()`.

```
typedef struct {
    int function;                /* logical operation */
    unsigned long plane_mask;    /* plane mask */
    unsigned long foreground;    /* foreground pixel */
    unsigned long background;    /* background pixel */
    int line_width;              /* line width */
    int line_style;     /* LineSolid, LineOnOffDash,
                           LineDoubleDash */
    int cap_style;      /* CapNotLast, CapButt,
                           CapRound, CapProjecting */
    int join_style;     /* JoinMiter, JoinRound, JoinBevel */
    int fill_style;     /* FillSolid, FillTiled,
                           FillStippled, FillOpaqueStippled */
    int fill_rule;      /* EvenOddRule, WindingRule */
    int arc_mode;       /* ArcChord, ArcPieSlice */
```

```
    Pixmap tile;          /* pixmap for tiling operations */
    Pixmap stipple;       /* 1 plane pixmap for stippling */
    int ts_x_origin;      /* offset for tile or stipple operations */
    int ts_y_origin;
    Font font;            /* default text font for text operations */
    int subwindow_mode;       /* ClipByChildren, IncludeInferiors */
    Bool graphics_exposures; /* should exposures be generated? */
    int clip_x_origin;        /* origin for clipping */
    int clip_y_origin;
    Pixmap clip_mask;         /* bitmap clipping; other calls
                                 for rects */
    int dash_offset;          /* patterned/dashed line information */
    char dashes;
} XGCValues;
```

For more information on the meaning and use of each of the members, see Chapter 5, *The Graphics Context*, in Volume One, *Xlib Programming Manual*. The second argument of XtGetGC() is a mask that specifies which members of the structure are being set. See XtGCMask below for details.

XrmDatabase

A pointer to an internal resource manager datatype. Members of this structure should not be accessed directly. An XrmDatabase can be returned by the Xt calls Xt-Database() (a resource database) or XtGetErrorDatabase() (an error message database).

XrmOptionDescList

A structure used to define command line options, passed to XtAppInitialize(), XtDisplayInitialize(), or XtOpenDisplay(). The structure is defined as follows in *<X11/Xresource.h>*:

```
typedef struct {
    char           *option;   /* Option abbreviation in argv */
    char           *specifier;/* Resource specifier */
    XrmOptionKind argKind;    /* Which style of option it is */
    caddr_t        value;     /* Val to provide if XrmoptionNoArg */
} XrmOptionDescRec, *XrmOptionDescList;
```

The value for the argKind element is specified by one of the following enumerated values, defined in the same file:

```
typedef enum {
    XrmoptionNoArg,      /* Value specified in OptionDescRec.value */
    XrmoptionIsArg,      /* Value is the option string itself */
    XrmoptionStickyArg,  /* Value immediately follows option */
    XrmoptionSepArg,     /* Value is next argument in argv */
    XrmoptionResArg,     /* Resource and value in next arg in argv */
    XrmoptionSkipArg,    /* Ignore this opt and next arg in argv */
    XrmoptionSkipNArgs   /* Ignore this option and the next
                            OptionDescRec.value arguments in argv */
    XrmoptionSkipLine    /* Ignore this opt and rest of argv */
} XrmOptionKind;
```

XrmOptionDescRec

See XrmOptionDescList.

XrmOptionKind

See XrmOptionDescList.

XrmValue

A structure defined in *<X11/Xresource.h>*, used in XtConvert() and other resource conversion routines.

```
typedef struct {
    unsigned int    size;
    caddr_t         addr;
} XrmValue, *XrmValuePtr;
```

XrmValuePtr

See XrmValue.

XtAccelerators

A pointer to an opaque internal type, a compiled accelerator table. A pointer to an Xt-Accelerators structure is returned by a call to XtParseAccelerator-Table(). Usually, the compiled accelerator table is produced automatically by resource conversion of a string accelerator table stored in a resource file.

XtActionHookId

An opaque identifier returned by a call to XtAppAddActionHook(), and used thereafter to refer to a particular action hook procedure.

XtActionHookProc

The typedef for an action hook procedure. See XtActionHookProc(2) for details.

XtActionList

A typedef for _XtActionsRec, defined as follows in *<X11/Intrinsic.h>*:

```
typedef struct _XtActionsRec *XtActionList;
```

```
typedef struct _XtActionsRec{
    String      string;
    XtActionProc proc;
} XtActionsRec;
```

Actions are added by calls to XtAddActions() or XtAppAddActions(). By convention, the string and the function name are identical, except that the function name begins with an uppercase letter, as in the example:

```
static XtActionsRec two_quits[] = {
    {"confirm", Confirm},
    {"quit", Quit},
};
```

This mapping from strings to function pointers is necessary to allow translation tables to be specified in resource files, which are made up entirely of strings.

XtActionProc

The typedef for an action procedure. See XtActionProc(2) for details.

XtActionsRec

See XtActionList.

XtAddressMode

An enumerated type that specifies the possible values for the address_mode field of an XtConvertArgRec. See XtConvertArgList below for details.

XtAppContext

A pointer to an internal structure used to hold data specific to a particular application context. An XtAppContext can be returned by a call to XtCreate-ApplicationContext() or XtAppInitialize(). The application context being used by a widget can be returned by XtWidgetToApplicationContext(). The Xt routines that use a default application context are now superseded; almost all routines for handling explicit application contexts have names containing the string *App*.

XtArgVal

See ArgList.

XtCacheRef

An opaque converter cache identifier returned in the *cache_ref_return* argument of XtCallConverter(). The identifier reference count is decremented whenever the cached resource is released by a client.

XtCacheType

Identifies the type and amount of type converter caching to be used; specified in calls to XtAppSetTypeConverter() and XtSetTypeConverter(). Possible values are given by the following symbols:

```
#define XtCacheNone      0x001 /* never cache; always call converter */
#define XtCacheAll       0x002 /* reuse results of previous conversions
                                  if they match */
#define XtCacheByDisplay 0x003 /* reuse results, but remove value
                                  from cache if display is closed */
#define XtCacheRefCount  0x100 /* OR with above values to keep a
                                  count of times a conversion is used.
                                  When count falls to zero, remove
                                  conversion from cache */
```

XtCallbackList

A structure defined as follows in *<X11/Intrinsic.h>*:

```
    XtCallbackProc  callback;
    XtPointer       closure;
} XtCallbackRec, *XtCallbackList;
```

An XtCallbackList is statically defined just after the callback function itself is declared or defined. Then the callback list is used to set a callback resource with any of the calls that set resources, including XtCreateWidget(). In most documentation, the closure member is referred to as *client_data*. In application code, when Xt-AddCallback() and XtRemoveCallback() are used, an XtCallbackList is not required.

XtCallbackProc

The typedef for callback functions. See XtCallbackProc(2) for details.

XtCallbackRec

See XtCallbackList.

XtCallbackStatus

An enumerated type that defines the return values from `XtHasCallbacks()`:

```
typedef enum {
    XtCallbackNoList,   /* Callback resource doesn't exist */
    XtCallbackHasNone,  /* Resource exists, but no callbacks on it */
    XtCallbackHasSome   /* Resource exists, and callbacks
                           are registered for it */
} XtCallbackStatus;
```

XtCancelConvertSelectionProc

The typedef for a cancel selection conversion procedure registered by a call to `XtOwn-SelectionIncremental()`. See `XtCancelConvertSelectionProc(2)` for details.

XtCaseProc

The typedef for the case conversion procedure registered by a call to `XtRegister-CaseConverter()`. See `XtCaseProc(2)` for details.

XtConvertArgList

A structure used in calls to `XtAddConverter()`, `XtSetTypeConverter()`, and `XtAppSetTypeConverter()` to specify how the converter will get the arguments necessary to perform the conversion. The structure is defined as follows in *<X11/Intrinsic.h>*:

```
typedef struct {
    XtAddressMode   address_mode;
    XtPointer       address_id;
    Cardinal        size;
} XtConvertArgRec, *XtConvertArgList;
```

The enumerated type `XtAddressMode` specifies the possible values for the `address_mode` field, which controls how the `address_id` field should be interpreted.

```
typedef enum {
    XtAddress,              /* address */
    XtBaseOffset,           /* offset */
    XtImmediate,            /* constant */
    XtResourceString,       /* resource name string */
    XtResourceQuark         /* resource name quark */
    XtWidgetBaseOffset,     /* offset from ancestor */
    XtProcedureArg          /* procedure to call */
} XtAddressMode;
```

By specifying the address mode as `XtBaseOffset` or `XtWidgetBaseOffset` you can use `XtOffset()` or `XtOffsetOf()` to find the appropriate widget resource, much as you do in a resource list.

XtConvertArgRec

See `XtConvertArgList`.

XtConverter

The typedef for old-style resource converters. See `XtConverter(2)` for details.

XtConvertSelectionIncrProc

The typedef for the incremental selection conversion procedure. See `XtConvert-SelectionIncrProc(2)` for details.

XtConvertSelectionProc

The typedef for the selection conversion procedure registered by a call to `XtOwn-Selection()`. See `XtConvertSelectionProc(2)` for details.

XtDestructor

The typedef for a resource-cache-freeing procedure registered by a call to `XtAppSet-TypeConverter()` or `XtSetTypeConverter()`. See `XtDestructor(2)` for details.

XtEnum

A datum large enough to encode at least 128 distinct values, two of which are the symbolic values `True` and `False`.

XtErrorHandler

The typedef for low-level error or warning handlers. See `XtErrorHandler(2)` for details.

XtErrorMsgHandler

The typedef for high-level error or warning message handlers. See `XtErrorMsg-Handler(2)` for details.

XtEventHandler

The typedef for event handlers. See `XtEventHandler(2)` for details.

XtFilePredicate

The prototype for a filename evaluation procedure registered by the call to `XtFind-File()` or `XtResolvePathname()`. See `XtFilePredicate(2)` for details.

XtGCMask

A mask used in calls to `XtGetGC()` that indicates which fields in the `XGCValues` structure are to be used. The mask consists of a bitwise OR of the following symbols:

Member	Mask	Default
function	GCFunction	GXcopy
plane_mask	GCPlaneMask	All 1's.
foreground	GCForeground	0
background	GCBackground	1
line_width	GCLineWidth	0
line_style	GCLineStyle	LineSolid
cap_style	GCCapStyle	CapButt
join_style	GCJoinStyle	JoinMiter
fill_style	GCFillStyle	FillSolid
fill_rule	GCFillRule	EvenOddRule
tile	GCTile	Pixmap filled with foreground pixel.

Member	Mask	Default
stipple	GCStipple	Pixmap filled with 1's.
ts_x_origin	GCTileStipXOrigin	0
ts_y_origin	GCTileStipYOrigin	0
font	GCFont	(Implementation dependent)
subwindow_mode	GCSubwindowMode	ClipByChildren
graphics_exposures	GCGraphicsExposures	TRUE
clip_x_origin	GCClipXOrigin	0
clip_y_origin	GCClipYOrigin	0
clip_mask	GCClipMask	None
dash_offset	GCDashOffset	0
dashes	GCDashList	4 (i.e., the list [4, 4])
arc_mode	GCArcMode	ArcPieSlice

XtGeometryMask

See `XtWidgetGeometry`.

XtGeometryResult

An enumerated type used as the return value of the `XtQueryGeometry()`, `XtMakeGeometryRequest()`, and `XtMakeResizeRequest()` functions. It is defined as follows in *<X11/Intrinsic.h>*:

```
typedef enum {
    XtGeometryYes,      /* Request accepted */
    XtGeometryNo,       /* Request denied */
    XtGeometryAlmost,   /* Request denied but willing to take reply */
    XtGeometryDone      /* Request accepted and done */
} XtGeometryResult;
```

XtGrabKind

An enumerated type used in calls to `XtPopup()` to specify the nature of the grab to be asserted by the popup widget.

```
typedef enum {
    XtGrabNone,
    XtGrabNonexclusive,
    XtGrabExclusive
} XtGrabKind;
```

An exclusive grab constrains input to the widget actually making the grab (the latest widget in a popup cascade), while a non-exclusive grab allows input to any widget in the cascade.

XtInputCallbackProc

The typedef for the procedure registered by a call to `XtAppAddInput()`. See `XtInputCallbackProc`(2) for details.

XtInputId

A unique ID returned by a call to `XtAppAddInput()`; used to remove an input source with `XtRemoveInput()`.

XtInputMask

A mask used in calls to `XtProcessEvent()` to indicate which types of events should be processed. This mask is made up of a bitwise OR of the following symbols defined in *<X11/Intrinsic.h>*:

`XtIMXEvent`	Process X Events.
`XtIMTimer`	Process timeouts registered with `XtAppAddTimeout`.
`XtIMAlternateInput`	Process alternate input sources registered with `XtAppAddInput`.
`XtIMAll`	Process all three types of events.

An `XtInputMask` is returned by `XtPending()` to indicate what type of events are in the event queue. Don't confuse these values with `XtInputNoneMask`, `XtInput-WriteMask`, `XtInputReadMask`, and `XtInputExceptMask`, which are used in calls to `XtAddInput()` to indicate whether the file should be monitored for reads, writes, or exception conditions.

XtIntervalId

A unique ID returned by a call to `XtAppAddTimeout`; used to remove a timeout with `XtRemoveTimeout`. Remember that timeouts are automatically removed when the time expires.

XtKeyProc

The prototype for the keycode-to-keysym translation procedure registered in a call to `XtSetKeyTranslator()`. The default key translator is the Xt Intrinsics function `XtTranslateKey()`. See `XtKeyProc`(2) for more details.

XtLanguageProc

The prototype for the language or locale selection procedure registered in a call to `Xt-SetLanguageProc()`. See `XtLanguageProc`(2) and `XtSetLanguage-Proc()`(1) for more details.

XtListPosition

An enumerated type used in calls to `XtInsertEventHandler()` and `XtInsert-RawEventHandler()` to specify when the event handler is to be called relative to other previously registered handlers. It is defined as follows:

```
typedef enum {XtListHead, XtListTail} XtListPosition;
```

XtLoseSelectionIncrProc

The prototype for the lose selection procedure registered by a call to `XtOwn-SelectionIncremental()`. This optional procedure is called by Xt to inform the specified widget that it has lost the given selection. See `XtLoseSelectionIncr-Proc` for more details.

XtLoseSelectionProc

The typedef for the lose selection procedure registered by a call to `XtOwn-Selection()`. See `XtLoseSelectionProc`(2) for details.

XtPointer

A datum large enough to contain the largest of a char*, int*, function pointer, structure pointer, or long value. A pointer to any type or function, or a long, may be converted to an XtPointer and back again and the result will compare equal to the original value. In ANSI-C environments, it is expected that XtPointer will be defined as void.

XtPopdownID

A structure used by the built-in callback function XtCallbackPopdown(). This structure contains the Shell widget that is being popped down and the enabling widget that originally popped up the shell. XtPopdownID is defined as follows in *<X11/Intrinsics.h>*:

```
typedef struct {
    Widget   shell_widget;
    Widget   enable_widget;
} XtPopdownIDRec, *XtPopdownID;
```

XtRequestId

An opaque identifier for a particular incremental selection transfer request.

XtResource

See XtResourceList below.

XtResourceList

A structure used to declare widget or application resources, and to retrieve the current value of resources using XtGetSubresources(), XtGetSubvalues(), or XtGetResourceList(). It is defined as follows in *<X11/Intrinsic.h>*:

```
typedef struct _XtResource {
    String resource_name;       /* specify using XtN symbol */
    String resource_class;      /* specify using XtC symbol */
    String resource_type;       /* actual data type of variable */
    Cardinal resource_size;     /* specify using sizeof() */
    Cardinal resource_offset;   /* specify using XtOffset() */
    String default_type;        /* will be conv'ted to resource_type */
    XtPointer default_addr;     /* address of default value */
} XtResource, *XtResourceList;
```

See Volume Four, *X Toolkit Intrinsics Programming Manual*, for a detailed description of the XtResource structure.

XtSelectionCallbackProc

The typedef for the selection callback procedure registered by a call to XtGetSelectionValue() or XtGetSelectionValues(). See XtSelectionCallbackProc(2) for details.

XtSelectionDoneIncrProc

The prototype for the selection completion procedure registered by a call to XtOwnSelectionIncremental(). See XtSelectionDoneIncrProc (2) for details.

XtSelectionDoneProc

The typedef for the selection completion procedure registered by a call to `XtOwn-Selection()`. See `XtSelectionDoneProc(2)` for details.

XtTimerCallbackProc

The typedef for the procedure to be invoked after a timeout registered by a call to `XtAppAddTimeout`. See `XtTimerCallbackProc(2)` for details.

XtTranslations

A pointer to an opaque internal type, a compiled translation table. A pointer to an `XtTranslations` structure is returned by a call to `XtParseTranslationTable()`. Usually, the compiled translation table is produced automatically by resource conversion of a string translation table stored in a resource file.

XtTypeConverter

The prototype for new-style type converters as of R4. See `XtConverter` for a description of the obsolete R3 interface. The new interface provides more information to converters, supports conversion cache cleanup with resource reference counting, and allows additional procedures to be declared to free resources. See `XtTypeConverter`(2) for details.

XtValueMask

A mask used in calls to `XtCreateWindow()` to indicate which window attribute fields to use.

XtWidgetGeometry

A structure used to pass in and return data about widget geometry in calls to `XtQueryGeometry()` and `XtMakeGeometryRequest()`. It is defined as follows in *<X11/Intrinsic.h>*:

```
typedef struct {
    XtGeometryMask request_mode;
    Position x, y;
    Dimension width, height, border_width;
    Widget sibling;
    int stack_mode;
} XtWidgetGeometry;
```

The `request_mode` field specifies which of the other fields are to be used, or (for returned structures) contain valid values. It is made up of a bitwise OR of the following symbols defined in *<X11/X.h>*:

```
#define CWX                     (1<<0)
#define CWY                     (1<<1)
#define CWWidth                 (1<<2)
#define CWHeight                (1<<3)
#define CWBorderWidth           (1<<4)
#define CWSibling               (1<<5)
#define CWStackMode             (1<<6)
```

plus the following symbol from *<X11/Intrinsic.h>*:

```
#define XtCWQueryOnly           (1<<7)
```

which means that this call is a query only, and none of the values should be used; the return value should show what would happen if the geometry request were made. (In case you're wondering, the CW prefix stands for "ConfigureWindow"—these symbols are also used by the Xlib XConfigureWindow() call.)

The stack_mode field specifies the relationship between the current widget and a sibling widget specified in the same call. It is specified using one of the following symbols defined in <X11/X.h>:

Below	Place widget below sibling or on bottom of stack if no sibling.
TopIf	Place widget on top of stack if obscured.
BottomIf	Place widget on botton if it obscures sibling.
Opposite	If sibling occludes the widget, put widget on top of stack, but if widget occludes sibling, put widget on the bottom.

plus the following symbol from <X11/Intrinsic.h>:

XtSMDontChange	Don't change the stacking order.

If no sibling widget is specified in the call, the stacking order is relative to any sibling.

XtWorkProc

The typedef for the work procedure registered by a call to XtAppAddWorkProc(). See XtWorkProc(2) for details.

XtWorkProcId

The unique identifier returned by a call to XtAppAddWorkProc() and used as an argument in XtRemoveWorkProc().

This appendix describes each event in detail. It covers how the event is selected, what translation table symbols are valid for each event type, when each event occurs, the information contained in each event structure, and the side effects of the event, if any. Each event is described on a separate reference page.

Table C-1 lists each event mask, its associated event types, and the associated structure definition. See Chapter 8, *Events*, in Volume One, *Xlib Programming Manual*, for more information on events. See also Chapter 7, *Events, Translations, and Accelerators*, in Volume Four, *X Toolkit Intrinsics Programming Manual*.

Table C-1. Event Masks, Event Types, and Event Structures

Event Mask	Event Type	Event Structure
KeyPressMask	KeyPress	XKeyPressedEvent
KeyReleaseMask	KeyRelease	XKeyReleasedEvent
ButtonPressMask	ButtonPress	XButtonPressedEvent
ButtonReleaseMask	ButtonRelease	XButtonReleasedEvent
OwnerGrabButtonMask	n/a	n/a
KeymapStateMask	KeymapNotify	XKeymapEvent
PointerMotionMask PointerMotionHintMask ButtonMotionMask Button1MotionMask Button2MotionMask Button3MotionMask Button4MotionMask Button5MotionMask	MotionNotify	XPointerMovedEvent
EnterWindowMask	EnterNotify	XEnterWindowEvent
LeaveWindowMask	LeaveNotify	XLeaveWindowEvent
FocusChangeMask	FocusIn FocusOut	XFocusInEvent XFocusOutEvent

Table C-1. Event Masks, Event Types, and Event Structures (continued)

Event Mask	Event Type	Event Structure
ExposureMask	Expose	XExposeEvent
(selected in GC by qraphics_expose member)	GraphicsExpose NoExpose	XGraphicsExposeEvent XNoExposeEvent
ColormapChangeMask	ColormapNotify	XColormapEvent
PropertyChangeMask	PropertyNotify	XPropertyEvent
VisibilityChangeMask	VisibilityNotify	XVisibilityEvent
ResizeRedirectMask	ResizeRequest	XResizeRequestEvent
StructureNotifyMask	CirculateNotify ConfigureNotify DestroyNotify GravityNotify MapNotify ReparentNotify UnmapNotify	XCirculateEvent XConfigureEvent XDestroyWindowEvent XGravityEvent XMapEvent XReparentEvent XUnmapEvent
SubstructureNotifyMask	CirculateNotify ConfigureNotify CreateNotify DestroyNotify GravityNotify MapNotify ReparentNotify UnmapNotify	XCirculateEvent XConfigureEvent XCreateWindowEvent XDestroyWindowEvent XGravityEvent XMapEvent XReparentEvent XUnmapEvent
SubstructureRedirectMask	CirculateRequest ConfigureRequest MapRequest	XCirculateRequestEvent XConfigureRequestEvent XMapRequestEvent
(always selected)	MappingNotify	XMappingEvent
(always selected)	ClientMessage	XClientMessageEvent
(always selected)	SelectionClear	XSetSelectClearEvent
(always selected)	SelectionNotify	XSelectionEvent
(always selected)	SelectionRequest	XSelectionRequestEvent

Meaning of Common Structure Elements

Example C-1 shows the XEvent union and a simple event structure that is one member of the union. Several of the members of this structure are present in nearly every event structure. They are described here before we go into the event-specific members (see also Section 8.2.2 in Volume One, *Xlib Programming Manual*).

Example C-1. XEvent union and XAnyEvent structure

```
typedef union _XEvent {
    int type;                /* must not be changed; first member */
    XAnyEvent            xany;
    XButtonEvent         xbutton;
    XCirculateEvent      xcirculate;
    XCirculateRequestEvent xcirculaterequest;
    XClientMessageEvent  xclient;
    XColormapEvent       xcolormap;
    XConfigureEvent      xconfigure;
    XConfigureRequestEvent xconfigurerequest;
    XCreateWindowEvent   xcreatewindow;
    XDestroyWindowEvent  xdestroywindow;
    XCrossingEvent       xcrossing;
    XExposeEvent         xexpose;
    XFocusChangeEvent    xfocus;
    XNoExposeEvent       xnoexpose;
    XGraphicsExposeEvent xgraphicsexpose;
    XGravityEvent        xgravity;
    XKeymapEvent         xkeymap;
    XKeyEvent            xkey;
    XMapEvent            xmap;
    XUnmapEvent          xunmap;
    XMappingEvent        xmapping;
    XMapRequestEvent     xmaprequest;
    XMotionEvent         xmotion;
    XPropertyEvent       xproperty;
    XReparentEvent       xreparent;
    XResizeRequestEvent  xresizerequest;
    XSelectionClearEvent xselectionclear;
    XSelectionEvent      xselection;
    XSelectionRequestEvent xselectionrequest;
    XVisibilityEvent     xvisibility;
    long                 pad[24];
} XEvent;

typedef struct {
    int type;
    unsigned long serial;    /* # of last request processed by server */
    Bool send_event;         /* TRUE if this came from SendEvent request */
    Display *display;        /* display the event was read from */
    Window window;           /* window on which event was requested in
                              * event mask */
} XAnyEvent;
```

The first member of the XEvent union is the type of event. When an event is received (with XNextEvent, for example), the application checks the type member in the XEvent union. Then the specific event type is known and the specific event structure (such as xbutton) is used to access information specific to that event type.

Before the branching depending on the event type, only the XEvent union is used. After the branching, only the event structure that contains the specific information for each event type should be used in each branch. For example, if the XEvent union were called report, the report.xexpose structure should be used within the branch for Expose events.

You'll notice that each event structure also begins with a type member. This member is rarely used, since it is an identical copy of the type member in the XEvent union.

Most event structures also have a window member. The window member indicates the event window that selected and received the event. This is the window where the event arrives if it has propagated through the hierarchy as described in Section 7.2.1, in Volume Four, *X Toolkit Intrinsics Programming Manual*. One event type may have two different meanings to an application, depending on which window it appears in.

Many of the event structures also have a display and/or root member. The display member identifies the connection to the server that is active. The root member indicates which screen in the hierarchy links the window that received the event. Most programs use only a single screen and therefore don't need to worry about the root member. The display member can be useful since you can pass the display variable into routines by simply passing a pointer to the event structure, eliminating the need for a separate display argument.

All event structures include a serial member that gives the number of the last protocol request processed by the server. This is useful in debugging, since an error can be detected by the server but not reported to the user (or programmer) until the next routine that gets an event. That means several routines may execute successfully after the error occurs. The last request processed often indicates the request that contained the error.

All event structures also include a send_event flag, which if True indicates that the event was sent by XSendEvent (i.e., by another client rather than by the server).

The following pages describe each event type in detail. The events are presented in alphabetical order, each on a separate page (except for a few complementary pairs that are described together). Each page describes the circumstances under which the event is generated, the mask used to select it, the structure itself, its members, and useful programming notes. Note that the description of the structure members does not include those members common to many structures. If you need more information on these members, please refer to this introductory section.

ButtonPress, ButtonRelease

When Generated

There are two types of pointer button events: `ButtonPress` and `ButtonRelease`. Both contain the same information.

Translation Abbreviations

In translation tables, the event type `ButtonPress` or `ButtonRelease` may be used, or use one of the abbreviations shown in the following table.

Abbreviation	Description
BtnDown	Any pointer button pressed.
Btn1Down	Pointer button 1 pressed.
Btn2Down	Pointer button 2 pressed.
Btn3Down	Pointer button 3 pressed.
Btn4Down	Pointer button 4 pressed.
Btn5Down	Pointer button 5 pressed.
BtnUp	Any pointer button released.
Btn1Up	Pointer button 1 released.
Btn2Up	Pointer button 2 released.
Btn3Up	Pointer button 3 released.
Btn4Up	Pointer button 4 released.
Btn5Up	Pointer button 5 released.

Select With

May be selected separately, using `ButtonPressMask` and `ButtonReleaseMask`.

XEvent Structure Name

```
typedef union _XEvent {
    . . .
    XButtonEvent xbutton;
    . . .
} XEvent;
```

Event Structure

```
typedef struct {
int type;                /* of event */
unsigned long serial;    /* # of last request processed by server */
Bool send_event;         /* True if this came from a SendEvent request */
Display *display;        /* Display the event was read from */
Window window;           /* event window it is reported relative to */
Window root;             /* root window that the event occurred under */
Window subwindow;        /* child window */
Time time;               /* when event occurred, in milliseconds */
int x, y;                /* pointer coordinates relative to receiving
                          * window */
int x_root, y_root;      /* coordinates relative to root */
```

```
unsigned int state;      /* mask of all buttons and modifier keys */
unsigned int button;     /* button that triggered event */
Bool same_screen;        /* same screen flag */
} XButtonEvent;
typedef XButtonEvent XButtonPressedEvent;
typedef XButtonEvent XButtonReleasedEvent;
```

Event Structure Members

subwindow
: If the source window is the child of the receiving window, then the subwindow member is set to the ID of that child.

time
: The server time when the button event occurred, in milliseconds. Time is declared as unsigned long, so it wraps around when it reaches the maximum value of a 32-bit number (every 49.7 days).

x, y
: If the receiving window is on the same screen as the root window specified by root, then x and y are the pointer coordinates relative to the receiving window's origin. Otherwise, x and y are zero.

When active button grabs and pointer grabs are in effect (see Volume One, *Xlib Programming Manual*, Section 9.4), the coordinates relative to the receiving window may not be within the window (they may be negative or greater than window height or width).

x_root, y_root
: The pointer coordinates relative to the root window which is an ancestor of the event window. If the pointer was on a different screen, these are zero.

state
: The state of all the buttons and modifier keys just before the event, represented by a mask of the button and modifier key symbols: Button1Mask, Button2Mask, Button3Mask, Button4Mask, Button5Mask, ShiftMask, ControlMask, LockMask, Mod1-Mask, Mod2Mask, Mod3Mask, Mod4Mask, and Mod5Mask. If a modifier key is pressed and released when no other modifier keys are held, the ButtonPress will have a state member of 0 and the ButtonRelease will have a nonzero state member indicating that itself was held just before the event.

button
: A value indicating which button changed state to trigger this event. One of the constants: Button1, Button2, Button3, Button4, or Button5.

same_screen
: Indicates whether the pointer is currently on the same screen as this window. This is always True unless the pointer was actively grabbed before the automatic grab could take place.

Notes

Unless an active grab already exists, or a passive grab on the button combination that was pressed already exists at a higher level in the hierarchy than where the ButtonPress occurred, an automatic active grab of the pointer takes place when a `ButtonPress` occurs. Because of the automatic grab, the matching `ButtonRelease` is sent to the same application that received the `ButtonPress` event. If `OwnerGrabButtonMask` has been selected, the `ButtonRelease` event is delivered to the window which contained the pointer when the button was released, as long as that window belongs to the same client as the window in which the `ButtonPress` event occurred. If the `ButtonRelease` occurs outside of the client's windows or `OwnerGrabButtonMask` was not selected, the `ButtonRelease` is delivered to the window in which the `ButtonPress` occurred. The grab is terminated when all buttons are released. During the grab, the cursor associated with the grabbing window will track the pointer anywhere on the screen.

If the application has invoked a passive button grab on an ancestor of the window in which the `ButtonPress` event occurs, then that grab takes precedence over the automatic grab, and the `ButtonRelease` will go to that window, or it will be handled normally by that client depending on the `owner_events` flag in the `XGrabButton()` call.

CirculateNotify

When Generated

A `CirculateNotify` event reports a call to change the stacking order, and it includes whether the final position is on the top or on the bottom. This event is generated by `XCirculateSubwindows()`, `XCirculateSubwindowsDown()`, or `XCirculate-SubwindowsUp()`. See also the `CirculateRequest` and `ConfigureNotify` events.

Translation Abbreviations

In translation tables, the event type `CirculateNotify` may be used, or use the abbreviation `Circ`.

Select With

This event is selected with `StructureNotifyMask` in the `XSelectInput()` call for the window to be moved or with `SubstructureNotifyMask` for the parent of the window to be moved.

XEvent Structure Name

```
typedef union _XEvent {
    . . .
    XCirculateEvent xcirculate;
    . . .
} XEvent;
```

Event Structure

```
typedef struct {
    int type;
    unsigned long serial; /* # of last request processed by server */
    Bool send_event;      /* True if this came from SendEvent request */
    Display *display;      /* display the event was read from */
    Window event;
    Window window;
    int place;            /* PlaceOnTop, PlaceOnBottom */
} XCirculateEvent;
```

Event Structure Members

event   The window receiving the event. If the event was selected by `Structure-NotifyMask`, event will be the same as window. If the event was selected by `SubstructureNotifyMask`, event will be the parent of window.

window   The window that was restacked.

place   Either `PlaceOnTop` or `PlaceOnBottom`. Indicates whether the window was raised to the top or bottom of the stack.

CirculateRequest

When Generated

A CirculateRequest event reports when XCirculateSubwindows(), XCirculateSubwindowsDown(), XCirculateSubwindowsUp(), or XRestack-Windows() is called to change the stacking order of a group of children.

This event differs from CirculateNotify in that it delivers the parameters of the request before it is carried out. This gives the client that selects this event (usually the window manager) the opportunity to review the request in the light of its window management policy before executing the circulate request itself or to deny the request. (CirculateNotify indicates the final outcome of the request.)

Translation Abbreviations

In translation tables, the event type CirculateNotify may be used, or use the abbreviation CircRec.

Select With

This event is selected for the parent window with SubstructureRedirectMask.

XEvent Structure Name

```
typedef union _XEvent {
    . . .
    XCirculateRequestEvent xcirculaterequest;
    . . .
} XEvent;
```

Event Structure

```
typedef struct {
    int type;
    unsigned long serial; /* # of last request processed by server */
    Bool send_event;      /* True if this came from SendEvent request */
    Display *display;      /* display the event was read from */
    Window parent;
    Window window;
    int place;             /* PlaceOnTop, PlaceOnBottom */
} XCirculateRequestEvent;
```

Event Structure Members

parent   The parent of the window that was restacked. This is the window that selected the event.

window   The window being restacked.

place   PlaceOnTop or PlaceOnBottom. Indicates whether the window was to be placed on the top or on the bottom of the stacking order.

When Generated

A `ClientMessage` event is sent as a result of a call to `XSendEvent()` by a client to a particular window. Any type of event can be sent with `XSendEvent()`, but it will be distinguished from normal events by the `send_event` member being set to `True`. If your program wants to be able to treat events sent with `XSendEvent()` as different from normal events, you can check the `send_event` member, or you can provide a translation for `ClientMessage` events.

Translation Abbreviations

In translation tables, the event type `ClientMessage` may be used, or use the abbreviation `Message`.

The type of `ClientMessage` event (the `MessageType` field) can be specified as a detail in the translation (see `PropertyNotify`).

Select With

There is no event mask for `ClientMessage` events, and they are not selected with `XSelectInput()`. Instead `XSendEvent()` directs them to a specific window, which is given as a window ID, `PointerWindow`, or `InputFocus`.

XEvent Structure Name

```
typedef union _XEvent {
    . . .
    XClientMessageEvent xclient;
    . . .
} XEvent;
```

Event Structure

```
typedef struct {
    int type;
    unsigned long serial; /* # of last request processed by server */
    Bool send_event;      /* True if this came from SendEvent request */
    Display *display;      /* display the event was read from */
    Window window;
    Atom message_type;
    int format;
    union {
        char b[20];
        short s[10];
        long l[5];
    } data;
} XClientMessageEvent;
```

Event Structure Members

message_type   An atom that specifies how the data is to be interpreted by the receiving client. The X server places no interpretation on the type or the data, but it must be a list of 8-bit, 16-bit, or 32-bit quantities, so that the X server can correctly swap bytes as necessary. The data always consists of twenty 8-bit values, ten 16-bit values, or five 32-bit values, although each particular message might not make use of all of these values.

format   Specifies the format of the property specified by `message_type`. This will be one of the values `8`, `16`, or `32`.

ColormapNotify

When Generated

A `ColormapNotify` event reports when the colormap attribute of a window changes or when the colormap specified by the attribute is installed, uninstalled, or freed. This event is generated by `XChangeWindowAttributes()`, `XFreeColormap()`, `XInstall-Colormap()`, and `XUninstallColormap()`.

Translation Abbreviations

In translation tables, the event type `ColormapNotify` may be used, or use the abbreviation `Clrmap`.

Select With

This event is selected with `ColormapChangeMask`.

XEvent Structure Name

```
typedef union _XEvent {
    . . .
    XColormapEvent xcolormap;
    . . .
} XEvent;
```

Event Structure

```
typedef struct {
    int type;
    unsigned long serial; /* # of last request processed by server */
    Bool send_event;      /* True if this came from SendEvent request */
    Display *display;      /* display the event was read from */
    Window window;
    Colormap colormap;    /* A colormap or None */
    Bool new;
    int state;            /* ColormapInstalled, ColormapUninstalled */
} XColormapEvent;
```

Event Structure Members

window   The window whose associated colormap or attribute changes.

colormap The colormap associated with the window, either a colormap ID or the constant None. It will be None only if this event was generated due to an XFree-Colormap() call.

new   True when the colormap attribute has been changed, or False when the colormap is installed or uninstalled.

state   Either ColormapInstalled or ColormapUninstalled; it indicates whether the colormap is installed or uninstalled.

When Generated

A `ConfigureNotify` event announces actual changes to a window's configuration (size, position, border, and stacking order). See also the `CirculateRequest` event.

Translation Abbreviations

In translation tables, the event type `ConfigureNotify` may be used, or use the abbreviation `Configure`.

Select With

This event is selected for a single window by specifying the window ID of that window with `StructureNotifyMask`. To receive this event for all children of a window, specify the parent window ID with `SubstructureNotifyMask`.

XEvent Structure Name

```
typedef union _XEvent {
    . . .
    XConfigureEvent xconfigure;
    . . .
} XEvent;
```

Event Structure

```
typedef struct {
    int type;
    unsigned long serial;  /* # of last request processed by server */
    Bool send_event;       /* True if this came from SendEvent request */
    Display *display;      /* display the event was read from */
    Window event;
    Window window;
    int x, y;
    int width, height;
    int border_width;
    Window above;
    Bool override_redirect;
} XConfigureEvent;
```

Event Structure Members

event	The window that selected the event. The `event` and `window` members are identical if the event was selected with `StructureNotifyMask`.
window	The window whose configuration was changed.
x, y	The final coordinates of the reconfigured window relative to its parent.
width, height	The width and height in pixels of the window after reconfiguration.
border_width	The width in pixels of the border after reconfiguration.

above

If this member is None, then the window is on the bottom of the stack with respect to its siblings. Otherwise, the window is immediately on top of the specified sibling window.

override_redirect

The override_redirect attribute of the reconfigured window. If True, it indicates that the client wants this window to be immune to interception by the window manager of configuration requests. Window managers normally should ignore this event if override_redirect is True.

ConfigureRequest

When Generated

A `ConfigureRequest` event reports when another client attempts to change a window's size, position, border, and/or stacking order.

This event differs from `ConfigureNotify` in that it delivers the parameters of the request before it is carried out. This gives the client that selects this event (usually the window manager) the opportunity to revise the requested configuration before executing the `XConfigureWindow()` request itself or to deny the request. (`ConfigureNotify` indicates the final outcome of the request.)

Translation Abbreviations

In translation tables, the event type `ConfigureNotify` may be used, or use the abbreviation `ConfigureReq`.

Select With

This event is selected for any window in a group of children by specifying the parent window with `SubstructureRedirectMask`.

XEvent Structure Name

```
typedef union _XEvent {
    . . .
    XConfigureRequestEvent xconfigurerequest;
    . . .
} XEvent;
```

Event Structure

```
typedef struct {
    int type;
    unsigned long serial; /* # of last request processed by server */
    Bool send_event;      /* True if this came from SendEvent request */
    Display *display;     /* display the event was read from */
    Window parent;
    Window window;
    int x, y;
    int width, height;
    int border_width;
    Window above;
    int detail;           /* Above, Below, BottomIf, TopIf, Opposite */
    unsigned long value_mask;
} XConfigureRequestEvent;
```

Event Structure Members

parent   The window that selected the event. This is the parent of the window being configured.

window   The window that is being configured.

x, y	The requested position for the upper-left pixel of the window's border relative to the origin of the parent window.
width, height	The requested width and height in pixels for the window.
border width	The requested border width for the window.
above	None, Above, Below, TopIf, BottomIf, or Opposite. Specifies the sibling window on top of which the specified window should be placed. If this member has the constant None, then the specified window should be placed on the bottom.

Notes

The geometry is derived from the XConfigureWindow() request that triggered the event.

When Generated

A `CreateNotify` event reports when a window is created.

Translation Abbreviations

In translation tables, the event type `CreateNotify` may be used, or use the abbreviation `Create`.

Select With

This event is selected on children of a window by specifying the parent window ID with `SubstructureNotifyMask`. (Note that this event type cannot be selected by `StructureNotifyMask`.)

XEvent Structure Name

```
typedef union _XEvent {
    . . .
    XCreateWindowEvent xcreatewindow;
    . . .
} XEvent;
```

Event Structure

```
typedef struct {
    int type;
    unsigned long serial;     /* # of last request processed by server */
    Bool send_event;          /* True if this came from SendEvent
                               * request */
    Display *display;         /* display the event was read from */
    Window parent;            /* parent of the window */
    Window window;            /* window ID of window created */
    int x, y;                 /* window location */
    int width, height;        /* size of window */
    int border_width;         /* border width */
    Bool override_redirect;   /* creation should be overridden */
} XCreateWindowEvent;
```

Event Structure Members

`parent`	The ID of the created window's parent.
`window`	The ID of the created window.
`x, y`	The coordinates of the created window relative to its parent.
`width, height`	The width and height in pixels of the created window.
`border_width`	The width in pixels of the border of the created window.
`override_redirect`	The `override_redirect` attribute of the created window. If `True`, it indicates that the client wants this window to be immune to interception by the window manager of configuration requests.

Window managers normally should ignore this event if override_redirect is True.

Notes

For descriptions of these members, see the XCreateWindow() function and the XSet-WindowAttributes structure.

DestroyNotify

When Generated

A DestroyNotify event reports that a window has been destroyed.

Translation Abbreviations

In translation tables, the event type DestroyNotify may be used, or use the abbreviation Destroy.

Select With

To receive this event type on children of a window, specify the parent window ID and pass SubstructureNotifyMask as part of the event_mask argument to XSelect-Input(). This event type cannot be selected with StructureNotifyMask.

XEvent Structure Name

```
typedef union _XEvent {
    . . .
    XDestroyWindowEvent xdestroywindow;
    . . .
} XEvent;
```

Event Structure

```
typedef struct {
    int type;
    unsigned long serial; /* # of last request processed by server */
    Bool send_event;      /* True if this came from SendEvent request */
    Display *display;     /* display the event was read from */
    Window event;
    Window window;
} XDestroyWindowEvent;
```

Event Structure Members

event   The window that selected the event.

window   The window that was destroyed.

When Generated

`EnterNotify` and `LeaveNotify` events occur when the pointer enters or leaves a window.

When the pointer crosses a window border, a `LeaveNotify` event occurs in the window being left and an `EnterNotify` event occurs in the window being entered. Whether or not each event is queued for any application depends on whether any application selected the right event on the window in which it occurred.

In addition, `EnterNotify` and `LeaveNotify` events are delivered to windows that are *virtually crossed*. These are windows that are between the origin and destination windows in the hierarchy but not necessarily on the screen. Further explanation of virtual crossing is provided two pages following.

Translation Abbreviations

In translation tables, the event type `EnterNotify` and `LeaveNotify` may be used, or use one of the abbreviations shown in the following table.

Abbreviation	Description
`Enter`	Pointer entered window.
`EnterWindow`	Pointer entered window.
`Leave`	Pointer left window.
`LeaveWindow`	Pointer left window.

Normally, enter and leave events that occur because of grabs are treated just like normal enter and leave events. To handle them differently, you can use any of the abbreviations above together with a detail. For example, in the translation:

```
<Enter>Grab: grabbed()\n\
<Leave>Ungrab: ungrabbed()
```

The specified actions will be invoked only when the pointer enters or leaves the widget because of a grab or ungrab. The default is equivalent to the following to the following translation:

```
<Enter>Normal: allEvents()
```

The Core widget field `compress_enterleave` controls whether pairs of `EnterNotify` and `LeaveNotify` events with no intervening events are ignored. For more information, see Chapter 8, *More Input Techniques*, in Volume Four, *X Toolkit Intrinsics Programming Manual*.

Select With

Each of these events can be selected separately with `XEnterWindowMask` and `XLeaveWindowMask`.

XEvent Structure Name

```
typedef union _XEvent {
    . . .
    XCrossingEvent xcrossing;
    . . .
} XEvent;
```

Event Structure

```
typedef struct {
    int type;               /* of event */
    unsigned long serial;   /* # of last request processed by server */
    Bool send_event;        /* True if this came from SendEvent request */
    Display *display;       /* display the event was read from */
    Window window;          /* event window it is reported relative to */
    Window root;            /* root window that the event occurred on */
    Window subwindow;       /* child window */
    Time time;              /* milliseconds */
    int x, y;               /* pointer x, y coordinates in receiving
                             * window */
    int x_root, y_root;     /* coordinates relative to root */
    int mode;               /* NotifyNormal, NotifyGrab, NotifyUngrab */
    int detail;             /* NotifyAncestor, NotifyInferior,
                             * NotifyNonLinear, NotifyNonLinearVirtual,
                             * NotifyVirtual */
    Bool same_screen;       /* same screen flag */
    Bool focus;             /* Boolean focus */
    unsigned int state;     /* key or button mask */
} XCrossingEvent;
typedef XCrossingEvent XEnterWindowEvent;
typedef XCrossingEvent XLeaveWindowEvent;
```

Event Structure Members

subwindow	In a LeaveNotify event, if the pointer began in a child of the receiving window, then the child member is set to the window ID of the child. Otherwise, it is set to None. For an EnterNotify event, if the pointer ends up in a child of the receiving window, then the child member is set to the window ID of the child. Otherwise, it is set to None.
time	The server time when the crossing event occurred, in milliseconds. Time is declared as unsigned long, so it wraps around when it reaches the maximum value of a 32-bit number (every 49.7 days).
x, y	The point of entry or exit of the pointer relative to the event window.
x_root, y_root	The point of entry or exit of the pointer relative to the root window.

mode   Normal crossing events or those caused by pointer warps have mode `NotifyNormal`; events caused by a grab have mode `NotifyGrab`; and events caused by a released grab have mode `NotifyUngrab`.

detail   The value of the `detail` member depends on the hierarchical relationship between the origin and destination windows and the direction of pointer transfer. Determining which windows receive events and with which `detail` members is quite complicated. This topic is described in the next section.

same_screen   Indicates whether the pointer is currently on the same screen as this window. This is always `True` unless the pointer was actively grabbed before the automatic grab could take place.

focus   If the receiving window is the focus window or a descendant of the focus window, the `focus` member is `True`; otherwise, it is `False`.

state   The state of all the buttons and modifier keys just before the event, represented by a mask of the button and modifier key symbols: `Button1Mask`, `Button2Mask`, `Button3Mask`, `Button4Mask`, `Button5Mask`, `ShiftMask`, `ControlMask`, `LockMask`, `Mod1-Mask`, `Mod2Mask`, `Mod3Mask`, `Mod4Mask`, and `Mod5Mask`.

Virtual Crossing and the detail Member

Virtual crossing occurs when the pointer moves between two windows that do not have a parent-child relationship. Windows between the origin and destination windows in the hierarchy receive `EnterNotify` and `LeaveNotify` events. The `detail` member of each of these events depends on the hierarchical relationship of the origin and destination windows and the direction of pointer transfer.

Virtual crossing is an advanced topic that you should not spend time figuring out unless you have an important reason to use it. We have never seen an application that uses this feature, and we know of no reason for its extreme complexity. With that word of warning, proceed.

Let's say the pointer has moved from one window, the origin, to another, the destination. First, we'll specify what types of events each window gets and then the detail member of each of those events.

The window of origin receives a `LeaveNotify` event and the destination window receives an `EnterNotify` event, if they have requested this type of event. If one is an inferior of the other, the `detail` member of the event received by the inferior is `NotifyAncestor` and the detail of the event received by the superior is `NotifyInferior`. If the crossing is between parent and child, these are the only events generated.

However, if the origin and destination windows are not parent and child, other windows are *virtually crossed* and also receive events. If neither window is an ancestor of the other, ancestors of each window, up to but not including the least common ancestor, receive `LeaveNotify` events if they are in the same branch of the hierarchy as the origin and `EnterNotify` events, if they are in the same branch as the destination. These events can be used to track the motion of the pointer through the hierarchy.

- In the case of a crossing between a parent and a child of a child, the middle child receives a LeaveNotify with detail NotifyVirtual.

- In the case of a crossing between a child and the parent of its parent, the middle child receives an EnterNotify with detail NotifyVirtual.

- In a crossing between windows whose least common ancestor is two or more windows away, both the origin and destination windows receive events with detail Notify-Nonlinear. The windows between the origin and the destination in the hierarchy, up to but not including their least common ancestor, receive events with detail Notify-NonlinearVirtual. The least common ancestor is the lowest window from which both are descendants.

- If the origin and destination windows are on separate screens, the events and details generated are the same as for two windows not parent and child, except that the root windows of the two screens are considered the least common ancestor. Both root windows also receive events.

Table C-1 shows the event types generated by a pointer crossing from window *A* to window *B* when window *C* is the least common ancestor of *A* and *B*.

Table C-1. Border Crossing Events and Window Relationship

LeaveNotify	EnterNotify
Origin window (*A*).	Destination window (*B*).
Windows between *A* and *B* exclusive, if *A* is inferior.	Windows between *A* and *B*, exclusive, if *B* is inferior.
Windows between *A* and *C*, exclusive.	Windows between *B* and *C*, exclusive.
Root window on screen of origin if different from screen of destination.	Root window on screen of destination if different from screen of origin.

Table C-2 lists the detail members in events generated by a pointer crossing from window *A* to window *B*.

Table C-2. Event detail Member and Window Relationship

detail Flag	Window Delivered To
NotifyAncestor	Origin or destination when either is descendant.
NotifyInferior	Origin or destination when either is ancestor.
NotifyVirtual	Windows between *A* and *B*, exclusive, if either is descendant.
NotifyNonlinear	Origin and destination when *A* and *B* are two or more windows distant from least common ancestor *C*.

detail Flag	Window Delivered To
NotifyNonlinearVirtual	Windows between *A* and *C*, exclusive, and between *B* and *C*, exclusive, when *A* and *B* have least common ancestor *C*; also on both root windows if *A* and *B* are on different screens.

For example, Figure C-1 shows the events that are generated by a movement from a window (window *A*) to a child (window *B1*) of a sibling (window *B*). This would generate three events: a LeaveNotify with detail NotifyNonlinear for the window *A*, an EnterNotify with detail NotifyNonlinearVirtual for its sibling window *B*, and an EnterNotify with detail NotifyNonlinear for the child (window *B1*).

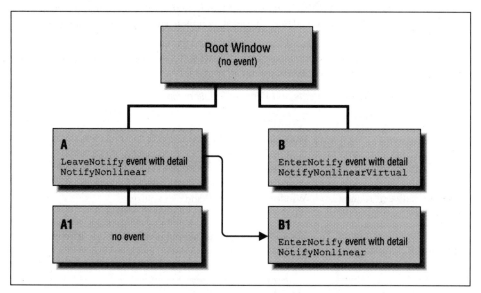

Figure C-1. Events generated by a move between windows

EnterNotify and LeaveNotify events are also generated when the pointer is grabbed, if the pointer was not already inside the grabbing window. In this case, the grabbing window receives an EnterNotify and the window containing the pointer receives a LeaveNotify event, both with mode NotifyUngrab. The pointer position in both events is the position before the grab. The result when the grab is released is exactly the same, except that the two windows receive EnterNotify instead of LeaveNotify and vice versa.

Figure C-2 demonstrates the events and details caused by various pointer transitions, indicated by heavy arrows.

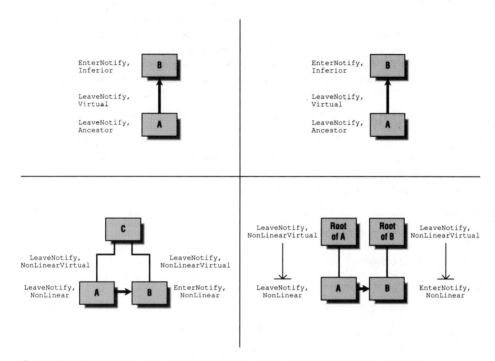

*Figure C-2. Border crossing events and detail member for pointer movement from
window A to window B, for various window relationships*

Expose

When Generated

An Expose event is generated when a window becomes visible or a previously invisible part of a window becomes visible. Only InputOutput windows generate or need to respond to Expose events; InputOnly windows never generate or need to respond to them. The Expose event provides the position and size of the exposed area within the window and a rough count of the number of remaining exposure events for the current window.

Translation Abbreviations

In translation tables, the event type Expose is the only valid string; there are no abbreviations.

The Core widget field compress_exposures controls whether contiguous Expose events are coalesced before calling a widget's expose() method. For more information, see Volume Four, *X Toolkit Intrinsics Programming Manual*.

Select With

This event is selected with ExposureMask.

XEvent Structure Name

```
typedef union _XEvent {
    . . .
    XExposeEvent xexpose;
    . . .
} XEvent;
```

Event Structure

```
typedef struct {
    int type;
    unsigned long serial;  /* # of last request processed by server */
    Bool send_event;       /* True if this came from SendEvent request */
    Display *display;      /* Display the event was read from */
    Window window;
    int x, y;
    int width, height;
    int count;             /* If nonzero, at least this many more */
} XExposeEvent;
```

Event Structure Members

x, y
: The coordinates of the upper-left corner of the exposed region relative to the origin of the window.

width, height
: The width and height in pixels of the exposed region.

count
: The approximate number of remaining contiguous Expose events that were generated as a result of a single function call.

Notes

A single action such as a window movement or a function call can generate several exposure events on one window or on several windows. The server guarantees that all exposure events generated from a single action will be sent contiguously, so that they can all be handled before moving on to other event types. This allows an application to keep track of the rectangles specified in contiguous Expose events, set the clip_mask in a GC to the areas specified in the rectangle using XSetRegion() or XSetClipRectangles(), and then finally redraw the window clipped with the GC in a single operation after all the Expose events have arrived. The last event to arrive is indicated by a count of 0. In Release 2, XUnionRectWith-Region() can be used to add the rectangle in Expose events to a region before calling XSetRegion().

If your application is able to redraw partial windows, you can also read each exposure event in turn and redraw each area.

When Generated

FocusIn and FocusOut events occur when the keyboard focus window changes as a result of an XSetInputFocus() call. They are much like EnterNotify and LeaveNotify events except that they track the focus rather than the pointer.

When a focus change occurs, a FocusOut event is delivered to the old focus window and a FocusIn event to the window which receives the focus. In addition, windows in between these two windows in the window hierarchy are virtually crossed and receive focus change events, as described below. Some or all of the windows between the window containing the pointer at the time of the focus change and the root window also receive focus change events, as described below.

Translation Abbreviations

In translation tables, the event type FocusIn and FocusOut may be used; there are no abbreviations.

By default, translations for focus change events detect focus changes due to grabs and XtSet-KeyboardFocus() or XSetInputFocus() calls. To distinguish these different types of focus change events, you can specify a detail in the translation. For example, to be notified only of focus changes resulting from grabs, you can use the translation:

```
<FocusIn>Grab: gotFocus()
```

For other types of focus events, you can use the details Ungrab, WhileGrabbed, and Normal.

Select With

FocusIn and FocusOut events are selected with FocusChangeMask. They cannot be selected separately.

XEvent Structure Name

```
typedef union _XEvent {
    . . .
    XFocusChangeEvent xfocus;
    . . .
} XEvent;
```

Event Structure

```
typedef struct {
    int type;              /* FocusIn or FocusOut */
    unsigned long serial;  /* # of last request processed by server */
    Bool send_event;       /* True if this came from SendEvent request */
    Display *display;      /* Display the event was read from */
    Window window;         /* Window of event */
    int mode;              /* NotifyNormal, NotifyGrab, NotifyUngrab,
                            * NotifyWhileGrabbed */
    int detail;            /* NotifyAncestor, NotifyVirtual, Notify-
                            * Inferior, NotifyNonLinear, NotifyNonLinear-
                            * Virtual, NotifyPointer, NotifyPointerRoot,
```

```
                        * NotifyDetailNone */
} XFocusChangeEvent;
typedef XFocusChangeEvent XFocusInEvent;
typedef XFocusChangeEvent XFocusOutEvent;
```

Event Structure Members

mode   For events generated when the keyboard is not grabbed, mode is Notify-Normal; when the focus change occurs while the keyboard is grabbed, mode is NotifyGrab; and when the focus change results from an ungrab, mode is NotifyUngrab.

detail   The detail member identifies the relationship between the window that receives the event and the origin and destination windows. It will be described in detail after the description of which windows get what types of events.

Notes

The *keyboard focus* is a window that has been designated as the one to receive all keyboard input irrespective of the pointer position. Only the keyboard focus window and its descendants receive keyboard events. By default, the focus window is the root window. Since all windows are descendants of the root, the pointer controls the window that receives input.

Most window managers allow the user to set a focus window to avoid the problem where the pointer sometimes gets bumped into the wrong window and your typing does not go to the intended window. If the pointer is pointing at the root window, all typing is usually lost, since there is no application for this input to propagate to. Some applications may set the keyboard focus so that they can get all keyboard input for a given period of time, but this practice is not encouraged.

Focus events are used when an application wants to act differently when the keyboard focus is set to another window or to itself. FocusChangeMask is used to select FocusIn and FocusOut events.

When a focus change occurs, a FocusOut event is delivered to the old focus window and a FocusIn event is delivered to the window which receives the focus. Windows in between in the hierarchy are virtually crossed and receive one focus change event each depending on the relationship and direction of transfer between the origin and destination windows. Some or all of the windows between the window containing the pointer at the time of the focus change and that window's root window can also receive focus change events. By checking the detail member of FocusIn and FocusOut events, an application can tell which of its windows can receive input.

The detail member gives clues about the relationship of the event receiving window to the origin and destination of the focus. The detail member of FocusIn and FocusOut events is analogous to the detail member of EnterNotify and LeaveNotify events but with even more permutations to make life complicated.

Virtual Focus Crossing and the detail Member

We will now embark on specifying the types of events sent to each window and the `detail` member in each event, depending on the relative position in the hierarchy of the origin window (old focus), destination window (new focus), and the pointer window (window containing pointer at time of focus change). Don't even try to figure this out unless you have to.

Table C-3 shows the event types generated by a focus transition from window A to window B when window C is the least common ancestor of A and B, and P is the window containing pointer. This table includes most of the events generated, but not all of them. It is quite possible for a single window to receive more than one focus change event from a single focus change.

Table C-3. FocusIn and FocusOut Events and Window Relationship

FocusOut	FocusIn
Origin window (A).	Destination window (B).
Windows between A and B, exclusive, if A is inferior.	Windows between A and B, exclusive, if B is inferior.
Windows between A and C, exclusive.	Windows between B and C, exclusive.
Root window on screen of origin if different from screen of destination.	Root window on screen of destination if different from screen of origin.
Pointer window up to but not including origin window if pointer window is descendant of origin.	Pointer window up to but not including destination window if pointer window is descendant of destination.
Pointer window up to and including pointer window's root if transfer was from `PointerRoot`.	Pointer window up to and including pointer window's root if transfer was to `PointerRoot`.

Table C-4 lists the `detail` members in events generated by a focus transition from window *A* to window *B*, with *P* being the window containing the pointer.

Table C-4. Event detail Member and Window Relationship

`detail` Flag	Window Delivered To
`NotifyAncestor`	Origin or destination when either is descendant.
`NotifyInterior`	Origin or destination when either is ancestor.
`NotifyVirtual`	Windows between *A* and *B*, exclusive, if either is descendant.
`NotifyNonlinear`	Origin and destination when *A* and *B* are two or more windows distant from least common ancestor *C*.
`NotifyNonlinearVirtual`	Windows between *A* and *C*, exclusive, and between *B* and *C*, exclusive, when *A* and *B* have least common ancestor *C*; also on both root windows if *A* and *B* are on different screens.
`NotifyPointer`	Window *P* and windows up to but not including the origin or destination windows.
`NotifyPointerRoot`	Window *P* and all windows up to its root, and all other roots, when focus is set to or from `Pointer-Root`.
`NotifyDetailNone`	All roots, when focus is set to or from `None`.

The following two pages show all the possible combinations of focus transitions and of origin, destination, and pointer windows and shows the types of events that are generated and their `detail` member. Solid lines indicate branches of the hierarchy. Dotted arrows indicate the direction of transition of the focus. At each end of this arrow are the origin and destination windows, windows *A* to *B*. Arrows ending in a bar indicate that the event type and detail described are delivered to all windows up to the bar.

In any branch, there may be windows that are not shown. Windows in a single branch between two boxes shown will get the event types and details shown beside the branch.

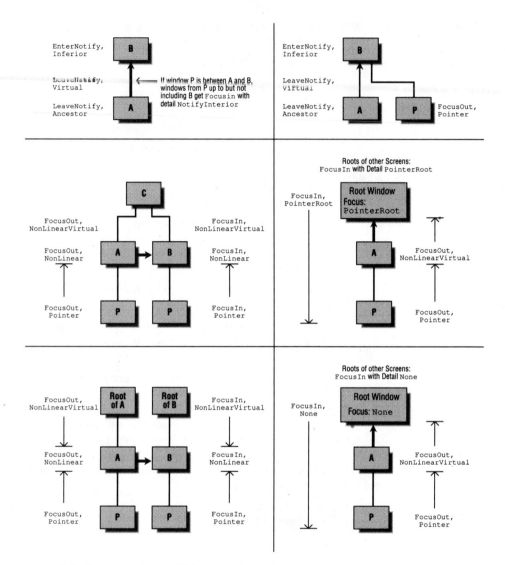

Figure C-3. FocusIn and FocusOut event schematics

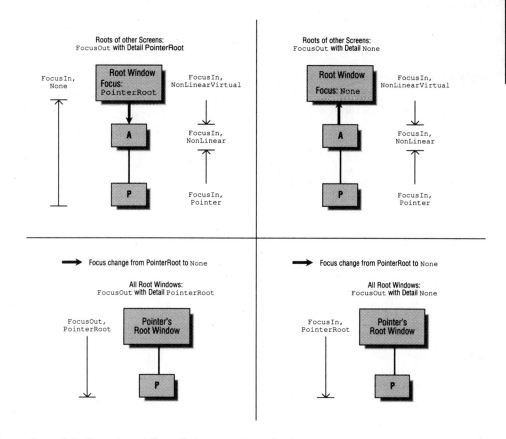

Figure C-3. FocusIn and FocusOut event schematics (cont'd)

FocusIn and FocusOut events are also generated when the keyboard is grabbed, if the focus was not already assigned to the grabbing window. In this case, all windows receive events as if the focus was set from the current focus to the grab window. When the grab is released, the events generated are just as if the focus was set back.

When Generated

GraphicsExpose events indicate that the source area for a XCopyArea() or XCopy-Plane() request was not available because it was outside the source window or obscured by a window. NoExpose events indicate that the source region was completely available.

Translation Abbreviations

In translation tables, the event types GraphicsExpose and NoExpose may be used, or use the abbreviations GrExp or NoExp.

Select With

These events are not selected with XSelectInput() but are sent if the GC in the XCopy-Area() or XCopyPlane() request had its graphics_exposures flag set to True. If graphics_exposures is True in the GC used for the copy, either one NoExpose event or one or more GraphicsExpose events will be generated for every XCopyArea() or XCopyPlane() call made.

XEvent Structure Name

```
typedef union _XEvent {
    . . .
    XNoExposeEvent xnoexpose;
    XGraphicsExposeEvent xgraphicsexpose;
    . . .
} XEvent;
```

Event Structure

```
typedef struct {
    int type;
    unsigned long serial; /* # of last request processed by server */
    Bool send_event;      /* True if this came from SendEvent request */
    Display *display;     /* Display the event was read from */
    Drawable drawable;
    int x, y;
    int width, height;
    int count;            /* if nonzero, at least this many more */
    int major_code;       /* core is X_CopyArea or X_CopyPlane */
    int minor_code;       /* not defined in the core */
} XGraphicsExposeEvent;

typedef struct {
    int type;
    unsigned long serial; /* # of last request processed by server */
    Bool send_event;      /* True if this came from SendEvent request */
    Display *display;     /* Display the event was read from */
    Drawable drawable;
    int major_code;       /* core is X_CopyArea or X_CopyPlane */
    int minor_code;       /* not defined in the core */
} XNoExposeEvent;
```

Event Structure Members

drawable   A window or an off-screen pixmap. This specifies the destination of the graphics request that generated the event.

x, y   The coordinates of the upper-left corner of the exposed region relative to the origin of the window.

width, height   The width and height in pixels of the exposed region.

count   The approximate number of remaining contiguous GraphicsExpose events that were generated as a result of the XCopyArea() or XCopy-Plane() call.

major_code   The graphics request used. This may be one of the symbols X_Copy-Area or X_CopyPlane or a symbol defined by a loaded extension. These symbols are defined in *<X11/Xproto.h>*.

minor_code   Zero unless the request is part of an extension.

Notes

Expose events and GraphicsExpose events both indicate the region of a window that was actually exposed (x, y, width, and height). Therefore, they can often be handled similarly.

GravityNotify

When Generated

A `GravityNotify` event reports when a window is moved because of a change in the size of its parent. This happens when the `win_gravity` attribute of the child window is something other than `StaticGravity` or `UnmapGravity`.

Translation Abbreviations

In translation tables, the event type `GravityNotify` may be used, or use the abbreviation `Grav`.

Select With

This event is selected for a single window by specifying the window ID of that window with `StructureNotifyMask`. To receive notification of movement due to gravity for a group of siblings, specify the parent window ID with `SubstructureNotifyMask`.

XEvent Structure Name

```
typedef union _XEvent {
    . . .
    XGravityEvent xgravity;
    . . .
} XEvent;
```

Event Structure

```
typedef struct {
    int type;
    unsigned long serial; /* # of last request processed by server */
    Bool send_event;      /* True if this came from SendEvent request */
    Display *display;      /* Display the event was read from */
    Window event;
    Window window;
    int x, y;
} XGravityEvent;
```

Event Structure Members

`event`   The window that selected the event.

`window`   The window that was moved.

`x, y`   The new coordinates of the window relative to its parent.

KeymapNotify

When Generated

A KeymapNotify event reports the state of the keyboard and occurs when the pointer or keyboard focus enters a window. KeymapNotify events are reported immediately after EnterNotify or FocusIn events. This is a way for the application to read the keyboard state as the application is "woken up," since the two triggering events usually indicate that the application is about to receive user input.

Translation Abbreviations

In translation tables, the event type KeymapNotify may be used, or use the abbreviation Keymap.

Select With

This event is selected with KeymapStateMask.

XEvent Structure Name

```
typedef union _XEvent {
    ...
    XKeymapEvent xkeymap;
    ...
} XEvent;
```

Event Structure

```
typedef struct {
    int type;
    unsigned long serial; /* # of last request processed by server */
    Bool send_event;      /* True if this came from SendEvent request */
    Display *display;      /* Display the event was read from */
    Window window;
    char key_vector[32];
} XKeymapEvent;
```

Event Structure Members

window   Reports the window which was reported in the window member of the preceding EnterNotify or FocusIn event.

key_vector A bit vector or mask, each bit representing one physical key, with a total of 256 bits. For a given key, its keycode is its position in the keyboard vector. You can also get this bit vector by calling XQueryKeymap().

Notes

The serial member of KeymapNotify does not contain the serial number of the most recent Protocol Request processed, because this event always follows immediately after FocusIn or EnterNotify events in which the serial member is valid.

KeyPress, KeyRelease

When Generated

KeyPress and KeyRelease events are generated for all keys, even those mapped to modifier keys such as Shift or Control.

Translation Abbreviations

In translation tables, the event types KeyPress and KeyRelease may be used, or use one of the abbreviations shown in the following table.

Abbreviation	Description
Key	Key pressed.
KeyDown	Key pressed.
Ctrl	KeyPress with Ctrl modifier.
Meta	KeyPress with Meta modifier.
Shift	KeyPress with Shift modifier.
KeyUp	Key released.

To execute an action in response to the press or release of an individual key, you can use any of the above abbreviations in combination with a detail. For example, in the translation:

```
<Key>a:    append()
```

the append action is invoked when the key "a" is pressed, regardless of which modifiers are being held. For more information on how to use translations to manage key events, see Chapter 7, *Events, Translations, and Accelerators*, in Volume Four, *X Toolkit Intrinsics Programming Manual*.

Select With

Each type of keyboard event may be selected separately with KeyPressMask and KeyReleaseMask.

XEvent Structure Name

```
typedef union _XEvent {
    ...
    XKeyEvent xkey;
    ...
} XEvent;
```

Event Structure

```
typedef struct {
    int type;              /* of event */
    unsigned long serial;  /* # of last request processed by server */
    Bool send_event;       /* True if this came from SendEvent request */
    Display *display;      /* Display the event was read from */
    Window window;         /* event window it is reported relative to */
    Window root;           /* root window that the event occurred on */
    Window subwindow;      /* child window */
    Time time;             /* milliseconds */
```

```
    int x, y;                  /* pointer coords relative to receiving window *
    int x_root, y_root;        /* coordinates relative to root */
    unsigned int state;        /* modifier key and button mask */
    unsigned int keycode;      /* server-dependent code for key */
    Bool same_screen;          /* same screen flag */
} XKeyEvent;
typedef XKeyEvent XKeyPressedEvent;
typedef XKeyEvent XKeyReleasedEvent;
```

Event Structure Members

subwindow	If the source window is the child of the receiving window, then the subwindow member is set to the ID of that child.
time	The server time when the button event occurred, in milliseconds. Time is declared as unsigned long, so it wraps around when it reaches the maximum value of a 32-bit number (every 49.7 days).
x, y	If the receiving window is on the same screen as the root window specified by root, then x and y are the pointer coordinates relative to the receiving window's origin. Otherwise, x and y are zero.
	When active button grabs and pointer grabs are in effect (see Volume One, *Xlib Programming Manual*, Section 9.4 and Volume Four, *X Toolkit Intrinsics Programming Manual*, Chapter 12, *Menus, Gadgets, and Cascaded Pop Ups*, Section 12.2.1), the coordinates relative to the receiving window may not be within the window (they may be negative or greater than window height or width).
x_root, y_root	The pointer coordinates relative to the root window which is an ancestor of the event window. If the pointer was on a different screen, these are zero.
state	The state of all the buttons and modifier keys just before the event, represented by a mask of the button and modifier key symbols: Button1Mask, Button2Mask, Button3Mask, Button4Mask, Button5Mask, ShiftMask, ControlMask, LockMask, Mod1-Mask, Mod2Mask, Mod3Mask, Mod4Mask, and Mod5Mask.
keycode	The keycode member contains a server-dependent code for the key that changed state. As such, it should be translated into the portable symbol called a keysym before being used. It can also be converted directly into ASCII with XLookupString(). For a description and examples of how to translate keycodes, see Volume One, Section 9.1.1, and Volume Four, Section 13.4.

Notes

Remember that not all hardware is capable of generating release events and that only the main keyboard (a-z, A-Z, 0-9), Shift, and Control keys are always found.

Keyboard events are analogous to button events, though, of course, there are many more keys than buttons and the keyboard is not automatically grabbed between press and release.

All the structure members have the same meaning as described for `ButtonPress` and `ButtonRelease` events, except that `button` is replaced by `keycode`.

MapNotify, UnmapNotify

When Generated

The X server generates MapNotify and UnmapNotify events when a window changes state from unmapped to mapped or vice versa. In most cases, Xt widgets are mapped in the final step of the process of realizing the application, initiated with XtRealizeWidget().

Translation Abbreviations

In translation tables, the event types MapNotify and UnmapNotify may be used, or use the abbreviations Map or Unmap.

Select With

To receive these events on a single window, use StructureNotifyMask in the call to XSelectInput() for the window. To receive these events for all children of a particular parent, specify the parent window ID and use SubstructureNotifyMask.

XEvent Structure Name

```
typedef union _XEvent {
    . . .
    XMapEvent xmap;
    XUnmapEvent xunmap;
    . . .
} XEvent;
```

Event Structure

```
typedef struct {
    int type;
    unsigned long serial;       /* # of last request processed by server */
    Bool send_event;            /* True if this came from SendEvent request */
    Display *display;           /* Display the event was read from */
    Window event;
    Window window;
    Bool override_redirect;     /* boolean, is override set */
} XMapEvent;

typedef struct {
    int type;
    unsigned long serial;       /* # of last request processed by server */
    Bool send_event;            /* True if this came from SendEvent request */
    Display *display;           /* Display the event was read from */
    Window event;
    Window window;
    Bool from_configure;
} XUnmapEvent;
```

Event Structure Members

event   The window that selected this event.

window   The window that was just mapped or unmapped.

override_redirect (XMapEvent () only)
> True or False. The value of the override_redirect attribute of the
> window that was just mapped.

from_configure (XUnmapEvent () only)
> True If the event was generated as a result of a resizing of the window's parent
> when the window itself had a win_gravity of UnmapGravity. See the
> description of the win_gravity attribute in Volume One, *Xlib Programming
> Manual*, Section 4.3.4. False otherwise.

When Generated

A `MappingNotify` event is sent when any of the following is changed by another client: the mapping between physical keyboard keys (keycodes) and keysyms, the mapping between modifier keys and logical modifiers, or the mapping between physical and logical pointer buttons. These events are triggered by a call to `XSetModifierMapping()` or `XSetPointer-Mapping()`, if the return status is `MappingSuccess`, or by any call to `XChange-KeyboardMapping()`.

This event type should not be confused with the event that occurs when a window is mapped; that is a `MapNotify` event. Nor should it be confused with the `KeymapNotify` event, which reports the state of the keyboard as a mask instead of as a keycode.

Translation Abbreviations

In translation tables, the event type `MappingNotify` may be used, or use the abbreviation `Mapping`. Xt handles `MappingNotify` automatically in most applications.

To detect only one of a modifier, keyboard, and pointer mapping changes, use a translation such as:

```
<Mapping>Pointer: pointerRemap()
```

Where `Pointer` can also be `Modifier` or `Keyboard`.

Select With

The X server sends `MappingNotify` events to all clients. It is never selected and cannot be masked with the window attributes.

XEvent Structure Name

```
typedef union _XEvent {
    ...
    XMappingEvent xmapping;
    ...
} XEvent;
```

Event Structure

```
typedef struct {
    int type;
    unsigned long serial;   /* # of last request processed by server */
    Bool send_event;        /* True if this came from SendEvent request */
    Display *display;       /* Display the event was read from */
    Window window;          /* unused */
    int request;            /* one of MappingModifier, MappingKeyboard,
                             * MappingPointer */
    int first_keycode;      /* first keycode */
    int count;              /* range of change with first_keycode*/
} XMappingEvent;
```

Event Structure Members

request
: The kind of mapping change that occurred: MappingModifier for a successful XSetModifierMapping() (keyboard Shift, Lock, Control, Meta keys), MappingKeyboard for a successful XChangeKeyboardMapping() (other keys), and MappingPointer for a successful XSetPointerMapping() (pointer button numbers).

first_keycode
: If the request member is MappingKeyboard or MappingModifier, then first_keycode indicates the first in a range of keycodes with altered mappings. Otherwise, it is not set.

count
: If the request member is MappingKeyboard or MappingModifier, then count indicates the number of keycodes with altered mappings. Otherwise, it is not set.

Notes

If the request member is MappingKeyboard, clients should call XRefreshKeyboardMapping().

The normal response to a request member of MappingPointer or MappingModifier is no action. This is because the clients should use the logical mapping of the buttons and modifiers to allow the user to customize the keyboard if desired. If the application requires a particular mapping regardless of the user's preferences, it should call XGetModifierMapping() or XGetPointerMapping() to find out about the new mapping.

When Generated

A MapRequest event occurs when the functions XMapRaised() and XMapWindow() are called.

This event differs from MapNotify in that it delivers the parameters of the request before it is carried out. This gives the client that selects this event (usually the window manager) the opportunity to revise the size or position of the window before executing the map request itself or to deny the request. (MapNotify indicates the final outcome of the request.)

Translation Abbreviations

In translation tables, the event type MapRequest may be used, or use the abbreviation MapReq.

Select With

This event is selected by specifying the window ID of the parent of the receiving window with SubstructureRedirectMask. (In addition, the override_redirect member of the XSetWindowAttributes structure for the specified window must be False.)

XEvent Structure Name

```
typedef union _XEvent {
    . . .
    XMapRequestEvent xmaprequest;
    . . .
} XEvent;
```

Event Structure

```
typedef struct {
    int type;
    unsigned long serial; /* # of last request processed by server */
    Bool send_event;      /* True if this came from SendEvent request */
    Display *display;      /* Display the event was read from */
    Window parent;
    Window window;
} XMapRequestEvent;
```

Event Structure Members

parent   The ID of the parent of the window being mapped.

window   The ID of the window being mapped.

When Generated

A `MotionNotify` event reports that the user moved the pointer or that a program warped the pointer to a new position within a single window.

Translation Abbreviations

In translation tables, the event type `MotionNotify` may be used, or use one of the abbreviations shown in the following table.

Abbreviation	Description
Motion	Pointer moved.
PtrMoved	Pointer moved.
MouseMoved	Pointer moved.
BtnMotion	Pointer moved with any button held down.
Btn1Motion	Pointer moved with button 1 held down.
Btn2Motion	Pointer moved with button 2 held down.
Btn3Motion	Pointer moved with button 3 held down.
Btn4Motion	Pointer moved with button 4 held down.
Btn5Motion	Pointer moved with button 5 held down.

To execute an action in response to motion hint events or normal motion events, you can use any of the abbreviations above, together with a detail. For example, in the translation:

```
<Motion>Normal:  allPositions()
```

the `allPositions` action will be called with all the motion events. On the other hand, if you specify:

```
<Motion>Hint:  lastPosition()
```

the `lastPosition` action will be called much less frequently—only when the pointer leaves the window or when a key or button changes state. The default, when you don't specify a detail, is to get normal motion events.

The Core widget field `compress_motion` also determines whether the widget gets all motion events or only periodic position updates. For more information, see Volume Four, *X Toolkit Intrinsics Programming Manual*.

Select With

This event is selected with `PointerMotionMask`, `PointerMotionHintMask`, `ButtonMotionMask`, `Button1MotionMask`, `Button2MotionMask`, `Button3-MotionMask`, `Button4MotionMask`, and `Button5MotionMask`. These masks determine the specific conditions under which the event is generated.

XEvent Structure Name

```
typedef union _XEvent {
    . . .
    XMotionEvent xmotion;
    . . .
} XEvent;
```

Event Structure

```
typedef struct {
    int type;                /* of event */
    unsigned long serial;    /* # of last request processed by server */
    Bool send_event;         /* True if this came from SendEvent request */
    Display *display;        /* Display the event was read from */
    Window window;           /* event window it is reported relative to */
    Window root;             /* root window that the event occurred on */
    Window subwindow;        /* child window */
    Time time;               /* milliseconds */
    int x, y;                /* pointer coords relative to receiving window */
    int x_root, y_root;      /* coordinates relative to root */
    unsigned int state;      /* button and modifier key mask */
    char is_hint;            /* is this a motion hint */
    Bool same_screen;        /* same screen flag */
} XMotionEvent;
typedef XMotionEvent XPointerMovedEvent;
```

Event Structure Members

subwindow
If the source window is the child of the receiving window, then the subwindow member is set to the ID of that child.

time
The server time when the button event occurred, in milliseconds. Time is declared as unsigned long, so it wraps around when it reaches the maximum value of a 32-bit number (every 49.7 days).

x, y
If the receiving window is on the same screen as the root window specified by root, then x and y are the pointer coordinates relative to the receiving window's origin. Otherwise, x and y are zero.

When active button grabs and pointer grabs are in effect (see Section 9.4 in Volume One, *Xlib Programming Manual*, and Section 12.2.1 in Volume Four, *X Toolkit Intrinsics Programming Manual*), the coordinates relative to the receiving window may not be within the window (they may be negative or greater than window height or width).

x_root, y_root
The pointer coordinates relative to the root window which is an ancestor of the event window. If the pointer was on a different screen, these are zero.

state
The state of all the buttons and modifier keys just before the event, represented by a mask of the button and modifier key symbols: Button1Mask, Button2Mask, Button3Mask, Button4Mask, Button5Mask, ShiftMask, ControlMask, LockMask, Mod1-Mask, Mod2Mask, Mod3Mask, Mod4Mask, and Mod5Mask.

is_hint
Either the constant NotifyNormal or NotifyHint. NotifyHint indicates that the PointerMotionHintMask was selected. In this case, just one event is sent when the mouse moves, and the current position can be found by calling XQueryPointer() or by examining the

motion history buffer with XGetMotionEvents(), if a motion history buffer is available on the server. NotifyNormal indicates that the event is real, but it may not be up to date, since there may be many more later motion events on the queue.

same_screen   Indicates whether the pointer is currently on the same screen as this window. This is always True unless the pointer was actively grabbed before the automatic grab could take place.

Notes

If the processing you have to do for every motion event is fast, you can probably handle all of them without requiring motion hints. However, if you have extensive processing to do for each one, you might be better off using the hints and calling XQueryPointer() or using the history buffer if it exists. XQueryPointer() is a round-trip request, so it can be slow.

EnterNotify and LeaveNotify events are generated instead of MotionNotify if the pointer starts and stops in different windows.

PropertyNotify

When Generated

A `PropertyNotify` event indicates that a property of a window has changed or been deleted. This event can also be used to get the current server time (by appending zero-length data to a property). `PropertyNotify` events are generated by `XChangeProperty()`, `XDeleteProperty()`, `XGetWindowProperty()`, or `XRotateWindow-Properties()`.

Translation Abbreviations

In translation tables, the event type `PropertyNotify` may be used, or use the abbreviation `Prop`.

To be notified of a change in a particular property, use the property name as a detail. For example, the translation:

```
<Prop>PRIMARY:    status()
```

results in the `status` action being called when the PRIMARY property (used in selections) is changed.

Select With

This event is selected with `PropertyChangeMask`.

XEvent Structure Name

```
typedef union _XEvent {
    . . .
    XPropertyEvent xproperty;
    . . .
} XEvent;
```

Event Structure

```
typedef struct {
    int type;
    unsigned long serial;    /* # of last request processed by server */
    Bool send_event;         /* True if this came from SendEvent request */
    Display *display;        /* Display the event was read from */
    Window window;
    Atom atom;
    Time time;
    int state;               /* NewValue, Deleted */
} XPropertyEvent;
```

PropertyNotify   *(continued)*

Event Structure Members

window   The window whose property was changed, not the window that selected the event.

atom   The property that was changed.

state   Either `PropertyNewValue` or `PropertyDeleted`. Whether the property was changed to a new value or deleted.

time   The `time` member specifies the server time when the property was changed.

ReparentNotify

When Generated

A ReparentNotify event reports when a client successfully reparents a window.

Translation Abbreviations

In translation tables, the event type ReparentNotify may be used, or use the abbreviation Reparent.

Select With

This event is selected with SubstructureNotifyMask by specifying the window ID of the old or the new parent window or with StructureNotifyMask by specifying the window ID.

XEvent Structure Name

```
typedef union _XEvent {
    ...
    XReparentEvent xreparent;
    ...
} XEvent;
```

Event Structure

```
typedef struct {
    int type;
    unsigned long serial;    /* # of last request processed by server */
    Bool send_event;         /* True if this came from SendEvent request */
    Display *display;        /* Display the event was read from */
    Window event;
    Window window;
    Window parent;
    int x, y;
    Bool override_redirect;
} XReparentEvent;
```

Event Structure Members

window
: The window whose parent window was changed.

parent
: The new parent of the window.

x, y
: The coordinates of the upper-left pixel of the window's border relative to the new parent window's origin.

override_redirect
: The override_redirect attribute of the reparented window. If True, it indicates that the client wants this window to be immune to meddling by the window manager. Window managers normally should not have reparented this window to begin with.

ResizeRequest

When Generated

A `ResizeRequest` event reports another client's attempt to change the size of a window. The X server generates this event type when another client calls `XConfigureWindow()`, `XResizeWindow()`, or `XMoveResizeWindow()`. If this event type is selected, the window is not resized. This gives the client that selects this event (usually the window manager) the opportunity to revise the new size of the window before executing the resize request or to deny the request itself.

Translation Abbreviations

In translation tables, the event type `ResizeRequest` may be used, or use the abbreviation `ResReq`.

Select With

To receive this event type, specify a window ID and pass `ResizeRedirectMask` as part of the `event_mask` argument to `XSelectInput()`. Only one client can select this event on a particular window. When selected, this event is triggered instead of resizing the window.

XEvent Structure Name

```
typedef union _XEvent {
    ...
    XResizeRequestEvent xresizerequest;
    ...
} XEvent;
```

Event Structure

```
typedef struct {
    int type;
    unsigned long serial;   /* # of last request processed by server */
    Bool send_event;        /* True if this came from SendEvent request */
    Display *display;       /* Display the event was read from */
    Window window;
    int width, height;
} XResizeRequestEvent;
```

Event Structure Members

window   The window whose size another client attempted to change.

width, height   The requested size of the window, not including its border.

SelectionClear

When Generated

A SelectionClear event reports to the current owner of a selection that a new owner is being defined.

Translation Abbreviations

In translation tables, use the event type SelectionClear, or use the abbreviation SelClr.

However, all selection events are normally handled automatically by Xt's selection mechanism, and therefore no translations are needed.

When translations are used, the name of the selection property can be specified as a detail (see PropertyNotify).

Select With

This event is not selected. It is sent to the previous selection owner when another client calls XSetSelectionOwner() for the same selection.

XEvent Structure Name

```
typedef union _XEvent {
    . . .
    XSelectionClearEvent xselectionclear;
    . . .
} XEvent;
```

Event Structure

```
typedef struct {
    int type;
    unsigned long serial;   /* # of last request processed by server */
    Bool send_event;        /* TRUE if this came from SendEvent request */
    Display *display;       /* Display the event was read from */
    Window window;
    Atom selection;
    Time time;
} XSelectionClearEvent;
```

Event Structure Members

window   The window that is receiving the event and losing the selection.

selection   The selection atom specifying the selection that is changing ownership.

time   The last-change time recorded for the selection.

SelectionNotify

When Generated

A `SelectionNotify` event is sent only by clients, not by the server, by calling `XSend-Event()`. The owner of a selection sends this event to a requestor (a client that calls `XConvertSelection()` for a given property) when a selection has been converted and stored as a property or when a selection conversion could not be performed (indicated with property `None`).

Translation Abbreviations

In translation tables, use the event type `SelectionNotify`, or its abbreviation `Select`.

However, all selection events are normally handled automatically by Xt's selection mechanism, and therefore no translations are needed.

When translations are used, the name of the selection property can be specified as a detail (see `PropertyNotify`).

Select With

There is no event mask for `SelectionNotify` events, and they are not selected with `XSelectInput()`. Instead `XSendEvent()` directs the event to a specific window, which is given as a window ID: `PointerWindow`, which identifies the window the pointer is in, or `InputFocus`, which identifies the focus window.

XEvent Structure Name

```
typedef union _XEvent {
    . . .
    XSelectionEvent xselection;
    . . .
} XEvent;
```

Event Structure

```
typedef struct {
    int type;
    unsigned long serial;   /* # of last request processed by server */
    Bool send_event;        /* TRUE if this came from SendEvent request */
    Display *display;       /* Display the event was read from */
    Window requestor;
    Atom selection;
    Atom target;
    Atom property;          /* Atom or None */
    Time time;
} XSelectionEvent;
```

Event Structure Members

This structure's mambers have the values specified in the `XConvertSelection()` call that triggers the selection owner to send this event, except that the `property` member either returns the atom specifying a property on the requestor window with the data type specified in `target` or will return `None`, indicating that the data could not be converted into the `target` type.

SelectionRequest

When Generated

A SelectionRequest event is sent to the owner of a selection when another client requests the selection by calling XConvertSelection().

Translation Abbreviations

In translation tables, the event type SelectionRequest may be used, or use the abbreviation SelReq.

However, all selection events are normally handled automatically by Xt's selection mechanism, and therefore no translations are needed.

When translations are used, the name of the selection property can be specified as a detail (see PropertyNotify).

Select With

There is no event mask for SelectionRequest events, and they are not selected with XSelectInput().

XEvent Structure Name

```
typedef union _XEvent {
    ...
    XSelectionRequestEvent xselectionrequest;
    ...
} XEvent;
```

Event Structure

```
typedef struct {
    int type;
    unsigned long serial;  /* # of last request processed by server */
    Bool send_event;       /* TRUE if this came from SendEvent request */
    Display *display;      /* Display the event was read from */
    Window owner;          /* must be next after type */
    Window requestor;
    Atom selection;
    Atom target;
    Atom property;
    Time time;
} XSelectionRequestEvent;
```

Event Structure Members

The members of this structure have the values specified in the XConvertSelection() call that triggers this event.

The owner should convert the selection based on the specified target type, if possible. If a property is specified, the owner should store the result as that property on the requestor window and then send a SelectionNotify event to the requestor by calling XSendEvent(). If the selection cannot be converted as requested, the owner should send a SelectionNotify event with property set to the constant None.

VisibilityNotify

When Generated

A `VisibilityNotify` event reports any change in the visibility of the specified window. This event type is never generated on windows whose class is `InputOnly`. All of the window's subwindows are ignored when calculating the visibility of the window.

Translation Abbreviations

In translation tables, the event type `VisibilityNotify` may be used, or use the abbreviation `Visible`.

Most widgets do not need to provide a translation for this event, because the Core widget field `visible_interest` provides a simplified form of the same information. For more information, see Chapter 8, *More Input Techniques*, in Volume Four, *X Toolkit Intrinsics Programming Manual*.

Select With

This event is selected with `VisibilityChangeMask`.

XEvent Structure Name

```
typedef union _XEvent {
    ...
    XVisibilityEvent xvisibility;
    ...
} XEvent;
```

Event Structure

```
typedef struct {
    int type;
    unsigned long serial;   /* # of last request processed by server */
    Bool send_event;        /* TRUE if this came from SendEvent request */
    Display *display;       /* Display the event was read from */
    Window window;
    int state;
                            /* VisibilityUnobscured, */
                            /* VisibilityPartiallyObscured, or */
                            /* VisibilityFullyObscured */
} XVisibilityEvent;
```

Event Structure Members

state
: A symbol indicating the final visibility status of the window: `Visibility-Unobscured`, `VisibilityPartiallyObscured`, or `Visibility-FullyObscured`.

Notes

Table C-5 lists the transitions that generate `VisibilityNotify` events and the corresponding `state` member of the `XVisibilityEvent` structure.

VisibilityNotify *(continued)*

Table C-5. The State Element of the XVisibilityEvent Structure

Visibility Status Before	Visibility Status After	State Member
Partially obscured, fully obscured, or not viewable.	Viewable and completely unobscured.	`VisibilityUnobscured`
Viewable and completely unobscured, viewable and fully obscured, or not viewable.	Viewable and partially obscured.	`VisibilityPartially-Obscured`
Viewable and completely unobscured, or viewable and partially obscured, or not viewable.	Viewable and partially obscured.	`VisibilityPartially-Obscured`

Intrinsics Error and Warning Messages

The two sections below summarize the common error and warning messages that the Intrinsics can generate. Additional implementation-dependent messages are permitted. The information has this form:

Message Name
Message Type   Default message

Note that many messages have more than one type; however, all Intrinsics errors and warnings have class `XtToolkitError`.

Error Messages

allocError
calloc
malloc   Cannot perform calloc.
realloc   Cannot perform malloc.
                                        Cannot perform realloc.

communicationError
select
                                        Select failed.

internalError
shell
                                        Shell's window manager interaction is broken.

invalidArgCount
xtGetValues
xtSetValues
                                        Argument count > 0 on NULL argument list in XtGetValues.
                                        Argument count > 0 on NULL argument list in XtSetValues.

invalidClass
constraintSetValue
                                        Subclass of Constraint required in CallConstraintSet-Values.
xtAppCreateShell
xtCreatePopupShell   XtAppCreateShell requires non-NULL widget class.
xtCreateWidget   XtCreatePopupShell requires non-NULL widget class.
xtPopdown   XtCreateWidget requires non-NULL widget class.
xtPopup   XtPopdown requires a subclass of shellWidgetClass.
                                        XtPopup requires a subclass of shellWidgetClass.

invalidDimension
  xtCreateWindow
  shellRealize

Widget %s has zero width and/or height.
Shell widget %s has zero width and/or height.

invalidDisplay
  xtInitialize

Cannot open display.

invalidGeometryManager
  xtMakeGeometryRequest

XtMakeGeometryRequest – parent has no geometry manager.

invalidParameter
  removePopupFromParent
  xtAddInput

RemovePopupFromParent requires non-NULL popuplist.
Invalid condition passed to XtAddInput.

invalidParameters
  xtMenuPopupAction

MenuPopup wants exactly one argument.

invalidParent
  realize
  xtCreatePopupShell
  xtCreateWidget
  xtMakeGeometryRequest

  xtMakeGeometryRequest
  xtManageChildren
  xtUnmanageChildren

Application shell is not a windowed widget?
XtCreatePopupShell requires non-NULL parent.
XtCreateWidget requires non-NULL parent.
XtMakeGeometryRequest – NULL parent. Use SetValues instead.
XtMakeGeometryRequest – parent not composite.
Attempt to manage a child when parent is not Composite.
Attempt to unmanage a child when parent is not Composite.

invalidProcedure
  inheritanceProc
  realizeProc

Unresolved inheritance operation.
No realize class procedure defined.

invalidWindow
  eventHandler

Event with wrong window.

missingEvent
  shell

Events are disappearing from under Shell.

noAppContext
  widgetToApplication-
    Context

Couldn't find ancestor with display information.

noPerDisplay
  closeDisplay
  getPerDisplay

Couldn't find per display information.
Couldn't find per display information.

noSelectionProperties
  freeSelectionProperty

Internal error: no selection property context for display.

nullProc
  insertChild

NULL insert_child procedure.

subclassMismatch
  xtCheckSubclass

Widget class %s found when subclass of %s expected: %s.

translationError

merginTablesWithCycles — *Trying to merge translation tables with cycles, and cannot resolve this cycle.*

Warning Messages

ambigiousParent

xtManageChildren
xtUnmanageChildren

Not all children have same parent in XtManageChildren.
Not all children have same parent in XtUnmanageChildren.

communicationError

windowManager

Window Manager is confused.

conversionError

string

Cannot convert string "%s" to type %s.

displayError

invalidDisplay

Cannot find display structure.

grabError

grabDestroyCallback

XtAddGrab *requires exclusive grab if* spring_loaded *is* TRUE.

grabDestroyCallback

XtAddGrab *requires exclusive grab if* spring_loaded *is* TRUE.

xtRemoveGrab

XtRemoveGrab *asked to remove a widget not on the grab list.*

initializationError

xtInitialize

Initializing Resource Lists twice.

invalidArgCount

getResources

Argument count > 0 on NULL *argument list.*

invalidCallbackList

xtAddCallbacks
xtCallCallback
xtOverrideCallback
xtRemoveAllCallback
xtRemoveCallbacks

Cannot find callback list in XtAddCallbacks.
Cannot find callback list in XtCallCallbacks.
Cannot find callback list in XtOverrideCallbacks.
Cannot find callback list in XtRemoveAllCallbacks.
Cannot find callback list in XtRemoveCallbacks.

invalidChild

xtManageChildren
xtUnmanageChildren

NULL *child passed to* XtManageChildren.
NULL *child passed to* XtUnmanageChildren.

invalidDepth

setValues

Cannot change widget depth.

invalidGeometry

xtMakeGeometryRequest

Shell subclass did not take care of geometry in XtSetValues.

invalidParameters

compileAccelerators
compileTranslations

String to AcceleratorTable *needs no extra arguments.*
String to TranslationTable *needs no extra arguments.*

| mergeTranslations | MergeTM to TranslationTable needs no extra arguments. |
| xtMenuPopdown | XtMenuPopdown called with num_params != 0 or 1. |

invalidParent
xtCopyFromParent

CopyFromParent must have non-NULL parent.

invalidPopup
unsupportedOperation

Popup menu creation is only supported on ButtonPress or EnterNotify events.

xtMenuPopup

Cannot find pop up in _XtMenuPopup.

xtMenuPopdown

Cannot find pop up in _XtMenuPopdown.

invalidProcedure
deleteChild

NULL delete_child procedure in XtDestroy.

inputHandler

XtRemoveInput: Input handler not found.

set_values_almost

set_values_almost procedure shouldn't be NULL.

invalidResourceCount
getResources

Resource count > 0 on NULL resource list.

invalidResourceName
computeArgs

Cannot find resource name %s as argument to conversion.

invalidShell
xtTranslateCoords

Widget has no shell ancestor.

invalidSizeOverride
xtDependencies

Representation size %d must match superclass's to override %s.

invalidTypeOverride
xtDependencies

Representation type %s must match superclass's to override %s.

invalidWidget
removePopupFromParent

Widget not on parent list.

missingCharsetList
cvtStringToFontSet

Missing charsets in String to FontSet conversion.

noColormap
cvtStringToPixel

Cannot allocate colormap entry for "%s".

registerWindowError
xtRegisterWindow

Attempt to change already registered window.

xtUnregisterWindow

Attempt to unregister invalid window.

translation error
nullTable

Cannot remove accelerators from NULL table.

nullTable

Tried to remove non-existant accelerators.

translationError
ambiguousActions

Overriding earlier translation manager actions.

mergingNullTable

Old translation table was null, cannot modify.

nullTable

Cannot translate event through NULL table.

`unboundActions`	Actions not found: %s.
`xtTranslateInitialize`	Initializing Translation manager twice.

translationParseError

`showLine`	... found while parsing "%s".
`parseError`	Translation table syntax error: %s.
`parseString`	Missing "\".

typeConversionError

`noConverter`	No type converter registered for "%s" to "%s" conversion.

versionMismatch

`widget`	Widget class %s version mismatch: widget %d vs. intrinsics %d.

wrongParameters

`cvtIntOrPixelToXColor`	Pixel-to-color conversion needs screen and colormap arguments.
`cvtIntToBool`	Integer-to-Bool conversion needs no extra arguments.
`cvtIntToBoolean`	Integer-to-Boolean conversion needs no extra arguments.
`cvtIntToFont`	Integer-to-Font conversion needs no extra arguments.
`cvtIntToPixel`	Integer-to-Pixel conversion needs no extra arguments.
`cvtIntToPixmap`	Integer-to-Pixmap conversion needs no extra arguments.
`cvtIntToShort`	Integer-to-Short conversion needs no extra arguments.
`cvtStringToBool`	String-to-Bool conversion needs no extra arguments.
`cvtStringToBoolean`	String-to-Boolean conversion needs no extra arguments.
`cvtStringToCursor`	String-to-cursor conversion needs screen argument.
`cvtStringToDisplay`	String-to-Display conversion needs no extra arguments.
`cvtStringToFile`	String-to-File conversion needs no extra arguments.
`cvtStringToFont`	String-to-font conversion needs screen argument.
`cvtStringToFontSet`	String-to-FontSet conversion needs screen argument.
`cvtStringToFontStruct`	String-to-cursor conversion needs screen argument.
`cvtStringToInt`	String to Integer conversion needs no extra arguments.
`cvtStringToPixel`	String-to-pixel conversion needs screen and colormap arguments.
`cvtStringToShort`	String-to-Integer conversion needs no extra arguments.
`cvtStringToUnsignedChar`	String-to-Integer conversion needs no extra arguments.
`cvtXColorToPixel`	Color-to-Pixel conversion needs no extra arguments.

E
Resource File Format

A resource file contains text representing the default resource values for an application or set of applications.

The format of resource files is defined in *Xlib – C Language X Interface* and is reproduced here for convenience only.

The format of a resource specification is:

ResourceLine	Comment | IncludeFile | ResourceSpec | <empty line>
Comment	"!" {<any character except null or newline>}
IncludeFile	"#" WhiteSpace "include" WhiteSpace FileName WhiteSpace
FileName	<valid filename for operating system>
ResourceSpec	WhiteSpace ResourceName WhiteSpace ":" WhiteSpace Value
ResourceName	[Binding] {Component Binding} ComponentName
Binding	"." | "*"
WhiteSpace	{<space> | <horizontal tab>}
Component	"?" | ComponentName
ComponentName	NameChar {NameChar}
NameChar	"a"-"z" | "A"-"Z" | "0"-"9" | "_" | "-"
Value	{<any character except null or unescaped newline>}

Elements separated by vertical bar (|) are alternatives. Curly braces ({...}) indicate zero or more repetitions of the enclosed elements. Square brackets ([...]) indicate that the enclosed element is optional. Quotes ("...") are used around literal characters.

If the last character on a line is a backslash (\), that line is assumed to continue on the next line.

To allow a Value to begin with whitespace, the two-character sequence "*space*" (backslash followed by space) is recognized and replaced by a space character, and the two-character sequence "*tab*" (backslash followed by horizontal tab) is recognized and replaced by a horizontal tab character.

To allow a Value to contain embedded newline characters, the two-character sequence "\n" is recognized and replaced by a newline character. To allow a Value to be broken across multiple lines in a text file, the two-character sequence "*newline*" (backslash followed by newline) is recognized and removed from the value.

To allow a Value to contain arbitrary character codes, the four-character sequence "\nnn", where each n is a digit character in the range of "0"–"7", is recognized and replaced with a single byte that contains the octal value specified by the sequence. Finally, the two-character sequence "\\" is recognized and replaced with a single backslash.

F
Translation Table Syntax

Notation

Syntax is specified in EBNF notation with the following conventions:

[a]	Means either nothing or "a"
{ a }	Means zero or more occurrences of "a"
(a | b)	Means either "a" or "b"
\n	Is the newline character

All terminals are enclosed in double quotation marks (" "). Informal descriptions are enclosed in angle brackets (< >).

Syntax

The translation table has the following syntax:

translationTable	= [directive] { production }
directive	= { "#replace" | "#override" | "#augment" } "\n"
production	= lhs ":" rhs "\n"
lhs	= (event | keyseq) { "," (event | keyseq) }
keyseq	= """ keychar {keychar} """
keychar	= ["^" | "$" | "\"] <ISO Latin 1 character>
event	= [modifier_list] "<"event_type">" ["(" count["+"] ")"] {detail}
modifier_list	= (["!"] [":"] {modifier}) | "None"
modifier	= ["~"] modifier_name
count	= ("1" | "2" | "3" | "4" | ...)
modifier_name	= "@" <keysym> | <see ModifierNames table below>
event_type	= <see Event Types table below>
detail	= <event specific details>
rhs	= { name "(" [params] ")" }
name	= namechar { namechar }
namechar	= ("a"-"z" | "A"-"Z" | "0"-"9" | "_" | "-")
params	= string {"," string}.

string	= quoted_string | unquoted_string
quoted_string	= """ {<Latin 1 character> | escape_char} ["\\"] """
escape_char	= "\""
unquoted_string	= {<Latin 1 character except space, tab, ",", \n, ")">}

The *params* field is parsed into a list of `String` values that will be passed to the named action procedure. A *quoted string* may contain an embedded quotation mark if the quotation mark is preceded by a single backslash (\). The three-character sequence "\"" is interpreted as "single backslash followed by end-of-string"

Modifier Names

The modifier field is used to specify standard X keyboard and button modifier mask bits. Modifiers are legal on event types `KeyPress`, `KeyRelease`, `ButtonPress`, `ButtonRelease`, `MotionNotify`, `EnterNotify`, `LeaveNotify`, and their abbreviations; however, parsing a translation table that contains modifiers for any other events generates an error.

- If the modifier list has no entries and is not `None`, it means "don't care" on all modifiers.

- If an exclamation point (!) is specified at the beginning of the modifier list, it means that the listed modifiers must be in the correct state and no other modifiers can be asserted.

- If any modifiers are specified and an exclamation point (!) is not specified, it means that the listed modifiers must be in the correct state and "don't care" about any other modifiers.

- If a modifier is preceded by a tilde (˜), it means that that modifier must not be asserted.

- If `None` is specified, it means no modifiers can be asserted.

- If a colon (:) is specified at the beginning of the modifier list, it directs the Intrinsics to apply any standard modifiers in the event to map the event KeyCode into a KeySym. The default standard modifiers are Shift and Lock, with the interpretation as defined in Volume Zero, *X Protocol Reference Manual*. The resulting KeySym must exactly match the specified KeySym, and the non-standard modifiers in the event must match the modifier_list. For example, `:<Key>a` is distinct from `:<Key>A`, and `:Shift<Key>A` is distinct from `:<Key>A`.

- If both an exclamation point (!) and a colon (:) are specified at the beginning of the modifier list, it means that the listed modifiers must be in the correct state and that no other modifiers except the standard modifiers can be asserted. Any standard modifiers in the event are applied as for colon (:) above.

- If a colon (:) is not specified, no standard modifiers are applied. Then, for example, "<Key>A" and "<Key>a" are equivalent.

In key sequences, a circumflex (^) is an abbreviation for the Control modifier, a dollar sign ($) is an abbreviation for Meta, and a backslash (\) can be used to quote any character, in particular a double quote ("), a circumflex (^), a dollar sign ($), and another backslash (\).

Briefly:

No modifiers:	None <event> detail
Any modifiers:	<event> detail
Only these modifiers:	! mod1 mod2 <event> detail
These modifiers and any others:	mod1 mod2 <event> detail

The use of `None` for a `modifier_list` is identical to the use of an exclamation point with no modifers.

Table F-1. Modifier Keys

Modifier	Abbreviation	Meaning
Ctrl	c	Control modifier bit.
Shift	s	Shift modifier bit.
Lock	l	Lock modifier bit.
Meta	m	Meta key modifier.
Hyper	h	Hyper key modifier.
Super	su	Super key modifier.
Alt	a	Alt key modifier.
Mod1		Mod1 modifier bit.
Mod2		Mod2 modifier bit.
Mod3		Mod3 modifier bit.
Mod4		Mod4 modifier bit.
Mod5		Mod5 modifier bit.
Button1		Button1 modifier bit.
Button2		Button2 modifier bit.
Button3		Button3 modifier bit.
Button4		Button4 modifier bit.
Button5		Button5 modifier bit.
None		No modifiers.
Any		Any modifier combination.

A key modifier is any modifier bit one of whose corresponding KeyCodes contains the corresponding left or right KeySym. For example, *m* or *Meta* means any modifier bit mapping to a KeyCode whose KeySym list contains `XK_Meta_L` or `XK_Meta_R`. Note that this interpretation is for each display, not global or even for each application context. The Control, Shift, and Lock modifier names refer explicitly to the corresponding modifier bits; there is no additional interpretation of KeySyms for these modifiers.

Because it is possible to associate arbitrary KeySyms with modifiers, the set of modifier key modifiers is extensible. The "@" <KeySym> syntax means any modifier bit whose corresponding KeyCode contains the specified KeySym name.

A `modifier_list`/KeySym combination in a translation matches a modifiers/KeyCode combination in an event in the following ways:

- If a colon (:) is used, the Intrinsics call the display's XtKeyProc with the KeyCode and modifiers. In order to match, the value of:

  (modifiers & ~modifiers_return)

  must equal modifier_list, and keysym_return must equal the given KeySym.

- If (:) is not used, the Intrinsics mask off all "don't care" bits from the modifiers. This value must be equal to modifier_list. Then, for each possible combination of "don't care" modifiers in the modifier list, the Intrinsics call the display's XtKeyProc with the KeyCode and that combination ORed with the cared-about modifier bits from the event. keysym_return must match the KeySym in the translation.

Event Types

The event type field describes XEvent types. In addition to the standard Xlib symbolic event type names, the following event type synonyms are defined:

Table F-2. EventType Values

Type	Meaning
Key	KeyPress
KeyDown	KeyPress
KeyUp	KeyRelease
BtnDown	ButtonPress
BtnUp	ButtonRelease
Motion	MotionNotify
PtrMoved	MotionNotify
MouseMoved	MotionNotify
Enter	EnterNotify
EnterWindow	EnterNotify
Leave	LeaveNotify
LeaveWindow	LeaveNotify
FocusIn	FocusIn
FocusOut	FocusOut
Keymap	KeymapNotify
Expose	Expose
GrExp	GraphicsExpose
NoExp	NoExpose
Visible	VisibilityNotify
Create	CreateNotify
Destroy	DestroyNotify
Unmap	UnmapNotify
Map	MapNotify
MapReq	MapRequest
Reparent	ReparentNotify
Configure	ConfigureNotify
ConfigureReq	ConfigureRequest

Type	Meaning
Grav	GravityNotify
ResReq	ResizeRequest
Circ	CirculateNotify
CircReq	CirculateRequest
Prop	PropertyNotify
SelClr	SelectionClear
SelReq	SelectionRequest
Select	SelectionNotify
Clrmap	ColormapNotify
Message	ClientMessage
Mapping	MappingNotify

The supported abbreviations are listed in Table F-3.

Table F-3. Modifier Key Abbreviations

Abbreviation	Meaning
Ctrl	KeyPress with Control modifier.
Meta	KeyPress with Meta modifier.
Shift	KeyPress with Shift modifier.
Btn1Down	ButtonPress with Button1 detail.
Btn1Up	ButtonRelease with Button1 detail.
Btn2Down	ButtonPress with Button2 detail.
Btn2Up	ButtonRelease with Button2 detail.
Btn3Down	ButtonPress with Button3 detail.
Btn3Up	ButtonRelease with Button3 detail.
Btn4Down	ButtonPress with Button4 detail.
Btn4Up	ButtonRelease with Button4 detail.
Btn5Down	ButtonPress with Button5 detail.
Btn5Up	ButtonRelease with Button5 detail.
BtnMotion	MotionNotify with any button modifier.
Btn1Motion	MotionNotify with Button1 modifier.
Btn2Motion	MotionNotify with Button2 modifier.
Btn3Motion	MotionNotify with Button3 modifier.
Btn4Motion	MotionNotify with Button4 modifier.
Btn5Motion	MotionNotify with Button5 modifier.

The detail field is event-specific and normally corresponds to the detail field of the corresponding event as described by the X Protocol specification. The detail field is supported for the following event types:

Table F-4. Event Types That Support a detail Field

Event	Event Field
KeyPress	KeySym from event detail (KeyCode).
KeyRelease	KeySym from event detail (KeyCode).
ButtonPress	button from event detail.
ButtonRelease	button from event detail.
MotionNotify	event detail.
EnterNotify	event mode (not detail).
LeaveNotify	event mode (not detail).
FocusIn	event mode (not detail).
FocusOut	event mode (not detail).
PropertyNotify	atom.
SelectionClear	selection.
SelectionRequest	selection.
SelectionNotify	selection.
ClientMessage	type.
MappingNotify	request.

If the event type is KeyPress or KeyRelease, the detail field specifies a KeySym name in standard format that is matched against the event as described above; for example, <Key>A.

For the events PropertyNotify, SelectionClear, SelectionRequest, SelectionNotify, and ClientMessage, the detail field is specified as an atom name; for example, <Message>WM_PROTOCOLS. For the events MotionNotify, EnterNotify, LeaveNotify, FocusIn, FocusOut, and MappingNotify, either the symbolic constants as defined by the X Protocol specification or the numeric values may be specified.

If no detail field is specified, then any value in the event detail is accepted as a match.

A KeySym can be specified as any of the standard KeySym names, a hexadecimal number prefixed with *0x* or *0X*, an octal number prefixed with *0*, or a decimal number. A KeySym expressed as a single digit is interpreted as the corresponding Latin 1 KeySym. For example, *0* is the KeySym XK_0. Other single character KeySyms are treated as literal constants from Latin 1, for example, *!* is treated as 0x21. Standard KeySym names are as defined in *<X11/keysymdef.h>* with the XK_ prefix removed. (See Appendix H, *Keysyms*, in Volume Two, *Xlib Reference Manual*.)

Canonical Representation

Every translation table has a unique, canonical text representation. This representation is passed to a widget's `display_accelerator()` procedure to describe the accelerators installed on that widget. The table below shows the canonical representation of a translation table. (See also the section on "Syntax" earlier in this appendix.)

translationTable	= { production }
production	= lhs ":" rhs "\n"
lhs	= event { "," event }
event	= [modifier_list] "<"event_type">" ["(" count["+"] ")"] {detail}
modifier_list	= ["!"] [":"] {modifier}
modifier	= ["~"] modifier_name
count	= ("1" | "2" | "3" | "4" | ...)
modifier_name	= "@" <keysym> | <see canonical modifier names below>
event_type	= <see canonical event types below>
detail	= <event specific details>
rhs	= { name "(" [params] ")" }
name	= namechar { namechar }
namechar	= { "a"-"z" | "A"-"Z" | "0"-"9" | "_" | "-" }
params	= string {"," string}.
string	= quoted_string
quoted_string	= """ {<Latin 1 character> | escape_char} ["\\"] """
escape_char	= \"

The canonical modifier names are:

Button1	Mod1	Ctrl
Button2	Mod2	Shift
Button3	Mod3	Lock
Button4	Mod4	
Button5	Mod5	

The canonical event types are:

ButtonPress	DestroyNotify	KeyPress	PropertyNotify
ButtonRelease	EnterNotify	KeyRelease	ReparentNotify
CirculateNotify	Expose	LeaveNotify	ResizeRequest
CirculateRequest	FocusIn	MapNotify	SelectionClear
ClientMessage	FocusOut	MappingNotify	SelectionNotify
ColormapNotify	GraphicsExpose	MapRequest	SelectionRequest
ConfigureNotify	GravityNotify	MotionNotify	UnmapNotify
ConfigureRequest	KeymapNotify	NoExpose	VisibilityNotify
CreateNotify			

Examples

- Always put more specific events in the table before more general ones:

```
Shift <Btn1Down> : twas()\n\
<Btn1Down> : brillig()
```

- For double-click on Button1 up with Shift, use this specification:

```
Shift<Btn1Up>(2) : and()
```

This is equivalent to the following line with appropriate timers set between events:

```
Shift<Btn1Down>,Shift<Btn1Up>,Shift<Btn1Down>,Shift<Btn1Up> : and()
```

- For double-click on Button1 down with Shift, use this specification:

```
Shift<Btn1Down>(2) : the()
```

This is equivalent to the following line with appropriate timers set between events:

```
Shift<Btn1Down>,Shift<Btn1Up>,Shift<Btn1Down> : the()
```

- Mouse motion is always discarded when it occurs between events in a table where no motion event is specified:

```
<Btn1Down>,<Btn1Up> : slithy()
```

This is taken, even if the pointer moves a bit between the down and up events. Similarly, any motion event specified in a translation matches any number of motion events. If the motion event causes an action procedure to be invoked, the procedure is invoked after each motion event.

- If an event sequence consists of a sequence of events that is also a noninitial subsequence of another translation, it is not taken if it occurs in the context of the longer sequence. This occurs mostly in sequences like the following:

```
<Btn1Down>,<Btn1Up> : toves()\n\
<Btn1Up> : did()
```

The second translation is taken only if the button release is not preceded by a button press or if there are intervening events between the press and the release. Be particularly aware of this when using the repeat notation, above, with buttons and keys because their expansion includes additional events, and when specifying motion events because they are implicitly included between any two other events. In particular, pointer motion and double-click translations cannot coexist in the same translation table.

- For single click on Button1 up with Shift and Meta, use this specification:

```
Shift Meta <Btn1Down>, Shift Meta<Btn1Up>: gyre()
```

- For multiple clicks greater than or equal to a minimum number n, a plus sign (+) may be appended to the final (rightmost) count in an event sequence. The actions will be invoked on the nth click and on each subsequent click arriving within the multi-click time interval. For example:

```
Shift <Btn1Up>(2+) : and()
```

- To indicate `EnterNotify` with any modifiers, use this specification:

  ```
  <Enter> : gimble()
  ```

- To indicate `EnterNotify` with no modifiers, use this specification:

  ```
  None <Enter> : in()
  ```

- To indicate `EnterNotify` with Button1 down and Button2 up and "don't care" about the other modifiers, use this specification:

  ```
  Button1 ~Button2 <Enter> : the()
  ```

- To indicate `EnterNotify` with Button1 down and Button2 down exclusively, use this specification:

  ```
  ! Button1 Button2 <Enter> : wabe()
  ```

You do not need to use a tilde (~) with an exclamation point (!).

Defined Strings

This appendix lists the contents of the *StringDefs.h* header file. The contents are classified by resource names, class types, representation types, and constants. In all cases, the value of each symbol is a character string identical to the symbol except without the XtN, XtC, XtR, or XtE prefix.

Table G-1. Resource Names

XtNaccelerators	XtNmenuEntry
XtNallowHoriz	XtNname
XtNallowVert	XtNnotify
XtNancestorSensitive	XtNnumChildren
XtNbackground	XtNorientation
XtNbackgroundPixmap	XtNparameter
XtNbitmap	XtNpixmap
XtNborderColor	XtNpopupCallback
XtNborder	XtNpopdownCallback
XtNborderPixmap	XtNresize
XtNborderWidth	XtNreverseVideo
XtNcallback	XtNscreen
XtNchildren	XtNscrollProc
XtNcolormap	XtNscrollDCursor
XtNdepth	XtNscrollHCursor
XtNdestroyCallback	XtNscrollLCursor
XtNeditType	XtNscrollRCursor
XtNfile	XtNscrollUCursor
XtNfont	XtNscrollVCursor
XtNfontSet	XtNselection
XtNforceBars	XtNselectionArray
XtNforeground	XtNsensitive
XtNfunction	XtNshown
XtNheight	XtNspace
XtNhighlight	XtNstring
XtNhSpace	XtNtextOptions
XtNindex	XtNtextSink

XtNinitialResourcesPersistent	XtNtextSource
XtNinnerHeight	XtNthickness
XtNinnerWidth	XtNthumb
XtNinnerWindow	XtNthumbProc
XtNinsertPosition	XtNtop
XtNinternalHeight	XtNtranslations
XtNinternalWidth	XtNunrealizeCallback
XtNjumpProc	XtNupdate
XtNjustify	XtNuseBottom
XtNknobHeight	XtNuseRight
XtNknobIndent	XtNvalue
XtNknobPixel	XtNvSpace
XtNknobWidth	XtNwidth
XtNlabel	XtNwindow
XtNlength	XtNx
XtNlowerRight	XtNy
XtNmappedWhenManaged	

Table G-2. Class Types

XtCAccelerators	XtCOrientation
XtCBackground	XtCParameter
XtCBitmap	XtCPixmap
XtCBoolean	XtCPosition
XtCBorderColor	XtCReadOnly
XtCBorderWidth	XtCResize
XtCCallback	XtCReverseVideo
XtCColormap	XtCScreen
XtCColor	XtCScrollProc
XtCCursor	XtCScrollDCursor
XtCDepth	XtCScrollHCursor
XtCEditType	XtCScrollLCursor
XtCEventBindings	XtCScrollRCursor
XtCFile	XtCScrollUCursor
XtCFont	XtCScrollVCursor
XtCFontSet	XtCSelection
XtCForeground	XtCSensitive
XtCFraction	XtCSelectionArray
XtCFunction	XtCSpace
XtCHeight	XtCString
XtCHSpace	XtCTextOptions
XtCIndex	XtCTextPosition
XtCInitialResourcesPersistent	XtCTextSink

Table G-2. Class Types (continued)

XtCInsertPosition	XtCTextSource
XtCInterval	XtCThickness
XtCJustify	XtCThumb
XtCKnobIndent	XtCTranslations
XtCKnobPixel	XtCValue
XtCLabel	XtCVSpace
XtCLength	XtCWidth
XtCMappedWhenManaged	XtCWindow
XtCMargin	XtCX
XtCMenuEntry	XtCY
XtCNotify	

Table G-3. Representation Types

XtRAcceleratorTable	XtRInitialState
XtRAtom	XtRInt
XtRBitmap	XtRJustify
XtRBool	XtRLongBoolean
XtRBoolean	XtRObject
XtRCallback	XtROrientation
XtRCallProc	XtRPixel
XtRCardinal	XtRPixmap
XtRColor	XtRPointer
XtRColormap	XtRPosition
XtRCursor	XtRScreen
XtRDimension	XtRShort
XtRDisplay	XtRString
XtREditMode	XtRStringArray
XtREnum	XtRStringTable
XtRFile	XtRUnsignedChar
XtRFloat	XtRTranslationTable
XtRFont	XtRVisual
XtRFontSet	XtRWidget
XtRFontStruct	XtRWidgetClass
XtRFunction	XtRWidgetList
XtRGeometry	XtRWindow
XtRImmediate	

Boolean Enumeration:
  XtEoff
  XtEfalse
  XtEno
  XtEon
  XtEtrue
  XtEyes

Orientation Enumeration:
  XtEvertical
  XtEhorizontal

Text Edit Enumeration:
  XtEtextRead
  XtEtextAppend
  XtEtextEdit

Color Enumeration:
  XtExtdefaultbackground
  XtExtdefaultforeground

Font:
  XtExtdefaultfont

Changes Between
Release 4 and Release 5

This appendix summarizes the changes to Xt and related libraries between Release 4 and Release 5.

Determining Release Level

The file *<X11/Intrinsic.h>* defines the symbol `XtSpecificationRelease`. In Release 4, this symbol had the value 4, and in Release 5, it has the value 5. You can use it in C preprocessor directives to conditionally compile code that depends on a particular release of Xt.

New Functions

There are four new Xt functions in Release 5. They are `XtAllocateGC()`, `XtGet-ActionList()`, `XtScreenDatabase()`, and `XtSetLanguageProc()`. These new functions are documented in Section 1 of this book. There is also one new prototype procedure defined: `XtLanguageProc()`. It is documented in Section 2.

Changed Arguments

The functions `XtAppInitialize()`, `XtVaAppInitialize()`, `XtOpenDisplay()`, `XtDisplayInitialize()`, and `XtInitialize()` all require a pointer to a number of command-line arguments (i.e., `&argc`). In X11R4 these functions expected this argument to be of type `Cardinal *` which, to guarantee portability, required an annoying typecast: `(Cardinal *)&argc`. In X11R5, these functions were changed to expect an argument of type `int *`. This does not affect the binary compatibility of clients, but programs which perform the explicit cast to `Cardinal *` will need to be changed to avoid compilation warnings with the X11R5 Xt header files. The `Cardinal *` type continues to be used in a number of places, including the `XtAppErrorMsg()` and `XtAppWarningMsg()` functions, type converter functions, and the `initialize` and `set_values` widget methods.

Resource Handling

The most significant changes to Xt in Release 5 all have to do with the handling of resources and the resource database.

There are a number of new Xrm functions in the Xlib library. In addition, the resource file syntax has been extended to support a '?' wildcard character and a #include directive. See the Third Edition of Volume One, *Xlib Programming Manual* for details.

In X11R5, the Intrinsics read the customization resource from the database or the -customization command-line argument, and use its value when determining which app-defaults files to read for an application. See XtDisplayInitialize() in Section 1 for more information.

In X11R5, Xt builds a separate resource database for each screen of a display. This means that an application that opens windows on two different screens can get different resources for them; this is important if, for example, one screen is color and one is monochrome. The new function XtScreenDatabase() returns the resource database for a specified screen. See XtDisplayInitialize() in Section 1 for more information on how the resource database is built for a screen.

The X11R5 Resource Manager supports a new function XrmPermStringToQuark() which creates an XrmQuark without copying the source string. To allow Xt to take advantage of the memory savings possible through this function, the Xt specification has been changed to require that the strings used for resource and constraint resource names, classes, and types all be permanent strings (i.e. they must be string constants, or at least must not be modified or freed during the lifetime of the application). The strings used for widget class names and action procedure names must also be permanently allocated.

The algorithm for building the resource database for an application has been substantially changed to accomodate internationalization and the new customization resource. See XtDisplayInitialize() in Section 1 for a detailed description of the new algorithm.

The XtNbaseTranslations Resource

In Release 5, the Xt Intrinsics determine the translations for a widget by merging the default translations of the widget class with the new XtNbaseTranslations resource and the standard XtNtranslations resource. This new XtNbaseTranslations resource is intended to give application programmers a way to customize a widget's default translations without making it difficult for a user to customize the application's default translations.

Note that this new resource is handled internally by the Intrinsics and does not correspond to any actual widget field. See Chapter 10 of Volume Four, *X Toolkit Intrinsics Programming Manual* for more information.

Internationalization

There were many changes in Release 5 at the Xlib level for internationalization. In the X Toolkit, however, there is only one function for internationalization. `XtSetLanguage-Proc()` is called to set the function that sets the locale when an application starts up. It is documented in Section 1. Most internationalized applications applications should call it just before `XtAppInitialize()`, using three `NULL` arguments. This instructs Xt to use the default locale-setting function.

Implementation Changes

Prior to X11R5, the Xt string constants (the `XtN`, `XtC`, and `XtR` names) were macros for constant strings. With many compilers, each occurrence of a constant string is compiled into the object file, even when there are multiple instances of the same string. In the X11R5 MIT implementation of Xt, these macros have been changed to pointers into a single large array of characters (with embedded null characters dividing the array into individual strings). Under this new scheme, all of the Xt strings are embedded in every application once, but none more than once. Since these strings are almost always used anyway, this results in an overall memory savings.

A common problem resulting from this change occurs if you compile a program using the X11R5 header files and link with the X11R4 libraries. If you do this, your linker will complain that the symbols `XtStrings` and `XtShellStrings` are undefined.

The Translation Manager was completely reimplemented. The new version is significantly smaller and more efficient.

Prior to X11R5, the MIT implementation of *<X11/Intrinsic.h>* included the file *<X11/Xos.h>*. This inclusion was a violation of the specification, and the file is no longer included. *<X11/Xos.h>* defines System V and BSD-style string indexing functions (`index` and `strchr`), includes the appropriate time-handling header file, and hides other, more obscure, operating system dependencies. The most likely problem to result from this change in *<X11/Intrinsic.h>* is that programs that unknowingly relied on macro definitions of `index` or `strchr` from *<X11/Xos.h>* will now fail to compile. These programs may be compiled with the `-DXT_BC` flag which will restore the pre-X11R5 behavior.

Substantial effort has been put into the MIT X11R5 implementation to make it comply with ANSI-C and POSIX standards. All references to the type `caddr_t` have been changed to `XtPointer` because `caddr_t` is not part of the ANSI-C standard.

New standard header files have been defined that make it easier to write portable X applications. They are *<X11/Xfuncs.h>*, *<X11/Xfuncproto.h>*, and *<X11/Xosdefs.h>*. See the Third Edition of Volume One, *Xlib Programming Manual* for more information on these files.

New Widgets

There are four new widgets in the Xaw widget library: Panner, Porthole, Repeater, and Tree. They are documented in Section 5.

New Xmu Converters

The Xmu library contains several new type converter functions in Release 5 that will be useful to Xt programmers. They are `XmuCvtStringToColorCursor()`, `XmuCvtStringToGravity()`, and `XmuNewCvtStringToWidget()`. They are documented in Section 6.

Editres

There is a new client, *editres*, which allows a user or programmer to interactively edit the widget resources of any running application that participates in the Editres protocol. The default VendorShell widget registers an event handler procedure that understands this protocol and will communicate with the `editres` client. This even handler, `_XEditRes-CheckMessages()`, is part of the Xmu library; you can register it explicitly when programming with Motif or other widget sets that do not register it by default. See Section 6 of this book for documentation of the Xmu function, and Chapter 14 of Volume Four, *X Toolkit Intrinsics Programming Manual* for more information on the *editres* client.

Index

Index

events (cont'd)
VisibilityNotify, 859-860
XEvent, union, 805
XtAppNextEvent, 101
XtAppPending, 103, 301
(see also expose.)
expose, Expose events, 59
exposure, XtAddExposureToRegion, 59
method, 561-566
Expose event, 828-829

F

fatal error, (see error)
files
file input, registering file, 77-78
searching for, 182
FocusIn event, 830-835
FocusOut event, 830-835
font conventions, in this book, xi
Form widget, 631-634
child resources, 632
resources, 631-632
freeing storage block, (see storage block)
function pointers, converting to an
XtCallbackList, 747
functions, list of, 769
new in R5, 1

G

GCs, (see graphics contexts)
geometry management, 621
about, 797
changes, 264-267
changing (XtMakeGeometryRequest),
264-267
constraints on children, 631-634
geometry_manager method, 567
querying, XtQueryGeometry, 307-311
root_geometry_manager method, 601
scrollable widget, 732-734
set_values_almost, 612
(see also methods, change_managed.)
get_values_hook, 221, 574-576
grabs, about, 797
XtAddGrab, 60-62
XtRemoveGrab, 326
graphics contexts, 68, 160, 199, 319
deallocating, 319
destroying, 160
freeing, 160

obtaining, 68-70, 199-200
sharable, 199-200
sharable and modifiable, 68-70
(see also XtAllocGC; XtDestroyGC;
XtGetGC; XtReleaseGC.)
GraphicsExpose event, 59, 836-837
GravityNotify event, 806, 838
Grip widget, resources, 635-636

I

initialization, XtToolkitInitialize, 368
initialization procedure, registering, 739
initialize method, 579-582
initialize_hook method, 585
initializer functions, calling, 740
input queue, determining events, 103, 301
examining head, 102, 300
XtAppNextEvent, 101
XtAppPeekEvent, 102
XtAppPending, 103, 301
XtPeekEvent, 300
InputOutput window, 828
insert_child method, 586
internationalization, in R5, 3
Intrinsics, selection timeout, 110

J

JumpProc, 674

K

key translation, registering, 346
XtSetKeyTranslator, 346
keyboard
keyboard focus, 347, 547
redirecting input, 347-348;
(see also accept_focus; XtSetKeyboard-
Focus.)
mapping, 845
keyboard focus window, 830
keycodes, translating, keycode-to-keysym,
370-373
XtTranslateKey, 370-371;
XtTranslateKeycode, 372-373
KeymapNotify event, 839
KeyPress event, 840-842
KeyRelease event, 840-842
keysyms, determining case, 147
in action procedures, 185

Q

query_geometry method, 589

R

R5, changed arguments, 1
  changes from R4, 1-4
  how resources handled in, 2
  implementation changes, 3
  internationalization, 3
  new functions in, 1
  new widgets in, 4
  new Xmu converters, 4
raw event handlers, 64-65
realize method, 594-597
RectObj, 517
regions, 59, 562
registering, actions (see actions)
  callbacks, 50-54
  converters, 55, 74-76, 316
  event handlers, 57-58
  fatal error handlers, 107-108
  nonfatal error handlers, 116-117
  raw event handler, 64-65
  work procedure, 80
removing, callbacks, 321-323
  grabs, 326
  input, 327
  raw event handlers, 328-329
  timeouts, 330
ReparentNotify event, 853
Repeater widget, 666
ResizeRequest event, 854
resizing, resize method, 598
resources, application resources, 189
  constraint, 499
  copying, XtSetValues, 360-362
  database, obtaining, 158
  database of screen, obtaining, 340
  file format, 867
  getting constraint resource list, 195
  getting resource list, 203
  how handled in R5, 2
  obtaining subpart values, 218-219
  querying, XtGetValues, 220-222
  resource conversion, XtDirectConvert,
    163
  resource list, copying, 356, 356-357;
    updating, 215, 215-217
  setting application values, 189
  type conversion, XtConvert, 142-143
  widget, 759;

obtaining, 760
XtGetResourceList, 203

S

scrollbars, controlling scrolling area,
    670-676
  Scrollbar widget, 670-676;
    resources, 671-673
  scrollbarWidgetClass, 670-676
  setting thumb values, 675
searching for files, (see XtFindFile)
SelectionClear event, 855
SelectionNotify event, 856-857
SelectionRequest event, 858
selections, data, 207, 211
  obtaining, 211-212;
  XtDisownSelection, 165;
  XtOwnSelection, 292;
  (see also XtGetSelectionValue; XtGet-
    SelectionValues.)
  selection data; obtaining, 207
  timeout, 90, 110, 353
  (see also timeouts.)
sensitivity, checking state, XtIsSensitive,
    253
  setting state, XtSetSensitive, 354
set_values method, 360, 603-608
  (see also XtSetValues.)
set_values_almost method, 612-614
set_values_hook method, 615
Shell widget, 522
  types, 522-523
    ApplicationShell, 523;
    OverrideShell, 522;
    Shell, 523;
    TopLevelShell, 522;
    TransientShell, 522;
    VendorShell, 523;
    WMShell, 523
  XtIsShell, 254
Simple widget, class, resources, 677-678
SimpleMenu widget, creating, 684
  resources, 679-682
SmeBSB object, resources, 687-688
standard selection target types, 742
storage, allocating
  XtMalloc, 269
  XtNew, 281
  freeing (XtFree), 184
  resizing (XtRealloc), 314
strings, converting to various types, 748

converting to widgets, 756
copying (XtNewString), 282
defined, 879
error message (XtStringConversionWarning), 366
StringDefs.h header file, 879
StripChart widget, class, about, 692-694
structure, 285
determining field's byte offset, 285
(see also XtOffset.)
subpart resources, obtaining values, 218-219
SubstitutionRec structure, 183, 338

T

target types, converting to standard selection, 742
Template widget, 695-702
templateWidgetClass, 695-702
Text widget, 703-722
creating, 717
default bindings, 714-715
edit modes, 704
resources, 704-709
timeouts, invoking procedure after timeout, 79
selection timeout value, 90, 110
XtAppAddTimeOut, 79
XtAppGetSelectionTimeout, 90
XtAppSetSelectionTimeout, 110
XtRemoveTimeOut, 330
XtSetSelectionTimeout, 353
Toggle widget, 723-728
resources, 723-725
toolkits, changes between R4 and R5, 1-4
XtInitialize, 235-236
TopLevelShell, 527
TransientShell, 530
translations, 72
compiling, table, 299
merging, 121, 291
overriding, 291
removing, 380
translation table, 869
XtAugmentTranslations, 121
XtOverrideTranslations, 291
XtUninstallTranslations, 380
(see also actions.)
Tree widget, 729
types, SubstitutionRec, 183, 338

U

UnmapNotify event, 843-844

V

VendorShell, 533
Viewport widget, 732-734
destroying, 734
removing child, 734
resources, 732-734
ViewportWidgetClass, 732-734
virtual crossing, 824
VisibilityNotify event, 859-860

W

warning handler, 119, 404
calling high-level, 119-120, 404
(see also XtAppWarningMsg; XtWarningMsg.)
warnings, listing, 861
RectObj, 517
Shell, 522
TransientShell, 530
VendorShell, 533
WMShell, 536
widget nodes, initializing arrays of, 762
looking up by name, 764
widgets, 677, 703
accept_focus method, 123
adding to parent list, 270-272
Box, 621
callback list (see callbacks)
child widget, creating/managing, 150
class
determining subclass (XtIsSubclass), 255;
obtaining (XtClass), 139;
verifying (XtCheckSubclass), 138;
XtIsComposite, 246;
XtIsConstraint, 247;
XtIsShell, 254;
XtIsSubclass, 255
Command, 624
converting strings to, 756
creating, 82, 149-150, 153-155;
additional top-level, 149;
custom widget, 695-702, 696;
independent widget trees, 82-83;
window, 156-157;

X

About the Editor

David Flanagan is a consulting programmer and principal of Dovetail Systems, a company specializing in user interface and widget development. He has been programming with X and Xt since their early days at MIT, and is also an expert on the Motif widgets. David holds an S.B. degree in Computer Science and Engineering from the Massachusetts Institute of Technology.

Volume 0: X Protocol Reference Manual for X11 Release 4 and Release 5

Edited by Adrian Nye
3rd Edition, February 1992

Volume 0, X Protocol Reference Manual, describes the X Network Protocol which underlies all software for Version 11 of the X Window System. The manual is updated for R5. Contents are divided into three parts:

Part One provides a conceptual introduction to the X Protocol. It describes the role of the server and client and demonstrates the network transactions that take place during a minimal client session.

Part Two contains an extensive set of reference pages for each protocol request and event. It is a reformatted and reorganized version of the Consortium's Protocol specification. All material from the original document is present in this manual, and the material in the reference pages is reorganized to provide easier access. Each protocol request or event is treated as a separate, alphabetized reference page. Reference pages include the encoding requests and replies.

Part Three consists of several appendixes describing particular parts of the X Protocol, along with several reference aids. It includes the most recent version of the ICCCM and the Logical Font Conventions Manual.

The Third Edition of Volume 0 can be used with any release of X.

516 pages, ISBN: 1-56592-008-2

Volume 1: Xlib Programming Manual for X11 Release 4 and Release 5

By Adrian Nye
3rd Edition, July 1992

Newly updated to cover X11 Release 5, *Volume 1, Xlib Programming Manual* is a complete guide to programming to the X library (Xlib), the lowest level of programming interface to X. New features include introductions to internationalization, device-independent color, font service, and scalable fonts.

Includes chapters on:

* X Window System concepts
* Simple client application
* Window attributes
* The graphics context
* Graphics in practice
* Color and Events
* Interclient communication
* The Resource Manager
* A complete client application
* Window management

824 pages, ISBN: 1-56592-002-3

Volume 2: Xlib Reference Manual for X11 Release 4 and Release 5

By Adrian Nye
3rd Edition, June 1992

Volume 2, Xlib Reference Manual, is a complete programmer's reference for Xlib, updated for X11 Release 4 and Release 5.

Includes:

* Reference pages for Xlib functions
* Reference pages for event types
* Permuted links to Xlib functions
* Description of macros and reference pages for their function versions
* Listing of the server-side color database
* Alphabetical index and description of structures
* Alphabetical index and description of defined symbols
* KeySyms and their meaning
* Illustration of the standard cursor font
* Function group index to the right routine for a particular task
* Reference pages for Xlib-related Xmu functions (miscellaneous utilities)
* 4 single-page reference aids for the GC and window attributes

New features in the 3rd Edition include:

* Over 100 new manpages covering Xcms, internationalization, and the function versions of macros
* Updating to the R5 spec
* New "Returns" sections on all the functions which return values, making this information easier to find

1138 pages, ISBN: 1-56592-006-6

X BOOKS FROM O'REILLY & ASSOCIATES, INC.

Volume 3: X Window System User's Guide for X11 Release 4

By Valerie Quercia and Tim O'Reilly
3rd Edition, May 1990

Volume 3, X Window System User's Guide, orients the new user to window system concepts and provides detailed tutorials for many client programs, including the xterm terminal emulator and window managers.

Building on this basic knowledge, later chapters explain how to customize the X environment and provide sample configurations.

This popular manual is available in two editions, one for users of the MIT software, one for users of Motif. The Standard Edition uses the twm manager in most examples and illustrations, and has been updated for X11 Release 4.

Topics include:

- Starting the system and opening windows
- Using the xterm terminal emulator and window managers
- Most standard release clients, including programs for graphics, printing, font manipulation, window/display information, removing windows, as well as several desktop utilities
- Customizing the window manager, keyboard, display, and certain basicfeatures of any client program
- Using and customizing the mwm window manager, for those using the OSF/Motif graphical user interface
- System administration tasks, including managing fonts, starting X automatically, and using the display manager, xdm, to run X on a single or multiple display

Standard Edition: 752 pages, ISBN: 0-937175-14-5

Volume 3M: X Window System User's Guide OSF/Motif Edition

By Valerie Quercia and Tim O'Reilly
2nd Edition, January 1993

Newly revised for Motif 1.2 and X11 Release 5, this alternative edition of the User's Guide highlights the Motif window manager and graphical interface. It will be the first choice for the many users with the Motif graphical user interface.

Topics include:

- Overview of the X Color Management System (Xcms)
- Using the X font server
- Bitmap and xmag
- Tear-off menus and drag-and-drop
- Starting the system and opening client windows
- Using the xterm terminal emulator
- Using standard release clients
- Using Motif's mwm window manager
- Customizing the keyboard, display and basic features of any client program
- Performing system administration tasks, such as managing fonts, starting X automatically, and using the display manager to run X on single or multiple displays

Motif Edition: 956 pages, ISBN: 1-56592-015-5

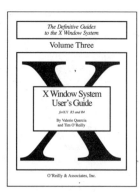

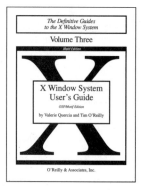

Volume 4: X Toolkit Intrinsics Programming Manual for X11 Release 4

By Adrian Nye and Tim O'Reilly
Standard: 2nd Edition, September 1990
Motif: 2nd Edition, August 1992

Volume 4 is a complete guide to programming with the X Toolkit Intrinsics, the library of C language routines that facilitate the design of user interfaces, with reusable components called widgets. It provides concepts and examples that show how to use the various X Toolkit routines. The first few chapters are devoted to using widgets; the remainder of the book covers the more complex task of writing new widgets.

Volume 4 is available in two editions. The Standard Edition uses Athena widgets in examples for X11 Release 4 to demonstrate how to use existing widgets but provides a good introduction to programming with any widget set based on Xt. The Motif Edition uses the Motif 1.2 widget set in examples, and has been updated for X11 Release 5. Both books include:

- Introduction to the X Window System
- Building applications with widgets
- Constructing a bitmap editor with widgets
- Basic widget methods
- Events, translations, and accelerators
- Event handlers, timeouts, and work procedures
- Resource management and type conversion
- Selections and window manager interaction
- Geometry management
- Menus, gadgets, and cascaded pop-ups
- Miscellaneous techniques
- Comparison of Athena, OSF/Motif, and AT&T OPEN LOOK widgets
- Master index to volumes 4 and 5

This book is designed to be used with *Volume 5, X Toolkit Intrinsics Reference Manual*, which provides reference pages for each of the Xt functions and the widget classes defined by Xt.Volume 5.

Standard Edition: 624 pages, ISBN: 0-937175-56-0

Motif Edition: 714 pages, ISBN 1-56592-013-9

Volume 5: X Toolkit Intrinsics Reference Manual for X11 Release 4 and Release 5

Edited by David Flanagan
3rd Edition, April 1992

Volume 5, X Toolkit Intrinsics Reference Manual, is a complete programmer's reference for the X Toolkit. It provides reference pages for each of the Xt functions as well as the widget classes defined by Xt and the Athena widgets.

This volume is based on Xt documentation from MIT and has been re-edited, reorganized, and expanded. Contents include:

- Reference pages for each of the Xt Intrinsics and macros, organized alphabetically for ease of use
- Reference pages for the interface definitions of functions registered with other Xt functions
- Reference pages for the Core, Composite, and Constraint widget methods
- Reference pages for the Object, RectObj, Core, Composite, Constraint, and Shell widget classes defined by Xt
- Reference pages for Athena widget classes
- Reference pages for Xt-related Xmu functions
- Permuted index
- Many appendixes and quick reference aids
- Index

The 3rd Edition of Volume 5 has been completely revised. In addition to covering Release 4 and Release 5 of X, all the man pages have been completely rewritten for clarity and ease of use, and new examples and descriptions have been added throughout the book.

916 pages, ISBN: 1-56592-007-4

Volume 6: Motif Programming Manual for OSF/Motif Version 1.1

By Dan Heller
1st Edition, September 1991

The *Motif Programming Manual* is a source for complete, accurate, and insightful guidance on Motif application programming. There is no other book that covers the ground as thoroughly or as well as this one.

The *Motif Programming Manual* describes how to write applications using the Motif toolkit from the Open Software Foundation (OSF). The book goes into detail on every Motif widget class, with useful examples that will help programmers to develop their own code. Anyone doing Motif programming who doesn't want to have to figure it out on their own needs this book.

In addition to information on Motif, the book is full of tips about programming in general, and about user interface design.

Contents include:

- An introduction to the Motif programming model, how it is based on the X Toolkit Intrinsics, and how it differs from them

- Chapters on each of the Motif widget classes, explaining them in depth, with useful examples that will help you to improve your own code. For example, the chapter on menus shows how to develop utility functions that generalize and simplify menu creation. All of the code shown in the book is available free of charge over the Internet or via UUCP

- Complete quick reference appendices on Motif functions, widgets, and gadgets

This one book can serve both your tutorial and reference needs. The book assumes competence with the C programming language, as well as familiarity with fundamental X Window System concepts. The *Motif Programming Manual* is not only the most comprehensive guide to writing applications with Motif, it is an integral part of the most widely used series of books on

X as a whole. It complements and builds upon the earlier books in the X Window System Series from O'Reilly & Associates, as well as on OSF's own Motif Style Guide. Does not cover UIL.

1032 pages, ISBN: 0-937175-70-6

Volume 7: XView Programming Manual and XView Reference Manual

Edited by Dan Heller
Programming Manual: 3rd Edition, September 1991
Reference Manual: 1st Edition, September 1991

Volume 7, XView Programming Manual, has been revised and expanded for XView Version 3. XView was developed by Sun Microsystems and is derived from Sun's proprietary programming toolkit, SunView. It is an easy-to-use object-oriented toolkit that provides an OPEN LOOK user interface for X applications.

For XView Version 3, the major additions are:

- Internationalization support for XView programs

- A new Drag and Drop package that lets the user transfer data between applications by dragging an interface object to a region

- A mouseless input model that means XView applications can be controlled from the keyboard without a mouse. Soft function keys are also supported

- The Notices package has been completely rewritten to incorporate Notice objects

- The Selection package has been rewritten, replacing the SunView-style selection service

- New panel items such as multiline text items and drop target items have been included. The Panels chapter has been reworked to clarify and simplify panel usage

- Panel item extensions are now covered in XView Internals to allow programmers to build custom panel items

The Attribute Summary from the previous edition of the *XView Programming Manual* has been expanded and is now published as a companion volume, the *XView Reference Manual*. It contains complete alphabetical listings of all XView attributes, functions, and macros, as well as other reference information essential for XView programmers.

XView Programming Manual:
798 pages, ISBN: 0-937175-87-0

XView Reference Manual:
266 pages, ISBN: 0-937175-88-9

XView Programming and Reference Manual Set:
1064 pages, ISBN: 0-937175-89-7

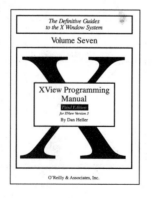

The Definitive Guides to the X Window System
Volume Six
Motif Edition
Motif Programming Manual
For OSF/Motif Version 1.1
By Dan Heller
O'Reilly & Associates, Inc.

The Definitive Guides to the X Window System
Volume Seven
XView Programming Manual
Third Edition
for XView Version 3
By Dan Heller
O'Reilly & Associates, Inc.

Volume 8: X Window System Administrator's Guide for X11 Release 4 and Release 5

By Linda Mui and Eric Pearce
1st Edition, October 1992

As X moves out of the hacker's domain and into the "real world," users can't be expected to master all the ins and outs of setting up and administering their own X software. That will increasingly become the domain of system administrators. Even for experienced system administrators X raises many issues, both because of subtle changes in the standard UNIX way of doing things and because X blurs the boundaries between different platforms. Under X, users can run applications across the network, on systems with different resources (including fonts, colors, and screen size) than the applications were designed for originally. Many of these issues are poorly understood, and the technology for dealing with them is in rapid flux. This book is the first and only book devoted to the issues of system administration for X and X-based networks, written not just for UNIX system administrators but for anyone faced with the job of administering X (including those running X on stand-alone workstations).

The book includes:

- An overview of X that focuses on issues that affect the system administrator's job
- Information on obtaining, compiling, and installing the X software, including a discussion of the trade-offs between vendor-supplied and the free MIT versions of X
- How to set up xdm, the X display manager, which takes the place of the login program under X and can be used to create a customized turnkey X session for each user
- How to set up user accounts under X (includes a comparison of the familiar shell setup files and programs to the new mechanisms provided by X)
- Issues involved in making X more secure. X's security features are not strong, but an understanding of what features are available can be very important, since X makes it possible for users to intrude on each other in new and sometimes unexpected ways.
- How fonts are used by X, including a description of the font server
- A discussion of the issues raised by running X on heterogenous networks
- How colors are managed under X and how to get the same colors across multiple devices with different hardware characteristics
- The administration issues involved in setting up and managing X terminal

- How to use PC and Mac X servers to maximize reuse of existing hardware and convert outdated hardware into X terminals
- How to obtain and install additional public domain software and patches for X
- Covers features new in R5, including the font server and Xcms

The *X Window System Administrator's Guide* is available either alone or packaged with the X CD. The CD will provide X source code to complement the instructions for installing the software.

Without CD-ROM, 372 pages, ISBN: 0-937175-83-8
With CD-ROM, ISBN: 1-56592-052-X

X Window System Administrator's Guide CD-ROM

The CD-ROM contains the source code for MIT's public domain X Window System, and will be offered with the X Window System's Administrator's Guide. It contains pre-compiled binaries for popular platforms, and comes complete with an installation system that allows custom installation of the CD-ROM.

The CD includes:

- Rock Ridge CD-ROM drivers from Young Minds, so you can install the CD as a UNIX filesystem on several popular UNIX platforms
- Complete "core" source for MIT X11 Release 4 and 5. This includes the new R5 features, such as the fontserver and XCMS.
- Complete "contrib" source for MIT X11 Release 5. This includes some programs not available in the MIT distribution, such as 'xtici', the Tektronics Color Editor.
- Complete examples and source code for all the books in the X Window System Series.
- Programs and files that are discussed in Volume 8. These were previously available only to administrators with Internet access.
- Pre-compiled X11 Release 5 binaries for Sun3, Sun4, and IBM RS6000 platforms. (The RS6000 server supports the Skyway adaptor, not the new GT3 adaptor.)

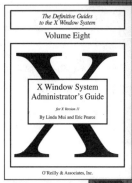

The Definitive Guides to the X Window System

Volume Eight

X Window System Administrator's Guide
for X Version 11
By Linda Mui and Eric Pearce

O'Reilly & Associates, Inc.

Programmer's Supplement for R5 of the X Window System, Version 11

By David Flanagan
1st Edition, November 1991

This book is for programmers who are familiar with Release 4 of the X Window System and want to know how to use the new features of Release 5. It is intended as an update for owners of Volumes 1, 2, 4, and 5 of the O'Reilly and Associates' X Window System series, and provides complete tutorial and reference information to all new Xlib and Xt toolkit functions.

It includes:

- Overview of the R5 changes as they affect application programming
- How to write an internationalized application---one that anticipates the needs of a language and culture other than English
- How to use scalable fonts and the fonts provided by the new font server
- How to get consistent color on any display by using the X Color Management System
- Overview of PEX, the new three-dimensional graphics extension for X
- Reference pages for all new and modified Xlib and Xt functions and Athena widgets

Together with Volume 2 and Volume 5, owners of the *Programmer's Supplement for Release 5* have a complete set of reference pages for the current MIT X Consortium standards for Xlib and Xt.

390 pages, ISBN: 0-937175-86-2

The X Window System in a Nutshell

Edited by Ellie Cutler, Daniel Gilly, and Tim O'Reilly
2nd Edition, April 1992

Once programmers have mastered the concepts behind X and learned how to program in Xlib and Xt there is still a mass of details to remember. *The X Window System in a Nutshell* fills this gap. Experienced X programmers can use this single-volume desktop companion for most common questions, keeping the full X Window System series of manuals for detailed reference. X in a Nutshell contains essential information in a boiled-down quick-reference format that makes it easy to find the answers needed most often:

- Command line options and resources for the standard MIT X clients
- Calling sequence for all Xlib and Xt functions and macros
- Detailed description of structures, enums, and other X data types used as arguments or return values in Xlib or Xt functions
- Description of the code inside a basic widget quick reference to the event structures
- Font name syntax, color names, resource file and translations table syntax, and cursors
- Xlib and Xt error messages

This book has been newly updated to cover R5 but is still useful for R4. The descriptions of the functions have been expanded and clarified, with improved cross-referencing to important related functions. Includes material on Xcms and the internationalization features of R5.

424 pages, ISBN: 1-56592-017-1

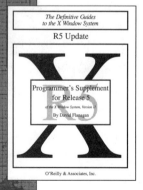

PHIGS Programming Manual: 3D Programming in X

By Tom Gaskins
1st Edition, February 1992

A complete and authoritative guide to PHIGS and PHIGS PLUS programming, this book documents the PHIGS and PHIGS PLUS graphics standards and provides full guidance regarding the use of PHIGS within the X environment. The discussions of PHIGS and PHIGS PLUS are fully integrated in this text, which takes as its starting point the PEX Sample Implementation (or PEX-SI)—the publicly available and most widely established base for commercial PHIGS products. In addition, the *PHIGS Programming Manual* explains, at both elementary and advanced levels, how to integrate your PHIGS applications with standard X (Xlib) functions. Window management, event handling, input-output, even lower-level drawing functions---all of these can be made part of your PHIGS programs. Besides Xlib itself, there are detailed examples and explanations based on the Motif, OLIT, and XView toolkits.

The *PHIGS Programming Manual*:

- Offers a clear and comprehensive introduction to PHIGS: output primitives, attributes, color, structure, and all you need to know to begin writing PHIGS programs
- Offers technical know-how. Author Tom Gaskins has for many years been an implementor of PHIGS and is also a key contributor to the international PHIGS standardization efforts.
- Shows how to use PHIGS in your X Window System applications
- Illustrates the concepts of PHIGS and PHIGS PLUS with over 200 figures
- Clearly explains the subtleties of viewing, lighting, and shading, complete with practical code examples, each of them modular and simple to understand, but virtually none of them merely a "toy" program
- Includes the DIS ISO C binding, the closest in existence to the coming ISO standard
- Demonstrates the use of PHIGS and PHIGS PLUS in interactive programs, so that you can do more than merely display pictures
- Fully describes all the PHIGS and PHIGS PLUS functions
- Has a companion reference manual. Taken together, these books are the only documentation you'll need for a product that is changing the way the X world thinks about graphics.

Whether you are starting out in 3D graphics programming or are a seasoned veteran looking for an authoritative work on a fast-rising 3D graphics standard, this book will serve your purposes well.

Softcover: 968 pages, ISBN: 0-937175-85-4
Hardcover: 968 pages, ISBN: 0-937175-92-7

PHIGS Reference Manual: 3D Programming in X

Edited by Linda Kosko
1st Edition, October 1992

The definitive and exhaustive reference documentation for the PHIGS/PEX Sample Implementation ("PEX-SI"). Contains all the reference pages from the MIT X Consortium release, but in upgraded form, with additional reference materials. Together with the *PHIGS Programming Manual*, this book is the most complete and accessible documentation currently available for both the PEX-SI and the PHIGS and PHIGS PLUS standards.

The *PHIGS Reference Manual* is the definitive and exhaustive reference documentation for the PHIGS/PEX Sample Implementation ("PEX-SI"). It contains all the reference pages from the MIT X Consortium release, but in upgraded form. It also contains additional reference materials.

1116 pages, ISBN: 0-937175-91-9

PEXlib Programming Manual

By Tom Gaskins
1st Edition, December 1992

The world of workstations changed dramatically with the release of the X Window System. Users can finally count on a consistent interface across almost all makes and models of computers. At the same time, graphics applications become easily portable.

Until recently, X supported only 2D graphics. Now, however, by means of the PEX extensions to X together with the PEXlib applications programming interface, native, 3D graphics have come to the X Window System. PEXlib allows the programmer to create graphics programs of any complexity, and also provides the basis for higher-level graphics systems and toolkits.

The *PEXlib Programming Manual* is the definitive programmer's guide to PEXlib, covering both PEX versions 5.0 and 5.1. Containing over 200 illustrations and 19 color plates, it combines a thorough and gentle tutorial approach with valuable reference features. Along the way, it presents the reader with numerous programming examples, as well as a library of helpful utility routines—all of which are available online. You do not need to have prior graphics programming experience in order to read this manual.

Written by Tom Gaskins—the widely recognized authority who also authored the O'Reilly and Associates' *PHIGS Programming Manual*—this book is the only programming guide to PEXlib you will ever need.

1154 pages, ISBN: 1-56592-028-7

PEXlib Reference Manual

By O'Reilly & Associates
1st Edition, December 1992

The *PEXlib Reference Manual* is the definitive programmer's reference resource for PEXlib, and contains complete and succinct reference pages for all the callable routines in PEXlib version 5.1. The content of the *PEXlib Reference Manual* stands, with relatively few changes, as it was created by the MIT X Consortium.

The *PEXlib Reference Manual* is a companion volume to the O'Reilly and Associates' *PEXlib Programming Manual*, written by Tom Gaskins. The *Programming Manual* is a thorough tutorial guide to PEXlib, and includes valuable reference features. Together, these books offer the most complete and accessible documentation available for PEXlib version 5.1.

577 pages, ISBN: 1-56592-029-5

About The X Resource

The X Resource is a quarterly working journal for X programmers that provides practical, timely information about the programming, administration, and use of the X Window System. *The X Resource* is the Official Publisher of the MIT X Consortium Technical Conference Proceedings, which form the January issue. Issues can be purchased separately or by subscription.

The X Resource: Issue 2, April 1992

Edited by Adrian Nye

190 pages, ISBN: 0-937175-97-8

The X Resource: Issue 3, July 1992

Edited by Adrian Nye

220 pages, ISBN: 0-937175-98-6

The X Resource: Issue 4, October 1992

Edited by Adrian Nye

276 pages, ISBN: 0-937175-99-4

The X Resource: Issue 5, January 1993

Edited by Adrian Nye

272 pages, ISBN: 1-56592-020-1

NAME _____
COMPANY _____
ADDRESS _____
CITY _____ STATE _____ ZIP _____

BUSINESS REPLY MAIL
FIRST CLASS MAIL PERMIT NO. 80 SEBASTOPOL, CA

POSTAGE WILL BE PAID BY ADDRESSEE

O'Reilly & Associates, Inc.

103 Morris Street Suite A
Sebastopol CA 95472-9902

NAME _____
COMPANY _____
ADDRESS _____
CITY _____ STATE _____ ZIP _____

BUSINESS REPLY MAIL
FIRST CLASS MAIL PERMIT NO. 80 SEBASTOPOL, CA

POSTAGE WILL BE PAID BY ADDRESSEE

O'Reilly & Associates, Inc.

103 Morris Street Suite A
Sebastopol CA 95472-9902

NO POSTAGE
NECESSARY IF
MAILED IN THE
UNITED STATES